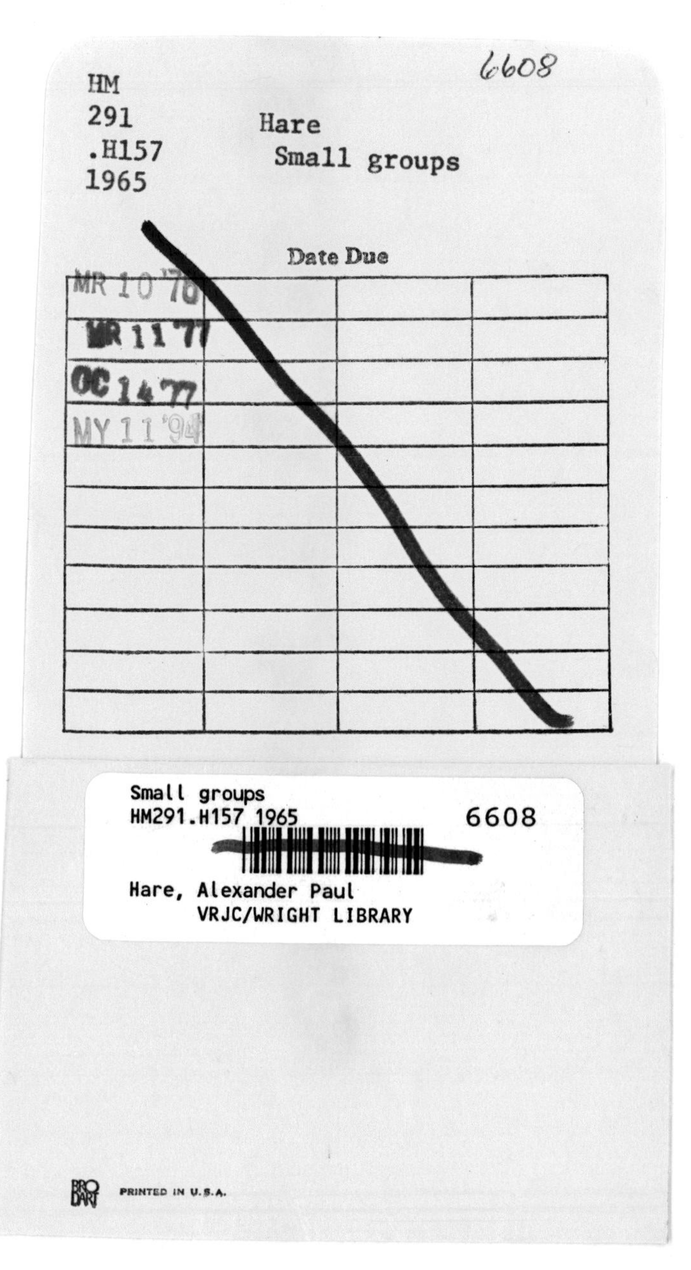
6608
HM
291
.H157
1965
Hare
Small groups
Date Due
MR 10 '76
MR 11 '77
OC 14 '77
MY 11 '94
Small groups
HM291.H157 1965
6608
Hare, Alexander Paul
VRJC/WRIGHT LIBRARY
BRODART
PRINTED IN U.S.A.

SMALL GROUPS

STUDIES IN SOCIAL INTERACTION

SMALL GROUPS

STUDIES IN SOCIAL INTERACTION

Edited by

A. PAUL HARE
HAVERFORD COLLEGE

EDGAR F. BORGATTA
THE UNIVERSITY OF WISCONSIN

ROBERT F. BALES
HARVARD UNIVERSITY

Revised Edition

ALFRED·A·KNOPF *NEW YORK*

L. C. CATALOG CARD NUMBER: 65–11960

THIS IS A BORZOI BOOK,
PUBLISHED BY ALFRED A. KNOPF, INC.

PUBLISHED 1955
REVISED EDITION PUBLISHED 1965
897

Preface to the Revised Edition

THE STUDY of small groups is important not only to those who specialize in social science, but also to those of us who want to understand better our own behavior and the behavior of our fellows. In the study of small groups the events we are interested in relating to each other occur within a limited range of space and time. It becomes possible to make the actual observations required by our theories without encountering many of the difficulties present in examining similar phenomena on a larger scale. As Homans puts it in *The Human Group*, one stands some chance to "get all the way around" a small group, and to relate a diversity of factors to each other.

Small groups are often so called because they have the same advantage for the participant that they do for the scientist studying the group—they are groups that are small enough so that the individual participant can "get all the way around" and fill out his relationship to each other person by some direct interaction with him. One can assemble small groups in the laboratory or observe them in the field, and obtain a large range of information about overt behavior, perception of members, attitudes toward each other, values and consensus on values, degrees of satisfaction, and so on, in a degree of detail not possible when the number of persons involved is too large to be held within the mind of the single participant. The study of social interaction and its related causes and effects in small groups is a microscopic method in more senses, perhaps, than has commonly been recognized. The idea that a small group may bear many general resemblances to larger-scale social systems is fairly common by now. However, the idea that the content analysis of discussion in a small group such as, for example, a therapy group can be a microscopic method of studying culture is not so common. In the study of small groups we are concerned with the microscopic study of sub-cultures, just as we are concerned with the microscopic study of small social systems. Similarly, in the total process which goes on in small groups we are observing the process by which personality elements are developed and elaborated in the individual.

The study of small groups is thus a method for the study of social systems, of culture, and of personality—all three. Its strategic significance in the development of social science generally is that it relates all three of these types of structure to a common base—the social process out of which they arise and through which they change. This field of research does not "belong" to any one of the recognized social sciences alone. It is the common property and concern of all. It has historical roots in each of them, and, as it develops, may be expected to contribute to each of them. Small group research is more than the study of one concrete "compartment" of social phenomena among many others. It is the study of the generic social process on the microscopic level.

Most of the social sciences and a number of applied disciplines are vitally involved in small group research at the present time. Quite a number of *social psychologists* are working in the field, both with a *psychological* and a *sociological* emphasis. From *clinical psychology* there are a number of workers interested in problems of *interviewing, counseling,* and *psychotherapy.* A large number of workers of different disciplines who study the roles of *family* members, the *socialization of the child,* and the internal dynamics of the family may be considered students of small groups. Still another historical root may be found in a line of speculation and later research concerned with the process of *group thinking, group problem-solving,* and the *operation of seminars, boards, panels,* and *decision-making committees.* There is a very lively interest among *educational psychologists* in classroom and instructional groups. Still other interest stems from problems of administration in all sorts of settings—*educational, recreational, religious, governmental, industrial,* and *military.* The conviction seems to be growing that problems of *administration, human relations on the face to face level, leadership, job training,* and the like are pretty much the same no matter what the concrete job of the organization.

In the social process we may expect to find the seeds, at least, of the organizations of activities that we view on a more general level as personality, society, and culture. And similarly, in various patterned aspects of the social process we may expect to find the concrete referents of many of the higher-order abstractions we use to describe these more fully developed and complicated structures. The study of small groups may perform a clarifying service in showing us how certain of our common concepts in social science, such as status, role, function, motivation, trait, culture pattern, and the like, are really only useful abstractions from the same concrete events—the behavior of individuals in interaction with each other. We often express the desirability of translation from one frame of reference to another, say from a sociological to a psychological to a cultural. The translation can probably best be made, not from one set of abstractions directly to the other, but by relating each of them to the more microscopic level of process which provides the basic reference material with which all are concerned.

The book is divided into three parts. The first part is concerned with the historical and theoretical background of the field. The second contains a collection of studies which view the social process from the perspective of the single individual in a social situation. The third contains studies in which the perspective is more that of an external observer viewing the group as a system of social interaction and describing its characteristics.

There is a saying that "it is a wise child that knows its own father." The field of small group research is so new that it has not yet recognized sufficiently even the more important of its ancestors. It is our hope to make a beginning in this direction in Chapters 1 and 2, where we have included some of the early theoretical and empirical classics of the field. In Chapter 3 on current theory we have tried to obtain a more or less representative selection of points of view which are either current and thriving in the field at present, or have been influential in the development of current theory and research.

In Parts II and III we have in general tried to include substantial empirical studies which contain source data from which further theorizing may be done. We hope that the studies we have chosen carry enough information so that the creative reader of the book will be able to make generalizations that have not previously been stated, and perhaps even new discoveries. It is our opinion that the facts and empirical generalizations available even now are adequate for a new and powerful synthesis, in mathematical form, of certain basic aspects of the interaction process. Simmel's reluctant apology of fifty years ago that such an attempt "during the foreseeable future . . . would be a wholly fantastic enterprise" stands as a prediction which has been seriously undermined by now.

Although the line of division is not absolutely distinct, there is a difference in perspective that may be recognized between the studies in Part II and those in Part III. When one tries to understand the immediate motives for behavior, it is more or less natural to take the point of view of the acting *subject*, as an individual facing a social situation, being influenced by factors in that situation, and in turn attempting to influence it through his behavior. One can do this for a specific subject, for each of the subjects in the group taken as a series, or try to arrive at some kind of average. This, generally speaking, is the perspective of Part II.

On the other hand, when one tries to understand how the situation gets to be what it is for a given subject at a given time, it is natural to take the perspective of an *observer* who takes into account the reciprocal orientation and behavior of two or more persons who adjust and readjust their relation over the course of time by some series of interactions. From this perspective one sees uniformities in the patterns of relationship and communication as they are developed and maintained between the individuals viewed as an interdependent system. This, in general, is the perspective of Part III.

One should not suppose that either perspective excludes the other.

They are both abstracted from the same process. It may be true that persons differ in the perspective which seems most natural to them, but the student of human behavior should be able to take either or both, as required by the problem.

The ease of taking a given perspective is certainly influenced by the research techniques that are available. One of the impressions that emerges strongly from a study of the history of the field is a sense of the intimate connection between the discovery or development of methods of research and the development of new bodies of theory. It is no accident that the problem of "together and apart" was a very early theoretical preoccupation; it rested on perhaps the simplest of all methods of experimental manipulation. The sociometric theory of likes and dislikes rests on a basically simple questionnaire, and the more recent upsurge of interest in social perception rests on an extension—the use of questions in which the subject is asked to predict how others will answer. The experimental manipulation of exposing the same individual to a series of relationships and the ability to reduce large masses of observations to simpler form by statistical methods are essential to the development of substantial theory of the consistency of individuals. Studies featuring these techniques are included in Part II.

The perspective of Part III, which views the group as a system of interaction, is equally dependent upon the development of research methods. A whole area of theory concerning the properties of various types of communication networks hinges around the fact that one can experimentally manipulate the channels of communication between members of a group. A new dimension of theoretical development opens up when one is able to obtain measurements of a set of interdependent variables through a long time series, as one can in the observation of overt interaction or other sorts of content analysis of communication. Indeed, the very concept of a system can have little reality unless a series of measurements through time can be visualized. Similarly, for this order of conceptualization, one must be able to visualize a number of different sorts of variables each measured separately. One cannot go far in the development of theory about how and why the roles of members in a group become differentiated from each other without the prior development of many methods of measurement: personality measures, interaction measures, perception measures, and rating and choice measures.

The problem of leadership appears early and late. Of all the perennials in the field, this one is the hardiest. No matter which perspective one takes, it looms prominently. From the individual perspective it is perhaps the most salient form of influencing and being influenced by others in the social situation. From the perspective of the group as a differentiated system, it is perhaps the most salient form of role differentiation. Theory about leadership ranges from the most simple-minded notions to the most complex and subtle. Hardly any variable is easier to manipulate, by appointment, choice, or instruction, but hardly any is harder to analyze and control. This is true in practical affairs as in the scientific laboratory. But as the problem is difficult, the rewards of solving it are great. It is a safe prediction that leadership will continue to be a focus of much small group research.

Our comments for this preface have required practically no change since the 1955 edition. The changes we have made in the volume are largely extensions, but the core of the volume remains relatively the same. In some cases, we have substituted new materials for older ones, particularly where summaries of cumulative work have become available. There is a large addition to the text, however, consisting of 20 new articles. Much of the space for this additional text comes from omission of the annotated bibliography of the 1955 edition. The bibliography is still recommended to those interested in a survey of research, which is possible because of the indexing provided. But, at this point there are sufficient copies of the older edition in libraries so that retaining the bibliography in the current edition is not warranted. Additional major bibliographic work has been published to which readers may wish to refer, especially A. P. Hare's *Handbook of Small Group Research* (Glencoe, Illinois: The Free Press, 1962) and E. F. Borgatta's trend report and bibliography on *Small Group Research* (*Current Sociology*, Vol. IX, No. 3, 1960).

In the present revision we have omitted the chapter "Together and Apart" and added chapters on "Group Influence," "Group Size," and "Group Composition, Coalitions, and Subgroups."

Finally, we are indebted to the authors who have given us permission to include their work in this volume, and to the American Psychological Association, American Sociological Society, *Sociometry*, *Human Relations*, and the other organizations and publishers who have given permission to reprint their materials.

A. PAUL HARE
Haverford College

EDGAR F. BORGATTA
The University of Wisconsin

ROBERT F. BALES
Harvard University

November 1964

Contents

PART I

HISTORICAL AND THEORETICAL BACKGROUND

Introduction 3

CHAPTER 1 : Early Theory

Division of Labor 5
EMILE DURKHEIM

The Significance of Numbers for Social Life 9
GEORG SIMMEL

Primary Groups 15
CHARLES H. COOLEY

The Social Foundations and Functions of Thought and Communication 20
GEORGE H. MEAD

CHAPTER 2 : Early Research

A Preliminary Study of the Psychology and Pedagogy of Leadership 24
LEWIS M. TERMAN

The Influence of the Group upon Association and Thought 31
FLOYD H. ALLPORT

Aggressive Behavior in a Small Social Group 35
ETHEL M. RIDDLE

The Gang 38
FREDERIC M. THRASHER

Test Room Studies in Employee Effectiveness 44
C. E. TURNER

CHAPTER 3 : Current Theory

The Equilibrium of Groups 54
ELIOT D. CHAPPLE and CARLETON S. COON

The Analysis of Situational Fields in Social Psychology 57
LEONARD S. COTTRELL, JR.

Group Emotion and Leadership 71
FRITZ REDL

The Principles and Traits of Leadership 87
CECIL A. GIBB

"Subjective" and "Objective" Elements in the Social Field: The Three Step Procedure 95
KURT LEWIN

Contributions of Sociometry to Research Methodology in Sociology 99
J. L. MORENO

Concepts and Methods in the Measurement of Group Syntality 107
RAYMOND B. CATTELL

Adaptive and Integrative Changes as Sources of Strain in Social Systems 127
ROBERT F. BALES

An Approach to the Study of Communicative Acts 132
THEODORE M. NEWCOMB

A Theory of Social Comparison Processes 146
LEON FESTINGER

Social Behavior as Exchange 170
GEORGE C. HOMANS

Theory of Organizational Decision-Making 184
JAMES G. MARCH

PART II

THE INDIVIDUAL IN SOCIAL SITUATIONS

Introduction 195

CHAPTER 4 : Social Perception

A Scale for the Measurement of Empathic Ability 197
ROSALIND F. DYMOND

The Relative Abilities of Leaders and Non-Leaders to Estimate Opinions of Their Own Groups 206
KAMLA CHOWDHRY and THEODORE M. NEWCOMB

Relational Analysis: An Extension of Sociometric Method with Emphasis upon Social Perception 217
RENATO TAGIURI

Assumed Similarity Measures as Predictors of Team Effectiveness 223
FRED E. FIEDLER

Conceptual and Methodological Problems in Interpersonal Perception 236
N. L. GAGE and LEE J. CRONBACH

A Test of Interactionist Hypotheses of Self-Conception 250
S. FRANK MIYAMOTO and SANFORD M. DORNBUSCH

CHAPTER 5 : Consistency of the Individual

Individual Differences in the Social Atom 258
HELEN H. JENNINGS

Mother-Child Interaction and the Social Behavior of Children 267
BARBARA MERRILL BISHOP

Validity and Constancy of Choices in a Sociometric Test 270
EUGENE BYRD

The Consistency of Subject Behavior and the Reliability of Scoring in Interaction Process Analysis 277
EDGAR F. BORGATTA and ROBERT F. BALES

Recording and Evaluating the Performance of Individuals as Members of Small Groups 282
LAUNOR F. CARTER

The Influence of Individual Members on the Characteristics of Small Groups 287
WILLIAM HAYTHORN

The Stability of Interpersonal Judgments in Independent Situations 298
EDGAR F. BORGATTA

Role-playing Specification, Personality, and Performance 308
EDGAR F. BORGATTA

CHAPTER 6 : Group Influence

Opinions and Social Pressure 318
SOLOMON E. ASCH

Effects of Different Conditions of Acceptance upon Conformity to Group Norms 325
JAMES E. DITTES and HAROLD H. KELLEY

The Perpetuation of an Arbitrary Tradition Through Several Generations of a Laboratory Microculture 339
ROBERT C. JACOBS and DONALD T. CAMPBELL

PART III

THE GROUP AS A SYSTEM OF SOCIAL INTERACTION

Introduction 355

CHAPTER 7 : Communication Network

The Distribution of Participation in Small Groups: An Exponential Approximation 358
FREDERICK F. STEPHAN and ELLIOT G. MISHLER

Interaction of Individuals in Reconstituted Groups 370
EDGAR F. BORGATTA and ROBERT F. BALES

Personality and Group Position 387
LEONARD BERKOWITZ

Techniques for the Study of Group Structure and Behavior: Empirical Studies of the Effects of Structure in Small Groups 400
MURRAY GLANZER and ROBERT GLASER

Seating Position and Small Group Interaction 427
A. PAUL HARE and ROBERT F. BALES

CHAPTER 8 : Interaction and Equilibrium

Some Effects of Feedback on Communication 434
HAROLD J. LEAVITT and RONALD A. H. MUELLER

The Equilibrium Problem in Small Groups 444
ROBERT F. BALES

Task and Interaction Process: Some Characteristics of Therapeutic Group Discussion 477
GEORGE A. TALLAND

Interaction Process Analysis of the Mediation of Labor-Management Disputes 483
HENRY A. LANDSBERGER

CHAPTER 9 : Group Size

Size of Group as a Factor in the Interaction Profile 495
ROBERT F. BALES and EDGAR F. BORGATTA

Twenty Questions: Efficiency in Problem Solving as a Function of Size of Group 513
DONALD W. TAYLOR and WILLIAM L. FAUST

Effects of Group Size 525
EDWIN J. THOMAS and CLINTON F. FINK

CHAPTER 10 : Group Composition, Coalitions, and Subgroups

On the Dimensions of Group Behavior 537
EDGAR F. BORGATTA, LEONARD S. COTTRELL, JR., and HENRY J. MEYER

The Harvard Compatibility Experiment 555
WILLIAM C. SCHUTZ

A Theory of Coalition Formation 563
WILLIAM A. GAMSON

Coalitions in the Triad: Critique and Experiment 577
HAROLD H. KELLEY and A. JOHN ARROWOOD

CHAPTER 11 : Role Differentiation

Husband-Wife Interaction over Revealed Differences 591
FRED L. STRODTBECK

Some Consequences of Power Differences on Decision Making in Permanent and Temporary Three-Man Groups 600
E. PAUL TORRANCE

Role Differentiation in Small Groups 610
PHILIP E. SLATER

Sex Role Differentiation in Jury Deliberations 628
FRED L. STRODTBECK and RICHARD D. MANN

Compositional Effects, Role Systems, and the Survival of Small Discussion Groups 637
JAMES A. DAVIS

CHAPTER 12 : Leadership

An Experimental Approach to the Study of Autocracy and Democracy: A Preliminary Note 648
KURT LEWIN and RONALD LIPPITT

A Further Investigation of the Criteria of Leadership 655
LAUNOR F. CARTER, WILLIAM HAYTHORN, and MARGARET HOWELL

The Sociometry of Leadership in Temporary Groups 658
CECIL A. GIBB

Sharing Leadership in Small, Decision-Making Groups 675
LEONARD BERKOWITZ

Small Group Discussions with Participatory and Supervisory Leadership 688
A. PAUL HARE

Methods of Conducting Critiques of Group Problem-Solving Performance 692
E. PAUL TORRANCE

Some Findings Relevant to the Great Man Theory of Leadership 700
EDGAR F. BORGATTA, ARTHUR S. COUCH, and ROBERT F. BALES

PART I

Historical AND *Theoretical* *Background*

Introduction

THE HISTORICAL *origins of small group research are diffuse and diverse. Of the many pioneers, we have chosen a few to represent the rest. Most of the writers who have treated the development of social and cultural phenomena, as well as many who have been concerned with the development of the self and the internalization of social norms, have had something to say about small groups. They found that in some way the origins of the phenomena they were seeking could be seen on the small group level, or that the comparison of small with large groups gave them a more generalized perception than could be had by confining their interest to groups of larger size.*

Simmel, who was writing about groups of two and three persons at the turn of this century, is a particularly good example of a theorist whose urge toward generalized theory led him to a long, clear look at the factor of size itself as a determinant of the form of social relationships. Durkheim, Cooley, and Mead, as well as Simmel, all in their own ways, were deeply concerned with the problem of the social control of behavior and saw the phenomenon of "internalization" as intimately tied up with the interaction of the individual with others in small groups. Indeed, if there is any preoccupation which has been more characteristic of small group theory than the interest in leadership, it is the more general theme of social control—an interest in the social conditions under which the motivation of individuals is most effectively developed, maintained, and changed.

Most of the early research in the field is easily associated with this theme. Among the earliest relevant experimental studies are those of Triplett in 1898, concerned with a curious facilitating or "dynamogenic" effect that occurred when people were together and in competition rather than alone. The alone and together theme was given a new impetus in the early twenties by the experiments of F. H. Allport, and is still active today. The study of child development by first hand observation is another important source of small group research which goes back at least to the turn of the century. We have chosen Terman's 1904 study of the "Psychology and Pedagogy of Leadership" among children as an early landmark. Terman's study is classic in its foreshadowing of methods and themes that were to be developed later in the work of Goodenough, Anderson, D. S. Thomas, Pigors, and many others. Piaget's work on children's games is almost in a class by itself as an exemplification of the study of the small group as the creator and carrier of a sub-culture. Here, also, the theme of social control is prominent.

The failure of social control in the larger society and its re-establishment with reversed content in the small group has provided the motive for many important studies. We have taken the work of Thrasher on the gang to represent the work in the field of gangs of other pioneers, such as Puffer, Furfey, and Whyte. Riddle's study, in 1925, of aggressive behavior in a small social group is still ahead of much present-day laboratory research in the use of physiological measures, although some research of this type is now being done in hospital settings. Current developments in the theory of games and economic behavior are likely to give rise to small group studies that will look back to Riddle's work as a pioneer effort. Although systematic observations of individual and group behavior in the factory had been made in the early part of the century by F. K. Taylor and other proponents of scientific management, the Western Electric researches, described here in an early article by Turner, are generally regarded as the classic studies in the industrial area of small group research.

In Chapter 3 we present a series of selections in current theory representing a number of different points of view. Current theory in the technical sense is still far from unified, in spite of the widespread conviction that it can and will be. Differences in language, imagery, and interpretive thought-models always present a certain amount of difficulty. But the difficulties are, after all, familiar. All the traditional dilemmas and puzzles that have been encountered by the behavioral sciences in their struggle toward an understanding of human behavior are encountered in small group theory. Small group research may well be the setting in which many of the traditional dilemmas will be resolved and the divergent perspectives merged. This hope, as much as the desire to obtain answers to practical problems, is probably a major factor in the widespread appeal of the field. We believe that, in spite of the fact that the pieces have not yet been completely fitted together, the serious reader of Chapter 3 can hardly fail to gain a sense of an emerging congruence, and feel a sense of this hope.

CHAPTER 1 EARLY THEORY

Division of Labor

EMILE DURKHEIM

¶ WHILE *Durkheim's* Division of Labor *centers on societal problems, the reference frequently is to group organization in a generic sense. His analysis of the division of labor has many modern counterparts in the emphases on concepts such as role differentiation and the problem of equilibrium. Here we have reproduced three very brief sections which summarize major points of relevance for small group (and large group) organizational theory.*

WE KNOW, in effect, that, wherever organic solidarity is found, we come upon an adequately developed regulation determining the mutual relations of functions. For organic solidarity to exist, it is not enough that there be a system of organs necessary to one another, which in a general way feel solidary, but it is also necessary that the way in which they should come together, if not in every kind of meeting, at least in circumstances which most frequently occur, be predetermined. Otherwise, at every moment new conflicts would have to be equilibrated, for the conditions of equilibrium can be discovered only through gropings in the course of which one part treats the other as an adversary as much as an auxiliary. These conflicts would incessantly crop out anew, and, consequently, solidarity would be scarcely more than potential, if

FROM *Division of labor*. Glencoe, Ill.: Free Press, 1947. Reprinted by permission of the publisher.

mutual obligations had to be fought over entirely anew in each particular instance. It will be said that there are contracts. But, first of all, all social relations are not capable of assuming this juridical form. We know, moreover, that a contract is not self-sufficient, but supposes a regulation which is as extensive and complicated as contractual life itself. Besides, the links which have this origin are always of short duration. A contract is only a truce, and very precarious; it suspends hostilities only for a time. Of course, as precise as this regulation may be, it will always leave a place for many disturbances. But it is neither necessary nor even possible for social life to be without conflicts. The role of solidarity is not to suppress competition, but to moderate it.

Moreover, in the normal state, these rules disengage themselves from the division of labor. They are a prolongation of it. Assuredly, if it only brought together individuals who united for some few moments to exchange personal services, it could not give rise to any regulative action. But what it brings face to face are functions, that is to say, ways of definite action, which are identically repeated in given circumstances, since they cling to general, constant conditions of social life. The relations which are formed among these functions cannot fail to partake of the same degree of fixity and regularity. There are certain ways of mutual reaction which, finding themselves very conformable to the nature of things, are repeated very often and become habits. Then these habits, becoming forceful, are transformed into rules of conduct. The past determines the future. In other words, there is a certain sorting of rights and duties which is established by usage and becomes obligatory. The rule does not, then, create the state of mutual dependence in which solidary organs find themselves, but only expresses in clear-cut fashion the result of a given situation. In the same way, the nervous system, far from dominating the evolution of the organism, as we have already said, results from it (2, p. 746). The nerve-cords are probably only the lines of passage which the streams of movements and excitations exchanged between different organs have followed. They are the canals which life has hewed for itself while steadily flowing in the same direction, and the ganglia would only be the place of intersection of several of these lines (3, pp. 438 ff.). Because they misunderstood this aspect of the phenomena, certain moralists have claimed that the division of labor does not produce true solidarity. They have seen in it only particular exchanges, ephemeral combinations, without past or future, in which the individual is thrown on his own resources. They have not perceived the slow work of consolidation, the network of links which little by little have been woven and which makes something permanent of organic solidarity.

We are now in a position to solve the practical problem that we posed for ourselves at the beginning of this work.

If there is one rule of conduct which is incontestable, it is that which orders us to realize in ourselves the essential traits of the collective type. Among lower peoples, this reaches its greatest rigor. There, one's first duty is to resemble everybody else, not to have anything personal about one's beliefs or actions. In more advanced societies, required likenesses are less numerous; the absences of some likenesses, however, is still a sign of moral failure. Of course, crime falls into fewer different categories; but today, as heretofore, if a criminal is the object of reprobation, it is because he is unlike us. Likewise, in lesser degree, acts simply immoral and prohibited as such are those which evince dissemblances less profound but nevertheless considered serious. Is this not the case with the rule which common morality expresses when it orders a man to be a man in every sense of the word, which is to say, to have all the ideas and sentiments which go to make up a human conscience? No doubt, if this formula is taken literally, the man prescribed would be man in general and not one of some particular social species. But, in reality, this human conscience that we must integrally realize is nothing else than the collective conscience of the group of which we are a part. For what can it be composed of, if not the ideas and sentiments to which we are most attached? Where can we find the traits of our model, if not within us and around us? If we believe that this collective ideal is that of all humanity, that is because it has become so abstract and general that it appears fitting for all men indiscriminately. But, really, every people makes for itself some particular conception of this type which pertains to its personal temperament. Each represents it in its own image. Even the moralist who thinks he can, through thought, overcome the influence of transient ideas, cannot do so, for he is impregnated with them, and no matter what he does, he finds these precepts in the body of his deductions. That is why each nation has its own school of moral philosophy conforming to its character.

On the other hand, we have shown that this rule had as its function the prevention of all agitation of the common conscience, and, consequently, of social solidarity, and that it could accomplish this role only by having a moral character. It is impossible for offenses against the most fundamental collective sentiments to be tolerated without the disintegration of society, and it is necessary to combat them with the aid of the particularly energetic reaction which attaches to moral rules.

But the contrary rule, which orders us to specialize, has exactly the same function. It also is necessary for the cohesion of societies, at least at a certain period in their evolution. Of course, its solidarity is different from the preceding, but though it is different, it is no less indispensable. Higher societies can maintain themselves in equilibrium only if labor is divided; the attraction of like for like less and less suffices to produce this result. If, then, the moral character of the first of these rules is necessary to the playing of its role, it is no less necessary to the second. They both correspond to the same social need, but satisfy the need differently, because the conditions of existence in the societies themselves differ. Consequently, without speculating concerning the first principle of ethics, we can induce the moral value of one from the moral value of the other. If, from certain points of view, there is a real antagonism between them, that is not because they serve different ends. On the contrary, it is because they lead to the same end, but through opposed means. Accordingly, there is no necessity for choosing between them once for all nor of condemning one in the name of the other.

But if the division of labor produces solidarity, it is not only because it makes each individual an *exchangist,* as the economists say (1, p. 248); it is because it creates among men an entire system of rights and duties which link them together in a durable way. Just as social similitudes give rise to a law and a morality which protect them, so the division of labor gives rise to rules which assure pacific and regular concourse of divided functions. If economists have believed that it would bring forth an abiding solidarity, in some manner of its own making, and if, accordingly, they have held that human societies could and would resolve themselves into purely economic associations, that is because they believed that it affected only individual, temporary interests. Consequently, to estimate the interests in conflict and the way in which they ought to equilibrate, that is to say, to determine the conditions under which exchange ought to take place, is solely a matter of individual competence; and, since these interests are in a perpetual state of becoming, there is no place for any permanent regulation. But such a conception is, in all ways, inadequate for the facts. The division of labor does not present individuals to one another, but social functions. And society is interested in the play of the latter; in so far as they regularly concur, or do not concur, it will be healthy or ill. Its existence thus depends upon them, and the more they are divided the greater its dependence. That is why it cannot leave them in a state of indetermination. In addition to this, they are determined by themselves. Thus are formed those rules whose number grows as labor is divided, and whose absence makes organic solidarity either impossible or imperfect.

But it is not enough that there be rules; they must be just, and for that it is necessary for the external conditions of competition to be equal. If, moreover, we remember that the collective conscience is becoming more and more a cult of the individual, we shall see that what characterizes the morality of organized societies, compared to that of segmental societies, is that there is something more human, therefore more rational, about them. It does not direct our activities to ends which do not immediately concern us; it does not make us servants of ideal powers of a nature other than our own, which follow their directions without occupying themselves with the interests of men. It only asks that we be thoughtful of our fellows and that we be just, that we fulfill our duty, that we work at the function we can best execute, and receive the just reward for our services. The rules which constitute it do not have a constraining force which snuffs out free thought; but, because they are rather made for us and, in a certain sense, by us, we are free. We wish to understand them; we do not fear to change them. We must, however, guard against finding such an ideal inadequate on the pretext that it is too earthly and too much to our liking. An ideal is not more elevated because more transcendent, but because it leads us to vaster perspectives. What is important is not that it tower high above us, until it becomes a stranger to our lives, but that it open to our activity a large enough field. This is far from being on the verge of realization. We know only too well what a laborious work it is to erect this society where each individual will have the place he merits, will be rewarded as he deserves, where everybody, accordingly, will spontaneously work for the good of all and of each. Indeed, a moral code is not above another because it commands in a drier and more authoritarian manner, or because it is more sheltered from reflection. Of course, it must attach us to something besides ourselves but it is not necessary for it to chain us to it with impregnable bonds.

REFERENCES

1. de Molinari. *La morale economique.*
2. Perrier. *Colonies animales.*
3. Spencer. *Principles of biology.* Vol. II.

The Significance of Numbers for Social Life

GEORG SIMMEL

THE PRESENT studies begin by examining forms of social life, combinations and interactions among individuals. But they do so in one respect only: the bearing which the mere *number* of sociated individuals has upon these forms of social life. It will immediately be conceded on the basis of everyday experiences, that a group upon reaching a certain size

FROM Kurt H. Wolff, *The sociology of Georg Simmel.* Glencoe, Ill.: Free Press, 1950. Reprinted by permission of the translator and publisher.

must develop forms and organs which serve its maintenance and promotion, but which a smaller group does not need. On the other hand, it will also be admitted that smaller groups have qualities, including types of interaction among their members, which inevitably disappear when the groups grow larger. This quantitative determination of the group, as it may be called, has a twofold function. Negatively speaking, certain developments, which are necessary or at least possible as far as the contents or conditions of life are concerned, can be realized only below or above a particular number of elements. Positively, certain other developments are imposed upon the group by certain purely quantitative modifications. Yet not even these developments emerge automatically, for they also depend on other than numerical characteristics. The decisive point, however, is that they are not the result of these characteristics alone, for they emerge only under certain numerical conditions.

The Quantitative Determination of Group Divisions and of Certain Groups

OBVIOUSLY, the notions "large" and "small" groups are extremely crude scientific designations, indeterminate and vague. They are useful, really, only as a suggestion that the sociological form of the group depends upon its quantitative aspects. But they are quite insufficient to show the real connection between the two in any more precise manner. Yet it is perhaps not always impossible to determine this relation more exactly. To be sure, during the foreseeable future in the development of our knowledge, it would be a wholly fantastic enterprise if we wanted to express the formations and relations so far discussed in exact numerical values. Nevertheless, within modest limits, namely in regard to characteristic sociations among small numbers of persons, certain traits can be indicated even at this stage of our knowledge. As transitions from complete numerical determinateness, I shall discuss some cases in which the quantitative determination of the group is already of some sociological significance but is not yet fixed in every detail.

NUMERICALLY EQUAL SUBDIVISIONS

The number operates as a classificatory principle within the group. That is, parts of the group which are formed through enumeration function as relative units. At this point, I merely emphasize this general principle; later I shall discuss the significance of particular individual numbers. The division of a unified group, and more especially, its division not only from top to bottom, in terms of ruling and being ruled, but among its coordinated members, is one of the most extraordinary advances made by mankind. It is the anatomical structure which forms the basis of the higher organic and social processes. The classification may derive from ancestry, or from associations based on voluntary pledges, or from identity of occupation, or from grouping by local districts. All these principles of classification are combined with the quantitative principle: the mass of existing men or families is divided by a certain number and thus yields numerically equal subdivisions. To each of them, the whole has approximately the same relation as each subdivision has to its component individuals. This principle is, however, so mechanical that in order to operate it must be combined with a more concrete one: numerical equal subdivisions are composed either of persons who are somehow related—relatives, friends, neighbors—or of equals or unequals who supplement one another. Yet the numerical identity constitutes the formal principle of classification, even though it never decides *alone*. But it always plays its role, which may be very important, or may be almost negligible.

The Isolated Individual and the Dyad

OUR STATEMENTS up to this point concerned social formations which depend on the number of their component elements. But our insight was incapable of formulating this dependence in a way which would have allowed us to derive sociological consequences from certain specific numbers. This is not impossible, however, if we content ourselves with sufficiently simple structures. If we begin with the lower limit of the numerical series, there appear arithmetically definite magnitudes as the unequivocal presuppositions of characteristic sociological formations.

THE ISOLATED INDIVIDUAL

The numerically simplest structures which can still be designated as social interactions occur between two elements. Nevertheless, there is an externally even simpler phenomenon that belongs among sociological categories, however paradoxical and in fact contradictory this may seem —namely, the isolated individual. As a matter of fact, however, the processes that shape elements in the *dual* are often simpler than those required for the sociological characterization of the *singular*. For this, two phenomena are above all relevant here: isolation and freedom. The mere fact that an individual does not interact with others is, of course, not a sociological fact, but neither does it express the whole idea of isolation. For, isolation, in so far as it is important to the individual, refers by no means only to the absence of society. On the contrary, the idea involves the somehow imagined, but then rejected, existence of society. Isolation attains its unequivocal, positive significance only as society's effect at a distance—whether as lingering-on of past relations, as anticipation of future contacts, as nostalgia, or as an intentional turning away from society. The isolated man does not suggest a being that has been the only inhabitant of the globe from the beginning. For his condition, too, is determined by sociation, even though negatively. The whole joy and the whole bitterness of isolation are only different reactions to socially experienced influences. Isolation is interaction between two parties, one of which leaves, after exerting certain influences. The isolated individual is isolated only in reality, however; for ideally, in the mind of the other party, he continues to live and act.

A well-known psychological fact is very relevant here. The feeling of isolation is rarely as decisive and intense when one actually finds oneself physically alone, as when one is a stranger, without relations, among many physically close persons, at a "party," on a train, or in the traffic of a large city. The question whether a group favors or even permits such loneliness in its midst is an essential trait of the group structure itself. Close and intimate communities often allow no such intercellular vacuums. When we speak of anti-social phenomena like wretched persons, criminals, prostitutes, suicides, etc., we may refer to them as a social deficit that is produced in a certain proportion to social conditions. In a similar way, a given quantity and quality of social life creates a certain number of temporarily or chronically lonely existences, although they cannot as easily be ascertained by statistics as can these others.

ISOLATION

Isolation thus is a relation which is lodged within an individual but which exists between him and a certain group or group life in general. But it is sociologically significant in still another way: it may also be an interruption or periodic occurrence in a given relationship between two or more persons. As such, it is especially important in those relations whose very nature is the denial of isolation. This applies, above all, to monogamous marriage. The structure of a particular marriage, of course, may not even involve the finest and most intimate nuances of the mates. But where it does, there is an essential difference between the case in which they have preserved the joy of individual isolation in spite of the perfect happiness of their life in common, and the case in which the relation is never interrupted by devotion to solitude. The second case may have various reasons. Habituation to the life in common may have deprived isolation of its attractiveness; or insufficient certainty of love may make interruption by solitude feared as unfaithfulness or, what is worse, as a danger to faithfulness. At any rate, it is clear that isolation is not limited to the individual and is not the mere negation of association. It also has a positive sociological significance. As a conscious feeling on the part of the individual, it represents a very specific relation to society. And furthermore, its occurrence changes the nature of both large and very intimate groups, whereby it may be the cause as well as the effect of this change.

THE DYAD

We see that such phenomena as isolation and freedom actually exist as forms of sociological relations, although they often do so only by means of complex and indirect connections. In view of this fact, the simplest sociological formation, methodologically speaking, remains that which operates between two elements. It contains the scheme, germ, and material of innumerable more complex forms. Its sociological significance, however, by no means rests on its extensions and multiplications only. It itself is a sociation. Not only are many general forms of sociation realized in it in a very pure and characteristic fashion; what is more, the limitation to two members is a condition under which alone several forms of relationship exist. Their typically sociological nature is suggested by two facts. One is that the greatest variation of individualities and unifying motives does not alter the identity of these forms. The other is that occasionally these forms exist as much between two groups—families, states, and organizations of various kinds—as between two individuals.

Everyday experiences show the specific character that a relationship attains by the fact that only two elements participate in it. A common fate or enterprise, an agreement or secret between two persons, ties each of them in a very different manner than if even only three have a part in it. This is perhaps most characteristic of the secret. General experience seems to indicate that this minimum of two, with which the secret ceases to be the property of the one individual, is at the same time the maximum at which its preservation is relatively secure. A secret religious-political society which was formed in the beginning of the nineteenth century in France and Italy, had different degrees among its members. The real secrets of the society were known only to the higher degrees; but a discussion of these secrets could take place only between any two members of the high degrees. The limit of two was felt to be so decisive that, where it could not be preserved in regard to knowledge, it was kept at least in regard to the verbalization of this knowledge. More generally speaking, the difference between the dyad [1] and larger groups consists in

1 Never Simmel's term, but shorter and more convenient than his, which here, for instance, is "*Zweierverbindung*" (union of two).—Tr.

the fact that the dyad has a different relation to each of its two elements than have larger groups to *their* members. Although, for the outsider, the group consisting of two may function as an autonomous, super-individual unit, it usually does not do so for its participants. Rather, each of the two feels himself confronted only by the other, not by a collectivity above him. The social structure here rests immediately on the one and on the other of the two, and the secession of either would destroy the whole. The dyad, therefore, does not attain that super-personal life which the individual feels to be independent of himself. As soon, however, as there is a sociation of three, a group continues to exist even in case one of the members drops out.

THE EXPANSION OF THE DYAD: THE TRIAD VS. THE DYAD

This peculiar closeness between two is most clearly revealed if the dyad is contrasted with the triad.[2] For among three elements, each one operates as an intermediary between the other two, exhibiting the twofold function of such an organ, which is to unite and to separate. Where three elements, A, B, C, constitute a group, there is, in addition to the direct relationship between A and B, for instance, their indirect one, which is derived from their common relation to C. The fact that two elements are each connected not only by a straight line—the shortest—but also by a broken line, as it were, is an enrichment from a formal-sociological standpoint. Points that cannot be contacted by the straight line are connected by the third element, which offers a different side to each of the other two, and yet fuses these different sides in the unity of its own personality. Discords between two parties which they themselves cannot remedy, are accommodated by the third or by absorption in a comprehensive whole.

Yet the indirect relation does not only strengthen the direct one. It may also disturb it. No matter how close a triad may be, there is always the occasion on which two of the three members regard the third as an intruder. The reason may be the mere fact that he shares in certain moods which can unfold in all their intensity and tenderness only when two can meet without distraction: the sensitive union of two is always irritated by the spectator. It may also be noted how extraordinarily difficult and rare it is for three people to attain a really uniform mood—when visiting a museum, for instance, or looking at a landscape—and how much more easily such a mood emerges between two. A and B may stress and harmoniously feel their *m*, because the *n* which A does not share with B, and the *x* which B does not share with A, are at once spontaneously conceded to be individual prerogatives located, as it were, on another plane. If, however, C

2 Again not Simmel's term, but again more convenient than "*Verbindung zu dreien*" (association of three) and the like.—Tr.

joins the company, who shares *n* with A and *x* with B, the result is that (even under this scheme, which is the one most favorable to the unity of the whole) harmony of feeling is made completely impossible. Two may actually be *one* party, or may stand entirely beyond any question of party. But it is usual for just such finely tuned combinations of three at once to result in three parties of two persons each, and thus to destroy the unequivocal character of the relations between each two of them.

The sociological structure of the dyad is characterized by two phenomena that are absent from it. One is the intensification of relation by a third element, or by a social framework that transcends both members of the dyad. The other is any disturbance and distraction of pure and immediate reciprocity. In some cases it is precisely this absence which makes the dyadic relationship more intensive and strong. For, many otherwise undeveloped, unifying forces that derive from more remote psychical reservoirs come to life in the feeling of exclusive dependence upon one another and of hopelessness that cohesion might come from anywhere but immediate interaction. Likewise, they carefully avoid many disturbances and dangers into which confidence in a third party and in the triad itself might lead the two. This intimacy, which is the tendency of relations between two persons, is the reason why the dyad constitutes the chief seat of jealousy.

Primary Groups

CHARLES H. COOLEY

BY PRIMARY groups I mean those characterized by intimate face-to-face association and cooperation. They are primary in several senses, but chiefly in that they are fundamental in forming the social nature and ideals of the individual. The result of intimate association, psychologically, is a certain fusion of individualities in a common whole, so that one's very self, for many purposes at least, is the common life and purpose of the group. Perhaps the simplest way of describing this wholeness is by saying that it is a "we"; it involves the sort of sympathy and mutual identification for which "we" is the natural expression. One lives in the feeling of the whole and finds the chief aims of his will in that feeling.

It is not to be supposed that the unity of the primary group is one of mere harmony and love. It is always a differentiated and usually a competitive unity, admitting of self-assertion and various appropriative passions; but these passions are socialized by sympathy, and come, or tend to come, under the discipline of a common spirit. The individual will be ambitious, but the chief object of his ambition will be some desired place in the thought of the others, and he will feel allegiance to common standards of service and fair play. So the boy will dispute with his fellows a place on the team, but above such disputes will place the common glory of his class and school.

The most important spheres of this intimate association and cooperation—though by no means the only ones—are the family, the play-group of children, and the neighborhood or community group of elders. These are practically universal, belonging to all times and all stages of development; and are accordingly a chief basis of what is universal in human nature and human ideals. The best comparative studies of the family, such as those of Westermarck (7) or Howard (5), show it to us as not only a universal institution, but as more alike the world over than the exaggeration of exceptional customs by an earlier school had led us to suppose. Nor can anyone doubt the general prevalence of play-groups among children or of informal assemblies of various kinds among their elders. Such association is clearly the nursery of human nature in the world about us, and there is no apparent reason to suppose that the case has anywhere or at any time been essentially different.

As regards play, I might, were it not a matter of common observation, multiply illustrations of the universality and spontaneity of the group discussion and cooperation to which it gives rise. The general fact is that children, especially boys after about their twelfth year, live in fellowships in which their sympathy, ambition and honor are engaged even more, often, than they are in the family. Most of us can recall examples of the endurance by boys of injustice and even cruelty, rather than appeal from their fellows to parents or teachers—as, for instance, in the hazing so prevalent at schools, and so difficult, for this very reason, to repress. And how elaborate the discussion, how cogent the public opinion, how hot the ambitions in these fellowships.

Nor is this facility of juvenile association, as is sometimes supposed, a trait peculiar to English and American boys; since experience among our immigrant population seems to show that the offspring of the more restrictive civilizations of the continent of Europe form self-governing play-groups with almost equal readiness. Thus Miss Jane Addams, after pointing out that the "gang" is almost universal, speaks of the interminable discussion which every detail of the gang's activity receives, remarking that "in these social folk-motes, so to speak, the young citizen learns to act upon his own determination." (1, p. 177)

Of the neighborhood group it may be said, in general, that from the time men formed permanent settlements upon the land, down, at least, to the rise of modern industrial cities, it has played a main part in the primary, heart-to-heart life of the people. Among our Teutonic forefathers the village community was apparently the chief sphere of sympathy and mutual aid for the commons all through the "dark" and middle ages, and for many purposes it remains so in rural districts at the present day. In some countries we still find it with all its ancient vitality, notably in Russia, where the mir, or self-governing village group, is the main theatre of life, along with the family, for perhaps fifty millions of peasants.

In our own life the intimacy of the neighborhood has been broken up by the growth of an intricate mesh of wider contacts which leaves us strangers to people who live in the same house. And even in the country the same principle is at work, though less obviously, diminishing our economic and spiritual community with our neighbors. How far this change is a healthy development, and how far a disease, is perhaps still uncertain.

Besides these almost universal kinds of primary association, there are many others whose form depends upon the particular state of civilization; the only essential thing, as I have said, being a certain intimacy and fusion of personalities. In our own society, being little bound by place, people easily form clubs, fraternal societies and the like, based on congeniality, which may give rise to real intimacy. Many such relations are formed at school and college, and among men and women brought together in the first instance by their occupations—as workmen in the same trade, or the like. Where there is a little common interest and activity, kindness grows like weeds by the roadside.

But the fact that the family and neighborhood groups are ascendant in the open and plastic time of childhood makes them even now incomparably more influential than all the rest.

Primary groups are primary in the sense that they give the individual his earliest and completest experience of social unity, and also in the sense that they do not change in the same degree as more elaborate relations, but form a comparatively permanenent source out of which the latter are ever springing. Of course they are not independent of the larger society, but to some extent reflect its spirit; as the German family and the German school bear somewhat distinctly the print of German militarism. But this, after all, is like the tide setting back into creeks, and does not commonly go very far. Among the German, and still more among the Russian, peasantry are found habits of free cooperation and discussion almost uninfluenced by the character of the state; and it is a familiar and well-supported view that the village commune, self-governing as regards local affairs and habituated to discussion, is a very widespread institution in settled communities, and the continuator of a similar autonomy previously existing in the clan. "It is man who makes monarchies and establishes republics, but the commune seems to come directly from the hand of God." (4, ch. 5)

In our own cities the crowded tenements and the general economic and social confusion have sorely wounded the family and the neighborhood, but it is remarkable, in view of these conditions, what vitality they show; and there is nothing upon which the conscience of the time is more determined than upon restoring them to health.

These groups, then, are springs of life, not only for the individual but for social institutions. They are only in part moulded by special traditions, and, in larger degree, express a universal nature. The religion or government of other civilizations may seem alien to us, but the children or the family group wear the common life, and with them we can always make ourselves at home.

By human nature, I suppose, we may understand those sentiments and impulses that are human in being superior to those of lower animals, and also in the sense that they belong to mankind at large, and not to any particular race or time. It means, particularly, sympathy and the innumerable sentiments into which sympathy enters, such as love, resentment, ambition, vanity, hero-worship, and the feeling of social right and wrong.[1]

Human nature in this sense is justly regarded as a comparatively permanent element in society. Always and everywhere men seek honor and dread ridicule, defer to public opinion, cherish their goods and their children, and admire courage, generosity, and success. It is always safe to assume that people are and have been human.

It is true, no doubt, that there are differences of race capacity, so great that a large part of mankind are possibly incapable of any high kind of social organization. But these differences, like those among individuals of the same race, are subtle, depending upon some obscure intellectual deficiency, some want of vigor, or slackness of moral fiber, and do not involve unlikeness in the generic impulses of human nature. In these all races are very much alike. The more insight one gets into the life of savages, even those that are reckoned the lowest, the more human, the more like ourselves, they appear. Take for instance the natives of Central Australia, as described by Spencer and Gillen (6), tribes having no definite government or worship and scarcely able to count to five.[2] They are generous to one another, emulous of virtue as they understand it, kind to their children and to the aged, and by no means harsh to women. Their faces as shown in the photographs are wholly human and many of them attractive.

1 These matters are expounded at some length in Cooley (2).
2 Compare also Darwin's views. (3, ch. 7)

And when we come to a comparison between different stages in the development of the same race, between ourselves, for instance, and the Teutonic tribes of the time of Cæsar, the difference is neither in human nature nor in capacity, but in organization, in the range and complexity of relations, in the diverse expression of powers and passions essentially much the same.

There is no better proof of this generic likeness of human nature than in the ease and joy with which the modern man makes himself at home in literature depicting the most remote and varied phases of life—in Homer, in the Nibelung tales, in the Hebrew Scriptures, in the legends of the American Indians, in stories of frontier life, of soldiers and sailors, of criminals and tramps, and so on. The more penetratingly any phase of human life is studied the more an essential likeness to ourselves is revealed.

To return to primary groups: the view here maintained is that human nature is not something existing separately in the individual, but a *group-nature or primary phase of society*, a relatively simple and general condition of the social mind. It is something more, on the one hand, than the mere instinct that is born in us—though that enters into it—and something less, on the other, than the more elaborate development of ideas and sentiments that makes up institutions. It is the nature which is developed and expressed in those simple, face-to-face groups that are somewhat alike in all societies; groups of the family, the playground, and the neighborhood. In the essential similarity of these is to be found the basis, in experience, for similar ideas and sentiments in the human mind. In these, everywhere, human nature comes into existence. Man does not have it at birth; he cannot acquire it except through fellowship, and it decays in isolation.

If this view does not recommend itself to common sense I do not know that elaboration will be of much avail. It simply means the application at this point of the idea that society and individuals are inseparable phases of a common whole, so that wherever we find an individual fact we may look for a social fact to go with it. If there is a universal nature in persons there must be something universal in association to correspond to it.

What else can human nature be than a trait of primary groups? Surely not an attribute of the separate individual—supposing there were any such thing—since its typical characteristics, such as affection, ambition, vanity, and resentment, are inconceivable apart from society. If it belongs, then, to man in association, what kind or degree of association is required to develop it? Evidently nothing elaborate, because elaborate phases of society are transient and diverse, while human nature is comparatively stable and universal. In short the family and neighborhood life is essential to its genesis and nothing more is.

Here as everywhere in the study of society we must learn to see mankind in psychical wholes, rather than in artificial separation. We must see and feel the communal life of family and local groups as immediate facts, not as combinations of something else. And perhaps we shall do this best by recalling our own experience and extending it through sympathetic observation. What, in our life, is the family and the fellowship; what do we know of the we-feeling? Thought of this kind may help us to get a concrete perception of that primary group-nature of which everything social is the outgrowth.

REFERENCES

1. Addams, Jane. *Newer ideals of peace.*
2. Cooley, C. H. *Human nature and the social order.*
3. Darwin, C. *Descent of man.*
4. De Tocqueville, A. *Democracy in America.* Vol. 1.
5. Howard. *A history of matrimonial institutions.*
6. Spencer, & Gillen. *The native tribes of Central Australia.*
7. Westermarck. *The history of human marriage.*

The Social Foundations and Functions of Thought and Communication

GEORGE H. MEAD

MEAD'S *theoretical conceptualization in* Mind, Self and Society *is today one of the landmarks of social psychology. Here we have reproduced a small section on communication and social organization.*

THE PRINCIPLE which I have suggested as basic to human social organization is that of communication involving participation in the other. This requires the appearance of the other in the self, the identification of the other with the self, the reaching of self-consciousness through the other. This participation is made possible through the type of communication which the human animal is able to carry out—a type of communication distinguished from that which takes place among other forms which have not this principle in their societies. I discussed the sentinel, so-called, that may be said to communicate his discovery of the danger to the other members, as the clucking of the hen may be said to communicate to the chick. There are conditions under which the gesture of one form serves to place the other forms in the proper attitude toward external conditions. In one sense we may say the one form communicates with the other, but the difference between that and self-conscious communication is evident. One form does not know that communication is taking place with the other. We get illustrations of that in what we term mob-consciousness, the attitude which an audience will take when under the influence of a great speaker. One is influenced by the attitudes of those about him, which are reflected back into the different members of the audience so that they come to respond as a whole. One feels the general attitude of the whole audience. There is then communication in a real sense, that is, one form communicates to the other an attitude which the other assumes toward a certain part of the environment that is of importance to them both. That level of communication is found in forms of society which are of lower type than the social organization of the human group.

In the human group, on the other hand, there is not only this kind of communication but also that in which the person who uses this gesture and so communicates assumes the attitude of the other individual as well as calling it out in the other. He himself is in the role of the other person whom he is so exciting and influencing. It is through taking this role of the other that he is able to come back on himself and so direct his own process of communication. This taking the role of the other, an expression I have so often used, is not simply of passing importance. It is not something that just happens as an incidental result of the gesture, but it is of importance in the development of cooperative activity. The immediate effect of such role-taking lies in the control which the individual is able to exercise over his own response.[1] The control of the action of the individual

1 From the standpoint of social evolution, it is this bringing of any given social act, or of the total social process in which that act is a constituent, directly and as an organized whole into the experience of each of the individual organisms implicated in that act, with reference to which he may consequently regulate and govern his individual conduct, that constitutes the peculiar value and significance of self-consciousness in these individual organisms.

We have seen that the process or activity of thinking is a conversation carried on by the individual between himself and the generalized other; and that the general form and subject matter of this conversation is given and determined by the appearance in experience of some sort of problem to be solved. Human intelligence, which expresses itself in thought, is recognized to have this character of facing and dealing with any problem of environmental adjustment which confronts an organism possessing it. And thus, as we have also seen, the essential characteristic of intelligent behavior is delayed responses—a halt in behavior while thinking is going on; this delayed response in a cooperative process can take place in the conduct of the individual himself if he can take the role of the other. It is this control of the response of the individual himself through taking the role of the other that leads to the value of this type of communication from the point of view of the organization of the conduct in the group. It carries the process of cooperative activity farther than it can be carried in the herd as such, or in the insect society.

And thus it is that social control, as operating in terms of self-criticism, exerts itself so intimately and extensively over individual behavior or conduct, serving to integrate the individual and his actions with reference to the organized social process of experience and behavior in which he is implicated. The physiological mechanism of the human individual's central nervous system makes it possible for him to take the attitudes of other individuals, and the attitudes of the organized social group of which he and they are members, toward himself, in terms of his integrated social relations to them and to the group as a whole; so that the general social process of experience and behavior which the group is carrying on is directly presented to him in his own experience, and so that he is thereby able to govern and direct his conduct consciously and critically, with reference to his relations both to the social group as a whole and to its other individual members, in terms of this social process. Thus he becomes not only self-conscious but also self-critical; and thus, through self-criticism, social control over individual behavior or conduct operates by virtue of the social origin and basis of such criticism. That is to say, self-criticism is essentially social criticism, and behavior controlled by self-criticism is essentially behavior controlled socially.[2] Hence social control, so far from tending to crush out the human individual or to obliterate his self-conscious individuality, is, on the contrary, actually constitutive of and inextricably associated with that individuality; for the individual is what he is, as a conscious and individual personality, just in as far as he is a member of society, involved in the social process of experience and activity, and thereby socially controlled in his conduct.

The very organization of the self-conscious community is dependent upon individuals taking the attitude of the other individuals. The development of this process, as I have indicated, is dependent upon getting the at-

---

and the thinking for the purposes of which it is delayed (including the final selection, as the result of the thinking, of the best or most expedient among the several responses possible in the given environmental situation) being made possible physiologically through the mechanism of the central nervous system, and socially through the mechanism of language.

2 Freud's conception of the psychological "censor" represents a partial recognition of this operation of social control in terms of self-criticism, a recognition, namely, of its operation with reference to sexual experience and conduct. But this same sort of censorship or criticism of himself by the individual is reflected also in all other aspects of his social experience, behavior, and relations—a fact which follows naturally and inevitably from our social theory of the self.

titude of the group as distinct from that of a separate individual–getting what I have termed a "generalized other." I have illustrated this by the ball game, in which the attitudes of a set of individuals are involved in a cooperative response in which the different roles involve each other. In so far as a man takes the attitude of one individual in the group, he must take it in its relationship to the action of the other members of the group; and if he is fully to adjust himself, he would have to take the attitudes of all involved in the process. The degree, of course, to which he can do that is restrained by his capacity, but still in all intelligent processes we are able sufficiently to take the roles of those involved in the activity to make our own action intelligent. The degree to which the life of the whole community can get into the self-conscious life of the separate individuals varies enormously. History is largely occupied in tracing out the development which could not have been present in the actual experience of the members of the community at the time the historian is writing about. Such an account explains the importance of history. One can look back over that which took place, and bring out changes, forces, and interests which nobody at the time was conscious of. We have to wait for the historian to give the picture because the actual process was one which transcended the experience of the separate individuals.

Occasionally a person arises who is able to take in more than others of an act in process, who can put himself into relation with whole groups in the community whose attitudes have not entered into the lives of the others in the community. He becomes a leader. Classes under a feudal order may be so separate from each other that, while they can act in certain traditional circumstances, they cannot understand each other; and then there may arise an individual who is capable of entering into the attitudes of the other members of the group. Figures of that sort become of enormous importance because they make possible communication between groups otherwise completely separated from each other. The sort of capacity we speak of is in politics the attitude of the statesman who is able to enter into the attitudes of the group and to mediate between them by making his own experience universal, so that others can enter into this form of communication through him.

CHAPTER 2

EARLY RESEARCH

A Preliminary Study of the Psychology and Pedagogy of Leadership

LEWIS M. TERMAN

THE section of Terman's study presented below represents one of the earliest systematic experimental and observational researches reported in the literature of this country. The focus on suggestability, deriving directly from the work of Binet, was expanded in this study. Readers will note that the design of experiment and sophistication of interpretation are "modern."

LEADERSHIP AMONG CHILDREN

Experimental

THE FOLLOWING experimental study was made. It is in part a repetition of some work done by Binet (1, p. 330 ff.). It seemed, however, that the study should embrace a much larger number of pupils [1]

ABRIDGED from the article of the same title in *Pedagogical Seminary*, 1904, II, 413–451. Reprinted by permission of the author and publisher.

1 Binet used only 24.

and should also be made more intensive. That is, facts concerning the pupils should be gained from other sources than the tests.

One hundred pupils of the Bloomington, Indiana, public schools acted as subjects. They were distributed as follows:

Grade 2,	12 boys	and	12 girls		
" 4,	12 "	"	12 "		
" 6,	8 "	"	12 "		
" 8,	8 "	"	8 "		

In addition, 8 boys and 8 girls, in the colored school, ranging from the 5th to the 8th grade, were tested separately.

The general aim was to discover those pupils who might be termed "leaders" of their fellows, and to ascertain the qualities whereby they held this ascendency. It is evident that without long personal acquaintance with each pupil, and without opportunity for long and careful observations of their actions during work and play, the outcome of the study must be meager enough. The results are not claimed to have a high degree of absolute value.

The tests were as follows: on a heavy cardboard about 16 x 24 inches were fastened pictures and objects, to the number of ten. The pupils were withdrawn, four at a time, to an unoccupied and quiet room. To throw them off their guard they were told that they were to engage in a memory test. It was further explained that the cardboard would be turned so that they could view for ten seconds the objects and pictures pasted on the other side. After the removal of the cardboard from sight they were to answer a number of questions concerning what they had seen. They were given to understand that we would record the reply of each pupil and the order in which it was given. They were therefore urged to reply both quickly and correctly. The answers were given with loud voice. The instructions were always repeated till they were clearly understood.

Binet used only three pupils in each group. On consideration, it seemed best to have more. Groups of five were first tried but the order of the replies being too difficult to get, the number was reluctantly reduced to four. Binet also chose one member of each group to act as chairman of that group, allowing him to read the questions, to record the answers, and at the same time to act as subject himself. To say nothing of the relative disadvantage thus thrown on such pupil, it appeared that even so slight an exhibition of preference on the part of the experimenter would likely affect the group spirit. Accordingly all were allowed to stand on equal footing, either myself or an assistant asking the questions while the other kept the records. The girls and the boys were tested separately. Moreover, except in the colored school, the pupils of any group were chosen from a single grade.

Twenty-three questions were asked concerning the objects and pictures, 11 of which were catch questions; that is, they asked about things which were not on the cardboard. These were intended to serve as a test of the pupils' suggestibility. It was found somewhat difficult to hit upon the right sort of catch questions and to locate them properly in the series. Two extremes were to be avoided. The traps must not be too glaring, else the suspicions of the subject would be aroused. Neither must they be so easily led up to that none would escape them. Usually they were separated by fair questions, and the more obvious ones were placed toward the latter part of the list, since we hoped by that time to have won the confidence of the pupils.

When all the 100 subjects had been thus tested in groups of 4, a second series was begun in an exactly analogous way, with a new set of objects on the cardboard and a new set of 23 questions, 9 of which were catches. Eighty of the former 100 pupils participated. For this series of experiments the former groups were broken up and new ones formed. In the latter, the pupils were intentionally so chosen that each group would contain at least one pupil who had shown himself a leader, and one who had appeared to be an automaton in the previous tests. It could thus be determined whether the rank of a pupil in any group of the first series had wholly a relative, or to some extent an absolute meaning.

In elaborating the results the following points were noted for each pupil:

1. The number of times his reply was first, second, third, or fourth.
2. Originality.
3. The number of times each pupil of a group imitated each of the others.
4. Total number of imitations made by each.
5. Total number of times each pupil was imitated, by all the others.
6. Suggestibility, as measured by the number of times the subject fell into the trap.

The arbitrary use of some of the above terms must be explained. "Originality" means that the answer could not have been influenced by the answer of any other pupil. This does not, however, preclude its being suggested by a trap question. The "originality" can be shown in two ways: First, by answering before all the others; second, by giving an answer which, though not first, differed from the preceding answers in such a way that it could not have been influenced by them. Here, it must be acknowledged, there was often room for doubt, since it was not always possible to calculate just how far contrary suggestion was at work. "Suggestibility" was computed in per cent. If the pupil fell into all the traps his "suggestibility" was reckoned 100%. If into 4 out of a total of 8, 50%, etc. The other items will be made clear by the following illustration: Suppose that in answer to a question the same reply was given by all, A, B, C, and

D, in a group. If A answers first, he is "original." B answers second, and since his answer is the same as A's, he is credited with one "imitation." C answers third and therefore "imitates" A and B once each. D answers fourth and therefore "imitates" A, B, and C once each. That is, A makes no "imitation," B makes one, C makes two, and D makes three. A was "imitated" three times, B twice, and C once.

As expected, certain of the pupils answered first nearly always, while others were generally last and were content to repeat exactly or with slight variation the answer of another. For example, in one group:

	FIRST	SECOND	THIRD	FOURTH
A answered	1	4	8	10
C "	9	6	5	2

It soon became evident that not always could those who answered first be called "leaders." Fifteen times it occurred that the group rank of pupils in quickness and in number of times "imitated" differed radically, *i.e.*, by as much as two places. Here, we have an unmistakable exhibition of personal preference. Those who have not the initiative for framing an answer of their own, will prefer to repeat the answer of one pupil rather than that of another. The first reply is a stimulus which always tends to result in an activity of the other pupils suggested by it or imitative of it, but in the above fifteen cases the tendency was generally overcome by some inhibition. It likewise happened several times that the quickest were not the most "original." With twelve pupils there was a wide divergence between the group rank in "originality," and that in number of times "imitated." Another, and perhaps more significant result was the fact that low "originality" often accompanied low "suggestibility," and vice versa in fact the average "suggestibility" of the *leaders* was slightly greater than that of the *automatons*, the percentage being 62 and 59 respectively. Their comparative "originality," however, was 13.4 and 5.6, out of a total of 23 questions answered. This fact may have been due to the intense desire of the leaders to answer first, though the subjects were repeatedly reminded that it was as important to answer correctly as to answer quickly.

A greater number than expected, namely, 19 out of 80, obtained in the second series of tests a radically different rank from what they had gained in the first series. Of 22 leaders in the second series, 12 had been leaders in the first series, and five had occupied very low rank. Out of 32 automatons in the second series, 18 had been so in the first series, and 7 had occupied very high rank.

The following table shows the grade and sex differences for "originality." Each number represents the number of original answers out of the total set of 23.

GRADE	2	4	6	8	COLORED	AVERAGE FOR EACH SEX	
boys	8.50	8.33	9.25	10.12	9.50	9.14	Series I
girls	7.16	6.91	8.00	10.62	9.62	8.50	
boys	9.85	7.25	8.00	10.00	7.12	8.44	Series II
girls	6.37	5.87	8.00	9.62	8.87	7.75	
Average for each grade	7.97	7.09	8.31	10.09	8.78	8.45	

The following table shows the percentage of "suggestibility."

GRADE	2	4	6	8	COLORED	AVERAGE FOR EACH SEX	
boys	50	77	77	45	73	64	Series I
girls	66	76	77	52	77	69	
boys	72	76	91	45	78	72	Series II
girls	86	97	90	55	61	78	
Average for each grade	68.5	81.5	83.7	49.2	72.2	71	

The second part of our task was to get further facts about the pupils that would throw light on the cases of leadership among them. This the teachers were kind enough to furnish by answering 22 questions in regard to each pupil. They are as follows:

1. Age? 2. Size, in relation to grade? 3. Dress? 4. Is dress gaudy? 5. Any physical peculiarity or deformity? 6. Health? 7. Are parents wealthy or otherwise prominent? 8. Is it an only child? 9. Quality of school work? 10. Notable for boldness or daring? 11. A leader in games or pranks? 12. If so, is it by forcing others or by natural attraction? 13. Liked or disliked by other pupils? 14. Why? 15. Fluent of speech in conversation? 16. Any dramatic qualities? 17. Looks? 18. Reads much or little? 19. Timid or forward? 20. High tempered or amiable? 21. Selfish or considerate? 22. Emotional or deliberate in temperament?

Questions like 2, 3, and 9 were graded on a scale of five. To illustrate, 1 = very large, 2 = large, 3 = average, 4 = small, 5 = very small. Questions like 16, 18, 19, and 20 were graded similarly on a scale of three. Some of the most important results are summed up in the following table.

	GRADE	2	4	6	8	COLORED	AVERAGE
Age in years	Leaders	7.67	10.43	13.20	14.75	14.00	12.01
	Automatons	7.40	10.17	12.60	14.80	14.60	11.91
Size, on scale of five	Leaders	2.16	2.62	2.33	3.20	2.00	2.46
	Automatons	3.11	3.00	2.80	3.00	3.00	2.98

	GRADE	2	4	6	8	COL-ORED	AVER-AGE
Dress, on scale of five	Leaders	2.50	3.28	1.83	1.80	2.50	2.38
	Automatons	2.70	3.25	2.40	2.00	2.60	2.59
Quality of work, scale of five	Leaders	2.40	2.14	2.50	2.20	3.00	2.41
	Automatons	2.50	3.50	2.60	3.00	2.60	2.84
Looks, scale of three	Leaders	2.25	1.62	1.50	1.20	2.00	1.72
	Automatons	2.11	2.12	2.20	1.75	2.20	2.09
Selfishness, scale of three	Leaders	2.20	1.56	2.00	1.20	2.25	1.84
	Automatons	2.00	2.00	2.00	2.25	2.00	2.05

Several of the questions do not furnish data to show anything clearly. To sum up the chief results, the pupils who were leaders in the tests are larger, better dressed, of more prominent parentage, brighter in their school work, more daring, more fluent of speech, better looking, greater readers, and less selfish than the automatons. It was found that a surprising number of times the leaders were graded on size, dress, and school work either as 5 or 1. To illustrate, in grade 4 the leaders are graded on school work as 1, 1, 5, 1, 1, 5, 1. The automatons of the same grade received the following ranks on the same question: 3, 4, 3, 3, 4, 3, 5, 3. This indicates that possibly there is a tendency for children to be influenced by what is unusual; that they are on the lookout for striking qualities of whatever sort; anything to get clear of tiresome mediocrity.

Finally, the same pupils, excepting those in grade 2, were allowed to answer the following questions:

What one of your schoolmates would you rather be like if you were not yourself? Why? Several other questions were asked calling for ideals, but the answers were so scattered that no well defined tendency could be made out. Above all it was desired to find out how much oftener, if any, those pupils stamped as leaders by the experiments would be chosen consciously as ideals by their mates, than would the automatons. The results show that they were chosen 4½ times as often. The fact is important as indicating the validity of the method of experimentation and the great importance of suggestion and imitation as elements in leadership.

Summary of Experimental Results

1. A large number maintain a well defined rank either as first or last in the groups.

2. The leaders in the tests were twice as often mentioned by the teachers as being leaders, and further were chosen 4½ times as often by their mates as ideals.

3. Suggestibility, as measured by these tests, rises from the second to the fourth grade and then falls rapidly in the succeeding grades. The

naïveté with which the smallest children gave correct answers to the catch questions was remarkable. It reminds one of the old story of the king who thought to appear in procession before his people in a magic garment, visible to all except the wicked, and whose nakedness was denounced only by a little child.

4. The pupils show marked choice in imitating the answers of others. Circumstances favor the quickest, but not always are these the most imitated.

5. The leaders have a high average suggestibility. This may indicate that there is some truth in the assertion, often made, that to be a leader it is more important to lead the way than to be right.

6. The group rank of many pupils in the second series was radically different from what it had been in the first. This does not seem to be due to a wide divergence between the average reaction time or "originality" of the second group as compared to the first. It is the group spirit as mirrored in the consciousness of each pupil. In one group a certain pupil *feels* himself inferior; he follows, therefore, the answers of the others. In another group the same pupil may *feel* himself superior, and be so regarded by the others. This recalls Emerson's words: "Who has more soul than I, masters me, though he should not raise his finger. . . . Who has less, I rule with like facility."

7. The leaders in the tests, according to the testimony of their teachers, are on the average larger, better dressed, of more prominent parentage, brighter, more noted for daring, more fluent of speech, better looking, greater readers, less emotional and less selfish than the automatons.

8. As regards the reasons given by the pupils for choosing certain of their schoolmates for ideals, intelligence increases in importance rapidly from the second to the eighth grade and goodness as rapidly falls.

9. According to the opinion of the teachers, such pupils are preferred most often for the following qualities, given in order of their importance: intelligence, congeniality, liveliness, and goodness.

10. The data were not suited to bring out race differences in the qualities of leadership.

REFERENCE

1. Binet, A. *La suggestibilité.*

The Influence of the Group upon Association and Thought

FLOYD H. ALLPORT

INTRODUCTION

IF SOCIAL psychology is to achieve the title of an independent science, it is high time that its many speculative theories and crude generalizations be subjected to experimental methods. The data of this science, it appears to the writer, may be for convenience subsumed under two heads, viz.: (1) the behavior of an individual in direct response to social stimulus, that is in response to some form of behavior in others, and, (2) behavior which is the response to a nonsocial stimulus, *e.g.*, a column of figures to be added, or a meal to be eaten, when such response is modified by the presence and actions of other persons. Responses to direct and incidental social stimuli are, in brief, the two classes of data for social psychology.

The following experiments bear upon certain problems of the second class of data mentioned. The method employed was to compare the mental processes (in this case association and thought) of the individual when alone with his reactions to similar and equivalent stimuli when a member of a "co-working or co-feeling" group. In this manner the part played by incidental or contributory social stimulation was determined.[1]

GENERAL METHOD

It was considered advisable to eliminate all incentives to rivalry which were not inherent in the very nature of the situation (*i.e.*, individuals working on similar tasks in one another's presence). The subjects were instructed not to regard their work as competitive; overt comparisons be-

FROM *Journal of Experimental Psychology*, 1920, 3, 159–182. Reprinted by permission of the author and the American Psychological Association, Inc.

1 A brief historical account of the study of the influence of the group upon the individual may be found in an article by Burnham (1).

tween individuals were also prohibited. The time given for the tests was constant, hence no one subject finished before the others. In this way rivalry, which is a distinct social problem and which should be studied separately, was reduced to its natural minimum. Each subject, however, was instructed to acquire the attitude of doing his best in both the group and the solitary work.

The subjects were arranged in groups, containing from 3 to 5 subjects each. The groups had no changes of personnel during a whole experiment. The subjects were upper classmen and graduate students in psychology at Harvard and Radcliffe Colleges. They were 26 in number, though not more than 15 were used in any single experiment. There were 24 men and 2 women. In age they ranged from 20 to 40 years, 26 being the average age.

In the group work the subjects were seated one on each side of a table 3 feet by 5 feet in dimensions. In groups of 5 two subjects sat at one of the longer sides. The same seats were retained by subjects throughout the course of an experiment. Care was taken to secure conditions, such as type of table, light, air, seating of the subjects, etc., in the rooms used for solitary work comparable to those conditions in the room where the subjects worked as a group.

The free chain associations which were to be written were started by a stimulus word, for example "building" or "laboratory," written at the top of a sheet of paper given to each subject. The same stimulus words were employed in the two conditions, *T* and *A*.[2] It was also emphasized in group work that the same stimulus word was given to all. It is not believed that the presence of the experimenter in the group work materially affected the results of the social influence.

In all experiments except the first constant intervals of time were given, in the group by spoken signal, and alone by buzzers placed in each room and tuned down to inobtrusive intensity. Control tests were given in the group, using the buzzer for signals in order to determine whether the buzzer itself played a part in the results. No difference was found in the average, between group tests given by the buzzer and those given by verbal signal. The writing materials (pen, pencil, etc.) used by each subject were kept as constant as possible throughout the experiment.

SUMMARY OF CONCLUSIONS

A. *The Influence of the Group upon Association*

I. QUANTITATIVE ASPECTS

1. The main result of the preceding experiments on association is the conclusion that the *presence of a co-working group is distinctly favorable*

2 *I.e.*, "Together" and "Alone."

to the speed of the process of free association. In various tests from 66 per cent to 93 per cent of the subjects show this beneficial influence of the group.

2. The beneficial group influence is *subject to variation according to the nature of the task.* In the more mechanical and motor requirements, such as writing *each word* associated, the group stimulus is more effective than in the more highly mental or more purely associational tasks such as writing only every *third* or *fourth* word.

3. There are *individual differences* in susceptibility to the influence of the group upon association. One type, who are nervous and excitable, may succumb to the distracting elements of the group activity and may show either no effect, or else a social decrement.

4. *In its temporal distribution* the beneficial effect of the group is greatest in the first part of the task and least toward the end of the task.

5. There is a tendency for the *slow individuals to be more favorably affected* in speed by the group co-activity than the more rapid workers. There are, however, certain striking exceptions.

6. *The variability in output* among the individuals varies generally with the social influence. Hence it is usually greatest in the group work. A striking exception to this occurs in the tests where rivalry is correlated with the social increment, and where only every third or fourth word is written. Here the variability is greatest in the solitary work. This result is in agreement with that of earlier investigators working on different processes.

7. There is suggestive but *not conclusive* evidence that the output of associations in a group where all the members are forming associations in the same category is greater than that in groups in which the members are divided in the trend of their associations between opposite or contrasted categories.

II. QUALITATIVE ASPECTS

8. A greater number of *personal associations* are *produced alone* than in the group.

9. In harmony with this fact is the tendency for subjects to produce *ideas suggested by their immediate surroundings* with *greater frequency in the group* than alone.

10. Less clear cut, but very probable, are the tendencies to produce a *greater number of "free rising" ideas in the group,* and to produce a greater number of words *suggested mainly by the initial stimulus word when working alone.*

III. FACTORS IN THE SOCIAL INFLUENCE

11. There are two opposing groups of factors in the influence of the social condition upon the association process. They are:

(1) Facilitating Factors:

(*a*) *Facilitation of movement* by perceptions or ideas of movements in others near us.

(*b*) *Rivalry* intrinsic in the bare social setting of a group working together. Rivalry is well correlated with the beneficial influence of the group in tests of a more mental sort (and less mechanical) such as writing every *fourth* word only. It is not so correlated when each word is written.

The beneficial effects of the group in experiments where the rivalry consciousness is closely correlated with this influence is less than in experiments where it is not so correlated, but where other factors—for example, motor facilitation—serve as the stimulus of the group.

(2) Impeding Factors: distraction, over-rivalry, emotions. Of the two groups, the facilitating is by far the more important in the total effect upon the work.

12. Beside the comparisons already indicated, we may note the general agreement of our work with that of earlier students in the *speed* improvement of mental operations, as shown by the quantity of the product, under conditions of working with others.

B. *The Influence of the Group upon the Thought Process*

13. In the highly controlled association of the thought process, as typified in written argument, more ideas are produced in the group than when working alone. Again we find an increased flow of thought owing to the social stimulus.

14. Among the ideas so produced, those of superior quality, however, are of relatively greater frequency in the solitary than in the group work. Ideas of a lower logical value are relatively more numerous in the group work.

15. More words are used in the arguments produced in the group than in those produced in solitude.

16. From the above facts, and also from the introspection of the subjects, we may conclude that the presence of the group influences the reasoner toward a more conversational and expansive form of expression. The more intense logical thinking of solitude gives way in the group to extensity of treatment.

17. These results appear to be related to the common observation that work requiring imagination or more concentrated and original thought is best performed in seclusion. There is also a connection suggested with the writer's experiments upon the social influence in attention and mental work. In that investigation, as well as in the present, the social influence was found to improve the quantity but not the quality of the mental performance.

REFERENCE

1. Burnham, W. H. The group as a stimulus to mental activity. *Science*, 1910, 31, 761–767.

Aggressive Behavior in a Small Social Group

ETHEL M. RIDDLE

RIDDLE'S *experiment with a group of six poker players is of great historical significance since it heralded the joining of several approaches of research. It was a combination of the group suggestibility experiment with psychometric measurement and introspective reports. We have reprinted the review given the research by Murphy, Murphy, and Newcomb since the original monograph is too long and detailed to be presented here.*

AN ELABORATE experimental approach to a highly competitive situation is Riddle's study of a series of poker games. Six college students participated. Each knew the others well, and within a short time all were accustomed to the situation of having their game in the laboratory. They agreed, furthermore, to various more or less disturbing or boring interruptions and distractions, such as the frequent recording of their feelings and attitudes, and the wearing of rubber stethograph tubes during the course of the experimental periods. They were, to be sure, paid for the time given to the experiment, but none showed any hesitation in betting his own money. The players were allowed to fix their own limits, a 5-cent ante and a 20-cent limit. This was higher than usual for most of them. By the time the experimenter was ready to take records, the players appear to have been able to lose themselves quite naturally in the game. For each draw, each player was required to fill out a "schedule A": "How anxious are you to beat each player?" (ratings from + 100 to − 100 for

FROM G. Murphy, Lois B. Murphy, & T. M. Newcomb, *Experimental social psychology*. New York: Harper & Bros., 1937. Reprinted by permission of the authors and publisher.

each of his antagonists). Schedule B asked, "Did you try to bluff anyone during this game?" and "Did anyone try to bluff you during this draw?"; and presented a scale for the emotional state ranging from + 100 (elated) to – 100 (gloomy). On schedule C was recorded the bodily state, from maximum excitement to maximum physical retardation.

A curious set of intercorrelations appears in which the three variables to be considered are: (1) the player's own hand; (2) the player's desire to win; (3) the player's own bet. The correlation between the first and third is + .62, and that between the first and second is + .53. Since the player's own hand can be only a cause and not a result of these other two factors, whereas the second and third factors may be causally related to each other, it becomes important to partial out the influence of one factor at a time in order to find the causal relations. When this is done, it turns out that the correlation between hand and bet falls to + .44, while that between hand and desire is + .09. The highest correlation of all, however, is between desire and bet, which is + .63. Riddle argues that the bet acts as a stimulus to desire rather than desire as a stimulus to bet.

A further problem in motivation appears in response to one's opponent's hand. By a similar technique Riddle shows that the opponent's bet correlates only + .05 with the player's own bet when the player's desire to win is partialed out. With this and much other statistical material, Riddle reaches the conclusion that the desire to win in this game situation is only to a slight extent aroused by the size of the player's own hand value. It is aroused more fully by the value of the opponent's hand. The influence of one's own hand is, of course, to increase one's own bet, and the effect of the opponent's hand is to inhibit one's bet. When, however, the balance has been struck and the bet made, this bet in turn duly determines the total strength of the desire to win. The method devised here seems entirely practicable in the study of even more complicated competitive situations.

A series of interesting individual differences appear among the six players. One, for example, has about the same desire to win over all of his opponents, whereas another's desire to win varies greatly with the particular opponent he is trying to beat at a given time. This leads to the question whether one player, who greatly stimulates the desire of other players to beat him, has any peculiar characteristics of his own which may explain the trend. He certainly has. A study of the number of times that a player bluffed and the number of times that his opponent knew he was bluffing shows that player A (the one whose bets aroused in other players such a desire to win) bluffed 31 times—far more than the number of times anyone else bluffed. Only seven times did the opponent against whom the bluff was aimed recognize that A was bluffing. Players B and C each tried only once to bluff during the whole experiment, and both were detected. On the other hand, the number of times a player suspected that he was being bluffed varied all the way from one to thirty. The number of times that this suspicion coincided with the actual attempt to bluff him was rather small, and only one of the six players seemed to be able to tell definitely when he was being bluffed.

It turns out that successful and unsuccessful efforts at bluffing are the very heart of the situation, and that precise quantitative analysis throws much light upon the causes of aggressive and defensive responses of the players. Correlations are worked out for size of bets, amount of bluffing, suspicion of being bluffed, amount won, etc., some of which are illuminating. The correlations between the average winning per draw and the tendency to be "bluffed against" is + .97. Whether a player wins or loses has, however, but little effect upon the opponent's judgment as to whether he is bluffing. The player who makes the highest bets, has the largest pile, and whose hands are running high, is, in general, thought by his opponents to bluff frequently. The player who is most successful in the game, who is most likely to win by good hands and a large pile, and who is most aggressive in his betting is the one against whom bluffs are most frequently directed. It turns out that the betters are not, in general, eager to win against those from whom they could most easily win; the weak player is not the one against whom the bluffs are directed. Quite contrary to the hedonistic interpretation, the goal here, even when measured in money terms, is very specific. It is not simply a desire to win money where it can be won most safely or in the largest amount, but rather, where an aggressive attitude and an exhibition of skill afford a direct challenge. On the other hand, the player who attempts to bluff most frequently is unlikely to be the one with the highest average desire to win, but rather the one whose desire varies most from game to game, and from opponent to opponent. The one who is really anxious to win seems to be definitely low in his willingness to risk money. The man "with the least adequate means of defense," whose pile and hands are low, is the one who most frequently thinks he is being bluffed.

The Gang

FREDERIC M. THRASHER

THRASHER'S The Gang *was one of the early systematic studies of small group informal organization. From this classic we have selected sections on size of gang, two and three boy gangs, and personality and role differentiation. Case materials, which are copiously presented in the text, are omitted here.*

The Size of the Gang

THE NECESSITIES of maintaining face-to-face relationships set definite limits to the magnitude to which the gang can grow. The size of Itschkie's group was determined by the number of boys readily able to meet together on the street or within the limited space of their hangout. The gang does not usually grow to such proportions as to be unwieldly in collective enterprises or to make intimate contacts and controls difficult.[1] Ordinarily, if all members are present, what is said by one of the group can be heard by all. Otherwise, common experience becomes more difficult and the group tends to split and form more than one gang. The number of "fringers" and hangers-on upon whom the gang can count for backing, however, may be larger, especially if it has developed a good athletic team.

Greater growth can be accomplished only through modifications of structure, such as those resulting from conventionalization. When a gang becomes conventionalized, assuming, for example, the form of a club, it may possibly grow to large proportions. The original gang, however, probably now becomes an "inner circle," remaining the active nucleus in

1 College fraternity policy, based on long years of experience in attempting to maintain intimate relationships and unity of purpose among its members, illustrates the necessity of controlling numbers. Thirty-five to forty members seems to be the maximum size for such a group if these conditions are to be maintained and communal life is to be carried on in the fraternity homes. If, for financial or other reasons, a fraternity grows to larger proportions, it is the custom to refer to its house satirically as a "hotel."

such cases. The additional members may develop their own cliques within the larger whole or maintain merely a more or less formal relationship to the organization. In many cases such a club is the result of the combination of two or more gangs.

Table 1 does not include the major portion of the gang clubs; these vary in number of members ordinarily from 20 or 25 to 75 or 100; only a few of the more prosperous clubs exceed 100 members. It will be seen

TABLE 1

Approximate Numbers of Members in 895 Gangs

NO. OF MEMBERS	NO. OF GANGS	PERCENTAGE OF TOTAL
From 3 to 5 (inclusive)	37	4.1
From 6 to 10	198	22.1
From 11 to 15	191	21.5
From 16 to 20	149	16.7
From 21 to 25	79	8.8
From 26 to 30	46	5.1
From 31 to 40	55	6.1
From 41 to 50	51	5.7
From 51 to 75	26	2.9
From 76 to 100	25	2.8
From 101 to 200	25	2.8
From 201 to 500	11	1.2
From 501 to 2,000	2	.2
Total gangs	895	100.0

that 806 of these gangs have memberships of 50 or under; these are largely of the non-conventionalized type. Most of the remaining 89 have memberships ranging from 51 to 2,000, though not all of them have been conventionalized.

The Two- and Three-Boy Relationship

What has been defined as a "two-boy gang" or an "intimacy" must not be overlooked in discussing the inner organization of the gang. In this type of relationship there is generally a subordination of one boy to the other. In one instance other members of the group expressed it in this way, "Jerry is running Alfred now." Hero-worship, open or tacit, plays an important part in such cases. Sometimes the abilities of one boy supplement those of the other.

In many of these cases one boy tends to become utterly enthralled by the other; and there grows up a devotion hardly to be excelled even in the cases of the most ardent lovers of opposite sexes.[2] While these in-

2 The intimacy in the gang provides a satisfaction for the boy's wish for response. One boy may fascinate another and the two be completely wrapped up in one another. While attachments such as these would probably be regarded as homosexual by the Freudians, they exist in most cases without definite sex impulses and are to be regarded as entirely normal and practically universal among boys.

timacies usually develop in pairs (the introduction of a third person many times making for complications and friction), yet it sometimes happens that the relationship may include three boys who cooperate in perfect congeniality.

It is relations of this sort, existing before the gang develops, that serve as primary structures when the group is first formed and that shape the growth of its future organization. The intimacy partly explains why many of the exploits of gang boys are carried out in pairs and trios. The boys often prefer to have a favored pal or two associated in an enterprise rather than bring in the whole gang.

The two- and three-boy relationship is often much more important to the individual boy than his relationship to the gang. In such cases a boy would doubtless forego the gang before he would give up his special pal or pair of pals. A series of such palships, one or two of which may be more highly prized than others, are characteristic of boys of the non-gang areas of the city and also of gangland boys who are not in gangs. In other words, under different conditions, the two- and three-boy relationship becomes a completely satisfactory substitute for the gang and the wish for recognition from a larger circle, if imperative, is gratified through membership in the family, the school, the club, and other groups and institutions to which the boy has access.

The "Organism" as a Whole

Each gang as a whole, and other types of social groups as well, may be conceived of as possessing an action pattern. Every person in the group performs his characteristic function with reference to others, or to put it another way, fills the individual niche that previous experience in the gang has determined for him. Lacking the group, personality in the sense here used would not exist. The action pattern of a group tends to become fixed and automatic in the habits of its members; it may persist long after the formal organization of the group has changed.

Yet the action pattern which characterizes each group can hardly be thought of as rigid and static; for it must be constantly changing to accommodate losses and additions of personnel, changes in its members due to growth and increasing experience, and other changes within and without the gang.

PERSONALITY AND THE ACTION PATTERN OF THE GANG

Every member of a gang tends to have a definite status within the group. Common enterprises require a division of labor. Successful conflict necessitates a certain amount of leadership, unreflective though it may be, and a consequent subordination and discipline of members. As the gang develops complex activities, the positions of individuals within the group are defined and social roles become more sharply differentiated. As a result of this process there arises a more or less efficient and harmonious organization of persons [3] to make possible a satisfactory execution of collective enterprises and to further the interests of the group as a whole. This is the action pattern of the gang.

The conflicts of the gang with outsiders and the execution of its other enterprises and activities result in a sort of social stratification in its membership. There are usually three, more or less well-defined, classes of members: the "inner circle," which includes the leader and his lieutenants; the rank and file, who constitute members of the gang in good standing; and the "fringers," who are more or less hangers-on and are not considered regular members.

The inner circle is usually composed of a constellation of especially intimate pals formed about the leader. The rank and file—the less enterprising and less capable—are subordinated to the inner circle, just as it, in turn, tends to be subordinated to the leader. Most gangs are not closed corporations, however, but have a certain group of hangers-on or associates—the fringers, who may be "kid followers" or admirers. They constitute a sort of nebulous ring, not to be counted on to go the full length in any exploit and likely to disappear entirely in case of trouble. Yet the gang usually tolerates them for their applause and their occasional usefulness. A gang in embryo sometimes forms in this fringe.

The Struggle for Status

Internally the gang may be viewed as a struggle for recognition.[4] It offers the underprivileged boy probably his best opportunity to acquire status and hence it plays an essential part in the development of his personality.

This struggle in the gang takes the form of both conflict and competition, which operate to locate each individual with reference to the others. As a result the gang becomes a constellation of personal interrelationships with the leader playing the central and guiding role. It may be considered as a "unity of interacting personalities"; but it may also be regarded as an accommodation of conflicting individualities more or less definitely subordinated and superordinated with reference to each other and the leader.

It is in these very roles, subordinate though they may be, that personality is developed. Any standing in the group is better than none, and there is always the possibility of improving one's status. Participation in gang

3 Like the family, the gang may be conceived of as a "unity of interacting personalities." See Burgess (1).

4 See Thomas (2, pp. 31–32).

activities means everything to the boy. It not only defines for him his position in the only society he is greatly concerned with, but it becomes the basis for his conception of himself. The gang boy might well say "I would rather be a fringer in the hang-out of the gang than to dwell in the swell joints of the dukes forever."

For this reason the gang boy's conception of his role is more vivid with reference to his gang than to other social groups. Since he lives largely in the present, he conceives of the part he is playing in life as being in the gang; his status in other groups is unimportant to him, for the gang is his social world. In striving to realize the role he hopes to take he may assume a tough pose, commit feats of daring or of vandalism, or become a criminal. Thus, his conception of his essential role as being in the gang helps to explain why the larger community finds difficulty in controlling him. If acquiring a court record, or being "put away" in an institution, gives him prestige in the gang, society is simply promoting his rise to power, rather than punishing or "reforming" him. Agencies which would attempt to redirect the boy delinquent must reach him through his vital social groups where an appeal can be made to his essential conception of himself.

The Process of Selection

There is a process of selection in the gang, as a result of the struggle for status, whereby the ultimate position of each individual is determined. The result of this process depends largely upon the individual differences—both native and acquired—which characterize the members of the group. Other things being equal, a big strong boy has a better chance than a "shrimp." Natural differences in physique are important and physical defects play a part. Natural and acquired aptitudes give certain individuals advantages. Traits of character, as well as physical differences, are significant; these include beliefs, sentiments, habits, special skills, and so on. If all members of the gang were exactly alike, status and personality could only be determined by chance differences in opportunity arising in the process of gang activity. In reality, both factors play a part.

That physical differences are important in determining status is indicated by the fact that the biggest boy or the strongest is often leader by virtue of that fact alone, for bulk usually means an advantage in fighting. Mere size, too, may enable a bully to gain control of the gang; his tenure as leader, however, is always uncertain.

Physical disabilities often help to determine status in the gang, as elsewhere, through the mechanism of compensation. The defect in such cases serves as a drive to some type of behavior whose excellence will make up for the lowered status which the boy feels himself likely to possess on account of his disability. Compensation arises, therefore, because of the discrepancy between his possible role and his conception of the role he feels he ought to play.

If a boy can compensate in some effective manner for a disability, it may not serve as an insurmountable barrier to leadership.

Fighting is one of the chief means of determining status in the gang; each member is usually rated on the basis of his fistic ability. In a fight to determine which of two contenders is the better, the gang usually guarantees fair play, equalizing the conditions as nearly as possible. In some gangs the best fighter is considered the leader; he can defend his title against all comers.

In addition to fighting, excelling in any other activity in which the gang engages is a method of gaining recognition. For most gangs this applies particularly in the field of athletic prowess, but it may apply equally to some form of daring or predatory activity. "Hardness" is frequently a means of getting prestige; usually the boy who has been arrested, has a court record, or has been put away to serve a sentence is looked upon with admiration.

Special Roles in the Gang

Besides leadership there are other social functions in the gang. Like leadership, these are also determined by individual qualities in the process of struggle and activity. They evolve as a result of group experience; they are determined by interaction in all of its complexities. The principal roles in the gang are sometimes distinguished from each other as being different types of leadership.[5]

If the imaginative boy does not have the qualities of geniality and physical force to give him pre-eminence, he may become the brains of the gang.

Like the jester of old, the "funny boy" is tolerated in spite of behavior that might otherwise be insulting. His irresponsibility is generally excused because of its humorous possibilities. This type of behavior is sometimes the result of an attempt to compensate for some trait—such as a high-pitched voice—which gives undesirable status in the gang.

A very undesirable status in the gang is that of a "sissy," a rating which may arise through effeminate traits, unwillingness to fight, or too much interest in books or other cultivated pursuits. It usually carries with it a girl's nickname. Ordinarily boys will go to any length to avoid such a role.

Another personality type which often emerges in the gang is the "show-off." He is the egotist, the braggart, the boaster, the bluffer, the "loud-mouth" of the group; and the other members usually discount him accordingly. He may resort to "loudness" to gain attention not otherwise

5 See Woods (3, pp. 115–116).

forthcoming, or, in his naïve conception of his role in the gang, he may simply be overestimating himself. His resulting status is certainly unforeseen by him and even unsuspected in certain cases.

Every gang usually has its "goat." He is a boy who is considered uncommonly "dumb"; he may be subnormal, as measured by psychological tests; and he can usually be depended upon to get caught if anybody does. Boys of this type are sometimes known as "goofy guys," if they combine some special peculiarity with their dumbness. Inexperienced boys are often used as "cats'-paws" in the exploits of the gang.

The nature, number, and variety of specialized roles, which in their interrelationships constitute the action pattern of the gang, must depend to a large extent upon the nature and complexity of the activities and enterprises undertaken. If the gang maintains a team, individual aptitudes play an important part in assigning places. Special abilities are useful in carrying out certain types of activities. The gang itself may become highly specialized (a functional type), as in the case of the development of some particular line of athletic sport or criminal pursuit. The more specialized the gang, the more highly differentiated is usually the division of labor among its members.

REFERENCES

1. Burgess, E. W. The family as a unity of interacting personalities. *Family*, 1926, 3-9.
2. Thomas, W. I. *The unadjusted girl.*
3. Woods. *The city wilderness.*

Test Room Studies in Employee Effectiveness

C. E. TURNER

THROUGH the courtesy of the Western Electric Company, a report is presented here upon the public health aspects of certain studies in the conduct of which the writer served as consultant. The investigations have been too extensive to be encompassed adequately in this

FROM *American Journal of Public Health*, 1933, 23, 577-584. Reprinted by permission of the author and publisher.

brief paper which will be limited to a description of this new type of industrial research and some of the major outcomes of the study.

The establishment of the test room study was the result of a 3-year investigation conducted by the company in cooperation with the National Research Council upon the relationship between illumination and the productivity of employees. A literal interpretation of the results would have suggested that poor illumination is desirable, for a comparison of two comparable groups of workers showed that those working with gradually reduced illumination had a higher output than those with ideal illumination. Such a conclusion would be obviously absurd.

What the investigation really showed was that the type of laboratory investigation which is possible in the exact sciences, where all but one factor can be controlled, is not possible in the study of human beings, and that other factors had entered the experiment which were more important than illumination. This suggested to G. A. Pennock, now Assistant Works Manager, the desirability of undertaking a study of employee effectiveness under test room conditions in which all of the factors affecting the physical and mental status of the worker could be observed with the greatest possible completeness. The company sought to learn those conditions under which people work best. We wished to study the human energy flowing into the product in order that we might deal with it more intelligently.

In April, 1927, 6 experienced female operators, chosen at random, were removed from the department in which they were working to a small test room in the corner of a regular shop. Their work was the assembly of telephone relays and involved putting together a coil, an armature, contact springs and insulators in a fixture, and securing the parts in position by means of four machine screws. The girls were invited to the office of the Superintendent in charge where the plan and objectives of the study were explained to them. Although shy at this first meeting, they readily consented to take part in the study. They were expressly cautioned to work at a comfortable pace and not to make a race out of the test.

The working equipment in the test room was like that in the regular department except that there was a hole in the bench at the right of each girl's position into which completed relays were dropped. The relay falls through a chute actuating a flapper gate. The opening of the gate closes an electrical circuit which controls a perforating device which in turn records the completion of the relay by punching a hole in a moving tape. This tape moves at the rate of ¼″ per minute and has space for a separate row of holes for each operator. The punched tape furnishes a complete output record for each girl for each instant of the day. The tape mechanism also carries a bank of 5 message registers giving a numerical record of the total number of relays completed by each operator.

As we began the test, our objectives were stated in the form of 6 questions:

1. Do employees actually get tired out?
2. Are rest pauses desirable?
3. Is a shorter working day desirable?
4. What is the attitude of employees toward their work and toward the company?
5. What is the effect of changing the type of working equipment?
6. Why does production fall off in the afternoon?

Fairly good answers have been secured to all of these questions except No. 5. New questions have constantly arisen and some of them have been satisfactorily answered.

Some description may well be given of the test room method as a means of research in industrial health and employee effectiveness. It is the observational method dealing simultaneously with many variables. Some factors can be controlled and made constant. One condition is changed at a time; but there are certain conditions which are not subject to experimental control. These must be watched carefully and interrelationships established. Too often scientists have been guilty of the *post hoc, ergo propter hoc* fallacy. They have changed one condition and regarded it as the cause of all subsequent events. Such factors as the physical or mental health or the attitude of the employee cannot, of course, be accurately measured quantitatively. Over long periods of time, however, many factors can be satisfactorily evaluated by means of proper statistical procedures.

Disregarding the problems of placement and working equipment, it has been our assumption that the effectiveness of an individual will vary with (a) his bodily status or physiological efficiency (health, skill, endurance); (b) his mental state (contentment and freedom from worry, fear, anger, hate, shame, or other morbid preoccupations); (c) his zest for work (determined by the enjoyment in performing the work, the feeling of justice in his treatment, and the desire for securing reward).

Certain specific changes having to do with the length of the working day or week, with the introduction of rest periods and with the sitting position of the operators have been made. These are described in Table 1.

At the beginning of the study, output records were kept for each girl in her regular department for 2 weeks without her knowledge. The girls were then moved to the test room where they worked for 5 weeks before any changes in working conditions were introduced. The intentional changes subsequently introduced have not by any means been the only ones studied. The following statement presents other differences which we have recognized between test room and shop conditions.

In the test room, the group piecework basis of payment paid each girl more nearly in proportion to her individual effort, since she was paid with a group of 6 instead of 100 or more. The girls in the test room assembled fewer different types of relays. The operators could read their exact output at any time from the recorder. The test room was not quieter; if anything, it was somewhat noisier than the regular department. New conditions of work provided an element of novelty. The girls realized that the experiment was receiving the attention of company officials, which meant that they were being noticed as individuals.

TABLE I

PERIOD NUMBER	PERIOD NAME	DURATION
1.	In Regular Department	2 weeks
2.	Introduction to Test Room	5 "
3.	Special Group Rate	8 "
4.	Two 5 Minute Rests	5 "
5.	Two 10 Minute Rests	4 "
6.	Six 5 Minute Rests	4 "
7.	15 Minute a.m. Lunch 10 Minute p.m. Rest	11 "
8.	Same as No. 7, but 4:30 stop	7 "
9.	Same as No. 7, but 4:00 stop	4 "
10.	Same as No. 7, (Check)	12 "
11.	Same as No. 7, but Sat. a.m. off	9 "
12.	Same as No. 3, (No Lunch or Rests)	12 "
13.	Same as No. 7, but operators furnish own lunch. Company furnishes beverage	31 "
14.	Same as No. 11	9 "
15.	Same as No. 13	31 "
16.	Same as No. 13, except operators change position	4 "
17.	Same as No. 16, except 4:15 stop and Sat. a.m. off	25 "
18.	Same as No. 17, except Friday p.m. off	15 "

Beginning with Period 7, rest periods have begun at 9:30 in the morning and 2:30 in the afternoon.

There has been a fundamental change in supervision. There was no group chief in the test room, but instead a "friendly observer" of the experiment. Discipline was secured through leadership and understanding. The girls were allowed to talk and to leave the bench whenever they liked; they were not compelled to pick up parts from the floor at the time they were dropped. An *esprit de corps* grew up within the group.

The girls were given physical examinations every 6 weeks. They objected to this at first but later each trip to the hospital became a "party."

Three types of records are kept in the test room in order that changes may be determined in (1) output, (2) the individual, (3) conditions of work.

1. *Changes in production* may be accurately measured and constitute one evidence of the effectiveness of the worker. By means of a conversion factor, all output data were expressed in terms of a single type of relay. From the

output records previously mentioned, we have determined for each operator (1) the daily output; (2) the average hourly output at different times of day, for different days of the week and for different periods of the study; (3) average weekly output; (4) the number of defective relays; (5) the amount of repair work done. During the first few periods of the study, 15-minute output records were computed in order to study variability or uniformity of performance.

2. Data concerning *changes in the health, the habits, or the attitudes* of the operators have been secured from (1) physical examinations, (2) the comments of operators, (3) attendance irregularities, (4) occasional series for blood pressure and pulse rate records, (5) vascular skin reaction readings, (6) records of the hours of sleep, (7) social case records, (8) intelligence and dexterity tests, (9) questionnaires to reflect attitude toward working conditions, (10) diet records over certain periods.

3. *Changes in condition of work* have been indicated above. Records have also been kept of the types of relays assembled, the temperature and humidity of the room and any differences in the quality or methods of handling raw materials.

FINDINGS

The first specific problem which the test room sought to study was the effect of rest pauses which were introduced in Period 4. We did learn much concerning rest pauses but soon found that there was a continually rising output in the test room which was in large measure at least independent of rest pauses. At the end of 4 years, the individual operators had increased their output from 40 to 62 per cent. The relationship of this increase to rest pauses is shown in Chart 1. It will be seen that output rose appreciably in Period 3 before rest periods were introduced. In Period 12, rest periods were entirely eliminated and during 12 weeks, output reached a new height. This continued and the unexpected increase in production which was independent of hours of work showed the absurdity of any experiment in which rest periods are introduced and changes in output ascribed to this cause without checking to see whether other factors may have been responsible. With the reintroduction of rest pauses in Period 13, total output rose still further.

We inevitably became more and more concerned with the task of finding the explanations for the remarkably increased output. Was it because of better health or at the expense of health of the worker? Was it due to lessened fatigue? Was it due to changed pay incentive? Was it due to an improved mental state on the part of the worker, to the elimination of unhappy preoccupations, or a greater zest for work?

These studies gave us new knowledge of two types: (1) more information concerning the relative importance of fatigue, working conditions and mental attitudes as factors in the increased output; (2) specific information concerning the effect upon employee efficiency of certain specific factors like sleep, rest pauses, and sitting position.

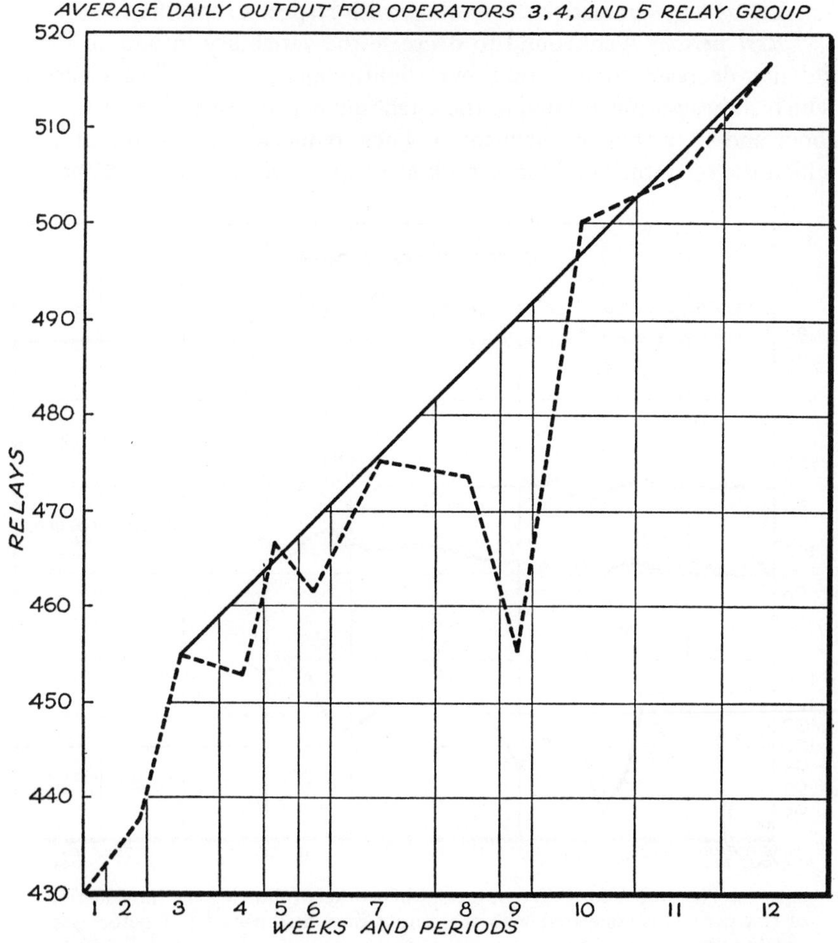

CHART 1. Solid line shows daily output increase from one full-day period to the next full-day period. Dotted line shows the actual average daily output. The work periods indicated at the bottom of the chart are as follows: (1) regular department (2 weeks), (2) test room (5 weeks), (3) special gang rate (8 weeks), (4) two 5-minute rests (5 weeks), (5) two 10-minute rests (4 weeks), (6) six 5-minute rests (4 weeks), (7) lunch rest (11 weeks), (8) lunch rest and 4:30 stop (7 weeks), (9) lunch rest and 4:00 stop (4 weeks), (10) same as period 7 (12 weeks), (11) lunch rest and Sat a.m. off (9 weeks), (12) same as No. 3 (12 weeks).

It is impossible to present here the detailed statistical evidence upon which conclusions are based. These data may be found in the Progress Reports issued by the company and it is probable that many of them will be included in a summarizing volume which is in preparation. We give a brief statement of the more important findings and ask the reader to check the statistical evidence from the Progress Reports if he wishes to do so.

Let us first summarize the findings with respect to specific factors:

Rest periods were found to decrease the variability in output. They did not decrease total output but slightly increased it. (See Chart 2, which shows output following the establishment of rest pauses in the test room and in 3 shop departments.) They reduced the amount of time which the operator voluntarily took away from her bench by about one

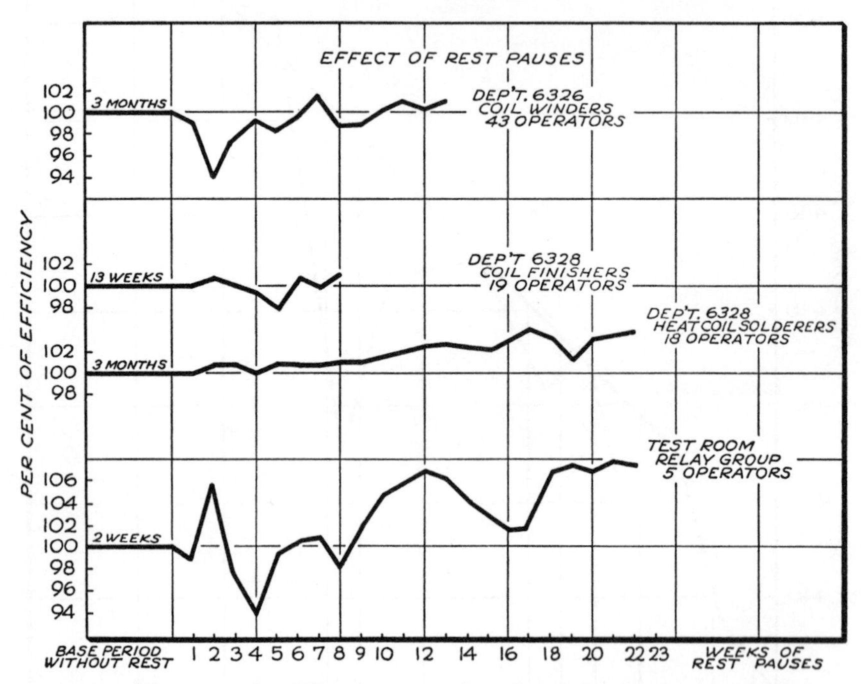

CHART 2. The output for different groups of workers following the introduction of rest periods is compared with the output of a base period just before rest pauses were put into effect.

half. Single 10- or 15-minute rest periods in the middle of the half day were preferred to more frequent shorter rest pauses.

The physical examinations showed that the increased output was not at the expense of the *health* of the worker. The health of the girls remained constant or improved slightly.

The question naturally arose as to whether the increased output was due to muscular *fatigue*. The study of the weekly output curve indicates that appreciable cumulative muscular fatigue does not exist. Vascular skin tests and pulse product readings were both taken to detect differences. They did not show cumulative fatigue and the latter test indicated less fatigue in this group than among workers in other occupations who had been tested elsewhere.

It seemed likely that the more satisfactory *basis of payment* may have been a factor in increasing output. We sought to check this by setting up 2 other test groups. One group of relay assemblers was left in the regular department but paid as a small group. A group of mica splitters who had always been paid on a straight piecework basis were put in a test room. With Group I, we administratively changed only the pay incentive, al-

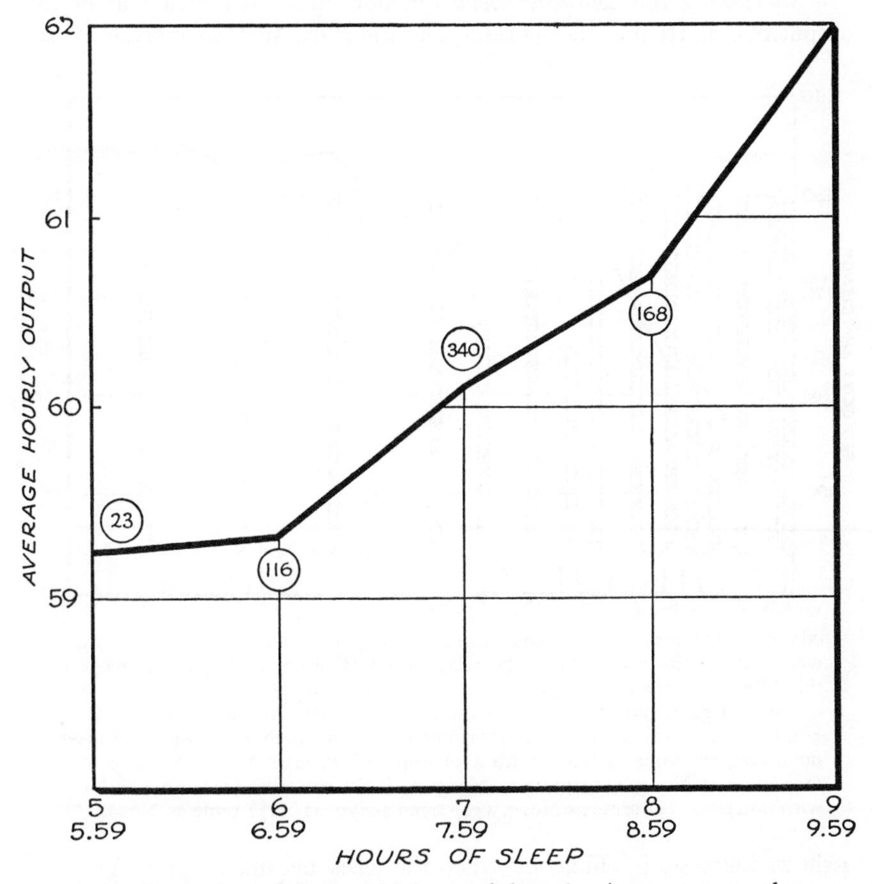

CHART 3. Comparison of output with hours of sleep showing an average of averages for 5 operators of the first relay assembly group. Figures in circles indicate the number of observations for each point.

though changes in attitude may also have taken place. With Group II, we provided test room conditions but did not change the pay incentive. The output in both groups went up over 10 per cent in a few months. We are inclined to believe that changed pay incentive may have been one factor in increasing output but it certainly was not the only factor.

An analysis of output on days following various amounts of *sleep* showed that sleep has a definite, though not a dominant effect on output. Chart 3.

A comparison of the output for the first hour after the operators changed from one type of relay to another with the average output for the first full day following such a change showed that there is not a decrease in output immediately after so slight a *change in the nature of the work.*

Shortening the working week did not show an increase in hourly output but shortening the working day did show such an increase. Chart

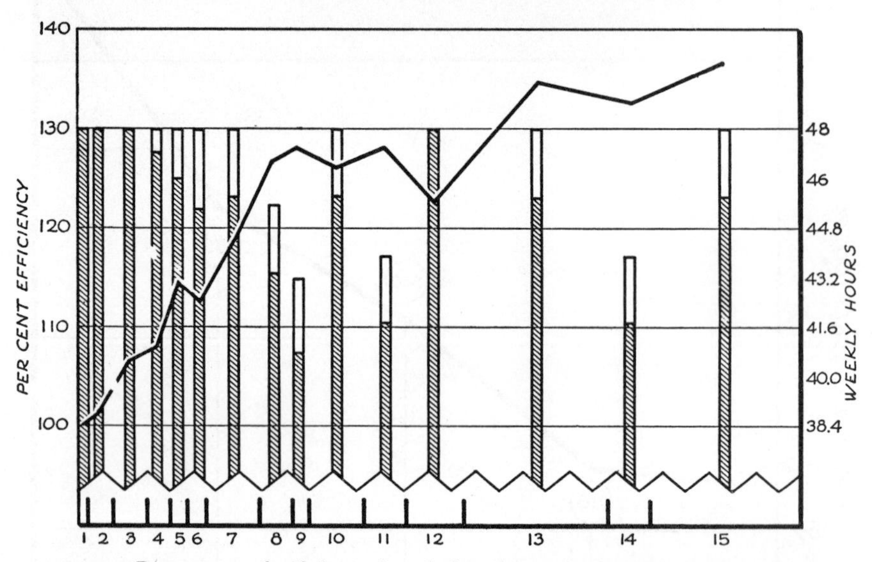

CHART 4. Percentage of efficiency in relationship to the length of the working week for operators 3 and 4 of the relay group. The types of working week in the different periods were as follows: (1) regular departments, (2) test room, (3) special gang rate, (4) two 5-minute rests, (5) two 10-minute rests, (6) six 5-minute rests, (7) a 15-minute morning rest with lunch and 10-minute afternoon rest, (8) same as No. 7 with 4:30 stop, (9) same as No. 7 with 4:00 stop, (10) same as No. 7, (11) same as No. 7 with Sat a.m. off, (12) same as No. 3 with no rests, (13) same as No. 7, (14) same as No. 11, (15) same as No. 13.

4 shows increases in efficiency when the week became shorter by reducing the length of the working day, but no increases when Saturday work was omitted. (Periods 11 and 14.)

The girls engaged in this type of work did not show a change in output during *menstrual periods.*

Changes in *sitting position* showed that the output of an operator is influenced by the workers sitting beside her.

Complete individual social case records were kept for test room employees. There is a definite relationship between output and satisfactory or unsatisfactory *home conditions and social relationships.*

We at first thought that the *novelty* of test room conditions might be partly responsible for increased output but the continuing increase in production over a 4-year period suggests that it was not of great importance. In the judgment of the girls themselves, certain elements of the test room situation were listed in the following order of importance: (1) the small group, (2) the type of supervision, (3) earnings, (4) novelty, (5) interest of the girls in the experiment, (6) the attention given in the test room by officials and investigators.

In order to test the effect which the test room observer himself might have upon the group, the one who had been in the test room since its beginning was removed and his assistant placed in charge. The supervision in the test room remained approximately the same; there seemed to be no measurable effect which could be assigned to the change in personalities.

CHAPTER 3

CURRENT THEORY

The Equilibrium of Groups

ELIOT D. CHAPPLE and CARLETON S. COON

A STATE of equilibrium may be defined as follows: if a small force is impressed upon a system, a change or adjustment takes place within the system, and once this force is removed, the system returns to approximately its previous state.

States of equilibrium are characteristic not only of individuals, but also of groups of individuals. In other words, the individuals of whom a group is composed adjust their interaction rates to each other; as they separately attain equilibrium, the group attains it likewise. Therefore a disturbance which upsets the equilibrium of one member will affect the others also.

If one of the members of a family becomes sick, we can observe how the relations of the group change in response to the new situation. This change is particularly evident if the sick person is one who works in an office and is habitually away from home most of the day. The daily visits of the doctor introduce a new person into the system of relations which we are studying, a person, furthermore, to whom all members of the family have to adjust. Secondly, the constant requirements of the patient greatly increase the frequency of interaction between him (or her) and the members of the family who live at home. In the third place, the normal

FROM *Principles of anthropology*. New York: Henry Holt & Co., 1942. Reprinted by permission of the authors and publisher.

interaction rates between the members of the family living at home are disturbed. As the patient's health improves, these disturbances of the family equilibrium decrease; when the patient returns to work, the quantitative character of the relations within the family becomes approximately what it was before the illness started.

At this point, it may be profitable to remind the reader that the equilibrium of the internal environment, the equilibrium of the individual in relation to others, and the equilibrium of the group are similar and related phenomena. We have pointed out that disturbances in the external environment produce consequent disturbances in the internal environment, and vice versa. The actions of others stimulate the autonomic nervous system, and a change in the internal environment, as for example a severe illness accompanied by a rise in temperature, produces marked changes in the interaction rate between the affected individual and his group.

Since the equilibrium of an individual depends upon the differences between the interaction rates of the persons with whom he interacts, one of the commonest phenomena which can disturb his equilibrium is a change in the personnel of his group. Changes of this type include the loss of a member, the substitution of one member for another, and the addition of a new individual to the already existing personnel.

If one wishes to discover whether or not a given group of individuals (for example, five persons) has attained a state of equilibrium, he may do so by applying two tests. The first of these is to observe whether or not the rates of interaction between the individuals in the group are constant within clearly defined limits; that is, whether or not significant increases or decreases are taking place in the frequency of events, in the origin-response ratio, in the interaction rate within the event, and in the degree of synchronization. If the rates are constant and no such changes are taking place, equilibrium has been attained.

The second test is to see whether or not, after a disturbance takes place, the rates return to their previous values. They will do this if the group is in a state of equilibrium. When the personnel of such a group is changed, however, the previous state of equilibrium cannot be restored, unless the new member has exactly the same interaction rate as the person whom he has replaced, which rarely happens.

When one member of our group of five individuals dies, changes in the relations of all members must take place before the group can attain a new state of equilibrium. In the development of this new equilibrium, each individual must adjust his own rates in some way. Let us suppose that one of the members, A, has been interacting daily for about an hour a day at a given rate with B, the deceased member. If A is to maintain his state of equilibrium, or at least return to a state somewhat similar to his old one, he must find some outlet for the interaction to which he was accustomed. This means that, in order to make up for what he has lost, he will have to increase his interaction with one or more persons, either within the circle of the surviving members of the group, or outside it. His interaction rate, and the rates of the persons to whom he makes his new adjustment, must be synchronized if his previous equilibrium is to be restored. If this cannot be done, he will try to attain a new state of equilibrium at a different level of interaction.

Similar readjustments take place when a new individual is substituted for the deceased member. In this case, the new person will almost certainly have an interaction rate different from that of his predecessor, and he will consequently produce a different state of equilibrium in each of the other members. The amount of interaction which he contributes may be greater or smaller than that provided by the previous member; the new man may also have a much higher origin rate, or again, he may have a slow and phlegmatic rate of interaction. In any case, the other members of the group will be obliged to adjust to him, as he will to them. This process of mutual adjustment takes place slowly; the original members must be conditioned to the newcomer, and the reverse.

Let us consider a third situation, in which a new individual is added to the group without the loss of an original member. In this case, two results usually occur; the older members of the group adjust themselves to the newcomer, and the increase in the number of individuals concerned often causes a decrease in the individual interactions that take place. The resulting interaction rates represent a new distribution of the separate rates of the constituent individuals.

The process of adjustment which takes place within a group as the aftermath of a disturbance is marked by cyclical fluctuations; by days on which the members of the group fail to adjust, interrupt each other, become angry, and are unable to work together—days on which the regular routine, to which the members have been conditioned, is upset. As the group gradually regains its equilibrium, the range of these fluctuations decreases and the rhythm of the routine interactions becomes more constant.

As we can readily understand through our knowledge of the conditioning process, the degree to which a state of equilibrium becomes stable depends upon the length of time that the interaction rates, of which the equilibrium is composed, remain constant. This is equally true in respect to individuals and to groups. The longer, therefore, the individual or the group maintains his, or its, equilibrium, the more fixed and automatic will the conditioning of the individual, or individuals, concerned become.

The degree of stablity has an important bearing on the ability of the individual or group to withstand disturbances of equilibrium; as a rule, the greater the stability, the stronger and, at the same time, less elastic is the state of equilibrium. For example, a group with a high interaction rate and a long history of continued stability will maintain its equilibrium under the impact of powerful external forces, but an internal change, such as the loss of a member, will produce serious effects, and its adjustment to a new equilibrium after the loss will be a slow and difficult process, if such an adjustment can be made at all.

There is, therefore, a great difference between groups, as well as between the individuals of whom they are composed, in their ability to withstand major changes of environment; and this ability depends in part, as we have seen above, on the relative stability of the states of equilibrium concerned.

The Analysis of Situational Fields in Social Psychology

LEONARD S. COTTRELL, JR.

IN COMMON with many others operating in the vague and complex field of social psychology, I find it impossible at this juncture to produce a logically rigorous system of assumptions and concepts with which to analyze and interpret human social interaction. Notwithstanding the rickety condition of the present formulation, I deem it worthwhile to expose it for critical examination by fellow workers in the hope of gaining new perspectives on it myself.[1]

There are no essentially new terms in this formulation. I am particularly aware of the influence on my own thinking of the work of Charles H. Cooley, George H. Mead, Ellsworth Faris, Sigmund Freud, and Kurt Lewin. Those familiar with recent developments in social psychology will also see that the present statement is in line with a general current which is also manifest in the work of H. S. Sullivan, R. D. Lasswell, J. L. Moreno, Karen Horney, Erich Fromm, W. L. Warner, and many others.

In what follows, I shall be taking the position, familiar to most sociologists, (1) that any item of social behavior is understood only as it is

FROM *American Sociological Review*, 1942, 7, 370-382. Reprinted by permission of the author and publisher.

1 I wish to express my appreciation for the many helpful suggestions I have received from Ruth Gallagher Goodenough, Ward H. Goodenough, and Ralph White with whom I have frequently discussed the ideas in this paper.

seen as a functional part of a situation composed of interacting selves; (2) that in functioning in an interactive system, the organism not only develops the response patterns representing its part in such an interact but actually incorporates the response patterns of the other(s) in its reactive system; and (3) that when one elaborates the two foregoing assumptions into a working system of social psychology, he finds it necessary to modify radically the atomistic methods of traditional psychology which treat of reflexes, traits, motives, and various other behavioral syndromes which are referred to the individual with a minimum of attention to precise specification of the interactive context.[2]

I. ILLUSTRATIVE MATERIAL

I shall begin this discussion by introducing some very simple concrete materials to which it may be convenient to refer later. These materials will also serve to indicate a few of the problems of interpretation for which I believe the situational approach offers a possible solution.

First Illustration. *B* (aged 14 months) was as curious about his environment as most children of his age. The knobs on the gas cook stove were particularly fascinating. The mother, though usually rather patient and indulgent toward his explorations, met these particular manipulative efforts with very firm "No! No's!," pulling him away and starting him off in other directions. After this interact had been repeated several times, *B* found the field clear for another try. He pulled up to the knobs and as he started to take hold he suddenly let loose a torrent of "No! No! No's!" with vigorous shaking of his head; whereupon he backed off to survey the situation. He seemed a little surprised at hearing the parental admonition when no parent was present but he took another look and repeated the whole act again. He finally crashed through this rudimentary conscience and twisted the forbidden knobs, at which point adult intervention ended the scene.

This performance is interpreted here as a simple instance in which the child manifested an incorporated (introjected) act of the other and responded to his own action with the action of the other. At a later stage in his career, he may refer to certain of such "other" parts of self-other patterns as his conscience.

Second Illustration. At a later age (26 months), the child mentioned above put on more complicated performances which may be regarded as manifestations of his introjection of more complex "other" activity. A fairly typical instance may be cited.

One late afternoon near the dinner hour, *B* knotted his face into something of a scowl and pitched his normally low voice into something approaching an infant growl.

2 This type of treatment has its uses and is entirely suitable for many purposes but not for analysis of social interactional phenomena.

"I want some meat for my supper," he said to his mother. Then added, "I'm daddy and I've come home from work." The mother took the cue and addressed him as daddy, asked how his little boy *B* was, etc., etc.

At the table, he insisted on taking his father's place at the head of the table, assigning the displaced parent to the high chair. He wished to serve but had to submit (after some protest) to being assisted in this part of his role. He admonished "*B*" not to spill his "brown milk" referring to the father's coffee. He referred to his milk as "white coffee," saying only big people could drink white coffee. After the meal, *B* continued to act in his capacity as daddy and "read" a story to his "son" and finally undertook to put him to bed. The father finally balked at being put in the crib, giving as his reason that the crib might break down. The two then agreed to "pretend" to put the father in the crib.

It is interesting to note that if the father acted out of character, *B* prompted him with very definite direction as to how "*B*" should act. Moreover if the mother or the maid did not treat *B* himself as father and the father as *B*, they were peremptorily put back into the proper relationship by *B*.

Third Illustration. *Y*, a woman aged 35, was the second of three children. The oldest child was a boy and the youngest, a girl. The father was a very adequate person and a benevolent patriarch. All the family seemed devoted to him, but *Y* was his favorite child from the time of her birth. When the younger daughter was born, *Y*, at that time about four, became very ill and the father gave her all of his attention. From that time on, *Y* was practically an invalid. She consistently regarded herself as weak, helpless, and dependent. She expected and received the appropriate solicitous behavior from family and friends. She was suspected of tuberculosis, anemia, etc. No positive findings were made and no treatment was effective. Meanwhile, the father gave most of his time and interest to his sick daughter. If the daughter improved a little and essayed a trip, she would become ill and her father would have to go for her and bring her home. There grew up between father and daughter a very intimate bond of communication and understanding. This "conditioning" of *Y* went on until she was nearly 30 years of age. At that time, her father died suddenly after a brief illness.

The day after his death, *Y*, who for nearly 30 years could hardly climb the stairs, got up, took the dazed family in hand, directed arrangements for the funeral, supervised the settling of the estate, and went off to take a short business course in order to prepare herself for a job. She already knew much about her father's business and, with her special preparation, she brushed her older brother aside and took over the supervision of the father's business and made a success of it. She has become the "father" of the family, and is now locally famous for her advocacy of vigorous living. Her father had been quite a water sportsman; she became an even better one. In many ways, she manifested her vigorous responsibility-assuming attitudes in her relations with others.

Apparently her illness was functional rather than organic. But leaving aside this and other interesting problems in the case, we are interested here in interpreting the shift in personality as a manifestation of a rather complete incorporation of the father's role. With this interpretation, *Y's* behavior becomes intelligible. For example, she does not expect her brother and the other members of her family to become independent. She expects them to be dependent upon her for leadership and aid. With the suggested interpretation, we are not surprised at this attitude toward the other members of her family. Nor shall we be surprised if she should show a reversion to her former dependent, cared-for self if she ever falls in love with an adequate, solicitous older man. On the other hand, she may well marry or otherwise take unto herself a very dependent to-be-cared-for person to fuss over.

Fourth Illustration. The following experiment was tried in a class in social psychology.

A case study was broken up into descriptions of behavior of the person in different areas of his life activity. Each separate description was read to the class and the students were asked to rate the subject on a few traits on the basis of the single description. The raters were told that each description was of a different person. This may be illustrated by giving two condensed descriptions and the resulting median ratings from one case.

Description of *A*, aged 10: "The parents complain that *A*, their oldest child, is a very difficult child at home. He is moody, sulks a lot, refuses to cooperate, does his work under protest, fights and bullies the younger children, and is frequently very cruel to them. He is always causing a quarrel or a fight and is stubborn and defiant in his attitude toward the parents . . . , etc."

Description of *B*, aged 10: "When the teachers referred *B* to the clinic, he was described as a very isolated and shy child. He did what he was required to do in class work but was very timid and diffident about participating in discussions or volunteering to do anything. He was always on the sidelines in anything the class or play groups did. He was frequently bullied by children smaller and younger than himself, and never seemed to stand up for himself with his equals or superiors. He cried easily and seemed to have a general feeling of inferiority. He frequently daydreamed in class . . . , etc."

The group of raters was then told that the excerpts represented rating on the same personality. The group was then asked to rate the person on the basis of their knowledge of him in all of the different situations from which the various descriptions of him were derived. This assignment was found to be very difficult and no one was satisfied with his ratings. The ratings showed more scatter than did the ratings on separate situations. When questioned as to how they decided on a general rating some were found to have struck some kind of informal average; others rated the person on what was probably his most frequently manifested behavior; still others rated the person on what they decided was his "truest" self.

If time permitted us to present an analysis of this case, it could be shown that the different behavior patterns of the child in question were functionally related to the particular roles or positions he had in the different situations. The adjustive work which was intensive and resulted in considerable success was chiefly a matter of establishing the child in a different relationship to the situations in which he was having difficulty, partly by situational changes and partly by helping him to redefine his situations.

Fifth Illustration. A university personnel office referred a secretary for consultation. The difficulty seemed to be that although a very skillful worker, she couldn't or wouldn't hold a position very long. The interviews revealed that no matter what the job situation appeared to be when she started it, she would very shortly establish a relationship with the other members of the staff in which she perceived herself to be the object of antagonism and injustice. The interpretation drawn from her history rested chiefly on the rigid conception of a self-other pattern in which she expected rejection and hostility and reacted by retaliative behavior. This frame of relationships she projected on every new situation.

II. SOME PROPOSITIONS CONCERNING INTERPERSONAL BEHAVIOR

The foregoing concrete instances suggest certain ideas which may be stated in the form of propositions. The general point of view may be tested by determining the truth or falsity of these propositions. They are presented not as proved principles but as propositions to be tested.

The following propositions refer to interpersonal activity. Later we shall indicate the way this frame of reference may be applied to interaction of groups.

I. When human organisms respond to each other over a period of time, the activity of each becomes the stimulus pattern for a more or less stabilized response pattern in the other(s), assuming that the motivational components remain essentially unchanged.

Definition 1. A series of conditioned acts comprising the reciprocal responses of all members of a social situation is referred to as an interact pattern.

Definition 2. An internally consistent series of conditioned responses by one member of a social situation which represents the stimulus pattern for the similarly internally consistent series of conditioned responses of the other(s) in that situation is called a role.

II. The impact upon one human organism, *A*, of the activities of another, *B*, not only stimulates and conditions a response pattern of *A* to *B* but also conditions in *A* the response pattern of *B* to *A as A has perceived that action*, and vice versa. The latter pattern is not necessarily manifested overtly but must be assumed to exist at least in incipient or attitudinal form.

(This process of responding by reproducing the acts of the other(s) has been referred to by various writers as taking the role of the other, identification, introjection, sympathy, empathy, imitation.)

Definition 3. This process of "double conditioning" is referred to as the incorporation or internalization of an interact pattern.

Definition 4. An internalized interact is referred to as a self-other pattern.

III. It follows from II that each member of an interpersonal relationship is not only conditioned to respond to the acts of the other(s) with his own act series but is conditioned to respond to his own response series as a stimulus series with actions he incorporates from the other(s).

Hence, after the interactive experience has been repeated enough times, it is possible for each member to carry out the entire interact alone, at least in incipient form.

Propositions I–III may be crudely represented schematically in the following diagrams.

1. Assume two unconditioned organisms *A* and *B* with motives S_A^D and S_B^D respectively. Assume further that the activities of each become a stimulus series for the other. This condition can be represented thus:

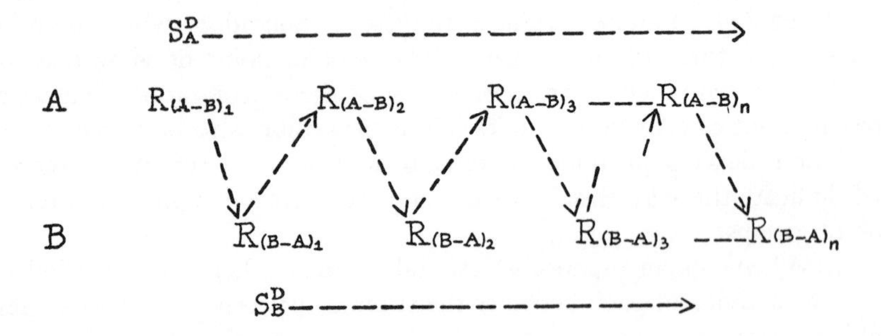

where S^D is the motivational component and $R_{(A-B)}$ and $R_{(B-A)}$ are the responses of *A* to *B* and *B* to *A* respectively.

2. Let the conditions in 1 be repeated a number of times and by proposition II, we have:

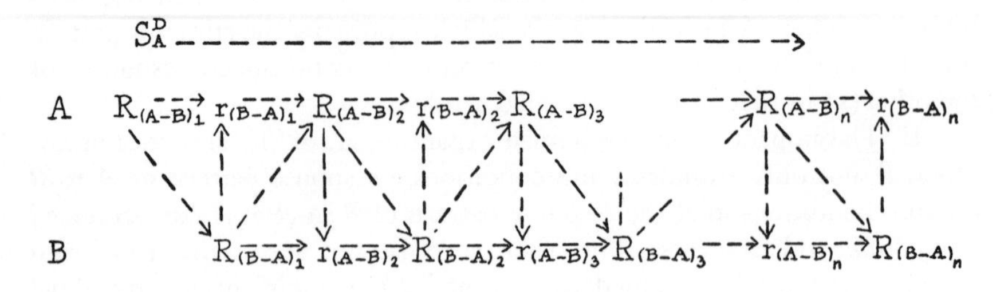

where *r* represents the incorporated response of the other.

The responses of each have now been incorporated by the other as expected "other" responses to the own-self responses.

3. When responses represented in 2 have been established, it is then possible for each member of the pair to carry out the interact in incipient form, thus:

$$S_A^D \dashrightarrow$$

$$(A \leftarrow\!-\!\rightarrow B') \qquad r_{(\overline{A}-\overline{B})_1} \dashrightarrow r_{(\overline{B}-\overline{A})_1} \dashrightarrow r_{(\overline{A}-\overline{B})_2} \dashrightarrow r_{(\overline{A}-\overline{B})_n} \dashrightarrow r_{(B-A)_n}$$

and $(B \leftrightarrow A')$ can be similarly represented. Where B' and A' represent the incorporated response series of B into A and A into B respectively.

The instances cited above in First and Second Illustrations will serve as very simple illustrations of the processes considered in Propositions I–III.

If these propositions can be proved, then in analyzing or treating personalities, it becomes necessary to assume that the reactive system includes not only those response patterns the person has manifested but also the response patterns of the others of his life situations. Thus, from this point of view the rebellious child is also in part the authoritarian parent; the saint is part sinner; the communist is part capitalist; the Southern White is part Negro psychologically.

IV. The self-other patterns of each member of an interact system are frequently not congruent. The more intimate the contact through time, the greater will be the tendency for the patterns to coincide. (Exceptions to this latter statement will be found in cases where personality structures are extremely rigid such as those found among neurotics.)

V. A self-other pattern once established tends to persist either as a dynamic tendency (if motivational components remain integrated with it) or as a latent pattern which can be reproduced, given appropriate situational and motivational conditions. (See Third and Fourth Illustrations above.)

VI. A self-other pattern once established tends to be projected on new interact situations unless the components and structure of the field are very unlike that in which the pattern was developed. Projection means here, that if through interaction, *A* has developed a self-other pattern of $(A \leftrightarrow B')$, then if *A's* contact with *C* is not too unlike that with *B*, *A* will expect B' behavior from *C* and will behave toward *C* in terms of those expectations. If *C* does not fit the pattern, an exploratory period will yield a self-other pattern in *A* of $(A \leftrightarrow C')$.

Under certain conditions, the personality is rendered so insecure by having to develop new relational patterns that it clings rigidly to those it has even where they are maladaptive to the objective situation as seen by an observer. (See Fifth Illustration above.)

VII. Self-other patterns established early in the life of the organism are more likely to be persistent and pervasive than are those acquired later.

1. The earlier patterns are projected on a wider variety of new, later, situations. By reacting to anticipated "other" responses, the person is more likely to receive the responses he expects. This process reinforces the previous self-other pattern.

2. Feelings of anxiety arising from having to function in an unknown pattern of interaction will tend to reinforce those patterns which have already been established even though they may appear to an observer to result in frustrations.

VIII. From I, II, and III it follows that every interact series that becomes established as an incorporated self-other pattern provides the organism with two or more (depending on the number of roles in the pattern) response systems or roles. The interact ($A \leftrightarrow B$) produces a self-other pattern in A of A and B' and in B of A' and B. Under certain conditions, A will act overtly in the role B' rather than as A.

This fact is of considerable importance in accounting for or predicting major changes in personality. (See Second and Third Illustrations.)

IX. The human organism will incorporate a limited number of self-other patterns with which it functions in the series of situational fields in which it exists.

Definition 5. Personality is the population of self-other patterns and their intra-personal organization. (See Fourth Illustration.)

X. The personality system includes self-other patterns developed by other persons and acquired through the process of identification.

Propositions concerning the factors which govern the selection of identification patterns cannot be presented now. Motivational factors, personality structure and situational pressures all operate in determining the selection.

XI. The self-other patterns composing a personality are not all given direct overt expression with equal frequency or completeness. Certain patterns will dominate the system while others remain latent or gain indirect expression.

Propositions covering the determinants of dominance cannot be presented here. The three general factors mentioned in connection with Proposition X are the important ones.

XII. All personality systems are subject to internal stress due to the activity of contradictory roles. The greater the number of incompatible roles and the more overlapping the situations are which evoke them, the greater the amount of conflict in the personality.

XIII. Persons seek to minimize conflict by: (1) living within a restricted and simply structured field; (2) keeping separated those situations requiring incompatible roles; (3) remaining "unconscious" of contradictory roles by such mechanisms as projection, reaction formation, conversion, etc.; (4) developing a master definition of the situation such as a philosophy of history, a theology, or a philosophy of life which gives consistency, meaning, and integration to their various patterns.

XIV. The person responds in a social situation according to his own definition of the situation.

This definition will usually deviate from that of an observer, unless or until the latter is closely identified with the former. (See Proposition II.)

Definition 6. By the social situation is meant the system of self-other patterns comprising a given interact. (The terms social situation and social interact as used here are equivalent and may be used interchangeably.)

Definition 7. By definition of the situation is meant the system of expected "other" responses aroused in a given personality by a given situation.

From Definitions 6 and 7 it is evident that a social situation as seen by an observer may not coincide with a given participant's definition of it. Moreover, the various participants will necessarily have differing definitions of the situation. This raises the interesting questions of how consensus is achieved, how communication takes place, and how we understand another person. These are subjects which call for the formulation and testing of additional propositions.

XV. It follows from the foregoing propositions that understanding the behavior of a personality requires an observer to comprehend its several definitions of the situation. This calls for a partial identification with the subject.

XVI. It follows further that items of behavior such as attitudes, traits, etc., studied apart from the context provided by the actor's definition of the situation, yield meaningless results.

If these propositions are valid, they call for a radical shift in much of our methodology in social psychology. (See Fourth Illustration above.)

III. APPLICATION TO ANALYSIS OF COLLECTIVE BEHAVIOR

The foregoing propositions have been aimed at the analysis of interpersonal relations. If space permitted, we could show that with slight modifications, the same general propositions would hold when applied to behavior in and between groups. To discuss group interaction, we do not need to desert the vocabulary we have found useful in describing individual personality phenomena. Groups of individuals occupy functional positions in relation to other groups, and the overt behavior characteristics, ideologies, and frames of reference which individual members show are functionally related to these positions.

This approach to group interaction focuses attention upon the way an individual actually participates in intergroup relations, upon the meaning of these relations to the individuals involved. Symbols have meaning when they arouse an incorporated structure of acts. Group interaction is mediated by symbolic tags, which serve to identify self and "other" roles for groups. These tags, or symbols of identification, refer to an act and counteract structure in which the "I" or self role is actually a "we" role, and the role of the other is the behavior expected from any member of a group of others, or a "they" role.

The average individual in our society is able to act in the name of many such symbolized groups. His role for some of them is laid down in very early interaction, for instance his role as a member of a particular family in the community, or the roles appropriate to sex or class positions. Other worlds of secondary symbolic participation open up to him as he matures, so that he comes to have as many symbolized selves as there are groups which claim his allegiance. Which of these selves gains overt expression at a given time depends upon the way in which self-other relations of a particular moment are perceived by the actor. In times of international crisis, the individual's attention is directed consistently toward the stage on which national symbols represent the acting roles. He interprets the acts of other national groups from his position as an American or as a Briton or as a German. He feels insecure when a hostile national group increases its armed strength, or he feels righteous and belligerent when his personal surrogate is able to wave the Big Stick. Similarly his attention is drawn to a field dominated by the symbols "capital" and "labor," when he becomes aware of his interests involved on that front. His identification with one or the other of these groups provides him with a role position from which to perceive and interpret events and actions in this particular field.

Group interaction of this sort can be arrested at almost any degree of inclusiveness, simply by defining a dominant "we-they" relationship. A skillful employer can block attempts to organize his workers if he can keep racial, national, or religious antagonisms alive. Indeed, the formula "divide and rule," expressed in situational terms, means to prevent effective opposition by defining the field for interaction about irrelevant or less inclusive symbols. The Ministry of Propaganda of the German Reich uses this technique to disable the nations it opposes, while at the same time it subordinates every other symbol of identification within Germany to establish the supremacy of the national symbol.

Propaganda, from this point of view, is simply a technique for defining fields of group interaction and for keeping the focus of attention on these fields. Groups that play for high stakes of power and prestige must develop refined propaganda methods, first of all to hold group interaction in desired areas of "we-they" relationships, and then to control the specific expectancy patterns of those relationships.

Space does not allow for further elaboration of the application of situational analyses to collective behavior. Enough has been said to indicate the general line along which such applications might proceed.

IV. THE SOCIAL ACT

The discussion thus far has been centered on the patterning of a series of reciprocally related responses of two or more social selves. Motivational components of these acts have been indicated but the integration of a theory of motivation and the present theory has not been made explicit. The limits of this paper permit of only a bare indication of the way this problem may be approached.

An adequate conception of the social act and the ways it may be analyzed seems to me to furnish an excellent lead to the desired integration. A social act is conceived of here as a series of reciprocally related acts by units called selves, which series forms a dynamic perceptual unit. The general form consists of a beginning or precipitating condition, the definition of goals or end relations toward which the interacting units conceive themselves to be moving, a series of relevant intermediate activities, and finally some kind of end-state of relationship of the implicated selves.[3] This end-state varies in its degree of permanence. A social act is usually not perceived in the same way by actors and observers of the social act. Thus, a social act which one may describe as a parent disciplining his child may be perceived by the child as an unwarranted aggression by a stupid but powerful bully, by the parent as an unpleasant part of the task of fitting the child for participation in larger social acts of the family and community life, and by an observer as an overt expression of jealousy which the parent holds toward the child and rationalizes as parental duty. The social act of a strike or a war is too obviously a differently defined experience by participants to need elaboration here. To understand the behavior of a participant, it is therefore necessary to perceive the social act as he does—his notion of how it started, the goals he perceives for himself and the other selves implicated and the functional relevance he assigns to the intermediate activity.

This conception of the social act calls for two supplementary modes of analysis which, used separately, yield incomplete knowledge but together provide a relatively complete frame of reference which will make intelligible most if not all behavior with which the social psychologist is concerned.

1. Human social activity may be analyzed as motivated or goal-directed actions. The analytical problem is to determine the motives and goals.

3 It should be noted that a social act may take place intrapersonally among the selves composing a part or all of a single personality.

2. Goal-seeking activity which concerns the social psychologist always implicates more than one self. Hence, the motivational analysis must be supplemented by an analysis of the self-other patterns which emerge out of and function in the interaction of motivated organisms. Two organisms may both need affection but the self-other pattern into which this motive has been integrated may differ widely.

It may be well to add the caution that motive-goal analysis when used alone tends to reify such terms as affection, security, etc., as entities the organism wants. It must always be kept in mind that satisfactions or goal responses classed as affection, security, etc., involve a set of responses that must be made to the self's acts. Hence, the goal is not a "thing" but a reciprocal system of activity. Barriers which block the organism are not static elements of a maze he must learn but are responses which other interacting selves make to his acts. These barriers may be overt responses from others objectively present or introjected patterns within the personality system.

From this discussion it will be seen that the boundaries of a social act are determined with respect (1) to goals, and (2) to the interacting self-other patterns implicated in the activity. On the goal-directed axis, we may say a social act begins when a terminal or goal response is defined. The end point in the act lies between two points on the continuum. The first is that point at which, if the action is stopped, the symptoms of frustration would be at a maximum. The second is that point at which, if the action is stopped, the symptoms of frustration would be minimal.

On the interact axis, the social act is limited by what we have called the person's definition of the situation. (See Definition 7.)

A great many important implications for social psychological analysis emerge from this view of the social act but discussion of them must be omitted.

V. SOME IMPLICATIONS

The theoretical orientation suggested in this paper implies a good many changes in research method as well as in practical techniques in therapeutic procedures, in education for social living, as well as in the way people approach the actual problems of living together in the family, the community, and the world.

Research Method. The theoretical position outlined here does not require one to question the value for many purposes of much experimental work and measurement of abstracted trait attributes which may justifiably be called atomistic and which have passed for social psychological research. However, it makes it necessary to insist that such work be deliberately and self-consciously oriented to a situational frame of reference. Attitudes, motives, traits, emotions, opinions, and national, and racial group characteristics can no longer be studied in abstraction or with vague references to "the general social situation" if results are to have any meaning. The behavior indicated by such terms must be tied to a specifically defined social interact frame. Predictions of behavior must be made in terms of probable behavior in a specified situational context as perceived by the actor. This of course requires a vocabulary adapted to situational description. It also requires an enormous amount of research to establish major types of social situational patterns in which the persons must function.

Perhaps the most important methodological implication is the one calling for skills by which an investigator can assimilate himself to the acting perspective of his subject, individual or group. Such skills are sometimes referred to as intuition, sympathetic or empathetic introspection, identification-projection, role taking, etc. Whatever the name and whatever the actual process, the proposed orientation requires that the processes involved be made as explicit as possible and as subject to testing, verification, and operational formulation as possible. The way this method is made more explicit and subject to testing may not, to be sure, be the same way in which other methodological devices are handled, but that does not essentially alter the requirement.

Therapeutic Method. The marked shifts in phrasing the therapeutic problem and in therapy itself may be appreciated by a review of the recent work of Fromm (1), Horney (2, 3), Moreno (4, 5), and Sullivan (6). Instead of seeking for the traumatic cyst in the psyche, the complex, or the strayed libido, the focus is on the self-other patterns and their genesis, distortions, projection, etc., as seen in actual operation in the interview, on the clinical stage, and as reported from extraclinical experiences. Problem behavior is not given a clinical name and treated as a disease entity but is regarded as a function of the situational fields and the positions in them which the subject represents. The various innovators in psychiatric therapeutic work state their orientation and therapeutic procedures differently, but it is not hard to see that they all point in the direction of a situational orientation.

Education. There are obviously many implications for formal as well as informal education relevant to the development of a healthy basic self-other orientation. I wish to suggest what this view of human behavior implies for education for citizenship. One of the deepest problems of modern society is to deal with the profound and dangerous cleavages that threaten the basic consensus on which the society rests. Totalitarianism is one answer to the intransigent oppositions generated in western cultures. A democratic solution of the problem requires that the citizens interacting in their roles as members of opposing groups become increasingly able to take the roles of their opponents. It is only through this ability that integrative solution of conflict rather than armed truces can be arrived at. Education for citizenship must develop content and techniques in social studies that will enable the child and youth readily to see the community and the world through the eyes of persons occupying many different functional positions in his society. This is important not only in education for living with and solving problems with different race, class, and national groups, but in education for marriage and family living as well.

I suspect that a major shift must take place from teaching mere abstract knowledge about society to greater emphasis on the presentation of life experiences of many different persons with whom the student may become identified and thus experience the world and its problems as others of his society experience it.

Social Adjustments. The opportunity to observe persons operating in marriage, parent-child, and local community relations has left me with a very definite opinion that facility for seeing situational relations and a wide range of genuine (not merely verbal) role taking ability greatly increases the probabilities that conflicts and maladjustments will be dealt with integratively and constructively rather than in repressive destructive ways. Attribute thinking about and diagnoses of social problems leads to witch-hunting and futile efforts to exterminate the bad. Situational thinking and role taking skill open up broad possibilities for creative inventions of techniques and social arrangements for treating and preventing disintegrative and destructive processes.

REFERENCES

1. Fromm, E. Die psychoanalytische Characterologie und ihre Bedeutung für die Socialpsychologie. *Z. f. Soc. Forsch.*, 1932, 1, 252–277.
2. Horney, Karen. Conceptions and misconceptions of the analytical method. *J. nerv. ment. Dis.*, 1935, 81, 399–410.
3. Horney, Karen. *New ways in psychoanalysis*. New York, 1939.
4. Moreno, J. L. Interpersonal therapy and the psychopathology of inter-personal relations. *Sociometry*, 1937, 1, 9–76.
5. Moreno, J. L. Psychodramatic treatment of marriage problems. *Sociometry*, 1939, 3, 1–23.
6. Sullivan, H. S. Conceptions of modern psychiatry. *Psychiatry*, 1940, 3, 1–117.

Group Emotion and Leadership

FRITZ REDL

FREUD'S article on *Group Psychology and the Analysis of the Ego* has influenced psychoanalytic literature since 1921, mainly in two directions. A series of valuable attempts have been made to expand psychoanalytic explorations through the application of sociological, anthropological, and socio-economic theory. Then, in the field of education some of the later publications in the *Zeitschrift für Psychoanalytische Pädagogik* clearly recognize the growing importance of group psychology, especially for educational practice. Strictly speaking, however, Freud's article has not found supplementation on the same level on which the author started his investigation of the problem.

This is all the more surprising, because people during the last decade have been more interested in these problems. They clearly understand how futile it is to attempt to interpret events in the world at large without more thorough group psychological consideration. In addition, there is no doubt that Freud's article is incomplete, and that it does invite more supplementation than any of his other writings. The methodological equipment used and the material to which it is being applied chiefly characterizes his paper.

The *methodological equipment* is markedly different from the one he would have used had he written the article after his concepts and fundamental theories had undergone their later changes. This would be especially true if it were applied to the following points:

His concept of the *ego-ideal*—frequently called *ideal-ego*—is not yet differentiated into the two components which he later distinguished as elements derived through an incorporation of parental threats—conscience—and the residues of a narcissistic cathexis of personality traits—*ego-ideal*—in the later meaning of the term. He used the term *ego-ideal* in a way which comprised both functions indiscriminately.

ABRIDGED from *Psychiatry*, 1942, 5, 573–596. Copyright, 1942, by the William Alanson White Psychiatric Foundation, Inc. Reprinted by permission of the author and publisher. The reprinted portion represents approximately the first half of the article as it appears in *Psychiatry*.

In his use of the term *identification* Freud changed his meaning several times during the course of the article. In some places, he distinguished between the "establishment of an object in the ego-ideal" on the one hand, and the "identification of the group members 'in their ego' " on the other hand. Elsewhere, he used the term in its later meaning.

Freud's article appeared shortly before he developed his theory of the differentiation of love-drives and aggressive drives. There is no doubt that the application of these concepts would make considerable difference. It seems especially promising to apply this differentiation to the chapter on group psychological explanations of the army.

The *material* Freud used for his discussion is also responsible for some of the peculiarities of his publication. He applied the insight gained out of rich experience in handling individual patients and used these to draw analogies with situations in "the church," "the army," and other group psychological phenomena. The generality of some of his formulations is clearly due to the fact that he did not compare concrete personality experience with equally direct group psychological experience. This is why his formula reads: "Such a (primary) mass is a number of individuals, who have put one and the same individual in the place of their ego-ideal and have, through doing so, identified with each other in their ego."

In general, there can be little doubt of the validity of this formula, but there is serious doubt of its adequacy for every group formation found in practice. Of course, Freud purposely excluded from his investigation those group formations which occur without the influence of a "leader." Even if one follows him in this limitation of the problem, it seems highly probable that this formula needs modification and supplementation. It must, perhaps, be partly replaced by other formulæ, if it is to cover the rich field of practical group formations around a *central* person of some kind.

This investigation tries to supplement Freud's study in the points just mentioned. It attempts to utilize the methodological equipment developed after 1921; it applies this equipment on such group psychological observations which could be gained from practical work with groups of children and adolescents, in school and camp situations. Nevertheless, the fundamental object of investigation remains strictly the same: an attempt to examine the intra-psychical emotional and instinctual events in the members of groups, especially those which happen "round" some *central* person, and are constituent factors in group formative processes.

PSYCHOANALYTIC EXPLORATION AND SOCIOLOGY

The final word about the relationship between the two fields has not been written—nor should this study be weighted with such an attempt. However, methodological considerations of this sort are sufficiently vital that a clear statement as to the author's position might well help to avoid a number of possible misunderstandings. This can easily be done.

A psychoanalytic study of *group emotion* is not identical with a psychoanalytic study of *the group* or *groups*. It is only the first which is being attempted. To try the second seems nonsensical. "Groups" are phenomena containing so many different ingredients that the attempt to bring them to any one formula by the technique of psychoanalytic exploration must remain futile. Indeed, an attempt to do so seems analogous to the idea that any one person could be understood by psychoanalytic methods exclusively, eliminating all the data about this person's organic structure, for example. The importance of understanding the manifold factors constituting group life—psychological, socio-economic, and all others—is, therefore, fully recognized, but this paper does not attempt to deal with all of them. It purposely singles out only one of the aspects of group life, the emotional and instinctual relationships between persons who constitute a group. This is, therefore, an attempt to supplement, not to substitute, work with other or wider aspects of the problem.

Neither is this an attempt to mix psychoanalytic with "sociological" viewpoints. Such mixtures are frequently offered as an advanced development. Attempts at keeping the psychoanalytic technique in its *pure form* are threatened with the stigma of narrow-mindedness and lack of "sociological sensitivity." Yet, this study obviously confines its scope to the merely psychoanalytic sphere for the following reasons.

It is hoped that some blend between psychoanalytic and sociological insights may eventually be created. However, it is definitely felt that the time is not yet ripe. One cannot mix two things before one has them. Today, there is a *Sociology of the Group* on the one hand and a *Psychoanalytical Psychology of the Person* on the other. These two do not blend. The product of such mixing is either a sociology with a certain number of friendly complements to the contribution of psychoanalytic thought, or a psychoanalytic study with more or less eager recognition of the importance of sociological research. The desirable blend would first require a *Psychoanalytic Psychology of the Group*. To develop this, following the steps made in that direction by Freud's article, seems to be the first task. Only after exhaustive studies will there be some meaningful integration between sociology and psychoanalysis.

DEFINITIONS AND BASIC ASSUMPTIONS

Group Emotion

The term *emotion* is used here with the same wide meaning that is implied in phrases like "the emotional development of children," for example. In all these cases emotion "proper" is not alone intended, drives as well are included. Since the word *drive* does not have an adequate adjective, a further complication has been introduced into these formulations. The term *instinctual* will be used as adjective for drive. The summarizing of emotions and drives under the same phrase is a deplorable shortcoming, but it corresponds to a widespread scientific habit based on terminological tradition and convenience.

When "group emotions" are discussed, it is realized that they do not occur in a vacuum, but they are events that take place within and among the persons who constitute a group. In all probability they are composed of the same ingredients found in any "emotion," although they occasionally seem to obey their own special laws. The term *group* does not seem to designate some special quality, but rather, the "conditions for their arousal." *Thus, by "group emotions," reference shall be made to instinctual and emotional events taking place within persons under the pressure of group formative processes.*

From this definition it is obvious that further distinctions should be made. Not all of the emotion people have while they are in a group is really "group" emotion. Thus, for example, a pair of lovers holding hands in a political propaganda meeting might justly refuse to have the love emotion in which they participated considered under the category of group-emotion. Where it seems necessary this difference can be taken care of by calling emotions which are not the result or cause of the group formative process going on concurrently, just *"individual" emotions*—although it is realized that this term is misleading insofar as any emotion is, basically, a process happening within a personal situation. Furthermore, not all group emotions are equally *basic* to the process of group formation. Some, for example, are the source of group formation. The adoration one hundred people have for one and the same person may make this person their leader. It is basic for the formation of the group. On the other hand, on the basis of this group formation, a number of other emotional relationships may develop between these persons which might not otherwise have been experienced. These emotions are the result of, rather than the cause for, group formative processes. Thus, for example, *A* may begin to distrust *B*, without any highly "personal" hate against him, merely on the basis of a general group aversion which has developed through the role *B* has played within his group. In that case *A's* feeling toward *B* is the product of a special group emotional constellation. The following distinction will therefore be made:

Constituent group emotions are instinctual and emotional events in the potential members of a group which are basic to the group formative processes; *secondary group emotions* are such instinctual and emotional procedures within and among the members of a group as have developed on the basis of some group formative processes.

Of course, any emotion may be constituent in one situation and secondary in another. The diagnosis as to the one or the other situation is not always easy, although vital for the judgment and influence of group formative processes.

The Central Person

Freud called the person around whom the group formative process crystallizes the "leader," following a well rooted linguistic habit. However, since 1921, quite a few things have happened which make all more sensitive to the tremendous differences of meaning which this word assumes under certain circumstances. This investigation, especially, led to the discovery of a number of types of group formation, which do occur "around a central person," but for the designation of which the word "leader" simply does not lend itself. It is therefore necessary to begin with a terminological correction, reserving the word "leader" for only one type of role of the person central for group formation and relationships with members, giving different names to the other forms.

By *central person* is meant person "around whom" group formative processes take place, the "crystallization point" of the whole affair. The word "central" is simply willful and should not be taken literally. "Focal" might be better for logical reasons, but for linguistic purposes, it is unsatisfactory.

The term *central person* designates the one through emotional relationship to whom the group formative processes are evoked in the potential group members.

Ten types of "leadership"—ten different roles which this *central person* may play in group formation—can easily be distinguished.

The object of this investigation must be recognized as the study of drive-relationships and emotional procedures within each member of a group, on the basis of which group formative processes are evoked.

Freud's limitation of the topic to those types of group formation which occur "around some person," is followed, excluding other mass psychological investigations from this study.

The weight of the study is on the constituent group emotions, the secondary consequences of group formation on the emotional relationships between the members are only alluded to occasionally for the purpose of illustration. The interpersonal relations should provide the basis for another study, equally important for the purpose of education.[1]

1 Studies made by Kurt Lewin of the University of Iowa, and Ronald Lippitt of New York, furnish data on this topic.

Basic Assumptions

The methodological equipment developed by Freud is used in this study. During this work two further assumptions are suggested, both of a metapsychological character. They are the assumption of the *guilt-and-fear-assuaging effect of the initiatory act*, and the assumption of the infectiousness of the unconflicted on the conflicted personality constellation, or of the *spatial repetition compulsion.* These two assumptions will be explained in detail; a partial attempt at their justification will be made in this study.

TEN TYPES OF GROUP FORMATION

All the *Ten Types* presented deal with group formation "around" a central person. The difference between the ten types lies in the different role of the central person for the basic processes of group formation. The method which has been used to present these ten types is somewhat involved. Its peculiarity for the whole problem will become a topic of discussion later. Let it suffice at this point to say that an attempt has been made to present each type by describing one or more "illustrative examples." The explanation and formula which is thought to differentiate the type from others is then given. This summarizes the nature of the constituent group formative processes at work.

The "examples" are not necessarily identical with clinical material, nor are they to be used as "proof" for the formula which follows them. The examples are intended as illustrations for the purpose of introduction and explanation of each type. In condensing many observations into a composite picture, a host of practically irrelevant items were discarded in order to isolate one process. These illustrative examples will be best understood if they are taken as graphic slides. They all claim to be based on concrete reality experiences, but none of them pretends to be a photograph. Problems of frequency and actuality—for example—will be taken up in "discussion" of the ten types immediately following their presentation.

Type 1: "The Patriarchal Sovereign"

Illustrative Example: This group is composed of approximately ten-year-old children, most of whom are just at that point in their development where they most fully represent the end states of "childhood" immediately before the outbreak of preadolescent symptoms. In charge of them is a teacher who fits the following description: "He is an elderly gentleman of stern but not unfriendly exterior, decided but fundamentally mild in his manner. He stands for 'order and discipline' but they are values so deeply ingrained in him that he hardly thinks of them explicitly, nor does it occur to anyone to doubt them in his presence. He believes in good and thorough work, knows very clearly what he expects and leaves no doubt about it in the minds of his students." The atmosphere of the classroom may be easily described. The children accept his values without question. Their emotions about him are a mixture of love and adoration, with an element of anxiety in all those instances in which they are not quite sure of his approval. As long as they behave according to his code they feel happily secure—sheltered. Thoughts and imaginations which do not comply with his code are suppressed in his presence. The jokes he makes, or acknowledges, are funny. If one youngster is not quite so ready as the others to concentrate his filial adoration upon this type of a teacher, makes unfitting remarks, unruly gestures, or shows lack of submission, the others will experience a deep feeling of moral indignation—even though they may have enjoyed this youngster's jokes a few minutes previously during the recreation period. They all love their teacher and trust him infinitely, but certain thoughts must never enter their minds in his presence. When questioned or doubted by this teacher, tears come more easily than words; behind the happy security felt in his presence there is a nagging fear of its loss which streams into awareness every once in a while without apparent cause.

Explanation: These youngsters love their teacher, but that is not all that occurs. Their love is of a type which leads to "identification." It would be absurd to say that they want to be like their teacher, but they want to behave so that their teacher will approve of them.

Formula: These children become a group because they incorporate the "super-ego"—conscience—of the central person, into their own. On the basis of this similarity between them, they develop group emotions toward each other.

Type 2: "The Leader"

Illustrative Example: This group of boys are between fifteen and seventeen years of age. Most of them are far beyond their preadolescence—at the verge of transition from earlier adolescence into later adolescence. The teacher in charge of them is, or has the appearance of being, very young. He has an attractive exterior. He is somewhat juvenile but not too unpleasantly so in his views and behavior. He also stands for "work and discipline," and gets his youngsters to comply without much outward pressure. However, the basis on which he gets them to accept his authority is a little different. He differs from the patriarch mainly in that he strongly sympathizes with the drives of the children. They are clearly aware of it. He plays a dual role in his teaching. In his own super-ego, he is identified with the order and the demands of the school which he represents; but he is keenly aware of the instinctual demands of the youngsters. In order to combine both he has to display considerable technical skill. If he succeeds, he makes his class feel secure and happy; if he fails, they are frightened either of him or of their own drives. The children adore him, but they also accept what he stands for without much question. The boy who misbehaves is not the greatest danger to the emotional equilibrium of the group. He elicits moral pity rather than indignation from the others. The danger is the boy who tries to get a more intensive emotional counter response from the teacher than the others, while less ready to pay for it by conscientious output of work. He is hated and despised by them. A single youngster in that group, feeling negatively viewed by the teacher, is unhappy rather than frightened. Undesirable thoughts and actions still remain confessable. To be "understood"—accepted—is the minimum requirement of group happiness in this class.

Explanation: A central person of this kind appeals to the love emotions as well as to the narcissistic tendencies in the children. However, it would be difficult to say that they put the teacher in the place of their "conscience." Rather they place him in the other part of their super-ego, in what is usually called their "ego-ideal," which means that they start wishing to become the type of person he is.

Formula: The children become a group because they incorporate the teacher's personality into their ego-ideal. On the basis of this similarity they develop group emotions toward each other. This formula coincides most closely with that of Freud in *Group Phychology and the Analysis of the Ego.*

Type 3: "The Tyrant"

Illustrative Example: This is a class of children approximately ten years old, near the verge of preadolescence. In charge of them is an elderly, or middle-aged teacher, among whose motives for teaching were one or both of the following: He is compulsively bound to repeat a certain pattern of "discipline" against the children because this is the only way he can prove late obedience to some of the demands of his own parents; or, his most intensive drive satisfactions lie in the direction of sadism, and he has to use the children as objects for that purpose. This teacher will not "stand for" anything, but has to "impose" some kind of capricious "order" or "discipline" all the time. Nor will he be satisfied to do so quietly. He will require a noisy machinery of special tricks, rules, and revenge techniques. His concept of discipline, too, will be of the most compulsive, unrealistic sort; the way he works it out is as "unchild-minded" as possible. In short, there is a "regular tyrant" in charge of this class. Everyday psychology might tempt one to expect children to hate the teacher and fight him as much as they dared. Indeed, this does happen in a few examples, which I will describe later. The entirely different reaction from the youngsters is surprising. These children submit easily. They rebel against the silly pedantry of this tyrant less vehemently than other groups do against the reasonable demands of their beloved leader. Nor do they submit only temporarily. What they show is genuine "identification." How strong is this identification? This is illustrated by the youngster who does dare to rebel in such a class. He has a difficult time. He has everyone against him, the teacher, the other youngsters, and himself. The others show intensive signs of moral indignation, eventually becoming afraid of the child.

However, one difference seems obvious. The emotional relations these youngsters develop among themselves seem less intensive than in the other illustrations. Children of such classes develop little "comradeship"—unlike those who just hate their teacher without identifying with him—and they seem to be afraid of each other, and distrustful. They seem to fear that too much intimacy might endanger the successful repression of their hostility and might force them to realize what cowards they are.

Explanation: Doubtless, the identification of these children with their tyrant is genuine. He is the central person for that group. Unlike the two previous illustrations, this identification occurs from a different motive. It is not love which causes them to identify, but fear. Of course, not all fear leads into identification, but it does in the type just described.

Formula: These children incorporate the super-ego of the central person into their own by way of identification, the outgrowth of fear of the aggressor, and on this basis establish group emotions between each other.

Type 4: The Central Person as Love Object

Freud mentioned an example of group formation which he exempted from the leadership type. It fits into the pattern according to the broadened concept of the *central person* I have introduced.

Imagine a number of women who are in love with a singer or pianist and crowd around him after his performance. Certainly each of them would prefer to be jealous of all the others. However, considering their large number and how impossible it is for them to reach the aim of their infatuation, they resign and instead of pulling each other's hair, they act like a uniform group. They bring ovations to their idol in common actions and would be glad to divide his locks among themselves (2).

The life in the school class furnishes two similar examples for illustration.

Illustrative Example, 1: There is a group of sixteen-year-old girls in a class of a girls' high school. In charge of them is a male teacher—young, attractive, but narcissistic enough so that they are not too greatly frightened sexually from the outset. It is known that in some such cases "the whole class falls in love with him." From that moment on, they will act like a group in many ways along the line of Freud's example. Despite their infatuation for him, it would not be surprising if the teacher complained that he had trouble with discipline—that these girls did not obey him or follow his wishes without pressure. It seems that this kind of "being in love" with the central person does not make for "identification" described in *Type 2.*

Illustrative Example, 2: In a coeducational class of approximately sixteen-year-old children, there is one especially pretty girl, rather narcissistic. In similar situations one frequently finds a whole cluster of boys loving and adoring her in various ways, but equally unsuccessful insofar as their wish for exclusive possession goes. The girl is equipped with special skill for keeping them all equidistant and yet equally near. Symptoms of dense group formation may sometimes be observed among these boys. They seem very close to each other, and yet their relationship is not genuine friendship. It is on a group emotional basis. This becomes evident when the girl ultimately decides in favor of one of her suitors. The other boys then begin to hate him as their rival, with the exception perhaps of the one or two who may move even closer to the successful colleague and, thus, enjoy some of the satisfactions denied to them *via* the mechanism of *altruistic concession* (1).

Explanation: There is no doubt that the group emotional symptoms are genuine and that the teacher in *Example 1* and the girl in *Example 2* are playing the role of the central person without whose presence this type of group formative process would not have been evoked. However, it is also evident that these central persons could not be called "leaders" by any interpretation of the term—that the other children do not "identify" with them. Nor do they incorporate their central person's standards. The central person remains "outside" but does call out a display of group emotional symptoms in these children.

Formula: The children choose one and the same person as an object of their love, and on the basis of this similarity they develop group emotions between each other.

Type 5: The Central Person as Object of Aggressive Drives

Illustrative Example, 1: A type of teacher similar to the one described under the heading of "tyrant" is less intensive in his sadism, less superior in the rest of his personality traits. He is in charge of a group of rather problematic adolescents in a school setup which is so well regimented through an established system of suppressive rules that no one dares to rebel, because it would be too futile. These children obey their teacher under the constant application of pressure. They behave sufficiently well to keep out of trouble, but they do so grudgingly. They neither identify with the teacher nor with what he represents. Their relationship toward him—with the possible exception of a "sissy" in the class—is one of intensive hatred, of piled-up aggression which is kept from exploding only by their reality-insight. And yet, although they do not identify with the teacher, the emotions they develop toward each other will be truly positive and strong. The amount of "comradeship" these children display is enormous—greater than in any of the other groups. He who dares to identify with the hated oppressor is an outcast—arouses a lynching attitude in the rest of the class. Their feeling toward him is one of moral indignation, but its content it different from the other examples. It is moral indignation "from beneath," to use one of Nietzsche's terms.

Illustrative Example, 2: Here is a group of children who have developed no special group structure. There is no person in charge of them with a sufficiently outspoken personality to encourage any of the previously mentioned types of group formation. A new youngster suddenly enters the class who differs from them in that he is a very outspoken type. This new youngster is especially narcissistic, defiant, lofty, and unskilled in handling other people's weaknesses. If he is intellectually superior, he need not even be of a different ethnic group. Everyone's aggression is immediately turned against him. At the same time one may observe that his entrance into the class has indirectly influenced group formative processes. They move closer together; their common aggression against him seems to "bind" them, and they become more of a "group" than they were before.

Explanation: This new youngster cannot be called a "leader." The others neither like him nor "identify" with him. They do quite the contrary; and yet, he does apparently become the focal point of their group formative procedures, much as the teacher did in *Example 1.*

Formula: The children choose one and the same person as an object of their aggressive drives and through this similarity develop group emotions about each other.

Type 6: The Organizer

Illustrative Example: In a class of approximately thirteen-year-old boys there are five who find clandestine enjoyment of the cigarette as a symbol of adulthood. And yet, all five are of the type who have decided worries about how they can obtain cigarettes. They have neither the money to buy them, the courage to do so, nor the impudence to steal them from their fathers. Preadolescent revolt against adult concepts of what a good child should be has not progressed far enough. A new boy, for whom smoking is no great problem, enters the class. He neither invites, instigates nor encourages the others in this enterprise. They all know that he can get the desired cigarettes for them if they but ask. I have seen cases where hardly any other factor was involved. The boys neither loved nor admired this youngster; on the contrary, he was rather looked down upon as socially inferior. They did not fear him nor did he use any direct or indirect pressure upon them. Yet, by the mere fact of getting them the cigarettes, they suddenly eventuated into a regular "group," held together on the basis of their participation in the same forbidden pleasure.

Explanation: Perhaps this example seems more complicated—less credible—than the others, being unaccustomed to finding this function of the organizer isolated. Usually, it is coupled with other roles which the central person assumes for the potential group members. Although there are not many clear examples of this type, they cannot be reduced to any of the other types because neither love, hatred, nor identification is involved.

Formula: The central person renders an important service to the ego of the potential group members. He does so by providing the means for the satisfaction of common undesirable drives and thus prevents guilt feelings, anxieties, and conflicts which otherwise would be involved in that process for them. On the basis of this service, the latent undesirable drives of these youngsters can manifest openly. Through this common conflict-solution, group emotions develop in the interpersonal situation.

Type 7: The Seducer

Illustrative Example, 1: In a group of thirteen-year-old boys, six, involved in "group masturbation," are apprehended. The first superficial examination by school authorities reveals apparent, unequal participation. Some were onlookers, none were mutually active; all agreed that one of them was the "leader" of the gang. After thorough investigation the following situation was revealed. The obvious "culprit" was most "actively" engaged in masturbation. He was the "first to start it." However, he was not at all active in encouraging the others to join or to perform likewise. He was a little more developed than any of them; he masturbated freely at home without special guilt feelings. Masturbation meant something entirely different for him than for them, nor did he need the group from the standpoint of sex satisfaction. He gained nothing from the group situation, except prestige. He was not homosexual in the usual sense of the term; more surprising, perhaps, is the fact that the others neither especially loved nor feared him. They were more infantile than he. They had sufficiently conquered their anxieties about sex curiosity to take the first step in active experimentation on a highly pregenital level. However, they might not have done so alone, since that would have made them feel guilty about it. Actually, they used this boy for the purpose of "seduction." They needed him and the group situation allowed them to overcome their restrictions. Only after he was the "first one to do it" were they ready and able to join.

Illustrative Example, 2: A class of fifteen-year-old children, in high spirits toward the end of their morning sessions, wait for their teacher to arrive. He is somewhat late. He is the "leader" type, with a slight patriarchal tendency. Recently, at an examination period, a considerable amount of tension and dissatisfaction was extant. The relationship between them and their teacher was rather strained. He now enters the room. They stand at attention as was expected. Suddenly, one youngster, neither much liked, respected, nor feared by the others, starts yelling aggressively in a much more rebellious manner than anyone would have expected, especially toward this teacher. There is a moment of surprise. Before the teacher can react manifestly, they all join in. The whole class is in an uproar, more intensively so than any of them can afterwards "understand."

Explanation: Both examples beyond doubt represent group formation through the existence of a central person. In both cases the potential group members had much in common before the group formative processes began. It is also evident that they did not start before the central person committed the "first act." Apparently what evoked the group emotional reactions was the fact that these central persons committed an "initiatory" act. Through this act, the satisfaction of undesirable drives became possible in others, who would otherwise not have openly expressed them.

This concept of the "initiatory act" is not an invention but the description of a procedure observed so frequently in school and adult life that it does not require proof. It needs, however, to be explained. Thus far, I do not attempt to show why the "first act" may have such magical power over other people's suppressed drives. I simply allude to the fact here and keep its explanation for a later presentation.

What occurred in these children is here described. There is a strong increase in the intensity of undesirable drives—sex, in *Example 1*, aggressions, in *Example 2*. The personal super-ego of these children remains strong enough to suppress any possibility of the drives becoming overt. The ego of these children is in a predicament. Pressed with equal strength from oppressed drives and super-ego demands, it knows not what to do. Anxiety and uneasiness are the usual emotional accompaniments of such disturbances to balance. It is on the basis of such a situation that the effect of an "initiatory act" seems to take place.

Formula: The central person renders a service to the ego of the potential group members. He does this by committing the "initiatory act" and thus prevents guilt feelings, anxieties, and conflicts. On the basis of this service, the latent drives of these children manifest openly. Through this common conflict-solution, they develop group emotions.

Type 8: The Hero

Illustrative Example: This is the same tyrant-group described under *Type 3*—where all the children were fully identified with their oppressor—at a later interval. These children have developed further into preadolescent rebelliousness. Their reality insight begins to fade in important issues: yet sufficiently frightened, they keep their defensive identification against rebellious wishes. The tyrant now begins to make deplorable mistakes. He chooses, for example, one child as the preferable object of his sadism and persecutes him more and more persistently. The others almost pity the child, but pity would imply criticism of their tyrant, and that would tend to revive their own dangerously rebellious feelings against him. So, they hold as tightly to their protective identification with the oppressor as they can. However, one of them has more courage. Something in his history makes him less able to endure this—or, perhaps, his insight into the real dangers implied by rebellion dwindles more rapidly. In any event, he is one day unable to tolerate the teacher's attack upon his victim. This boy defends his colleague and is considered "fresh" and reckless. The whole class gasps with surprise. They expect something fearful to happen. Surely the teacher will kill that child, or lightning will strike out of the clear sky. But no avenging stroke of lightning descends to quell the rebellion. The teacher is evidently too surprised or frightened momentarily to know what to do. When he demonstrates his fury, it is too late. The "hero" has worked his miracle. All the youngsters have altered their sentiments, at least secretly. Now they adore him and even start identifying with him. He takes his punishment, but remains victorious.

Explanation: The situation is similar to the one previously described, but events now move in the opposite direction. These youngsters suffer similarly from a number of suppressed tendencies—such as just rebellion in favor of a suffering colleague—however, they are too fearful of the realistic consequences of such feelings. Their personal cowardice hinders them from doing what they feel is right, but what would have awful consequences for them. Again the hero commits the "initiatory act." Through his demonstration of courage the others suddenly discard anxieties and dare—if not to act, then, at least—to feel what their own standard of justice has long wanted them to experience.

Formula: The central person renders a service to the ego of the potential group members. He does so by committing the "initiatory act" and thus saves them anxieties and conflicts. The "initiatory act," however, leads in the direction of moral values *versus* cowardly self-protection this time. On the basis of this service the undesirable tendencies toward cowardly submission in these children are conquered. Through this common conflict-solution group psychological emotions are evoked.

Type 9: The "Bad Influence"

There are children in many classes who are constantly being accused of being "undesirable elements" by all teachers, parents, and by the other children, too. And yet, they can scarcely be accused of "having an evil" influence. Usually what they are accused of is unclear but it is assumed that their mere presence in the classroom affects the others badly—"brings out the worst in them." And yet it would be embarrassing to say how they do this. Accusations made against them often have to be withdrawn, because no definite basis exists in fact. Nothing can be proved. Sometimes, admittedly, these children are not so difficult to manage; they are better than the influence they are accused of having on the others. Fundamentally, this is an accusation of seduction through magic. Apparently belief in the infectiousness of something within these children seems absurd, and yet, it is not. The background upon which the accusations are made is usually true. These children do affect the others, not overtly—quite in contrast to the "seducer type"—but, by their presence in the same room, something happens to these youngsters which makes them unruly, full of "dirty" ideas, or just difficult to manage. What supports this?

Illustrative Example: In a botany class of eleven-year-old children, a word is mentioned which reminds those who "know" of a sex situation. About a dozen are preoccupied with associations of this sort. When the word is mentioned, they all look at one boy, then at each other. They grin. He grins back. The whole room, at this moment, is divided in two. The threads of this little clique are spread like a net over it. Next day a nearly identical situation recurs. However, that boy happens to be absent from class. Nothing happens. The children fail to make the same association as the day before. Their little "gang" remains submerged in the group without interruption.

Explanation: This type again is very similar to that of the "seducer"; the difference, however, rests in the technique used for "seduction." Nothing like the "initiatory act" is implied here. The explanation has to be reduced to a more descriptive statement to show how the "bad influence" works. The dynamic explanation must be considered later.

With the inner constellation of the potential group members similar to that described in the seduction type, it can apparently be said that they possess a number of undesirable drives which seek expression; their super-ego is in command of the situation, so that satisfaction of these undesirable drives is impossible without the penalty of remorse and anxiety; and, the ego of these children is in a "bad jam," squeezed between the urges of their drives and the demands of a strong super-ego.

The inner constellation of the "bad influence" type of a central person is different from that of the group members. In him there is no conflict. His drives in the same direction do not set loose conflicts and problems for him. He faces them and does not care. Alertness, on the part of the others to this event seems sufficient encouragement for the expression of what they had just been trying to suppress. This really means the assumption of a definite process which might best be described by saying that the "unconflicted" personality constellation has an infectious influence on the conflicted whenever they meet. This again is the description of an easily observable fact, which by itself provides no understanding of the process. However, it is enough to explain the group formative processes in these cases. It is important to realize that these examples of so-called "bad influence" are usually group psychological procedures.

Formula: The central person renders a service to the ego of the potential group members. He does so by virtue of the "infectiousness of the unconflicted personality constellation upon the conflicted one." Through this, he saves them the expense of guilt feelings, anxieties, and conflicts. On the basis of this service, the latent undesirable drives of these children can manifest openly. Through this common conflict solution, these children develop group emotions in relationship with each other.

Type 10: The "Good Example"

Illustrative Example: The same class as the one mentioned in the previous example contains another group of boys who "gang up" with each other even more intensively than do the undesirable ones. Nevertheless, the teacher would hesitate to call them a "gang" or even a group. They are just a bunch of very good friends, he would say. However, one of them is the obvious center, and he "has a marvelous influence" upon the others. They are much nicer when he is around. If pressed, the teacher could hardly explain how that boy manages to influence them for he obviously does nothing. In looking at this group more closely, the following situation is discovered. These children are not "friends" in the personal meaning of this term. All are at that stage where they are full of new curiosities of which they are afraid, because they would feel guilty in satisfying them. This one boy, however, is far removed from any undesirable thought or act.

Explanation: The inner constellation in the potential group members shows a number of undesirable drives seeking expression, the super-ego is decidedly against this but scarcely able to maintain its position for long, and the ego is in a "bad jam" about how to maintain balance in such a situation. The inner constellation of the central boy in this situation contains no conflict of this kind. The mere idea of expressing undesirable thoughts in his presence is impossible. So, the group moves closer to him; in his presence they feel secure. What they fear is their own drives; what they look for is some support for their endangered super-ego. The situation is the exact reverse of the "Bad Influence" example.

Formula: The central person renders a service to the ego of the potential group members. He does so by virtue of the "infectiousness of the unconflicted personality constellation upon the conflicted one." Through this, he saves them the necessity to face their own drives of which they are afraid, and conflicts resulting from this. This time, however, the solution leads in the direction of moral values instead of undesirable drives. On the basis of this service, the children can suppress their undesirable drives according to the command of their own super-ego. Through this common conflict solution they develop group emotions in the relationship with each other.

SUMMARY

For the purpose of rapid summary, these ten types can be grouped into three main categories and tabulated.

The Role of the Central Person for the Group Formative Process

The Central Person as an Object of Identification	
On the basis of love	
Incorporation into conscience	Type 1
Incorporation into the "ego ideal"	Type 2
On the basis of fear	
Identification with the aggressor	Type 3
The Central Person as an Object of Drives	
As an object of love drives	Type 4
As an object of aggressive drives	Type 5
The Central Person as an Ego Support	
Providing means for drive satisfaction	Type 6
Dissolving conflict situations through guilt-anxiety assuagement	
Through the technique of the initiatory act in the service of drive satisfaction	Type 7

and in the service of drive defense — Type 8
Through the "infectiousness of the unconflicted personality constellation over the conflicted one" in the service of drive satisfaction — Type 9
and in the service of drive defense — Type 10

REFERENCES

1. Freud, Anna. *The ego and the mechanisms of defense.* London: Hogarth, 1922.
2. Freud, S. *Group psychology and the analysis of the ego.* London: Hogarth, 1922.

The Principles and Traits of Leadership

CECIL A. GIBB

INTRODUCTION

THE PROBLEM of leadership as a psychological phenomenon is closely related with considerations of the nature of personality and achieves some clarity if the relation between the two concepts is briefly considered. Psychologists have defined personality generally in one of two ways: (*a*) as the effect the individual has on other people or (*b*) as the total pattern of habits of cognition, affection, and conation. The latter use is that more frequently chosen. Personality in this sense is an abstraction from observed behavior and the apparent relations of this behavior to the individual's needs and to the environment. As Burt has recently pointed out (2),

> [the individual is never an isolated unit and] what the psychologist has to study are the interactions between a "personality" and an "environment"–the behavior of a dynamic mind in a dynamic field of which it forms a part.

ABRIDGED from *Journal of Abnormal and Social Psychology,* 1947, 42, 267–284. Reprinted by permission of the author and the American Psychological Association, Inc.

The writer is indebted to Emeritus Professor H. T. Lovell and to Professor W. M. O'Neil for a critical reading of a draft of this paper.

"Leadership" is a concept applied to the personality-environment relation to describe the situation when one, or at most a very few, personalities are so placed in the environment that his, or their, "will, feeling, and insight direct and control others in the pursuit of a cause" (9).

Leadership has usually been thought of as a specific attribute of personality, a personality trait, that some persons possess and others do not, or at least that some achieve in high degree and others scarcely at all. The search for leaders has often been directed toward finding those persons who have this trait well developed. The truth would seem, however, to be quite different. In fact, viewed in relation to the individual, leadership is not an attribute of the personality but a quality of his role within a particular and specified social system.[1] Viewed in relation to the group, leadership is a quality of its structure. And, depending upon the definition of "group," this particular quality may become a "*sine qua non*." Without leadership, there is no focus about which a number of individuals may cluster to form a group. A group is here defined as two or more people in a state of social interaction. Group activity means that individuals are acting together in some fashion; that there is some order of the different lines of individual action. There is a division of labor within a group that is accepted by all members of the group. In a discussion group, for example, the speaker performs a task different from that of other members. Both he and the members act in expected ways, and yet their behavior may be collective. The coherence occurs because of the common understandings or cultural traditions as to how they should behave. Similarly, the concept of leadership as a cultural norm plays a considerable part in the emergence of a leader. And this would seem to be the significance of Warren's parenthetic statement that "leadership depends on attitudes and habits of dominance in certain individuals and submissive behavior in others" (11). It is not implied that these are instincts variously strong in some individuals and weak in others, but that these are accepted ways of behaving within the cultural framework and that therefore they tend to determine the field forces acting in a group situation.

LEADERSHIP THEORY

This dynamic conception of groups composed of dynamic entities or personalities interacting will accord well with Lewin's notion (7) that the individual's characteristics and actions change under the varying influence of "the social field." It does not seem unreasonable to claim that groups have

1 "The place in a particular system which a certain individual occupies at a particular time will be referred to as his *status* with respect to that system" (8, p. 76). "In so far as it represents overt behavior, a *role* is the dynamic aspect of a status: what the individual has to do in order to validate his occupation of the status" (8, p. 77).

a capacity to propel to leadership one or more of their number; and, what is more, the choice of a specific individual for the leadership role will be more dependent upon the nature of the group and of its purpose than upon the personality of the individual; but it will be most dependent upon the relation between the personality and the group at any particular moment. That is to say, in Linton's terms, that the group choice of a leader will be determined by the status of individual members. This claim does not lose sight of the nature of the individuals who constitute the group, and it does not assert that any member may be propelled to leadership nor does it suggest that the social situation alone makes the leader. Leadership is both a function of the social situation and a function of personality, but it is a function of these two in interaction; no additive concept is adequate to explain the phenomenon. There is no justification for saying that personality qualities which make for leadership exist in a latent form when not being exercised in a social situation. Any qualities of personality common to leaders in varying situations may also exist in persons who never achieve leadership status. What might be called the attributes of leaders are abstracts from a total interactional situation and are qualities of a particular social role. In the absence of this kind of social situation the latent existence of the same pattern of qualities cannot be inferred. Again, this does not mean that there can be no potential leaders, but it does mean that the potentiality cannot be directly known any more than capacity can be known except as a back-inference from expressed ability.

Leadership is not usually an enduring role unless an organization is built up which enables an individual to retain the role after he ceases to be qualified for it. In this case leadership becomes domination or mere headship. In the absence of such an artificial restriction, the interaction within the group is very fluid and the momentary group leader is that person who is able to contribute most to progress toward the common goal. Ten men previously unknown to each other are set a common problem, such as transporting heavy radio equipment to the top of a steep cliff. In the initial stages they are ten individuals thinking of possible solutions. One may find a solution which he communicates to the others. Usually this establishes interaction. The ten now become one group and the group focus is the man, A, who offered the solution. He is the leader at the moment. He is in the position of influencing their behavior more than they influence his. He is in the role of initiator of group action, which at this point consists of discussion. If now his plan is accepted, the group goal changes. It has been the choice of a plan and for that phase A occupied the leadership role. The goal now, however, is the execution of the plan. Two things may happen. A, by virtue of a prestige he has acquired, may continue in the role of leader or he may find another individual, B, naturally taking over. The group problem is now more practical, and B may, by virtue of his different innate capacities or previous experiences, be better able to contribute to the group project. Leadership then passes naturally to B, and, if difficulties are met and a third man, C, offers a solution, the role may pass to him. On the other hand, it is possible that all of these individuals, A, B, and C, may find their retention of the leadership role very short lived and even momentary only because another member of the group, D, rises to a more permanent occupancy of the role by virtue of his ability to translate suggestions into working orders, and by virtue of his greater social effectiveness.

Observation of group behavior in this way strongly supports the contention that leadership is not an attribute of personality or of character. It is a social role, the successful adoption of which depends upon a complex of abilities and traits. But even more, the adoption of a leadership role is dependent upon the specific situation. The same individual in the same group may alternate between the role of leader and follower as the group goal changes. Most frequently the individual is propelled into a position of leadership by virtue of his capacity for interpersonal contribution in the specific situation. There is, however, a generic aspect to leadership as Du Vall (3) has pointed out. This is indicated by the fact that the person of all-round superiority is more frequently in situations in which he is able to make a contribution.

The first main point to be made, then, in leadership theory is that leadership is relative always to the situation. Men may come together and yet not constitute a group. Until the individuals of the aggregation are given a common object or goal, there will be no social interaction and consequently no group formation. Each may face an individual problem and achieve an individual solution. But when many face a common problem and one or more of the individual solutions is communicated to others then there is interaction, and, if that interaction is focused upon one or two individuals in the group, then he or they are leaders for the time being. Clearly, in order that such a situation may develop, it is necessary that there should be a problem, and that it should be such a problem as to afford an opportunity for the play of individual differences in its solution. The circumstances must be such as to require a choice. As Schneider (10) has pointed out, it is the social circumstances which make particular attributes of personality attributes of leadership. While the social circumstances are such as to demand the original formulation of a plan, inventing ability will be an attribute of personality determining the adoption of a leadership role. But, the plan having been formulated, the social circumstances then demand not invention but social effectiveness as an attribute of personality essential for the leadership role. And, unless the same individual possesses both attributes, the leadership passes from one to another. The situation determines which of many attributes of personality will be attributes of leadership at any given moment. That is why Pigors (9) observes that, "whenever an obstacle physical or mental prevents the flow of action, the group welcomes any manifestation of individual difference that tends to resolve this uncertainty or to facilitate group action."

Leadership, then, is always relative to the situation (*a*) to the extent that a certain kind of situation is required before the leadership relation will appear at all, and (*b*) in the sense that the particular set of social circumstances existing at the moment determines which attributes of personality will confer leadership status and consequently determines which members of a group will assume the leadership role, and which qualities of personality function to maintain the individual in that role. This was one of the things indicated by Thrasher's study of juvenile gangs in Chicago. Leadership seemed to be a quality that came out as the group moved about together–it was the result of the social situation. This is, in fact, the second principle of leadership theory. It is that individual accession to the leadership role is dependent upon the group goal and upon the capacity of the individual to contribute to the achievement of the goal. Pigors says:

> It is nonsense to talk of leadership in the abstract since no one can just lead without having a goal. Leadership is always *in* some sphere of interest, and *toward* some objective goal seen by leader and follower (9).

Only in so far as the individual can contribute to group progress in the required direction has he any claim to a hearing, and, unless he can establish himself with his fellow members, he will not receive recognition as their leader. This is, of course, to raise the question whether the leader can exercise a creative influence upon the group's goals and activities or whether he can do no more than express and exemplify already accepted ideals and contribute to progress in the direction of an accepted goal perhaps by pin pointing and clarifying a previously vague conception. Klineberg (5) suggests that a compromise is indicated in that "the leader has great influence but only on certain groups under certain conditions. Change these or change him," he says, "and the resulting behavior is markedly altered." Schneider (10), on the other hand, claims that the "new" history as written by Marx, Turner, Beard, and others, "sees leaders as a product of the times and leadership as a function of the circumstances of the moment." The problem seems to be indeterminate because there is no denying that the "great men" of history have been responsible for changes in the social situation of which they were a part but there is no way of telling to what extent these changes would have occurred anyway or under the leadership of another group-chosen personality.

The third characteristic of the leadership process to which attention may be drawn is that its basic psychology is that of social interaction. There can be no leadership in isolation, it is distinctly a quality of a group situation. There can be no leader without followers. An individual's intellectual quality may be very superior and his individual solution of a group problem may be excellent but he is not a leader until his solution is communicated, and then not until other people are associated with him in giving expression to his ideas. Leader and follower must be united by common goals and aspirations and by a will to lead, on one side, and a will to follow, on the other, i.e., by a common acceptance of one another. From this it follows that the individual must have membership character in the group which makes him its leader, because leaders and followers are interdependent. This is the first of Brown's (1) "field dynamical laws of leadership," and the first of Du Vall's (3) criteria of the leadership process. The leader must be a member of the group; he must share the group objectives and aspirations. Stated in other words, this principle of mutual interaction between the leader and the group implies that the individual chosen leader must have certain qualities of personality which, derived as they are from his group-membership-character, confer upon him a certain social effectiveness and determine his acceptability.

Having group-membership-character, it is upon individual differences that one depends for election to leadership status. It is because there are individual differences of capacity and skill that one, and usually only one, of a group emerges having a pattern of qualifications superior to others for meeting present group needs. But these "superior" persons must not be too different. Followers subordinate themselves not to an individual who is utterly different but to a member of their group who has superiority at this time and who is fundamentally the same as they are, and who at other times is prepared to be a follower just as they are.

For Jennings (4):

> Leadership is definable by a manner of interacting with others. . . . Both isolation and leadership were found to be products of interpersonal interaction and not of attributes residing within the persons. . . . No simple variable such as the length of time the individual had been in the community or his chronological age relative to other members, or his intelligence or even his greater opportunity for contacting others, appears to account for the particular choice-status accorded him. Instead the reciprocal interplay maintaining between the individual and those in the same field and constituting the individual's personality as the latter view him appears to be the underlying basic explanation of isolation and leadership.

The determination of the role to be played by the individual is the group reaction to his interpersonal contribution. The close relation between leader and followers is therefore apparent.

The leader inevitably embodies many of the qualities of the followers. Any individual's personality at a given point in time reflects the field forces with which it is interacting. The personality which most adequately reflects those forces is the one most likely to be propelled to leadership. Thus it is that La Piere and Farnsworth (6) are led to make the point that because there is such close interaction between the leader and the led it is often difficult to determine just who affects whom and to what extent. For this reason it is possible for leadership to be nominal only. This possibility is emphasized by a carry-over of prestige from one point in time to another. The fact that individual A in our earlier example was intellectually quickest with a suggested solution of the group problem established him as a focus of attention in the minds of the others. Momentarily, at any rate, he became their leader and they became followers. A definite interactional pattern was established. A social-cultural evaluation was made of him by the others. That is precisely what is meant by prestige. Prestige is a distinction attaching to a person in the minds of others. It depends, as we have now seen, on the qualities ascribed to the individual by other members of the group. As Young points out, prestige is a special case of the point

> that a man's personality reflects others' image and recognition of him. A leader's prestige rests upon the apperceptive background of the followers. The leader takes on the qualities which his adherents project on him (12).

This, too, is Brown's (1) second "field dynamical law of leadership," that the "leader must represent a region of high potential in the social field," i.e., that he must have prestige and this he acquires by symbolizing the ideals of all members of the group. In some instances it may be said that prestige within a group is acquired by virtue of an external appointment or by virtue of a certain status in an institution which embraces that group, as in the case of a parish priest. In such a case the assumption of a leadership role is made easier, but it is still true that it will be retained only while the individual so appointed is able to symbolize the ideals of the group members. In other words, the personality thus "made" leader must so reflect the field forces within the group with which it is interacting as to have had potential leadership status if membership without leadership could have been granted by the appointment.

Reviewing leadership theory one may say, then, that its three most important principles are, first, that leadership is always relative to the situation—relative, that is, in two senses: (*a*) that leadership flourishes only in a problem situation and (*b*) that the nature of the leadership role is determined by the goal of the group; and this is, in fact, the second principle of leadership, that it is always toward some objective goal. The third principle is that leadership is a process of mutual stimulation—a social interactional phenomenon in which the attitudes, ideals, and aspirations of the followers play as important a determining role as do the individuality and personality of the leader.

These principles lead us to accept Pigors' (9) definition of leadership as a "process of mutual stimulation which, by the successful interplay of relevant individual differences controls human energy in the pursuit of a common cause." And any person may be called a leader "during the time when and in so far as, his will, feeling, and insight direct and control others in the pursuit of a cause which he presents."

As Jennings says:

> the "why" of leadership appears not to reside in any personality trait considered singly, nor even in a constellation of related traits, but in the interpersonal contribution of which the individual becomes capable in a specific setting eliciting such contribution from him (4).

provided that the individual superiority is not so great as to preclude solidarity of purpose.

Such a theory of the leadership process excludes such group situations as those organized for professional tuition, expert advice, management, and the like, and excludes the concept of headship. When once the group activity has become dominated by an established and accepted organization, leadership tends to disappear. Even if this organization originally served the leadership role, any continuance of the organization as such, after the causal set of circumstances has ceased to exist, represents a transition to a process of domination or headship, where headship is regarded, as Warren (11) defined it, as "a form of authority determined by caste, class or other factors than popular selection and acceptance," and where domination is defined by Pigors (9) as

> a process of social control in which accepted superiors assume a position of command and demand obedience from those who acknowledge themselves as inferiors in the social scale; and in which by the forcible assumption of authority and the accumulation of prestige a person (through a hierarchy of functionaries) regulates the activities of others for purposes of his own choosing.

The characteristics of this process of domination as distinct from that of leadership are that: (*a*) the position of headship is maintained through an organized system and not by the spontaneous recognition of the individual contribution to the group goal; (*b*) the group goal is arbitrarily chosen by the autocratic head in his own self-interest and is not internally determined; (*c*) there is not really *a group* at all, since there is no sense of shared feeling or joint action; and (*d*) there is in this process a wide social gap between the group members and the head, who strives to maintain this social distance as an aid to his coercion of the group through fear.

This concept of domination and headship is important because it is so different from that of leadership and because so much so-called leadership in industry, education, and in other social spheres is not leadership at all, but is simply domination. It is not, however, necessary that headship should preclude leadership.

REFERENCES

1. Brown, J. F. *Psychology and the social order.* New York: McGraw-Hill, 1936.
2. Burt, C. The assessment of personality. *Brit. J. educ. Psychol.*, 1945, 15, 107–121.
3. Du Vall, E. W. *Personality and social group work.* New York: Association Press, 1943.
4. Jennings, Helen H. *Leadership and isolation.* London: Longmans Green, 1943.
5. Klineberg, O. *Social psychology.* New York: Holt, 1940.
6. La Piere and Farnsworth. *Social psychology.* (2nd Ed.) New York: McGraw-Hill, 1942.
7. Lewin, K. *A dynamic theory of personality.* New York: McGraw-Hill, 1935.
8. Linton, R. *The cultural background of personality.* New York: Appleton-Century, 1945.
9. Pigors, P. *Leadership or domination.* Boston: Houghton-Mifflin, 1935.
10. Schneider, J. Social class, historical circumstances and fame. *Amer. J. Sociol.*, 1937, 43, 37–56.
11. Warren, H. C. *Dictionary of psychology.* Boston: Houghton Mifflin, 1934.
12. Young, Kimball. *Social psychology.* (2nd Ed.) New York: Crofts, 1945.

"Subjective" and "Objective" Elements in the Social Field: The Three Step Procedure

KURT LEWIN

ONE last point concerning conceptualization and general methodology may be mentioned. To predict the course of a marriage, for instance, a psychologist might proceed in the following way. He might start by analyzing the life space of the husband H. This analysis would involve the relevant physical and social facts in the husband's surroundings, including the expectations and character of his wife W, all represented in the way the husband, H, perceives them. Let us assume that this analysis is sufficiently complete to permit the derivation of the resultant forces on

FROM Kurt Lewin, Frontiers in group dynamics: Concept, method and reality in social science; social equilibria and social change. *Human Relations*, 1947, 1, 5–41. Reprinted by permission of Mrs. Gertrude W. Lewin and the publisher.

the husband (Fig. 1a). This would be equivalent to a prediction of what the husband actually will do as his next step. The data about the life space of the husband might be sufficiently elaborate to determine the resultant force on the wife W, as he sees her (Fig. 1a). This resultant force, however, would not indicate what the wife will actually do but merely what the husband expects his wife to do.

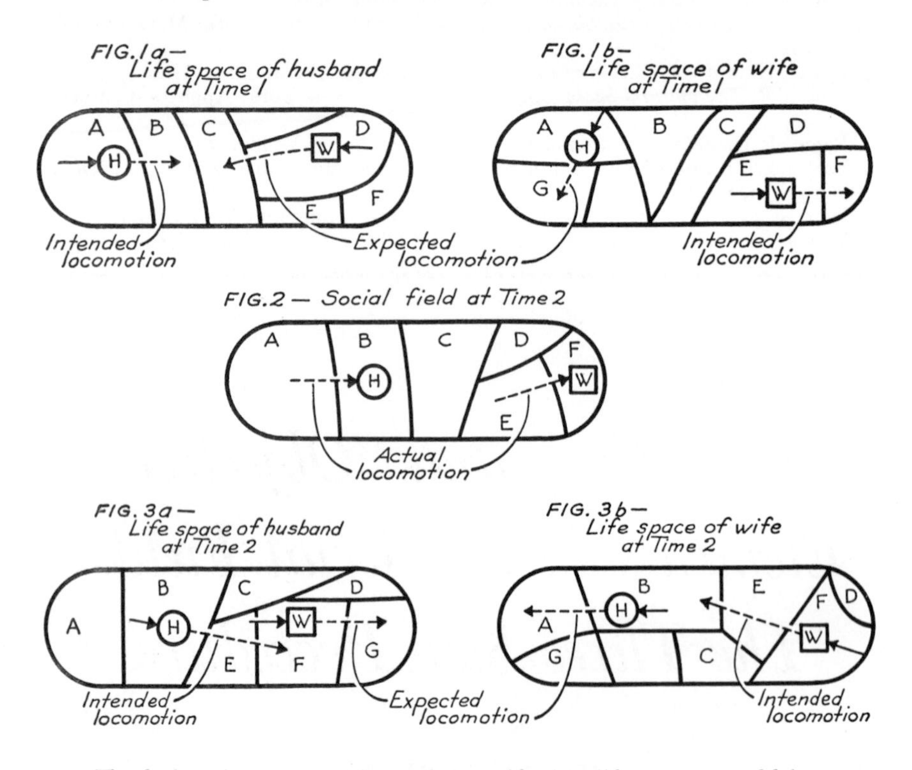

To derive the next conduct of the wife, her life space would have to be analyzed (Fig. 1b). Usually the wife will see the situation, including herself, W, and her husband, H, somewhat differently from her husband. Let us assume she sees her husband located in an area corresponding to his own perception of himself; that she perceives her own position, however, as being in region e rather than d; and that the cognitive structure of the intermediate regions b and c are for her, too, somewhat different from what they are for her husband. Corresponding to this difference between the life spaces of the husband and wife, the resultant force on the wife, W, may point to the region f rather than to c. This means that the wife will actually move forward f rather than toward c as her husband expected.

The considerations thus far give the basis for predicting the next moves of husband and wife to the region b and f respectively (Fig. 2):

analyzing the two psychological ("subjective") fields gives the basis for predicting the actual ("objective") next step of behavior.

But how do we proceed from here if we are to answer the social problem of the fate of the marriage? Neither husband nor wife had expected their partner to behave as he or she actually did. Obviously, the next step will depend largely on how each will react to this surprise, how each will interpret the conduct of the other, or, more generally speaking, how each will "perceive" the new situation.

The husband who has expected his wife to move from d to c and now sees her moving in the opposite direction, to f, may interpret this to mean that his wife has "changed her mind." In this case he may expect her next move to proceed in the same direction, namely toward g (Fig. 3a). Furthermore, the behavior of his wife is likely to change for him the "meaning" of c, that is, the cognitive structure of the situation. The wife who sees her husband move to b rather than g may perceive this to be an excursion to an activity which would be completed in a certain time after which he would return to a (Fig. 3b). She therefore decides to join her husband in b (Fig. 3b), whereas her husband, having a different perception of the situation (Fig. 3a), intends to move on to f, which he perceives as being closer to his wife.

Obviously, husband and wife will soon be in trouble if they do not "talk things over," that is, if they do not communicate to each other the structure of their life spaces with the object of equalizing them.

This analysis of the history of a marriage has proceeded in a series of three steps: first, a separate analysis of the psychological situation of the husband and that of the wife, at time 1 with the purpose of deriving the next behavior of each. Second, representing the resultant sociological ("objective") situation at time 2. Third, deriving with the help of the laws of perception the resultant psychological situation for husband and wife at time 2. This would give the basis for the next sequence of three steps, starting with the analysis of the psychological situation of the persons involved predict their actual next step.

Such a procedure looks involved, particularly if we consider groups composed of many members. Is it possible to eliminate the "objective," or the "subjective," aspect of this analysis? Actually, social science faces here two types of question; one concerning the size of units, the other concerning the role of perception in group life. It would be prohibitive if the analysis of group life always had to include analysis of the life space of each individual member.

Analysis of group life, can proceed rather far on the basis of relatively larger units. In the end, of course, the theory of small and large units has to be viewed in social science as well as in physical science, as one theoretical system. But this stage can be reached only after an attack on both the larger and the smaller units.

Unfortunately, treating groups as units does not eliminate the dilemma between "subjective" and "objective" aspects of social fields. It seems to be impossible to predict group behavior without taking into account group goals, group standards, group values, and the way a group "sees" its own situation and that of other groups. Group conflicts would have quite different solutions if the various groups concerned did not perceive differently the situation existing at a given time. To predict or to understand the steps leading to war between two nations A and B it seems to be essential to refer to the group life space of A and to the different group life space of B. This means that the analysis of group interaction has again to follow a three-step procedure, moving from the separate analysis of the life space of each group to the group conduct in the total social field and from there back again to the effect on the group life space.

This procedure of analysis which swings from an analysis of "perception" to that of "action," from the "subjective" to the "objective," and back again is not an arbitrary demand of scientific methodology, nor is it limited to the interaction between groups or between individuals. The procedure mirrors one of the basic properties of group life. Any kind of group action or individual action, even including that of the insane, is regulated by circular causal processes of the following type: individual perception or "fact-finding"—for instance, an act of accounting—is linked with individual action or group action in such a way that the content of the perception or fact-finding depends upon the way in which the situation is changed by action. The result of the fact-finding in turn influences or steers action.

Certain schools in psychology, sociology, and economics have had the tendency to eliminate the problems of perception. The analysis of all social sciences, however, will have to take into account both sections of this circular process.

Contributions of Sociometry to Research Methodology in Sociology

J. L. MORENO

TWO THESES spearheaded my original program of research in social science, (*1*) "The whole of human society develops in accord with definite laws" (6, p. 4), (*2*) "A truly therapeutic procedure cannot have less an objective than the whole of mankind" (6, p. 3). From the point of view of "system" the two theses led logically to the differentiation between Sociometry and Sociatry.[1]

According to Sociometry, society systems are preference or attraction-repulsion systems. This is claimed to be true not only of human, but also of non-human societies. It also claimed that human preferential systems cannot be examined adequately by the old methods of fact-finding objectivity as statistical methods and observational methods, but that the methods themselves and the instruments derived from them have to undergo a process of *subjectification* in order to return to the researcher endowed with a more profound objectivity, having gained a grasp of the social processes on the depth level. This new *sociometric objectivity* can well be contrasted with the old *positivistic* objectivity of Comte.

It is due to this striving of sociometric method towards a superior and more complete objectivity that we gave systematic emphasis:

FROM *American Sociological Review*, 1947, 12, 287–292. Reprinted by permission of the author and publisher.

1 "The imbalances within the social atom and their reflection upon the development of psychological currents and networks give social psychiatry a nosological basis and differentiate it as a discipline from psychiatry proper. Psychiatric concepts as neurosis and psychosis are not applicable to socioatomic processes. A group of individuals may become *sociotic* and the syndrome producing this condition can be called a *sociosis*" (6, p. 192). See also Moreno (8).

(a) To the study of social structures in statu nascendi (concept of the moment).

(b) To the shift from the gross examination of social aggregates to minute atomistic events, from the macroscopic to the microscopic method (6, pp. 134–164, ch. 9) of investigation.

(c) To the development of situational sociology (situation and role analysis).

(d) To operational and measurement procedures, and above all,

(e) To a revolution of the relationship between the investigator and his subjects.

They themselves were thus motivated to be and turned into researchers of each other. A community of a thousand people for instance, became animated by sociometric devices to account for their social feelings and possibly to correct them. Sociometry became then, paraphrasing the famous saying of Lincoln: *the sociology of the people, by the people, and for the people.* The operation of sociological research became itself socio (mass) centered instead of individual centered.

It is due to this reorientation in research methodology that new instruments of a great variety have been invented and their number is still rapidly growing. They have been differentiated in accord with their particular focus, in (*1*) sociometric tests, (*2*) action tests, (*3*) situation tests, (*4*) role tests, (*5*) spontaneity tests, (*6*) psycho-dramatic tests, (7) sociodramatic tests. The new and provocative material required original forms of presentation. The chief innovations have been (a) the sociogram (1931), (b) the sociomatrix, and (c) the "action matrix" (1923).

We have contrasted the macrosociologies of Comte, Marx, Sumner, etc., with the "micro-sociologies" among which sociometry is the most conscious representative. By sociomicroscopic configurations we do not mean only the informal small groups, but the dynamic social units of which they are comprised, the pattern variants of social atoms, the clustering of social atoms into larger associations invisible to the eye of the human observer (social molecules), psychosocial networks, the clustering of numerous such networks into more comprehensive formations; finally the study of dyads, triangles, quadrangles, pentagons, and chains of persons. We assumed that the study of these primary atomic structures of human relations is the preliminary and indispensable groundwork to most macrosociological investigations.

Sociology owes to Sociometry a few genuine generalizations among which are most prominent (a) the law of social gravitation or mobility,[2] (b) the sociogenetic law,[3] (c) the sociodynamic law,[4] (d) the reality test

2 Stated by Moreno (6) and furthered by Deutschberger, along sociometric lines (3), approached from a different angle by Stouffer (14), Stewart (12, 13), Thorndike (15), and Bassett (1). See also Moreno (6, ch. 20, pp. 342–345).

3 Stated by Moreno (6), furthered by Jennings (5) and Criswell (2).

4 The idea of a sociodynamic law has been formulated by Moreno (6, 7, 8).

of social configurations (11), (e) the law of the social atom,[5] and (f) the tele phenomenon.[6]

(A) THE LAW OF SOCIAL GRAVITATION OR MOBILITY

My first formulation of a law of social gravity was: "Mankind is a social and organic unity.—Tendencies must emerge between the different parts of this unity drawing them at one time apart and drawing them another time together.—These attractions and repulsions or their derivatives may have a near or distant effect not only upon the immediate participants in the relation but also upon all other parts of that unity which we call mankind.—Its organization develops and distributes itself in space apparently according to a law of social gravity which seems to be valid for every kind of grouping irrespective of the membership (6, p. 3).

This was thirteen years ago. Since then a number of studies have been advanced in which the idea of such a law was postulated. It may be worthwhile to compare the methods brought forth by non-sociometric [2] sociologists, Stouffer (1940), Stewart (1941), Thorndike (1942), with the methods proposed by sociometrists from Moreno (1934) to Deutschberger (1946). According to my formulation the movements of populations are propelled by two processes. One process draws the groups apart; the other process draws the groups together. The sociometric formula of social gravitation states:

> People 1 (P1) and People (P2) move towards each other—between a locality X and a locality Y—in direct proportion to the amount of attraction given (a1) or received (a2), in inverse proportion to the amount of repulsion given (r1) or received (r2), the physical distance (d) between the two localities being constant, the facilities of communication between X and Y being equal.

The formulas of Stouffer and Stewart, based on statistical analysis of number and distance, even if correct in themselves, are unsatisfactory because of their symbolic character, leaving the people out, the dynamics of inter-personal and inter-group relations. Stewart's finding can be easily integrated into the sociometric formula which then would read as follows:

> People 1 (P1) and People (P2) move towards each other in direct proportion to the amount of attraction given (a1) or received (a2), in inverse proportion to the amount of repulsion given (r1) or received (r2) and in inverse proportion to the physical distance (d) between locality X and locality Y, the residences of P1 and P2 respectively, the facilities of communication between X and Y being constant.

I applied the sociometric findings in a small community to the macrosociological phenomenon of inter-state migration.[4] Comparing the census

5 Stated by Moreno (6). See also Jennings (4).
6 Stated by Moreno (6).

figures of spontaneous migration of people from one state to the other, from east to west, from the south to the north, within a given period, with the sociometrically explored migrations in a small community, I suggested that the same law which determines the migratory movements in a small community dominates the spontaneous migration of people throughout the territory of the United States. Sociometric evidence further indicated that the desire for migration (the number of potential and frustrated attempts) is many times larger than the migration which becomes manifest. It indicates, too, that the parts of the country towards which these potential unfulfilled migrations tend, are important phenomena in the analysis of social gravitation. Census reports provide us only with the end results. They do not register the full process, the invisible processes of migration, from the statu nascendi of an embryonic striving on, all the intermediary stages of a plan up to the act of migration itself. A full understanding of migratory movements cannot be attained without their recognition.[7]

(B) THE SOCIOGENETIC LAW

Another important generalization introduced by sociometry (6, pp. 65–66) is usually called the sociogenetic law. It states that the highest forms of group organization have evolved from simple ones: between the simplest patterns of groups formed by infants and the most complex formed by adults there are numerous intermediary stages. Parallel with this process of social differentiation a characteristic differentiation and growth of socio-sexual structure takes place within the group. The course of differentiation may differ from one culture to another, from a pre-literate to a modern society, but a common basic core of evolutionary patterns and a parallel trend should be found in all of them. From a sociatric point of view, the sociogenetic law is a challenge to the therapist. It is probable that a comparative study of cultures will show a great degree of variety in the evolutionary trend taken by their infant groups moving up to their adult groups, but it is doubtful that the trend itself can be abolished. The sociogenetic and social gravity laws both are merely symptoms of societies which are basically preference systems. Abolishing the laws entirely would mean that these systems of preference themselves have vanished and that human nature and human society have turned into forms which must be considered as unreal to our comprehension.

(C) THE SOCIODYNAMIC LAW

The sociodynamic law is divided into a first and a second part. The first part (6, p. 74) states that the income of emotional choices per capita is

7 Deutschberger furthered the study of social gravitation in terms defined by mathematical procedures by directly submitting U.S. census tracts to sociometric tests and comparing the patterns of attracting in changing neighborhoods.

unevenly divided among the members of the group regardless of its size or kind; comparatively few get a lion's share of the total output of emotional choices, out of proportion with their needs and their ability to consummate them; the largest form an average income of choice group within their means to consummate them and a considerable number remain unchosen or neglected. The scores when plotted form a J curve, about two-thirds of the population receiving scores below chance and a relatively few obtaining high scores. Though an equal number would have been expected on the basis of chance the proportion of isolates was generally greater than the proportion of stars.

The second part states that if the opportunities of being chosen are increased by increasing the size of the group and the number of choices per capita, the volume of choices continue to go to those at the top end of the range (the "stars") in direct proportion to the size of the group and to the number of choices permitted per capita, furthering the gap between the small star group, the average group, and the neglected group. The excess "profit" gained by the already overchosen members must be ascribed to a chain and network effect which operates in cases of non-acquaintance (with the chosen individual) in addition to the score based on acquaintance (with the chosen individual). The direct factor is proximity choice, the indirect factor, a symbolic choice. An individual, A, may score high in his face to face group, but because of his "role" (he may be a baseball player, an actor, or a senator) his ultimate score may turn out to be a multiple of the initial score (role corresponds here to what is usually meant by status; status is too much of an abstraction, but role implies a living and concrete function).

The sociodynamic law affects all human relations, it operates, (a) on the inter-personal level and (b) on the inter-group level. It is found in some degree in all social aggregates whatever their kind, whether the criterion is search for mates, search for employment, or in socio-cultural relations. Its effect may change in degree but it is universally present, appearing like a halo effect, *inherent in every* social structure. A particularly significant effect takes place on the level of economic relations. The "surplus" choice becomes analogous to the surplus value observed by Marx in the process of accumulation and production of capital. The distorted profit picture in economic relations is a reflection of the distorted choice picture on the inter-personal and inter-group level. The social revolution on the class struggle is therefore a displacement from the microscopic to the macroscopic level. Social revolution on the macrosociological level is only *part* of the struggle. Marx was operating on the gross, macrosociological level of events. He often used intuitively near-sociometric ideas—a "macro" sociometrist. He was therefore rarely altogether wrong, but also rarely altogether right. Being unaware of the social microscopy of modern sociometry, he committed many grave errors (9) of insight. It would be interesting to envision what effect this knowledge would have had upon his theory and method of social revolution. It appears at least that the place of revolutionary action should have been reoriented towards the smallest units of human relations, the social atoms, the primary receptacles of "preferentiation," in order to become truly and permanently effective. The sociodynamic effect does not cease to be effective in a socialistic system of society. It assumes only different forms. The sociodynamic law offers, from a sociatric point of view, a most serious challenge to the therapist. It can be argued that it is not a law of nature but a manifestation of our present cultural values. The fact that there are very few extremely high scores may be due to the cultural factor of the value we place on competition and skill. But according to sociometric tenets, laws of nature are not absolute but themselves products of nature and vulnerable to change. It considers the spontaneity or plasticity of the universe, physical and social, as preliminary to all laws of nature. The chances are that the sociodynamic effect can be *reduced* by therapeutic devices, like sociometric group reconstruction and spontaneity training applied on a world wide scale.

(D) THE REALITY TEST OF SOCIAL CONFIGURATIONS

A further contribution has been made by sociometry towards foundations of an objective sociology by formulating in terms defined by mathematical procedures a measure of social configurations. Based on their varying deviation from chance the degree of social significance of social configurations can be calculated. The generalizations resulting from this test should become a fruitful field for all sociological investigations dealing with the integration and disintegration of groups.

(E) THE LAW OF THE SOCIAL ATOM

The old sociological term socius, metaphorically and vaguely used in pre-sociometric literature, has regained in my discovery of the social atom a precise definition and has opened the way for fruitful hypotheses and practical research. The hypothesis states that as the individual projects his emotions into the groups around him and as the members of these groups in turn project their emotions toward him, a pattern of attractions and repulsions, as projected from both sides, can be discerned on the threshold between individual and group. This pattern is called his "social atom." "Every individual's social atom retains a significant *consistency* in its ratio of positive reciprocation and its interchoice ratio between two time points. The incidence of patterns at one time and at a later time in the same community is a relatively constant factor in the structure of attractions and in the structure of rejections which characterize it. There are found, in a given community, specific choice and rejection patterns and they show an orderly distribution within it. Yet, while the incidence of certain patterns may be relatively constant, the findings further show that the individuals occupying particular patterns at one time may or may not be the same individuals who occupy them at the later time."

(F) THE TELE PHENOMENON

I defined Tele as *the socio-gravitational factor responsible for the degree of reality of a social configuration above chance*. It operates between individuals, drawing them to form *more* positive or negative pair-relations, triangles, quadrangles, polygons, etc., than by chance. The factor responsible for the degree of irreality of social configurations *near or below* chance, can be called transference. Tele and transference (the pathological distortion of tele) became thus amenable to a sociometric type of quantification. Sociometrists differentiate therefore three types of relationships: reality produced relations (often described as coexistential, co-operational, two way or objectified relations), delusional relations, and esthetic relations. The reality produced relations are tele phenomena; it is upon them that the solidity and permanency of social relations depend. The delusional relations are transference phenomena and play a role in psychopathology. The esthetic relations are empathy phenomena, empathy being the one-way "Einfuehlung" into objects. It is harmful to stretch the meaning of transference to cover all human relationships beyond the definition given to it by its coiner. It is particularly meaningless because if we make transference an over-all term we would have to differentiate three types of transference, reality bound transference, delusional transference, and esthetic transference. This gives lip service to the "word" transference but it does not change the facts. It is preferable therefore, to have for every operation a specific term expressing it. In this manner the three phenomena, tele, transference, empathy, which were dormant and inherent in Mesmer's animal fluid, have been identified by sociometrists as independent functions and again brought together and shown in combined operation. Studies of the warming up process of individuals towards each other have revealed that the importance which psychoanalysis has given to transference is exaggerated. The tele phenomenon is operating already in the first meeting of two individuals. The longer a relationship lasts the more it becomes dominated by tele and not by transference. Even if the transference portion was large to begin with, it vanishes often as the relationship goes on. This is found to be true of all inter-individual relations, even of the relation between physician and patient. As the relationship endures the projectional aspects recede and the real attributes of the physician are perceived. In other words, true transference, in the psychoanalytic sense, diminishes in quantity and intensity as individuals mature and as groups gain in cohesion and integration. The effect of social catharsis is to increase tele production and to decrease transference production between members of groups. Tele, therefore, can be defined as the group binder, transference as the group *disintegrator*. That the factor tele operates between persons has been demonstrated by sociometric methods (11). It operates, (a) between persons like A B, who are mere acquaintances, (b) between persons like A B, who are not only mere acquaintances but who are attracting or rejecting one another in reference to one or more specific criteria, (c) between persons like A B, who are *unacquainted* persons but related to each other via a criterion; like A B, who are unacquainted *and* unrelated to each other by a criterion.

(G) SOCIOMETRIC TEST OF INTERGROUP RELATIONS

The most promising new development is the application of sociometric methods to intergroup relations. The one method now widely used is the *sociodrama* (10), stemming from psychodrama which studies interpersonal relations. Sociodrama studies intergroup relations by means of action methods. Psychodrama and sociodrama tests explore two different areas found interwoven in every group.

Another method suggested by the writer is a new sociometric test modified for the measurement of intergroup relations. The new sociometric test of inter-group relations differs from its twin test of interpersonal relations by the *systematic and gradual reduction of the choice area* permitted. Whereas for instance, in the interpersonal test the tendency was to extend for the individual the area of choice to a maximum, a maximum of self-expression, in order to gain insight into the endo-social thresholds, the tendency of the inter-group test is gradually to limit the choice area and focus his attention upon the restricted area. A sociometrist of a neighborhood may direct the inhabitants to choose their associates *only* among the Negroes, the Spanish, and the refugees and leave themselves, the American born out of being chosen. The expression of preference is then limited to the three minority groups. Or he may direct the inhabitants to choose their associates only among representatives of certain vocations, physicians, teachers, and lawyers, for instance, leaving all other vocations out. Through the data received, role (intergroup) preference instead of only individual preference comes to expression. Without losing the specificity of individual choice, the more varied and reduced the areas are, the more the results will gain a group categorical character. In proportion to the degree to which choice areas are reduced, there will result a scale ranging from a maximum degree of individual choice expression, to a maximum of group characterizations of its choice.

The *rapprochement* between sociometry and the social sciences is rapidly increasing. These are signposts indicating the trend, but there are many more. It means an advance of the combat forces against the threat of sociometric cultism, to an extent indispensable with any pioneering endeavor. This development, however, is in itself a case illustration of the law of gravity operating between sociometry and the social sciences. The progressive factors are increasing, the retarding factors are shrinking.

REFERENCES

1. Bassett, R. E. *Sociometry*, 1946, 9.
2. Criswell, Joan H. A sociometric study of race cleavage in the classroom. *Arch. Psychol.*, 1939, No. 235.
3. Deutschberger, P. Patterns of attraction in changing neighborhoods. *Sociometry*, 1946, 9, No. 4.
4. Jennings, Helen H. Experimental evidence of the social atom. *Sociometry*, 1942, 5, 135–145.
5. Jennings, Helen H. *Leadership and isolation.* London: Longmans, Green, 1943.
6. Moreno, J. L. *Who shall survive?* 1934.
7. Moreno, J. L. *Statistics of social configurations*, 1937–8.
8. Moreno, J. L. Sociometry and the cultural order. *Sociometry*, 1943, 6, 299–344.
9. Moreno, J. L. Marxism, Comtism and sociometry. *Sociometry*, 8, No. 2.
10. Moreno, J. L. Sociodrama. *Psychodrama Monogr.*, No. 1. Beacon House, N.Y.
11. Moreno, J. L., & Jennings, Helen H. Sociometric statistics of social configurations. *Sociometry*, 1938, 1, 342–374.
12. Stewart, J. Q. The gravitation or geographical drawing power of a college, 1941.
13. Stewart, J. Q. Influence of a population at a distance. *Sociometry*, 1942.
14. Stouffer, S. A. Intervening opportunities. *Amer. sociol. Rev.*, 1940.
15. Thorndike, E. L. The causes of inter-state migration. *Sociometry*, 1942.

Concepts and Methods in the Measurement of Group Syntality

RAYMOND B. CATTELL

I. FIRST THINGS FIRST IN SOCIAL PSYCHOLOGY

NOW THAT social psychology has recognized its major concern to be the psychology of groups—in relation to one another and to individuals—the time is ripe to discuss research methods and concepts for arriving at *the description of group behavior.*

FROM *Psychological Review*, 1948, 55, 48–63. Reprinted by permission of the author and the American Psychological Association, Inc.

It is to be hoped that history will not repeat itself by recapitulating in social psychology the unnecessarily wayward and wasteful course of individual psychology. The development of an exact science of prediction in relation to individual personality required, as in other biological sciences, the prior provision of accurate description, measurement, and classification of phenomena. Actually amateur speculation and incontinent "explanation," remote from actualities of measurement or observation, ran riot and sadly delayed progress by deflecting the attention of researchers, until recent years, from the basic and unescapable discipline of a true science of personality measurement.

This contribution to social psychology begins, therefore, with the challenge that the solution of the vital practical and theoretical social problems now clamoring for attention requires scientific workers to restrain themselves from superficial "research" until a correct foundation for the meaningful description and measurement of groups has been achieved. It then proceeds to propound concepts, methods, and experiments for this foundation. It asserts, as a logical premise, that to arrive at laws governing the development and interaction of groups, we must first have some accurate means of defining a group at a given moment.

We have, in short, to establish a branch of psychology concerned with the "personality" of groups. "Establish" is used advisedly; for at present—in spite of much talk about "culture patterns"—methods and concepts simply do not exist. The sociologists, recognizing that a group cannot be defined in merely political or economic terms, have turned to the psychologist for a science of the living group entity, but, for reasons evident in the following section, they have yet done so in vain. Mannheim (24), typical of sociologists disappointed in constructive synthesis by the psychologists' impotence, well says "The main reason for our failure in this branch of human studies is that up till now we have had no historical or sociological psychology."

II. THE DIMENSIONS OF SYNTALITY

By "personality," in the individual, we mean "that which will predict his behavior in any given, defined situation" (8). Mathematically we take a pattern of indices which defines the personality and another set defining the situation, arriving therefrom at an estimate of the ensuing behavior. Psychologically we speak of the former—the personality indices—as a structure of traits—a set of more or less permanent "readinesses," which function behaviorally under the impact of a stimulus situation.

For the corresponding structure in the group an unambiguous term is needed. Examination of many possible verbal roots indicates *syntality* as best indicating the "togetherness" of the group, while having sufficient suggestive parallelism to "personality" and "totality." Further, we may perhaps speak appropriately of the syntality of a group as inferred from the "synaction" of its members—the group action as defined below. Syntality covers dynamic, temperamental, and ability traits of the group.[1]

The measurement of syntality can profit greatly from the technical advances gained in the measurement of personality. The early failures of personality study mentioned above came not only from an attempt to abort the descriptive phase of psychology, but from an inability, once the necessity of description was admitted, to find any better foundation for measurement than the numberless shifting sands of arbitrary "traits" in poorly designed *ad hoc* "tests." All that has been altered, by the original work of Spearman, Burt (5), Thurstone (35) and many others, which made the concept of the unitary trait meaningful. Although this work has yet scarcely affected applied psychology it has, in the last fifteen years, delivered psychology already from a confused impasse. It first enlightened the measuring of abilities, and later, by the work of Guilford, Mosier, Reyburn, and others on questionnaire response and the present writer's analyses of surface and source traits, was carried to those unitary traits of temperamental and dynamic nature which could complete the description of personality.

It is easy to see now that if factorial methods had been applied from the beginning to the description and measurement of personality, using R-technique for common traits and P-technique (8) for unique traits, a true perspective of the important dimensions would have been obtained much earlier than by the hit-or-miss methods of clinical "intuition." The measurement of abilities, for example, would have been saved many a discouraging, profitless circuit of "philosophical" debate as to the nature of various abilities, as well as many acrimonious, ineffectual arguments as to the criteria against which measures should be validated. The disillusionment of students with overburdened lists of personality "types"—each peculiar to the university at which he happened to be studying—would also have been avoided.

Social psychology now stands where the study of individual personality then stood. In effect psychologists have accumulated a few fragmentary aspects of group syntality from various isolated studies. They have chanced upon "morale" (although the label probably covers such different variables as group persistence against difficulties and mean level of individual idealism), aggressiveness, authoritarian-democratic stucture, isolationism, degree of freedom from internal dissension, etc. Mostly these "dimensions" of group behavior have been seized upon in response to the

1 Apparently the only other use of syntality, a specialized and remote one, is in C. Morris's *Signs, language and behavior*, New York: Prentice Hall, 1946. The derived term, synergy, employed below, has been used (apart from its physiological use) in sociology by Lester Ward (37) but again in a far wider and less technical, defined sense than here. These contexts are so remote that no danger of confusion arises.

suggestion of some immediate practical problem, without regard to any over-all theory or to long-term scientific needs in social psychology. The slightest consideration of the whole natural history of groups would probably suggest more important variables than these for describing their total behavior.

An embarrassing harvest of muddle, moreover, is likely to be reaped if the application of large terms for small variables continues very long with respect to the labeling of group traits. Is it fitting, for example, to describe experimental groups as Totalitarian or Democratic (in science as distinct from journalism) when no proof is offered that these are unitary patterns or when the variables actually measured are perhaps the least important for defining that total pattern, if it exists as a single pattern?

It would seem better to stick to modest, less interpretive, more contingent labels for more completely definable experimental variables, until the true patterns emerge and are confirmed.

Social psychology, therefore, now awaits its foundation of accurately described syntalities, alike at the level of culture patterns, of institutional groups, and of small committees. That foundation can be achieved *by factor analysis of a "population" of groups, on a suitably chosen collection of group behavior variables.* Our purpose here is not to present particular results but to examine the promise and the limitations of this novel application of factorization and discuss the conditions under which it is valid. Nevertheless, the discussion will be guided at least by certain rough and qualitative observations already possible on the first two studies now proceeding in the field, and to be reported elsewhere (11, 12). The first is a study of 60 nations, factorizing 40 variables by R-technique, checked by two small sample studies employing Q- and P-techniques (8, 11). The second (12) factorizes a rich variety of group performances from 25 groups of six people each, i.e., of "committee size." For effective exploration with the new method requires that it be brought to bear on widely different group sizes and forms.

A general requirement of the method is that the variables shall be chosen with the utmost catholicity to cover all aspects of group behavior. The application of this principle to individual personality in the "personality sphere" concept (8) has already rewarded us with factors which not only clarify long familiar, previously foggy, clinical syndromes, but also reveal important dimensions which were never conceptualized. By attention to this principle in the realm of social psychology we can expect similarly to discover those factors which will describe most of the differences of groups in terms of relatively few unitary traits or meaningful dimensions. They may turn out to be familiar dimensions such as morale, democratic organization, industrialization, etc. or may open our eyes to functionally new "wholes" or dimensions of groups. Thereafter, by assigning measurements on these primary dimensions to any given culture pattern we can accurately define its syntality, as the necessary basis for developmental and causal studies.

III. THE FACTORIZABLE CHARACTERISTICS OF GROUPS: LOGICAL ANALYSIS

As we concentrate on the choice of variables we run into certain problems of assortment which can perhaps be solved to a certain degree by armchair reflection. This and the following section constitute attempts thus to achieve the maximum clarity of experimental design and problem formulation, with the adoption of definite hypotheses.

Out of deference to majority opinion we ought perhaps to ask at the outset the supposedly devastating question whether such a thing as a group mentality exists at all. It is of historical if not of scientific importance that McDougall's penetrating pioneer analysis (25) of "the group mind" was badly received by a certain section of American psychologists. In the descendants of this sectional opposition the allergic reaction to his expression is still so strong as to paralyze thought, and writers who pander [2] to irrationality have for years operated with McDougall's concept by circumlocutions. The rejection was not due to opposition to Hegelianism, for McDougall's able philosophical preamble explicitly refuted Hegelian mysticism and accepted Hobhouse's searching anti-idealist criticisms. The probably correct, but more trivial explanation was that this contribution to social psychology was launched at an unfortunate moment. For a large number of callow students in psychology were unable at that time to recognize any manifestation of mind unless formally, or often actually, reduced to the twitching of a dog's hind leg. From the drouth of this sterile atomism they presently rushed, with undiminished lack of judgment, down a steep place into the sea of ineffable, unmeasurable—but far from inaudible—Gestalt.

Fortunately a steady nucleus of naturalistic observation and methodological constructiveness survived and developed, despite those local setbacks, and despite the disturbances from the clamorous medieval tournaments among the pseudo-philosophical "isms" of psychology. Meanwhile the idea was further developed by Gurwitch (18) in sociology, and, in more vague terms, by Whitehead and by Roethlisberger in industrial psychology. Finally, the main line of development in pure psychology has given us better technical methods, notably factor analysis and its variants, for investigating behavioral wholes and dynamic patterns.

It could be argued that any study of total organisms, such as McDougall proposed, should have been postponed until new methods had been

2 To the objection that many psychologists misconceive the term one must reply as Freud did to Max Eastman's similar objection to the precisely defined notion of the Unconscious, "Cannot they correct their misconceptions?"

invented, but this is quite different from asserting (a) that reflexology is capable of explaining the behavior of organisms as such, or (b) that wholes do not exist. Of the difficulties of the social psychologist at that juncture McDougall wrote (25, p. x), ". . . to the obscure question of fact with which he deals, it is in the nature of things impossible to return answers supported by indisputable experimental proofs. In this field the evidence of an author's approximation towards truth can consist only in his success in gradually persuading competent opinion of the value of his views." His optimism about the existence of a large reservoir of competent opinion proved unjustified. But the vigor of prejudice has one virtue: that it forces the development of precision methods from the conclusions of which the prejudiced cannot escape.

McDougall himself, unfortunately, failed to develop the method here described, but many of his conclusions about group behavior are likely to prove correct, and his basic contention that it is rewarding to deal with groups as single entities remains the springboard whence we take off into new research fields. His arguments for treating the group as an organism or mind which have never been refuted, are set out below [3] together with

3 The behavior of a group has more formal resemblance to the behavior of an individual organism than to any other natural entity, principally in the following respects:

(1) A group preserves characteristic behavior habits and structure despite the continual replacement of actual individuals.

(2) It shows memory for group experiences and learning.

(3) It is capable if responding as a whole to stimuli directed to its parts, i.e., it tends to solve problems of individuals and sub-groups by group action.

(4) It possesses drives which become more or less integrated in executive functions of nutrition, acquisition, aggression, defense, etc. Groups vary in dynamic integration analogously to the variation of individuals in character.

(5) It experiences "moods" of expansiveness, depression, pugnacity, etc. which modify characteristic behavior and energy output as do emotional states in the individual.

(6) It shows collective deliberation, a process highly analogous to the trial-and-error thinking of the individual, when held up in a course of action. Similarly the act of collective volition, through legislatures and executives, is closely analogous to the resolution of conflicting dynamic demands in the individual.

A group also tends to exercise some choice on admission or rejection of those who aggregate towards it. This, like some few other basic characteristics of groups, has no analogy in the individual mind, except the remote one of selective learning and attention.

Against these it can be urged (a) that the grey matter or total nervous system is more dispersed than that associated with the single biological organism, and (b) that there is no group consciousness corresponding to individual consciousness. Both of these are doubtful objections, but in any case they are outside the realm of psychological observation. They *may* account for the systematic differences research will undoubtedly find between the "group mind" and the individual mind; they do not jeopardize the aim of using the group as a behavioral unity and reference point in psychological research. A less bald outline of the theoretical arguments over the group mind has been set out by the present writer elsewhere (7). Extremely few "experimental" (as distinct from historical) treatments of groups as unitary organisms yet exist to demonstrate the practicability of the hypothesis; but Thorndike's treatment of cities (34), showing them to have persistent characteristic traits, already offers some pragmatic proof. Characteristic (c) above—that all parts react adjustively (perhaps homeo-

certain new observations on the question. That some psychologists should ever have congratulated themselves on their "realism" (rather than on mere concrete thinking and failure of abstraction) in rejecting the group as an organic entity, is still more surprising when one observes that hard-headed lawyers, politicians, and statesmen deal operationally with groups *as* groups every day.

As to the behavior from which the group mentality is to be inferred, however, there runs alike through McDougall's and other psychologists' writings what we consider a rather serious confusion of characteristics. On grounds of logical analysis we suggest that there are *three* aspects or "panels" to be taken into account in defining a group.

(*1*) *Syntality Traits* (Behavior of the group as a group). The group behavior recorded here concerns any effect the group has as a totality, upon other groups or its physical environment. Just as the individual may show more willed (conscious), and less organized (neurotic symptom, temperament) behavior, so the group behavior will range from action by (a) whatever organized will and executive agencies the group processes, to (b) less organized, uncontrolled elements and so to (c) unorganized mass action, expressing largely the average individual as under (*3*) below. For example, the sheer amount of food the group eats would be largely a function of this last kind.

A catalogue of syntality traits, analogous to the personality sphere, as advocated above, is not easy to obtain, since there is no dictionary as of personality traits. We have proceeded by (a) making an exhaustive study of the many incisive writings on group characteristics, e.g., Benedict (1), Brogan (3), Cole (13), Keyserling (23), Mead (26), Siegfried (32), and Münsterberg (29), and of the characterizations found in history and (b) by using the *personality sphere* (8) as a guide to possibly important areas of behavior in syntality.

Most of these traits will be inferred from external behavior of the group, but the executive will of the group can manifest its properties also in *internal action*, e.g., in deliberately changing internal organization, suppressing internal revolt. Examples of syntality traits are: aggressiveness against groups (e.g., acts of declaration of war), efficiency in exploitation of natural resources, isolationism, energy in trading, reliability in commitments, proneness to trade cycles or to revolutions.

(*2*) *Characteristics of Internal Structure.* These concern the *relationships among the members of the group*. The character of unification and of government is primary, and this may vary from a practically unstructured crowd through horde leadership and the incipient democratic leadership in Moreno's (27) vague "tele or the movement of feeling to-

---

statically) to stimuli affecting limited segments—will be taken as the primary definition of the group.

ward leader individuals" to a highly organized legislature and executive. Internal structure characters issue in syntality traits but they are not themselves the behavior of the group.

Examples of structural characters are: all sorts of indices expressing degree of heterogeneity in various characteristics, indices of class structure, pattern of institutions and organs such as church, army, family, modes of government, and communication.

(3) *Population Traits.* These are mere aggregate values—definitions of the personality of the *average* (or typical, modal) member of the group. It is noticeable that in the literature of group characteristics the bulk of observations actually concern the typical member of the population rather than the group syntality.

Examples of population characteristics are: average intelligence, crime incidence, attitudes on moral and religious questions, and all that is usually gathered by population polls.

The probable relationship among these three [4] panels is that if we knew all the laws of social psychology we could predict the first from the second and third. Alternatively, if we knew the third and the environment of the group we could predict the second, i.e., the type of group structure which would emerge, and therefore, ultimately, the first, i.e., the group behavior. This is no denial of the principle that the mind of the group is fashioned by individuals and in turn fashions the individual mind. In the extreme instance of the second where we are dealing with a practically unstructured crowd, the first and third become practically identical.

From the interim observations available in our experiments we can already generalize the hypothesis that the changes in syntality traits produced by changes in population traits will be qualitatively as well as quantitatively different from the latter. For example, an increment in average intelligence may change character-like qualities in the group, while a difference between groups in average emotional stability of the population may appear as a difference in the ability of the group *per se* to solve cognitive complexities. This we shall call the *theory of emergents* (or syntal emergents).

IV. SEVEN THEOREMS ON THE DYNAMICS OF SYNTALITY

The implicit conception of group which most people unconsciously adopt in such discussions as the above is of an aggregate composed of a number of individuals whose *whole existence* is bound up with the group. Real

4 It may be objected that we overlook a fourth ingredient in the definition of the group—namely the group tradition. It is true that this "momentum" of the group is as important as its material existence and that groups of any maturity are composed of the dead as much as of the living. These traditions, however, exist in the minds of the living—the constitution of the United States, for example, would be ineffective if no one knew about it—and are adequately included in all three panels above.

groups are rarely of this kind and for the most profitable application of the new method to general group investigation it behooves us first to analyze as far as possible what the situation is with regard to varieties of groups and the modifications of method required to cope with them. This analysis turns principally on the dynamic relations within and between groups, for temperamental and ability characters do not differ in any systematic way, as far as we can see, from those known in individuals.

Sociologists have written a good deal about group classification and, more tangentially, about dynamics, and we must first glance at the evolution of opinion among outstanding representatives. Gumplowicz in his classical treatment (16) outdistanced most of the psychologists of a generation later by conceiving that laws can be formed about the behavior of groups ("The behavior of collective entities is determined by natural laws") but failed to agree with the present integrative psychological position by maintaining somewhat unnecessarily that this behavior had no relation to "the motives and natural qualities of (constituent) individuals." Ross (30) proceeded to carry the study of groups into a classificatory system which included "Fortuitous groups" (crowds), "Natural groups" (families, clans), "Interest groups" (states, confederacies, guilds), and also, but less happily, "Likeness groups" (professions, classes) in which presumably nothing dynamic but only a logical bond might hold the members together. Gillin and Gillin (15) adopt a somewhat similar classification, but descriptively and without implying fundamental psychological differences. To the psychologist a merely logical classification is untenable. *Every* group is an interest group—in the sense that its existence arises from a dynamic need—or else it is not, in any psychological sense, a group. Sorokin and Zimmerman's (33) distinction between "systems" and "congeries" seems to be a statement of this issue in other terms.[5]

Even when sociologists, however, have recognized that a group exists only because and so long as it satisfies psychological needs, they have failed to appreciate the nature of the ergic (10) and the metanergic needs that are involved in its support. Hayes (20), Hart (19), Von Wiese (36), and others stress or dwell wholly upon security, as if small groups form, and then aggregate into larger groups, only under threat. This may be a common motive—indeed fear and gregariousness may account for practically all association in the lower animals. But in man, with his power of learning ways of long-circuited satisfaction, the whole gamut of primary ergs—hunger, escape, self assertion, curiosity, sex, gregariousness, etc.—may participate in group formation. The sheer fact of groups needing to have adequate dynamic basis, obvious though it may now be, needs em-

5 The satisfaction of a need through the physical existence of the group is the basic definition of existence of a psychological group. The definition that a group exists when there is "internal interaction" of individuals seems less fundamental to the present writer, and indeed derivative from the above primary condition.

phasis at this juncture in social psychology because the extension of group experiment of the present kind brings the risk that, in the artificial situation of experiments, groups will be employed which are not created by a real purpose of the participants.

Beyond this fundamental character the psychologist has next to recognize the fact of *dynamic specialization*, a phenomenon tied up with the almost universal occurrence of overlapping groups. For the simplification of a first experimental approach we have chosen, as described above, self-contained groups: nations, which have relatively shadowy loyalties beyond themselves, and committee groups in a control "vacuum" situation in which no other loyalties of the members are brought into action or conflict. But the great majority of existing social groups, other than nations, are overlapping, in the sense that individuals belong simultaneously to several groups. This situation exists because, as Cole succinctly puts it (13), "an association (group) can always be made specific in function, while man can never be made so."

From this arise some intricate but important relations among groups and between group structure and the dynamic structure of the individual. For brevity and precision we shall formulate these relations in *seven theorems concerning the psychodynamics of groups*, the first of which will simply state the conclusion of the above few paragraphs' discussion.

Theorem 1. The Dynamic Origin of Groups: Definition of Synergy. Groups are devised for achieving individual satisfaction and exist only when they provide a means to the ends of individual ergic goals.

The interest, "ergic investment," or "need satisfaction" tied up with the existence of the group must be clearly conceived as having three parts or modifications: (*1*) First there is the total individual energy going into the group—absorbed by its activities—which we have called the group *synergy*. (*2*) As Rousseau (31) pointed out, however, "the general will" is not the same as "the will of all." In Bosanquet's (2) phrase, the individual wills "cancel one another" resulting in "sovereignty." In our vectorial theory of dynamic traits certain components nullify one another, as shown by the difference between the resultant expressing the dynamic interest of the group and the non-vectorial sum of the individual interests. The unified attitude which emerges as the dynamic intention of the group *per se* we shall call the *effective synergy* or effective investment. It is the energy expressed in gaining the outside goals for which the group has come together (*3*). The difference between the total synergy and the effective synergy is absorbed in internal friction and in maintaining cohesion of the group. This we may call the *intrinsic* or *group maintenance synergy*. It is a loss by internal friction and absorption. Without more space than can be given here it is not possible to analyze the rather complex transformations in group maintenance. This synergy absorbs not only selfish, anti-social and aggressive motivations, which "cancel out," but also the self-submissive and self assertive satisfactions of leader-follower activity and the needs of the gregarious drive. The latter is usually satisfied wholly in the group and does not pass on into effective synergy, though, like some other intrinsic synergy expenditures, it does "effective" work in the sense of preserving group cohesion.

Though the magnitude of the intrinsic synergy normally has to be inferred from the difference of (*1*) and (*2*), it manifests itself directly as an active resistance when attempts are made to dissolve the group. Intrinsic synergy is *relatively* (not absolutely) great, in comparison with effective synergy, in a recreational club interested in sociability; effective synergy is relatively great in a political party, a scientific institute, or a religious missionary society. However, in the special situation of an attempt to dissolve the group *all* the energy may be thrown back into cohesive activities, so that the last statement will no longer be true.

Theorem 2. The Vectorial Measurement of Group Synergy. To measure the total vectorial intrinsic and effective investment in a given group, i.e., the total group *synergy*, we have to take account of (*1*) the number of people interested; (*2*) the intensity or strength of the satisfaction each gains; (*3*) the ergic quality (vector direction (10)) of the satisfactions, and (*4*) the subsidiation relations of these satisfactions with respect to other groups and other purposes of the individuals concerned.

The number of people interested in a group will depend partly on the demostatic level or percolation range (6) of the idea involved, from the point of view of intelligence level, and partly on the dynamic needs it sets out to satisfy. For the present we can set aside this mere number, as a multiplier of whatever other measurements we make.

The measurement of dynamic quantity and quality has been treated systematically elsewhere (10). An attitude is a vector quantity defined as to direction (quality) by: (aF_1) (bF_2) (cF_3) . . . etc., where F_1, F_2, etc. are coordinates corresponding to basic drives (ergs) or to general sentiment structures (and therefore common social institutions) and a, b, etc. are coefficients for the particular attitude, expressing the extent of its subsidiation to each of these common and basic goals. The strength of the attitude is expressed by

$$S = aF_1 + bF_2 + cF_3 \ldots \text{etc.},$$

where a, b, and c are as above, and F_1, F_2, etc. have satisfaction values specific for that group.

The synergy of the group is the vectorial resultant of the attitudes toward the group of all its members. Individual attitudes will vary slightly in direction and some of this deviation will be cancelled in the vectorial sum–in other words, it will be lost in the internal friction of the group.

The rest will appear either as intrinsic investment, constituting the basic strength of cohesion of the group, or as effective investment, constituting the interest of the group as such.

The effective synergy of the group can finally be expressed as a vector quantity on the same coordinates as for individual attitudes.

Theorem 3. Syntal Subsidiation and the Dynamic Lattices of Groups. The effective synergy of any group goes out to purposes which are outside the group and consequently sets up habits of reacting which are subsidiary (10), with respect to some ultimate goal of the group's activity. The formation or partial support of other (mostly ancillary) groups is generally part of the subsidiation chain. For example, a nation sets up an army as a means to its goal of security or aggression, and a country club may set up a committee to engineer a swimming pool as part of its synergy purpose of providing recreation. The use of group B as a tool by group A is not incompatible with the use of A by B, and, as in personal subsidiation (10), paths will form a complex, *dynamic lattice* with transflux and retroaction.

Some typical syntal subsidiations in the group and individual habits which form institutions are illustrated in the dotted lines in the following diagram. The nation supports universities because they are on its subsidiation chain to the goal of an educated democracy. It favors the family as maintaining population stability, while cities contribute to its desire for revenue and prestige. Both the family and the city, as groups, in turn have need of the nation, which satisfies their need for protection, etc. The army, in pursuit of its purposes, founds an Army Air Force and this in turn sets up a psychological Personnel Section. Although these latter accord with the will of the nation they are not directly in the subsidiary chain of the nation's purpose of self defence, but draw their origin from separate successive synergies of Army and Army Air Force. The nation, as it were, delegates synergy to the army and, as a group, has no sense of these further purposes.

Syntal dynamic lattices are quite different and distinct from the dynamic lattice patterns of individuals, even of the particular individuals who happen to constitute chief executives of groups. (Compare dotted with continuous lines in the diagram.) This happens increasingly with the growth of specialized labor and of general currency. Nevertheless the two sets of dynamic lattices necessarily add up to the same activities and the same energy total–save for the loss between intrinsic and effective synergy.

Problems of relationship of syntal lattices and personal lattices will be different for overlapping and non-overlapping groups. Some groups, e.g., nations, demand a sovereignty which will not permit members to belong to other, generally similar, groups, or to experience subjection to the purposes of other groups. Most groups, however, have overlapping personnel, and this creates dynamic problems in connection with syntal subsidiation more complex than for non-overlapping groups.

Syntal subsidiation chains will not normally end in ergic goals, as do those of individuals. The basic goals of the group concern the preservation

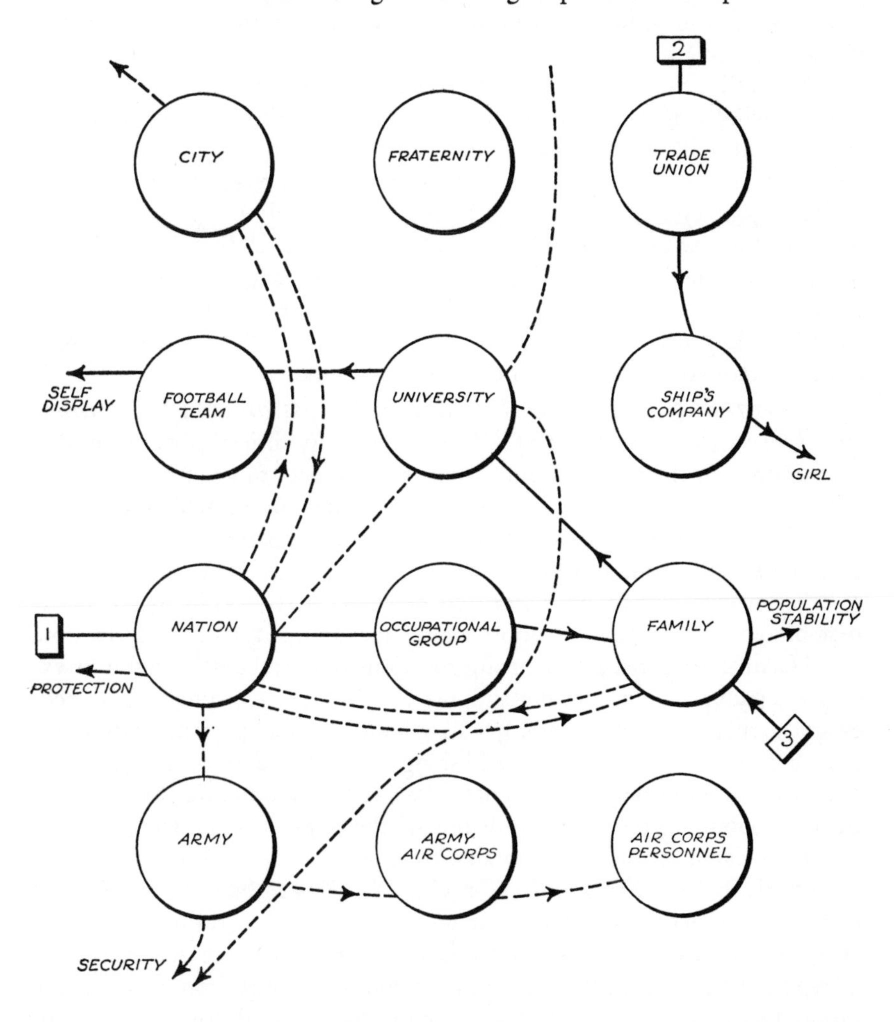

and expansion of the group. They can be resolved into ergic goals, by analysis, but they are not individual biological goals in themselves.

Theorem 4. Personal Subsidiation of Groups in the Individual Dynamic Lattice. The subsidiation chains occurring in the dynamic lattice of the individual (10) often include groups as "links." For example, an *émigré* doctor may acquire citizenship (Group 1) in order that he may belong to his professional group (Group 2) in order that he may maintain his family (Group 3). (Chain 1 in the diagram.) Or a man may belong to a trade union (Group 2), in order to be able to join a ship's company (Group 2) in order to travel to see his girl. (Chain 2 in the diagram.) Or, to illustrate a different direction, a young man half in mind to leave the parental roof may maintain his belonging to the family in order to be sent to a university in order to get onto the university football team. (Chain 3 in the diagram.)

Naturally, the personal subsidiation chains, like the syntal chains, will not run wholly among groups ("girl" in 2), nor will they run in one direction, but will curve back on themselves. Also like subsidiary chains generally (10), they will split at frequent intervals. For example, the motivation to join a university will not be sustained wholly by the satisfactions in connection with joining the football team (even in this day and age) but also by the prospect of joining a fraternity, acquiring professional standing, etc. Consequently calculation of the investment in any group, by the adding up of the dynamic energies of subsidiation chains, must heed the redistribution which occurs at each link.

Theorem 5. Patterns of Loyalty, Subsidiation, and Subordination Determined by Law of Effect. Like any other pattern of dynamic behavior the habits of individuals with respect to groups are formed either by insightful or by trial and error behavior, in which the most rewarded reactions become stabilized.[6] The final pattern of syntal and personal subsidiation, as well as other characteristics discussed below, is, in other words, *settled by conditions of external reality*, in that it is the best pattern discovered for approaching maximum dynamic satisfaction.

Harmful or unnecessary group reactions tend to be removed. For example, a group which does not support (by its effective synergy) its necessary ancillary groups fails; a group which tolerates parasitic subgroups fails; a group which errs in establishing correct orders of loyalty, e.g., family more important than country, fails—and these failures break down the corresponding faulty group habits of the population concerned.

How far it would be profitable to deal with syntal learning by the law of effect applied to groups as a whole remains to be seen. Two transformations between syntal and personal adjustments to reality can, however, be indicated. (*1*) The rewards and punishments of individuals in group modification are different in kind and magnitude from those of the group. For example, the defeat of a nation may mean death to some, economic loss to others, loss of self regard for all. The "death" of a nation—its total disintegration—may mean no more than the necessity for the individual to acquire new language and other habits. (*2*) Not only are individual rewards different, but they are also often delayed, indirect and harder to associate, insightfully, with their group causes. Since group learning eventually takes place through this "secondary" learning of indi-

6 If any proof of this is needed, it is offered, for example, by Mowrer's neat experiments on the social behavior of the rat (28).

viduals it is not surprising that the acquisition of intelligently adapted and integrated group behavior is a slower and more painful process than similar learning with respect to the purposes of individuals.

In referring to the group behavior that has to get adapted to reality we have spoken of a hierarchy of loyalty, as well as of the previously described personal subsidiation lattice and syntal subsidiation (or "subordination") lattice. The relation of these to one another is tentatively discussed in the next section.

That personal, individual behavior shall fit in with the requirements of syntal subsidiation and integration is assured mainly by (a) the creation of forces in the individual super ego which augment personal subsidiation trends usually of a more purely ergic level, and (b) the shifting of rewards to "artificial" points by money and other tokens exchangeable for dynamic satisfaction. Thus when many desire the defense of a country but few volunteer for the army an army of mercenaries may be made "loyal" to the country by rewards transferred from the money representing and created by the dynamic attachments of others to their country. Money is thus one way, the principal way, of transferring dynamic energy from one point to another. This needs to be taken into account in any attempt at dynamic calculus and offers one of the bridges from psychology to economics.

Theorem 6. Synergic Constancy in a Closed System (Fixed Population) with Overlapping Groups. By reason of the principle of constancy of individual mental energy (on which we proceed in such matters of individual dynamics as learning or neurosis) certain relations follow in the synergies of overlapping groups.

Chief among these deduced relations is that of *constancy of total synergy in overlapping groups*, providing certain conditions are maintained. Not all of the individual's energy goes into groups, so condition (*1*) is that the non-group investment remain constant. Condition (*2*) is that the group activities remain on the same level with regard to long circuiting (or goal distance). This is necessary for two reasons. First, the individual's energy becomes expressed more readily if he is permitted less long circuited satisfaction. Since some groups occasion less suppression and internal conflict in individuals than others, releasing more of the individual's total energy for external expression, this condition is not easily satisfied. Secondly, new groups can be linked on to a personal subsidiation chain of groups without calling on fresh energy, provided the population has not reached its toleration limit for long circuiting. For example, if a man has interest in a golf club he may be induced to join a society for the preservation of the golf course, without drawing on any new springs of interest. But this long circuiting may strike him as a bore. There are probably further conditions related to his interest in golf which will only become evident when the principle of constancy of individual mental energy is more accurately worked out. For example, we are arguing on the condition of constancy of what psychoanalysts would call "object libido investment," not of total energy, and certain social changes might alter the ratio of object libido to the total energy.

A corollary on this theorem is that the liquidation of any group structure will then automatically create—for psychological reasons alone and without regard for social needs and real conditions—a readjustment among the synergies of the remaining overlapping groups. They must alter their patterns to give new qualities of satisfaction—or else the residue must be taken up by some new group, equivalent in synergy, if not in intellectual content, to the lost group. For example, the dissolution of football teams might result in the activities of political parties taking on the characteristics of street fighting. A calculus of group readjustment could thus be founded on the ergic mensuration of vectors of synergy.

Theorem 7. Isomorphism of Syntality Change and Personality Change. Although the structures and functions of groups, overlapping or non-overlapping, are always ultimately shaped by the conditions of reality (as in Theorem 5 above), their form at any moment depends also on the readiness of individual minds to learn quickly or to depart quickly from that structure which is, realistically, optimum.

There will thus be a close parallelism (modified by the nature of the intrinsic relations within the groups) between syntality traits and personality traits of the population, especially those concerned with learning and dynamic stability. For example, the immediate cause of stability of group structures is the stability of the corresponding attitudes and sentiments in the individual mind. Nothing prevents an army marching to the capital and taking charge of a nation except the higher loyalty of the patriotic sentiment, in relation to the army sentiment, in the minds of the individual soldiers. (In fact Roman legionaries abroad sometimes experienced such a growth of the sentiment toward their army fellows that unscrupulous generals could use them to overpower the Republic.) The "realistic" checks ultimately make this unrewarding (to the army and to the nation), but the immediate check is only the inherent stability (disposition rigidity) of sentiments in the individual mind.

Among the chief parallel characteristics that may be suggested are syntal conservatism (resistance to gradual change) and personal, individual *disposition rigidity;* syntal integration and personal intelligence level; syntal freedom from fashions and boom-depression cycles and individual emotional maturity; syntal democratic political conflict and personal tolerance for internal mental conflict (since group conflict in overlapping groups brings parallel personal mental conflict), and so on. Some evidence that the first of these relations can be demonstrated in data already available has been set out by the present writer elsewhere (9). In so far as this theorem operates, the advance of social psychology as an exact science is limited by the advance of personality measurement.

V. SYNTALITY MEASUREMENT AND THE DYNAMIC RELATIONS OF GROUPS

The implications of the above theorems for the design of experiments directed to determining the dimensions of syntality are numerous and we have space to emphasize only a few.

In the first place, the dynamic makeup (synergy) of groups will vary far more than that of individuals, both in strength and quality. Consequently it may be profitable to sort groups into classes of more comparable kinds before starting experiments. Sorokin, Zimmerman, and Galpin (33) have already proceeded with group classification essentially on this basis, into "elementary groups" which satisfy a single need and "cumulative groups" which hold their members by many ties. The dynamic vectorial methods suggested here simply carry this to greater quantitative meaning and exactness.

Secondly, group syntality will usually be far more narrow in dynamic content than the dynamic expression of individuals. Groups can fight, ally, acquire, fear, protect, submit, assert themselves, seek food, etc., but sexually directed behavior, for example, is rare (the rape of the Sabines, and matrimonial agencies, apart). The choice of dynamic variables for factorization therefore needs to aim at more dense representation in narrow ergic directions.

Theorem 2 above, that synergy can be expressed with regard to the ergic coordinates used for individuals leaves open the possibility that factorization may show synergy to be conveniently expressible also in terms of some relatively basic goals of groups *per se*. For example, the interests of an insurance company or a library may be as intelligible, if not as apt for dynamic calculus, when expressed in terms of service to a few basic social institutions as of basic human ergs.

This remains to be clarified by our initial experiments, as also does the question whether any laws systematically relate syntal and personal dynamic lattices and the hierarchy of typical individual loyalty to groups discussed in Theorem 5. There are concepts here which can only be tentatively defined and interrelated. Is "loyalty" to a group determined by "duty" (super ego investment) or by total synergy? Is the order of loyalty the same as the order of "social distance" (17) among people in the various groups, or, more likely, the same as the syntal subsidiation order? Can the correct order of syntal subsidiation be determined by asking "Could this group exist at all without that?" or must a situation always be arranged in which some conflict between the groups, from the standpoint of individual loyalties, exists? Is it possible that groups can only conflict in so far as their subsidiation paths are different? These questions will be dealt with elsewhere. Thirdly, because of the sensitive interdependence of groups, in regard to synergic quantity and quality, the synergy of most groups and especially the smaller, subordinate ones, will be much more liable to gross fluctuations than the total dynamic traits of the individual. So great a "function fluctuation" makes factorization more difficult but no less worth while. It requires "snapshot" measurement by R-technique, or the special use of P-technique. Measurement of the changing synergies of groups offers the true basis for discovery of the laws governing syntal subsidiation and other group interrelationships.

The measurement of syntalities with respect to their dynamic make-up and subsidiation relationships offers the prospect not only of putting the description of group behavior on an altogether higher level of exactness, but of making possible a new branch of study employing a kind of "dynamic bookkeeping" with respect to overlapping groups and the energy investments of individuals. From this "bookkeeping" the data for a whole field of new laws regarding the psychodynamics of groups emerge. For example, many overlapping groups are approximately isomorphous (in the sense of mathematical group theory) so that their synergies would behave as approximately complementary.

Pursuit of measurable relationships in the dynamics of personalities and syntalities opens up also two extremely important developments of psychology—ethics and economics. A good deal of the morality of individual behavior is admittedly weighed in terms of the effects of the latter on the welfare of groups (whether or not we accept the whole theoretical basis of Mill and Bentham). Indeed, the calculations of discrepancy between constituent individual attitudes and group synergies become in effect an estimation of individual morality—if the general position of Mill and Evolutionary Ethics (7) is accepted.

Similarly the key to the whole relationship of psychology and economics lies in these calculations. For groups to achieve their objects it is necessary to transmit interest energy from place to place. Transmission along a subsidiation chain takes place for groups and for individuals principally by tokens (money) but the process is perhaps clearer for groups. As frequently mentioned in sociology the most consistent characteristics of existing primary groups (other than behaving as a totality) are (*1*) order and (*2*) taxation. Synergy expresses itself most frequently through the latter. Members of a group tax themselves, proportionally to the strength of their interest in the existence of the group. This money is at once a measure of the strength of their individual attitudes and of the group synergy; for, generally it is not by work on the part of the members themselves that the group synergy expresses itself, but by the work of others paid for by the taxation of the group. That cost could be used as a measure of desire, thus uniting economic and psychodynamic measures, is not a new idea but an old one which was found wanting (8, 10). Only when it is considered in the total setting of group dynamics, apparently, can it be made workable.

These theoretical vistas in group dynamics can be glanced along but not followed, here. For the dynamic traits of groups are only one aspect of the total syntality and have been examined more analytically only because it appears that syntality differs from personality more in dynamic structure than in ability or temperament traits. However, the upshot of our examination is that dynamic characteristics, especially if they are sampled with proper regard to the nature of group synergies, can profitably be included in the same factorization with measures of group temperament and group abilities.

VI. SUMMARY

(1) Social psychological research can advantageously be centered on the behavior of groups as organic, functionally integrated entities. Group syntality has more resemblances than differences with regard to individual personality, suggesting profitable transfer of research methods from one to the other.

(2) Effective research on the development, abnormalities, and interrelations of groups can proceed only on a foundation of syntality measurement. The dimensions of syntality can be found by factor analysis.

(3) Factor analysis must rest on an even sampling of a wide range of group characteristics. The characteristics of groups have to be sought at three levels: (1) Syntality—the behavior of the group; (2) Structure—the relations of individuals in the group; (3) Population personality traits—the individual characteristics averaged.

(4) Groups differ from individuals most radically in their dynamic make-up or synergy, especially because of the structural possibilities of overlapping groups. This does not invalidate the factorization of group characteristics but it introduces complications requiring special attention to the design of investigation.

(5) The dynamic relationships which have to be heeded in the design of experiments to investigate group syntalities, and which require investigation in their own right as prime determiners of the behavior of groups, have been expressed in seven theorems. These theorems may be briefly labelled: (1) Dynamic origin of groups; (2) Vectorial measurement of synergy; (3) Subsidiation in the syntal lattice; (4) Subsidiation in the personal lattice; (5) Hierarchies of loyalty from the law of effect; (6) Synergic constancy in a system of overlapping groups; and (7) Isomorphism of syntality change and personality change.

REFERENCES

1. Benedict, R. *Patterns of culture*. New York: Houghton Mifflin, 1934.
2. Bosanquet, B. *The philosophical theory of the state*. London: Macmillan, 1910.
3. Brogan, D. W. *The American character*. New York: Knopf, 1945.
4. Buell, R. L. *International relations*. New York: Holt, 1929.
5. Burt, C. *Factors of the mind*. London: Univer. of London Press, 1940.
6. Cattell, R. B. Some changes in social life in a community with a falling intelligence quotient. *Brit. J. Psychol.*, 1938, 28, 430–450.
7. Cattell, R. B. *Psychology and the religious quest*. New York: Nelson, 1938.
8. Cattell, R. B. *The description and measurement of personality*. New York: World Book Co., 1946.
9. Cattell, R. B. The riddle of perseveration. II. Solution in terms of personality structure. *J. Person.*, 1946, 14, 239–268.
10. Cattell, R. B. The ergic theory of attitude and sentiment measurement. *Educ. Psychol. Measmt.*, 1947, 7, 221–246.
11. Cattell, R. B. The syntality of national culture patterns: I. R-technique on 63 nations. (Unpublished.)
12. Cattell, R. B. & Wispe, L. The dimensions of syntality in structured groups ot six persons. (Unpublished.)
13. Cole, G. D. H., & Cole, M. *A Guide to modern politics*. London: Gollancz, 1934.
14. Cole, G. D. H. *Social theory*. New York: Frederick Stokes, 1920.
15. Gillin, J. L., & Gillin, J. P. *Introduction to sociology*. New York: Macmillan, 1946.
16. Gumplowicz, L. *Outlines of sociology* (trans. by F. H. Moore). Philadelphia: American Academy of Political and Social Science, 1899.
17. Gurnee, H., & Baker, E. The social distances of some common social relationships. *J. abnorm. soc. Psychol.*, 1938, 33, 265–269.
18. Gurwitch, A. *The sociology of law*. New York: Philosophical Library, 1942.
19. Hart, H. N. *Science of social relations*. New York: Holt, 1931.
20. Hayes, E. C. *Principles of sociology*. New York: Appleton, 1923.
21. Hobhouse, L. T. *The metaphysical theory of the state*. New York: Macmillan, 1918.
22. Jennings, H. Structure of leadership–development and sphere of interest. *Sociometry*, 1938, 1, 99–143.
23. Keyserling, H. *Das Spektrum Europas*. Berlin: Deutsche Verlags-Anstalt, 1928.
24. Mannheim, K. *Man and society*. New York: Harcourt, Brace, 1940.
25. McDougall, W. *The group mind*. New York: Putnam, 1920.
26. Mead, M. *And keep your powder dry*. New York: Morrow, 1943.
27. Moreno, J. L., & Jennings, Helen H. Statistics of social configurations. *Sociometry*, 1938, 1, 342–374.
28. Mowrer, O. H. *An experimentally produced "social problem."* (Film, obtainable Harvard Educ. Dept.), 1939.
29. Münsterberg, H. *The Americqus*. Garden City: Doubleday, 1914.
30. Ross, E. A. *Foundations of sociology*. New York: Macmillan, 1905.
31. Rousseau, J. J. *Du contrat social*. Amsterdam: Rey, 1762.
32. Siegfried, A. *France, a study in nationality*. London: H. Milford, Oxford Univer. Press, 1930.
33. Sorokin, R. A., Zimmerman, C. C., & Galpin, C. J. *A systematic source book in rural sociology*. Minneapolis: Univer. of Minnesota Press, 1930.
34. Thorndike, E. L. *Your city*. New York: Harcourt, Brace, 1939.
35. Thurstone, L. L. *The vectors of the mind*. Chicago: Univer. of Chicago Press, 1935.
36. Von Wiese, L. *Systematic sociology* (trans. by H. Becker). New York: John Wiley, 1932.
37. Ward, L. F. *Pure sociology*. New York: Macmillan, 1903.

Adaptive and Integrative Changes as Sources of Strain in Social Systems

ROBERT F. BALES

THE STUDY of complete societies suggests a number of tentative generalizations which may be useful to the student of small groups. In order to take advantage of what is known, however, one needs first to abstract from complete societies those aspects of structure which are also found in small groups. Second, one needs to infer from the kinds of structural variation found in societies, both historically and cross culturally, what the mechanisms underlying changes from one state of structure to another may be, so that useful hypotheses about changes in the structure of a single group, within a small time span, can be deduced.

Looking at large scale systems in a very abstract way, one can form an idea of two "chains of events" or "series of strains" starting from opposite poles and proceeding in opposite directions, tending to cancel each other out, and each in its terminal effects tending to set off the opposite chain of events. One chain of events has its starting point in the necessities of adaptation to the outer situation and proceeds in its series of strains through changes in the division of labor, changes in the distribution of property, authority, and status and has its malintegrative terminal effects in the disturbance of the existing state of solidarity. The other chain of events has its starting point in the necessities of integration or reintegration of the social system itself and proceeds in its series of strains through a reactive (or perhaps aboriginal) emphasis on solidarity which exerts a dissolving, undermining, equalizing, or curbing effect on the differential distribution of status, on differences in authority, differences in distribu-

FROM R. F. Bales, *Interaction process analysis: A method for the study of small groups*. Cambridge: Addison-Wesley, 1949. Reprinted by permission of the author and publisher.

tion of property, and differences in functional roles in the division of labor, with an ultimate terminal effect that may be maladaptive. The social system in its organization, we postulate, tends to swing or falter indeterminately back and forth between these two theoretical poles: optimum adaptation to the outer situation at the cost of internal malintegration, or optimum internal integration at the cost of maladaptation to the outer situation.

The series of hypotheses below is an attempt to state our conception of these interconnections in the most general way possible, for all sorts of small groups:

As particular functional problems (instrumental, adaptive, integrative, or expressive) become more acute, pressing, or continuous, more demanding in time and effort, strains are created toward the definition of specific social roles, differentiated in terms of particular persons, who are given the implicit or explicit responsibility of meeting and solving the specific functional problems as they arise in the group. Furthermore:

As the felt importance of the specific function performed by a particular person increases, strains are created toward an increase in his generalized social status. Conversely, as the felt importance of the particular function decreases, strains are created toward a decrease in his generalized social status.

As the functional social roles in a group become more specific, differentiated, and formal, more demanding in time and effort of the particular individuals performing the roles, strains are created toward a more individualistic and inequalitarian distribution of access to resources and rewards, both in terms of access to the instrumentalities involved in the performance of the function and in terms of some reward or compensation for the loss of time and effort and the value rendered to the group. Furthermore:

As the felt advantage of a particular person in the distribution of access to resources increases, strains are created toward an increase in his generalized social status. Conversely, as the advantage of the particular person decreases, strains are created toward a decrease in his generalized social status.

As the functional social roles in a group become more specific, differentiated, and formal, strains are created toward a more differentiated and centralized exercise of directive control in order to coordinate and regulate these special functions. Furthermore:

As the directive control of a given person increases, strains are created toward an increase in his generalized social status. Conversely, as his directive control decreases, strains are created toward a decrease in his generalized social status.

Moreover, to point up the significance of the foregoing tendencies, as status differences between persons increase, strains are created toward a less solid (more neutral, indifferent, or antagonistic) relation between them. Thus, to conclude, as the functional roles performed by persons in a group become more specific, differentiated, and formal, strains are created toward a less solidary relation between them.

This is a conception of a series of changes in social relationships "set off" by changes in the functional problems which the group faces in its problem solving process. It is a somewhat more abstract statement of the kinds of relationships we tend to find in larger social systems between the occupational system and the institutions of property, authority, social stratification, and solidarity, each of which finds its more abstract statement in the series of hypotheses above.

The phenomena in one way or another associated with this series of changes in the larger social system are extremely varied and interesting. This is not the place to attempt to present a convincing analysis, but they would include, as we view it, the institutionalization of a certain "indifference," "impersonality," "impartiality," or "emotional neutrality" as an explicit obligation in the performance of certain roles, such as those of the judge, the doctor, the administrator, the foreman, etc.; compulsive tendencies toward absenteeism, migration, isolation, refusal to communicate; the formation of sects, schisms, minority sub-groups, etc. In another direction they may include the practice of black magic, witchcraft, and sorcery; compulsive striving for and retention of symbols of achievement, wealth, power, authority, and prestige; compulsive striving for symbols of love, acceptance, solidarity; ritual and symbolic attempts to increase the solidarity of the whole group; fantasy about and romanticization of desired symbols of security, such as symbols of achievement, wealth, power, authority, prestige, love, acceptance, solidarity; etc. In still another direction, the phenomena may include active attacks on or modifications of the existing division of labor, and the existing system of property and authority; compulsive competitiveness and rebelliousness; passive resistance and non-cooperation; the designation of specific targets for aggression, such as scapegoats within or outside the group; the permission of aggressive displays in certain contexts, such as in drinking, warfare, or punishment of transgressors; the prohibition and inhibition of aggressive tendencies such as complaining, agitating, "conniving," and meeting in secret; the establishment of certain modes of self-aggression, such as mutilation, flagellation, asceticism; etc.

The series of hypotheses above have to do with certain changes which are "set off," as it were, by changes in the division of labor which, in turn, is closely related to the task demands facing the group. There is a complementary or contrary series of changes, we hypothesize, which are "set off" by changes in the state of solidarity of the group. The general terminal effect of the first chain of events is to produce strains toward a lesser solidarity. One of the possible reactions to this strain is a reactive, compulsive attempt to secure and retain symbols of love, acceptance, solidarity, and the initiation of rituals and fantasies on this theme, as mentioned above. However, this reaction may go so far as to create difficulties in its own right. From the point of view of the overall functioning of social systems in terms of the various kinds of flexibilities they need to have, *either* marked uncontrolled antagonism or marked uncontrolled solidarity has its "dangers." In general, both tend to be regulated and controlled as to when, toward whom, and to what degree they may be expressed in action or institutionalized in a social relationship. A very strong relationship of solidarity (as well as a marked antagonism) between persons or within sub-groups or even of the group as a whole, may interfere with the adaptation and integration of the whole group by the following "chain of events":

As solidarity between persons of different status increases, strains are created toward a merging, or equalization of their status, both as they view the relation and as others view the relation. In general, members of solidary groups tend to be classed together in the scale of stratification, and individual mobility in the scale of stratification involves some loosening or breaking of former ties of solidarity. Solidarity and status differences are in certain respects incompatible. However:

The adaptation of the social system to its outer situation requires a certain degree of neutrality, mobility, and recognition of status differences in certain social relationships since:

As solidarity between persons performing specific, differentiated, and formal roles increases, strains are created toward a more diffuse, less differentiated, and less formalized performance of functional social roles, which in turn may be accompanied by a loss of efficiency and responsibility, a loss of the inducement of increased status, a perversion of function from group ends to the individual ends of the persons immediately involved, and so may threaten the adaptation and integration of the group as a whole. (Nepotism, favoritism, particularism, etc.)

Similarly:

As solidarity between persons having different advantages in the distribution of property rights increases, strains are created toward a more "communal," "equalitarian" distribution of property rights, which may tend to interfere with the adaptation and integration of the whole group by the dissociation of reward from functionally specific tasks, and consequent reduction of motivation to the efficient performance of explicit functions on behalf of the group.

Similarly:

As solidarity increases between those in authority and those subjected to control, strains are created toward a more diffuse, less differentiated, and less formal exercise of authority, which in turn may interfere with the adaptation and integration of the whole group by making it difficult or impossible for the persons in authority to require or demand that which is necessary but unpleasant, difficult, or dangerous.

Thus, to sum up, as sub-group or interpersonal solidarity increases in the contexts mentioned above (i.e., in functionally specific, differentiated, and formal contexts), strains are created toward insecurity through the threat of a less effective adaptation of the system as a whole to the outer situation, and various reactive attempts to remove or express this insecurity may be expected. In larger social systems there are various interesting phenomena which are apparently associated with this series of strains. Again, simply to give some examples, we would include: limitation of contact, by avoidance or physical segregation; institutionalization of "impersonality" or "impartiality," as mentioned above; prohibition (in functionally specific contexts where they might be disruptive) of certain activities which symbolize or tend to create solidarity, such as sexual approach (note incest taboos), performance of personal favors, eating together (note food taboos), drinking together, marrying, loaning of money or other articles, similarity in dress, speech, etc. In another direction, the damaging effects of over-strong sub-solidarities may be counteracted to some extent by communal rituals directed toward the maintenance and creation of sentiments which will (1) secure the allegiance and obligations of individuals and sub-groups to the group as a whole, (2) make for a conscientious performance of specialized function, and (3) justify the existing differentiation of property, authority, and status, in terms of a more general overarching system of major values and hierarchical sub-values. In still another direction, the damaging effects of malintegrative sub-solidarities may be combatted by creating an emphasis on some threat to the group as a whole and by making an aggressive attack on personal or impersonal aspects of the outer situation in such a way as to increase the overall solidarity at the expense of sub-group solidarities.

An Approach to the Study of Communicative Acts

THEODORE M. NEWCOMB

THIS paper points toward the possibility that many of those phenomena of social behavior which have been somewhat loosely assembled under the label of "interaction" can be more adequately studied as communicative acts. It further points to the possibility that, just as the observable forms of certain solids are macroscopic outcomes of molecular structure, so certain observable group properties are predetermined by the conditions and consequences of communicative acts.

The initial assumption is that communication among humans performs the essential function of enabling two or more individuals to maintain simultaneous orientation toward one another as communicators *and* toward objects of communication. After presenting a rationale for this assumption, we shall attempt to show that a set of propositions derived from or consistent with it seems to be supported by empirical findings.

CO-ORIENTATION AND THE A–B–X SYSTEM

Every communicative act is viewed as a transmission of information, consisting of discriminative stimuli, from a source to a recipient.[1] For present purposes it is assumed that the discriminative stimuli have a discriminable object as referent. Thus in the simplest possible communicative act one person, A, transmits information to another person, B, about something, X. Such an act is symbolized here as AtoBreX.

The term "orientation" is used as equivalent to "attitude" in its more

FROM *Psychological Review*, 1953, 60, 393–404. Reprinted by permission of the author and the American Psychological Association, Inc.

1 This statement is adapted from G. A. Miller's definition: " 'information' is used to refer to *the occurrence of one out of a set of alternative discriminative stimuli.* A discriminative stimulus is a stimulus that is arbitrarily, symbolically, associated with something (or state, or event, or property) and that enables the stimulated organism to discriminate this thing from others" (9, p. 41).

inclusive sense of referring to both cathectic and cognitive tendencies. The phrase "simultaneous orientation" (hereinafter abbreviated to "co-orientation") itself represents an assumption; namely, that A's orientation toward B and toward X are interdependent. A–B–X is therefore regarded as constituting a system. That is, certain definable relationships between A and B, between A and X, and between B and X are all viewed as interdependent. For some purposes the system may be regarded as a phenomenal one within the life space of A or B, for other purposes as an "objective" system including all of the possible relationships as inferred from observation of A's and B's behavior. It is presumed that a given state of the system exists when a given instance of AtoBreX occurs, and that as a result of this occurrence the system undergoes some change (even though the change be regarded as only a reinforcement of the pre-existing state).

The minimal components of the A–B–X system, as schematically illustrated in Fig. 1, are as follows:

1. A's orientation toward X, including both attitude toward X as an object to be approached or avoided (characterized by sign and intensity) and cognitive attributes (beliefs and cognitive structuring).
2. A's orientations toward B, in exactly the same sense. (For purposes of avoiding confusing terms, we shall speak of positive and negative *attraction* toward A or B as persons, and of favorable and unfavorable *attitudes* toward X.)
3. B's orientation toward X.
4. B's orientation toward A.

In order to examine the possible relationships of similarity and difference between A and B, we shall make use of simple dichotomies in regard to these four relationships. That is, with respect to a given X at a given time, A and B will be regarded as cathectically alike (++ or −−) or different (+− or −+) in attitude and in attraction; and as cognitively alike or different. We shall also make use of simple dichotomies of degree–i.e., more alike, less alike. We shall refer to lateral similarities of A's and B's orientations to X as *symmetrical* relationships.

This very simple system is designed to fit two-person communication. In the following discussion these additional limitations will be imposed, for simplicity's sake: (*a*) communicative acts will be treated as verbal ones, in face-to-face situation; (*b*) initiation of the communicative act is considered to be intentional (i.e., such acts are excluded as those which the actor assumes to be unobserved); (*c*) it is assumed that the "message" is received–i.e., that the communicative act is attended to by an intended recipient, though not necessarily with any particular degree of accuracy; and (*d*) A and B are assumed to be group members, characterized by continued association.

The assumption that co-orientation is essential to human life is based upon two considerations of complementary nature. First, the orientation of any A toward any B (assuming that they are capable of verbal communication) is rarely, if ever, made in an environmental vacuum. Even in what seems the maximally "pure" case of two lovers oblivious to all but each other, both singly and both jointly are dependent upon a common environment; and their continued attachment is notoriously contingent upon the discovery or development of common interests beyond themselves. It is not certain that even their most person-oriented communications (e.g., "I love you") are devoid of environmental reference. The more intense one person's concern for another the more sensitive he is likely to be to the other's orientations to objects in the environment.

Second, the orientation of any A capable of verbal communication about almost any conceivable X is rarely, if ever, made in a social vacuum. There are few if any objects so private that one's orientations toward them

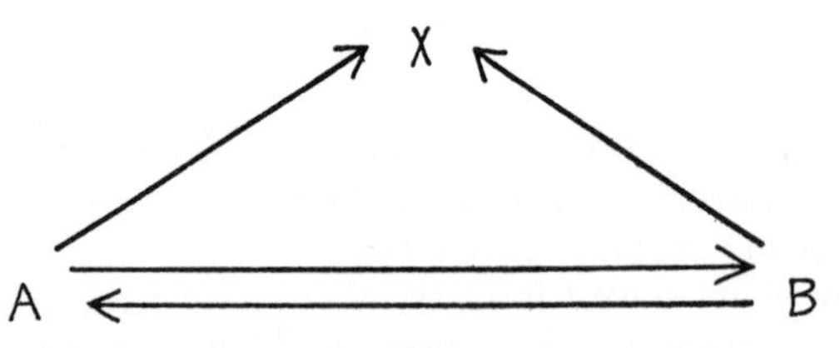

FIG. 1. Schematic illustration of the minimal A–B–X system

are uninfluenced by others' orientations. This is particularly true with regard to what has been termed "social reality" (3); i.e., the less the possibility of testing one's assumptions by observing the physical consequences of those assumptions, the greater the reliance upon social confirmation as the test of what is true and valid. And even when assumptions can be put to the direct test (e.g., the child can find out for himself about the stove which he has been told is hot), social reality is often accepted as the quicker or the safer test. As various linguists have pointed out, moreover, a good deal of social reality is built into the very language with which we communicate about things. Under the conditions of continued association which we are assuming, A and B as they communicate about X are dependent upon each other, not only because the other's eyes and ears provide an additional source of information about X, but also because the other's judgment provides a testing ground for social reality. And to be dependent upon the other, in so far as such dependence influences behavior, is to be oriented toward him.

In short, it is an almost constant human necessity to orient oneself toward objects in the environment and also toward other persons oriented toward those same objects. To the degree that A's orientation either toward X or toward B is contingent upon B's orientation toward X, A is motivated to influence and/or to inform himself about B's orientation toward X. Communication is the most common and usually the most effective means by which he does so.

SYMMETRY OF ORIENTATION

Much of the remainder of this paper will deal with the relationships between A's and B's orientations toward X, within the postulated A–B–X system. The implications of this model are: (*a*) that while at any given moment the system may be conceived of as being "at rest," it is characterized not by the absence but by the balance of forces; and (*b*) that a change in any part of the system (any of the four relationships portrayed in Fig. 1) may lead to changes in any of the others. We shall also make the assumption (not inherent in the model) that certain forces impinging upon the system are relatively strong and persistent, and that thus there are "strains" toward preferred states of equilibrium.

This assumption, related to the initial one concerning the co-orientation function of communication, is as follows. To the degree that A's orientation toward X is contingent upon B's orientation toward X, A's co-orientation will be facilitated by similarity of his own and B's orientation toward X. The first advantage of symmetry—particularly of cognitive symmetry—is that of ready calculability of the other's behavior; the more similar A's and B's cognitive orientations, the less the necessity for either of them to "translate" X in terms of the other's orientations, the less the likelihood of failure or error in such "translations," and thus the less difficult and/or the less erroneous the co-orientation of either. Second, there is the advantage of validation of one's own orientation toward X; the more similar A's and B's orientations, either cognitive or cathectic (particularly in the many areas where validation is heavily dependent upon "social reality"), the more confident each of them can be of his own cognitive and evaluative orientations. Co-orientation is of course possible with little or no symmetry, but the facilitative value of symmetry for co-orientation is considerable.

If these advantages are commonly experienced as such, communicative acts resulting in increased symmetry are likely to be rewarded, and symmetry is likely to acquire secondary reward value. This is the basis of our assumption of a persistent "strain toward symmetry," under the conditions noted.

These assumptions may now be brought together in terms of the following inclusive postulate: *The stronger the forces toward A's co-orientation in respect to B and X,* (*a*) *the greater A's strain toward symmetry with B in respect to X;* and (*b*) *the greater the likelihood of increased symmetry as a consequence of one or more communicative acts.* The latter part of the postulate assumes the possibility of modified orientations toward X on the part of both A and B, who over a period of time exchange roles as transmitters and receivers of information.

Several testable propositions are derivable from this postulate. First, if the likelihood of instigation to and achievement of symmetry varies as a function of forces toward co-orientation, the latter varies, presumably, with valence of the objects of co-orientation—i.e., of intensity of attitude toward X and of attraction toward B. That is, under conditions such that orientation toward either B or X also demands orientation toward the other, the greater the valence of B or of X the greater the induced force toward co-orientation, and thus the greater the likelihood of both instigation toward and achievement of symmetry.

Such research findings as are known to the writer are in support of these predictions. Experimental results reported by Festinger and Thibaut (5), by Schachter (12), and by Back (1) indicate that attempts to influence another toward one's own point of view vary as a function of attraction. In the second of these studies it is shown that communications within a cohesive group are directed most frequently toward those perceived as deviates, up to a point where the deviate is sociometrically rejected (i.e., attraction decreases or becomes negative), beyond which point communication to them becomes less frequent. It is also shown in this study that frequency of influence-attempting communication varies with degree of interest in the topic of group discussion.

Some of these same studies, and some others, present data concerning symmetry as a consequence of communication. Thus Festinger and Thibaut, varying "pressure toward uniformity" and "perception of homogeneous group composition," found actual change toward uniformity following a discussion to be a function of both these variables, but some change toward uniformity took place in every group, under all conditions. Back found that subjects who started with different interpretations of the same material and who were given an opportunity to discuss the matter were influenced by each other as a direct function of attraction.

Findings from two community studies may also be cited, as consistent with these laboratory studies. Newcomb (10), in a replicated study of friendship choices as related to political attitudes in a small college community, found on both occasions that students at each extreme of the attitude continuum tended to have as friends those like themselves in attitude. Festinger, Schachter, and Back (4), in their study of a housing project, found a correlation of +.72 between a measure of attraction and a measure of "conformity in attitude." No direct observations of communication are made in these two studies; the relevance of their findings for the present point depends upon the assumption that frequency of communication is a function of attraction. This assumption is clearly justified in these two particular investigations, since in both communities there was complete freedom of association. As noted below, this assumption is not justified in all situations.

Other testable propositions derivable from the general postulate have to do with A's judgments of existing symmetry between himself and B with respect to X. Such judgments (to which the writer has for some time applied the term "perceived consensus") are represented by the symbol *B–X*, within A's phenomenal A–B–X system. Such a judgment, under given conditions of demand for co-orientation with respect to a given B and a given X, is a major determinant of the likelihood of a given AtoBreX, since strain toward symmetry is influenced by perception of existing symmetry. Such a judgment, moreover, is either confirmed or modified by whatever response B makes to AtoBreX. The continuity of an A–B–X system thus depends upon perceived consensus, which may be viewed either as an independent or as a dependent variable.

According to the previous proposition, the likelihood of increased symmetry (objectively observed) as a consequence of communicative acts increases with attraction and with intensity of attitude. The likelihood of perceived symmetry presumably increases with the same variables. Judgments of symmetry, like other judgments, are influenced both by "reality" and by "autistic" factors, both of which tend, as a function of attraction and intensity of attitude, to increase the likelihood of perceived consensus. Frequency of communication with B about X is the most important of the "reality" factors, and this, as we have seen, tends to vary with valence toward B and toward X. As for the "autistic" factors, the greater the positive attraction toward B and the more intense the attitude toward X, the greater the likelihood of cognitive distortion toward symmetry. Hypothetically, then, perceived symmetry with regard to X varies as a function of intensity of attitude toward X and of attraction toward B.

A considerable number of research studies, published and unpublished, are known to the writer in which subjects' own attitudes are related to their estimates of majority or modal position of specified groups. Only a minority of the studies systematically relate these judgments to attraction, and still fewer to intensity of attitude. Among this minority, however, the writer knows of no exceptions to the above proposition. The most striking of the known findings were obtained from students in several university classes in April of 1951, in a questionnaire dealing with the very recent dismissal of General MacArthur by President Truman:

	PRO-TRUMAN *Ss* WHO . . .	ANTI-TRUMAN *Ss* WHO . . .
attribute to "most of my closest friends"		
pro-Truman attitudes	48	2
anti-Truman attitudes	0	34
neither	4	4
attribute to "most uninformed people"		
pro-Truman attitudes	6	13
anti-Truman attitudes	32	14
neither	14	13

If we assume that "closest friends" are more attractive to university students than "uninformed people," these data provide support for the attraction hypothesis. Comparisons of those whose own attitudes are more and less intense also provide support, though less strikingly, for the hypothesis concerning attitude intensity.

Perceived symmetry, viewed as an independent variable, is obviously a determinant of instigation to symmetry-directed communication. Festinger (3), with specific reference to groups characterized by "pressures toward uniformity," hypothesizes that "pressure on members to communicate to others in the group concerning item *x* increases monotonically with increase in the perceived discrepancy in opinion concerning item *x* among members of the group," as well as with "relevance of item *x* to the functioning of the group," and with "cohesiveness of the group." And, with reference to the choice of recipient for communications, "The force to communicate about item *x* to a particular member of the group will increase as the discrepancy in opinion between that member and the communicator increases [and] will decrease to the extent that he is perceived as not a member of the group or to the extent that he is not wanted as a member of the group" (3, p. 8). Support for all of these hypotheses is to be found in one or more of his and his associates' studies. They are consistent with the following proposition: the likelihood of a symmetry-directed AtoBreX varies as a multiple function of perceived discrepancy (i.e., inversely with perceived symmetry), with valence toward B and with valence toward X.

Common sense and selected observations from everyday behavior may also be adduced in support of these propositions. For example, A observes that an attractive B differs with him on an important issue and seeks symmetry by trying to persuade B to his own point of view; or A seeks to reassure himself that B does not disagree with him; or A gives information to B about X or asks B for information about X. From all these acts we may infer perception of asymmetry and direction of communication toward symmetry. Selected observations concerning symmetry as a consequence of communication are equally plentiful; there is, in fact, no social phenomenon which can be more commonly observed than the tendency for freely communicating persons to resemble one another in orientation toward objects of common concern. The very nature of the communicative act as a transmission of information would, on a priori grounds alone, lead to the prediction of increased symmetry, since following the communication both A and B possess the information which was only A's before. B will not necessarily accept or believe all information transmitted by A, of course, but the likelihood of his doing so presumably varies not only with attraction toward A but also with intensity of attitude toward X, since in the long run the more important X is to him the more likely it is that he will avoid communicating with A about X if he cannot believe him. Thus the propositions have a considerable degree of face validity.

But everyday observation also provides instances to the contrary. Not all communications are directed toward symmetry, nor is symmetry an inevitable consequence of communication, even when attraction is strong and attitudes are intense. A devoted husband may refrain from discussing important business matters with his wife, or two close friends may "agree to disagree" in silence about matters of importance to both. People who are attracted toward one another often continue to communicate about subjects on which they continue to disagree—and this is particularly apt to happen with regard to attitudes which are intense, contrary to our theoretical prediction.

In sum, the available research findings and a considerable body of everyday observation support our predictions that instigation toward, perception of, and actual achievement of symmetry vary with intensity of attitude toward X and attraction toward B. The readiness with which exceptions can be adduced, however, indicates that these are not the only variables involved. The propositions, at best, rest upon the assumption of *ceteris paribus;* they cannot account for the fact that the probabilities of A's instigation to communicate about a given X are not the same for all potential B's of equal attraction for him, nor the fact that his instigation to communicate to a given B are not the same for all Xs of equal valence to him. We shall therefore attempt to derive certain further propositions from our basic assumption that both instigation to and achievement of symmetry vary with strength of forces toward co-orientation in the given situation.

DYNAMICS OF CO-ORIENTATION

The foregoing propositions represent only a slight extrapolation of Heider's general principle (6) of "balanced states" in the absence of which "unit relations will be changed through action or through cognitive reorganization." In a later paper devoted specifically to the implications of Heider's hypotheses for interrelationships among attitudes toward a person and toward his acts, Horowitz et al. (8) note the following possible resolutions to states of imbalance: (*a*) the sign-valence of the act is changed to agree with that of the actor; (*b*) the reverse of this; and (*c*) the act is cognitively divorced from the actor; in addition, of course, the disharmony may be tolerated.

Orientations as attributed by A to B are here considered as equivalent to acts so attributed, in Heider's sense, and symmetry is taken as a special case of balance. Assume, for example, the following asymmetry in A's phenomenal system: +A:X, +A:B, −*B*:*X*, +*B*:*A* (i.e., A has positive attitude toward X, positive attraction toward B, perceives B's attitude toward X as negative, and B's attraction toward A as positive). Any of the following attempts at "resolution," analogous to those mentioned by

Heider, are possible: (*a*) −A:X; (*b*) −A:B, or (*c*) cognitive dissociation. These can occur in the absence of any communication with B. Attempts at harmony (symmetry) may also be made via communications directed toward +*B*:*X*. And, if such attempts fail, the three alternatives mentioned as possible without communication are still available. Finally, there is the possibility of compromise, following communication (e.g., agreement on some mid-point), and the possibility of "agreeing to disagree."

Such acts of resolution are made necessary, according to the present theory, by the situational demands of co-orientation on the one hand and by the psychological strain toward symmetry on the other. But symmetry is only a facilitating condition for co-orientation, not a necessary one. While (as maintained in the preceding propositions) the probabilities of symmetry vary, *ceteris paribus*, with demand for co-orientation, the theory does not demand that a symmetry-directed AtoBreX occur in every instance of strong demand for co-orientation. On the contrary, the theory demands that it occur only if, as, and when co-orientation is facilitated thereby. We must therefore inquire more closely into the nature of the forces toward co-orientation as related to possible forces against symmetry.

One kind of situational variable has to do with the nature of the forces which result in association between A and B. Of particular importance are constrained (enforced) vs. voluntary association, and association based upon broad as contrasted with narrow common interests. The range of Xs with regard to which there is demand for co-orientation is presumably influenced by such forces. The relevant generalization seems to be as follows: *The less the attraction between A and B, the more nearly strain toward symmetry is limited to those particular Xs, co-orientation toward which is required by the conditions of association.* This would mean, for example, that as attraction between two spouses decreases, strain toward symmetry would increasingly narrow to such Xs as are required by personal comfort and conformity with external propriety; similarly, the range of Xs with regard to which there is strain toward symmetry is greater for two friendly than for two hostile members of a chess club.

The problem of constraint has already been noted. In some of the studies cited above it was assumed that frequency of communication varies with attraction, but this is not necessarily true under conditions of forced association. Two recent theoretical treatises deal with this problem.

Homans, one of whose group variables is "frequency of interaction" (though not communication, specifically), includes the following among his other propositions: "If the frequency of interaction between two or more persons increases, the degree of their liking for one another will increase, and vice versa"; and "The more frequently persons interact with one another, the more alike in some respects both their activities and their sentiments tend to become" (7, p. 120). (The latter proposition, which closely resembles the one here under consideration, apparently takes a much less important place in Homans' system than the former.) Almost immediately, however, the latter proposition is qualified by the statement, "It is only when people interact as social equals and their jobs are not sharply differentiated that our hypothesis comes fully into its own." In nearly every chapter, moreover, Homans (whose propositions are drawn *post hoc* from various community, industrial, and ethnological studies) points to the limitations which are imposed by constraining forces—particularly those of rank and hierarchy—upon the relations among attraction, similarity of attitude, and communication.

Blake manages to incorporate these considerations in a more rigorous proposition. Noting that hostility cannot be considered as the simple psychological opposite of positive attraction, he proposes to substitute a curvilinear for Homans' linear hypothesis: ". . . when pressures operate to keep members of a group together, the stresses that drive toward interaction will be stronger in *both* positive and negative feeling states than in neutral ones" (2). This proposition seems consistent with the present argument to the effect that demands for co-orientation are likely to vary with the nature and degree of constraints upon association; hence communicative acts, together with their consequences, will also vary with such constraints.

Another situational variable deals with the fact that, under conditions of prescribed role differentiation, symmetry may take the form of "complementarity" (cf. 11) rather than sameness. For example, both a man and his small son may (following a certain amount of communication of a certain nature) subscribe to the *same norms* which prescribe *differentiated behavior* for man and boy with respect to a whiskey and soda. If the father drinks in the son's presence, there are demands upon both of them for co-orientation; but there is strain toward symmetry only with respect to "the code," and not with respect to personal orientation toward the whiskey and soda. The code becomes the X with regard to which there is strain toward symmetry. In more general terms, *under conditions of differentiation of A's and B's role prescriptions with regard to X, the greater the demand for co-orientation the greater the likelihood of strain toward symmetry with respect to the role system* (rather than with respect to X itself).

A third situational variable has to do with the possibility that symmetry may be threatening. Particularly under circumstances of shame, guilt, or fear of punishment there are apt to be strong forces against a symmetry-directed AtoBreX, even though—in fact, especially when—attitude toward X (the guilty act) and attraction toward B (a person from whom it is to be concealed) are strong. Under these conditions it is the demand for co-orientation which creates the problem; if A could utterly divorce X (his own act) from B, he would not feel guilty. Forces toward symmetry, however, are opposed by counterforces. Demand for co-orientation induces strain toward symmetry, but does not necessarily lead to a symmetry-directed AtoBreX.

A theoretically analogous situation may result from the omnipresent fact of multiple membership groups. That is, strains toward symmetry with B_1 in regard to X may be outweighed by strains toward symmetry with B_2, whose orientations toward X are viewed as contradictory with those of B_1. This is often the case when, for example, two good friends "agree to disagree" about something of importance to both. Thus in one study (14) it was found that those members least influenced by reported information concerning their own group norms were those most attracted to groups whose norms were perceived as highly divergent from those of the group in question.

Communicative acts, like others, are thus subject to inhibition. Such "resolutions" as "agreement to disagree," however, represent relatively stressful states of equilibrium. It is therefore to be expected, in ways analogous to those noted by Lewin in his discussion of the quasi-stationary equilibrium, that A–B–X systems characterized by such stress will be particularly susceptible to change. Such change need not necessarily occur in the particular region of the system characterized by maximal strain.

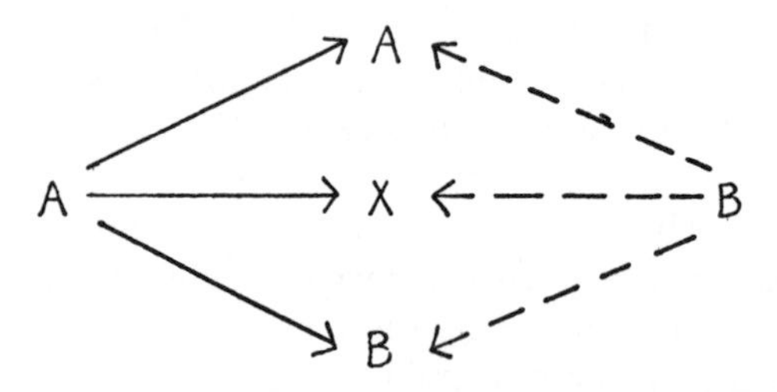

FIG. 2. Schematic illustration of A's phenomenal A–B–X system

The dynamics of such a system are by no means limited to those of strains toward symmetry, but must include changes resulting from acceptance of existing asymmetry. The possible range of dynamic changes is illustrated in Fig. 2. (In this figure, the A and B at either side represent persons as communicators; the A and B in the center represent the same persons as objects of co-orientation. The broken lines represent A's judgments of B's orientations.) Given perceived asymmetry with regard to X, and demand for co-orientation toward B and X, the possibilities for A are such that he can:

1. achieve, or attempt to achieve, symmetry with regard to X
   a. by influencing B toward own orientation,
   b. by changing own orientation toward B's,
   c. by cognitively distorting B's orientation;

2. introduce changes in other parts of the system
   a. modify his attraction toward B,
   b. modify his judgment of own attraction for B,
   c. modify evaluation of (attraction toward) himself (A),
   d. modify his judgment of B's evaluation of himself (B);
3. tolerate the asymmetry, without change.

As suggested by this listing of possible "solutions," the perception of asymmetry, under conditions of demand for co-orientation, confronts A with a problem which he can attempt to solve behaviorally (i.e., by communicative acts) and/or cognitively (i.e., by changing either his own orientations or his perception of B's orientations). Whatever his chosen "solution," it has some effect upon A's phenomenal A–B–X system—either to reinforce it or to modify it. As a result of repeatedly facing and "solving" problems of co-orientation with regard to a given B and a given X, a relatively stable equilibrium is established. If A is free either to continue or not to continue his association with B, one or the other of two eventual outcomes is likely: (*a*) he achieves an equilibrium characterized by relatively great attraction toward B and by relatively high perceived symmetry, and the association is continued; or (*b*) he achieves an equilibrium characterized by relatively little attraction toward B and by relatively low perceived symmetry, and the association is discontinued. This "either-or" assumption under conditions of low constraint presupposes a circular relationship between attraction and the perception of symmetry. The present theory demands this assumption of circularity, and empirical evidence (under conditions of relative freedom from constraint) seems to support it.

Under conditions of little or no freedom to discontinue association, no such circularity is assumed. The conditions which dictate continued association also dictate the requirements for co-orientation, which are independent of attraction. The empirical data suggest that the degree to which attraction is independent of symmetry varies with the degree of *perceived* (rather than the degree of objectively observed) constraint.

GROUP PROPERTIES

It follows from the preceding assumptions and propositions that there should be predictable relationships between certain properties of any group and variables having to do with communicative behavior within that group. A group's structural properties, for example, viewed as independent variables, may create problems and may provide solutions to other problems of communication. Viewed the other way around, many properties of a group are outcomes of its communicative practices. Evidence from many sources points to distinctive properties of groups which are precisely those which the foregoing considerations would lead us to expect, either as conditions for or as consequences of a given kind and frequency of communicative acts.

Three kinds of properties are briefly noted. Each of them is hypothetically related (either as dependent or as independent variable) to the probabilities of the occurrence of a given kind of communicative act.

1. *Homogeneity of orientation* toward certain objects. All descriptive accounts of interacting groups note this property, in one way or another and by one label or another. As applied to behavior, it does not necessarily refer to similarity of action on the part of all group members, but only of demand or expectation; e.g., all expect each to take his own differentiated role. In order to account for the observed facts it is necessary to make the assumptions (not previously made in this paper) that information may be transmitted in non-verbal ways, and with or without intention to do so—e.g., a person's behavior with regard to a given object informs observers about his orientation to it.

If communication is thus broadly defined, then the degrees of homogeneity of orientation of a given group with respect to specified objects are presumably related to communication variables with respect to those objects. It is not hypothesized that homogeneity is an invariable function of any single index of communication (frequency, for example), but rather that it varies in accordance with the dynamics of A–B–X systems. While there are often extra-group determinants of homogeneity of orientation, it seems reasonable to view this very important group property as an outcome of the conditions and consequences of communicative acts.

2. *Homogeneity of perceived consensus* (i.e., homogeneity of judgments of homogeneity of orientation). This property, though not often specifically mentioned in the literature on groups, is usually implicitly assumed. Most communication presupposes a considerable degree of perceived as well as objective homogeneity of orientation. The very fact of using language or gesture presupposes the assumption of consensus among communicants as to the information transmitted by the use of symbols.

Homogeneity of orientation and of perceived consensus do not, in spite of implicit assumptions to the contrary, have an invariant relationship; judgments of homogeneity may be of any degree of accuracy. If, as in the village reported by Schanck (13), each of many dissenters from a supposed norm believes himself the only dissenter, this state of pluralistic ignorance is an important group property, and is plausibly described by the author as an outcome of certain practices of communication. Any degree of homogeneity of perceived consensus, representing any degree of accuracy, is hypothetically an outcome of previous communicative acts and a determinant of future ones.

3. *Attraction among members.* Relationships of positive attraction of some degree invariably characterize continuing groups under conditions

of minimal constraint, and are commonly found even under conditions of considerable constraint. This is so commonly the case that Homans (7) ventures the almost unqualified hypothesis that "liking" increases with frequency of interaction, and vice versa. Viewed in the light of the hypothetical dynamics of A–B–X systems, Homans' proposition would be amended to the effect that interpersonal attraction varies with the degree to which the demands of co-orientation are met by communicative acts.

These are not, of course, the only group properties of significance, nor are these properties outcomes exclusively of intragroup communication. (Some properties of almost any group, particularly at early stages of its history, derive largely from individual characteristics which its members bring to it.) It appears to be the case, nevertheless, that the hypothetical conditions and consequences of communicative acts are not limited to groups of two, and that some of the important properties of observed groups are consistent with the hypothetical dynamics of A–B–X systems.

SUMMARY

Communicative acts, like other molar behaviors, may be viewed as outcomes of changes in organism-environment relationships, actual and/or anticipated. Communicative acts are distinctive in that they may be aroused by and may result in changes anywhere within the system of relations between two or more communicators and the objects of their communication. It seems likely that the dynamics of such a system are such that from an adequate understanding of its properties at a given moment there can be predicted both the likelihood of occurrence of a given act of communication and the nature of changes in those properties which will result from that act.

Some of the most significant of group properties are those which, hypothetically, vary with intragroup communicative acts. It should therefore be rewarding to discover whether support for the present hypotheses, as apparently provided by the scattered evidence now available, can be confirmed in more systematic ways. If so, there are promising possibilities of investigating the phenomena of social interaction by viewing them as events within communication systems.

REFERENCES

1. Back, K. The exertion of influence through social communication. *J. abnorm. soc. Psychol.*, 1951, 46, 9–23.
2. Blake, R. R. The interaction-feeling hypothesis applied to psychotherapy groups. *Sociometry*, 1953, 16, 71–77.
3. Festinger, L. Informal social communication. In L. Festinger, K. Back, S. Schachter, H. H. Kelley, & J. Thibaut, *Theory and experiment in social communication.* Ann Arbor Institute for Social Research, Univer. of Michigan, 1950.

4. Festinger, L., Schachter, S., & Back, K. *Social pressures in informal groups.* New York: Harper, 1950.
5. Festinger, L., & Thibaut, J. Interpersonal communications in small groups. *J. abnorm. soc. Psychol.*, 1951, 46, 92–99.
6. Heider, F. Attitudes and cognitive organization. *J. Psychol.*, 1946, 21, 107–112.
7. Homans, G. C. *The human group.* New York: Harcourt, Brace, 1950.
8. Horowitz, M. W., Lyons, J., & Perlmutter, H. V. Induction of forces in discussion groups. *Hum. Relat.*, 1951, 4, 57–76.
9. Miller, G. A. *Language and communication.* New York: McGraw-Hill, 1951.
10. Newcomb, T. M. *Personality and social change.* New York: Dryden, 1943.
11. Parsons, T., & Shils, E. A. (Eds.) *Toward a general theory of action.* Cambridge: Harvard Univer. Press, 1951.
12. Schachter, S. Deviation, rejection and communication. *J. abnorm. soc. Psychol.*, 1951, 46, 190–207.
13. Schanck, R. L. A study of a community and its groups and institutions conceived of as behaviors of individuals. *Psychol. Monogr.*, 1932, 43, No. 2 (Whole No. 195).
14. White, M. S. Attitude change as related to perceived group consensus. Unpublished doctoral dissertation, Univer. of Michigan, 1953.

A Theory of Social Comparison Processes

LEON FESTINGER

IN THIS paper we shall present a further development of a previously published theory concerning opinion influence processes in social groups (7). This further development has enabled us to extend the theory to deal with other areas, in addition to opinion formation, in which social comparison is important. Specifically, we shall develop below how the theory applies to the appraisal and evaluation of abilities as well as opinions.

Such theories and hypotheses in the area of social psychology are frequently viewed in terms of how "plausible" they seem. "Plausibility" usually means whether or not the theory or hypothesis fits one's intuition or

FROM *Human Relations*, 1954, 7, 117–140. Reprinted by permission of the author and publisher.

The development of this theory was aided by a grant from the Behavioral Sciences Division of the Ford Foundation. It is part of the research program of the Laboratory for Research in Social Relations.

one's common sense. In this meaning much of the theory which is to be presented here is not "plausible." The theory does, however, explain a considerable amount of data and leads to testable derivations. Three experiments, specifically designed to test predictions from this extension of the theory, have now been completed (5, 12, 19). They all provide good corroboration. We will in the following pages develop the theory and present the relevant data.

Hypothesis I: There exists, in the human organism, a drive to evaluate his opinions and his abilities.

While opinions and abilities may, at first glance, seem to be quite different things, there is a close functional tie between them. They act together in the manner in which they affect behavior. A person's cognition (his opinions and beliefs) about the situation in which he exists and his appraisals of what he is capable of doing (his evaluation of his abilities) will together have bearing on his behavior. The holding of incorrect opinions and/or inaccurate appraisals of one's abilities can be punishing or even fatal in many situations.

It is necessary, before we proceed, to clarify the distinction between opinions and evaluations of abilities since at first glance it may seem that one's evaluation of one's own ability is an opinion about it. Abilities are of course manifested only through performance which is assumed to depend upon the particular ability. The clarity of the manifestation or performance can vary from instances where there is no clear ordering criterion of the ability to instances where the performance which reflects the ability can be clearly ordered. In the former case, the evaluation of the ability does function like other opinions which are not directly testable in "objective reality." For example, a person's evaluation of his ability to write poetry will depend to a large extent on the opinions which others have of his ability to write poetry. In cases where the criterion is unambiguous and can be clearly ordered, this furnishes an objective reality for the evaluation of one's ability so that it depends less on the opinions of other persons and depends more on actual comparison of one's performance with the performance of others. Thus, if a person evaluates his running ability, he will do so by comparing his time to run some distance with the times that other persons have taken.

In the following pages, when we talk about evaluating an ability, we shall mean specifically the evaluation of that ability in situations where the performance is unambiguous and is known. Most situations in real life will, of course, present situations which are a mixture of opinion and ability evaluation.

In a previous article (7) the author posited the existence of a drive to determine whether or not one's opinions were "correct." We are here stating that this same drive also produces behavior in people oriented toward obtaining an accurate appraisal of their abilities.

The behavioral implication of the existence of such a drive is that we would expect to observe behavior on the part of persons which enables them to ascertain whether or not their opinions are correct and also behavior which enables them accurately to evaluate their abilities. It is consequently necessary to answer the question as to how persons go about evaluating their opinions and their abilities.

Hypothesis II: To the extent that objective, non-social means are not available, people evaluate their opinions and abilities by comparison respectively with the opinions and abilities of others.

In many instances, perhaps most, whether or not an opinion is correct cannot be immediately determined by reference to the physical world. Similarly it is frequently not possible to assess accurately one's ability by reference to the physical world. One could, of course, test the opinion that an object was fragile by hitting it with a hammer, but how is one to test the opinion that a certain political candidate is better than another, or that war is inevitable? Even when there is a possible immediate physical referent for an opinion, it is frequently not likely to be employed. The belief, for example, that tomatoes are poisonous to humans (which was widely held at one time) is unlikely to be tested. The situation is similar with respect to the evaluation of one's abilities. If the only use to which, say, jumping ability was put was to jump across a particular brook, it would be simple to obtain an accurate evaluation of one's ability in this respect. However, the unavailability of the opportunity for such clear testing and the vague and multipurpose use of various abilities generally make such a clear objective test not feasible or not useful. For example, how does one decide how intelligent one is? Also, one might find out how many seconds it takes a person to run a certain distance, but what does this mean with respect to his ability—is it adequate or not? For both opinions and abilities, to the extent that objective physical bases for evaluation are not available, subjective judgments of correct or incorrect opinion and subjectively accurate assessments of one's ability depend upon how one compares with other persons.

Corollary II A: In the absence of both a physical and a social comparison, subjective evaluations of opinions and abilities are unstable.

There exists evidence from studies on "level of aspiration" which shows clearly the instability of evaluations of abilities in the absence of comparison with other persons (13, 15, 20, 21, 23). The typical situation in an experiment designed to study "level of aspiration" is as follows: a person is given a task to perform which is serial in nature. This may be a series of trials of throwing darts at a target or a series of information tests or a series of puzzles or the like. After each trial the person is told what he scored (how many points he made or how many correct answers or how long it took) and is asked to state what score he expects to get or will try for on the next trial. These experiments have previously been interpreted in terms of goal directed behavior. If we examine the situation closely, however, it is apparent that the individual's stated "level of aspiration" is actually a statement of what he considers a good performance to be. In other words, it is his evaluation, at that time, of what score he should get, that is, his evaluation of his ability. The data show clearly that if the person scores as well as he said he expected to do, he feels he has done well (experiences success) and if he scores less than his "aspirations" he feels he has done poorly (experiences failure) (17).

Let us examine, then, the stability of these evaluations in a situation where the person performing the task has no opportunity for comparison with others. The data from these studies show that the "level of aspiration" fluctuates markedly as performance fluctuates. If the person makes a score better than his previous one, then what was formerly considered a good performance is no longer good and his "level of aspiration" goes up. If his performance drops, his "level of aspiration" drops. Even after a person has had a good deal of experience at a task, the evaluation of what is good performance continues to fluctuate.

Similar instability is found in the case of opinions. When, using the autokinetic effect, persons are asked to make judgments of how far the point of light moves, these judgments continue to fluctuate before there are any comparison persons.[1]

To the extent, then, that there are relevant data available, they tend to confirm *Corollary II A* concerning the instability of evaluations in the absence of comparisons.

Corollary II B: When an objective, non-social basis for the evaluation of one's ability or opinion is readily available persons will not evaluate their opinions or abilities by comparison with others.

Hochbaum (18) reports an experiment concerning the effect of knowledge of others' opinions on one's own opinion which corroborates *Corollary II B*. Half of the subjects in this experiment were persuaded by the experimenter that they were extremely good at being able to make correct judgments concerning things like the issue they were to discuss. The other half of the subjects were made to feel that they were extremely

1 Although published material on the autokinetic effect does not present the data in this form, it is clearly shown in special analysis of data from an experiment by Brehm, J. W., A quantitative approach to the measurement of social influence. Honors thesis, Harvard University, 1952.

poor in making such judgments. They were then asked to write their opinions down and were handed back a slip of paper presumably reporting to them the opinions of each other person in the group. In this way the subjects were made to feel that most of the others in the group disagreed with them. Those subjects who were given an objective basis for feeling that their opinion was likely to be correct did not change their opinions very often in spite of the disagreement with others in the group. Those who had an objective basis for feeling their judgments were likely to be poor changed their opinion very frequently upon discovering that others disagreed with them.

Hypothesis III: The tendency to compare oneself with some other specific person decreases as the difference between his opinion or ability and one's own increases.

A person does not tend to evaluate his opinions or his abilities by comparison with others who are too divergent from himself. If some other person's ability is too far from his own, either above or below, it is not possible to evaluate his own ability *accurately* by comparison with this other person. There is then a tendency not to make the comparison. Thus, a college student, for example, does not compare himself to inmates of an institution for the feeble minded to evaluate his own intelligence. Nor does a person who is just beginning to learn the game of chess compare himself to the recognized masters of the game.

The situation is identical with respect to the evaluation of opinions. One does not evaluate the correctness or incorrectness of an opinion by comparison with others whose opinions are extremely divergent from one's own. Thus, a person who believes that Negroes are the intellectual equals of whites does not evaluate his opinion by comparison with the opinion of a person who belongs to some very anti-Negro group. In other words, there is a self-imposed restriction in the range of opinion or ability with which a person compares himself.

Corollary III A: Given a range of possible persons for comparison, someone close to one's own ability or opinion will be chosen for comparison.

There is some evidence relevant to this corollary from an experiment by Whittemore (24). The purpose of the study was to examine the relation between performance and competition. Subjects were seated around a table and given tasks to work on. There was ample opportunity to observe how the others were progressing. After the experimental session, in introspective reports, the subjects stated that they had almost always spontaneously selected someone whose performance was close to their own to compete against.

Corollary III B: If the only comparison available is a very divergent one, the person will not be able to make a subjectively precise evaluation of his opinion or ability.

There is evidence supporting this corollary with respect to abilities but no relevant evidence in connection with opinions has been found.

Hoppe (20) in his experiment on level of aspiration reports that when subjects made a score very far above or very far below their level of aspiration they did not experience success or failure respectively. In other words, this extremely divergent score presented no grounds for self evaluation. Dreyer (5) performed an experiment in which high school children were made to score either: very far above the reported average for boys like themselves; at the reported average; or very far below the reported average. After a series of trials they were asked, "How well do you feel you did on the test?" There were five possible categories of response. The top two were good or very good; the bottom two were poor or very poor. In the middle was a noncommittal response of fair. Both those who scored very far below and those who scored very far above the reported group average gave the response "fair" significantly more often than did those who scored at the reported group average. Also, on the average, the persons who had scored at the reported average felt they had done better than did those scoring far above the group. Again the data support the hypothesis.

We may then conclude that there is selectivity in comparison on abilities and opinions and that one major factor governing the selectivity is simply the discrepancy between the person's own opinion or ability and that of another person. Phenomenologically, the appearance of this process is different for opinions and for abilities but conceptually it is exactly the same process. In dealing with opinions one feels that those with whom one does not compare oneself are different kinds of people or members of different groups or people with different backgrounds. Frequently this allegation of difference, to support the non-comparability, is made together with some derogation. In the case of abilities, the phenomenal process is that of designation of status inferior or superior to those persons who are non-comparable to oneself. We will elaborate on this later.

Derivation A (from I, II, III): Subjective evaluations of opinions or of abilities are stable when comparison is available with others who are judged to be close to one's opinions or abilities.

Derivation B (from I, II, III): The availability of comparison with others whose opinions or abilities are somewhat different from one's own will produce tendencies to change one's evaluation of the opinion or ability in question.

There are also data to show the effect which knowledge of group opinions or group abilities has on the person's evaluations which were initially formed privately. If the evaluation of an opinion or an ability formed in the absence of the possibility of comparison with others is indeed unstable, as we have presumed, then we would expect that, given an opportunity to make a comparison with others, the opportunity would be taken and the comparison would have a considerable impact on the self evaluation. This is found to be true for both abilities and opinions. "Level of aspiration" experiments have been performed where, after a series of trials in which the person is unable to compare his performance with others, there occurs a series of trials in which the person has available to him the knowledge of how others *like himself* performed on each trial (1, 4, 6, 17). When the "others like himself" have scores different from his own, his stated "level of aspiration" (his statement of what he considers is good performance) almost always moves close to the level of the performance of others. It is also found that under these conditions the level of aspiration changes less with fluctuations in performance, in other words, is more stable. When the reported performance of others is about equal to his own score, the stability of his evaluation of his ability is increased and, thus, his level of aspiration shows very little variability. Dreyer, in an experiment specifically designed to test part of this theory (5), showed clearly that the variance of the level of aspiration was smaller when the subject scored close to the group than when he scored far above or far below them. In short, comparison with the performance of others specifies what his ability should be and gives stability to the evaluation.

Festinger, Gerard, et al. (10) find a similar situation with respect to opinions. When a person is asked to form an opinion privately and then has made available to him the consensus of opinion in the group of which he is a member, those who discover that most others in the group disagree with them become relatively less confident that their opinion is correct and a goodly proportion change their opinion. Those who discover that most others in the group agree with them become highly confident in their opinion and it is extremely rare to find one of them changing his opinion. Again, comparison with others has tended to define what is a correct opinion and has given stability to the evaluation. This result is also obtained by Hochbaum (18).

We may then conclude that *Derivations A* and *B* tend to be supported by the available data.

Derivation C (from I, III B): A person will be less attracted to situations where others are very divergent from him than to situations where others are close to him for both abilities and opinions.

This follows from a consideration of *Hypothesis I* and *Corollary III B*. If there is a drive toward evaluation of abilities and opinions, and if this evaluation is possible only with others who are close enough, then there should be some attraction to groups where others are relatively close with respect to opinions and/or abilities. There are data confirming this for both opinions and abilities.

Festinger, Gerard, et al. (10) report an experiment in which after each person had written down his opinion on an issue he was handed back a slip of paper presumably containing a tabulation of the opinions in the group. Some in each group were thus given the impression that most of the others in the group held opinions close to their own. The rest were given the impression that most others in the group held opinions quite different from their own. After the experiment they were each asked how well they liked the others in the group. In each of the eight different experimental conditions those who thought that the others held divergent opinions were less attracted to the group.[2]

The previously mentioned experiment by Dreyer (5) has as one of its main purposes the testing of this derivation in connection with abilities. He used a "level of aspiration" situation and falsified the scores he reported to the subjects so that some thought they were scoring very far above the group, some thought they were scoring very far below the group, while others thought they were scoring about the same level as the average of others like them. After each trial they were asked whether they wanted to continue for another trial or whether they would prefer to stop. The reasoning was that if those scoring well above or well below the group average were not able to evaluate their ability accurately, the situation would be less attractive to them and they would stop sooner. On the average, those scoring very much above the group stop after the fifth trial, while those scoring below or at the average of the group stop after the ninth trial.[3] There is no difference between those scoring at and those scoring well below the average of the group. The derivation in the case of abilities seems confirmed for deviation from the group in one direction then but not in the other. This is probably due to the presence of another pressure which we shall discuss in detail later, namely, the value placed in our culture on being better and better with the result that the subjects scoring below the group wanted to, and felt that they might, improve and achieve comparability with the group average.

This result from the experiment by Dreyer (5) is also corroborated in the previously mentioned experiment by Hochbaum (18). It will be recalled that half the subjects were made to feel that their ability in judging situations of the kind they were to discuss was extremely good and very superior to the abilities of the others in the group. The other half of the subjects were made to feel that their ability was poor and consider-

2 This result is not reported in the article cited. It was obtained by analyzing the data for this particular purpose.

3 It is interesting to note that on this point, the usual theory of level of aspiration (21) would lead to a quite different prediction, namely, that those scoring consistently below the group would stop earliest.

ably worse than the ability of the others in the group. At the end of the experiment all the subjects were asked whether, if they returned for another session they would like to be in the same group or a different group. Of those who felt they were very much above the others in the group, only 38 per cent wanted to return to the same group. Of those who felt that they were considerably inferior to the others, 68 per cent wanted to return to the same group.

With the qualification concerning the asymmetry with regard to abilities the derivation may be regarded as confirmed. We will discuss the unidirectional drive upwards for abilities, which produces the asymmetry, in more detail later.

Derivation D (from I, II, III): The existence of a discrepancy in a group with respect to opinions or abilities will lead to action on the part of members of that group to reduce the discrepancy.

We have stated in *Hypotheses I, II, and III* and in the corollaries to these hypotheses that there is a drive to evaluate accurately one's opinions and abilities, that this evaluation is frequently only possible by comparison with others and that the comparison tends to be made with others who are close to oneself on the particular ability or opinion in question. This implies that the drive to evaluate one's ability or opinion will lead to behavior which will produce for the person a situation where those with whom he compares himself are reasonably close to him, in other words, there will be action to reduce discrepancies which exist between himself and others with whom he compares himself.

Before we can discuss the data relevant to this derivation it is necessary to point out two important differences between opinions and abilities which affect the behavioral manifestations of the action to reduce discrepancies. We will state these differences in the form of hypotheses.

Hypothesis IV: There is a unidirectional drive upward in the case of abilities which is largely absent in opinions.

With respect to abilities, different performances have intrinsically different values. In Western culture, at any rate, there is a value set on doing better and better which means that the higher the score on performance, the more desirable it is. Whether or not this is culturally determined, and hence culturally variable, is an important question but one with which we will not occupy ourselves here.[4]

With respect to most opinions, on the other hand, in the absence of comparison there is no inherent, intrinsic basis for preferring one opinion

4 There is some evidence, for example, that among the Hopi Indians this preference for better performance is absent (2).

over another. If we thought of opinions on some specific issue as ranging along a continuum, then no opinion in and of itself has any greater value than any other opinion. The value comes from the subjective feeling that the opinion is correct and valid.

Hypothesis V: There are non-social restraints which make it difficult or even impossible to change one's ability. These non-social restraints are largely absent for opinions.

If a person changes his mind about something, deserts one belief in favor of another, there is no further difficulty in the way of consummating the change. It is true that there are sometimes considerable difficulties in getting someone to change his mind concerning an opinion or belief. Such resistance may arise because of consistency with other opinions and beliefs, personality characteristics that make a person lean in one direction or another and the like. But the point to be stressed here is that once these resistances are overcome, there is no further restraint which would make it difficult for the change to become effective.

There are generally strong non-social restraints, however, against changing one's ability, or changing one's performance which reflects this ability. Even if a person is convinced that he should be able to run faster or should be more intelligent, and even if he is highly motivated to improve his ability in this respect, there are great difficulties in the way of consummating the change.

We may now examine the implications of *Derivation D*. Considering *Hypothesis IV* it is clear that the action to reduce the discrepancy which exists is, in the case of opinions, a relatively uncomplicated pressure towards uniformity. When and if uniformity of opinion is achieved there is a state of social quiescence. In the case of abilities, however, the action to reduce discrepancies interacts with the unidirectional push to do better and better. The resolution of these two pressures, which act simultaneously, is a state of affairs where all the members are relatively close together with respect to some specific ability, but not completely uniform. The pressures cease acting on a person if he is just slightly better than the others. It is obvious that not everyone in a group can be slightly better than everyone else. The implication is that, with respect to the evaluation of abilities, a state of social quiescence is never reached.

Competitive behavior, action to protect one's superiority, and even some kinds of behavior that might be called cooperative, are manifestations in the social process of these pressures which do not reach quiescence. We shall now elaborate this further in considering the specific nature of the social action arising from pressures toward uniformity. There are three major manifestations of pressure toward uniformity which we shall list below together with the relevant data.

Derivation D_1: When a discrepancy exists with respect to opinions or abilities there will be tendencies to change one's own position so as to move closer to others in the group.

Derivation D_2: When a discrepancy exists with respect to opinions or abilities there will be tendencies to change others in the group to bring them closer to oneself.

Considering *Hypothesis V* in relation to the above two subderivations we can see that a difference is implied between the resulting process for opinions and for abilities. Since opinions are relatively free to change, the process of changing the positions of members of a group relative to one another is expressed in action which is predominantly socially oriented. When differences of opinion exist, and pressures toward uniformity arise, these pressures are manifested in an influence process. Members attempt to influence one another, existing opinions become less stable and change occurs. This process of social influence, as we have mentioned before, ceases if and when uniformity of opinion exists in the group.

When pressures toward uniformity exist with respect to abilities, these pressures are manifested less in a social process and more in action against the environment which restrains movement. Thus, a person who runs more slowly than others with whom he compares himself, and for whom this ability is important, may spend considerable time practising running. In a similar situation where the ability in question is intelligence, the person may study harder. But, needless to say, movement toward uniformity may or may not occur. Even if it occurs, it will take much, much longer than in the case of opinions.

This process would, of course, not be competitive if it were not for the simultaneous operation of the unidirectional push upward which is stated in *Hypothesis IV*. Because of this unidirectional push and the pressure toward uniformity, the individual is oriented toward some point on the ability continuum slightly better than his own performance or the performance of those with whom he is comparing himself. If uniformity concerning an ability were reached this would not lead to a cessation of competition as long as the unidirectional push upward is operating.

There are data which corroborate the two derivations with regard to both abilities and opinions. Back (3), Festinger and Thibaut (9), Festinger, Gerard, et al. (10) and Gerard (14) have shown clearly that the presence of disagreement in a group concerning some opinion leads to attempts to influence others who disagree with them and also to tendencies to change own opinion to agree more with the others in the group. The effect of this process is to have the group move closer and closer to agreement. In groups where uniformity concerning some issue is reached the influence process on that issue ceases.

In the case of abilities the evidence is less direct for a number of reasons. First, there have been fewer studies conducted relevant to this point. Second, since the process resulting from pressure to reduce discrepancies concerning abilities is not clearly shown in a social process, and since it is complicated by the drive to do better and better, it is harder to identify. Some evidence is available from the literature on level of aspiration (21). It has been shown that in most situations, an individual's level of aspiration is placed slightly above his performance. When told the average performance of others like himself, the level of aspiration is generally set slightly above this reported group average. These results are what we would expect if the resolution of the simultaneous unidirectional drive upward and the pressure towards uniformity is indeed a drive to be slightly better than the others with whom one compares oneself. These data can then be viewed as an indication of the desire to change one's position relative to others.

An experiment by Hoffman, Festinger, and Lawrence (19) specifically designed to test parts of the present theory, shows this competitive process clearly. In a performance situation where one of three persons is scoring considerably above the other two, these two can and do act so as to prevent the high scorer from getting additional points. Thus, when the situation is arranged such that the performance of each person is controllable by the others in the group, action is taken to change the position of the members to reduce the discrepancies which exist.

Let us also examine what we would expect of the behavior of someone whose performance is considerably higher than the other members of the group and who has no other possible comparison group to turn to for his evaluation of this ability. Since the others are considerably poorer, they will not effectively serve as a comparison for his own evaluation. The pressure acting on him toward comparability can manifest itself in two ways. It is possible that under these conditions his performance will actually deteriorate slightly over a period of time. It is also possible that he will devote considerable time and effort to trying to improve the performance of the others in the group to a point where at least some of them are close to, but not equal to, him. This could take the form of helping them practice, coaching them, motivating them to improve and the like. Once comparability has been achieved, however, the process should change to the familiar competitive one.

There is some indirect corroboration of this from experimental evidence. Greenberg (16) reports a study in competition in which pairs of children, seated together at a table, were to construct things out of "stones" (blocks) which were initially all in one common pile. Grabbing blocks from the pile was one of the indications of competition while giving blocks to the others was taken as one indication of lack of competition. The author reports the case of two friends, E. K. and H. At a time when E. K.'s construction was clearly superior to that of H., H. asked for "stones" and was freely given such by E. K. Subsequently E. K. asked H. whether or not she wanted more "stones." At the end of the session, although privately the experimenter judged both constructions to be nearly equal, when the children were asked "whose is better?" E. K. said "mine" and H., after a moment, agreed.

From many such pairs the author summarizes as follows: "Sometimes when a child gave another a 'stone,' it was not at all an act of disinterested generosity, but a display of friendly competition and superior skill."

Derivation D_3: When a discrepancy exists with respect to opinions or abilities there will be tendencies to cease comparing oneself with those in the group who are very different from oneself.

Just as comparability can be achieved by changing the position of the members with respect to one another, so can it also be achieved by changing the composition of the comparison group. Thus, for example, if pressures toward uniformity exist in a group concerning some opinion on which there is a relatively wide discrepancy, there is a tendency to redefine the comparison group so as to exclude those members whose opinions are most divergent from one's own. In other words, one merely ceases to compare oneself with those persons.

Here again we would expect the behavioral manifestation of the tendency to stop comparing oneself with those who are very divergent to be different for opinions and for abilities. This difference arises because of the nature of the evaluation of opinions and abilities and because of the asymmetry introduced by the unidirectional push upward for abilities. We will consider these in order.

It will be recalled that opinions are evaluated in terms of whether or not subjectively they are correct while abilities are evaluated in terms of how good they seem. In other words, the existence of someone whose ability is very divergent from one's own, while it does not help to evaluate one's ability, does not make, in itself, for discomfort or unpleasantness. In the case of opinions, however, the existence of a discrepant opinion threatens one's own opinion since it implies the possibility that one's own opinion may not be correct. *Hypothesis VI,* which we will state below, leads us then to expect that the process of making others incomparable (ceasing to compare oneself with others) will be accompanied by hostility or derogation in the case of opinions but will not, generally, in the case of abilities.

Hypothesis VI: The cessation of comparison with others is accompanied by hostility or derogation to the extent that continued comparison with those persons implies unpleasant consequences.

Thus, in the case of opinions we expect the process of making others incomparable to be associated with rejection from the group. In the case of abilities, this may or may not be the case. It would be plausible to expect that there would rarely be derogation in making those below oneself incomparable. When making those above oneself incomparable, the presence of unidirectional push upward might lead to derogation in some instances.

The asymmetry introduced in the case of abilities is another difference we may expect to find. While in the case of opinions, deviation on either side of one's own opinion would lead to the same consequences, in the case of abilities there is a difference. The process of making others incomparable results in a "status stratification" where some are clearly inferior and others are clearly superior.

Corollary VI A: Cessation of comparison with others will be accompanied by hostility or derogation in the case of opinions. In the case of abilities this will not generally be true.

Festinger, Schachter, and Back (8) and Schachter (22) have shown that when there is a range of opinion in a group there is a tendency to reject those members of the group whose opinions are very divergent from one's own. This rejection tends to be accompanied by a relative cessation of communication of those who are rejected. This is undoubtedly another evidence of the cessation of comparison with those persons.

There are data relevant to this point in connection with abilities from the experiment by Hoffman, Festinger, and Lawrence (19). In this experiment, one out of a group of three persons was made to score very much higher than the other two on a test of intelligence. When the nature of the situation allowed, the two low scoring subjects ceased to compete against the high scorer and began to compete against each other. When they did this they also rated the intelligence of the high scorer as considerably higher than their own, thus acknowledging his superiority. In those conditions where they continued to compete against the high scorer they did not rate his intelligence as higher than their own. In other words, when the situation allowed it they stopped comparing their scores with the score of someone considerably higher than themselves. This cessation of comparison was accompanied by an acknowledgment of the others' superiority. A number of sociometric questions showed no hostility toward or derogation of the high scorer.

Having discussed the manifestations of the "pressure toward uniformity" which arises from the drive to evaluate opinions and abilities, we will now raise the question as to the factors which determine the strength of these pressures.

Derivation E (from I, II, and III): Any factors which increase the strength of the drive to evaluate some particular ability or opinion will increase the "pressure toward uniformity" concerning that ability or opinion.

Hypothesis VII: Any factors which increase the importance of some particular group as a comparison group for some particular opinion or ability will increase the pressure toward uniformity concerning that ability or opinion within that group.

To make the above statements relevant to empirical data we must of course specify the factors involved. The corollaries stated below will specify some of these factors. We will then present the data relevant to these corollaries.

Corollary to Derivation E: An increase in the importance of an ability or an opinion, or an increase in its relevance to immediate behavior, will increase the pressure toward reducing discrepancies concerning that opinion or ability.

If an opinion or ability is of no importance to a person there will be no drive to evaluate that ability or opinion. In general, the more important the opinion or ability is to the person, the more related to behavior, social behavior in particular, and the more immediate the behavior is, the greater will be the drive for evaluation. Thus, in an election year, influence processes concerning political opinions are much more current than in other years. Likewise, a person's drive to evaluate his intellectual ability will be stronger when he must decide between going to graduate school or taking a job.

The previously mentioned experiment by Hoffman, Festinger, and Lawrence (19) corroborates the *Corollary to Derivation E* with respect to abilities. It will be recalled that this experiment involved groups of three persons who took an "intelligence test." The situation was arranged so that one of the subjects (a paid participant) started out with a higher score than the other two. From then on the two subjects could completely control how many points the paid participant scored. The degree to which they prevented him from scoring points was taken as a measure of the extent to which they were competing against him and hence as an indication of the strength of the pressure toward uniformity acting on them. Half of the groups were told that this test which they were to take was an extremely valid test and hence a good measure of intelligence, an ability which these subjects considered important. The other half of the groups were told that it was a very poor test and the research was being done to demonstrate conclusively that the test was no good. For these subjects their performance was consequently not important. The results showed that the competition with the high scorer was significantly greater for the high importance than for the low importance condition.

Unfortunately there are no relevant data from experiments concerning opinions. The *Corollary to Derivation E* applies to opinions also, however, and is testable.

The data which we have presented refer to changing the position of members in the group. As the pressure toward uniformity increases there should also be observed an increase in the tendency to cease comparison with those who are too different from oneself. Specifically, this would mean that the range within which appreciable comparison with others is made should contract as the pressure toward uniformity increases. This leads to an interesting prediction concerning abilities which can be tested. The more important an ability is to a person and, hence, the stronger the pressures toward uniformity concerning this ability, the stronger will be the competition about it and also the greater the readiness with which the individuals involved will recognize and acknowledge that someone else is clearly superior to them. And just as in influence processes, where, once rejection has taken place there tends to be a cessation of communication and influence attempts toward those who have been made incomparable (10, 22), so we may expect that once inferior or superior status has been conferred, there will be a cessation of competition with respect to those who have been thus rendered incomparable.

Thus, for example, let us imagine two individuals who are identical with respect to some particular ability but differ markedly in how important this ability is to them personally. The prediction from the above theory would say that the person for whom the ability is more important would be more competitive about it than the other; would be more ready to allocate "inferior status" to those considerably less good than he; and would be more ready to allocate "superior status" to those considerably better than he. In other words, he would be more competitive within a narrower range.

Corollary VII A: The stronger the attraction to the group the stronger will be the pressure toward uniformity concerning abilities and opinions within that group.

The more attractive a group is to a member, the more important that group will be as a comparison group for him. Thus the pressure to reduce discrepancies which operate on him when differences of ability or opinion exist will be stronger. We would expect these stronger pressures toward uniformity to show themselves in all three ways, increased tendency to change own position, increased effort to change the position of others, and greater restriction of the range within which appreciable comparison is made.

There are a number of studies which corroborate *Corollary VII A* with regard to opinions. Back (3) showed that in groups to which the members were highly attracted there were more attempts to influence others than in groups to which the members were less attracted. This greater exertion of influence was accompanied by more change of opinion in the highly attractive groups. Festinger, Gerard, et al. (10) showed a tendency for members of highly attractive groups to change their opinions more frequently than members of less attractive groups upon discovering that most others in the group disagreed with them. This change of opinion was before any influence had actually been exerted on them by other members of the group. They also found that there was more communication attempting to influence others in the high than in the low attractive groups.

Schachter (22) showed that this same factor, attraction to the group, also increased the tendency to cease comparison with those who differed too much. Members of his highly attractive groups rejected the deviate significantly more than did members of the less attractive groups.

Festinger, Torrey, and Willerman (12) report an experiment specifically designed to test *Corollary VII A* with respect to abilities. If, given a range of performance reflecting some ability, the comparison, and hence the competition, in highly attractive groups would be stronger than in less attractive groups, then this should be reflected in the feelings of having done well or poorly after taking the tests. If *Corollary VII A* is correct we would expect those scoring slightly below others to feel more inadequate in the high than in the low attractive groups. Similarly we would expect those scoring equal to or better than most others to feel more adequate in the high than in the low attractive groups. Groups of four persons were given a series of tests supposed to measure an ability that these persons considered important. One of the subjects was caused to score consistently slightly below the others. The other three were made to score equally well. Those members who were highly attracted to the group, and scored below the others, felt they had done worse than similar persons who were not attracted to the group. Those who were attracted to the group and had scored equal to the others felt that they had done better than did similar persons who were not attracted to the group. Thus the results of the experiment corroborate the corollary for abilities.

Corollary VII B: The greater the relevance of the opinion or ability to the group, the stronger will be the pressure toward uniformity concerning that opinion or ability.

The conceptual definition of relevance of an opinion or an ability to a group is not completely clear. There are, however, some things one can state. Where the opinion or ability involved is necessary or important for the life of the *group* or for the attainment of the satisfactions that push the members into the group, the need for evaluation in that group will be strong. Groups will thus differ on what one may call their "realm of relevance." A group of men who meet every Friday night to play poker, and do only this together, will probably have a narrow "realm of relevance." The abilities and opinions for which this group serves as a comparison will be very restricted. The members of a college fraternity, on the other hand, where the group satisfies a wider variety of the members' needs will have a wider "realm of relevance."

In spite of the conceptual unclarity which is involved it is possible to create differences in relevance of an issue to a group which are clear and unambiguous. Thus Schachter (22) created high and low relevance conditions in the following manner. Groups which were to discuss an issue relevant to the group were recruited specifically for that purpose. Other groups were recruited ostensibly for very different kinds of things and on a pretext were asked to discuss the particular issue in question. They were promised this would never happen again in the life of the group thus making this issue of low relevance to that particular group. Schachter found, confirming *Corollary VII B*, that the tendency to reject deviates was stronger in the high relevance condition than in the low relevance condition.

No other evidence bearing on *Corollary VII B* has been located.

Thus far we have discussed only factors which, in affecting the pressure toward uniformity, affect all three manifestations of this pressure in the same direction. There are also factors which affect the manifestations of pressure toward uniformity differentially. We will discuss two such factors.

Hypothesis VIII: If persons who are very divergent from one's own opinion or ability are perceived as different from oneself on *attributes consistent with the divergence*, the tendency to narrow the range of comparability becomes stronger.

There is evidence supporting this hypothesis with respect to both abilities and opinions. In the previously mentioned experiment by Hoffman, Festinger, and Lawrence (19) half the groups were told that the three persons in the group had been selected to take the test together because, as far as could be determined, they were about equal in intelligence. The other groups were told that one of the three was very superior to the others. This was reported in a manner which made it impossible for either of the subjects to suppose that he himself was the superior one. In the "homogeneous" condition the subjects continued to compete against the paid participant who was scoring considerably above them. In the condition where they thought one of the others was clearly superior they competed considerably less with the paid participant and tended to compete with each other. In other words, when there was the perception of a difference consistent with the fact that the paid participant was scoring above them, they ceased comparison with him.

There is additional evidence on this point from level of aspiration experiments. Festinger (6) reports an experiment where, on an intellectual task, subjects (college students) were told they were scoring considerably above another group which they ordinarily considered inferior to themselves (high school students) or were told they were scoring considerably below a group which they considered superior to themselves (graduate students). In these circumstances there is practically no effect on the level of aspiration. Thus, the knowledge of this other group's being divergent in a direction consistent with the label of the group had no effect on their evaluation. It is interesting to note in this same experiment that if the reported direction of difference is inconsistent with the level of the group this destroys the incomparability and the effect on the level of aspiration is very great.

The evidence concerning opinions relating to *Hypothesis VIII* comes from experiments reported by Gerard (14) and Festinger and Thibaut (9). In both of these experiments discussions were carried on in a group of persons with a considerable range of opinion on the issue in question. In each experiment, half of the groups were given the impression that the group was homogeneous. All the members of the group had about equal interest in and knowledge about the issue. The other half of the groups were given the impression that they were heterogeneously composed. There was considerable variation among them in interest in and knowledge about the problem. In both experiments there was less communication directed toward those holding extremely divergent opinions in the heterogeneous than in the homogeneous condition. In other words, the perception of heterogeneity on matters related to the issue enabled the members of the groups to narrow their range within which they actively compared themselves with others.

It is interesting, at this point, to look at the data from these two experiments in relation to *Hypothesis III* which stated that the tendency to compare oneself with others decreased as the divergence in opinion or ability increased. In both the Gerard experiment (14) and the Festinger and Thibaut experiment (9) it was found that most communication was directed toward those whose opinions were most different from the others. Since we have just interpreted a reduction in communication to indicate a reduction in comparison with others, it is necessary to explain the overall tendency to communicate most with those holding divergent opinions in the light of *Hypothesis III*.

From *Hypothesis III* we would expect comparison to be made mainly with those closest to oneself. This is indeed true. The support one gets for one's opinion is derived from those close to one's own. However, it will be recalled that, in the case of opinions, comparison with others who are divergent represents a threat to one's own opinion. It is for this reason that communication is directed mainly toward those most divergent but still within the limits where comparison is made. This communication represents attempts to influence them. Reduction in communication to these extreme opinions indicates that the existence of these extreme opinions is less of a threat to one's own opinion. In other words, one is comparing oneself less with them. In the case of abilities we would not expect to find any such orientation toward very divergent persons. Comparison behavior in the case of abilities would follow very closely the simple relation stated in *Hypothesis III.*

Hypothesis IX: When there is a range of opinion or ability in a group, the relative strength of the three manifestations of pressures toward uniformity will be different for those who are close to the mode of the group than for those who are distant from the mode. Specifically, those close to the mode of the group will have stronger tendencies to change the positions of others, relatively weaker tendencies to narrow the range of comparison and much weaker tendencies to change their own position compared to those who are distant from the mode of the group.

Some data are available to support this hypothesis, with reference to opinions, from experiments by Festinger, Gerard, et al. (10) and by Hochbaum (18). In both of these experiments some persons in each group were given the impression that the rest of the group disagreed with them while others were given the impression that most of the group agreed with them. In both experiments there was considerably more change of opinion among the "deviates" than among the conformers. In both experiments there were considerably more attempts to influence others made by the conformers than by the deviates. While there exist no adequate data relevant to the tendency to narrow the range of comparison, corroboration is suggested in the experiment by Festinger, Gerard, et al. (10). In this experiment it was found that the deviates actually communicated less to those holding most divergent opinions than to those somewhat closer to their own position. The conformers showed the more familiar pattern of communicating most to those with extremely divergent opinions in the group.

The question may also be raised as to the determinants of the extent to which the group actually does move closer toward uniformity when pressures in this direction exist. In part, the degree of such movement toward uniformity will be dependent upon the strength of the pressures. In part they will be dependent upon other things. In the case of opinions it will be dependent upon the resistances to changing opinions, and upon the power of the group to successfully influence its members. The theory concerning the determinants of the power of the group to influence its members is set forth elsewhere (7). We will not repeat it here since the power of the group to influence its members is relatively unimportant with regard to abilities. The social process itself, no matter how much power the group has, cannot achieve movement toward uniformity on abilities. The power of the group successfully to influence its members will be effective only insofar as changing members' values concerning a given ability and increasing motivations can be effective. With respect to values and motivations concerning the ability the situation is identical with the social process that goes on concerning opinions.

IMPLICATIONS FOR GROUP FORMATION AND SOCIETAL STRUCTURE

The drive for self evaluation concerning one's opinions and abilities has implications not only for the behavior of persons in groups but also for the processes of formation of groups and changing membership of groups. To the extent that self evaluation can only be accomplished by means of comparison with other persons, the drive for self evaluation is a force acting on persons to belong to groups, to associate with others. And the subjective feelings of correctness in one's opinions and the subjective evaluation of adequacy of one's performance on important abilities are some of the satisfactions that persons attain in the course of these associations with other people. How strong the drives and satisfactions stemming from these sources are compared to the other needs which people satisfy in groups is impossible to say, but it seems clear that the drive for self evaluation is an important factor contributing to making the human being "gregarious."

People, then, tend to move into groups which, in their judgment, hold opinions which agree with their own and whose abilities are near their own. And they tend to move out of groups in which they are unable to satisfy their drive for self evaluation. Such movement in and out of groups is, of course, not a completely fluid affair. The attractiveness to a group may be strong enough for other reasons so that a person cannot move out of it. Or there may be restraints, for one or another reason, against leaving. In both of these circumstances, mobility from one group to another is hindered. We will elaborate in the next section on the effects of so hindering movement into and out of groups.

These selective tendencies to join some and leave other associations, together with the influence process and competitive activity which arise when there is discrepancy in a group, will guarantee that we will find relative similarity in opinions and abilities among persons who associate with one another (at least on those opinions and abilities which are relevant to that association). Among different groups, we may well expect to find relative dissimilarity. It may very well be that the segmentation into groups is what allows a society to maintain a variety of opinions within it and to accommodate persons with a wide range of abilities. A society or town which was not large enough or flexible enough to permit such segmentation might not be able to accommodate the same variety.

The segmentation into groups which are relatively alike with respect to abilities also gives rise to status in a society. And it seems clear that when such status distinctions are firmly maintained, it is not only members of the higher status who maintain them. It is also important to the members of the lower status to maintain them for it is in this way that they can relatively ignore the differences and compare themselves with their own group. Comparisons with members of a different status group, either higher or lower, may sometimes be made on a phantasy level, but very rarely in reality.

It is also important to consider whether or not the incomparability consequent upon group segmentation is a relatively complete affair. The conferring of status in the case of abilities or the allegation of "different kind of people" in the case of opinions may markedly lower the comparability but may not completely eliminate it. The latter is probably the more accurate statement. People are certainly aware, to some extent, of the opinions of those in incomparable groups. To the extent that perfect incomparability is not achieved, this has important bearing on differences in behavior to be expected from members of minority groups. Members of minority groups, if they are unable to achieve complete incomparability with other groups, should be somewhat less secure in their self evaluations. One might expect from this that within a minority group, the pressures toward uniformity would be correspondingly stronger than in a majority group. The minority group would seek stronger support within itself and be less well able to tolerate differences of opinion or ability which were relevant to that group.

In connection with opinion formation, there is experimental evidence that this is the case (14). Subgroups which were in the minority within larger experimental groups showed evidence of stronger pressures toward uniformity within the subgroup than did the majority subgroups. In minority groups where particular abilities were relevant, we would, by the same line of reasoning, also expect stronger pressures toward uniformity and hence fiercer competition with respect to that ability than in majority groups.

We may recall that stronger pressure toward uniformity also implies the existence of stronger tendencies to regard as incomparable those who deviate markedly. Since others are made incomparable with respect to opinions by means of rejection from the group, this gives us a possible explanation of the persistent splitting into smaller and smaller factions which is frequently found to occur in minority groups which are under strong pressure from the majority segments of the population.

CONSEQUENCES OF PREVENTING INCOMPARABILITY

There are predominantly two kinds of situations in which comparability is forced despite the usual tendencies not to compare oneself with those who deviate markedly. One such situation occurs when the attraction of the group is so strong, for other reasons, that the member continues to wish to remain in the group in spite of the fact that he differs markedly from the group on some opinion or ability. If, together with this state of affairs, he has no other comparison group for this opinion or ability, or if the opinion or ability is highly relevant to that group, then comparability is forced to a great extent. The psychological tendencies to make incomparable those who differ most will still be present but would not be as effective as they might otherwise be.

Under these circumstances where the attraction to the group remains high, the group has power to influence the member effectively and, in the case of opinion difference, we would expect an influence process to ensue which would be effective enough to eliminate the difference of opinion. In short, there would be movement toward uniformity. But what happens in the case of an ability? Here, while the group will probably succeed in motivating the member concerning this ability it is quite likely that the ability itself may not be changeable. We have then created a situation where a person's values and strivings are quite out of line with his performance and we would expect, if he is below others, deep experiences of failure and feelings of inadequacy with respect to this ability. This is certainly not an unusual condition to find.

The other major situation in which comparability is forced upon a person is one in which he is prevented from leaving the group. The theory concerning the effect of this situation on opinion formation is spelled out elsewhere (11). We will touch on the main points here in order to extend the theory to ability evaluation. In circumstances where a person is restrained from leaving a group either physically or psychologically, but otherwise his attraction to the group is zero or even negative, the group does not have the power to influence him effectively. Uniformity can, however, be forced, in a sense, if the group exerts threats or punishment for non-compliance. In the case of opinions, we may here expect to find overt compliance or overt conformity without any private acceptance on the part of the member. Thus a boy who is forced to play with some children whom he does not particularly like would, in such circumstances, where threat was employed, agree with the other children publicly while privately maintaining his disagreement.

Again, when we consider abilities, we find a difference which arises because abilities may be difficult if not impossible to change on short notice. Here the deviating member who is restrained from leaving the group may simply have to suffer punishment. If he deviates toward the higher end of the ability scale, he can again publicly conform without privately accepting the evaluations of the group. If he deviates toward the lower end of the ability scale this may be impossible. Provided he has other comparison groups for self evaluation on this ability he may remain personally and privately quite unaffected by this group situation. While publicly he may strive to perform better, privately his evaluations of his ability may remain unchanged.

SUMMARY

If the foregoing theoretical development is correct, then social influence processes and some kinds of competitive behavior are both manifestations of the same socio-psychological process and can be viewed identically on a conceptual level. Both stem directly from the drive for self evaluation and the necessity for such evaluation being based on comparison with other persons. The differences between the processes with respect to opinions and abilities lie in the unidirectional push upward in the case of abilities, which is absent when considering opinions and in the relative ease of changing one's opinion as compared to changing one's performance.

The theory is tentatively supported by a variety of data and is readily amenable to further empirical testing. One great advantage, assuming the correctness of the theory, is that one can work back and forth between opinions and ability evaluations. Some aspects of the theory may be more easily tested in one context, some in the other. Discoveries in the context of opinions should also hold true, when appropriately operationally defined, in the context of ability evaluation.

REFERENCES

1. Anderson, H. H., & Brandt, H. F. Study of motivation involving self-announced goals of fifth grade children and the concept of level of aspiration. *J. soc. Psychol.*, 1939, 19, 209–232.
2. Asch, S. E. Personality developments of Hopi children. Unpublished manuscript referred to in Murphy, Murphy, & Newcomb, *Experimental social psychology*. New York and London: Harper, 1931, 1937 (Rev. Ed.).
3. Back, K. The exertion of influence through social communication. *J. abnorm. soc. Psychol.*, 1951, 46, 9–24.
4. Chapman, D. W., & Volkmann, J. A., A social determinant of the level of aspiration. *J. abnorm. soc. Psychol.*, 1939, 34, 225–238.
5. Dreyer, A. Behavior in a level of aspiration situation as affected by group comparison. Ph.D. thesis, Univer. of Minnesota, 1953.
6. Festinger, L. Wish, expectation and group standards as factors influencing level of aspiration. *J. abnorm. soc. Psychol.*, 1942, 37, 184–200.
7. Festinger, L. Informal social communication. *Psychol. Rev.*, 1950, 57, 271–282.
8. Festinger, L., Schachter, S., & Back, K. *Social pressures in informal groups*. New York: Harper, 1950.
9. Festinger, L., & Thibaut, J. Interpersonal communications in small groups. *J. abnorm. soc. Psychol.*, 1951, 46, 92–100.
10. Festinger, L., Gerard, H., et al. The influence process in the presence of extreme deviates. *Hum. Relat.*, 1952, 5, 327–346.

11. Festinger, L. An analysis of compliant behavior. In M. Sherif (Ed.), *Group relations at the crossroads.* New York: Harper, 1953.
12. Festinger, L., Torrey, J., & Willerman, B. Self-evaluation as a function of attraction to group. *Hum. Relat.*, 1954, 7, 2.
13. Gardner, J. W. Level of aspiration in response to a prearranged sequence of scores. *J. exp. Psychol.*, 1939, 25, 601–621.
14. Gerard, H. The effect of different dimensions of disagreement on the communication process in small groups. *Hum. Relat.*, 1953, 6, 249–272.
15. Gould, R. An experimental analysis of "Level of aspiration." *Genet. Psychol. Monogr.*, 1939, 21, 1–116.
16. Greenberg, P. J. Competition in children: An experimental study. *Amer. J. Psychol.*, 1932, 44, 221–248.
17. Hilgard, E. R., Sait, E. M., & Magaret, G. A. Level of aspirations as affected by relative standing in an experimental social group. *J. exp. Psychol.*, 1940, 27, 411–421.
18. Hochbaum, G. M. Certain personality aspects and pressures to uniformity in social group. Ph.D. thesis, Univer. of Minnesota, 1953.
19. Hoffman, P. J., Festinger, L., & Lawrence, D. H. Tendencies toward comparability in competitive bargaining. *Hum. Relat.*, 1954, 7, 2.
20. Hoppe, F. Erfolg und Misserfolg. *Psychol. Forsch.*, 1930, 14, 1–62.
21. Lewin, K., Dembo, T., Festinger, L., & Sears, P. S. Level of aspiration. In *Personality and the behavior disorders.* Vol. 1. New York: Ronald Press, 1944. Pp. 333–378.
22. Schachter, S. Deviation, rejection and communication. *J. abnorm. soc. Psychol.*, 1951, 46, 190–208.
23. Sears, P. S. Levels of aspiration in academically successful and unsuccessful children. *J. abnorm. soc. Psychol.*, 1940, 35, 498–536.
24. Whittemore, I. C. The influence of competition on performance. *J. abnorm. soc. Psychol.*, 1925, 20, 17–33.

Social Behavior as Exchange

GEORGE C. HOMANS

THE PROBLEMS OF SMALL-GROUP RESEARCH

THIS ESSAY will hope to honor the memory of Georg Simmel in two different ways. So far as it pretends to be suggestive rather than conclusive, its tone will be Simmel's; and its subject, too, will be one of his. Because Simmel, in essays such as those on sociability, games, coquetry, and conversation, was an analyst of elementary social behavior, we call him an ancestor of what is known today as small-group research. For what we are really studying in small groups is elementary social behavior: what

Reprinted from *American Journal of Sociology*, 1958, 63, 597–606, by permission of The University of Chicago Press and the author.

happens when two or three persons are in a position to influence one another, the sort of thing of which those massive structures called "classes," "firms," "communities," and "societies" must ultimately be composed.

As I survey small-group research today, I feel that, apart from just keeping on with it, three sorts of things need to be done. The first is to show the relation between the results of experimental work done under laboratory conditions and the results of *quasi*-anthropological field research on what those of us who do it are pleased to call "real-life" groups in industry and elsewhere. If the experimental work has anything to do with real life—and I am persuaded that it has everything to do—its propositions cannot be inconsistent with those discovered through the field work. But the consistency has not yet been demonstrated in any systematic way.

The second job is to pull together in some set of general propositions the actual results, from the laboratory and from the field, of work on small groups—propositions that at least sum up, to an approximation, what happens in elementary social behavior, even though we may not be able to explain why the propositions should take the form they do. A great amount of work has been done, and more appears every day, but what it all amounts to in the shape of a set of propositions from which, under specified conditions, many of the observational results might be derived, is not at all clear—and yet to state such a set is the first aim of science.

The third job is to begin to show how the propositions that empirically hold good in small groups may be derived from some set of still more general propositions. "Still more general" means only that empirical propositions other than ours may also be derived from the set. This derivation would constitute the explanatory stage in the science of elementary social behavior, for explanation *is* derivation.[1] (I myself suspect that the more general set will turn out to contain the propositions of behavioral psychology. I hold myself to be an "ultimate psychological reductionist," but I cannot know that I am right so long as the reduction has not been carried out.)

I have come to think that all three of these jobs would be furthered by our adopting the view that interaction between persons is an exchange of goods, material and non-material. This is one of the oldest theories of social behavior, and one that we still use every day to interpret our own behavior, as when we say, "I found so-and-so rewarding"; or "I got a great deal out of him"; or, even, "Talking with him took a great deal out of me." But, perhaps just because it is so obvious, this view has been much neglected by social scientists. So far as I know, the only theoretical work that makes explicit use of it is Marcel Mauss's *Essai sur le don*, published in 1925, which is ancient as social science goes.(5) It may be that the tradition of neglect is now changing and that, for instance, the psychologists

1 See Braithwaite (4).

who interpret behavior in terms of transactions may be coming back to something of the sort I have in mind.[2]

An incidental advantage of an exchange theory is that it might bring sociology closer to economics—that science of man most advanced, most capable of application, and, intellectually, most isolated. Economics studies exchange carried out under special circumstances and with a most useful built-in numerical measure of value. What are the laws of the general phenomenon of which economic behavior is one class?

In what follows I shall suggest some reasons for the usefulness of a theory of social behavior as exchange and suggest the nature of the propositions such a theory might contain.

AN EXCHANGE PARADIGM

I start with the link to behavioral psychology and the kind of statement it makes about the behavior of an experimental animal such as the pigeon. (15) As a pigeon explores its cage in the laboratory, it happens to peck a target, whereupon the psychologist feeds it corn. The evidence is that it will peck the target again; it has learned the behavior, or, as my friend Skinner says, the behavior has been reinforced, and the pigeon has undergone *operant conditioning*. This kind of psychologist is not interested in how the behavior was learned: "learning theory" is a poor name for his field. Instead, he is interested in what determines changes in the rate of emission of learned behavior, whether pecks at a target or something else.

The more hungry the pigeon, the less corn or other food it has gotten in the recent past, the more often it will peck. By the same token, if the behavior is often reinforced, if the pigeon is given much corn every time it pecks, the rate of emission will fall off as the pigeon gets *satiated*. If, on the other hand, the behavior is not reinforced at all, then, too, its rate of emission will tend to fall off, though a long time may pass before it stops altogether, before it is *extinguished*. In the emission of many kinds of behavior the pigeon incurs *aversive stimulation*, or what I shall call "cost" for short, and this, too, will lead in time to a decrease in the emission rate. Fatigue is an example of a "cost." Extinction, satiation, and cost, by decreasing the rate of emission of a particular kind of behavior, render more probable the emission of some other kind of behavior, including doing nothing. I shall only add that even a hard-boiled psychologist puts "emotional" behavior, as well as such things as pecking, among the unconditioned responses that may be reinforced in operant conditioning. As a statement of the propositions of behavioral psychology, the foregoing is, of course, inadequate for any purpose except my present one.

2 In social anthropology D. L. Oliver is working along these lines, and I owe much to him. See also Newcomb (11).

We may look on the pigeon as engaged in an exchange—pecks for corn—with the psychologist, but let us not dwell upon that, for the behavior of the pigeon hardly determines the behavior of the psychologist at all. Let us turn to a situation where the exchange is real, that is, where the determination is mutual. Suppose we are dealing with two men. Each is emitting behavior reinforced to some degree by the behavior of the other. How it was in the past that each learned the behavior he emits and how he learned to find the other's behavior reinforcing we are not concerned with. It is enough that each does find the other's behavior reinforcing, and I shall call the reinforcers—the equivalent of the pigeon's corn—*values,* for this, I think, is what we mean by this term. As he emits behavior, each man may incur costs, and each man has more than one course of behavior open to him.

This seems to me the paradigm of elementary social behavior, and the problem of the elementary sociologist is to state propositions relating the variations in the values and costs of each man to his frequency distribution of behavior among alternatives, where the values (in the mathematical sense) taken by these variables for one man determine in part their values for the other.[3]

I see no reason to believe that the propositions of behavioral psychology do not apply to this situation, though the complexity of their implications in the concrete case may be great indeed. In particular, we must suppose that, with men as with pigeons, an increase in extinction, satiation, or aversive stimulation of any one kind of behavior will increase the probability of emission of some other kind. The problem is not, as it is often stated, merely, what a man's values are, what he has learned in the past to find reinforcing, but how much of any one value his behavior is getting him now. The more he gets, the less valuable any further unit of that value is to him, and the less often he will emit behavior reinforced by it.

THE INFLUENCE PROCESS

We do not, I think, possess the kind of studies of two-person interaction that would either bear out these propositions or fail to do so. But we do have studies of larger numbers of persons that suggest that they may apply, notably the studies by Festinger, Schachter, Back, and their associates on the dynamics of influence. One of the variables they work with they call *cohesiveness,* defined as anything that attracts people to take part in a group. Cohesiveness is a value variable; it refers to the degree of reinforcement people find in the activities of the group. Festinger and his colleagues consider two kinds of reinforcing activity: the symbolic be-

3 See Skinner (16). The discussion of "double contingency" by T. Parsons and E. A. Shils (12) could easily lead to a similar paradigm.

havior we call "social approval" (sentiment) and activity valuable in other ways, such as doing something interesting.

The other variable they work with they call *communication* and others call *interaction.* This is a frequency variable; it is a measure of the frequency of emission of valuable and costly verbal behavior. We must bear in mind that, in general, the one kind of variable is a function of the other.

Festinger and his co-workers show that the more cohesive a group is, that is, the more valuable the sentiment or activity the members exchange with one another, the greater the average frequency of interaction of the members (1). With men, as with pigeons, the greater the reinforcement, the more often is the reinforced behavior emitted. The more cohesive a group, too, the greater the change that members can produce in the behavior of other members in the direction of rendering these activities more valuable (14). That is, the more valuable the activities that members get, the more valuable those that they must give. For if a person is emitting behavior of a certain kind, and other people do not find it particularly rewarding, these others will suffer their own production of sentiment and activity, in time, to fall off. But perhaps the first person has found their sentiment and activity rewarding, and, if he is to keep on getting them, he must make his own behavior more valuable to the others. In short, the propositions of behavioral psychology imply a tendency toward a certain proportionality between the value to others of the behavior a man gives them and the value to him of the behavior they give him (16).

Schachter also studied the behavior of members of a group toward two kinds of other members, "conformers" and "deviates" (15). I assume that conformers are people whose activity the other members find valuable. For conformity is behavior that coincides to a degree with some group standard or norm, and the only meaning I can assign to *norm* is "a verbal description of behavior that many members find it valuable for the actual behavior of themselves and others to conform to." By the same token, a deviate is a member whose behavior is not particularly valuable. Now Schachter shows that, as the members of a group come to see another member as a deviate, their interaction with him—communication addressed to getting him to change his behavior—goes up, the faster the more cohesive the group. The members need not talk to the other conformers so much; they are relatively satiated by the conformers' behavior: they have gotten what they want out of them. But if the deviate, by failing to change his behavior, fails to reinforce the members, they start to withhold social approval from him: the deviate gets low sociometric choice at the end of the experiment. And in the most cohesive groups—those Schachter calls "high cohesive-relevant"—interaction with the deviate also falls off in the end and is lowest among those members that rejected him most strongly, as if they had given him up as a bad job. But how plonking can we get? These findings are utterly in line with everyday experience.

PRACTICAL EQUILIBRIUM

At the beginning of this paper I suggested that one of the tasks of small-group research was to show the relation between the results of experimental work done under laboratory conditions and the results of field research on real-life small groups. Now the latter often appear to be in practical equilibrium, and by this I mean nothing fancy. I do not mean that all real-life groups are in equilibrium. I certainly do not mean that all groups must tend to equilibrium. I do not mean that groups have built-in antidotes to change: there is no homeostasis here. I do not mean that we assume equilibrium. I mean only that we sometimes *observe* it, that for the time we are with a group—and it is often short—there is no great change in the values of the variables we choose to measure. If, for instance, person A is interacting with B more than with C both at the beginning and at the end of the study, then at least by this crude measure the group is in equilibrium.

Many of the Festinger-Schachter studies are experimental, and their propositions about the process of influence seem to me to imply the kind of proposition that empirically holds good of real-life groups in practical equilibrium. For instance, Festinger *et al.* find that, the more cohesive a group is, the greater the change that members can produce in the behavior of other members. If the influence is exerted in the direction of conformity to group norms, then, when the process of influence has accomplished all the change of which it is capable, the proposition should hold good that, the more cohesive a group is, the larger the number of members that conform to its norms. And it does hold good (6).

Again, Schachter found, in the experiment I summarized above, that in the most cohesive groups and at the end, when the effort to influence the deviate had failed, members interacted little with the deviate and gave him little in the way of sociometric choice. Now two of the propositions that hold good most often of real-life groups in practical equilibrium are precisely that the more closely a member's activity conforms to the norms the more interaction he receives from other members and the more liking choices he gets from them too. From these main propositions a number of others may be derived that also hold good.[4]

Yet we must ever remember that the truth of the proposition linking conformity to liking may on occasion be masked by the truth of other propositions. If, for instance, the man that conforms to the norms most

4 For propositions holding good of groups in practical equilibrium see Homans (8), and Riecken and Homans (13).

closely also exerts some authority over the group, this may render liking for him somewhat less than it might otherwise have been.[5]

Be that as it may, I suggest that the laboratory experiments on influence imply propositions about the behavior of members of small groups, when the process of influence has worked itself out, that are identical with propositions that hold good of real-life groups in equilibrium. This is hardly surprising if all we mean by equilibrium is that all the change of which the system is, under present conditions, capable has been effected, so that no further change occurs. Nor would this be the first time that statics has turned out to be a special case of dynamics.

PROFIT AND SOCIAL CONTROL

Though I have treated equilibrium as an observed fact, it is a fact that cries for explanation. I shall not, as structural-functional sociologists do, use an assumed equilibrium as a means of explaining, or trying to explain, why the other features of a social system should be what they are. Rather, I shall take practical equilibrium as something that is itself to be explained by the other features of the system.

If every member of a group emits at the end of, and during, a period of time much the same kinds of behavior and in much the same frequencies as he did at the beginning, the group is for that period in equilibrium. Let us then ask why any one member's behavior should persist. Suppose he is emitting behavior of value A_1. Why does he not let his behavior get worse (less valuable or reinforcing to the others) until it stands at $A_1 - \triangle A$? True, the sentiments expressed by others toward him are apt to decline in value (become less reinforcing to him), so that what he gets from them may be $S_1 - \triangle S$. But it is conceivable that, since most activity carries cost, a decline in the value of what he emits will mean a reduction in cost to him that more than offsets his losses in sentiment. Where, then, does he stabilize his behavior? This is the problem of social control (7).

Mankind has always assumed that a person stabilizes his behavior, at least in the short run, at the point where he is doing the best he can for himself under the circumstances, though his best may not be a "rational" best, and what he can do may not be at all easy to specify, except that he is not apt to think like one of the theoretical antagonists in the *Theory of Games*. Before a sociologist rejects this answer out of hand for its horrid profit-seeking implications, he will do well to ask himself if he can offer any other answer to the question posed. I think he will find that he cannot. Yet experiments designed to test the truth of the answer are extraordinarily rare.

I shall review one that seems to me to provide a little support for

5 See Homans (8), pp. 244–248, and Bales (2)

the theory, though it was not meant to do so. The experiment is reported by H. B. Gerard, a member of the Festinger-Schachter team, under the title "The Anchorage of Opinions in Face-to-Face Groups" (7). The experimenter formed artificial groups whose members met to discuss a case in industrial relations and to express their opinions about its probable outcome. The groups were of two kinds: high-attraction groups, whose members were told that they would like one another very much, and low-attraction groups, whose members were told that they would not find one another particularly likable.

At a later time the experimenter called the members in separately, asked them again to express their opinions on the outcome of the case, and counted the number that had changed their opinions to bring them into accord with those of other members of their groups. At the same time, a paid participant entered into a further discussion of the case with each member, always taking, on the probable outcome of the case, a position opposed to that taken by the bulk of the other members of the group to which the person belonged. The experimenter counted the number of persons shifting toward the opinion of the paid participant.

TABLE 1

Percentage of Subjects Changing Toward Someone in the Group

	AGREEMENT	MILD DISAGREEMENT	STRONG DISAGREEMENT
High attraction	0	12	44
Low attraction	0	15	9

TABLE 2

Percentage of Subjects Changing Toward the Paid Participant

	AGREEMENT	MILD DISAGREEMENT	STRONG DISAGREEMENT
High attraction	7	13	25
Low attraction	20	38	8

The experiment had many interesting results, from which I choose only those summed up in Tables 1 and 2. The three different agreement classes are made up of people who, at the original sessions, expressed different degrees of agreement with the opinions of other members of their groups. And the figure 44, for instance, means that, of all members of high-attraction groups whose initial opinions were strongly in disagreement with those of other members, 44 per cent shifted their opinion later toward that of others.

In these results the experimenter seems to have been interested only in the differences in the sums of the rows, which show that there is more shifting toward the group, and less shifting toward the paid participant, in the high-attraction than in the low-attraction condition. This is in line with a proposition suggested earlier. If you think that the members of a group can give you much—in this case, liking—you are apt to give them much—in this case, a change to an opinion in accordance with their views—or you will not get the liking. And, by the same token, if the group can give you little of value, you will not be ready to give it much of value. Indeed, you may change your opinion so as to depart from agreement even further, to move, that is, toward the view held by the paid participant.

So far so good, but when I first scanned these tables, I was less struck by the difference between them than by their similarity. The same classes of people in both tables showed much the same relative propensities to change their opinions, no matter whether the change was toward the group or toward the paid participant. We see, for instance, that those who change least are the high-attraction, agreement people and the low-attraction, strong-disagreement ones. And those who change most are the high-attraction, strong-disagreement people and the low-attraction, mild-disagreement ones.

How am I to interpret these particular results? Since the experimenter did not discuss them, I am free to offer my own explanation. The behavior emitted by the subjects is opinion and changes in opinion. For this behavior they have learned to expect two possible kinds of reinforcements. Agreement with the group gets the subject favorable sentiment (acceptance) from it, and the experiment was designed to give this reinforcement a higher value in the high-attraction condition than in the low-attraction one. The second kind of possible reinforcement is what I shall call the "maintenance of one's personal integrity," which a subject gets by sticking to his own opinion in the face of disagreement with the group. The experimenter does not mention this reward, but I cannot make sense of the results without something much like it. In different degrees for different subjects, depending on their initial positions, these rewards are in competition with one another: they are alternatives. They are not absolutely scarce goods, but some persons cannot get both at once.

Since the rewards are alternatives, let me introduce a familiar assumption from economics—that the cost of a particular course of action is the equivalent of the foregone value of an alternative (17)—and then add the definition: Profit = Reward − Cost.

Now consider the persons in the corresponding cells of the two tables. The behavior of the high-attraction, agreement people gets them much in the way of acceptance by the group, and for it they must give up little in the way of personal integrity, for their views are from the start in accord with those of the group. Their profit is high, and they are not prone to change their behavior. The low-attraction, strong-disagreement people are getting much in integrity, and they are not giving up for it much in valuable acceptance, for they are members of low-attraction groups. Reward less cost is high for them, too, and they change little. The high-attraction, strong-disagreement people are getting much in the way of integrity, but their costs in doing so are high, too, for they are in high-attraction groups and thus foregoing much valuable acceptance by the group. Their profit is low, and they are very apt to change, either toward the group or toward the paid participant, from whom they think, perhaps, they will get some acceptance while maintaining some integrity. The low-attraction, mild-disagreement people do not get much in the way of integrity, for they are only in mild disagreement with the group, but neither are they giving up much in acceptance, for they are members of low-attraction groups. Their rewards are low; their costs are low too, and their profit—the difference between the two—is also low. In their low profit they resemble the high-attraction, strong-disagreement people, and, like them, they are prone to change their opinions, in this case, more toward the paid participant. The subjects in the other two cells, who have medium profits, display medium propensities to change.

If we define profit as reward less cost, and if cost is value foregone, I suggest that we have here some evidence for the proposition that change in behavior is greatest when perceived profit is least. This constitutes no direct demonstration that change in behavior is least when profit is greatest, but if, whenever a man's behavior brought him a balance of reward and cost, he changed his behavior away from what got him, under the circumstances, the less profit, there might well come a time when his behavior would not change further. That is, his behavior would be stabilized, at least for the time being. And, so far as this were true for every member of a group, the group would have a social organization in equilibrium.

I do not say that a member would stabilize his behavior at the point of greatest conceivable profit to himself, because his profit is partly at the mercy of the behavior of others. It is a commonplace that the shortrun pursuit of profit by several persons often lands them in positions where all are worse off than they might conceivably be. I do not say that the paths of behavioral change in which a member pursues his profit under the condition that others are pursuing theirs too are easy to describe or predict; and we can readily conceive that in jockeying for position they might never arrive at any equilibrium at all.

DISTRIBUTIVE JUSTICE

Yet practical equilibrium is often observed, and thus some further condition may make its attainment, under some circumstances, more probable than would the individual pursuit of profit left to itself. I can offer evidence for this further condition only in the behavior of subgroups and not in that of individuals. Suppose that there are two subgroups, working close together in a factory, the job of one being somewhat different from that of the other. And suppose that the members of the first complain and say: "We are getting the same pay as they are. We ought to get just a couple of dollars a week more to show that our work is more responsible." When you ask them what they mean by "more responsible," they say, if they do their work wrong, more damage can result, and so they are under more pressure to take care (9). Something like this is a common feature of industrial behavior. It is at the heart of disputes not over absolute wages but over wage differentials—indeed, at the heart of disputes over rewards other than wages.

In what kind of proposition may we express observations like these? We may say that wages and responsibility give status in the group, in the sense that a man who takes high responsibility and gets high wages is admired, other things equal. Then, if the members of one group score higher on responsibility than do the members of another, there is a felt need on the part of the first to score higher on pay too. There is a pressure, which shows itself in complaints, to bring the *status factors,* as I have called them, into line with one another. If they are in line, a condition of *status congruence* is said to exist. In this condition the workers may find their jobs dull or irksome, but they will not complain about the relative position of groups.

But there may be a more illuminating way of looking at the matter. In my example I have considered only responsibility and pay, but these may be enough, for they represent the two kinds of things that come into the problem. Pay is clearly a reward; responsibility may be looked on, less clearly, as a cost. It means constraint and worry—or peace of mind foregone. Then the proposition about status congruence becomes this: If the costs of the members of one group are higher than those of another, distributive justice requires that their rewards should be higher too. But the thing works both ways: If the rewards are higher, the costs should be higher too. This last is the theory of *noblesse oblige,* which we all subscribe to, though we all laugh at it, perhaps because the *noblesse* often fails to *oblige.* To put the matter in terms of profit: though the rewards and costs of two persons or the members of two groups may be different, yet the profits of the two—the excess of reward over cost—should tend to equality. And more than "should." The less-advantaged group will at least try to attain greater equality, as, in the example I have used, the first group tried to increase its profit by increasing its pay.

I have talked of distributive justice. Clearly, this is not the only condition determining the actual distribution of rewards and costs. At the same time, never tell me that notions of justice are not a strong influence on behavior, though we sociologists often neglect them. Distributive justice may be one of the conditions of group equilibrium.

EXCHANGE AND SOCIAL STRUCTURE

I shall end by reviewing almost the only study I am aware of that begins to show in detail how a stable and differential social structure in a real-life group might arise out of a process of exchange between members. This is Peter Blau's description of the behavior of sixteen agents in a federal law-enforcement agency (3).

The agents had the duty of investigating firms and preparing reports on the firms' compliance with the law. Since the reports might lead to legal action against the firms, the agents had to prepare them carefully, in the proper form, and take strict account of the many regulations that might apply. The agents were often in doubt what they should do, and then they were supposed to take the question to their supervisor. This they were reluctant to do, for they naturally believed that thus confessing to him their inability to solve a problem would reflect on their competence, affect the official ratings he made of their work, and so hurt their chances for promotion. So agents often asked other agents for help and advice, and, though this was nominally forbidden, the supervisor usually let it pass.

Blau ascertained the ratings the supervisor made of the agents, and he also asked the agents to rate one another. The two opinions agreed closely. Fewer agents were regarded as highly competent than were regarded as of middle or low competence; competence, or the ability to solve technical problems, was a fairly scarce good. One or two of the more competent agents would not give help and advice when asked, and so received few interactions and little liking. A man that will not exchange, that will not give you what he has when you need it, will not get from you the only thing you are, in this case, able to give him in return, your regard.

But most of the more competent agents were willing to give help, and of them Blau says:

> A consultation can be considered an exchange of values: both participants gain something, and both have to pay a price. The questioning agent is enabled to perform better than he could otherwise have done, without exposing his difficulties to his supervisor. By asking for advice, he implicitly pays his respect to the superior proficiency of his colleague. This acknowledgment of inferiority is the cost of receiving assistance. The consultant gains prestige, in return for which he is willing to devote some time to the consultation and permit it to disrupt his own work. The following remark of an agent illustrates this: "I like giving advice. It's flattering, I suppose, if you feel that others come to you for advice" (3).

Blau goes on to say: "All agents liked being consulted, but the value of any one of very many consultations became deflated for experts, and the price they paid in frequent interruptions became inflated" (3). This implies that, the more prestige an agent received, the less was the increment of value of that prestige; the more advice an agent gave, the greater was the increment of cost of that advice, the cost lying precisely in the foregone value of time to do his own work. Blau suggests that something of the same sort was true of an agent who went to a more competent colleague for advice: the more often he went, the more costly to him, in feelings of inferiority, became any further request. "The repeated admission of his inability to solve his own problems . . . undermined the self-confidence of the worker and his standing in the group" (3).

The result was that the less competent agents went to the more competent ones for help less often than they might have done if the costs of repeated admissions of inferiority had been less high and that, while many agents sought out the few highly competent ones, no single agent sought out the latter much. Had they done so (to look at the exchange from the other side), the costs to the highly competent in interruptions to their own work would have become exorbitant. Yet the need of the less competent for help was still not fully satisfied. Under these circumstances they tended to turn for help to agents more nearly like themselves in competence. Though the help they got was not the most valuable, it was of a kind they could themselves return on occasion. With such agents they could exchange help and liking, without the exchange becoming on either side too great a confession of inferiority.

The highly competent agents tended to enter into exchanges, that is, to interact with many others. But, in the more equal exchanges I have just spoken of, less competent agents tended to pair off as partners. That is, they interacted with a smaller number of people, but interacted often with these few. I think I could show why pair relations in these more equal exchanges would be more economical for an agent than a wider distribution of favors. But perhaps I have gone far enough. The final pattern of this social structure was one in which a small number of highly competent agents exchanged advice for prestige with a large number of others less competent and in which the less competent agents exchanged, in pairs and in trios, both help and liking on more nearly equal terms.

Blau shows, then, that a social structure in equilibrium might be the result of a process of exchanging behavior rewarding and costly in different degrees, in which the increment of reward and cost varied with the frequency of the behavior, that is, with the frequency of interaction. Note that the behavior of the agents seems also to have satisfied my second condition of equilibrium: the more competent agents took more responsibility for the work, either their own or others', than did the less competent ones, but they also got more for it in the way of prestige. I suspect that the same kind of explanation could be given for the structure of many "informal" groups.

SUMMARY

The current job of theory in small-group research is to make the connection between experimental and real-life studies, to consolidate the propositions that empirically hold good in the two fields, and to show how these propositions might be derived from a still more general set. One way of doing this job would be to revive and make more rigorous the oldest of theories of social behavior—social behavior as exchange.

Some of the statements of such a theory might be the following. Social behavior is an exchange of goods, material goods but also nonmaterial ones, such as the symbols of approval or prestige. Persons that give much to others try to get much from them, and persons that get much from others are under pressure to give much to them. This process of influence tends to work out at equilibrium to a balance in the exchanges. For a person engaged in exchange, what he gives may be a cost to him, just as what he gets may be a reward, and his behavior changes less as profit, that is, reward less cost, tends to a maximum. Not only does he seek a maximum for himself, but he tries to see to it that no one in his group makes more profit than he does. The cost and the value of what he gives and of what he gets vary with the quantity of what he gives and gets. It is surprising how familiar these propositions are; it is surprising, too, how propositions about the dynamics of exchange can begin to generate the static thing we call "group structure" and, in so doing, generate also some of the propositions about group structure that students of real-life groups have stated.

In our unguarded moments we sociologists find words like "reward" and "cost" slipping into what we say. Human nature will break in upon even our most elaborate theories. But we seldom let it have its way with us and follow up systematically what these words imply (10). Of all our many "approaches" to social behavior, the one that sees it as an economy is the most neglected, and yet it is the one we use every moment of our lives—except when we write sociology.

REFERENCES

1. Back, K. W. The exertion of influence through social communication. In L. Festinger, K. Back, S. Schachter, H. H. Kelley, & J. Thibaut, (Eds.), *Theory and experiment in social communication.* Ann Arbor, Mich.: Research Center for Group Dynamics, Univer. of Michigan, 1950.
2. Bales, R. F. The equilibrium problem in small groups. In A. P. Hare, E. F. Borgatta, & R. F. Bales (Eds.), *Small groups.* New York: A. A. Knopf, 1955.
3. Blau, P. M. *The dynamics of bureaucracy.* Chicago: Univer. of Chicago Press, 1955.

4. Braithwaite, R. B. *Scientific explanation.* Cambridge: Cambridge Univer. Press, 1953.
5. Cunnison, I. *The Gift*, trans. by M. Mauss. Glencoe, Ill.: The Free Press, 1954.
6. Festinger, L., Schachter, S., & Back, K. *Social pressures in informal groups.* New York: Harper, 1950.
7. Gerard, H. B. The anchorage of opinions in face-to-face groups. *Hum. Relat.*, 1954, 7, 313–325.
8. Homans, G. C. *The human group.* New York: Harcourt, Brace, 1950.
9. Homans, G. C. Status among clerical workers. *Hum. Org.*, 1953, 12, 5–10.
10. Homans, G. C. *The white-collar job.* Ann Arbor, Mich.: Survey Research Laboratory, Univer. of Michigan, 1953.
11. Newcomb, T. M. The prediction of interpersonal attraction. *Amer. Psychologist*, 1956, 11, 575–586.
12. Parsons, T., & Shils, E. A. (Eds.), *Toward a general theory of action.* Cambridge, Mass.: Harvard Univer. Press, 1951.
13. Riecken, H. W., & Homans, G. C. Psychological aspects of social structure. In G. Lindzey (Ed.), *Handbook of social psychology.* Cambridge, Mass.: Addison-Wesley, 1954, 786–832.
14. Schachter, S., Ellertson, N., McBride D., & Gregory, D. An experimental study of cohesiveness and productivity. *Hum. Relat.*, 1951, 4, 229–238.
15. Schachter, S. Deviation, rejection, and communication. *J. abnorm. soc. Psychol.*, 1951, 46, 190–207.
16. Skinner, B. F. *Science and human behavior.* New York: Macmillan, 1953.
17. Stigler, G. J. *The theory of price.* New York: Macmillan, 1952 (Rev. Ed.).

Theory of Organizational Decision-Making

JAMES G. MARCH

ORGANIZATIONS are ubiquitous institutions. They appear to consort freely with many aspects of the political, social, and eco-

FROM A. Ranney (Ed.), *Essays on the Behavioral Study of Politics.* Urbana, Ill., University of Illinois Press, 1962. pp. 191–208.

This paper draws heavily on the work of a number of my colleagues. In particular, the ideas expressed depend on my collaboration with Richard M. Cyert in the development of a behavioral theory of the firm and with Herbert A. Simon in work on organization theory. Either or both of these estimable gentlemen should properly have been coerced into co-authorship of the paper were it not for the fact that either or both of them would probably object to some of the things that are said and almost certainly to how I say them. For treatments of the same general subject, see March & Simon (9) and Cyert & March (6).

nomic systems. This generality of organizational phenomena has led to anomalies within the various academic disciplines. One of the most important studies of a political organization is by a sociologist (11). Two political scientists have written a recent book dealing extensively with business organizations (9). A psychologist is working on a biological model of some economic organizations (8).

One of the consequences of such promiscuity is a tendency to underestimate the significance of differences between governmental organizations and nongovernmental organizations, to assume that the same theory will do for all types of organizations. Though I recognize at least some of the difficulties involved, I am sympathetic with such tendencies. As a result, neither the theoretical nor the methodological ideas expressed below distinguish between the study of political organizations and the study of other kinds of decision-making systems. Perhaps they should; I am inclined to think they should not.

THE THEORY OF ORGANIZATIONAL DECISION-MAKING

Organization theory is a collection of incongruous elements. In fact, a recent symposium on "modern organization theory" is an impressive monument to heterogeneity (8). Such a state of affairs does not distinguish organization theory from many other theories, but it leads to problems for general discussions of the study of organization. Either we attempt the substantial task of theoretical integration or we condemn ourselves to parochialism.

With apologies to my co-workers in the field, this is a parochial essay. It is concerned with that part of organizational theory dealing with the analysis, prediction, and explanation of human behavior in large, complex, more or less purposive organizations. Thus, it excludes from consideration the important tradition of prescriptive organization theory. Even within the field of positive organization theory, the paper is parochial. It is concerned with the study of organizations as information-handling and decision-making systems. Thus, on this score it excludes significant recent work on the internal dynamics of organizational systems, particularly as those dynamics are reflected in growth and decay.

The classic theory of organizational decision-making suffers from two critical deficiencies. First, it consists of largely unverified propositions about how organizations behave. Some of these propositions are empirically meaningless, some are simply wrong, some are probably correct. Second, the theory lacks a language of sufficient power to permit anything more than the simplest derivations of its empirical implications. Neither the language of poetry (analogies, paradoxes, puns, etc.) nor the language of classical mathematics has been adequate for examining the implications of the theory.

Thus, the theory of organizational decision-making has traditionally lacked models that combine substantive sensibility with formal power. In large part, we lacked models having either attribute until roughly twenty-five years ago. Since that time, field studies of various kinds have provided information that allows us to formulate at least some rudimentary notions of a sensible literary model. In turn, these substantive developments have permitted the use of new methods for dealing with the verification and the model-construction needs of the theory. On the basis of recent work, I will argue that major advances seem to be promised by substantive revision of the theory, by the introduction of computer program models, and by the utilization of laboratory experimentation and structured field studies in the verification of theoretical propositions.

DEVELOPMENTS IN SUBSTANTIVE THEORY

Revisions and Elaborations of the Concept of Organizational Goals (4)

Few organization theories escape the need for postulating a concept either labeled as, or analogous to, organizational goals. In normative organization theory, the efficiency criterion obviously relates to costs and returns measured in terms of goal achievement. The difficulties in developing a useful criterion of efficiency are notorious, not only in the case of public organizations but also in the case of such presumably uncomplicated institutions as business firms. On the one hand, the traditional organizational engineer is likely to measure efficiency in terms of such factors as the clip-to-paper ratio without concerning himself much with the implications such a measure has for the content of organizational goals. On the other hand, the sophisticated observer is likely to equate what the organization is currently achieving with organization goals, thereby reducing the question of efficiency to a giant tautology.

Positive theorists face a related problem. The problem can be paraphrased in terms of the following: (1) People (i.e., individuals) have goals; collectivities of people do not. (2) To develop a positive theory of organizational decision-making, we seem to need something analogous —at the organizational level—to individual goals at the individual level. For the moment, let us assume that we accept these propositions. Not everyone does. The theorist's problem then becomes one of introducing some concept of organization goals that is consistent with the apparent denial of their existence. There are two classic solutions to the problem. The entrepreneurial solution is to describe an organization as consisting of an entrepreneur (either the top of the managerial hierarchy or some external control group, such as stockholders, or congress) and a staff. The goals of the organization are then defined to be the goals of the entrepreneur. Conformity to these goals is purchased by payments (wages, interest, love, etc.) made by the entrepreneur to the staff and by a system of internal control that informs the staff of the entrepreneurial demands. This solution to the problem is characteristic of the economic theory of the firm, some political theories of public bureaucracies, and most theories of management.

The second classic solution to the problem is to identify a common or consensual goal. This is a goal that is shared by the various participants in the organization. It may be *a priori* sharing, as in many theories of political institutions in which the goal of "public interest" or "social welfare" is introduced. Or it may be *a posteriori* sharing, as in some theories of small group goal-formation through discussion. In either case, conflict is eliminated through consensus.

Neither solution is entirely happy. As a number of observers have pointed out, the existence of unresolved conflict is a conspicuous feature of organization. Organizations seem to have one goal at one time and another at another time. Different parts of the organization seem to have different goals at the same time. It is exceedingly difficult to construct a useful, positive theory of organizational decision-making if we insist on goal-consistency, either from subunit to subunit or from time to time.

As a result, recent theories of organizational objectives describe goals as the consequence of a continuous bargaining-learning process. In this process we can distinguish three subprocesses. The first is bargaining among the potential members of the organization. The organization is a coalition, and it gradually changes its composition through arriving at bargains with new members and rescinding bargains with old ones. In the course of such coalition formation, side payments are exchanged, much as is anticipated in the entrepreneurial theory of goals. What distinguishes most organizations, however, is that many of these side payments are not monetary payments but policy commitments and that internal consistency is not maintained.

Where bargaining is in terms of policy rather than money, some of the familiar framework of game theory seems less useful than it might be with respect to coalition formation where side payments satisfy the requirements of unrestricted transferability and conservation of utility. Rather, we require some way of describing the complementaries among various subsets of policy demands and some procedure for predicting which subsets of demands will be met. For the decisions on meeting demands are, in fact, the decisions on organizational goals.

The second subprocess is the internal organizational procedures through which objectives are stabilized and elaborated. We have ample reasons from field studies of organizations to specify that a theory of organizational objectives must take account of the powerful institutional forces directed toward stabilizing policy commitments and elaborating them through secondary bargaining. The allocation of functions, the use of budgets, the maintenance of precedents, the institution of standard operating procedures all serve to reinforce existing policy commitments.

The third subprocess is the process by which objectives change as a function of experience. On the one hand, organizational objectives are subject to the usual aspiration level phenomena. Thus, the quantitative level of a particular objective is a function of past achievement by the organization and past achievement by other organizations with which it is compared. On the other hand, since the organization has a rather large number of demands, experience affects which among the total set of potential demands are considered at a particular point in time and by whom. Different subunits will attend to different demands at different times.

If we adopt such a theory of organizational goals, we can tentatively explain some of the conspicuous features of organizational goals as we observe them in actual organizations. In particular, we can predict the rather crude internal rationalization of goals, the widespread use of non-operational goals, the shifts of objectives over time, and the sequential attention to goals within organizations.

Revisions and Elaborations of the Theory of Organizational Expectations (1, 2, 3, 13)

Organizations have some quality of purposiveness. As has been suggested above, it is a purposiveness having certain exotic characteristics. But it is possible to talk meaningfully about organizational goals. Consequently, a theory of organizational decision-making ordinarily postulates some connection between the choices made by the system and the objectives pursued by the system.

The classic theory of decision-making is built on three basic postulates of rationality: (1) all alternatives are known; (2) all consequences of all alternatives are known; and (3) a unique preference order exists over the set of consequences and all subsets of consequences. The organization chooses that alternative that has as its consequence the most preferred subset of consequences.

Empirical studies of organizations, however, indicate a wide disparity between the information requirements indicated by such a theory and the actual information used by an organization in making a decision. In particular, there have been four major objections to the classic concepts of expectations in organizational decision-making. First, the classical theory implies a continuous competition at the margin among all alternatives for organizational resources with extensive use of expectational data and planning. Observations of organizational decision-making suggest, however, that (within some relatively loose constraints) decisions will reflect local adaptation to local problems rather than adjustment through overall marginal planning. Feedback is often substituted for planning. Second, the theory makes information-seeking simply one of the alternative courses of action to be evaluated by the organization and selected or rejected in terms of its expected cost and expected return. Empirical observations seem to indicate that search activity is stimulated by failure, that some alternatives are more conspicuous to an organization than others, that alternatives are considered sequentially rather than simultaneously, and that only crude comparisons are made between search costs and potential returns. Third, the theory implies substantial computational ability on the part of the organization and the use of rather refined tools of comparison. Actual observation indicates that most organizations use very limited computational techniques, that they treat various considerations as independent constraints rather than reduce them to a single dimension, and that the informational demands they make are quite modest. Fourth, the theory seems to imply that the process by which information is obtained and processed is entirely neutral. This appears unlikely. Organizational information is likely to be replete with a full complement of conscious and unconscious selective perceptions and bias.

The major implication of these comments on the classic theory of expectations and choice is that an adequate theory of organizational decision-making must include a well-defined theory of search. Information is not given; it is obtained. Before it can be obtained, there must be motivation for the organization to obtain the information—motivation either on the part of the organization, some subunit of the organization, or some external information source. A theory of search must answer three major questions: (1) When will an organization institute search activities? (2) When will it stop? (3) Where will it search?

Recent theories of organization search suggest at least partial answers to each of these questions. In simplest terms, the theories specify that an organization will search for new alternatives when its current goals exceed its current achievement; that it will examine alternatives sequentially and in a more or less predictable order until a satisfactory one is obtained; and that it will then stop searching.

Unfortunately, the theory of search is not well developed with respect to the order of search. Perhaps the most interesting proposition (with respect to organizational search—there is a related but different theory with respect to individual problem-solving) builds upon the general characteristics of the division of labor in an organization. If we postulate that the division of labor in an organization is used ordinarily as the basis for dividing an organization problem into subproblems and, furthermore, that the subunits established by such a division of labor will tend to become the organizational guardians of particular subgoals, we can predict a form of local adaptation. Problems that are perceived to arise in one sector of the organization will have solutions sought in the same sector.

In addition, we can predict a kind of free market in alternatives. While some subunits in the organization have problems for which they seek solutions, other subunits have solutions for which they seek problems. Similarly, within a subunit, pet projects will tend to be defined as solutions to conspicuous problems.

Revisions and Elaborations of the Concept of Organizational Learning (5)

"Organizational learning" has the same taint as the concept of organizational goals. To assume that organizations go through the same processes of learning as do individual human beings seems unnecessarily naive. But organizations do exhibit (as do other social institutions) adaptive behavior over time. These adaptations certainly use individual members of the organization as instruments, but the results of the learning process involved seem to be independent of individual characteristics and to proceed substantially uninterrupted through repeated changes in organizational personnel.

Recent work on organizational learning has focused on learning with respect to four different phases in the decision process: learning with respect to decision rules; learning with respect to attention rules; learning with respect to search rules; learning with respect to information coding rules.

In contrast to at least some theories of organizational decision-making, observations of organizations making decisions suggest considerable uncertainty (at least initially) about proper decision rules. Typically this reflects not poor organizational design but some mixture of conflict, uncertainty, and passivity within the organizational coalition. The "details" have to be worked out through a trial and error process that reminds one of a rat in a maze. A good theory will include decision-rule learning functions to explain such phenomena.

Similarly, organizations learn what parts of their environment to attend to. There have been attempts, in recent models of organizational decision-making, to introduce considerations of the following sort: Let us suppose that an organization subunit has responsibility for a particular organizational goal. Since this goal is ordinarily stated in relatively non-operational terms, the subunit must develop some observable indices of performance on the goal. Among the indices objectively available to the subunit, which will be used? Observation suggests that this is a typical case of learning. Subunits in the short run do not change indices significantly. But there are long run shifts toward indices that produce generally satisfactory results (i.e., in this case, usually show the subunit to be performing well).

Search rules also change. As has already been pointed out, a modern theory of organizational choice includes a theory of search. In such a theory the sequential character of alternative consideration is of prime importance. There now is considerable suggestion that the order in which alternatives are considered is not fixed but changes as the organization experiences search success or failure. Such phenomena need to be reflected in the theory.

Finally, we can observe organizational learning with respect to information coding rules. Any decision-making system develops codes for communicating information about the environment. Any such code partitions all possible states of the world into a relatively small number of classes of states. Learning consists in changes in the partitioning. In general, we would want to have a theory that predicted the gradual development of an efficient code in terms of the decision rules currently in use. Thus, if a decision rule is designed to choose between two alternatives, the information code will tend to reduce all possible states of the world to two classes. If the decision rules changes, the theory should predict a change in the information code, but only after a time lag reflecting the rate of learning. The short-run consequences of incompatibilities between the coding rules and the decision rules form some of the more interesting dynamic features of an organizational, decision-making model.

General Implications of These Substantive Changes in the Theory

The implications of these substantive results for the development of models of organizational decision-making are reasonably clear:

(1) We require models that, in contrast with classical models, assume multiple, changing, acceptable-level goals.

(2) We require models that, in contrast with classical models, deal explicitly with the problem of internal conflict.

(3) We require models that, in contrast with classical models, include a theory of search and information handling.

(4) We require models that, in contrast with classical models, permit adaptation and change through organizational learning.

This is no small order. Empirical studies of organizational behavior have persistently posed large problems for theory construction. To a limited extent, the problems have been straightforward, and certain aspects of organizational decision-making have been amenable to conventional mathematical approaches. In particular, we can cite productive work, drawing on mathematical economics (10), game theory (12), and servo-mechanism theory (7).

But classical mathematics is not designed to deal effectively with the kind of theory outlined earlier in this paper. Consequently, it is no accident that the relatively complicated, branching models developed in the past few years and explorations in the potential utility of electronic computer programs to represent such models have reinforced each other. The major methodological advance of the past decade has been the development of the computer as an instrument of theory construction. This is, of course, a development that organization theory has shared with a large number of social science fields.

REFERENCES

1. Cyert, R. M., Dill, W. R., & March, J. G. The role of expectations in business decision making. *Admin. sci. Quart.*, 1958, 3, 307–340.
2. Cyert, R. M., & March, J. G. Organizational structure and pricing behavior in an oligopolistic market. *Amer. econ. Rev.*, 1955, 45, 129–139.
3. Cyert, R. M., & March, J. G. Organizational factors in the theory of oligopoly. *Quart. J. Econ.*, 1956, 70, 44–64.
4. Cyert, R. M., & March, J. G. A behavioral theory of organizational objectives. In M. Haire (Ed.), *Modern organization theory*. New York: Wiley, 1959.
5. Cyert, R. M., & March, J. G. Business operating procedures. In B. von H. Gilmer (Ed.), *Industrial psychology*. New York: McGraw-Hill, 1961.
6. Cyert, R. M., & March, J. G., *A behavioral theory of the firm*. Englewood Cliffs, N.J.: Prentice-Hall, 1963.
7. Haberstroh, C. J. Processes of internal control in firms. Unpublished doctoral dissertation, Univer. of Minnesota, 1957.
8. Haire, M. Biological models and empirical histories of the growth of organizations. In M. Haire (Ed.), *Modern organization theory*. New York: Wiley, 1959.
9. March, J. G., & Simon, H. A. *Organizations*. New York: Wiley, 1958.
10. Marschak, J. Efficient and viable organizational forms. In M. Haire (Ed.), *Modern organization theory*. New York: Wiley, 1959.
11. Selznick, P. *TVA and the grass roots*. Berkeley: Univer. of California Press, 1949.
12. Shubik, M. *Strategy and market structure*. New York: Wiley, 1959.
13. Simon, H. A. A behavioral model of rational choice, *Quart. J. Econ.* 1955, 69, 99–118.

PART II

THE *Individual* IN *Social Situations*

Introduction

EACH OF US *intuitively understands the perspective of the individual in a social situation, since it is the same perspective from which each of us views his own world. We may not understand how the situation got to be what it is at present, and we may not be able to anticipate accurately how the action we take now will ultimately affect the situation we will face sometime in the future. Similarly, we may not understand just why we feel as we do in the present, and may have a very poor perception of how others are thinking and feeling. But we all have a feeling that there is a part of the world that is "really real." That part is the fact of our present experience. We may doubt the reality of some of the objects we create through our experience, but that we do experience we "really know."*

Similarly, most of us have a strong conviction that our experience is an important part or aspect of the process that controls our behavior. We know very well that we do some things unintentionally, that many things go on in our mind and body which we do not ordinarily experience, and that often we wish or will to do something without being able to do so. But nearly every moment of our waking lives convinces us that our experience of deciding to do something or not has a good deal to do with whether or not we later experience ourselves doing it. We feel that what goes on in our experience is a real and important mediating link between the events that we perceive in our situation and the behavior we address to it.

Consequently, we are all concerned with the accuracy of our perception—that it should report the world to us now as we shall later find it. Indeed, our concern goes beyond avoiding errors which nature may later point out to us. Most of us realize, though sometimes dimly, that, by acting on our assumptions, we make our world in part, as we go along—particularly that part of it which has to do with our ability to experience and act and the way others will experience and act. These parts of reality are sometimes called "subjective reality" and "social reality." As W. I. Thomas *so succinctly put it: "If men define situations as real, they are real in their consequences."*

The line is very dim, at times, between that which is real because the physical events of nature will later convince us; that which is real because we subjectively experience it as so, and act irrevocably upon it; and that which is real because others say it is real and act upon their assumptions. We are all dependent, usually more than we know or care to admit, upon consensus with our fellows in drawing the lines between these different sorts of reality. Even more disturbing—or perhaps hopeful—is the realization that our very ability to experience, to decide, and to control our own behavior through our decisions is dependent in many subtle and involuntary ways on our relationship and interaction with our fellows.

This is a problem that is infinitely complex. It is quite as alive in the social sciences as in philosophy and the humanities, though it is not always recognized or stated in quite this form. This is the problem of motivation and social control as seen from the subjective side, from the perspective of the individual in a social situation. The studies in this part are all in one way or another concerned with it. How does the individual perceive or infer what others are thinking and feeling, and how is this related to his position in the group? This is the theme of the studies in Chapter 4. How much is the individual affected by others in the group, especially when other members attempt to change, directly or indirectly, his opinions and behavior, and how much does he tend to maintain a consistency of his own and affect others? These are the problems considered in Chapters 5 and 6.

The social situation for a given individual may be another individual, or a relationship with a series of other individuals, or it may be, as he conceives it in his own mind, a relationship between himself and the group as a whole. Similarly, in making measurements of perception, liking, disliking, behaving, the individual may be measured against another individual, a series, or against the group average. One can even measure each individual in a group in turn, with each compared to the average of all the others, and still not get beyond the perspective of "the individual" in a generalized sense, compared to "all those others." The work in social perception begins to get beyond this, however. As one obtains data on the prediction of each individual as to how each other individual will rate or choose him, the situation immediately begins to assume complexity. The situation is what it is because each individual makes it so by his choices, which each of the others takes into account in making his predictions. At least two steps of a process of interaction between the individuals is represented, and one is led naturally to the perspective of the group as a system of interaction, the perspective of Part III.

CHAPTER 4

SOCIAL PERCEPTION

A Scale for the Measurement of Empathic Ability

ROSALIND F. DYMOND

IN A PREVIOUS article (2) the writer made some suggestions concerning the importance of the empathic process in the understanding and creation of the state clinicians call "insight." A rudimentary attempt was made to measure the empathic ability of a small group of students and to relate this ability to the degree of insight they had into their interpersonal relations.

Although the term "empathy" has been in the psychological literature for some time, it has had several different usages. For this reason it is important that the term be defined before it is used further. Empathy will be used in this paper to denote the imaginative transposing of oneself into the thinking, feeling and acting of another and so structuring the world as he does.

Recently there have been suggestions from several different sources that empathy may be one of the underlying processes on which our understanding of others is built. This is sometimes phrased as, "fellow-feeling," "social awareness," "sympathy" or "insight." Lois Murphy (4) in her work on the development of sympathy in young children says:

FROM *Journal of Consulting Psychology*, 1949, 13, 127–133. Reprinted by permission of the author and the American Psychological Association, Inc.

In the case of sympathy, probably general thresholds for being affectionate, for seeing similarities between other's situations and our own, and for empathic responsiveness underlie sympathic habits. . . . If we could find measures for susceptibility to empathic responses, if such they be, we might well find the basis for the most important individual differences in sympathy.

In a very different context, Roy G. Hoskins, (3, pp. 102, 165) speaking of schizophrenia says:

It throws open the possibility that the primary defect in schizophrenia, a defect from which the remainder of the symptomatology stems–is inadequate empathy.
Perhaps as fundamentally characteristic as anything about the psychosis is the failure of the subject either to achieve or retain adequate breadth or depth of empathy.

L. S. Cottrell (1, p. 374) in his work on the analysis of situational fields holds that empathy is the basic process in all social interaction.

The impact of one human organism, A, on the activities of another, B, not only stimulates and conditions a response pattern of A to B but also conditions in A the response pattern of B to A as A has perceived that action and vice versa. (This process of responding by reproducing the acts of the other(s) has been referred to by various writers, as, taking the role of the other, identification, introjection, sympathy, empathy or imitation.)

D. L. Watson (5) in his paper on the nature of insight says:

To have correct insight is to share the feeling of him you are observing, to attach the significance appropriate to his part in events.

Although these and others have touched on the importance of the empathic process, there has been little or no systematic work done on the process itself. Many important questions suggest themselves immediately.

1. Can empathic ability be isolated and measured?
2. What is the normal range of the individual differences?
3. Does the development of this ability follow an age curve?
4. What is the relation of this ability to other personality and life history factors, such as intelligence, sociometric position, type of family atmosphere in which the individual was raised, etc.
5. Are there various dimensions to this ability, such as depth, (the degree to which one empathizes with any one individual), and breadth, (the number of individuals with whom one can empathize)?

Before any of the other questions can be dealt with it is necessary that question 1 be answered. A standardized test must be devised which requires the subject to empathize with others and which provides a measure of his accuracy. The remainder of this paper will deal with an attempt to construct such a scale and with the results obtained with it.

The test was made up of four parts, each containing the same six items. In the first part the individual was asked to rate himself, on a five point scale, on each of six characteristics. In the second part he was asked to rate some other individual on the same six traits. In the third he was asked to rate the other individual as he believes this other would rate himself. In the fourth he must rate himself as he thinks the other would rate him. In other words, if two individuals A and B are being tested for their empathy with each other, the procedure would be as follows:

A. Part 1. A rates himself, (A)
  2. A rates B as he (A) sees him.
  3. A rates B as he thinks B would rate himself.
  4. A rates himself (A) as he thinks B would rate him.

B. Part 1. B rates himself, (B)
  2. B rates A as he (B) sees him.
  3. B rates A as he thinks A would rate himself.
  4. B rates himself (B) as he thinks A would rate him.

Therefore a measure of A's empathic ability can be derived by calculating how closely his predictions of B's ratings, (A3 and A4), correspond with B's actual ratings (B1 and B2). Similarly a measure of B's empathy with A can be obtained by calculating how closely his predictions of A's rating, (B3 and B4), correspond to A's actual ratings (A1 and A2).

The six traits which were used as the items in all four parts of the test were:

1. self-confidence
2. superior-inferior
3. selfish-unselfish
4. friendly-unfriendly
5. leader-follower
6. sense of humour

Although the usual objections to such trait-ratings were recognized, this procedure was followed none the less because the ratings were not being used to determine the personality of the subjects nor to determine how accurate the others were in their estimation of this. The test was designed to answer the question how well can the subject transpose himself into the thinking, feeling and acting of the others. If he can do this he should be able to predict how the others will behave in certain defined situations. The situation chosen to test this ability was the subject's ability to predict how others will rate themselves and how they will rate him on these six traits.

The test was designed for use with a social psychology class which was studying the structuring and functioning of groups. There were 53 subjects in all, 29 females and 24 males. The class members were divided in a random way into five groups of seven members each and three groups of six members. All groups were composed of both sexes and in no cases were friends members of the same group. These groups met once a week to discuss and plan a class project. In each case one member was designated Group Observer. The Group Observer took no part in the group's activities, his sole duty being to keep records of how the group structured itself and how it functioned.

The empathy test or Rating Test, as it was called, was first given after these groups had met three times. Each student was required to rate himself on the six characteristics, to rate each of his group members in turn on these traits, and then to make the two types of prediction for each group member: (*1*) how each group member will rate him, and (*2*) how each group member will rate himself. This would seem to require that the individual take the role of the others, or empathize with them in order to see himself as others see him and in order to see others as they look to themselves. Since each rating is made on a five point scale, the test can be scored in terms of the total number of points the individual is in error in his predictions. This was called the Deviation Score and was the one commonly used. Another method of scoring was occasionally used for particular problems. This was called the Right Score and involved counting the number of predictions which coincided exactly with the actual rating.

The first calculation which was made was a comparison of the Right Scores with the number of right predictions which could be expected if chance alone were operating. The number right on each of the two types of prediction (3 and 4) and on both combined was much higher than could be expected if chance alone were the only factor operating in the making of these predictions, (the differences being significant at the 1 per cent level). Therefore it seems likely that this test is measuring some ability, other than chance, to predict what others will do under certain circumstances which involves taking the role of the other or empathizing with him.

In order to discover if the scores would improve as the subjects were in contact with each other over a longer period, the test was given again six weeks later after the groups had met eight times. Table 1 compares the scores obtained on the two tests. Both the Deviation Scores and the Right Scores are quoted although they have opposite interpretations. In terms of deviation the lower the score the more accurate the prediction, whereas in terms of the Right Score the higher score represents the greater accuracy.

An examination of Table 1 shows that some individuals did better on the second test than they had previously, but some did less well. On the whole there was a slight but not significant improvement. Only ten of the fifty-three subjects changed their scores significantly; nine of these were significantly improved and one was significantly poorer. It would appear,

TABLE 1

A Comparison of the Mean Scores Obtained on Test 1 and Test 2 (Retest)

	DEVIATION SCORES			RIGHT SCORES		
	RANGE	MEAN	S. D.	RANGE	MEAN	S. D.
Test 1	37–70	51.3	8.0	18–39	28.8	6.5
Test 2	29–75	48.0	9.0	18–46	31.3	7.5

then, that the longer contact did not significantly affect the scores and that therefore there was no real increase in the understanding of each other, on the whole, by the group members over this period of time. However when a breakdown was made according to sex an interesting difference was noted.

Although the difference between the males and females was not significant on the first test in terms of either method of scoring, on the second test the females were more accurate than the males in terms of both types of scoring. Also when each sex is considered separately, the males did not increase their scores significantly from Test 1 to Test 2 whereas the females did. Although the females did not have any initial advantage in their ability to empathize with others, for some reason they did, on the whole, learn to understand other group members better over the experimental period, whereas the males did not.

TABLE 2

Comparison of Mean Scores of Males and Females on Rating Test 1 and Test 2 (Retest)

	MEAN DEVIATION SCORE		MEAN RIGHT SCORE	
	MALES	FEMALES	MALES	FEMALES
Test 1	52.1	51.4	28.5	29.0
Test 2	50.9	45.6	30.0	36.0

From the Group Observers' reports it was learned that there were large qualitative differences in the groups themselves. Some groups functioned very smoothly, some were deadlocked in struggles for leadership and others were characterized by apathy. A good many of these differences were reflected in the group scores.

Group One was characterized by smooth relationships, a high degree of interest in their project, and a good deal of cooperative effort. Group Eight stood at the other end of the scale. It was broken into two antagonistic factions and accomplished no real work as a result of personal feuding. This group's attempts to empathize with each other were actually less successful, on the average, the second time than the first. This test

TABLE 3

Mean Scores and Ranking by Groups, Test 1 and Test 2

GROUP	TEST 1	TEST 2	RANK (1)	RANK (2)
1.	43.4	42.2	1	1
2.	55.4	50.5	7	6
3.	52.1	42.8	5	2
4.	49.7	46.0	3	3
5.	64.5	53.7	8	7
6.	50.1	47.2	4	4
7.	47.8	49.1	2	5
8.	52.5	54.1	6	8

does seem to reveal and corroborate in a quantitative manner some of the qualitative differences reported by the Group Observers.

A further calculation was made to determine whether there was any significance to the pattern of the deviations. For the most part the subjects would sometimes overestimate the others in their predictions and sometimes underestimate them so that the deviations did not differ significantly from chance expectancy. However there were some cases in which the errors were so large in one direction as to be significant, (more than 2 S. D.).

There were thirteen individuals in the sample who had distortions in their perceptions of themselves or others, or both, which lasted over the two tests. These people appear to enter their personal relations with a dis-

TABLE 4

Deviations Significant for Their Consistency of Direction

	UNDERESTIMATIONS OF WHAT OTHERS WILL SAY ABOUT:		OVERESTIMATIONS OF WHAT OTHERS WILL SAY ABOUT:	
	THEMSELVES	THE SUBJECT	THEMSELVES	THE SUBJECT
Test 1	14	9	4	11
Test 2	11	8	6	10
Repeats	4	4	2	5

tortion which causes them to feel that others either look down on them or up to them more than they actually do, or that others either think better or worse of themselves than they actually do. This test gives a measure of the direction and extent of these distortions of perception in personal relations which have been recognized in both psychology and common sense as feelings of inferiority or superiority.

One criterion which any new test must meet is that of validity. As this is the only test purporting to measure empathic ability which is known to the author, the simple solution of correlating the results of this test with those obtained with some other test of empathy was inapplicable. The problem of finding some other measure of the ability in question was partially solved by utilizing the same method as reported in the previous paper (2).

Ten subjects from the original sample of fifty-three were asked to take the Thematic Apperception Test (TAT). These subjects were unaware that they represented the five highest and the five lowest scores on the Rating Test. The TAT's were administered by another psychologist (Mrs. Helen Wait), who then turned them over to the author for blind analysis with only an identifying number. The stories were analyzed in terms of how well the subjects took the role or empathized with the characters they introduced into their stories. The five individuals whose scores

TABLE 5

Correlations of Observers' Rating of Empathic Ability of Their Group Members and the Test Results

	CORRELATION COEFFICIENT
Observers With High Empathy (in deciles 1–5) N=4	r = +.61
Observers With Low Empathy (in deciles 6–10) N=4	r = +.14

on the Rating Test classified them as highly empathic also rated as highly empathic on the TAT analysis. Four of those whose scores on the Rating Test were very low, also showed low empathy in their stories. Only one whose empathy seemed low on the Rating Test appeared to be highly empathic on the TAT analysis. Although this is hardly sufficient evidence on which to state that this is a valid test of empathic ability, the two types of evidence do tend to corroborate each other.

A further attempt to establish the validity of the test was made by correlating the Group Observers' ratings of the empathic ability of their group members with the test results. This correlation was too low to be of any significance. However when the Observers themselves were divided into two groups according to their empathic ability, an interesting difference was noted.

Although the number of judges is too small for this evidence to be conclusive, Table 5 seems to show that those with good empathic ability are better judges of the empathy of others than those with low ability. A parallel case would be if judges rating the intelligence of others made better judgments when they themselves had good intelligence.

A further criterion which a new test must meet is that of reliability. Actually a high degree of reliability was not anticipated with this test, as it was expected that the scores would change as the individuals got better acquainted. Therefore the correlation of +.60 between Test 1 and Test 2 was not surprising. Although this coefficient is not high enough to warrant the statement that there is good test-retest reliability over this period, it is sufficiently high to say that there is a fairly strong tendency for the empathy ratings to be stable. Since the predictions of what others would say was expected to vary, the individual's own concept of himself was next taken as a measure of the reliability of the test. In other words, it was not expected that the individual's own ratings of themselves would vary

TABLE 6

Amount and Direction of Change from Test 1 to Test 2 in Concept of Self

NO. OF POINTS CHANGED	NO. OF JUDGMENTS CHANGED	PERCENTAGE
+4	2	.6
+3	0	.0
+2	3	.9
+1	50	15.8
0	213	67.0
−1	45	14.2
−2	5	1.5
−3	0	.0
−4	0	.0
	318	100.0

very considerably within the six week period. The reliability coefficients of the six items were as follows:

(1) .82; (2) .71; (3) .73; (4) .80; (5) .62; (6) .77.

It is interesting to note that the lowest of these (.62) was the item concerning leadership ability. The individual's own conception of his ability in this regard was subject to some change after being thrown into an unstructured group situation.

Another technique for demonstrating the reliability of the test was to calculate the actual change in number of points of the concept of self. Since fifty-three subjects made six judgments about themselves there was a total of three hundred and eighteen judgments made. Table 6 shows the number of these judgments which were changed and the amount and direction of this change, (on a five point scale).

Table 6 shows that 97 per cent of the judgments that the individuals made about themselves were exactly the same on the second test as on the first or varied only one scale place in either direction. This appears to show a high degree of reliability for these judgments. Although this too fails to be sufficient evidence of the reliability of the test as a whole, it does point to the likelihood of the test meeting this criterion satisfactorily.

To return to the problem of the relation of insight and empathy with which the previous article (2) was concerned, an interesting relationship was noted. At the close of the experiment each subject was asked to rate himself according to his own judgment of the amount of empathy he had in comparison with the others in this experimental group. Each rated himself on a five point scale varying from Very High to Very Low. The group was then divided into deciles according to their scores on the last Rating Test. Next the relation between the individual's self-rating and the

TABLE 7

Relation of Rating Test Scores and Subject's Own Judgment of His Empathic Ability

	HIGH EMPATHY DECILES 1–5 N = 27	LOW EMPATHY DECILES 6–10 N = 26
Ratings Coincide	33%	8%
Subject 1 scale position off	41%	27%
Subject 2 scale positions off	18%	34%
Subject 3 scale positions off	2%	27%
Subject 4 scale positions off	0%	4%
	100%	100%

test's rating was determined. Those falling in deciles 1–5 (on the Rating Test) were designated as the High Empathy Group, and those in deciles 6–10 as the Low Empathy Group. The High Empathy Group's ratings of themselves corresponded closer to the test's ratings of them than did those of the Low Empathy Group.

Table 7 shows that 74 per cent of the High Empathy Group placed themselves in the same fifth of the group as the test did or were only one placement off. Only 35 per cent of the Low Empathy Group corresponded to this degree. It seems that those whose empathic ability is high, as measured by this test, have better insight into the fact that they are high, than those who are low have into the fact that they are low. (This, of course assumed the validity of the test.) It seems very likely that the ability to take the role of another, (empathy), is positively related to the ability to understand ourselves, (insight). This latter state seems to involve the ability to stand off and look at ourselves from another's point of view.

To sum up, this paper has reported an attempt to develop a test for the measurement of empathic ability and the results of this test on a group of fifty-three students. Although the work is too preliminary for there to be any final claim made concerning the validity or reliability of the test, the evidence reported does seem to point to this possibility. The ability that is concerned here, seeing things from the other person's point of view, is one in which individuals obviously differ from one another. Some of us are highly sensitive and perceptive of what the other fellow is thinking and how he is feeling, while others are very obtuse and slow about picking up these clues. What accounts for these differences? Can this ability be trained? These are important questions still to be solved. This paper is merely an attempt to define the area as an important one for further study, and to try to provide some techniques for its exploration.

REFERENCES

1. Cottrell, L. S. The analysis of situational fields in social psychology. *Amer. sociol. Rev.*, 1942, 7, 370–382.
2. Dymond, Rosalind. A preliminary investigation of the relation of insight and empathy. *J. consult. Psychol.*, 1948, 4, 228–233.
3. Hoskins, R. G. *The biology of schizophrenia.* New York: Norton, 1946.
4. Murphy, Lois. *Social behavior and child personality: An exploratory study of some roots of sympathy.* New York: Columbia Univer. Press, 1937.
5. Watson, D. L. On the role of insight in the study of mankind. *Psychoanal. Rev.*, 1938, 25, 358–371.

The Relative Abilities of Leaders and Non-Leaders to Estimate Opinions of Their Own Groups

KAMLA CHOWDHRY
and
THEODORE M. NEWCOMB

ACCORDING to modern social psychological theory, individuals are not selected for positions of leadership merely because they possess personal qualities which fit them for leadership in general. We must, on the other hand, assume that individual characteristics *in a particular*

FROM *Journal of Abnormal and Social Psychology*, 1952, 47, 51–57. Reprinted by permission of the authors and the American Psychological Association, Inc.

The full data upon which this partial report is based are to be found in the first-named author's *Leaders and their Ability to Estimate Group Opinion*, 1948, University of Michigan Library.

group situation have something to do with the selection of leaders. Every group is characterized by a set of interests shared by its members, and with regard to these common interests every group has a set of standards which are important determiners of their members' attitudes. Attitudes toward other things, not closely related to the common interests of a particular group, may be expected to be less homogeneous than attitudes toward objects of common interest. It is likely, however, that in every group there is some diversity of attitudes, even with regard to matters of most focal interest in the group.

Other things equal, those members of a group will be most effective leaders who are most familiar with its standards, and most familiar with the degree to which those standards are shared by the group's members. It seems likely, too, that such familiarity with the group is considered desirable by members as they choose their leaders. If so, then chosen leaders should be more accurate than non-leaders in their estimates of the attitudes of other members toward issues relevant to the group's interest. There is no reason, however, to conclude that leaders should judge more accurately than non-leaders the attitudes of members on issues irrelevant to their own groups. On the contrary, if we assume that the characteristics of leaders are more or less specific to particular group situations, we shall expect chosen leaders to be better than average judges of other members' attitudes on relevant, but not on irrelevant issues. It might, of course, turn out that chosen leaders are superior judges of members' attitudes toward irrelevant as well as toward relevant issues; in that event we should have to conclude that leadership is a function of a *general* capacity to judge the attitudes of associates, but not a function of the particular standards of particular groups.

This study therefore attempts to test the hypothesis that chosen leaders of a group are superior to non-leaders in estimating group opinion on issues of high relevance to that group, but not superior to them on issues of little relevance. This hypothesis makes no assumptions as to the components of interest, social skill, or personality dynamics which go to make up ability to judge group opinion. Nothing is hypothesized beyond the covariance of two variables: frequency of being chosen for positions of leadership, and ability to judge group opinion on issues of varying relevance to the group. The confirmation of the hypothesis, however, would tend to support a theory of leadership which presupposes interaction among group members who share interests and standards. The rejection of the hypothesis would tend to support a theory of leadership based primarily upon individual differences in skills and capacities.

The hypothesis is one that can be tested either by creating groups in the laboratory, or by obtaining the appropriate information from "natural," existing groups; only the latter procedure was employed in this study. Four groups were selected upon the basis of the following criteria:

1. That they be organized around definite interest patterns, like religion or politics.

2. That each group provide a basis for face-to-face interaction, so that the phenomena of leadership and isolation could emerge.

3. That the members be sufficiently familiar with each other and the opinions of the group to be able to evaluate group opinion.

4. That each group be an example of a common interest group in our society.

A religious group, a political group, a medical fraternity, and a medical sorority were chosen for the investigation. Each of these four groups satisfied the above criteria, though in varying degrees. The medical fraternity and sorority were somewhat different from the religious and political groups, in having a wider range of common interests and experience. They had in common social as well as medical interests, whereas the political and religious groups, according to available information, were more nearly limited to a single interest.

METHOD

Each group was administered a different attitude questionnaire which was subdivided into three parts. These three parts were designed to get at three different levels of relevance to the group's common interests. The first part of the questionnaire dealt with issues with which the group was familiar, and which were presumed to be relevant to the group's goals. The third part consisted of issues which were not only little discussed in the group, but which did not seem to be connected with the basic interest pattern of the group. The second part was intermediate in familiarity and relevance.

For the religious group, the first part consisted of items dealing with historic Christian doctrines and practices. The second part included items dealing with the church as a social institution, and the attitudes of Christians toward war. The third part included items dealing with general economic and political issues. Almost all the items in this questionnaire were taken from a previously published "Inventory of Religious Concepts" (1).

For the political group, the first part of the questionnaire consisted of items which the Wallace Progressive group was interested in at that time (1948), and which they were discussing in their meetings. It included such issues as civil liberties, the Palestine question, the Czechoslovakian *coup*, Wallace as a presidential candidate, and nationalization of natural resources. The second part dealt with general economic and political issues, and the third part consisted of items dealing with the church as a social institution, and the attitudes of Christians toward war. The second and third parts of the questionnaire were the same as those used for the religious group.

For the medical fraternity and the medical sorority the items in the first part of the questionnaire were selected (with the help of men and women medical students from other groups) to be representative of those usually discussed in the "bull sessions" of medical students, both men and women. The items dealt with the role of professional women at home, the desirability of medical women as wives, the problems of abortion and euthanasia, of equal opportunity of admission for women and Jews to medical schools, etc. These items were taken from a number of sources, the major one being Kirkpatrick's scale on Feminism (3) and Symonds' Social Attitude questionnaire (5). The second part consisted of general economic and political items, and the third part consisted of religious items dealing with the church as a social institution, and the attitudes of Christians towards war. The second and third parts had also been used in both the religious and political groups.

Sociometric data were also collected in each group according to four criteria of leadership. The questions asked were:

1. Who are the three persons who, in your opinion, are most capable of acting as president of your group?

2. Who are the three persons who, in your opinion, most influence the opinions of the group?

3. Who are the three persons who, in your opinion, are most worthy of acting as representatives of this group to a convention? (The convention was specified according to the nature of the group.)

4. Who are the three persons in this group with whom you would most like to be friends?

Personal information, including name, age, sex, educational status, length of group membership, and positions in previous groups, was also collected.

TABLE I

Correlation between the Total and Each of the Four Sociometric Criteria

GROUP	CRITERION I	CRITERION II	CRITERION III	CRITERION IV
Religious	.95	.89	.81	.67
Political	.96	.97	.84	.95
Fraternity	.87	.70	.53	.86
Sorority	.96	.93	.61	.68

Each member of the group was requested to make two replies to every item in the questionnaire. The first was a response indicating his own reaction to the statement by encircling "A" if he definitely agreed, encircling "D" if he definitely disagreed, encircling "a" if he had a tendency to agree rather than disagree, and encircling "d" if he had a tendency to disagree rather than agree, with the statement. Secondly, each member was requested to give the percentage of the group which he believed agreed with the statement. The latter procedure has been used by Newcomb (4) and Travers (6) in their investigations.

From the sociometric data the group status of each individual was determined. Those individuals were arbitrarily designated leaders who received the highest fifth of the total choices on the four criteria. The rest were called non-leaders, and among the non-leaders those who did not receive a single vote on any of the four criteria were termed isolates. The use of total choices for differentiating group status was justified by the high correlation of choices received, according to each of the four criteria. Table 1 gives the correlations between the total and each of the four sociometric criteria, in each of the four groups. All the correlations are significant at high levels of confidence.

Measurement of Sensitivity

To determine the individual's ability to judge group opinion, or his sensitivity to group opinion, a mean error score for each individual was computed, as follows. First, actual group opinion was calculated for each item of the questionnaire by taking the percentage of people who actually agreed to each item. ("Definite agreement" was combined with "tendency to agree.") Secondly, the average error score was calculated for each individual by subtracting his estimate from the actual group opinion concerning each item, and averaging the divergences. The algebraic signs were not taken into consideration because we were not interested in the direction of the error, but only in the magnitude of error.

RESULTS

Comparison of Estimates

In Table 2 the leaders of each of the four groups are compared to non-leaders and isolates with respect to their ability to evaluate group opinion at the three levels of relevance. The mean error score of the leader group is compared to that of the non-leader and isolate groups, and the significance of difference between the groups is tested.

In the *religious group* on part A (items assumed to be most relevant) the leaders are superior to non-leaders and isolates. The difference between leaders and non-leaders is significant at the .05 level, and between leaders and isolates at the .01 level. On part B (items assumed to be of intermediate relevance) the leaders again have a tendency to be better evaluators than non-leaders and isolates. The difference between leaders and non-leaders is not significant, but the difference between leaders and isolates is significant at the .05 level. On part C (items assumed to be of least relevance) there is hardly any difference in the error scores of leaders, non-leaders, and isolates.

In the *political group* on part A the mean error score of leaders is again the least. The difference between leaders and non-leaders is significant at the .07 level, and between leaders and isolates at the .02 level. On parts B and C there are no significant differences in the mean error scores of leaders, non-leaders, and isolates.

In the *fraternity* on part A the mean error of leaders in evaluating group opinion is less than that of non-leaders or of isolates. The differences in mean error of leaders and non-leaders, and of leaders and isolates, are both significant at the .01 level. On part B the difference between the mean errors of non-leaders is not significant; the difference between leaders and

TABLE 2

Differences in the Degree to which Leaders, Non-Leaders and Isolates Can Estimate Group Opinion

GROUPS COMPARED	A ITEMS			B ITEMS			C ITEMS		
	DIFF. IN MEAN ERR.	DIFF. IN STD. ERR.	t	DIFF. IN MEAN ERR.	DIFF. IN STD. ERR.	t	DIFF. IN MEAN ERR.	DIFF. IN STD. ERR.	t
Religious Group									
6 Leaders vs. 20 Non-leaders	6.13	2.52	2.38 *	4.36	3.53	1.24	2.95	2.34	1.26
6 Leaders vs. 8 Isolates	9.00	2.96	3.04 **	9.87	3.50	2.82	2.47	2.89	.85
Political Group									
5 Leaders vs. 18 Non-leaders	4.98	2.58	1.93	3.10	3.60	.86	2.57	4.35	.59
5 Leaders vs. 7 Isolates	9.93	3.66	2.71 *	5.32	4.64	1.16	6.09	7.00	.87
Medical Fraternity									
6 Leaders vs. 24 Non-leaders	6.76	2.50	2.70 **	2.31	2.66	.86	2.80	3.02	.91
6 Leaders vs. 6 Isolates	7.22	1.71	4.22 **	6.72	2.93	2.29 *	3.10	3.01	1.00
Medical Sorority									
8 Leaders vs. 32 Non-leaders	4.08	2.39	1.71	6.80	2.50	2.72 **	1.23	2.77	.44
8 Leaders vs. 6 Isolates	2.67	1.98	1.35	7.66	2.73	2.81 **	2.88	4.15	.69

* .05 level.
** .01 level.

isolates is significant at the .05 level. On part C the difference in mean errors is too small to be significant.

In the *medical sorority* on part A the leaders make a smaller average error than non-leaders and isolates, but the differences are not significant. On part B, however, the differences in error scores of leaders and non-leaders, and of leaders and isolates are both significant at the .01 level. On part C the differences in the mean errors of leaders, non-leaders, and isolates are small enough to be accounted for by chance variations.

In the medical sorority we used the same questionnaire as we did for the medical fraternity. The leaders in the fraternity are superior to non-leaders and isolates in their knowledge of group opinion on part A, but this superiority on the same issues is not shown by the sorority leaders. The latter finding is opposite to the hypothetical prediction. On the other hand, the sorority leaders are significantly superior to non-leaders and isolates in their ability to evaluate group opinion on part B. This superiority on part B is not shared by the fraternity leaders. On part C, however, neither the fraternity nor the sorority leaders are better in evaluating group opinion than non-leaders and isolates. There seem to be two possible explanations of this difference of results on parts A and B in the fraternity and the sorority. First, our assumption that the same type of things are familiar and relevant to the fraternity and sorority members may be wrong. It is possible that items on part A were more discussed and more relevant to the members of the fraternity, and the items on part B were more discussed and more relevant to the members of the sorority. Secondly, the fraternity was a much more homogeneous group than the sorority; the sorority included Chinese, Filipinos, Negroes, and South Americans. The fraternity included only white North Americans. It is possible that evaluating group opinion of a homogeneous group is easier than evaluating group opinion of a comparatively heterogeneous one.

In summarizing the results of the four groups in sensitivity to group opinion we may say that, on issues designed to be familiar and relevant to the group (A), the leaders are superior to non-leaders and isolates in their ability to evaluate group opinion, the differences between leaders and isolates usually being greater than between leaders and non-leaders. On issues designed to be relatively nonfamiliar and nonrelevant (C), there are no differences in leaders, non-leaders, and isolates in their ability to evaluate group opinion. On issues intermediate in nature to the above two, there are no consistent results.

Supplementary Data from Other Groups

Data from two quite different groups (Bennington College students and a C.I.O. local) were obtained concerning relevant issues only. In the former group, the mean error score of leaders was smaller than that of both non-leaders and isolates, at the .01 level of confidence. Similar differences were obtained in the C.I.O. group at the .03 level.

Chronological Age

The average age of religious leaders (twenty-six) is about three years greater than that of non-leaders and isolates in the same group, while political leaders are on the average two years younger (thirty) than other members of the same group. Neither of these differences is statistically significant. In the fraternity and in the sorority the average age of leaders (twenty-five) is only a few months greater than that of all other members of the same groups. Chronological age is thus not related to leadership and isolation in these data, and evidently has no relation to ability to evaluate group opinion.

Length of Membership in Group

The longer a person has been a member of a group the more likely it is, other things equal, that he will be able to evaluate group opinion accurately. Is it possible that leaders in these groups were those individuals whose memberships were of relatively long duration, and who, therefore, knew more members and their opinions?

TABLE 3

Average Months of Membership in Various Groups

GROUP	LEADERS	NON-LEADERS	ISOLATES
Religious	11.5	21.2	22.5
Political	5.2	4.7	8.0
Fraternity	33.6	25.7	21.2
Sorority	30.9	29.0	25.1

Table 3 shows that leaders in the religious group have a shorter period of membership, while leaders in the fraternity and sorority groups have a little longer period of membership in their groups than non-leaders and isolates. In the political group the leaders' length of membership is intermediate between that of non-leaders and of isolates.

Length of membership, in these groups, is not consistently related to leadership and isolation, nor to an individual's ability to evaluate group opinion. Travers' data (6) confirm this finding.

Academic Status

Since all or most members of all groups were college students, it is possible to note whether academic status of a person is connected with his status in the group. The chi-square test of significance was used to test whether graduates and seniors were more often in the leader group than in the non-leader and isolate groups. None of the relationships found was significant, indicating that there is no association between leadership and the academic status of an individual, in these groups.

Relations of Elected Positions in Other Groups and Present Status

The chi-square test was again used to see whether there was any significant association between past and present status. Only in the fraternity and sorority groups did we find that leaders have occupied elected positions in other groups significantly more often than non-leaders and isolates ($p<.02$). The other leadership positions held by fraternity and sorority leaders were (according to own statements) predominantly in social and recreational organizations. Such findings suggest that leadership may be "transferable" among similar kinds of groups.

INTERPRETATION

It was found that leaders of a group are significantly superior to non-leaders and isolates in their ability to judge group opinion on familiar and relevant issues, the difference between leaders and isolates being usually greater than the difference between leaders and non-leaders. This differential ability on the part of leaders, non-leaders, and isolates to judge group opinion is, however, not evident in unfamiliar or less familiar or less relevant issues.

It is possible that leaders are accorded the leader status because of this superior ability in evaluating group opinion, and that isolates sink into psychological isolation because of this lack of understanding of the group. An alternative explanation might be that leaders have a superior knowledge of the group because of the greater opportunities afforded to them in their official position, since they come into greater contact with the members and can therefore evaluate their opinions better. That familiarity alone is not a sufficient explanation for the greater understanding of leaders is evidenced by a number of facts gathered from other studies, as well as from some of the preceding data.

In the community studied by Jennings (2) some individuals, because of the work situations they had chosen, had greater opportunities of social contact than others. These individuals who had a greater opportunity to know and be known by others were not more often chosen than ones who lacked similar opportunities; 35 per cent (13/37) of the overchosen subjects were individuals of the high opportunity group, whereas 65 per cent

(24/37) attained a similar status without having the same kind of exceptional opportunities.

Further relevant evidence is to be found in the Bennington College data, which show that individuals who later acquire prestige and leadership status are those who possess more than the average amount of sensitivity to group opinion. "Entering freshmen who later acquire leader status have less conservative attitudes than those who are later to achieve little or no prestige. This is significant primarily by way of showing that the histories and the personal characteristics of entering freshmen are such that they are impelled to varying degrees of leadership and prestige, and that *within a few weeks of entering college they have already sized up the dominant community trends*, toward which they adapt themselves in proportion to their habits of seeking leadership and prestige" (4). Those freshmen who had ability enough to "size up" the situation were the individuals who later acquired the leader status.

Group understanding or knowledge, then, seems to be an important factor in the status that an individual may acquire in the group. Understanding or knowledge presupposes communication between individuals, and it seems that some individuals have a better ability to keep these channels of communication open than others. Jennings (2) says, "Each [leader] appears able to establish rapport quickly and effectively with a wide range of other personalities. . . . By contrast, the isolates and near-isolates appear relatively 'self-bound,' unable to bridge the gap between their own personalities and those of other persons."

Also the leaders seem to possess attitudes and personality characteristics which make it possible for them to be in fuller communication with the members of the group. According to Jennings (2), "The overchosen individuals are personalities who are not concerned with personal problems, but direct their energies to group problems. The underchosen individual is self-centered and is not outgoing in emotional expansiveness."

This suggests that certain personality traits of the overchosen make it possible for them to be in fuller communication with the members than can be said of the underchosen. The leaders' thinking is in terms of the group, and this attitude makes it necessary for them to keep the channels of communication open. The isolates, on the other hand, are "self-centered" and "relatively self-bound." Their channels of communication do not operate in both directions, and are often blocked entirely. They are relatively incapable of going out of themselves to understand the groups' problems. There is a lack of group understanding on their part because they fail to establish a two-way communication.

The ability to function as an effective group member would also seem to be related to the ability to perceive the opinions and attitudes of the group. The more awareness an individual has of an environment, the more satisfactorily he can adjust to it, other things equal. Each individual adjusts to the situation according to the way he perceives it, and not as it "really" is. Since the leaders' perceptions of the prevailing attitude trends existing in a group tend to be more realistic than those of non-leaders and isolates, the chances of their adequate adjustment are greater than those of the non-leaders and isolates.

Our evidence, thus interpreted, suggests that group status, understanding, communication, and adjustment are interdependent variables; it seems likely that better understanding, ready communication, adequate adjustment, and high status are apt to be associated, whereas relative lack of understanding and adjustment, blocked communication, and low status are similarly apt to be found together.

It seems reasonable to conclude, therefore, that leaders of groups like these are chosen, in part at least, because of recognized qualities of "sensitivity" to other members of the group. If so, such qualities may or may not be *potentially* of a general nature. That is, the same ability which enables an individual to be a good judge of others' religious attitudes in a religious group might also enable him to be a good judge of political attitudes in a political group. The fact is, however, that leaders excel primarily in judging attitudes of special reference to their own groups. They are not just good judges of others' attitudes in general; if they have the ability to become such all-around good judges, they are not motivated to develop it equally in all directions.

And so we conclude that in groups like these the ability to be a good judge of others' attitudes is a necessary but not a sufficient condition of being chosen for leadership. A further necessary condition is that the ability be demonstrated within the confines of a specific membership-character. Leadership *potentiality* may be adaptable to a wide range of membership characters. But leaders of particular groups seem to be chosen because their potentialities have been developed in particular directions, as called for by the differentiated interests of group members.

REFERENCES

1. Dunkel, H. B. *General education in the humanities.* Washington, D.C.: American Council on Education, 1947.
2. Jennings, Helen H. *Leadership and isolation.* New York: Longmans, Green, 1943.
3. Kirkpatrick, C. Belief pattern scale for measuring attitudes towards feminism. *J. soc. Psychol.*, 1936, 7, 423–426.
4. Newcomb, T. M. *Personality and social change.* New York: Dryden, 1943.
5. Symonds, P. M. A Social Attitude Questionnaire. *J. educ. Psychol.*, 1925, 16, 316–322.
6. Travers, R. M. V. A study in judging the opinions of groups. *Arch. Psychol.*, 1941, No. 266.

Relational Analysis: An Extension of Sociometric Method with Emphasis upon Social Perception

RENATO TAGIURI

AT A BROAD level of generality, understanding of an interpersonal relationship depends upon the availability of information regarding two of its aspects: the first of these is the nature of the response of each person to the other. The second aspect consists of the *perception* that each person has of the other person's response toward him. The analysis of any interpersonal relationship must consider these two components.

Standard sociometric procedures provide simultaneously two types of data about any member of a group: (a) information about *his* affective response to the others and (b) information about others' affective response to him. Since the latter is the result of the choices and rejections of *all the other* members of the group, one might add that the affective response of the group to the subject has a *consensual* nature. Behavior, however, does not consist of the response to the properties of the stimulus field objectively or consensually specified but, rather, of the reaction to what is perceived [1] by the subject. Therefore, while standard sociometric data constitute very useful information, understanding of behavior in interpersonal situations could be advanced further if, in addition to a consensual view

ABRIDGED from *Sociometry*, 1952, 15, 91–104. Reprinted by permission of the author and publisher.

1 "Perception" and "perceiving" in this paper are used in a broad sense to include inferences, and remembered stimuli, not necessarily present at the moment.

of the situation, one had access to information regarding the subject's view of it. One may find, for example, a highly chosen subject making only one choice, or, a highly rejected member making many choices. While various explanations are possible for either instance, the picture would acquire immediate transparence if one knew that this particular popular person is not aware of his success but, on the contrary, perceives himself as highly rejected. Similarly, the surprising response of the rejected subject could be understood better if it became apparent that this subject "felt" highly accepted. It must then be clear that the choice and rejection behavior of members of a group could be better comprehended if, in addition to an objective description of the social field (choices and rejections received by a subject) one also knew how the subject perceived this social field.

In this paper is described a method by means of which, in a single operation, data on the subject's perception of the situation can be gathered, together with the information usually obtained by standard sociometric procedures.

The method is an extension of the sociometric choice and rejection technique. The unusual features are the addition of a "guessing," or perceptual procedure and a special method for analyzing and utilizing the data.

THE "GUESSING" OR PERCEPTUAL PROCEDURE

By a "guessing" procedure is meant that subjects are required to *guess who will choose and reject them* in addition to the usual sociometric choices and rejections made by them. The number of choices, guesses, rejections, and guesses of rejection is left unrestricted. The guessing procedure adds the perceptual component to the standard sociometric method.

ANALYSIS AND UTILIZATION OF DATA BY MEANS OF A SPECIAL CLASSIFICATION OF DIADIC RELATIONSHIPS

After crosschecking the raw data obtained from each subject with those of every other subject, the following eight categories of information become available on each individual (S):

a. (——>) whom S chose,
b. (——<) who S guessed would choose him,
c. (<——) who chose S,
d. (>——) who guessed that S would choose him,
e. (----->) whom S rejected,
f. (-----<) who S guessed would reject him,
g. (<-----) who rejected S, and
h. (>-----) who guessed that S would reject him.

These eight components of the interaction between a subject and another member of the group will be referred to as "bonds" and will be represented by the symbols in brackets.

Any diad can be described in terms of those affective and perceptual elements of a two-person relationship that are expressed by choice, rejection, and their "guesses," and can be assigned to one of the eighty-one diadic categories possible. These constitute an empirical-theoretical *classification* of relationships between pairs of individuals. This feature of the method accounts for the name Relational Analysis given to it.

Theoretically, the eight bonds would combine in 256 ways.[2] On the logical ground, however, that subjects do not choose as well as reject the same individual, or guess that they are chosen as well as rejected by the same person, one can conclude that the total number of theoretically possible varieties of diads is equal to the sum of all combinations *not* containing incompatible bonds (e.g., choice and rejection). It thus becomes apparent that the most complex relationship is the one with only four bonds, since any fifth bond would be incompatible with one of the other four. This reduces the possible relationships from 256 combinations to 81, including the case where no bonds whatsoever exist between two individuals.[3]

Apart from being a convenient method for ordering the complex data of Relational Analysis this classification has several other useful features:

1. It is a way of describing a person, in terms of his perceived and actual relationships to other group members.
2. It is a method by means of which interpersonal relations between pairs of persons or sub-groups can be systematically classified and analyzed.
3. It provides a systematic way of comparing members of a group to one another.
4. It provides another method for describing, in a limited but important way, the cohesion of a group.
5. Study of deviations from the expected frequencies of the various types of diads have thrown light on certain regularities in the affective and perceptual aspects of interpersonal relationships.

2 $$\sum_{i=0}^{i=8} C_i^8 = 256$$

3 If the focus of attention is on the diad itself rather than on the members of the group, the number of different diads can be considered to be forty-five rather than eighty-one. If, however, the analysis is concerned with the subjects themselves, then it makes a difference whether subject S is related to Other by a choice (S——> O) or by a choice-received (S <——O). From an impersonal point of view on the other hand, the two diads above are identical.

While the purpose of this paper is to present the method, rather than the findings of specific studies in which it was used, it would, however, be difficult to give a clear idea of it without referring to some concrete data.

BEHAVIORAL AND REALITY DETERMINANTS OF THE PERCEPTION OF AFFECT

Since the focus of this method is upon adding the *perceptual dimension* of interpersonal relations to the information obtained by standard sociometric procedures, the bulk of the research done to date with this technique has been concerned with problems of perception of affect.

Several questions about the determinants of perception of affect can be answered by examining the data collected by means of the present method. In the present context one may speak of *external* determinants, i.e., actual positive or negative responses received, and of *internal* determinants, i.e., the factors within the subject that contribute to the nature of his perceptual hypotheses. The latter are represented in this method by the subject's own feelings (choice and rejection of Other). Internal and external determinants are, of course, conceived as being, by and large, simultaneously active.

We find that individuals have a realistic conception of who chooses them and rejects them. This, of course, is not surprising, since there is more order than chaos in interpersonal relations. According to modern theory, however, the perception of others' response should be a function not only of the behavior of the stimulus person, but also of the needs of the subject himself (1, 2). In other words, one would postulate that, *other things being equal*, the Subject's perception (guess) of Other's positive or negative feelings toward him would be related to the Subject's *own* feelings toward Other; or, that the strongest hypothesis would be the one with most motivational support. This is indeed true, and probably the major contribution of this method is to have permitted a quantitative and unequivocal demonstration of this fact. The relationship between the subject's own affect and the affect perceived by him is discussed more fully in another paper (9).

To give the reader an idea of this striking relationship some data will be presented that are related to it. In *all* groups studied it is found that relationships containing *inter*personally incongruent bonds (e.g., S——> >----O; S——> ≶----O; etc.) constitutes about 18 per cent of all relationships present. Relationships with *intra*personally inconsistent bonds (e.g., ——≷ ----< O; S----> ≷——<---- O; etc.), equally likely in incidence, constitute however, *less than* 3 *per cent* of all relationships. This is one manifestation of the strong congruency between affect and perception discussed above. The tolerance for affective and perceptual inconsistency internal to the person is thus seen to be much lower than the tolerance for a similar inconsistency on reality bases, i.e., between the Subject and Other. The fact that perception of affect is simultaneously well based on reality and strongly determined by the Subject's *own* affects suggests the complex feed-back process of interpersonal actions and reactions leading to the concurrently adept external and internal adjustment. About thirty groups have been studied at the time of this writing and the relationship between perception of affect and affective response has been found to obtain generally, irrespective of the size of the group, the sex and the age of the subjects.

There are individuals who are exceptions to the good reality orientation of most subjects: some feel popular and are not, some feel isolated and are popular, some very grossly *mis*perceive affective responses. But there are practically no cases where there is a persistent lack of consistency in affect experienced for Other and affect perceived from Other.

RELIGIOUS ETHNOCENTRISM AND ITS RECOGNITION

A study of "recognition" of ethnocentrism between subgroups of adolescent boys in a large preparatory school (5, 9), will be summarized to illustrate the use of Relational Analysis in investigations of relationships *among* subgroups. In this particular case, only choices and guesses were obtained from the 676 subjects, and therefore, the variety of diadic relationships is limited to sixteen types. Criswell (3) among others, has shown that the standard choice-procedure of sociometry can be used to demonstrate cleavages that tend to subdivide groups in terms of some important variable such as sex, color, religion, and so on. Here it was supposed as a matter of course that some religious ingroup preference would appear in the population of the school studied. It was a matter of speculation, however, as to whether the subjects belonging to the different subgroups would be *aware* of the extent of the ethnocentrism of their own and of the other subgroups. Relational analysis answers this question unequivocally for the population studied, in the following manner.

One could assume, if there were *no* religious ingroup preference at all, that the choices allotted by each subgroup would be distributed among all subgroups in proportion to their size. It was found that such was not the case and that each subgroup preferred to choose from among its own members rather than from other subgroups. The choices *received* by the members of each subgroup constitute their social field. The guesses (of choices received) made by each subgroup would then constitute the subgroup's *perception* of the social field. It was found that the allotment of both choices and guesses among subgroups differed from a proportional distribution, but not from each other. In other words, the perception of the social field was congruent with the social field itself. It was concluded that, in general, members of subgroups directed their guesses *as if* they were aware of the actual subgroup preferences present in the population.

PERSONALITY ADJUSTMENT AND INTERPERSONAL RELATIONS

The relationship between personality adjustment and interpersonal relations was studied on the same group of preparatory school boys (9).

Modern theory of personality holds that personal adjustment is largely a function of "good" development in interpersonal relations; (4, 6, 7, 8, 10, Mowrer, 1950). It was thus postulated that well adjusted and maladjusted boys would differ in the adequacy of their social interaction and that such differences should be reflected in the relational analysis data. Two groups of students were selected from the experimental population: the first one consisted of 15 boys who were being seen by the school psychiatrist ("maladjusted") and the second included 20 students ("well-adjusted") who were outstanding in the sense that they seemed to be able to participate effectively in a variety of activities, from academic work to sports and hobbies.

The "well-adjusted" subjects differed significantly from the "maladjusted" ones in terms of:

a. their actual social situation (actual number of choices received is higher for the "well-adjusted").
b. their perceived social situation (average number of guesses). In other words, the "well-adjusted" "saw" more affection in their environment.
c. their "outgoingness" (average number of choices made).

In all the above instances the "well-adjusted" and the "maladjusted" had means respectively above and below those of the "average" boy in the school. It was concluded that the relationship between efficient psychological functioning and successful interpersonal relations held in this instance. Both groups responded to the perceptual part of the procedure (the "guess") *as if* they were aware of their respectively high and low social success.

The "maladjusted" subjects were also studied in terms of their accuracy in perceiving affect directed toward them. For this purpose they were matched, one by one, to "non-maladjusted" students who were comparable in terms of number of guesses made and number of choices received. The "maladjusted" did not differ at all from the subjects with whom they were matched in terms of their skill in recognizing affect.[4]

4 This finding should not be placed out of this context since its interpretation is complex and partly related to the fact that the very procedure for matching may have caused the selection of a somewhat unusual group of subjects. This matching procedure was necessary since the accuracy of the "guess" is partly a function of popularity as well as of number of guesses made.

REFERENCES

1. Bruner, J. S. Personality dynamics and the process on perceiving. In G. Ramsey, & R. R. Blake (Eds.), *Perception: An approach to personality*. New York: Ronald Press, 1951.
2. Bruner, J. S., & Postman, L. Symbolic value as an organizing factor in perception. *J. soc. Psychol.*, 1948, 27, 203–208.
3. Criswell, Joan H. A sociometric study of race cleavage in the classroom. *Arch. Psychol.*, 1939, No. 235.
4. Freud, S. *The problem of anxiety*. (American Ed.) New York: Norton, 1936.
5. Goodnow, R. E., & Tagiuri, R. Religious ethnocentrism and its recognition among adolescent boys. *J. abnorm. soc. Psychol.*, 1952, 47, 316–320.
6. Horney, K. *Our inner conflicts*. New York: Norton, 1945.
7. Moreno, J. L. *Who shall survive?* Beacon, N.Y.: Beacon House, 1934.
8. Sullivan, H. S. *Conceptions of modern psychiatry*. Washington, D.C.: William Alanson White Psychiatric Foundation, 1947.
9. Tagiuri, R. Related analysis: An extension of sociometric method. Unpublished doctoral dissertation, Harvard Univer., 1951.
10. White, R. W. *The abnormal personality*. New York: Ronald Press, 1948.

Assumed Similarity Measures as Predictors of Team Effectiveness

FRED E. FIEDLER

SMALL groups of individuals, working as teams, committees, or crews, conduct the overwhelming proportion of the nation's civic, industrial, and military business. The effectiveness with which these groups

FROM *Journal of Abnormal and Social Psychology*, 1954, 49, 381–388. Reprinted by permission of the author and the American Psychological Association, Inc.

The research reported here was carried out under Contract N6ori-07135 between the University of Illinois and the Office of Naval Research. The investigations were conducted by a group in which several members of the project staff played a part during various phases. In particular, the writer wishes to express his appreciation to Dr. L. J. Cronbach, then director of the project, and to Messrs. Walter Hartmann, S. A. Rudin, Mrs. Mary E. Ehart, Miss Vivian C. McCraven, and Dr. W. G. Warrington.

function is thus of practical as well as of theoretical concern in our society.

This paper reports a series of related investigations which deal with interpersonal relationships within a team as correlates of the team's total effectiveness.

Certain aspects of interpersonal perception have been investigated in previously published studies on therapeutic relationships (3) and interpersonal relations in a social group (5). These studies present techniques for obtaining the so-called "Assumed Similarity (*AS*) scores," which appear to be correlates of liking and warmth in interpersonal relationships. The present series of investigations relates these interpersonal perception variables to team effectiveness.

A first, frankly exploratory study used 14 high school basketball teams. The most promising measures which emerged from this study were then validated on a second group of 12 high school basketball teams (6). The hypotheses derived from both studies were later tested on teams which differed markedly from the first group, namely, three- and four-man surveying parties (4).

THE FIRST BASKETBALL STUDY

High school basketball squads are composed of from 9 to 18 players. These are chosen by the coach from a larger pool of interested boys competing for places on the first team. This study was conducted in the Midwest, where basketball is of considerable importance to high school players and coaches and where a large number of teams can be found.

The Instrument

The tests used in the basketball study were forced-choice questionnaires. These questionnaires consisted of 100 descriptive statements grouped into 20 blocks of five statements each. An attempt was made to construct the blocks so that, in the main, statements within each block would be equally acceptable to the subjects (*Ss*), but descriptive of different personality dimensions.

One block of statements is given as an example.

	MOST	LEAST
1*a*. I find it easy to understand what others are trying to tell me.		
b. People think I am a hard worker.	X	
c. I don't mind losing my temper when provoked.		
d. I like people who don't worry about me.		X
e. People often look to me for leadership.		

In a self-description *S* would answer these statements by making an X in the left square opposite the statement which *S* considered *most* characteristic of himself, and an X in the right square opposite the statement he considered to be *least* characteristic of himself.

Test procedure and instructions. So-called interpersonal perception scores were obtained by giving each *S* successively three separate questionnaires containing the same blocks of statements. Players were instructed as follows: (*a*) "describe yourself," (*b*) "predict how the person with whom you can cooperate best will describe himself," and (*c*) "predict how the person with whom you can cooperate least well will describe himself."

In addition to these interpersonal perception tests, players named the three team members—not necessarily the best players—with whom they could cooperate best, and the three with whom they could cooperate least well during games.[1]

Interpersonal Preception Scores

Conventional tests are scored by comparing *S*'s response with the "right" response of a key. Our scores are obtained by comparing two questionnaires of the same person. This comparison yields the so-called "Assumed Similarity" measures listed immediately below. Tentative interpretations are provided which are based in part on evidence from previous studies.

Assumed Similarity Scores

1. *ASp*—a measure of assumed similarity obtained by comparing (correlating) the *S*'s self-description with his prediction of the self-description of his *positive* choice, the best co-worker. High *ASp* appears to be related to personal liking and perhaps warmth for the chosen person (3, 5).[2]
2. *ASn*—a measure obtained by comparing the *S*'s self-description with his prediction of his *negative* choice. A high *ASn* score may, on the basis of the interpretation above, indicate a feeling of personal closeness and warmth for the negative choice.
3. *ASo*—a measure obtained by comparing *S*'s prediction for his positive choice with his prediction for his negative choice. This measure is interpreted as "set" to differentiate between people. Since *ASn* and *ASo* are highly correlated, we will concern ourselves here only with the scores *ASp* and *ASo*.

The Criterion

Group effectiveness was measured by proportion of games a team had won. The date used here was December 31, 1951,[3] before many changes in

1 This paper discusses only procedures pertinent to the present hypothesis. A detailed account of the studies is presented in (2, 6, 7, 9).

2 *AS* scores can be computed as correlations or as difference scores. To avoid possible confusion we will in this paper speak of high *AS* as meaning high assumed similarity, i.e., a high correlation between either the self and the predicted self of another person, or between the predicted self-descriptions of two other persons. In terms of *D* scores, this would imply small differences between the two descriptions on which *AS* is based.

3 The original report (5) deals with December 15 as the criterion date. Since some teams had at that time played fewer than 4 games, the December 31 date appears to be a better criterion estimate.

team personnel had taken place and by which time each team had played from 8 to 12 games.

In general, small schools are handicapped by having relatively few eligible students. However, teams generally compete with other neighboring schools of comparable size, thus equalizing some of the differences which would favor large schools. The criterion reliability was estimated by comparing the proportion of games a team had won during the first and second halves of the season. At this time it was possible only to estimate reliability for the second sample which was tested with end-of-season criteria. The corrected criterion reliability estimate for these 12 teams was .88. The corresponding reliability for the December 31 date could not be computed because too few games had been played, but it is undoubtedly lower (7).

Relation of Assumed Similarity Measures to Basketball Criteria

Our hypothesis states that interpersonal perception scores are related to the proportion of games a team wins. We tested whether team members of an effective team will, on the average, perceive each other differently

TABLE 1

Correlations between the Dec. 31, 1951 Criterion and Interpersonal Perception Scores in 14 Basketball Teams

	CORRELATION (rho)	
ASSUMED SIMILARITY MEASURE	MEDIAN SCORE IN TEAM AND CRITERION	SCORE OF MOST PREFERRED CO-WORKER AND CRITERION
ASp	—.25	—.63 *
ASo	—.03	—.69 **

* $p < .05$ according to Olds's tables (11).
** $p < .01$ according to Olds's tables (11).
The large number of exploratory tests run on this first sample does not allow interpretation of significance levels. These are here given only as a point of reference.

from members of ineffective teams. Here we correlated the team median of the *AS* scores with the criterion. As can be seen from the second column in Table 1, correlations between the criterion and median scores are generally near zero.

The group may, however, also express its attitude by the type of person whom most members of a team choose as their best co-worker. In order to get at this attitude we considered only the *AS* scores of those members of the various teams which had received the greatest number of "best co-worker" votes. As can be seen in Table 1, this procedure suggests that the *AS* scores of the team's "most preferred co-worker" correlate with the criterion in the negative direction.

In previous studies, high *ASp* seemed to be related to warm, empathic interpersonal relationships. We expected to find these relationships—hence also high *AS*—to be prevalent in effective teams. The present findings are thus in the direction opposite to that which was anticipated. They suggest that the most preferred cooperators in effective teams tend to be somewhat less warm and emotionally less involved with persons whom they choose as work companions than is the case of keymen in less effective teams.

The correlations in Table 1 are, of course, based on a small sample of teams, and on only moderately reliable scores, .62 and .61 for *ASp* and *ASo* respectively (9). In addition, they are the survivors of a considerable number of exploratory measures. A validation attempt, therefore, became essential.

VALIDATION STUDY ON BASKETBALL TEAMS

The second sample of teams was studied solely for the purpose of testing relationships which were significant at the .05 level in the first study, i.e., on measures *ASp* and *ASo* of the most preferred co-worker.

TABLE 2

Second Study: Point Biserial Correlations between the Criterion and Assumed Similarity Scores of Most Preferred Co-worker

ASSUMED SIMILARITY MEASURE	$r_{pt.\ bis.}$	t	p
ASp	−.20	.53	
ASo	−.58	2.20	.03

The only major modifications were in the method of choosing teams and testing significance. We selected, toward the end of the season, 9 teams which had had a predominantly winning season and 9 teams which had had a predominantly losing season, and requested their cooperation.[4] These came from the upper and lower third of a roster of over 50 teams. We tested 7 "good" teams and 5 "poor" teams which agreed to cooperate. Since the teams were dichotomously selected, point-biserial correlations were here used to estimate the degree of the relationship. The significance of the difference between the scores of "good" and "poor" teams was tested by the usual t test; inspection of the data indicated that the conditions for applying a t test were not violated. The small samples and the not very high reliability of the scores suggest caution in interpreting these data.

4 The writer gratefully acknowledges the invaluable assistance received from Clyde Knapp and Harry A. Combes of the University of Illinois.

As can be seen from Table 2, the point biserial correlation between the criterion and *ASo* of the team's most preferred co-worker is —.58. We attempted to validate two measures. Only one of these (*ASo*) reached significance. We are therefore not justified to consider the relation of *ASo* to team effectiveness in basketball as established. *ASp* of the teams' most preferred co-workers did not correlate significantly with the criterion even though the correlation is in the anticipated direction. We have plotted the measures *ASp* and *ASo* of the most preferred team members from good and poor teams. (See Fig. 1.)

	ASp			*ASo*	
Q CORRELATIONS	GOOD TEAMS	POOR TEAMS	Q CORRELATIONS	GOOD TEAMS	POOR TEAMS
.55			.55		
.50			.50		
.45	x	xx	.45		x
.40	x	x	.40		
.35			.35		x
.30	x	x	.30		
.25			.25	x	xx
.20	x		.20	x	x
.15	x	x	.15	x	
.10			.10	x	
.05			.05	x	
.00	x		.00		
—.05			—.05		
—.10			—.10	x	

FIG. 1. *ASo* and *ASp* of most preferred co-worker plotted against the criterion in the second sample

In addition, we also computed validities for the end of the season when all league games had been played. These validities are generally lower than those of December 31. It is clear from these data that *ASp* in contrast to *ASo* is not a promising predictor of team effectiveness (7).

STUDY ON SURVEYOR TEAMS [5]

The Hypothesis

The basketball team studies led to one major hypothesis: *Members of effective teams will prefer co-workers who assume relatively little similarity between the persons whom they choose and those whom they reject as their own co-workers.*

5 The writer is indebted to Prof. M. O. Schmidt, Civil Engineering Department, University of Illinois, whose interest and cooperation made this phase of the study possible.

Since we interpret high *AS* to be indicative of warmth toward, and acceptance of, others we also explored whether team effectiveness and congeniality are negatively related.

The following study was designed to test this hypothesis, and to obtain evidence regarding the additional question.

Selection of Groups

Student surveying parties work in teams of three to four men. The *S*s were 71 civil engineering students taking a required course in surveying. The course consists of two parts. The first part is taught on the university campus on a full-day basis, lasting three weeks; the second part covers five weeks. This is offered at a university-operated surveying camp in northern Minnesota where students concentrate on field problems in relatively difficult terrain. The camp is almost completely isolated and self-contained. Students as well as faculty members eat, sleep, and work there, and students are under practically continuous supervision of their instructors.

Organization of the course at camp. While at camp, the students were divided into six sections, one instructor remaining in charge of each of the sections throughout the camp period. Each section consisted of three or four parties, and each of the parties consisted of three or four men. A total of 22 surveying parties was formed.

Differences between basketball teams and surveying parties. Obviously basketball teams differ in many respects from surveying parties. The differences which we considered among the most important are the following:

a. Basketball teams require physical coordination, relatively little verbal interaction. Surveying is primarily an intellectual task requiring frequent verbal communication.

b. While basketball squads consist of 9–18 members, the surveying parties in our study were no larger than four men.

c. Basketball teams work under considerable time pressure. Speed in surveying is only of secondary importance.

d. Members of basketball teams are highly identified with the team, and personally involved with their team's success. This identification and involvement is almost completely absent in surveying teams. The students were graded individually, and no benefits were derived from being in a "good" surveying party. This is shown by the fact that none of the students were interested in their instructor's opinion of their *team.*

The Instrument

As in the basketball studies, *S*s responded to three identical questionnaires, predicting a preferred, and predicting a rejected co-worker. Unlike the forced-choice questionnaires used in the basketball study, the surveyor tests consisted of 60 statements, each of which was to be marked on a seven-point scale ranging from *definitely true* to *definitely untrue.* The statements were pretested on a

180-item questionnaire.[6] Statements were selected on the basis of an item analysis to obtain items with large variances on self-descriptions. Statements such as "I am very discriminating in my choice of friends," "I am not likely to admit defeat," or "when a person is a failure it is his own fault," were used. The instrument presents a considerable improvement over the tests used in the basketball studies. The reliabilities for *ASp* and *ASo* are .83 and .93 respectively (2). In addition, the tests require less time for administration.

By comparing the two tests by means of the statistic *D* (1), it is possible to obtain a score indicating how similarly any two of the questionnaires have been marked.

Test procedure and instructions. The instructions and administration of questionnaires followed those of the basketball studies, with a few, relatively minor, exceptions. The *S*s could predict their preferred and least preferred persons from among those with whom they had previously worked. These did not have to be persons at the camp. The *S*s again completed sociometrics regarding the three persons within their section (10–15 *S*s) whom they personally liked most and liked least. They similarly named three *S*s whom they preferred most, and the three whom they preferred least as co-workers.

The Criteria of Effectiveness

Instructors were asked to rank all teams in their section in terms of the following:

a. Accuracy with which surveying jobs were done by various parties.

b. Speed with which the jobs were done.

c. Congeniality of the teams in terms of lack of conflict and smooth-running field operations.

In addition, students in all sections were asked to "rank all parties in the section from best to poorest." This constitutes our *students' ratings* criterion.[7]

Accuracy is the main criterion in surveying. It was, therefore, the only criterion on which we attempted to validate the hypothesis derived from the basketball study. The one-tailed test of significance was applied, therefore, to the accuracy criterion only. Tests relating to other criteria were exploratory.

Each instructor could rank only the three or four surveying parties in his own section. Ranking of parties from different sections was standardized to permit comparison of all parties. *AS* scores for all 22 teams could then be correlated with the various criteria.

The fact that instructors' frames of reference differ decreases to some

6 We are indebted to Col. R. W. Faubion, Commanding Officer, Det. #3, Human Resources Research Center, Chanute Air Force Base, for permission to pretest this instrument.

7 Students' ratings of Section V could not be used. The *S*s in that section had been in more than one surveying party, and a number of students rated teams other than the main teams rated by the instructor of that section.

extent the criterion reliability. This would tend to obscure any relationships present, and it would increase the probability of accepting the null hypothesis when a true difference exists. Table 3 presents the intercorrelations of the four criteria used in this study for three- and four-man parties.

Relation of Assumed Similarity Measures to Criteria in Surveying

The accuracy criterion. Our major hypothesis states that the assumed similarity of most preferred co-workers in good teams will be relatively

TABLE 3

Intercorrelations (r) *of Criteria for Three- and Four-Man Surveyor Teams:* *

	ACCURACY	SPEED	CONGENIALITY RATINGS
Speed	.79		
Congeniality ratings	.15	.52	
Student ratings	−.34	.15	.39

* (See footnote 7.) Based on N's of 22, except correlations with the student rating criterion in which N's = 18.

low. The preferred co-workers in relatively poor teams will have high *ASo* scores.

Our population of teams consists of 22 surveying parties, divided into six different sections. This division presents difficulties in statistical treatment of the data since no criterion was available for comparing teams from different sections. We have here tested the hypothesis by two methods.

a. We compare the best and the poorest teams within each of the six sections. We can then ask whether the *AS* scores of the preferred co-worker in the best team from each section are lower than the *AS* scores of the preferred co-worker in the poorest team in each section. Since the two teams for each section are evaluated by the same instructor, the matched t test can here be used. This does, however, reduce to 12 the number of teams (cases) used in the analysis. (See Table 4.) As can be seen in Table 4, *ASo* differences are significant. *ASp* shows only a negligible difference.

b. A somewhat more satisfactory indication of the *degree* of relation comes from a second analysis. Citerion ratings were converted to z scores, and then correlated with the most preferred co-workers' *AS* scores, both *ASp* and *ASo*.

Table 4 also presents the r's between the primary criterion, accuracy, and these two *AS* scores. As can be seen, the hypothesized relationship has been found between the criterion and *ASo* of the most preferred co-worker. Hence, persons chosen as most preferred co-workers in effective (i.e., accurate) teams perceive a greater difference between those whom they prefer and those whom they reject as co-workers than keymen in less accurate teams. The findings thus are consistent with the hypothesis induced from the results which were obtained in the study on basketball teams.

The Secondary Criteria

No significant relation was found between *AS* scores and secondary criteria. The relation between *AS* scores on students' ratings is, however, in

TABLE 4

Comparison of AS *of Preferred Co-Workers in Teams Rated Highest and Lowest in Accuracy*

($N = 12$)

INTERPERSONAL PERCEPTION SCORES	MEAN OF HIGHEST TEAMS *	MEAN OF POOREST TEAMS	t	p	r ($N = 22$)
ASp	12.96	12.24	.56		
ASo	20.61	15.32	3.30	.025	—.51

* In terms of *D*'s. A high score indicates low assumed similarity.

the opposite direction of those found for accuracy and other criteria based on instructors' ratings. In other words, the students tended to rate those teams as better in which the preferred co-worker assumed relatively high similarity to his negative choice. This appears to lend some support to the interpretation that preference for a person with high *AS* is related positively to congeniality within the team. (See Table 3.)

The relation of congeniality and effectiveness was explored by one further step. An Intrateam Preference Index (*IPI*), defined as an index of congeniality, was devised and correlated with each of our four criterion ratings.

This measure of congeniality is based on the following considerations:

a. Each person had rated the other 10–15 members of his section in terms of how well he liked them as co-workers.

b. A subject worked in a three- or four-man team. He could choose his preferred co-workers within his own 3- or four-man team, or he could prefer others in his section who were not in the team.

c. We assume that a team whose members choose one another is more congenial than one whose members reject one another or choose outsiders.

The measure is computed by the formula:

Intrateam Preference Index (*IPI*) =

$$\frac{\left(\begin{matrix}\text{choices} \\ \text{within}\end{matrix} + \begin{matrix}\text{rejections} \\ \text{without}\end{matrix}\right) - \left(\begin{matrix}\text{choices} \\ \text{without}\end{matrix} + \begin{matrix}\text{rejections} \\ \text{within}\end{matrix}\right)}{nk - n}$$

n = number of men within the team
k = number of choices made by each individual

When this Intrateam Preference Index (*IPI*) was correlated with our four criterion ratings, the following relationships appeared: The correlation between accuracy and the *IPI* was negative (−.23), while other criterion ratings correlated positively with the *IPI*. The highest correlation was found between students' ratings and the *IPI* (.37). When we compare the most preferred co-worker's *ASo* scores of teams considered best and those considered poorest by students, we find higher *ASo* for teams rated high by students and lower *ASo* scores (greater perceived difference between most and least preferred work companions) for teams which students rated as poor. This relationship is not statistically significant (t = 2.24; t = 2.57 is required for significance of .05). The direction would tend to indicate, however, along with our other data, that effectiveness and congeniality may be inversely related in informal teams. This finding is in accord with the findings in the preceding basketball study. Moreover, it is supported by the results in Halpin's recent study of air crew leaders (8) and a paper by Schachter, Ellertson, and McBride on experimentally assembled student groups (10). The results are not in agreement with Van Zelst's study on construction workers (11). All in all, these data suggest that further study is needed to determine whether or not effectiveness and congeniality are inversely related.

DISCUSSION

Two interpersonal perception scores on assumed similarity were correlated with the criterion in each study. One relation reaches the prescribed significance level every time. The studies thus support the hypothesis that the interpersonal perception variable *ASo* plays a part in group effectiveness.

We feel that the present findings serve primarily to emphasize that research on interpersonal perception in task groups is a fruitful area for continued efforts. This discussion will, therefore, be largely concerned with the implications of these findings for further research.

Let us first examine the measure which yielded significant results.

ASo. This score was obtained by comparing *S*'s prediction of his positive choice for work companion with his prediction of his negative choice. It is thus the similarity which *S* assumes to exist between the person with whom he says he can, and the one with whom he says he cannot cooperate. According to our data, the most preferred co-worker in effective teams tends to perceive these two persons as relatively dissimilar. On the other hand, the most preferred co-worker in ineffective teams tends to perceive these persons as relatively similar. Low *ASo* (i.e., large perceived difference between most and least preferred work companions) may, therefore, reflect an evaluative, critical attitude toward others, as contrasted with warm, empathic interpersonal relations. (Further research is needed to clarify the meaning of this measure.) We have found that *AS* tends to correlate positively with reputed therapeutic competence (3); in subsequent studies it was shown that *S*s assume significantly more similarity to a person who is liked than to someone who is relatively disliked (5, 6). Since *ASo* and *ASn* (*AS* to the least preferred) are highly correlated, we believe that the person with low *ASo* is relatively unaccepting, and perhaps rejecting, to the person who is not a good work companion.

The most preferred co-worker. While *ASo* in key persons appears to measure relevant factors in team effectiveness, it also points to a phenomenon which may be of more general theoretical importance. Only the scores of the most preferred co-workers correlate with the criterion. When we correlated the team's median *ASo* with the criterion, no significant relationships were found. At present we are inclined to take these results as an indication that members of effective teams use a basis different from that of members of ineffective teams for choosing and rejecting others as cooperators. This interpretation is supported by the positive correlations between *ASo* of the most and of the second most preferred co-workers in basketball teams (.63 and .27 for the first and second samples, respectively). In light of our current interpretation of *ASo*, this would mean that members of effective teams prefer highly task-oriented persons as co-workers. Members of relatively ineffective teams list as their most preferred co-workers the more accepting, relationship-oriented team members. *ASo* in the most preferred team worker is thus possibly an indication of the entire team's attitude toward the task, e.g., an index of the team's morale. Whether or not these relations hold in radically different teams, e.g., formally structured groups, permanent crews, etc., remains to be established.

SUMMARY AND CONCLUSIONS

The present investigations test the hypothesis that group effectiveness is related to the interpersonal perceptions which members of the group have toward one another.

Interpersonal perceptions were measured by correlating identical questionnaires which subjects were instructed to fill out (*a*) describing themselves, (*b*) predicting the responses of their preferred co-worker, and (*c*) predicting the responses of their rejected co-worker.

The first studies used 14 high school basketball teams, tested at the beginning of the season. A second sample of 7 "good" and 5 "poor" teams was collected toward the end of the season for the purpose of verifying relations identified in the first study. A third sample consisted of 22 surveying teams.

The criterion of basketball team effectiveness was the proportion of games the teams had won (at midseason in the first sample, two weeks before the end of the season in the second sample). The criterion in the surveyor study was the instructor rating on accuracy. There was no correlation between the criterion and the median of any assumed similarity score within a team. The assumed similarity score, *ASo*, of the team's most preferred work companion was negatively correlated with the criterion in all three samples. The finding supports the hypothesis that *ASo* of the most preferred co-worker in surveying, and possibly also in basketball, is related to team effectiveness.

The interpersonal perception scores of the chosen person are believed to reflect his outlook on other persons and on the task. Low *ASo* is thought to reflect lack of emotional involvement with teammates and task-oriented attitudes. The group which chooses a differentiating person as preferred co-worker is thus likely to be more concerned with effective task performance, and correspondingly more successful. Some evidence suggests that the more effective surveying teams tend to be less congenial than relatively ineffective teams.

As in previous studies, we found that *S*s assumed greater similarity between themselves and their positive, than between themselves and their negative choices.

REFERENCES

1. Cronbach, L. J., & Gleser, Goldine C. *Similarity between persons and related problems of profile analysis.* Urbana, Ill.: Bureau of Research and Service, Univer. of Illinois, 1952. (Mimeo.) (Tech. Rep. No. 2, Contract N6ori-07135.)
2. Cronbach, L. J., Hartmann, W., & Ehart, Mary E. *Investigation of the character and properties of assumed similarity measures.* Urbana, Ill.: Bureau of Research and Service, Univer. of Illinois, 1953. (Mimeo.) (Tech. Rep. No. 7, Contract N6ori-07135.)
3. Fiedler, F. E. A method of objective quantification of certain counter-transference attitudes. *J. clin. Psychol.*, 1951, 7, 101–107.
4. Fiedler, F. E. *Assumed similarity measures as predictors of team effectiveness in surveying.* Urbana, Ill.: Bureau of Research and Service, Univer. of Illinois, 1953. (Mimeo.) (Tech. Rep. No. 6, Contract N6ori-07135.)
5. Fiedler, F. E., Blaisdell, F. J., & Warrington, W. G. Unconscious attitudes as correlates of sociometric choice in a social group. *J. abnorm. soc. Psychol.*, 1952, 4, 790–796.
6. Fiedler, F. E., Hartmann, W., & Rudin, S. A. *The Relationship of interpersonal perception to effectiveness in basketball teams.* Urbana, Ill.: Bureau of Research

and Service, Univer. of Illinois, 1952. (Mimeo.) (Suppl., Tech. Rep. No. 3, Contract N6ori-07135.)

7. Fiedler, F. E., Hartmann, W., & Rudin, S. A. *Correction and extension of the relationship of interpersonal perception to effectiveness in basketball teams.* Urbana, Ill.: Bureau of Research and Service, Univer. of Illinois, 1953. (Mimeo.) (Tech. Rep. No. 5, Contract N6ori-07135.)
8. Halpin, A. W. The relation between the crew's perception of the leadership behavior of airplane commanders and superiors' ratings of their combat performance. Paper read at Amer. Psychol. Ass., Washington, D.C., 1952.
9. Rudin, S. A., Lazar, I., Ehart, Mary E., & Cronbach, L. J. *Some empirical studies of the reliability of social perception scores.* Urbana, Ill.: Bureau of Research and Service, Univer. of Illinois, 1952. (Mimeo.) (Tech. Rep. No. 4, Contract N6ori-07135.)
10. Schachter, S., Ellertson, N., McBride, Dorothy, & Gregory, Doris. An experimental study of cohesiveness and productivity. *Hum. Relat.*, 1951., 4, 229–238.
11. Van Zelst, R. H. Sociometrically selected work teams increase production. *Personnel Psychol.*, 1952, 3, 175–185.

Conceptual and Methodological Problems in Interpersonal Perception

N. L. GAGE and LEE J. CRONBACH

IN STUDIES of interpersonal perception, the process most often investigated has been given such names as "empathy," "social sensitivity," "accuracy of social perception," "insight," and "diagnostic competence." Despite variations in terminology and method, the studies have

FROM Psychological Review, 1955, 62, 411–422. Reprinted by permission of the authors and the American Psychological Association, Inc.

One of the present writers has been engaged in empirical research on interpersonal perception, trying various testing techniques and methods of analysis (7, 8, 9, 10). The second writer has been investigating mathematical aspects of measures of interpersonal perception (2, 3).

A portion of this paper was presented by Gage as part of a symposium before the American Psychological Association, September, 1953. This work was supported in part by a research grant (M-650) from the Institute of Mental Health of the National Institutes of Health, Public Health Service.

similar aims. Knowledge about interpersonal perception is intended to be significant for social psychology and personality theory, as well as for practical problems in leadership, marital relations, clinical work, and teaching. Many difficulties, however, prevent clear interpretation of the results so far obtained. We attempt here to point out major pitfalls, to evaluate research procedures commonly used or recently advocated, and to suggest better designs for studies in this area.

NEED FOR SHARPENED CONCEPTUALIZATION

In studies of empathy and its sister traits, the basic variable has been only hazily conceptualized. This difficulty characterizes early research in any area; "intelligence," "attitude," and "adjustment" have all suffered from inadequacies of conceptualization comparable to those afflicting empathy. Writers have inadequately specified just what they mean to measure, or to what extent the variable they study overlaps the variables in other investigations. Thus, one test of empathy finds out how accurately subjects predict the ratings acquaintances will give them. Another test of empathy requires that subjects estimate the musical preferences of the average factory worker. Not surprisingly, these tests correlate only .02 (12).

Implicit Assumption of Generality

One fundamental question concerns degree of generality. Is understanding of others a highly generalized trait, or is it a collection of response patterns which have only a surface similarity? From the failure of many writers to delimit their concept, one gets the impression that they expect some people to be consistently good judges of others, and some people to be consistently poor judges; that is, a rather general trait is assumed to exist. If a Judge does well in predicting what response Others 1, 2, and 3 will give to stimuli *a*, *b*, and *c*, some investigators evidently would expect him to do well in predicting the responses of Others 4, 5, and 6 to stimuli *x*, *y*, and *z*. Only an expectation of this character would lead one to try predictions of musical tastes as a possible gauge of the effectiveness of a foreman, or to accept a test of ability to predict responses of office workers as a parallel form to a test of ability to predict responses of factory workers (15).

A generalized trait such as "empathic ability" may profitably be used as a construct if changes in the individual's behavior from situation to situation are small compared to differences between individuals in the same situation. The fact that mental tests correlate positively makes "general mental ability" a useful concept (though we can also differentiate that concept into more specific subtraits). "Resistance to stress" appears to be much less general; the general trait must be replaced by more specific traits describing resistance to particular stresses.

So, perhaps, with accuracy in interpersonal perception. Accuracy in predicting another's responses in one situation does correlate with accuracy in predicting another set of responses (7, 21). But it is questionable whether this accuracy must be ascribed to an "empathic" process, or even to genuine understanding (4, 21). It is therefore critically important to know just when measurements of empathy in one situation justify generalization to other situations or to a construct transcending particular situations. Until a general "ability to understand others" is established, workers should proceed with great caution, and define in any theoretical statement or interpretation of results just what facet is being discussed.

Nonequivalence of Alternative Operational Definitions

One reason why empathy is inadequately conceptualized is that many investigators have been content to rely on a simple "operational definition." Having invented a face-valid technique to measure the adequacy with which one person could understand another, investigators have neglected to inquire into its meaning. Entranced by the beauty of their operations, they have cloaked these limbs with barely enough conceptual analysis to provide some scientific respectability for their reports.

Most recent studies of interpersonal perception require a Judge to predict the responses of an Other. The predictions are scored for accuracy against the actual responses or characteristics of the Other. The responses to be predicted and the experimental conditions for obtaining scores have varied greatly from one study to the next. To clarify what present tests deal with, and thereby indicate the possible subdivisions of the field, we draw attention to four components of the typical experimental design:

a. The *Judge* whom the experimenter is attempting to measure.
b. The *Other(s)* whom the Judge is asked to interpret.
c. The *Input*, or information concerning the Other which is available to the Judge.
d. The *Outtake*, i.e., the statements or predictions about the Other obtained from the Judge.

The experimenter may, for example, decide to ask (*a*) kindergarten teachers to observe (*b*) children, and, using (*c*) cues obtained during observation, to predict (*d*) the sociometric choices each pupil will make.

Understanding another person may be regarded as having two stages, which suggest two continua for classifying investigations. First, the Judge must take in information, perhaps by observing the Other, or perhaps by dealing with him over a period of time; the first continuum therefore deals with the *degree of acquaintance* of the Judge with the Other. Second, the Judge must interpret the information in order to arrive at predictive statments; the second continuum therefore deals with the *degree of extrapolation* or inference required between Input and Outtake.[1] An experiment may be designed to make great demands on the intake process (little acquaintance) or the interpretative process (much extrapolation), or both, or neither. The extreme patterns are contrasted in Table 1.

This table makes it clear that understanding of other persons demands different things of the perceiver in different situations. If we ask a person questions about Others where he has had ample opportunity to learn the answers by experience (Pattern A), we are primarily measuring his knowledge. When we present him with questions which he cannot answer on the basis of past experience alone, we are measuring ability to acquire new knowledge. But different abilities are required, depending upon whether the difficulty he faces is that of gathering information (Pattern B), or of drawing inferences (Pattern C), or both (Pattern D). A Judge who performs well in one pattern might perform badly in another.

Classification of Studies According to Objects of Perception

It is also necessary to inquire just what "Others" are involved in any hypothesis; unless this is clearly delimited, it can only be assumed that the investigator is interested in a generalized ability to understand all other persons. Various studies have used quite different objects of perception, asking the Judge to predict:

a. how *persons in general* will behave;
b. how *a particular category of persons* deviates from the behavior of persons in general;
c. how *a particular group* deviates from the typical behavior of the particular category it belongs to;
d. how *an individual* deviates from the typical behavior of the particular group he belongs to;
e. how *an individual on a particular occasion* will deviate from his typical behavior.

1 Meehl (17, pp. 68–71) has used a parallel distinction in identifying two possible applications of the phrase "clinical intuition": (*a*) to the situation in which the clinician cannot be articulate about the *evidence* for his diagnosis; (*b*) to that in which the clinician cannot "show in what manner a particular hypothesis was *arrived at* from the stated evidence." These two aspects of intuition, namely, "evidence" and "manner of arriving at," seem to resemble our "acquaintance" and "extrapolation," respectively. With a high degree of acquaintance the judge would have a great deal of evidence, and a high degree of extrapolation would require what Meehl calls "the creative act of hypothesis-formation."

TABLE I

Four Types of Studies of Interpersonal Perception

	PATTERN A	PATTERN B	PATTERN C	PATTERN D
Judge-Other relationship	Much acquaintance	Little acquaintance	Much acquaintance	Little acquaintance
Input-Outtake relationship	Little extrapolation	Little extrapolation	Much extrapolation	Much extrapolation
Hypothesized process	When acquainted with an Other, the Judge has many opportunities to observe him; some Judges habitually take better advantage of these opportunities than do others, paying better attention to the Other and cumulating more information about him.	Encountering a stranger, the Judge has some opportunity to observe him; some Judges are better able than others to take advantage of this brief opportunity, hence cumulating more information.	When acquainted with an Other, the Judge has many opportunities to observe him; some Judges are better able than others to use the information thus acquired, together with some personality theory, to derive accurate statements about variables not observed directly.	Encountering a stranger, the Judge has some opportunity to observe him; some Judges are better able than others to use the information thus acquired, together with some personality theory, to derive accurate statements about variables not observed directly.
Illustration	Asking high school counselors to agree or disagree that "The majority of adolescents say they have conflict with their parents"	Having Judges interview strangers and then rate their command of English	Having husbands predict personality test responses of their wives	Asking clinicians to make predictions of scholastic success from projective tests
Quality represented in accuracy measure	Knowledge from past experience	Ability to observe	Ability to infer	Ability to observe and infer

We can show that each of these types of understanding may be useful. (*a*) General principles such as "All people have a need to be approved" are expectations which guide conduct. (*b*) The individual forms expectations about different categories of people: managers or labor leaders, for example. (*c*) The person discriminates within a category, to form expectations about a particular group he is associated with. An officer can make wise decisions about his men on the basis of a correct stereotype of enlisted men in general, but he can make even wiser decisions by taking the particular wishes of his own squadron into account. (*d*) One next comes down to describing the unique behavior of the individual Other, as in clinical diagnosis. (*e*) The final step, prediction of differences within the individual over occasions, is illustrated when a therapist decides that in certain sessions it is better to review than to introduce new interpretations.

Our five types of Others and four patterns point to 20 rather different ways in which an ability to understand Others may be defined. Though not all these combinations are equally significant, research plans and interpretations need to be specified in terms of some such concepts as these.

NEED FOR INTERPRETABLE SCORES

Comparing the Judge's predictions with the Other's actual behavior readily yields an accuracy score, but this score is difficult to interpret because a large number of processes may be postulated to explain it. This problem may best be described if we treat for the moment the simple situation where the prediction and the Other's actual behavior are reported dichotomously, and the prediction may therefore be scored as right or wrong. The conclusions would be modified only in detail if the score were based on magnitude of errors.

Controlling Effects of Real Similarity

Consider the study where we have (*a*) the Judge's self-description, (*b*) the Other's self-description, and (*c*) the Judge's prediction of *b*. The responses to any item have three aspects:

RS (real similarity): agreement of *a* and *b*
AS (assumed similarity): agreement of *a* and *c*
ACC (accuracy): agreement of *b* and *c*

Only two of these three are independent relations. That is, when two of these relations are known, the third may be inferred. Thus, if AS and RS on an item are scored 1 (denoting agreement), ACC must be 1. Scores for the three relational variables are obtained by summing the values obtained on single items. Any score may be considered a resultant of the other two. What we regard our test as measuring therefore depends on how we choose to conceptualize the problem, as has been pointed out by Tagiuri, Blake, and Bruner (22). Empirical studies have reported relations between the scores—for example, that Judges more typical of a group have higher accuracy in judging members of that group. But this may result merely from the linkage represented in the operations defining the scores, for when AS is constant and greater than RS, ACC and RS are correlated. Such a conclusion is a logical necessity, not a psychological finding regarding any superior insight on the part of the more typical Judge.

There is evidence that AS—perceiving Others as similar *to oneself*—is highly general over items. A person tends to assume similarity to the same degree throughout a questionnaire, despite marked variety in the apparent content of the items (20). Moreover, the tendency is somewhat general over preferred Others; if the Judge's AS score toward one friend is high, it will probably be high when he predicts the behavior of another friend (20). AS relative to a liked person, however, does not predict whether AS will be high or low when the Judge predicts for a disliked person (20). There is some justification, then, for regarding differences in the Judge's AS from Other to Other as a reflection of the Judge's attitude toward the Others (6). The AS score is to some extent a reflection of the Judge's general attitude toward other persons. But probably the AS score is also influenced by the Judge's set while taking the test; for example, Lundy (16) found that Judges who acquired facts about Other while interacting under a pay-attention-to-yourself set displayed more AS than did Judges instructed so as to have a pay-attention-to-the-Other set.

While the ACC score has a simple operational definition, it clearly does not correspond directly to any simple construct or trait. One possible solution is to obtain separate estimates of more elemental component variables (cf. 2). In making such analyses, however, the investigator risks embracing new confusions as he divorces the old.

Hastorf and Bender (13) have proposed to subtract AS from ACC (which they call "raw empathy") to estimate "refined empathy." This proposal has serious weaknesses, which may be clarified by considering the possible configurations of responses on dichotomous items. If *a* is the Judge's self-description, *b* is the Other's self-description, and *c* is the Judge's prediction, the patterns shown in Fig. 1 are possible. (With more than two response alternatives per item, the "WAD" cell contains two distinct patterns—*b* and *c* alike, or *b* and *c* different—which would modify the following argument.)

Following Kelly and Fiske (14, p. 108), we see that the total ACC score over all items is WAS plus WAD. The AS score is WAS plus UAS. When a Judge is predicting an Other, we may regard the real

	$a \neq b$ REAL DISSIMILARITY (RD)	$a = b$ REAL SIMILARITY (RS)
$a = c$ ASSUMED SIMILARITY (AS)	Unwarranted Assumed Similarity (UAS) $a = c \neq b$	Warranted Assumed Similarity (WAS) $a = b = c$
$a \neq c$ ASSUMED DISSIMILARITY (AD)	Warranted Assumed Dissimilarity (WAD) $a \neq b = c$	Unwarranted Assumed Dissimilarity (UAD) $a = b \neq c$

a = Judge's self-description; b = Other's self-description; c = Judge's prediction

FIG. 1. Possible combination of assumed and real similarity of any dichotomous item.

similarity or real dissimilarity of this pair on any item as fixed independently of any social perception by the Judge. Now we may ask, within the real similarity (RS) items: If the Judge predicts correctly, is he accurate? Or does he assume similarity? Obviously, these questions are operationally identical. The count of such items represents "warranted assumed similarity," and there is no way to distinguish whether this represents the mental set to assume similarity or the ability to judge accurately. In the Bender-Hastorf correction procedure, subtracting AS from ACC, we find that AS on RS items cancels ACC on RS items. Thus the RS items do not enter the refined empathy score.

Among real dissimilarity (RD) items where he predicts correctly, we might ask: Does the Judge recognize the dissimilarity or does he assume dissimilarity? These questions are both reflected in the count of WAD items. The Bender-Hastorf refined empathy score is equal to WAD − UAS. Therefore, the refined empathy score has a perfect negative correlation with AS, when RS is held constant. Furthermore, it has higher range when Judge and Other are dissimilar. Clearly, Bender and Hastorf did not arrive at a measure of accuracy independent of AS and RS.

The four categories of items in Fig. 1 have two degrees of freedom after the total number of RS items for a Judge-Other pair is established. We can take out two scores, and would like those scores to be independent. What score will be most meaningful depends on the correlation between the various cells. No single cell yields a good score as it stands, for the cell entry is influenced by RS.

One possibility is to employ the ratios WAS/RS and WAD/RD to summarize our information about the Judge. This procedure requires that enough items be used to keep the denominator large; otherwise, of course, the ratio becomes unreliable. In any case, however, the ratios for different Judges will be based on different items; this removes what may be an essential experimental control. The correlation between WAS/RS and WAD/RD should be determined. If these components are positively correlated, it follows that individual differences in prediction are more strongly determined by differences in ACC than by differences in AS tendency. The correlation will be negative if individual differences in prediction are more strongly influenced by AS than by ACC.

Distinguishing Stereotype and Differential Accuracy

The accuracy score may be divided in another manner (2, 7), yielding components which we may refer to as "stereotype accuracy" and "differential accuracy." The former refers to the individual's ability to predict the pooled responses of a given category of persons, whereas the latter refers to his ability to differentiate among individuals within the category.

Whatever score is used should reflect accuracy in predicting an Other at the intended level of specificity. If we are asking a Judge to predict the response of an individual to a personality inventory, we are probably interested in the fourth of our five types of Others, and want to measure "ability to predict how this individual deviates from the typical behavior of the particular group he belongs to." If accuracy is scored directly by comparing the prediction to the response of the individual, we are not distinguishing between two components which contribute to the Judge's success: his knowledge of the response that *any* individual in the subgroup is likely to give, and his knowledge of the way in which *this* individual deviates from the norm.

It is apparently desirable, when studying ability to predict at any one level, to obtain at least two scores: (*a*) ability to predict the typical behavior in the next-larger class to which Other belongs, and (*b*) ability to predict how Other deviates from the norm for this class. This would apply whether Other refers to an individual, a particular Army squadron, or some category such as "education majors."

There are three ways to measure differential and stereotype accuracy.

1. Where the Judge predicts the response of several Others, it is possible to determine the response of the average Other on each item, and the average of the Judge's predictions on that item. Thus we form an average profile of responses, and an average predicted profile. The distance between these two, possibly after removing differences in over-all average response, is a measure of stereotype accuracy (2). Here the stereotype that the Judge holds is inferred from his responses over many Others.

2. Where the Judge predicts for several Others, we can score each prediction for one Other against the responses of the remaining Others for whom the predictions were *not* intended (4, 7). Such "accidental" accuracy, when averaged over the unintended Others, reflects the understanding which is general over all members of the group of Others rather than specific to a particular Other. It provides a sort of "psychological

chance" base line. Accuracy measured in this way is closely related to stereotype accuracy of the first kind, but is also affected by the dispersions of predictions and self-descriptions (3, p. 472).

3. If we ask the Judge to indicate what proportion of a group will give a particular answer, or to mark the modal answer to be expected in a given group, his stereotype is expressed directly. This prediction can be compared with the actual responses of the group. It is quite possible that the stereotype obtained by this direct method would not coincide with the stereotype obtained by the other two methods. Such a discrepancy between what might be called the Judge's "conscious" and "unconscious" concept of the group could be of considerable interest, and studies obtaining both measures on the same Judge are called for.

In interpreting a stereotype accuracy score, a relation analogous to the assumed similarity-real similarity interaction may be noted. A person who is similar to the group, and who predicts that the group will in general give responses similar to his own, will almost certainly have high stereotype accuracy. A person who is atypical will have low stereotype accuracy if he assumes that other people give the same responses he does. If he assumes that others are different from himself, he may have either high or low stereotype accuracy, depending upon what differences actually occur.

The responses obtained in studies of social perception may be scored in many ways. The various scores so obtained are likely to be experimentally linked. Observed correlations are then likely to be artifacts of the experimental design, rather than relations among the traits the scores are named after. This type of difficulty is illustrated in a recent study (19). The Judges provided predictions of the norm, i.e., of what the average Other would say. This is c in Fig. 1. Empathy was defined as agreement between c and the true norm ($\bar{b}$). Reality was defined as agreement between c and the average prediction of all Judges ($\bar{c}$). If $\bar{b}$ agrees with $\bar{c}$ on more than half the items (as it surely would unless the Judges as a group are unrealistic in the extreme), then it necessarily follows that the empathy ($\bar{b}-c$) scores of individuals will be positively correlated with reality ($\bar{c}-c$) scores. The actual correlation was .77. No meaning can be attached to this result. There is an empirical fact underlying it, which is adequately described by the degree of overlap between the true norm ($\bar{b}$) and the average predicted norm ($\bar{c}$). Correlations among scores should not be interpreted in terms of higher order psychological constructs unless the operational variables are free from artifactual linkage.

NEED FOR INDEPENDENT CRITERIA OF SOCIAL SKILL

Many investigators have hypothesized that empathy, or accuracy of social perception, is correlated with effectiveness in interpersonal relations, and positive correlations have been found in several studies. In some research designs (e.g., 5, 11, 18), however, a linkage between accuracy score and criterion gives rise to an artifactual correlation. The obtained correlation cannot be interpreted.

For example, when sixth-grade pupils ranked each other sociometrically, and also estimated what ratings they would receive, accuracy in estimation correlated .50 with sociometric acceptance (5). But, as the authors report, pupils tended to predict that they would be highly accepted. Those who are indeed highly accepted automatically obtain better accuracy scores, and this fact alone would account for the observed correlation.

Another investigator (18) asked employees to rate their department supervisor. Then each supervisor predicted the ratings given by his department employees, and his predictive accuracy was scored. The correlation of accuracy with actual rating was .90. But we can expect a person to state that the group he is responsible for has good morale. This hypothesis alone is sufficient to account for the reported correlation, without introducing empathy or sensitivity as a construct. Suppose (to simplify) that the rating is on a 5-point scale, and that every supervisor predicts that his group will rate him 5 (very good). Now if each supervisor receives rating *b*, his accuracy score will be *5 minus b* (a low score representing high accuracy). Accuracy would obviously correlate *perfectly* with the actual rating. Random variations in the supervisors' predictions would lower the correlation, perhaps to the obtained value of .90. When findings can be explained parsimoniously as an artifact, investigators have the responsibility of making and reporting whatever analysis is necessary to preclude such possibilities.

Even if the predicted variate *b* is experimentally independent of the social effectiveness criterion X, X can have an artifactual correlation with predictive accuracy whenever *b* and X are correlated. In the study of supervisor's sensitivity (18), the rating by subordinates (*b*) correlated .86 with such a second criterion, executives' ratings of departmental production (X). This is a reasonable finding which we do not question. But if all supervisors made identical self-flattering predictions (*c*), their accuracy ($b-c$) in estimating workers' attitude would correlate .86 with this second criterion. The actual correlation was .82.

It is possible that accuracy in perceiving an Other improves one's effectiveness in dealing with that Other. But designs more subtle than that described above are required to establish such a relation. The response predicted by the Judge, on which the accuracy score is based, must not also be the effectiveness criterion of the study, nor may it be correlated with this criterion. One possible design would be to measure accuracy in estimating the *pattern* of Other's responses with elevation or social desirability eliminated (15, 23). A pupil's knowledge as to *which* Others will give him highest sociometric ratings should not be artifactually related to criteria of his popularity. The supervisor's or teacher's empathy might be assessed by determining if he knows in *which* respects his group is best satisfied. Another device is to use a "standard Other," requiring everyone whose accuracy is tested to make predictions for the same individual (21) or group (1). The investigator should take pains to test for the presence of artifacts by establishing whether the response-to-be-judged is uncorrelated with the criterion.

THE PROCESS OF SOCIAL PERCEPTION

The foregoing sections have emphasized the defects of recent conceptualizations and procedures in research on social perception. It would be unwise, however, to ignore the positive contributions stemming from this work: sharpened logical and psychological formulations and, particularly, insights concerning real and assumed similarity, stereotype and differential accuracy, and the dangers of artifactual relationships. These insights will apply to research on social perception in any kind of situation and with any kind of material—for example, even if the Judge is allowed to report freely on observations and interpretations of the real-life characteristics and behaviors of an Other.

Beyond this, some tentative substantive conclusions have begun to emerge, revealing what goes on when one person perceives another. Is the Judge's perception actually determined in any one-to-one fashion by cues he receives from the Other? Or is the reaction to the Other more "global"? Results with the kinds of data that have been collected to this point strongly suggest that the latter alternative is closer to the truth. Various global dispositions of the Judge appear to account for much of the variance in accuracy scores.

Two dispositions of this kind can be identified. First, Judges seem to differ significantly in their over-all tendencies to react favorably or unfavorably toward Others, both before and after the Others are observed. The Judge's favorability seems to determine his predictions or perceptions in a way that goes well beyond any identifiable stimuli coming from the Other. Then, if the Judge likes the Other, he will predict favorable, socially acceptable self-descriptions by the Other on a questionnaire or rating scale. If the Other does indeed describe himself favorably, the Judge will be accurate. But this accuracy stems more from a fortuitous concomitance of general favorability sets than from any differentiated perception of the Other.

A second kind of disposition has been termed the Judge's "implicit personality theory" (2); this consists of "built-in" correlations that the Judge consciously or unconsciously imposes on the traits, characteristics, or behaviors of Others. If the Judge is disposed to see trait B whenever he sees trait A, he will be accurate whenever traits A and B actually occur together in a given Other, and inaccurate when they do not. Judges have been found to differ in the closeness and direction of the associations they implicitly assume between traits. These differences among Judges influence their predictions of Others' responses, again in a way that seems to go far beyond any identifiable stimuli coming from the Others.

Hence, in the bulk of research to date, social perception as measured is a process dominated far more by what the Judge brings to it than by what he takes in during it. His favorability toward the Other, before or after he observes the Other, and his implicit personality theory, formed by his experiences prior to his interaction with the Other, seem to determine his perceptions. Most of the research that leads to this conclusion has been in situations where degree of acquaintance has been low. But this conclusion also seems to follow from studies where clinicians have been the judges, using the richest data that their diagnostic methods can provide, and from studies where husbands and wives have judged each other.

Probably we should not be surprised at this conclusion. It has its analogies, of course, in visual and aural perception. The process of perception is so laden with affect, and so highly over-learned in the course of socialization, that the dominant role of global dispositions might well be expected.

Research to test the limits of these conclusions readily suggests itself. We can begin with situations where degree of acquaintance is close, and only a small degree of extrapolation is required. Under these conditions we can get a base line in which specific identifiable cues dominate the perception. Then we can increase the degree of extrapolation and decrease the degree of acquaintance. At what point will the Judge's implicit personality theory and over-all favorability-unfavorability begin to appear and then to dominate? This question will not be researchable, of course, until it is put in operationally defined terms. Nonetheless, it appears at present that we shall not need to go far to find the perceiver rather than the stimulus determining the perception.

SUMMARY

This paper describes several conceptual and methodological problems in research on interpersonal perception and presents suggestions for dealing with them.

1. Sharpened conceptualizations of interpersonal perception processes are needed. It is often believed that accuracy in social perception constitutes a general trait. But accuracy has different operational definitions in different studies; this alone is sufficient to account for the contradictory evidence reported. Interpersonal perception makes different demands on the Judge, varying with the degree of acquaintance between the Judge and the Other, and with the degree of extrapolation required from Input to

Outtake. Five types of Other are identified in various types of research, ranging from persons in general to intraindividual variations. Each of the definitions of the problem requires separate study.

2. In measuring accuracy of interpersonal perception, research workers should take account of the altered meaning of accuracy scores as real similarity of the Judge to the Other varies. Faults in previously suggested "corrections" are noted.

3. Distinguishing between stereotype and differential accuracy should also make for more meaningful results.

4. Many reported relationships between accuracy of interpersonal perception and effectiveness in interpersonal relationships are contaminated by artifacts. Methods of avoiding artifacts are suggested.

5. Social perception, in most research to date, appears to be more a global process than a one-to-one response to cues received from the Other.

REFERENCES

1. Chowdhry, Kamla, & Newcomb, T. M. The relative abilities of leaders and nonleaders to estimate opinions of their own groups. *J. abnorm. soc. Psychol.*, 1952, 47, 51–57.
2. Cronbach, L. J. Processes affecting scores on "understanding of others" and "assumed similarity." *Psychol. Bull.*, 1955, 52, 177–193.
3. Cronbach, L. J., & Gleser, Goldine C. Assessing similarity between profiles. *Psychol. Bull.*, 1953, 50, 456–473.
4. Crow, W. J. A methodological study of social perceptiveness. Unpublished doctor's dissertation, Univer. of Colorado, 1954.
5. Dymond, Rosalind, F., Hughes, Ann S., & Raabe, Virginia L. Measurable changes in empathy with age. *J. consult. Psychol.*, 1952, 16, 202–206.
6. Fiedler, F. E. The psychological-distance dimension in interpersonal relations. *J. Pers.*, 1953, 22, 142–150.
7. Gage, N. L. Judging interests from expressive behavior. *Psychol. Monogr.*, 1952, 66, No. 18 (Whole No. 350).
8. Gage, N. L. Accuracy of social perception and effectiveness in interpersonal relationships. *J. Pers.*, 1953, 22, 128–141.
9. Gage, N. L., & Exline, R. V. Social perception and effectiveness in discussion groups. *Hum. Relat.*, 1953, 6, 381–396.
10. Gage, N. L., & Suci, G. J. Social perception and teacher-pupil relationships. *J. educ. Psychol.*, 1951, 42, 144–152.
11. Greer, F. L., Galanter, E. H., & Nordlie, P. G. Interpersonal knowledge and individual and group effectiveness. *J. abnorm. soc. Psychol.*, 1954, 49, 411–414.
12. Hall, H. E., & Bell, G. B. The relationship between two tests of empathy: Dymond's and Kerr's. *Amer. Psychologist*, 1953, 8, 361–362. (Abstract)
13. Hastorf, A. H., & Bender, I. E. A caution respecting the measurement of empathic ability. *J. abnorm. soc. Psychol.*, 1952, 47, 574–576.
14. Kelly, E. L., & Fiske, D. W. *The prediction of performance in clinical psychology.* Ann Arbor: Univer. of Michigan Press, 1951.
15. Kerr, W. A., & Speroff, B. J. *Measurement of empathy.* Chicago: Psychometric Affiliates, 1950.
16. Lundy, R. M. Assimilative projection in interpersonal perceptions. Unpublished doctor's dissertation, Ohio State Univer., 1954.
17. Meehl, P. *Clinical versus statistical prediction; a theoretical analysis and a review of the evidence.* Minneapolis: Univer. of Minnesota Press, 1954.

18. Nagle, B. F. Productivity, employee attitude, and supervisor sensitivity. *Amer. Psychologist,* 1953, 8, 408. (Abstract)
19. Norman, R. D., & Ainsworth, Patricia. The relationships among projection, empathy, reality, and adjustment, operationally defined. *J. consult. Psychol.,* 1954, 18, 53–58.
20. Rudin, S. A., Lazar, I., Ehart, Mary E., & Cronbach, L. J. Some empirical studies of the reliability of interpersonal perception scores. Unpublished manuscript, Univer. of Illinois, 1952. (Mimeo.)
21. Stone, G. C., Leavitt, G. S., & Gage, N. L. Generality of accuracy in perceiving standard persons. Unpublished manuscript, Bureau of Educational Research, Univer. of Illinois, 1954. (Mimeo.)
22. Tagiuri, R., Blake, R. R., & Bruner, J. S. Some determinants of the perception of positive and negative feelings in others. *J. abnorm. soc. Psychol.,* 1953, 48, 585–592.
23. Talland, G. A. The assessment of group opinion by leaders, and their influence on its formation. *J. abnorm. soc. Psychol.,* 1954, 49, 431–434.

A Test of Interactionist Hypotheses of Self-Conception

S. FRANK MIYAMOTO
and
SANFORD M. DORNBUSCH

GEORGE HERBERT MEAD constitutes something of a paradox for modern sociology. His works have been widely acclaimed for their fundamental importance to social-psychological and sociological theory. On the other hand, Mead's admirers have often encountered considerable difficulty in formulating research problems within the frame-

REPRINTED from *American Journal of Sociology,* 1956, 61, 399–403, by permission of The University of Chicago Press and the authors.

This paper reports part of the findings from a study of interpersonal perception, supported by the Agnes Anderson Fund, the Faculty Research Fund of the Graduate School of the University of Washington, and the Center for Advanced Study in the Behavioral Sciences. We are indebted to the following persons who were consulted at various stages of the research project: Charles E. Bowerman, S. Francis Camilleri, Samuel A. Stouffer, Robert E. L. Faris, William H. Sewell, Albert Hastorf, Stephen Richardson, David Gold, and Howard S. Becker. Statistical assistance was provided by Mrs. Joan Carlson, Elizabeth Johnson, John B. Hudson, Gerald Day, and Donald L. Garrity.

work of his views. True, during the last decade initial advances have been made in the empirical study of roles, role-taking, and role conflicts; however, the notions of self and self-conception—two additional key concepts in his system and the system of Cooley and others within this tradition—remain among the neglected problems of social psychology to which Leonard Cottrell (3) referred.

The aim of this paper is an empirical study of certain basic assumptions in the interactionist view of the self and self-conception. Essentially dynamic, the interactionist theory of the self is not easily translated into research operations. This paper does not study the ongoing process but concentrates instead on static consequences which can reasonably be deduced from Mead. The method here employed is too crude for investigating subtle aspects of Mead's theory, but improvements and refinements of the method are possible. Moreover, many interesting lines of inquiry into the self can be pursued with the method, such as it is.

Our concern is three problems suggested by the interactionist view of the self. First, a basic contribution of Mead and Cooley to the understanding of the self and self-conception lay in their emphasis upon the influence of the responses of others in shaping self-definitions. This principle, once recognized, may appear so self-evident as not to require empirical confirmation. However, it seems of interest to consider any empirical test which will confirm or deny the generalization.

Second, although it is Mead's habit to speak of "the response of the other" as providing the key to the definition of the self (5), the phrase is somewhat ambiguous, for a distinction may be drawn between (*a*) the actual response of the other and (*b*) the subject's perception of the response of the other. Mead often does not distinguish between these two; but it is consistent with his view that the perception of the other's response is the critical aspect. Will an empirical test support this assumption?

Finally, one of Mead's most illuminating analyses is his account of how the self may take the role of the generalized other. The "generalized other" refers to the individual's conception of the organized social process of which he is a part (5). This organized social process is composed of numerous specialized roles, and the individual identifies his own role in it and so fulfils his part as to enable the organized process to continue. On the other hand, individuals often enter into social relations wherein the organization of roles is obscure or minimal. In such a case, the individual cannot take the role of the generalized other in Mead's sense; yet, for the individual to act in the situation, some conception of the generalized other may be necessary. What kind of conception of self and others may be employed under these circumstances?

In our research we used social groups whose members were, at best, loosely joined by friendship and had no definite organized group activity within which to identify their respective roles. They were engaged as individuals, at the moment, in making empathic judgments about one another. It seemed reasonable to assume that the individual might be able to define—and would, in fact, use—a self-conception based on the *typical* attitudes of others toward him. Hence the third problem concerns the relation of self-conceptions to the perception of the typical attitudes of others toward one's self.

METHOD

Index of self-conception.—In recent years, due mainly to the renewed interest of psychologists in the study of the self, a number of methods have been developed for getting self-evaluations from experimental subjects. In one, subjects are requested to give self-characterizations by means of one of the following devices: checking appropriate words on an adjective check list of self-descriptive terms (7), responding to a standard personality inventory or to some other form of questionnaire that yields self-revealing responses, or writing out self-evaluative autobiographical sketches (1). These techniques are designed to reveal the content of individual self-conceptions.

A second method requires subjects to indicate their expected score on some test prior to taking the test—usually an aptitude or attitude scale—thus providing a picture of how an individual evaluates himself (8, 6). Here the unique feature is the objective measure of performance or attitude against which the individual's expectation (self-conception) may be compared.

A third approach that combines features of the previous two requires subjects in a group of limited size to rate themselves on specified personal characteristics, relative to the others. For example, in a study by Calvin and Holtzman, members of fraternity groups (about twenty members each) ranked all group members, including themselves, on characteristics such as leadership, adjustment, tolerance, drive, and so on (2). Not only was it possible to use the individuals' self-rankings as a measure of self-concept, but, because each member was rated by all others in the group, it was also possible to derive an average of the others' ratings against which the self-concept could be compared.

For the purpose of investigating interactionist hypotheses of the self, the latter provides the most satisfactory method. In the present study the index of self-conception was derived in the course of investigating a different problem, namely, the measuring of empathic ability, by means of an adaptation of a method developed by Rosalind Dymond and Leonard Cottrell (4). The Dymond-Cottrell method requires subjects in a group to give self-ratings as well as ratings on every other group member on a short list of specified personal characteristics.

Source of data.—Our data were gathered from 195 subjects in ten groups ranging in size from 8 to 48 persons. Four groups, totaling 63 subjects, consisted of volunteering members of two fraternities and two sororities. Each member had lived in his own club's house for at least three months. The other six groups, totaling 132 subjects, were classes in sociology, almost all class members of which participated in the study.

Definition of variables.—For convenience in identifying the four variables in this study, labels have been adopted and given specific meanings. Our terminology implies no more than is stated in our definitions.

1. "Self-conception": Each subject was asked to rate himself on a five-point scale for each of the following four characteristics: intelligence, self-confidence, physical attractiveness, and likableness. Subjects were told that the middle of the scale should be regarded as "average for *this* group." The analysis for each characteristic is separate, no summing operations being performed in the four ratings.

2. "Actual response of others": Each member of a group rated every other member of the group on the same four characteristics, using the five-point scale. The mean response to each subject was computed for each of the four characteristics.

The response of others as here defined does not correspond exactly with Mead's meaning of the term; he obviously refers to responses made in direct interpersonal relations, while our reference is to responses on a paper-and-pencil rating scale. It seems reasonable to assume, however, that the rating-scale response would tend to be a condensed symbolic version of real-life responses and that the two would correspond sufficiently for the purposes of this investigation. Mead himself often spoke of "the attitude of the other" interchangeably with the term "the role of the other."

3. "Perceived response of others": Each member of a group predicted how every other member would rate him on the scale. The mean prediction of each subject was found for each of the four characteristics.

4. "The generalized other": Each subject was asked to state, using the same scale, how he perceived *most* persons as viewing him. The specific question was: "How intelligent (self-confident, physically attractive, likable) do most people think you are?"

Method of analysis.—As in most studies of personal perception, good sampling was not easily achieved. Our sample was larger and more varied than those in most studies of this type, but our findings may not be reliable. Furthermore, data obtained as ours were, are not sufficiently sensitive to allow refined analyses. Because of these limitations in the design, we set restrictions upon our analysis.

First, since the groups are not a random sample from any known universe, statistical tests of significance are not employed, and the data are examined only for consistent tendencies from group to group. Second, we rely for our test upon inspection of gross differences. For each group, on each of the four characteristics, we determine whether the data support or do not support a specific hypothesis. Thus the ten groups and four characteristics yield forty results. If a hypothesis is supported forty times in the forty possible tests, we regard it as receiving perfect support; if the score is only twenty supporting tests out of the possible forty, the hypothesis is regarded as having no more than chance success.

The Findings

Hypothesis 1.—According to the interactionist view, the self-conceptions of most persons are likely to be determined by internalization of the behavior of others toward them. If so, those accorded high esteem by others

TABLE 1

CHARACTERISTIC	HYPOTHESIS SUPPORTED	HYPOTHESIS NOT SUPPORTED	TIE
Intelligence	9	0	1
Self-confidence	8	2	0
Physical attractiveness	9	1	0
Likableness	9	1	0
Total	35	4	1

should reflect a higher self-esteem than those poorly regarded. Stating this in the form of a testable hypothesis: *The mean of the actual responses of others to the subject will be higher for those persons with a high self-rating than for those with a low self-rating.* Sorting each group into high and low self-raters and comparing the means of the "actual responses of others" toward the subjects in each subclass, we get the results given in Table 1.

Analysis of the ten groups for all characteristics taken together shows that the hypothesis is supported ten out of ten times.

Hypothesis 2.—Earlier it was suggested that it is of interest to evaluate separately the effect on self-conception of the "actual response of other" and the "perceived response of others." As a first step in this analysis, the same procedure applied in the previous test to the "actual responses" may be applied to the "perceived responses." Again, after the high and low self-raters have been sorted, the hypothesis now reads: *The mean of the perceived responses of others will be higher for those persons with a high self-rating than for those with a low self-rating.* The results are shown in Table 2. Ten out of ten groups showed differences in the expected direction.

Hypothesis 3.—The next question is the relative effect on self-conception of the perceived response of others as compared to the effect of their actual responses. Social-psychological theory leads us to believe that the perceived behavior of others toward the self has a more direct

TABLE 2

CHARACTERISTIC	HYPOTHESIS SUPPORTED	HYPOTHESIS NOT SUPPORTED	TIE
Intelligence	10	0	0
Self-confidence	10	0	0
Physical attractiveness	10	0	0
Likableness	10	0	0
Total	40	0	0

TABLE 3

CHARACTERISTIC	HYPOTHESIS SUPPORTED	HYPOTHESIS NOT SUPPORTED	TIE
Intelligence	8	2	0
Self-confidence	9	0	1
Physical attractiveness	10	0	0
Likableness	7	3	0
Total	34	5	1

influence than their actual behavior. Hence the hypothesis: *Self-conception tends to be closer to the mean perceived response of others to the subject than to the mean actual response of others.* The findings are summarized in Table 3. Of the ten groups, nine showed a tendency to support the hypothesis, with one class of eleven persons indeterminate, confirming the hypothesis for two characteristics and not confirming for the other two.

Hypothesis 4.—It will be remembered that the index of the generalized other was determined by asking each subject, "How intelligent (etc.) do most people think you are?" In effect, the question which was used in testing Hypothesis 2, with respect to specific individuals in a specific group, was broadened to include all other social contacts of our subjects. Hence it is reasonable to assume that the line of thinking employed in developing the earlier hypothesis should apply here. Again using high and low self-raters to provide subclasses with differential self-conception, the following hypothesis is investigated: *Those persons who have high self-ratings on a characteristic will have a higher mean perception of the generalized other than will those with low self-ratings* (Table 4). Once

TABLE 4

CHARACTERISTIC	HYPOTHESIS SUPPORTED	HYPOTHESIS NOT SUPPORTED	TIE
Intelligence	9	0	1
Self-confidence	9	1	0
Physical attractiveness	10	0	0
Likableness	10	0	0
Total	38	1	1

again, all ten groups showed differences as anticipated.

Hypothesis 5.—In rating the "perceived responses of others," the subjects considered only those other persons present in the test group. However, self-conception emerges from interaction in divergent groups. Therefore, it should more closely reflect the way most persons are perceived as viewing the subject than the perception of the responses of any particular group of individuals to the subject. *Accordingly, self-conception should correspond more closely with the generalized other than with the mean of the perceived responses of others.* The results are shown in Table 5. The hypothesis is confirmed for thirty-five out of forty comparisons. Only for self-confidence is there any tendency to show marked deviations from the expected direction. Analysis of the ten groups shows all ten tending to confirm the hypothesis. A deficiency of the test of Hypothesis 5 is that both self-conception and generalized other are discrete variables, while mean perception is continuous. Essentially, the results show that self-conception and generalized other are usually given the identical rating.

TABLE 5

CHARACTERISTIC	HYPOTHESIS SUPPORTED	HYPOTHESIS NOT SUPPORTED	TIE
Intelligence	10	0	0
Self-confidence	5	4	1
Physical attractiveness	10	0	0
Likableness	10	0	0
Total	35	4	1

SUMMARY

The results of this research lend empirical support to the symbolic interactionist view of self-conception. Our findings indicate that the response, or at least the attitude, of others is related to self-conception; but they also indicate that the subject's perception of that response is even more closely related. We also find that an individual's self-conception is more closely related to his estimate of the generalized attitude toward him than to the perceived attitude of response of members of a particular group.

These empirical findings do little more than reinforce fundamental notions contained in the interactionist theory of self-conception. Beyond that, however, they suggest possibilities in studying self-conception within the symbolic interactionist framework.

REFERENCES

1. Bugental, J. F. T., & Zelen, S. L. Investigation into the self-concept. *J. Pers.*, 1950, 18, 483–498.
2. Calvin, A. D., & Holtzman, W. H. Adjustment and the discrepancy between self-concept and the inferred self. *J. consult. Psychol.*, 1953, 17, 39–44.

3. Cottrell, L. S. Some neglected problems in social psychology. *Amer. sociol. Rev.*, 1950, 15, 708–711.
4. Dymond, Rosalind F. A Scale for the measurement of empathic ability. *J. consult. Psychol.*, 1949, 13, 127–133.
5. Mead, G. H. *Mind, self, and society*. Chicago: Univer. of Chicago Press, 1934.
6. Newcomb, T. M. *Personality and social change*. New York: Dryden, 1943.
7. Sarbin, T. R. Role Theory. In G. Lindzey (Ed.), *Handbook of social psychology*. Cambridge, Mass.: Addison-Wesley, 1954.
8. Torrance, E. P. Rationalizations about test performance as a function of self-concepts. *J. soc. Psychol.*, 1954, 39, 211–217.

CHAPTER 5

CONSISTENCY OF THE INDIVIDUAL

Individual Differences in the Social Atom

HELEN H. JENNINGS

IN THE AREA of human interrelations—it goes without saying—the individual cannot be studied apart from the other individuals with whom he is interrelated.[1] Hence the problem of studying individual differences here involves not only the individual's emotional-social expression in choice and rejection of others but similarly the expression of other persons towards him. The sum of interpersonal structures resulting from the operation of reactions of choice and rejection centered about a given individual would comprise the individual's social atom, as defined by Moreno.[2] Obviously, if it is desired to study this sociometric unit, the social atom, in a given population, the psycho-social projections in choice and

ADAPTED by the author from Individual differences in the social atom. *Sociometry*, 1941, 4, 269–277. Reprinted by permission of the author and publisher.

1 The experimental material in this report is part of a study investigating individual differences in personal relationships and the character of the choice process (2).

2 Moreno defines the term as the "smallest constellation of psychological relations" comprising the "individual cells in the social universe," and consisting of "the psychological relations of one individual to those other individuals to whom he is attracted or repelled and their relation to him all in respect to a specific criterion" (3, p. 432).

rejection of each member of the population must be secured.[3] Assuming that by a sociometric investigation, the full expression of the members of a population towards one another are secured, the question then is: by what method of analysis can individual differences in the social atom be uncovered?

The method of attack upon this problem which is presented here was preceded by a study of individual differences in various expressions of the choice process in order to ascertain whether or not the various expressions are significantly correlated. If the findings should indicate that individual differences in any aspect of the choice process bear no relation to the differences in other aspects, it would then be futile to pursue a study of the social atom as a structural unit. Then, an investigator would be justified in examining *singly* the expression of the individual towards others and the expression of others towards the individual. Likewise, he would be justified in examining *singly* the expression of positive choice and the expression of rejection. Further, he might disregard whether choice or rejection are reciprocal, and treat as a simple sum the reactions of individuals towards one another.

To investigate the problem, three conditions of experimentation were considered necessary: (*1*) the experiment must test the population studied at two points in time sufficiently distant from each other to admit of structural changes taking place and being recorded; (*2*) the population must be allowed full, spontaneous expression, i.e., no limit must be put on the number of expressions the population gives by specifying a particular number, in order that the whole problem of expansiveness as it affects interrelation systems may be studied; if a given number of choices is specified, as has been done hitherto, it is not possible to study individual differences in expansiveness; and (*3*) negative expressions of rejection should be given the same importance as positive expressions of choice.

A sociometric experiment fulfilling the above conditions was carried out at the New York State Training School for Girls, Hudson, N.Y. The conditions of this experiment allowed unlimited expression of choice and rejection to the test-population comprising 443 persons at the time of Test I (January 1, 1938) and 457 persons at the time of Test II (September 3, 1938), and secured their expressions, positive and negative, towards one another on criteria[4] of significance to this population at two points in time separated by eight months.

3 The writer defines the social atom experimentally as: The constellation of psychosocial projections in positive choice and rejection by and towards the individual as secured under conditions permitting full expression for or against collaborating with others in common life situations (2, p. 324).

4 The criteria for choice and rejection were: (*1*) living in the same housing unit; (*2*) working in the same vocational group; (*3*) spending leisure or recreation together; and (*4*) studying in the same group. The findings relate to the 133 members of the population who were present for both Test I and Test II and living under like conditions in the community on both occasions; the findings are based on their reactions

Some of the findings relative to the choice process have in part been reported elsewhere (1) but may be repeated here as they bear on the present problem.

Choice and rejection as they are expressed by the individual or as they are directed towards him and the reciprocal structures found between the individual and the population indicate that the negative and positive aspects within the choice process are not two separate factors operating independently, either as they emanate from the individual or as they are focussed upon him by the population around him. Instead they form *one* choice process in which the negative and the positive aspects show particular relationships to each other.

Secondly, while the individual in his expression towards others shows increase or decrease on Test II in a manner that is not highly consistent with his expression on Test I, the average change in performance is insignificantly different from zero. (The critical ratio of the difference between the correlated means on the two tests is 1.65 for positive choice by the subject and −.50 for negative choice by the subject.)

Thirdly, the total impress of the individual upon the population, as measured by the sum of positive and negative reactions expressed by others for him, is significantly related at the two time points eight months apart. Fourthly, the positive expression of the population for the individual and the positive expression of the individual for the population shows only a very slight correlation on Test I and is insignificantly different from zero on Test II. This is likewise found for the sum of positive and negative expressions by the individual for the group compared with their expressions, positive and negative, for him, at the two time points. Fifthly, the positive reciprocations of the individual's choice expressions correlate fairly highly with the number of positive expressions for him, and also correlate significantly with the number of his positive choice expressions for others.

In addition to the findings just summarized, various other correlations between one or another aspect of the expression of choice and rejection, examined at the two time points, suggested that the choice process in a community does not vary randomly in its operation: when explored by comparing its expression within a population at one time with its expression at a later time, it is found to be characterized by a *particular manner of operation.*

It therefore appeared that the character of the choice process in its general operation throughout a population must similarly be reflected also in its particularized expression in the social atoms of the individual members of the community who were its "carriers." In the light of the evidence on the choice process it appeared that individual differences in in-

to the total population and the total population's reactions to them, at both periods, on criteria of uniform importance to the total membership.

terrelations within a social atom should be concomitantly examined on each of the six aspects found to be significantly related within the choice process: the positive and negative choice expression *by and towards* the individual together with the mutual expression (reciprocally positive or reciprocally negative) between the individual and others. The problem thus becomes one of examining individual differences in the individual's matrix of relationships in which he is the active focus and comparing it, as one unit, with the matrix formed around other individuals of which they are the active foci.

For this purpose, the positive expression of the subject for others, i.e., the number of individuals chosen by him for inclusion in his life situation, may be called his performance in emotional expansiveness towards others. Likewise the positive expression by others for the subject, i.e., the number of individuals choosing him for inclusion in their life situations, may be called the subject's performance in emotional expansiveness "achieved from" others. The positive reactions by the subject which are reciprocated by positive reactions from the individuals chosen may be called the subject's performance in positive reciprocation. The decision to include the measure of reciprocal reaction as an important performance (just as important as gross reaction by or towards the subject) rests on the finding previously reported that such performance is significantly related to several aspects of interrelations. The negative reactions by and towards the subject and reciprocated rejections may likewise be considered as three further performances in which the subject may be compared with other subjects. Each performance of the subject may then be studied as it ranks in respect to the respective performance of the other subjects, with the mean being taken as dividing subjects who have a plus (+) score in a given performance from subjects who have a minus (−) score in the respective performance. Whatever point is taken, there will be subjects who barely place within a + score or who barely place within a − score.

In the present analysis, it is convenient to describe the scores on positive emotional expansiveness in a given order: first, the expression of the subject towards others (number chosen by him); second, the expression of others towards the subject (number choosing him); and third, the reciprocal expressions between the subject and others (number reciprocating the subject's choice to them). Thus, the subject who has a − score in each of the above performances ranks below the respective average performance of the test-population. It is further convenient to follow the same order in describing the scores on negative reaction. Then, the total six performances may be called for brevity, the choice-and-rejection-pattern of the individual.

The presenting of the findings is simplified by referring to the first three performances (positive choice) as the individual's *choice pattern;* and the latter three performances (negative choice), as his *rejection pat-*

tern. Either the choice pattern or the rejection pattern, considered separately, gives a partial picture of the structure of the individual's total constellation given by his choice-and-rejection-pattern as a unit.

The individual may vary from average in a plus or minus direction in three scores on positive expansiveness; hence, there are eight possible choice patterns: −−−, +++, +−+, −+−, −−+, ++−, +−−, and −++. He may likewise vary in the same number of ways on rejection scores; hence, there are eight possible rejection patterns.

As any one of the eight possible choice patterns may be combined with any one of the eight possible rejection patterns, there are 64 technically possible choice-rejection patterns. However, in the test-population, counting both occasions, only 52 choice-rejection patterns appear: 12 do not occur on either Test I or Test II, given eight months later. Of the 64 choice-rejection patterns, only 10 are shown on Test I by five or more individuals; only 10 also are shown on Test II by five or more individuals; and 7 of the 10 are the same patterns. Such a finding was, of course, to be expected; the choice patterns and the rejection patterns cannot have a chance frequency since the choice process is characterized by significant correlations between one or another aspect of emotional expansiveness or of rejection.

The picture of choice-rejection patterns for the subjects as a whole is very complex and cannot be presented within the space limitations of this paper. Some of the findings related to the social atom of individuals while they are in a sociometric "leader-position," contrasted with the social atom of individuals while in a sociometric position of "isolated or near-isolated" will instead be included here as their patterns show a less complicated but equally interesting picture of interrelations.

For the purpose of examining patterns typical for the individuals towards whom the population as a whole shows unusual expansiveness in positive choice and towards whom they show unusually little expansiveness in positive choice, the subjects who respectively rank 1 S.D. above or below the mean may be compared, without regard to whether or not the position occurs on Test I or Test II or is shown by the same individual on both occasions. The position of 1 S.D. above the mean of the population may be referred to as a "leader-position" and that 1 S.D. below the mean of the population, as an "isolated or near-isolated" position, as the individuals occupying the respective positions are found in the one instance to be recognized and given "leadership" by the members of the community and in the other, to be hardly at all recognized even as participants by the population as a whole (2).

There are 43 leader-positions and 41 isolated-or-near-isolated-positions, as defined, found on Test I and Test II, counted together. The number occurring on Test I and Test II is in both instances approximately equal.

TABLE I

Choice-Rejection Patterns Shown by 41 Isolated-or-Near-Isolated-Positions *

TEST I AND TEST II

Positive Choice Pattern

Rejection Pattern		1 — — —	2 + + +	3 + — +	4 — + —	5 — — +	6 + + —	7 + — —	8 — + +	TOTAL	PERCENT
1	— — —	9						3		12	30
2	+ + +							7		7	17
3	+ — +							1		1	2
4	— + —	4								4	10
5	— — +	3								3	7
6	+ + —	1								1	2
7	+ — —							1		1	2
8	— + +	5						7		12	30
TOTAL		22						19		41	
PERCENT		54						46			100

* Ranking 1 S.D. below the mean in choices received: Test I and Test II. Each pattern represents the rank of the individual who shows an "isolated-or-near-isolated-position," as compared with the mean of the test-population (above the mean being indicated by + and below, by —), in three performances: the first + or — in a given pattern represents the individual's expression towards others; the second, the expression of others towards him; and the third, the reciprocal expression between the individual and others. For convenience the patterns are numbered.

Individuals in an isolated-or-near-isolated position could technically place in four possible choice patterns: −−−, +−+, −−+, or +−−. See Table 1. They are found, however, only in two of these patterns: 54 percent show a positive choice pattern of −−− and 4 percent, a positive choice pattern of +−−. They could technically place in any of the eight rejection patterns. Thirty percent show a −++ rejection pattern and 30 percent also a −−− rejection pattern, with the next most frequent pattern of rejection being +++. Their choice-rejection patterns are in order of frequencies: 9 −−− −−− ; 7 +−− +++ ; and 7 +−− −++. Thus only three choice-rejection patterns are found in 56 percent of the instances (23/41).

Individuals in a leader-position could technically place in four possible choice patterns: +++, −+−, ++−, or −++. They are found, however, in 49 percent of the instances to have a +++ pattern, in 35 percent to have a −++ pattern, and only rarely in either of the other two patterns. (See Table 2.) Thus at the time an individual has a leader-position he very likely will place above average in mutual positive choice with other individuals. On the other hand, the greatly above average positive expression of the population towards him may or may not be accompanied by an above average positive expression on his part towards the population. Similarly, as revealed in their positive choice patterns, there appears to be no relation between the extent of choice for others on the part of the individuals towards whom the population shows little if any positive expression: they show about equally often an above and a below average expression.

In marked difference from the isolated-or-near-isolated, the individuals in leader-positions show a +−− rejection pattern in 40 percent of the instances, a pattern shown only in 2 percent of the instances by the former group. Thus, in 40 percent of the instances, the individual in a leader-position in the test-community is above average in the number of persons he rejects while at the same time he is rejected by others to a smaller extent than the average member of the population and likewise has fewer than the average number of mutual rejection structures between himself and others in his constellation of interrelations. Furthermore, if all the patterns containing above average expression of rejection by the individual towards others are added together (rejection patterns #2, #3, #6 and #7 in Tables 1 and 2), it appears that 56 percent of the individuals in leader-positions, as contrasted with 23 percent of the individuals in isolated-or-near-isolated positions, are above average in the number of persons they reject. Thus above average rejection of others is found more often to characterize the interrelation pattern of individuals in the test-population who are very highly chosen by others than those who are very under chosen.

It is notable also that the −++ rejection pattern found for 30 percent of the isolated-or-near-isolated is totally absent for the individuals in

TABLE 2

Choice-Rejection Patterns Shown by 43 Leader-Positions *

TEST I AND TEST II

Positive Choice Pattern

Rejection Pattern		1 − − −	2 + + +	3 + − +	4 − + −	5 − − +	6 + + −	7 + − −	8 − + +	TOTAL	PERCENT
1	− − −		4		3				6	13	30
2	+ + +		1						1	2	5
3	+ − +		4							4	9
4	− + −		1						1	2	5
5	− − +		2						2	4	9
6	+ + −				1					1	2
7	+ − −		9				3		5	17	40
8	− + +									0	0
TOTAL			21		4		3		15	43	
PERCENT			49		9		7		35		100

* Ranking 1 S.D. above the mean in choices received: Test I and Test II. Each pattern represents the rank of the individual who shows a "leader-position," as compared with the mean of the test-population (above the mean being indicated by + and below, by —), in three performances: the first + or — in a given pattern represents the individual's expression towards others; the second, the expression of others towards him; and the third, the reciprocal expression between the individual and others. For convenience the patterns are numbered.

leader-positions. The two groups, however, equally often show the −−− rejection pattern (30 percent for either group). The most frequent choice-rejection pattern for the individual in a leader-position is +++ +−−, as compared with the most frequent pattern of −−− −−− found for the individual towards whom the population shows little or no positive choice. Other differences between the two groups of individuals may be seen by inspection of Tables 1 and 2.

It appears that individual differences in pattern within their respective total constellations of interrelations mark the individuals who as a group are shown to be relatively highly chosen members of the population or isolated-or-nearly-unchosen members of the population. Certain of the individual differences are consistently prevalent in their respective patterns. Yet, on the other hand, in still further aspects either group may resemble or differ from the other in its pattern of interrelations. In the latter instances, the aspects of the choice process are apparently not crucially related to the position the individual is accorded by those in contact with him.

The patterns reflect the total impress of others upon the individual and the total impress he in turn makes upon others. The individual differences in structure of constellations of interrelations are seen to be very much more complex than the view permitted by study of the character of the choice process in its general operation, apart from the individuals themselves from whom choice and rejection emanate and upon whom the choice and rejection of others impinge.

The implications of the findings are more fully evident, however, only by inspection of the extent to which individuals in the test-population as a whole are found to have particular patterns and the persistence or the fluctuation these patterns show. The results of this study are reported elsewhere (2). From the few findings presented in this paper, it may be concluded that individual differences in interrelations between well-chosen individuals and individuals who are unchosen-or-nearly-unchosen members of a population appear not to be limited to the contrasting degree to which they are chosen but are reflected in the social atom in such manner that it is structured by various patterns, some typical for the former group and some typical for the latter group.

The conclusion may be drawn that the social atom, for purposes of studying individual differences in interrelations, may be considered a structural unit resulting from the nature of the choice process. If it is a structural unit, in a wider sense than here described, it should be demonstrable that the social atom of *a given individual* as it undergoes change retains some consistency between its "internal structure" at one time and at a second time fairly distant. The evidence from such an analysis indicates this is the case (2).

REFERENCES

1. Jennings, Helen H. Sociometry and social theory. *Amer. sociol. Rev.*, 1941, 6, 512–522.
2. Jennings, Helen H. *Leadership and isolation.* New York: Longmans, Green, 1943. (2nd Ed. 1950).
3. Moreno, J. L. *Who shall survive? A new approach to the problem of human interrelations.* Collaborator: Helen H. Jennings. Washington, D.C.: Nervous and Mental Disease Publishing Co., 1934.

Mother-Child Interaction and the Social Behavior of Children

BARBARA MERRILL BISHOP

AN EXPERIMENT was designed to investigate factors in the interactive relationship between mother and child which might bear on the behavior and social learning of the child. Subjects for the study were 34 mothers and their respective children (17 boys and 17 girls) who attended the Preschool Laboratories of the Iowa Child Welfare Research Station. Ages of the children ranged from 3 years 4 months to 5 years 7 months. Each mother and child was observed for two half-hour sessions on different days in an experimental room which made available an assortment of play equipment for the child and magazines for the mother. The experimenter observed the session from an observation booth fitted with a one-way screen and recorded the behavior of both mother and child every five seconds in terms of a notational system based on a variety of behavior categories. The mothers were told that the purpose of the study was to investigate play behavior of children when adults are present, and that they were free to do as they wished during the period.

In order to investigate generalization of child behavior from that evidenced with the mother to that shown in social situations with other adults, each child was also tested for two 30-minute sessions, under the same experimental conditions, with a young woman who was socially unfamiliar to him and who has been termed the "neutral adult." The neutral

FROM *Psychological Monographs*, 1951, 65, No. 11 (Whole no. 328). Reprinted by permission of the author and the American Psychological Association, Inc.

adult was given a frequency range of the main behavior categories within which her behavior toward all the children should fall. Statistical analysis showed that her behavior in all 68 sessions, although somewhat variable, approached as satisfactory a degree of consistency as could be expected in a free-play, interactive situation. A subjective evaluation of her behavior would indicate that qualitatively her manner, attitude, and social responsiveness were constant from child to child.

In order to offset any factors associated with the order in which the child was tested with the adults, the 34 children were divided into two groups matched for age and sex. For one group of children the order of testing was two sessions with the mother, two sessions with the neutral adult; for the other group the order was reversed.

The categories which referred to the behavior of adults included 11 main types: lack of contact, interactive play, teaching, helping, praising, structurizing, directing, interfering, criticizing, cooperation, and non-cooperation. The last six categories were supplemented by numerical ratings expressing the qualitative nature of the behavior evidenced. The following are the categories descriptive of child behavior: bid for attention, bid for physical proximity, directing, interfering, criticizing, indications of anxiety, cooperation, non-cooperation, bid for praise, affection, asking for information, asking for permission, and asking for help. The first eight of these categories were also supplemented by qualitative ratings.

Statistical analysis showed that the mothers evidenced consistent behavior from the first to the second session. The children's behavior was also consistent from the first to the second session with the mother.

Positive correlations indicated that the children reflected directly in their own behavior the mother's use of directing-interfering-criticism, strong stimulation, and suggesting types of control, and also the tendency toward nonacceptance of stimulations.

A high degree of specificity of control, represented by high proportions of directing-interfering-criticism and strong stimulations in the behavior of the mother, showed positive relationships of from .45 to .71 with measures of non-cooperation and of inhibited and reluctant cooperation on the part of the child. Directing-interfering-criticism together with lack of contact from the mother yielded positive *r*'s from .42 to .62 with non-cooperation, with inhibited and reluctant cooperation, with a tendency toward high specificity of control, and with strong and aggressive stimulations and refusals by the child. Positive coefficients of the order of .6 were obtained between the mother's nonacceptance and the child's tendency to give strong and aggressive stimulations and refusals; strong and emotionally toned stimulations by the mother showed positive relationships of from .52 to .71 to negativism and to inhibited and reluctant cooperation on the part of the child.

Correlations ranging from +.43 to +.63 between categories of mother behavior indicated that the mothers who tended to remain out of contact with the child also tended to be more highly specific in their control and more unwilling to accept stimulations when interaction was in progress. Correlations of +.34 to +.44 between categories of child behavior suggested that the children who tended toward high specificity of control also tended to be more negativistic.

Analysis of the child's behavior from the first to the second session with the neutral adult yielded some significant differences. Evidence for generalization of the stimulus properties of the neutral adult from those of the mother was found in the case of the following child behavior categories: strong and aggressive stimulations, inhibited and reluctant cooperation, and non-cooperation. The direction of the change was a progressive increase from first to second session with the neutral adult to the average of the two sessions with the mother. In other words, as the child became more familiar with the neutral adult his behavior approached that displayed toward the mother. The children showed a trend toward differentiation of the stimulus properties of the neutral adult, as compared to the mother, in two types of behavior: asking permission, and directing-interfering-criticism. A decrease in asking permission occurred from the first to the second session with the neutral adult, which showed a correlation of +.41 with a tendency to give a high proportion of strong stimulations on the part of the mother. There was a significant increase in directing-interfering-criticism by the child from the first to the second session with the neutral adult which significantly exceeded in frequency that exhibited in the presence of the mother. This increase yielded positive correlations of from .33 to .42 with directing-interfering-criticism, strong stimulation, and lack-of-contact behavior patterns in the mother.

The order of testing with the adults did not affect these trends.

This study has presented a method for measuring the mother-child relationship under experimental conditions. It has also shown in broad outline some of the relationships which exist between mother and child behavior, viewed in terms of stimulus-response learning theory. Further research is needed to investigate these relationships in more detail and to discover other critical factors in this interactive relationship which are essential to the systematic understanding of personality development.

Validity and Constancy of Choices in a Sociometric Test

EUGENE BYRD

PROBLEM

THE PURPOSE of this study is to investigate the constancy of choice behavior as expressed on Moreno's sociometric tests and in a life situation. The degree to which observed choices in the life situation agree with reported choices on the sociometric test, when the criterion of choice is held constant, may be considered a measure of validity. In an effort to determine the degree of change in choice behavior that is known to occur over a period of time, the original sociometric test was readministered shortly following the observation of choosing in the life situation. Lack of validity would be indicated by a change greater than that expected and measured by the test-retest method.

BACKGROUND AND SETTING OF THE PROBLEM

The Moreno test has found extensive and intensive use in the fields of sociology, psychology, and education. Its fundamental purpose is to measure the social structure of a specified group. The sociometric test accomplishes this by requiring each individual of a specified group to select one or more individuals in that group on the basis of a stipulated criterion of choice. The standard method of obtaining choices in a sociometric test is the question-and-answer method (i.e., the individuals are asked to name their choices). These choices are usually written by the individual or, in cases of young children, may be written by the experimenter. Thus, by simply counting the total number of choices each individual receives from the other members of the group a rank order can be obtained and each in-

FROM *Sociometry*, 1951, 14, 175–181. Reprinted by permission of the publisher.

This study was made in connection with a research project being carried on under a grant from the Research Council of Florida State University.

dividual's relative position in that group may readily be ascertained. This is the basis of the group structure in sociometric studies.

The basic structure may be subdivided into groups of individuals on the basis of the number of choices received. Those individuals who receive the largest number of choices have been designated as *leaders, stars, most-chosen,* and *most-accepted.* Individuals receiving few or no choices have been called *isolates, unchosen, rejected, least-chosen,* and *least-accepted.* These names refer only to their sociometric status and may or may not agree with other behavioral criteria. One should use caution when using these terms to describe an individual as they are always relative to the group measured and the specific choice criteria used to determine the status. The status of an individual may also change and so an individual who is classified as an isolate on one sociometric test may not be so classified on another test or on the same test at a later date. It is important then to be able to know the degree of stability in sociometrically determined group status.

The following experiment was designed to investigate the validity of a sociometric test as measured by the degree to which observed choices agree with reported choices when the criterion of choice is held constant. In an effort to determine the expected degree of change in choice behavior the original sociometric test was readministered shortly following the observation of choosing in the life situation.

SUBJECTS

The subjects used in this experiment consist of twenty-seven pupils in the fourth grade class of the Florida State University Demonstration School. All subjects used in computing data were present at the administration of the sociometric tests.

METHODOLOGY

1. A sociometric test was administered to determine the group status. This test was of the paper and pencil type and the pupils wrote down their choices "privately." A single criterion of positive choice was used. No limit was set on the number of choices that could be expressed.

2. The subjects were next given the opportunity to make their choices in the life situation using the original choice criterion. On the basis of these choices group status was determined as in the sociometric test.

3. After all the subjects had expressed their choices in the life situation the original sociometric test was readministered and group status again determined.

PROCEDURE

Prior to administration of the first sociometric test the examiner was introduced to the class and with the help of the teacher discussed some of the things the children liked to do. Although the selection of presenting short psychodramas had been pre-selected by the examiner the suggestion of "doing some plays" came from the children themselves. The class then discussed some of the mechanics and manners that would be necessary for such plays. It was decided that the plays could be presented in the classroom with those not participating to act as an audience.

Situation I—The Sociometric Test

The examiner asked all the children to indicate the persons they would choose to be in their play.

When you give your play what classmates would you like to have in it? I want you to write down their names because you know them much better than I do. You may choose anyone you like and as many as you like. Write their names on the piece of paper you have. Miss B_______ or I will help you spell any names you need help with.

After the papers had been collected they were told:

You can be thinking about the play you would like to give. It may be about something you have done, something you are going to do, or about something you would like to do if you had the chance. It isn't necessary to write it all out but know what you want to do in case your turn comes first.

No further mention was made of their original choices.

Situation II—The Life Situation

After an interval of four days the dramas were presented at the average rate of two per one hour session; two sessions per week. No sessions were held when there were absences. Each child in turn was asked his choices privately by the examiner in order to obtain a higher degree of individual spontaneity and to avoid influence of a few individuals who exhibited obvious signs of wanting to be chosen in every play. No child with the exception of the last few knew when his turn would come.

After the choices were given, the examiner read off the names and those individuals chosen met in the corner of the room where the theme of the play and assigning of roles were given by each child who did the choosing. The play was then presented to the class. This procedure extended over an interval of eight weeks.

TABLE I

The Expression of Choices by a Fourth Grade in Three Situations Having the Same Choice Criterion

	CHOICES RECEIVED — PUPILS																											TOTAL CHOICES EXPRESSED SITUATION		
CHOICES EXPRESSED	AA	A	B	C	D	E	F	G	H	I	J	K	L	M	N	O	P	Q	R	S	T	U	V	W	X	Y	Z	I	II	III
AA		3	123		3	123	123	123	1		1 3	123		123				12										8	7	9
A	1 3		1	1 3		3				23		3				2	23				3		23					3	4	8
B	123	123		1 3	23	23	2	1		2		23					2											4	8	6
C	1 3	123			1	2	1			2					1 3	1	3							23			23	6	5	6
D	23	23	23			123	2		2			123	1					2	1									4	8	5
E	123	2	2		123		123	1	23			2						2	1									5	8	4
F	12	1	123		2	23		23	23		123	23		12				23										5	10	7
G	2	1					1 3				13	2		23							2		2					3	5	3
H	123	12			23	23				2		1 3					1											4	5	4
I	1 3	1 3	1 3	12	1	1 3		1			3	1 3			123		123	3	3	3					3		2	10	4	12
J	1		3		1 3	12	2	1 3	123			1						12										7	4	4
K	123	3	1 3	2	123	1	23		1 3									12										6	5	6
L	123	123	23				1				1	3			23		2				3				2			4	6	6
M	1 3	123	123	1	123	123	1 3		1	1		123			2													10	6	7
N	123	123	1 3			3			123	1	2		23									2			2			5	7	6
O	1 3	123	123	1	23						2	23						23				123						5	7	7
P	1 3	123	1		1	1				23			3			2							123					6	5	5
Q	123	23	123		23	2	12				23	23		1														4	8	6
R	3	3	1	1 3	123	1				3			3		1		2	2		123	2					2		6	6	7
S		123	1	1	1					123				1 3					123		12				123		23	9	6	6
T	1 3	123	3	1			23						1 2												3			4	3	5
U	3	123	3	1 3					12				1	2	1	123		23										6	5	6
V	1 3	1 3		123				123		2			3				123				3			2				5	5	7
W	1	12	2	23		1				1	1		1		3			2			2	3				3	3	6	5	5
X	1 3	123	1 3	2	2					12		2			2					1 3	3							5	6	5
Y	123	123	12		2	3				3	3		3				23	2					2					3	7	7
Z	123	123	123	1				1		123	1		1	1		123				3	1			1 3				12	5	7
TOTAL CHOICES REC'D I	21	19	15	11	9	9	7	6	6	6	6	6	5	5	4	3	3	3	3	2	2	1	1	1	1	0	0	155		
II	12	18	11	5	11	9	8	3	6	9	4	10	2	4	4	4	7	11	1	1	4	2	4	2	3	1	4		160	
III	21	20	15	6	10	10	6	4	5	6	6	11	5	3	4	2	5	4	2	4	4	2	2	2	3	1	3			166

Situation III—The Sociometric Retest

One week after the last drama was presented a second sociometric test was given. The children were told they would have an opportunity to give another play. The original sociometric test procedure was then repeated.

RESULTS

The choices made in all three situations are presented in Table 1. The subjects are listed in rank order of choices received on the first sociometric test in Situation I. The vertical columns contain the choices received. The horizontal rows contain the choices expressed. The numbers 1, 2, and 3 indicate the situation in which a choice was expressed. For example, pupil AA chose pupil B in all three situations. These choices are indicated by 1-2-3- under B's name. Since B also chose AA in all three situations these choices are indicated with 1-2-3- under AA's name. Individual totals in each situation, of choices received, and choices made are indicated.

CONSTANCY OF CHOICE EXPRESSION

The total number of choices made by the group are: Situation 1, 155; Situation II, 160; Situation III, 166. As a group the *number* of choices made tends to remain constant over a two month period.

In order to determine the extent to which the subjects choose the *same* individuals in any two situations a ratio was computed between the number of choices repeated in any two situations and the total number of choices expressed by the group in one of those situations. These results are presented in Table 2.

TABLE 2

Constancy of Choice Expression as Measured by Repeated Choices

SITUATION *	TOTAL NUMBER OF CHOICES MADE BY GROUP	CHOICE REPEATED		
		IN SITUATION	NUMBER	PERCENT
I	155	II	73	47
I	155	III	89	57
I	155	II & III	58	37
II	160	I	73	46
II	160	III	93	58
II	160	I & III	58	36
III	166	I	89	54
III	166	II	93	56
III	166	I & II	58	35

* Situation I—Sociometric Test
Situation II—Life Situation
Situation III—Sociometric Retest

Of 155 choices expressed in the original sociometric test (Situation I) 73 (47 percent) were reexpressed for the same individuals in the life situation (Situation II). Of 155 choices expressed in Situation I, 89 (57 percent) were reexpressed for the same individuals on the readministration of the sociometric test (Situation III). Of 160 choices expressed in the life situation 93 (58 percent) were expressed for the same individuals on the sociometric retest. Of 155 choices on the original sociometric test 58 (37 percent) were expressed for the same individuals in *both* the life situation and the sociometric retest.

These figures show that as a group about half of the choices expressed are for the same individuals from one situation to another regardless of whether they are written on paper or expressed in a life situation. This would suggest that the choice criterion was not psychologically different between the two situations as reflected by the group. How does this change in expression of choices affect the group status?

CONSTANCY OF CHOICE STATUS

In order to measure the degree of constancy of the group status from one situation to another the Spearman Rank-Difference correlation method was used.[1] Tied scores were given a common rank equal to the mean of the ranks involved. The coefficients found are as follows:

Situation I and II	Rho = .76 ± .09
Situation II and III	Rho = .80 ± .08
Situation I and III	Rho = .89 ± .04

If a t ratio of 2.0 is allowed then these three coefficients are not statistically significantly different. The coefficient of .89 ± .04 between the sociometric test-retest is relatively high. It also reflects the change in choice behavior we might expect from the changes observed in the expression of choices. Group status cannot change unless individuals change in their expression of choices. However, it is conceivable and likely that status is more stable than expression of choices. Leaders tend to remain leaders even though their choosers may vary. No attempt is made to demonstrate this hypothesis in this study.

It was stated that in order to measure validity of a sociometric test by observing the choice behavior in the life situation one must be prepared to measure the expected change in choice behavior that would occur during the interval between measurements. If the correlation between the sociometric test-retest is taken as a measure of this change then any increase in

[1] This method yields a coefficient designated by the Greek letter rho. For all practical purposes it is equivalent to the Pearson r. In no case does r exceed rho by more than .018. For the formulae and computation of rho and its standard error see Guilford, (1, pp. 227–231).

change in choice behavior due to lack of validity would tend to lower the coefficients of correlation between the sociometric tests and the life situation. It can be seen that these are lower but, as stated, not significantly so. This data suggests that there is little indication that change in choice behavior as measured by a sociometric test is due to lack of validity in the test. The greater part of the change is probably due to the dynamic aspect of choice behavior *per se*. This study should only be considered as exploratory. Only one group of children and one choice criterion were used. Further study is needed using other choice criteria and other groups differing in degree of cohesion before more decisive conclusions regarding the validity of sociometric tests are reached. Other methods of measuring validity that are not influenced by the intrinsic change should be investigated.

SUMMARY AND CONCLUSIONS

This study investigates the constancy of choice behavior as expressed on Moreno tests and in a life situation using the same choice criterion. This method is offered as an approach to the study of validity in sociometric tests. The sociometric test was readministered after choices were expressed in the life situation to determine the degree of expected change in choice behavior. The results of this study suggest that when a choice criterion has real meaning to the subjects, the degree of change in choice behavior between a sociometric test and a life situation is not significantly greater than that which occurs between a sociometric test and later readministration of the same test. The writer feels that the results of this study support the hypothesis that a sociometric test is valid insofar as the choice criterion has reality value for the subjects.

REFERENCE

1. Guilford, J. P. *Fundamental statistics in psychology and education.* New York: McGraw-Hill, 1942.

The Consistency of Subject Behavior and the Reliability of Scoring in Interaction Process Analysis

EDGAR F. BORGATTA
and
ROBERT F. BALES

WORK carried out by Bales and associates at Harvard has indicated that the *between observer reliability* (for highly skilled observers) by session by scoring category for initiated behavior is acceptably high, with correlations ranging between .75 and .95, depending on the scoring category (2). It may reasonably be inferred that for comparable conditions self-self observer reliability will be equally high or higher. For the self-self observer reliability to be lower, it would require, essentially, that the non-systematic errors of two observers consistently be in the same direction, which is relatively unlikely.

Adequate tests of self-self observer reliabilities will have to wait until series of standardized materials (such as films) are produced for scoring and then rescoring (test-retest). Tests of self-self observer reliability are restricted at present to recordings and written protocols. Experience in both these as reported by Bales and associates is satisfactory, but actual formal tests have been extremely limited since the demands on the observ-

FROM *American Sociological Review*, 1953, 18, 566–569. Reprinted by permission of the authors and publisher.

This research was supported in part by the United States Air Force under contract number AF 33(038)–12782 monitored by the Human Resources Research Institute, Maxwell Air Force Base, Alabama. Permission is granted for reproduction, translation, publication and disposal in whole or in part by or for the United States Government.

ers have been sufficiently great that repeat scoring is ordinarily defined as a luxury item. Repeat scoring by trainees has usually demonstrated satisfactory reliabilities after three to four months of relatively intensive training. In a recent research project with the Air Force, one observer (Borgatta) required estimates of self-self reliability with written protocols. The protocols were responses to the *Conversation Study*, a projective-type form in which ten pictures (depicting three-man groups) are presented and the subject is asked to write the conversation which is going on. The ordinary writing time is two hours. The *Conversation Study* forms of

TABLE 1

CATEGORY	TEST-RETEST PEARSON R.
1	.98
2	.93
3	.96
4	.81
5	.92
6	.96
7	.89
8	.65
9	.83
10	.70
11	.92
12	.88
Total	.92

eight subjects were scored and then rescored after an interval of more than four weeks. The scorer had had about four months of training at the time. The Pearsonian correlations are indicated in Table 1. Results of this order, while fairly satisfactory, are not considered to represent the best practically attainable. With greater experience specific improvement would be expected in terms of the establishment of more arbitrary criteria for making decisions, especially in terms of the categories in which known confusion of placement occurs.

It would appear, thus, that researchers may plan to utilize formal scoring techniques such as Bales' Interaction Process Analysis (1) with a reasonable confidence that training will produce observers who are reliable (or consistently arbitrary) in their scoring. A second question of reliability has not been considered in relation to Interaction Process Analysis, and this is that of the reliability of the "test" or *the consistency of the observed phenomena.* In raising this question it should be noted immediately that researchers working with the observation of groups would be greatly disturbed if they found extremely high reliability of the "test" or consistency of the observed phenomena under conditions which they suppose must vary. This is especially obvious in the analysis of phase changes within a given session, session to session changes, and more generally, in the expectations (or hypotheses) concerning the development of structure in the group over time. On the other hand, if common elements exist in the conditions under which the behavior occurs (i.e., the task, subjects, size of groups, etc.), a certain degree of consistency in the interaction pattern may be expected. It is apparent that in this type of study the term "reliability of the test" becomes inapplicable and the more correct identification is the "consistency of the observed phenomena." Few data have been produced in this area, although data which may be so analyzed in the future are currently being collected by Bales. Interest in the consistency of performance of subjects led to a limited treatment of some data in Bales' files. Five sets of data, each consisting of two or four sessions in which the same persons participated were analyzed to ascertain the stability with which each person maintained his position in relation to the other members of the session. In the case of four sessions, sessions 1 and 3, and 2 and 4, were combined directly. (A minor error is introduced in that the sessions were not exactly of the same length. This could have been corrected by conversion to time rates, but the additional work did not seem warranted by the additional accuracy which would have been evident.) The Pearsonian correlations are indicated in Table 2. The variance expected in correlations with such small N's is large, and in addition to this, the number of scores in certain categories is quite small as in the case with category 2. At the same time, the general picture of the correlations indicates that a positive

TABLE 2

NUMBER OF PARTICIPANTS (N)	3	5	5	4	5
NUMBER OF SESSIONS	2	2	4	4	4
Category 1	.40	—.14	.58	.26	.13
2	—.62	.67	.94	—.15	.50
3	.93	.91	.70	.95	.73
4	.26	.79	.83	.84	—.13
5	.87	.84	.94	.91	.58
6	.80	.79	.98	—.01	.76
7	.97	.39	.86	.01	.33
8	.92	.27	.99	.96	.19
9	—.03	.01	.33	.97	.61
10	—.53	.68	.69	.97	.74
11	.02	.85	.78	.89	.23
12	.00	—.25	.96	.00	1.00
Total	.99	.96	.85	.92	.56

relationship exists between the behavior of the same subject from one time to another in all the categories. This is not a sufficient test of the stability of individual performance, but is sufficiently good to give the researcher some confidence. The correlations may be viewed as depressed by certain known factors (session to session changes, development of a status hierarchy, task changes, and many additional "interference" factors).

Again, in connection with a research project for the Air Force, a sample of 126 subjects was observed, using Bales' scoring system. The sample was subdivided into 14 batches of nine subjects each. Within a batch of nine, each subject participated in groups of three four times, each session consisting of 48 minutes of observation time. Each subject participated with each of the eight other subjects of the batch of nine, two at a time. Each session was divided into six units of time and two general types of activity as follows:

Actual behavior–get acquainted–six minutes
Actual behavior–plan role playing–six minutes
Role playing behavior–role playing–twelve minutes
Actual behavior–plan role playing–six minutes
Role playing behavior–role playing–twelve minutes
Actual behavior–relax–six minutes

Data were collected by time unit, permitting collation under several plans. The "*actual behavior*" of each subject consisted of four units of six minutes each for each of four sessions (a total of 96 minutes). Each session involved the same type of task, but presented a different *social* situation for the subject since in each session he participated with two new persons for the first time. The 126 subjects may thus be examined under similar conditions for the stability (or consistency) of their social behavior (as scored by the Bales system) which may be attributable to individual personality factors. The stability of subjects was examined by two plans: (1) The patterns of behavior of the subjects in sessions one and three, and two and four, were combined and correlated. In this case we compare the behavior of the same individual in two situations with two other situations, masking changes that may be present within sessions and revealing stability between sessions that may be present (in the behavior of the individual) in spite of the fact that different persons are present in the group. (2) In the second plan we compare the behavior of the same subject in one half of each of the four sessions with his behavior in the other half, thus masking the changes between sessions and revealing the stability over time within sessions when the same two other persons are present. The correlations for initiated actual, initiated role playing, received actual, and received role playing behavior are indicated in Table 3.

The plan (1) correlations are ordinarily lower than the plan (2) correlations. This may be interpreted as evidence for the hypothesis that a

TABLE 3

Stability of Subjects by Category by Type of Behavior Observed (126 Subjects)

	INITIATED ROLE-PLAYING		INITIATED ACTUAL		RECEIVED ROLE-PLAYING		RECEIVED ACTUAL	
	PLAN (2)	PLAN (1)	PLAN (2)	PLAN (1)	PLAN (2)	PLAN (1)	PLAN (2)	PLAN (1)
Category								
1	.38	.33	.30	.23	.40	.23	.28	.26
2	.60	.15	.79	.43	.30	.25	.71	.14
3	.79	.64	.76	.63	.64	.22	.70	.41
4	.50	.46	.71	.61	.43	.31	.59	.34
5	.67	.47	.80	.59	.56	.29	.68	.49
6	.66	.65	.72	.57	.41	.28	.53	.29
7	.49	.28	.53	.53	.22	.13	.18	.07
8	.48	.46	.37	.34	.21	.14	.16	.09
9	.43	.13	.21	.00	.26	.08	.09	.10
10	.47	.44	.51	.32	.51	.31	.54	.27
11	.56	.34	.72	.43	.56	.29	.54	.36
12	.62	.11	.61	.02	.35	.13	.56	.10
Total	.79	.63	.81	.57	.57	.33	.78	.50

person will be more consistent, given the same amount of time, when interacting with the same individuals than when interacting with different individuals. The stability of subjects shown is sufficient to encourage us to believe that the interaction of an individual, as scored by this system, may tell us something about his personality, in spite of peculiarities due to the fact that he is interacting with particular other persons.

REFERENCES

1. Bales, R. F. *Interaction process analysis.* Cambridge, Mass.: Addison-Wesley, 1950.
2. Heinicke, C., & Bales, R. F. Developmental trends in the structure of small groups. *Sociometry*, 1953, 16, 7–38.

Recording and Evaluating the Performance of Individuals as Members of Small Groups

LAUNOR F. CARTER

THE MANY techniques for assessing individuals range from the simplest paper and pencil devices to intensive clinical appraisal. In the past few years there has been increasing interest in evaluating individuals in small group situations. Such assessment is thought to allow an exceptional opportunity to evaluate certain characteristics which are uniquely prominent in group interaction.

The major problem to be discussed in this paper attempts to answer one question, namely: What are the characteristics which can be evaluated by observing people interacting? In the use of small group observational techniques it seems probable that some such process as the following often occurs. The experimenter has a hypothesis he wishes to investigate. He desires to test this hypothesis in terms of variables he thinks observable in group behavior, and proceeds to develop a list of rating categories. Thus, in a study of leaders' behavior, my colleagues and I (1) attempted to rate nineteen variables such as the individual's cooperation, efficiency, confidence, prestige, insight, initiative, and leadership. During the last war the OSS Assessment Staff (7) tried to rate ten variables such as effective intelligence, leadership, interest, motivation, energy, and initiative. Recently, Hemphill and Coons (4) described leaders' behavior in terms of nine dimensions. Wherry (6) has described Army officers' behavior in terms of thirteen dimensions. Each group of investigators has attempted to examine "logically" the dimensions of behavior which might be observed, and then to build some instruments for recording this behavior. While good semantic distinctions can be made among quite a large number of sup-

FROM *Personnel Psychology*, 1954, 7, 477–484. Reprinted by permission of the author and publisher.

posed dimensions of behavior, the major theme of this paper will be that the actual number of dimensions which can be assessed is quite small. It will be contended that in assessing the behavior of individuals participating in small groups or situational tests, probably only three or at most four independent dimensions of behavior can be evaluated.

There are a number of empirical studies which support such a view. Arthur Couch and I (3) have some evidence suggesting that only three factors are needed to account for the variance obtained in ratings made on nineteen variables. We asked observers to make ratings on aggressiveness, cooperativeness, sociability, leadership, submissiveness, authoritarianism, task orientation, talkativeness, and many other logically distinguishable characteristics. It soon became apparent that our observers could not clearly distinguish nineteen independent characteristics in the subjects' behavior, although a logically sound case could be made that each variable represented a somewhat different way of behaving. Our problem was to discover how many psychologically independent factors need be defined to account for the variance in the nineteen ratings.

College men were formed into groups of eight or four members, and run on three different tasks: a reasoning task, a mechanical assembly task, and a discussion task. Some of the groups were run in emergent situations, and others in situations where the leader was appointed. At the end of each task, two independent observers rated the subject on the nineteen variables. Tables of intercorrelations of the trait characteristics for groups run under these conditions were obtained and factor analyzed. The main question we wished to answer was: How many factors are needed to account for most of the variance contained in the nineteen ratings?

In spite of considerable variation in group size, kind of task, and leadership practice, essentially the same factorial structure was found in each analysis. In all the analyses, three factors emerged. Table 1 shows the items which have higher loadings for each factor. The name given each factor is in capital letters, while the ratings identifying the factor appear under the factor name. This factorial composition came out essentially the same for eight independent analyses of group situations which differed in size, kind of task, and leadership structure. From an inspection of the factor loadings and their structure, the factors were identified as follows:

Factor I: Individual Prominence—the dimension of behavior which is interpreted as indicating the prominence of that individual as he stands out from the group. The behavior associated with the traits of aggressiveness, leadership, confidence, and striving for individual recognition seems to have a common element which is interpreted as the member's attempting to achieve individual recognition from the group.

Factor II: Group Goal Facilitation—the dimension of behavior which is interpreted as being effective in achieving the goal toward which the group is oriented. Efficiency, adaptability, cooperation, etc., all seem to have a common element which facilitates group action in solving the group's task.

TABLE I

Dimensions of Individual Behavior Observable in Small Groups

INVESTIGATOR	FACTOR I	FACTOR II	FACTOR III
Couch and Carter	INDIVIDUAL PROMINENCE	GROUP GOAL FACILITATION	GROUP SOCIABILITY
(Small groups. Ratings.)	Authoritarianism Confidence Aggressiveness Leadership Striving for recognition	Efficiency Cooperation Adaptability Pointed toward group solution	Sociability Adaptability Pointed toward group acceptance
Sakoda	PHYSICAL ENERGY	INTELLIGENCE	SOCIAL ADJUSTMENT
(OSS data. Various situations. Overall ratings.)	Energy and initiative Physical ability Leadership	Effective intelligence Observing and reporting Propaganda skills	Social relations Emotional stability "Security"
Hemphill and Coons	OBJECTIVE ATTAINMENT	GROUP INTERACTION FACILITATION	MAINTENANCE OF MEMBERSHIP
(Leader's behavior described by group members and leaders.)	"Related to output" "Initiation and organization"	"Enable group members to recognize their function"	"Behavior which is socially agreeable to group members"
Wherry	FORCEFUL LEADERSHIP AND INITIATIVE	PROPER ATTITUDE TOWARD JOB	SUCCESSFUL INTERPERSONAL RELATIONS
(Items describing Army officers' behavior completed by other officers.)	Bold Forceful Not timid Quick to take the lead JOB COMPETENCE AND PERFORMANCE Competent Alert Persevering	Sincere Helpful Cooperative	Genial Cordial Well liked
Clark	INDIVIDUAL PERFORMANCE	GROUP ORIENTATION	SOCIAL RELATIONS
(Sociometric items from combat squads.)	Scrounger Squad leader Cheerful	Helpful Work with Patrol with Share bunker with	Go on pass with
SUMMARY DESCRIPTION	INDIVIDUAL PROMINENCE AND ACHIEVEMENT	AIDING ATTAINMENT BY GROUP	SOCIABILITY

Factor III: Group Sociability—the dimension of behavior which is interpreted as indicating the positive social interaction of an individual in the group. The traits heavily loaded in this factor—sociability, striving for group acceptance, and adaptability—all have a common element which represents a friendly interpersonal behavior pattern of the individual toward the other group members.

The work of other investigators supports such a three dimensional interpretation. A short review of several relevant reports follows. The OSS Assessment Staff rated each participant on ten different variables. When Sakoda (5) factor analyzed the table of intercorrelations for these ratings, he also found that three factors accounted for the ten rating variables. His results are indicated on the table. While Sakoda has named these dimensions somewhat differently than we have, they seem to be similar in composition.

Hemphill and Coons (4) have recently published a monograph in which they describe the behavior of leaders. First they constructed a large number of items and had various group members rate the behavior of their group leaders. They also had leaders rate their own behavior. Members of the research staff then sorted the behavior descriptions into ten *a priori* dimensions. These dimensions were factor analyzed, and again three factors were obtained as indicated in the table.

Likewise in a study by Wherry (6), a limited number of dimensions were found. Several hundred Army officers each rated an immediate subordinate on 292 items describing the characteristics of the subordinate. The items were then sorted into thirteen logically distinct categories. The relationship of the items in these thirteen categories was analyzed by the Wherry-Gaylord Iterative Process. Wherry says, "After approximately four iterations in each case, the staff was surprised to discover that the items selected on the thirteen scales fell roughly into three groups or patterns." Feeling that more dimensions should be found, Wherry performed additional analyses. He reports, "Iteration of the (new) group of items resulted in a subtest which contained several new items. It was also tending to iterate toward one of the three groups, but iteration was stopped before it reached that stage. . . ." Here again, as can be seen in the table, three factors were found while a weak fourth one may have emerged.

Last winter a group led by Rodney Clark (2) studied rifle squads on the main line of resistance in Korea. As a part of the study, each squad member made sociometric choices relative to ten different activities. The choices were tabulated by item and the intercorrelation between types of activities obtained. As shown in the table, three factors were obtained, although the third factor is not well defined.

These studies point forcefully to the conclusion that descriptions of the behavior of individuals working in groups can be categorized into three dimensions. These same dimensions seem to be found whether the descriptions are made from the immediate observation of people working together, or from sociometric material, or from one individual describing the past behavior of another. It is quite possible to logically distinguish among a large number of disparate categories describing such behavior, but when reports of actual observations are obtained they can all be adequately included in three dimensions. It seems that these three dimensions can be described as follows:

FACTOR I: *Individual Prominence and Achievement*

These are behaviors of the individual related to his efforts to stand out from others and individually achieve various personal goals.

FACTOR II: *Aiding Attainment by the Group*

These are behaviors of the individual related to his efforts to assist the group in achieving goals toward which the group is oriented.

FACTOR III: *Sociability*

These are behaviors of the individual related to efforts to establish and maintain cordial and socially satisfying relations with other group members.

The implication of these conclusions for the rating of individuals in situational tests seems clear. Whatever system of rating is to be used, it should be designed to obtain a reliable estimate of each individual's behavior relative to these three factors. A large number of techniques have been employed to describe individuals' behavior in small groups. These techniques include subjective descriptions, rating scales, descriptive items, and recordings of the minutia of behavior. No general statement regarding the best methods can be made since the technique to be used depends upon the purpose for which the assessment is made and the degree of training and competence of the observers. Unfortunately, time does not permit a discussion of the advantages and limitations of the different systems.

There will be objection that, if assessment is to be made on the basis of the three factors proposed, it will not be possible to make statements regarding many customarily rated qualities, such as leadership, for example. After all, the impetus for situational testing has developed from leadership assessment. The results cited indicate that leadership is not a unitary trait, rather the behaviors usually subsumed under the term leadership seem to involve loadings on both Factor I, Individual Prominence, and Factor II, Group Goal Facilitation. In the Couch and Carter study the largest leadership loading was on Factor I, with a smaller loading on Factor II. In Sakoda's study, leadership was about equally loaded on these two factors, as it was in Clark's study. Leadership did not show a significant loading on the third factor, Group Sociability, in any of these studies. Thus it appears that leadership is not a single basic dimension but a composite of behaviors related to individual prominence and achievement, and of behaviors related to assisting the group in achieving group goals.

In conclusion, it seems apparent that the interaction behavior of individuals involved in small group situations can be adequately described by three factors. Using these three factors simplifies the conceptual problem of describing individual behavior, and may also clarify thinking regarding such concepts as leadership.

REFERENCES

1. Carter, L. F., Haythorn, W., Meirowitz, B., & Lanzetta, J. The relation of categorizations and ratings in the observation of group behavior. *Hum. Relat.*, 1951, 4, 239–254.
2. Clark, R. A. Analyzing the group structure of combat rifle squads. *Amer. Psychol.*, 1953, 8, 333.
3. Couch, A., & Carter, L. F. A factorial study of the rated behavior of group members. Paper read at meeting of Eastern Psychological Association, March 1952.
4. Hemphill, J., & Coons, A. *Leader behavior description.* Columbus: Personnel Research Board, Ohio State Univer., (undated).
5. Sakoda, J. M. Factor analysis of OSS situational tests. *J. abnorm. soc. Psychol.*, 1952, 47, 843–852.
6. Wherry, R. J. *Factor analysis of officer qualification form QCL-2B.* Columbus: Ohio State Univer. Research Foundation, 1950.
7. Office of Strategic Services Assessment Staff. *Assessment of men.* New York: Rinehart, 1948.

The Influence of Individual Members on the Characteristics of Small Groups

WILLIAM HAYTHORN

THERE has been increased emphasis in social psychology recently on the description and measurement of group characteristics. Hemphill and Westie (10) and Cattell and Wispé (6) have been particularly concerned with isolating dimensions along which groups vary. However,

FROM *Journal of Abnormal and Social Psychology*, 1953, 48, 276–284. Reprinted by permission of the author and the American Psychological Association, Inc.

The work described in this paper was done under a contract between the U.S. Navy, Office of Naval Research, and the University of Rochester. This is the eighth paper resulting from that work, and is a revision of a portion of a doctoral dissertation presented at the University of Rochester in 1952 (9). The work was under the general supervision of Dr. Launor F. Carter. Drs. Beatrice Shriver and John Lanzetta rendered invaluable service as observers and informal consultants.

little has been done to relate these group characteristics to the behavior of group members.

Cattell (4) has suggested that leadership be defined in terms of the effect the individual has on group "syntality," and has further hypothesized that each member of a group contributes something to the characteristics of the group. Redl (14) has discussed leadership in terms of the "central person" around whom group formative processes occur, the implication being that the central person is the primary factor in determining the nature of the group.

Other writers (12, 13, 15) in the area of group dynamics have theorized that group characteristics grow out of social interaction in the group, but to the author's knowledge there have been no experimental studies specifically focused on the relationships between the behavior of individual group members and the characteristics of the group. The present study attempts to explore some of these relationships.

METHOD

In order to isolate the effects an individual has on groups, it is necessary to have him work in several groups with different co-workers. Our experimental design, presented in Table 1, permits isolating the effect each subject (*S*) had on his groups, since each *S* worked in five unique groups; that is, no other *S* worked in more than one of them.

TABLE 1

Experimental Design

SESSION	GROUPS *			
1	ABCD	EFGH	IJKL	MNOP
2	AEIM	BFJN	CGKO	DHLP
3	AFKP	BELO	CHIN	DGJM
4	AGLN	BHKM	CEJP	DFIO
5	AHJO	BGIP	CFLM	DEKN

* Letters represent *S*s.

The *S*s were NROTC sophomores, all of whom volunteered and were paid one dollar per hour. They were brought to the laboratory in groups of four and asked to work on three different tasks—reasoning (R), mechanical assembly (MA), and discussion (D). The R and MA tasks are similar to those described in a previous publication (2). That is, the R task involved group solution of syllogistic reasoning problems, and the MA task involved building various structures from precut and predrilled lumber. Both tasks required a high degree of group participation and coordination. For the D task, TAT pictures were presented and the *S*s were asked to compose a story as a group (9, 11). This invariably touched off an active, lively discussion. Group agreement was required.

While the *S*s were working on the tasks, two observers (*O*s) independently watched and recorded behavior by a new recording technique, reported by Carter, *et al.* (3), in which the observers "categorize" and "type out" behavior as it occurs. At the end of each task the *O*s rated the *S*s on twelve behavioral characteristics such as cooperativeness, aggressiveness, and efficiency. Reliability of rating scales ranged from .10 (cooperativeness on the MA task) to .98 with an average reliability of .86.

At the end of the session, both *S*s and *O*s rated the group on eleven group characteristics such as morale, productivity, and cohesiveness. The average interobserver reliability for these ratings was .70, with a range from .20 to .92. The average correlation between ratings by *O*s and by *S*s, which provides another kind of reliability measure, was .64. Although these reliabilities are lower than one would wish, they are considered high enough to make the ratings of some value in an exploratory study such as this one.

In addition, the *S*s were asked to select the best and poorest leaders in the group, as well as the person with whom they liked best to work and the person with whom they liked least to work. Finally, after all groups had been run, *S*s were asked to fill out the Cattell Sixteen Personality Factor Questionnaire (5).

There were, then, the following measures of the behavior of individual group members:

1. The number of choices and rejections received by each *S* from his 15 co-workers on the two choice criteria. Because these were highly intercorrelated, a single measure of choice value was computed for each *S* by simply combining the two measures.
2. The ratings by two independent *O*s of each *S* on 12 variables on each of 3 tasks.
3. The behavioral or interaction categories recorded by *O*s for each *S*.
4. Scores on each of the 16 personality factors of the Cattell questionnaire.

For measures of characteristics of groups in which each *S* worked, two sets of scores were computed:

1. The ratings of group characteristics by each of the *S*'s 15 co-workers were summed. Thus, from Table 1 it can be seen that the average cohesiveness of groups in which subject A worked can be determined by summing the ratings of group cohesiveness by *S*s B_1, C_1, D_1, E_2, I_2, M_2, F_3, K_3, P_3, G_4, L_4, N_4, H_5, J_5, and O_5. The numeral subscripts indicate the session number.
2. The ratings of group characteristics by *O*s were summed over the five groups in which each *S* worked. The average morale, for example, of groups in which subject E worked can be determined by summing the ratings of group morale by the *O*s for groups EFGH, AEIM, BELO, CEJP, and DEKN.

RESULTS

Relationships between Ss' "Choice Values" and Characteristics of Groups in Which They Worked

Each *S*'s choice value was determined by counting all of the choices received by him from his co-workers, and subtracting from that all the rejections he received. Correlation coefficients between these scores and the average ratings of characteristics of groups in which each *S* worked (described above) were computed, and are presented in Table 2. The correlations with co-workers' ratings of group characteristics indicate statistically significant relationships between the degree to which an *S* was chosen by his co-workers and the extent to which co-workers rated groups in which he worked as high in morale, cooperativeness, cohesiveness, motivation, and interest in job completion. These results suggest

TABLE 2

Correlations between Subjects' Total Sociometric Scores and Ratings of Characteristics of Groups in which Subjects Worked

(N=16)

GROUP CHARACTERISTICS RATED	SOURCE OF RATINGS	
	CO-WORKERS	OBSERVERS
1. Talkativeness	—.24	.03
2. Morale	.68	.56
3. Competitiveness	—.10	—.18
4. Cooperativeness	.69	.38
5. Productivity	.36	.29
6. Cohesiveness	.52	.19
7. Motivation	.67	.27
8. Friendliness	.31	.09
9. Activity	.24	.14
10. Job Completion	.59	.49
11. Social Interaction	.30	.11

$r_{.05} = .49; r_{.10} = 43.$

that individuals who are highly chosen by co-workers "facilitate" group functioning, and that individuals who "depress" group functioning are not generally chosen by other members of the group. A possible alternative interpretation is that, since co-workers' ratings of group characteristics are correlated with co-workers' choices of group members, the results simply reflect halo in the co-workers' ratings. The former interpretation, however, is supported by the statistically significant correlations between *Ss*' choice-value scores and ratings by *Os* of group morale and interest in job completion.

Relationships between Rated Behavior of Ss and Rated Characteristics of Groups in Which Ss Worked

The preceding results suggest that highly chosen persons contribute to characteristics indicative of "smooth" group functioning. In order to determine what kinds of *behavior* facilitate or depress each of the group characteristics rated, correlations were computed between the average ratings of each *S* by the *O*s on each of the 12 behavioral traits and the ratings by co-workers of the characteristics of groups in which the *S*s worked.[1]

How the standard error of *r* should be determined is difficult to ascertain. There was an *N* of only 16 *S*s, but each *S* was observed in five different groups. An *N* of 80 gives an underestimation of standard error, since there were not 80 independent measures. An *N* of 16 gives an equally inaccurate overestimate of standard error, since there were 16 clusters of five scores each in the computations. However, since the latter gives a more conservative estimate, it was adopted.

With an *N* of 16 it is obvious that not many of the relationships are statistically significant. However, there are many factors depressing these correlations. For one thing, both sets of ratings include considerable error variance, and no correction for attenuation has been applied. Secondly, the correlations are between ratings of limited aspects of the *S*s' behavior and ratings of equally limited aspects of the group's characteristics. Presumably the *S*'s total behavioral pattern interacts with the total group in a more complicated manner than that indicated by these correlations. In the third place, the correlations indicate relationships between the rated behavior of single *S*s and the rated characteristics of groups in which the *S*s worked. It is more probable that the nature of a group is related to the behavior of all members and to the interaction between members. In view of this, and of the exploratory nature of the study, examining the obtained correlations for any suggested trends seems justified.

To discuss each of the correlations would be a tedious task, and would involve much repetition since the behavioral ratings are not completely independent. Carter and Couch (1) have factor analyzed ratings of similar traits rated under similar laboratory conditions, and have identified three factors which have been labelled Group Goal Facilitation, I; Striving for Individual Prominence, II; and Group Sociability, III. These factor analyses have been done with data from several experiments, using various *O*s and groups of various sizes and structures. There is, therefore, considerable reason to believe that most of the variance in the present 12 traits can be accounted for by the same three factors. Because of this, it is desirable to summarize the present results in terms of the factors.

If attention is directed to only those correlations significant at the .10 level or better, a definite pattern is evident. Of the 35 statistically significant correlations, 27 are between Factor I traits—cooperativeness, prestige, efficiency, and insight—and group characteristics indicating a smooth group functioning. Group morale, for instance, was correlated .66 with individual cooperativeness on the D task, .45 with prestige on the MA task, .52 with efficiency on the MA task, .47 with efficiency on the D task, .48 with insightfulness on the MA task, and .45 with insightfulness on the D task. The only other trait significantly related to group morale was

1 The table of correlations appears in detail in the original article.

leadership (.47 on the D task). This suggests that Factor I behavior as seen by *O*s "facilitated" group morale as seen by co-workers.

Similarly, co-workers' ratings of group cooperativeness correlated .47 with individual cooperativeness on the D task, .42 with prestige on the R task, .47 with prestige on the MA task, .48 with efficiency on the R task, .54 with efficiency on the MA task, .45 with efficiency on the D task, and .53 with insightfulness on the MA task. Factor I behavior, then, apparently facilitated group cooperativeness.

Group motivation correlated .45 with ratings of prestige on the MA task, .54 with efficiency on the D task, and .48 with insightfulness on the MA task. Group interest in job completion correlated .43 with prestige on the MA task, and .45 with insightfulness on the MA task. These findings suggest that individuals whom *O*s rate as efficient, insightful, and having prestige also increase the motivation of other members of the group.

Group talkativeness, which *S*s apparently considered inefficient activity, was negatively related to individual prestige on the R task (−.54) and on the MA task (−.47); to individual efficiency on the R task (−.49), and on the MA task (−.58); and to individual insightfulness on the R task (−.54) and on the MA task (−.54). Factor I behavior on the R and MA tasks significantly "depressed" group talkativeness, as rated by *S*s' co-workers.

Prestige and efficiency on the R task were also positively related to group interest in social interaction (.42 and .49 respectively). It would seem from all these *r*'s that when one member of a group engaged in a high degree of "group goal-facilitating" behavior, the entire group functioned better in terms of the measures obtained.

Group friendliness, however, was negatively related to most of the individual traits rated. Factor II traits—aggressiveness, initiative, confidence, authoritarianism, interest in individual solution, and leadership—tended especially to depress group friendliness. This factor—striving for individual prominence—seems to be somewhat similar to the self-oriented need behavior described by Fouriezos, Hutt, and Guetzkow (7). The finding that such behavior is negatively related to group friendliness is consistent with their finding that such behavior was negatively related to participant satisfaction with the meeting. Particularly relevant here is the correlation of −.56 between interest in individual solution and group friendliness.

There was some tendency for Factor III—sociability—to increase group talkativeness and interest in social interaction but the trend is not very significant statistically.

In summary it can be said that Factor I behavior—group goal-facilitation—was positively related to co-workers' ratings of group morale, cooperativeness, motivation, and interest in job completion. Factor II behavior—striving for individual prominence—tended to be negatively related to group friendliness. Factor III behavior—sociability—tended to be positively related to group talkativeness and interest in social interaction. Other specific findings, such as the correlation of .44 between individual submissiveness and group competitiveness, may suggest possible research leads for the future, but standing alone as they do here does not inspire much confidence in them.

Relationships between Personality Factors and Group Characteristics

It will be recalled that *S*s were given the Cattell Sixteen Personality Factor Questionnaire after all the groups had been run. Correlations were computed between scores on the 16 factors and ratings of group characteristics by *O*s (described above). These correlations are presented in Table 3.

TABLE 3

Correlations between Sixteen Personality Factor Questionnaire and Ratings of Group Characteristics by Observers

(N=16)

GROUP CHARACTERISTICS RATED	PERSONALITY FACTORS*										
	A	C	E	F	G	H	L	M	O	Q_2	Q_3
1. Morale	.24	.58				.10			−.49	−.11	
2. Competition	−.45										
3. Productivity	.17	.48	*−.16*	−.10	.19			−.61		.14	.41
4. Cohesiveness	.37		*.26*	.07		.29	−.69		−.33	*.15*	
5. Motivation		.27		−.25					−.26		
6. Friendliness			*.01*	.18		.17	−.57			−.33	
7. Job Completion		.43	*−.21*	−.21				−.43		.00	
8. Social Interaction			*.33*			.62				−.42	

$r_{.05} = .49$

* For descriptions of the personality factors, see the text and Cattell (5). Italics indicate cases in which the direction of the relationship was predicted incorrectly.

Before any of the correlations were computed, predictions were made about the directions of the relationships. The predictions were based chiefly on the general hypothesis that more mature, flexible, accepting persons would facilitate effective group functioning. A chi-square test of the hypothesis that there was no relationship between the predicted and computed signs of the correlations yielded a probability value of less than .001. That is, there is very little chance that the number of correct predictions resulted from chance. The alternate hypothesis that the directions of the relationships were predicted more accurately than chance by the general hypothesis stated must be considered tenable. The correlations in Table 3 therefore deserve a closer investigation. Only those correlations for which predictions were made were computed. Cases in which the direction of the relationship was incorrectly predicted are italicized. All of the 10 statistically significant correlations (.10 level) are in the expected directions.

Factor A, Cyclothymia vs. Schizothymia (Cattell's labelling), involves cooperativeness, trustfulness, and adaptability. The correlations are all in the expected directions, suggesting a tendency for groups in which A + *S*s worked to be rated as having high morale ($r=.24$), low competitiveness ($r=-.45$) and high cohesiveness ($r=.37$).

Factor C, Emotional Stability or Ego Strength vs. General Neuroticism, was expected to correlate positively with those group characteristics indicating efficient group functioning. The maturity and stability of high C *S*s were expected to lend stability and efficiency to groups in which C+ persons worked. The correlations between factor C scores and *O*s' ratings of group morale (.58), productivity (.48), and interest in job completion (.43) support these expectations.

Factor E, Dominance or Ascendance vs. Submission, was expected to be related positively to productivity and interest in job completion but negatively to group cohesiveness, friendliness, and interest in social interaction. All five correlations came out contrary to expectations. No satisfactory explanation of this prediction error has been achieved. The *S*s simply did not react to a dominant group member as the experimenter expected.

Factor F, Surgency vs. Desurgency, is said to describe persons "carefree, happy-go-lucky, fond of bustle and excitement, inclined to practical jokes and disinclined to occupations requiring close and accurate work" (5). It was predicted that scores on factor F would be positively related to ratings of group cohesiveness and friendliness, but negatively related to group productivity, motivation, and interest in job completion. The correlations are in the predicted directions, but low and insignificant.

Factor H, Adventurous Cyclothymia vs. Inherent Withdrawn Schizothymia, is described as a measure of the extent to which the respondent likes people. The expectation that factor H scores would be positively related to group cohesiveness and interest in social interaction was strongly supported by the correlations (.29 and .62 respectively).

Factor L, Paranoid Schizothymia vs. Trustful Accessibility, involves paranoid suspiciousness, jealousy, dourness, and rigidity. Persons scoring high on this factor were expected to depress group cohesiveness and friendliness. The correlations (−.69 and −.57 respectively) clearly tend to confirm this expectation.

Factor M, Bohemianism vs. Practical Concernedness, allegedly measures unconventionality, eccentricity and undependability. The M+ individual is described as one who "unconcernedly goes his own way in the community and does not feel much responsibility in practical matters"

(5). The correlations with *Os*' ratings of group productivity (−.61) and interest in job completion (−.43) lend strong support to the hypothesis that "practical, logical, conscientious" persons, low on factor M, facilitate group productivity while M+ individuals depress it.

Factor O, Worrying Suspiciousness vs. Calm Trustfulness, attempts to measure depressive tendencies, moodiness, etc. The correlations between factor O scores and *Os*' ratings of group morale (−.49), cohesiveness (−.33), and motivation (−.26) suggest that O+ persons detract from the pleasant feeling tone of the group.

Factor Q_2, Independent Self-Sufficiency vs. Lack of Resolution, is described as a measure of independence and resoluteness. A Q_2 person "prefers to work and make decisions in company with other people, likes social approval and admiration," etc. The correlations between factor Q_2 scores and *Os*' ratings of group friendliness (−.33) and interest in social interaction (−.42) suggest that individuals who are highly self-sufficient and do not particularly care for social approval tend to depress the social aspects of their groups.

In describing factor Q_3, Will Control and Character Stability, Cattell writes that ". . . it has been observed that when people who are high in this factor have been put together in groups, the general efficiency and objectiveness of the group is decidedly higher than in groups that are only average in the factor" (5, p. 16). The correlation (.41) with *Os*' ratings of the productivity of groups in which Q_3+ persons worked lends support to the hypothesis that such persons facilitate group productivity.

In summary of the results in Table 3, it seems probable that personality traits involving maturity, adaptability, and acceptance of others tend to facilitate or to be positively related to smooth and effective group functioning, while traits involving coolness, suspiciousness, eccentricity and the like tend to depress smooth group functioning (i.e., to be negatively related to ratings of group morale, cohesiveness, friendliness, etc.). This, of course, represents only a very general summary of the results, but it is felt that more specific conclusions cannot be drawn until much more research has been done. It seems clear, however, that *Ss*' responses to personality questionnaires are related to the effect *Ss* have on small groups, and that the characteristics of small groups are to some degree functions of the personality traits of individual group members.

DISCUSSION

The preceding results indicate that there are significant relationships between the behavior of individual group members and the characteristics of the total group, and that these relationships can be experimentally isolated. They also support Cattell's hypothesis that "every man in a group is to some extent a leader in so far as every man has some effect upon the syntality of a group" (4, p. 25). The present study suggests the possibility of studying leadership in terms of the relationships between individuals and group characteristics.

The results reported here are considered highly tentative. The lack of previous research in this area and the exploratory nature of this study greatly limit the extent to which the findings can be generalized. Within these limits, however, the following conclusions are considered tenable:

1. It is possible to isolate relationships between the behaviors of individual group members and the characteristics or "syntality" traits of small groups.

2. Individuals who are chosen by co-workers as good leaders or as persons with whom others like to work "facilitate" group functioning, while individuals who "depress" group functioning are not generally chosen by other members of the group.

3. Individual behavior patterns which include cooperativeness, efficiency, and insight—Factor I behavior—tend to "facilitate" or be positively related to effective group functioning as measured by ratings of group morale, cooperativeness, productivity, cohesiveness, motivation, and interest in job completion.

4. Individual behavior patterns which include aggressiveness, self-confidence, initiative, interest in individual solution, and authoritarianism —Factor II behavior—tend to be somewhat negatively related to ratings of group cohesiveness and friendliness.

5. Sociable behavior—Factor III—tends to reduce group motivation and competition, but to increase group talkativeness, friendliness, and interest in social interaction.

6. Personality traits involving maturity, adaptability, and acceptance of others tend to be positively related to smooth and effective group functioning.

7. Personality traits involving suspiciousness, eccentricity, and coolness toward others tend to be negatively related to smooth group functioning.

The results of this study support Cattell's (4) and Gibb's (8) suggestions that leadership be studied as relationships between individual group members and "syntality" traits of the group. At least in small groups of this nature it seems probable that each individual member makes some contribution to the characteristics of the total group. Such contributions can be investigated with a design similar to the one used here. Experimental studies utilizing such a design need to be conducted with a larger number of *S*s, different task situations, larger groups, and more refined measures of personality, behavior, and group characteristics. A knowledge of the effects of behavior of individuals on each other seems essential to an understanding of small group behavior.

SUMMARY

1. Sixteen male NROTC students met in groups of four. Each *S* worked with each other *S* once and only once, so that each *S* worked in five different groups. Each group worked on a Reasoning (R) task, a Mechanical Assembly (MA) task, and a Discussion (D) task.

2. The *S*s were observed by two independent *O*s who rated individual behavior and group characteristics. The *S*s also rated characteristics of their groups. Sociometric and personality data were obtained.

3. Relationships between measures of individuals and of groups were analyzed. Relationships were found, indicating that individual members significantly affect the characteristics of small groups. In general it was found that effective group functioning was facilitated by cooperativeness, efficiency, and insight, while behavior which we have called "striving for individual prominence" reduced group cohesiveness and friendliness.

4. Significant relationships in the predicted directions were also found between personality measures and ratings of group characteristics, suggesting that mature, accepting persons facilitate while suspicious, non-accepting persons depress group characteristics indicative of smooth functioning.

5. Some of the implications of this study for research on leadership and small group behavior were briefly discussed.

REFERENCES

1. Carter, L. F., & Couch, A. Factorial studies of the rated behavior of group members. Paper read at East. Psychol. Ass., March 1952.
2. Carter, L. F., Haythorn, W., & Howell, Margaret. A further investigation of the criteria of leadership. *J. abnorm. soc. Psychol.*, 1950, 45, 350–358.
3. Carter, L. F., Haythorn, W., Meirowitz, Beatrice, & Lanzetta, J. Note on a new technique of interaction recording. *J. abnorm. soc. Psychol.*, 1951, 46, 258–260.
4. Cattell, R. B. Determining syntality dimensions as a basis for morale and leadership measurement. In H. Guetzkow (Ed.), *Groups, leadership, and men.* Pittsburgh: Carnegie Press, 1951. Pp. 16–27.
5. Cattell, R. B., Saunders, D. R., & Stice, G. *Handbook for the sixteen personality factor questionnaire.* Champaign, Illinois: Institute for Personality and Ability Testing, 1949.
6. Cattell, R. B., & Wispé, L. G. The dimensions of syntality in small groups. *J. soc. Psychol.*, 1948, 28, 57–78.
7. Fouriezos, N. T., Hutt, M. L., & Guetzkow, H. Measurement of self-oriented needs in discussion groups. *J. abnorm. soc. Psychol.*, 1950, 45, 682–690.
8. Gibb, C. A. The research background of an interactional theory of leadership. *Aust. J. Psychol.*, 1950, 2, 19–42.
9. Haythorn, W. The influence of the individual group members on the behavior of coworkers and on the characteristics of groups. Ph.D. thesis, Univer. of Rochester, 1952.
10. Hemphill, J. K., & Westie, C. M. The measurement of group dimensions. *J. Psychol.*, 1950, 29, 325–342.
11. Henry, W. E., & Guetzkow, H. *Group projection sketches for the study of small*

groups. Publication No. 4 of the Conference Research Project. Ann Arbor: Univer. of Michigan, 1949.
12. Northway, M. L., Frankel, E. B., & Potashin, R. *Personality and sociometric status*. Sociometric Monographs, No. 11. New York: Beacon House, 1947.
13. Powell, J. W. The dynamics of group formation. *Psychiatry*, 1948, 11, 117–124.
14. Redl, F. Group emotion and leadership. *Psychiatry*, 1942, 5, 573–596.
15. Slavson, S. R. *An introduction to group therapy*. New York: The Commonwealth Fund, 1943.

The Stability of Interpersonal Judgments in Independent Situations

EDGAR F. BORGATTA

WHILE there are many problems involved in the use of ratings and rankings, their pervasiveness in social and psychological research attests to their importance. Thus, rather than to shy away from dealing with ratings and rankings, the need is for more systematic exploration and examination of their limitations. The study reported here brings together into a single experimental design several aspects that have generally received attention separately. The generic form of such a multitrait-multimethod design is discussed by Campbell and Fiske (5).

The research variables are stratified in three ways:

1. *Multitrait*. The research includes three dimensions of trait description. The scores representing these dimensions are based on prior work

FROM *Journal of Abnormal and Social Psychology*, 1960, 188–194. Reprinted by permission of the author and the American Psychological Association, Inc.

This study stems from the program of research titled, "The Variables and Conditions of Small Group Interaction" at New York University. Jonathan Robbin, technical associate, was in charge of machine analysis, and the research assistants were John Stimson, Robert Guerrin, Gerald Marwell, and Ardyth Stimson. This research was supported in whole or in part by the United States Air Force under Contract AF49(638)-195 monitored by the Air Force Office of Scientific Research of the Air Research and Development Command.

indicating that only a limited number of dimensions will account for most of the variance of interpersonal judgments.

2. *Multimethod.* It provides data on interpersonal judgments made in two independent situations.

3. *Multimethod.* It examines the interrelationship of self-ratings, self-rankings, and peer rankings.

The Dimensions of Interpersonal Judgments: Prior Work

An important emphasis in the use of sociometric ratings has been on the content of the criterion on which group members are asked to choose (or rate or rank) each other. Experience in use and direct research have led to a distinction between work (sociogroup) and the friendship (psychegroup) choices as relatively independent; that is, recognition has been given to the fact that the person who is chosen as the leader for a task situation might not be the same as the one with whom social activities might best be realized. Jennings (8, 9), for example, gave explicit attention to this analysis. Bales and Slater (1) and Slater (11) emphasized a similar distinction in the study of interaction process, under the rubrics of task and social-emotional specialists. In responses gathered after discussion meetings, however, organizing concepts included group member rankings on (*a*) contributing best ideas and (*b*) guiding the discussion, and ratings on (*c*) personal liking for the group members.

While there have been many other classifications of roles and of types of behavior, the above are particularly worthy of note since they stem from large bodies of empirical research. However, while the sets of concepts arising from both sociometry and interaction process analysis reflect an accumulated body of experience, the delineation of dimensions of ratings and rankings appears as a by-product rather than as a consequence of a direct inquiry such as Carter's (6). On the basis of factor analyses of his data, as well as a number of independently reported studies, Carter suggested that three categories account for most of the variance of individuals as seen in small group interaction: (*a*) individual prominence and achievement, (*b*) aiding attainment by the group, and (*c*) sociability. The relationship of these categories to the theoretical developments in sociometry and interaction process analysis is directly visible. Additional work undertaken to examine Carter's proposed three-factor system substantiates it at least in part, but the suggestion arises that four and possibly more factors may be required in order to account for the major portion of the variance of interpersonal judgments, with the dimensions organized around the concepts of individual assertiveness, sociability, intelligence, and emotionality (4).

We may at least conclude that propositions about the stability of judgments must be made with attention to the dimensions of content involved. The importance of this requirement has been particularly emphasized by Cronbach (7) in his analysis of discrepancy measures.

The Consistency of Peer Judgments: Prior Work

In the utilization of peer judgments, the question of the reliability of scores is a prominent and complex one. For example, if a person is said to have a high score on judgments made by peers on a sociability criterion, the question of reliability is not merely whether scores taken again in the same way for the same group will be relatively stable. Implicitly, the expectation is that the score identifies an attribute of the individual with some degree of generality. Still, it is quite another question to ask about the stability of such scores when they are taken in different groups or situations.

Referring particularly to sociometric measures, Mouton, Blake, and Fruchter (10) report only two studies of the consistency of judgments under conditions of experimental variation. The first is the study by Bell and French (3) that employed a single criterion (leadership), in which it was found that with a sample of 25 subjects (*S*s), organized as five-person groups in six successive 35-min. discussion sessions in which no two *S*s participated together more than once, the ranking scores of individuals were for any one session correlated on the average .75 with the average of the other sessions. The second study reported by Mouton, Blake, and Fruchter was their own, with a sample of 33 *S*s organized in three-person groups in two successive 15-min. discussion sessions, but in this case using 12 items or criteria. They concluded from their study that judgments of behavior can be made reliably under conditions of short-term interaction and indicated that the items most reliably judged in their study were leadership, contribution to group decision, and dominance position within the group.

Both these studies emphasize the consistency with which peers characterize the individual, particularly in terms of short-term contact, but they do not focus on the dimensions of content in judgments as such. In the second study just mentioned, the three items reported to be most reliably judged might be expected to correlate at a very high level and thus to represent only one dimension. Other studies that have touched on the consistency of judgments with varying composition of groups, such as that of Bass and Wuster (2), have reported positive findings but also have not been concerned with examining the problem of dimensions of judgment.

Self and Peer Judgments

In examining consistency over independent situations, there is as yet no systematic report on the relationship of self judgments with those of peers.

The data reported here permit the self and peer judgments to be examined in two independent discussion groups, with parallel analyses for three dimensions of judgment. Although the accuracy with which a person perceives the judgments of others of course enters these data indirectly, the data pertain to the correlation of the self-judgment with peer consensus. This is a measure of correspondence rather than of accuracy as such.

In addition, prior self-ratings representing an abstract frame of reference are compared with the judgments made in terms of the concrete sets of other persons in the two independent discussion situations. Thus, this design permits examination of the consistency of self-ratings made "alone" with self-rankings made in the context of specific others, as well as the comparison of self-ratings with peer rankings.

DESIGN OF THE ANALYSIS

The sample employed for this analysis consisted of 99 male *Ss*, college sophomores and juniors. Data were collected in three stages with from one to three months between each stage.

The first type of data collected was a self-rating check list of descriptive behavioral characteristics responded to as part of a general orientation test period for *Ss*. The check list represents 40 trait descriptions that have been developed and used in extensive research on the rating and ranking of behavior in interaction situations (4). The check list form asked the *S* to circle a number from 0 to 9 associated with a continuum running from "Definitely does not describe me" to "Definitely does describe me."

The second source of data was from a postmeeting questionnaire, based on the same 40 descriptive behavorial characteristics, that was completed after participation in a five-person discussion. *Ss* who were not acquainted participated in the interaction situation for 80 min., with four discussion topics. These topics were selected from an extensive attitude questionnaire called the General Orientations Profile that was administered previously at the orientation test period. Topics were chosen to represent orthogonal attitudinal content in the subject population. Thus, the successive alignments of agreements and disagreements on the topics occurred by chance within a session, and the opportunity was maximized for a person to find a topic in which he had some interest and on which he took some position. In this sense, also, the discussion situation was developed to maximize the possibilities for exposure to discussion participation on a variety of issues in a relatively short period of time. The questionnaire for ranking the group members was administered after the discussion. This provided self-rankings of the *Ss* on the descriptive behavioral characteristics and also the peer rankings (minus self-rankings) on the same characteristics.

The third source of data was similar to the second, but was carried out in a somewhat shorter discussion session (three new topics, 20 min. each, with the same orthogonal content as three of the previous topics), in three-person rather than five-person groups, and again in groups composed of persons who were not acquainted. Self and peer rankings on the characteristics were available from this source.

The three scores based on the ratings or rankings employed in this analysis are *Assertiveness, Sociability,* and *Emotionality.* Each score is composed of several highly intercorrelated variables found to be consistently associated with orthogonal clusters in factor analysis. The score in each case is the sum of the self-ratings, self-rankings, or peer rankings on the relevant items. The scores are composed of responses to the following items: Assertiveness (A)—Is very active, Initiative, Makes many suggestions, and Assertiveness; Sociability (S)—Shows solidarity and friendliness, Makes others feel he understands them, and Likeability; Emotionality (E)—Is very tense, Gets upset very easily, Tends to be very nervous, Emotionality. The remaining 29 items tend to be distributed on these factors or are involved in less well-defined factors.

RESULTS

Dependencies between the Contents

The matrix of product-moment intercorrelations for all scores in this analysis is presented in Table 1. Since the research focus requires comparisons of individuals in independent situations, the correlations were computed over all 99 *S*s. It would be possible, also, to make more limited examinations of the relationships among measures by computing, say, for each five-person group the intercorrelation matrix of the self-ratings, the five-person self-rankings and peer rankings, and the parallel scores each member received in the independent three-person groups. If this procedure were carried out it would be possible to describe directly the distribution characteristics of the observed relationships over the five-person groups. However, the procedure used appears appropriate in this context since the use of rankings holds constant the sum (or mean) of all ranks within the group, and the variability of group means of self-rankings and peer rankings is restricted within this dependency. Such variability would tend to attenuate relationships between the classes for the pooled data. Consistency of frame of reference between groups as well as within groups is necessary for relationships to be manifest in the pooled data.

A slight but significant relationship occurs among the three self-rating scores with Assertiveness and Sociability positively correlated ($r_{A_1S_1}=.23$) and both of these negatively correlated with Emotionality ($r_{A_1E_1}=-.21$; $r_{S_1E_1}=-.22$). In the self-rankings, both for the five- and three-person groups, Assertiveness and Sociability are positively correlated ($r_{A_2S_2}=.37$; $r_{A_4S_4}=.10$), although for the three-person group the correlation (.10) does not achieve the significance level. In the self-rankings, neither for the five- nor the three-person groups was the relationship between Assertiveness and Emotionality negative ($r_{A_2E_2}=.17$; $r_{A_4E_4}=.05$). On the other hand, the correlation of Sociability with Emotionality is negative and significant for both the five-person ($r_{S_2E_2}=-.20$) and the three-person groups ($r_{S_4E_4}=-.34$).

For the peer ranking scores in the five- and three-person groups, Assertiveness and Sociability are again positively correlated ($r_{A_3S_3}=.51$; $r_{A_5S_5}=.32$), and Sociability is negatively correlated with Emotionality ($r_{S_3E_3}=-.39$; $r_{S_5E_5}=-.41$). The relationship between Assertiveness and Emotionality is indicated to be positive, although slight and significant only for the three-person groups ($r_{A_3E_3}=.09$; $r_{A_5E_5}=.22$).

TABLE I

Intercorrelation Matrix
N = 99

	Five-Person Groups									*Three-Person Groups*					
	Self Ratings			*Self-Ranking*			*Peer Ranking*			*Self-Ranking*			*Peer Ranking*		
	A1	S1	E1	A2	S2	E2	A3	S3	E3	A4	S4	E4	A5	S5	E5
A1	—	*23*	*−21*	*43*	*31*	−06	*31*	*25*	−12	*22*	14	05	*23*	*31*	−03
S1		—	*−22*	11	*53*	*−21*	05	07	−19	02	*42*	*−27*	−01	08	−02
E1			—	−19	*−21*	*29*	10	−08	*22*	−02	*−25*	*26*	−06	−07	17
A2				—	*37*	17	*55*	*33*	13	*42*	03	07	*39*	10	11
S2					—	*−20*	05	*20*	*−27*	11	*51*	−16	15	*23*	*−21*
E2						—	*21*	−08	*43*	14	−17	*50*	*21*	−05	*22*
A3							—	*51*	09	18	−07	08	*38*	14	05
S3								—	*−39*	02	04	−05	*23*	*44*	*−23*
E3									—	05	−17	15	05	*−32*	*44*
A4										—	10	05	*61*	*22*	*28*
S4											—	*−34*	00	*27*	−14
E4												—	16	−08	15
A5													—	*32*	*22*
S5														—	*−41*
E5															

Note: Decimal points omitted. A, S, and E are the scores on dimensions of Assertiveness, Sociability, and Emotionality. Value of $|r| \geqq .20$ would satisfy a symmetric test of significance at the .05 level with 95 *df*. Significant values are italicized.

Although the measures for the three dimensions of content in the ratings and rankings were drawn from previous studies that indicated a high degree of independence among them, in this analysis the three contents tend to be related. The relationship probably depends in part on the fact that the groups had participated together only for a relatively short period of time and the opportunity to communicate had been somewhat restricted. In any set of peer judgments, as the group members get to know one another they should be better able to identify the characteristics of each person and to distinguish accurately between the characteristics in their rankings. When one knows an individual well enough, that is, one can *take into account* his other qualities in ranking him on a specific quality. Consider the following question, for example: "How high is an individual on Sociability?" Taking into account individual differences in activity levels appears to be implicit in the question.

Interrelationships of Self-Judgments Across Situations

The existence of some dependency among the three dimensions of content does not prohibit examining relationships across situations and types of measures. Thus, to begin with, the self-ratings made in terms of abstract reference points are predictive of the ranks *S*s assign to themselves in the five- and three-person groups. The self-rating score on Assertiveness is correlated with the parallel self-ranking score in both discussion groups ($r_{A_1A_2}=.43$; $r_{A_1A_4}=.22$); the self-rating score on Sociability is correlated with the parallel self-ranking scores ($r_{S_1S_2}=.53$; $r_{S_1S_4}=.42$); and the self-rating score on Emotionality is correlated with the parallel self-ranking scores ($r_{E_1E_2}=.29$; $r_{E_1E_4}=.26$). All these values are statistically significant and constitute the largest values, with only minor exception, in the vectors in the intersection matrices. The exception occurs for the correlation between the self-rating score on Sociability and the self-ranking score in the three-person group on Emotionality ($r_{S_1E_4}=-.27$). The negative relationships between Sociability and Emotionality from self-rating scores to self-ranking scores are statistically significant ($r_{S_1E_2}=-.21$; $r_{S_1E_4}=-.27$; $r_{E_1S_2}-.21$; $r_{E_1S_4}=-.25$). The additional significant relationship in these comparisons is a positive correlation of the self-rating score on Assertiveness with the self-ranking score on Sociability for the five-person group ($r_{A_1S_2}=.31$).

Stability of self-ranking scores may also be examined between the five- and the three-person groups. *S*s participated in these groups with different persons, and the restriction of comparison obviously differs when an *S* utilizes four other persons versus two other persons as the frame of reference in identifying characteristics. It is seen, however, that the self-ranking scores in the five-person group correlate with the self-ranking scores in the three-person groups quite substantially, in spite of the obvious restriction on variance involved in the limited number of comparisons in the groups ($r_{A_2A_4}=.42$; $r_{S_2S_4}=.51$; $r_{E_2E_4}=.50$).

The stability of self-ranking scores from situation to situation recalls the problem of contamination of measures that makes unraveling data of an interpersonal type quite challenging. Do the relatively stable indicators mean that a person has a well-defined and stable perception of his role among others or does it indicate, rather, that his place among others is indeed relatively stable and that he is able to identify what it is with some degree of accuracy? This question can be answered in part by examining the self-judgments in terms of the peer judgments, to which we will turn after considering the interrelationship of the peer rankings.

Interrelationship of Peer Rankings Across Situations

As we have already noted, the interrelationship among the dimensions of content used in the peer judgments borders on the substantial in both the five- and the three-person groups. However, when one examines the predictability of peer judgments from five- to three-person groups, one notes that the largest correlations in the intersection matrix occur in the main diagonal and each dimension best predicts itself. Thus, across the situations the correlations are for Assertiveness, $r_{A_3A_5}=.38$; for Sociability, $r_{S_3S_5}=.44$; and for Emotionality, $r_{E_3E_5}=.44$. Peer ranking scores on Sociability are significantly negatively correlated with peer ranking scores on Emotionality ($r_{S_2E_3}=-.23$; $r_{S_3E_2}=-.32$), but the magnitudes are below those of the main diagonal in the intersection matrix. An additional significant relationship occurs in this intersection matrix between the peer rankings on Sociability for the five-person group and the peer rankings on Assertiveness for the three-person group, although the relationship is small ($r_{S_3A_5}=.23$).

We may now examine the question of the predictability of peer ranking scores on the basis of self-rating and self-ranking scores. The peer scores, it should be recalled, do not involve self-rankings.

Self-Judgments as Predictors of Peer Judgments

Self-rating scores on Assertiveness are significantly correlated with corresponding peer ranking scores in the five- and the three-person groups ($r_{A_1A_3}=.31$; $r_{A_1A_5}=.23$). In both cases self-rating scores on Assertiveness are also significantly correlated with peer ranking scores on Sociability ($r_{A_1S_3}=.25$; $r_{A_1S_5}=.31$). Self-rating scores on Sociability, on the other hand, are not significantly associated with the peer ranking scores on Sociability ($r_{S_1S_3}=.07$; $r_{S_1S_5}=.08$). For the five-person groups, self-rating scores on Emotionality are significantly correlated with peer ranking scores on Emotionality ($r_{E_1E_3}=.22$), and the relationship is maintained in the three-person group ($r_{E_1E_5}=.17$) although it falls short of significance.

One notes first that self-judgments employing a specific group of individuals as a frame of reference lead to more substantial predictive correlations for the peer ranking scores in the groups than do self-ratings made in the abstract. Thus, for the five-person groups, self-ranking scores on Assertiveness are substantially correlated with peer ranking scores ($r_{A_2A_3}=.55$). Interestingly, these self-ranking scores in the five-person groups also are significantly correlated with peer ranking scores for the three-person groups, and again at a relatively substantial level ($r_{A_2A_5}=.39$).

The findings for self-rankings in the five-person groups in terms of Sociability and Emotionality parallel those of Assertiveness; that is, self-rankings on Sociability are significantly correlated with peer rankings in the five- and three-person groups ($r_{S_2S_3}=.20$; $r_{S_2S_4}=.23$), although for Sociability the magnitudes are smaller. Similarly, self-ranking scores on Emotionality for the five-person groups are correlated with peer ranking scores on Emotionality ($r_{E_2E_3}=.43$; $r_{E_2E_5}=.22$).

There are additional correlates as well: self-ranking scores on Assertiveness for the five-person groups are correlated with peer ranking scores on Sociability in the five-person groups ($r_{A_2S_3}=.33$); the parallel relationship occurs for three-person groups ($r_{A_4S_5}=.22$) but does not extend between self-ranking scores of the five-person groups and peer ranking scores for the three-person groups ($r_{A_2S_5}=.10$), or vice versa ($r_{A_3S_4}=-.07$). For the five-person groups, self-ranking scores on Emotionality are significantly correlated with peer ranking scores on Assertiveness ($r_{E_2A_3}=.21$), and also to peer ranking scores on Assertiveness in the three-person groups ($r_{E_2A_5}=.21$). However, the parallel relationships for self-ranking scores on Assertiveness for the three-person groups are not significant ($r_{E_4A_3}=.08$; $r_{E_4A_5}=.16$). Self-ranking scores on Sociability for the five-person groups are significantly negatively correlated with peer ranking scores on Emotionality for both the five- and the three-person groups ($r_{S_2E_3}=-.27$; $r_{S_2E_5}=-.21$); the parallel relationships for the three-person groups are not significant ($r_{S_4E_3}=-.17$; $r_{S_4E_5}=-.14$).

Examining now the self-rankings in the three-person groups, self-ranking scores on Assertiveness are positively correlated at a substantial level with peer ranking scores for the three-person groups ($r_{A_4A_5}=.61$) and, also, although at a much lower level, with the Sociability and the Emotionality peer ranking scores ($r_{A_4S_5}=.22$; $r_{A_4E_5}=.28$); self-ranking scores on Sociability are positively correlated with peer ranking scores on Sociability for the three-person groups ($r_{S_4S_5}=.27$); while the correlation between self and peer ranking scores on Emotionality is in the correct direction, the magnitude is not sufficient to satisfy the criterion of statistical significance ($r_{E_4E_5}=.15$).

Finally, self-rankings for the three-person groups do not appear to be efficient predictors of peer judgments in the five-person groups. It should be noted, however, in this intersection matrix all values in the main diagonal are positive although none are of sufficient magnitude to satisfy the significance criterion ($r_{A_4A_3}=.18$; $r_{S_4S_3}=.04$; $r_{E_4E_3}=.15$).

DISCUSSION AND SUMMARY

Self-rating scores appear to be direct predictors of the self-ranking scores that are made after five- and three-person discussion situations (median $r=.35$), independently of the dimensions of content. This finding could result simply from an individual's self-image or bias that he carries over into his self-perception when ranking himself in regard to any set of specific others. That is, if he judges himself to be relatively high in an abstract sense (self-rating), he may assign himself a rank that is high without attention to the qualities of others, whether he does this unconsciously or deliberately. This is not, it should be noted, the elevation problem that Cronbach (7) discusses, i.e., the tendency to rate all persons high, low, or at some given level, since the mean rank for each set of judgments is by definition the same.

The conception of an abstract self-image or bias in self-perception is not easily detached from the question of stability of qualities and accuracy of perception. If persons are stable in their qualities, the stability in independent situations would be dependent upon the equivalence of sets of persons in the different situations. Thus, the variation of the characteristics of sets of group members must be thought of as an important source of variance in the "unreliability" of judgments in independent situations. But beyond this consideration, in order for there to be reliability there must be accurate perception of the qualities of the group members in the independent situations. The prediction diagonal of peer judgments from five- to three-person groups (A_3A_5, S_3S_5, E_3E_5) tends to be positive and nontrivial (median $r=.44$), thus establishing the relative stability of ranks in independent groups, irrespective of the dimensions of content. Dependently, this also means that group members must view themselves consistently and with a common frame of reference. Since the prediction diagonals from self-rating and self-ranking scores to peer ranking scores (A_1A_3, S_1S_3, E_1E_3; A_1A_5, S_1S_5, E_1E_5; A_2A_3, S_2S_3, E_2E_3; A_2A_5, S_2S_5, E_2E_5; A_4A_3, S_4S_3, E_4E_3; and A_4A_5, S_4S_5, E_4E_5) tend to be positive and nontrivial (median $r=.22$), group members must also have accurate perception of their qualities according to the group consensus.

A point that needs to be emphasized here is that the respondents were not asked to predict how others would rate or rank them. Thus, except for logical dependency indicated, the ability of the person to predict judgments others make is not involved. This was not the task assigned.

As for the magnitudes of predictions, it appears that correlations of self-rating with self and peer rankings are larger for the five-person groups (A_1A_2, S_1S_2, E_1E_2; median $r=.43$, A_1A_3, S_1S_3, E_1E_3; median $r=.22$) than the three-person groups (A_1A_4, S_1S_4, E_1E_4; median $r=.26$; A_1A_5, S_1S_5, E_1E_5; median $r=.17$). This result accords with the view that the variation of sets of group members restricts the reliability of judgments, i.e., a more general base of judgment is available in five- than in three-person groups since sampling expectations dictate less variation in the means and variances of samples of larger size. In addition, of course, the concrete frame of reference for judgment is larger.

Since dimensions of content were employed that tend to be defined orthogonally in factor analytic studies, the generality of findings could be examined over these dimensions. In general, findings tended to occur in parallel, supporting the notion that principles may be observed without regard for the content but also emphasizing the need for specific and inclusive dimensions in describing characteristics of persons.

REFERENCES

1. Bales, R. F. & Slater, P. E. Role differentiation in small decision-making groups. In T. Parsons, R. F. Bales, et al. *Family, socialization and interaction process.* Glencoe, Ill.: Free Press, 1955.
2. Bass, B. M., & Wuster, C. R. Effects of the nature of the problem on LGD performance. *J. appl. Psychol.*, 1953, 37, 96–99.
3. Bell, G. B., & French, R. L. Consistency of individual leadership position in small groups of varying membership. *J. abnorm. soc. Psychol.*, 1950, 45, 764–767.
4. Borgatta, E. F. Cottrell, L. S., Jr., & Mann, J. H. The spectrum of individual interaction characteristics: An interdimensional analysis. *Psychol. Rep., Monogr. Suppl.* 4, 1958, 4, 279–319.
5. Campbell, D. T., & Fiske, D. W. Convergent and discriminant validation by the multitrait-multimethod matrix. *Psychol. Bull.*, 1959, 56, 81–105.
6. Carter, L. F. Recording and evaluating the performance of individuals as members of small groups. *Personnel Psychol.*, 1954, 7, 477–484.
7. Cronbach, L. J. Processes affecting scores on "understanding of others" and "assumed similarity." *Psychol. Bull.*, 1955, 52, 177–193.
8. Jennings, Helen H. Sociometric differentiation of the psychegroup and the sociogroup. *Sociometry,* 1947, 10, 71–79.
9. Jennings, Helen H. *Leadership and isolation.* (2nd Ed.) New York: Longmans, Green, 1950.
10. Mouton, Jane S., Blake, R. R., & Fruchter, B. The reliability of sociometric measures. *Sociometry*, 1955, 18, 7–48.
11. Slater, P. E. Role differentiation in small groups. *Amer. sociol. Rev.*, 1955, 20, 300–310.

Role-Playing Specification, Personality, and Performance

EDGAR F. BORGATTA

THE RESEARCH reported in this paper involves the following: Persons of known personality characteristics are asked to play assigned roles that involve characteristics designed to be (a) similar to and (b) different from their own. The report presents data on regularities

FROM *Sociometry*, 1961, 24, 218–233. Reprinted by permission of the author and the American Sociological Association, Inc.

This study stems from the research program, "The Variables and Conditions of Small Group Interaction," at New York University. This research was supported in whole or in part by the U..S. Air Force under contract AF 49 (638)—195, monitored by the Air Force Office of Scientific Research of the Air Research and Development Command (AFOSR TN 60–682).

associated with differences of personality characteristics, with differences of assigned role specifications, and also with the *congruency* between the previously measured personality characteristics and the assigned role specifications. Emphasis is placed on the specific personality measures used in the study. The effects that are observed are described through interaction process scores and through assessments, made immediately after each role-playing situation, on how well each person played and how much each person enjoyed the assigned role.

SELECTION OF PERSONALITY CHARACTERISTICS

Previous analysis indicates that much of the variance of scores based on peer judgments can be accounted for by a few concepts, particularly assertiveness, sociability, intelligence, and emotionality (1, 3, 4, 5). Further, a broad range of peer judgments has been studied in a variety of contexts, and the structure of such judgments has been replicated (1). For these reasons, it appeared desirable to use as personality characteristics in this study those derived from peer judgments and defined consistently in the replicated analysis of the structure of the judgments. The central concepts for analysis as personality characteristics in this study were two composite scores for the subjects derived from peer rankings after a five-man discussion session lasting 80 minutes and covering four topics for which group decisions were requested. Subjects were students at New York University, generally in the sophomore year at initial contact. The use of four independent topics permitted exposure of the individual in different contexts and in randomly distributed alliances, and thus, presumably, more broadly based peer judgments. Each composite peer score was the sum of peer rankings on four trait or behavior characteristic descriptions: *Assertiveness* was based on (a) Is very active, (b) Takes initiative, (c) Makes many suggestions, and (d) Shows assertiveness. *Emotionality* was based on (a) Is very tense, (b) Gets upset easily, (c) Tends to be very nervous, and (d) Emotionality. In the analyses of the peer judgments from which these data are drawn, the items included in the composite scores tend to be relatively pure in the two factors involved. The composite scores of Assertiveness and Emotionality were relatively independent: e.g., in an analysis of 155 male subjects from which the current samples were drawn, the correlation was .10.

RESEARCH DESIGN

On the basis of the prior Assertiveness score, the subjects were ordered in three units of approximately equal size. The principle of ordering was not revealed to the observers on the project until after the final stages of data collection for the entire project. The subjects, of course, had no knowledge of this ordering.

Approximately one year after the data for the composite scores were available, a series of three-man groups was constituted for role-playing sessions. With minor exception, each group was composed of the combination of High, Middle, and Low (H, M, and L) on prior Assertiveness score, and each group was composed so that members had no prior experimental contact in discussion groups. For this stage of analysis 29 groups or 87 subjects were recruited.

Each role-playing session involved three scenes. Each scene involved three persons with assigned roles to portray, and the directions were to carry on the role-playing for 20 minutes. The assigned roles were identified as Person 1, Person 2, and Person 3 in the directions; subjects who were H, M, and L were rotated through these identifications systematically by selection prior to the sessions. The order of the three scenes, however, was held constant.

Each scene involved status position identifications plus descriptions of characteristics considered to be consistent with the position. For example:

> Person 1 is a boy, 12 years old, who tends to be somewhat withdrawn. He is not particularly active, doesn't talk very much, and doesn't seem to mix well with others his age.
>
> Person 2 is the boy's mother, who is emotional, generally tense, and gets upset easily.
>
> Person 3 is the boy's father, who is an active and directive person, almost authoritarian in his manner.
>
> The scene is in the living room of the family's home. *You* are that family. You are discussing the boy's problems and the future.

In each of the scenes the persons described were designed to require (a) Assertive, (b) Submissive, and (c) Emotional performance. The role-playing specifications (assigned roles) were arranged so that each subject would perform under each type of requirement as he proceeded through the three scenes. Subjects appeared to respond to the instructions for role-playing without difficulty. It had been anticipated from prior experience that subjects would have no particular difficulties in taking the roles of the opposite sex, and this appeared to be the case here. Some indication of the ease with which the role-playing was undertaken may be seen in the high level of self-ratings on enjoyment discussed later in the paper.

The role-playing sessions were observed using a revision of Bales's scoring categories (3), here called Interaction Process Scores (IPS's). Table 2 presents a brief identification of the categories. In addition, after each role-playing scene, the participants completed a single-sheet rating form dealing primarily with how well each person performed and how much each person enjoyed playing the assigned role. Two observers also rated the role-players after each scene on the same questions.

When this stage of the data collection was completed, the identical design was repeated, using three additional but comparable scenes to provide a replication. The groups were composed on the same basis, again under the requirement of no prior experimental contact among the three-man group members. In this case, 24 groups or 72 of the 87 subjects constituted the sample size.

ANALYSIS OF THE DATA

Some of the findings from this study may be seen directly in Table 1. Series A, Series B, and Series A and B are the study, the replication, and the combined data.[1]

TABLE 1

*Total Interaction Process Score by Prior Peer Assertiveness Score and Role Specification**

		ROLE SPECIFICATION			
	ASSERTIVENESS SCORE	ASSERTIVE	SUBMISSIVE	EMOTIONAL	ALL
Series A	H	216.3	114.4	190.0	173.6
	M	208.8	96.3	172.2	159.1
	L	168.1	91.4	140.6	133.4
Series B	H	284.8	106.9	246.3	212.7
	M	255.0	91.0	223.1	189.7
	L	235.7	84.7	180.4	166.9
Series A+B	H	247.3	110.9	215.5	190.6
	M	229.7	93.9	195.3	173.0
	L	198.7	88.4	158.6	148.6

* Series A, 29 groups or 87 subjects; Series B, 24 groups or 72 subjects. Participation of a subject in each group was with persons with whom he never participated previously. High, Medium and Low Assertiveness scores were based on peer rankings in five-person discussion groups one year before role-playing. High, Medium and Low scores were defined by approximately equal thirds. The total interaction process scores are for 20 minutes in discussion (mean number of responses).

Note the following: Persons selected as H, M, and L in Assertiveness one year previously have on the average Total IPS's that correspond to this order not only generally, but also for each role specification, and this is true both in Series A and B. In other words, independent of the assigned role, Total IPS is a function of Assertiveness score.

That the assigned roles have differential meaning for the subjects is obvious in the consistent ordering of the roles by Total IPS as Assertive, Emotional, and Submissive.

1 Data for Series A and B are separately reported only for Table 1 to illustrate the parallel results.

That differential response is possible for subjects in these assigned roles is obvious in the substantially higher Total IPS's of the Low Assertive persons in the Assertive and Emotional assigned roles than of the High Assertive persons in the Submissive roles.

Note one additional incidental replicated finding in the comparison of Series A and B. The Total IPS's for the All column of Series B are higher, indicating a facilitation effect with practice. The increase arises only in the Assertive and Emotional assigned roles, and if anything, there is indicated a decreased rate for the Submissive assigned role. This might appear inconsistent, but this is what should be expected by facilitation when the instructions are for Submissive performance.

Aside from the variation noticeable on the Total IPS's, when Total IPS is controlled by converting the profile of separate IPS's into percentage rates, a number of qualitative differences are found. The largest differences are associated with the assigned roles (Table 2). For example, for the Series A and B in the Submissive assigned role (all subjects) only about 12 per cent of the total responses are IPS 17, *Shows antagonism,* in contrast to 28 per cent for the Assertive assigned role and 33 per cent for the Emotional assigned role. About 5 per cent of the Submissive assigned role responses are IPS 18, *Ego defensive,* compared to 3 per cent for the Emotional and 2 per cent for the Assertive assigned roles. About 17 per cent of the Submissive assigned role responses are IPS 15, *Shows inadequacy,* compared to 10 per cent for the Emotional and 4 per cent for the Assertive assigned roles. The profile for the Emotional assigned role is particularly characterized by high percentages of response in IPS 14, *Disagrees,* and IPS 17, *Shows antagonism,* while that of the Assertive assigned role has a high percentage of responses in IPS 06, *Procedural suggestion,* in addition to differences already noted.

Qualitative differences also occurred according to prior Assertiveness score. For example, the Low Assertiveness persons showed a greater proportion of agreement, both active and passive (IPS 04 and 05), asked for fewer opinions (IPS 13), showed less antagonism (IPS 17), but showed relatively more disagreement (IPS 14).

In Table 3, data are presented on the ratings of how well each person played and how much he enjoyed playing the assigned role. For the self-ratings, there is only a slight tendency for H, M, and L persons on prior Assertiveness scores to be ordered on either criterion. The self-ratings appear to be at a uniformly high level compared to peer and observer ratings, the only appreciable deviation being that H, M, and L persons all tended to rate enjoyment of the Submissive assigned role low.

Large differences are seen for H, M, and L persons, however, in the peer and observer ratings. While the ratings appear ordered on H, M, and L, the striking difference is in low ratings for Low Assertiveness persons. Low Assertiveness persons, however, get *relatively* high ratings

TABLE 2

IPS Percentage Profiles by Prior Peer Assertiveness Score by Role Specification (Series A+B)

PRIOR ASSERTIVENESS SCORE	HIGH				MEDIUM				LOW				TOTAL		
ROLE SPECIFICATIONS	A	S	E	TOTAL	A	S	E	TOTAL	A	S	E	TOTAL	A	S	E
NUMBER OF CASES	53	53	53	159	53	53	53	159	53	53	53	159	159	159	159
IPS 1 Social acknow.	0.1	0.0	0.1	0.1	0.1	0.2	0.1	0.1	0.1	0.0	0.1	0.1	0.1	0.1	0.1
IPS 2 Shows solidarity	1.5	1.0	1.0	1.2	1.0	1.7	0.7	1.0	1.4	1.5	1.2	1.3	1.3	1.4	1.0
IPS 3 Laughs	0.4	0.7	0.4	0.4	0.3	0.8	0.5	0.5	0.6	0.7	0.4	0.6	0.4	0.7	0.4
IPS 4 Acknowledges	0.6	0.9	0.7	0.7	0.6	0.9	0.3	0.5	0.9	0.5	0.7	0.8	0.7	0.8	0.5
IPS 5 Shows agreement	0.4	1.3	0.7	0.7	0.6	2.0	0.5	0.8	0.7	1.5	1.1	1.0	0.6	1.6	0.8
IPS 6 Procedural sugg.	6.5	4.0	3.2	4.8	6.5	3.2	3.3	4.7	7.1	4.8	4.1	5.6	6.7	4.0	3.5
IPS 7 Suggests solution	2.4	0.9	1.2	1.7	2.5	0.5	0.9	1.5	2.8	0.6	1.1	1.8	2.6	0.7	1.1
IPS 8 Gives evaluation	38.5	33.7	25.2	32.7	32.0	35.0	26.8	30.6	36.4	34.8	28.9	33.4	35.7	34.5	26.8
IPS 9 Self-analysis	0.0	0.1	0.0	0.0	0.0	0.0	0.0	0.0	0.0	0.2	0.0	0.0	0.0	0.1	0.0
IPS 10 Redirected agg.	0.4	0.3	0.2	0.3	0.1	0.7	0.4	0.3	0.3	0.4	0.5	0.4	0.2	0.4	0.3
IPS 11 Gives information	1.8	2.3	1.0	1.6	1.2	3.2	1.2	1.6	1.2	1.9	1.1	1.3	1.4	2.5	1.1
IPS 12 Draws attention	6.1	8.8	5.4	6.3	5.5	6.2	4.2	5.2	4.8	6.9	5.0	5.3	5.5	7.4	4.9
IPS 13 Asks evaluation	1.6	0.4	0.6	1.0	0.9	0.3	0.8	0.8	0.9	0.3	0.5	0.6	1.2	0.3	0.6
IPS 14 Disagrees	9.1	9.5	11.1	10.0	9.3	12.2	14.2	11.7	11.2	11.4	14.3	12.3	9.8	10.9	13.0
IPS 15 Shows inadequacy	4.1	16.9	11.8	9.2	3.7	16.8	8.1	7.7	3.7	17.7	9.0	8.4	3.9	17.1	9.8
IPS 16 Tension increase	0.1	0.5	0.0	0.2	0.1	0.3	0.2	0.2	0.3	0.1	0.2	0.2	0.2	0.3	0.1
IPS 17 Shows antagonism	24.1	13.4	34.5	26.0	32.8	11.0	34.6	29.5	25.9	11.3	28.6	24.0	27.6	12.0	32.9
IPS 18 Ego defensiveness	2.3	5.4	3.1	3.2	2.8	5.0	3.4	3.4	1.8	5.5	3.4	3.1	2.3	5.3	3.3
Total	100.0	100.1	100.2	100.1	100.0	100.0	100.2	100.1	100.1	100.1	100.2	100.2	100.2	100.1	100.2
Mean number responses for 20 min. session	247.3	110.9	215.5	190.6	229.7	93.9	195.3	173.0	198.7	88.4	158.6	148.6	225.3	97.7	189.8

TABLE 3

*Ratings on Role-Playing Ability and Enjoyment by Prior Peer Assertiveness Score and Role Specification (Series A+B)**

HOW WELL DO YOU FEEL EACH PERSON PLAYED THE PARTICULAR ROLE THAT WAS ASSIGNED?

	ASSERTIVENESS SCORE	ROLE SPECIFICATIONS ASSERTIVE	SUBMISSIVE	EMOTIONAL	ALL
Observer rating	H	1.94	1.79	1.81	1.85
	M	2.25	1.60	1.83	1.89
	L	.64	1.51	.89	1.01
Peer rating	H	1.94	2.23	2.04	2.07
	M	2.53	1.30	1.81	1.88
	L	1.36	1.40	1.21	1.32
Self-rating	H	2.87	2.91	2.89	2.87
	M	2.74	2.72	2.87	2.77
	L	2.57	2.68	2.64	2.63

HOW WELL DO YOU FEEL EACH PERSON ENJOYED PLAYING THE ROLE ASSIGNED?

	ASSERTIVENESS SCORE	ASSERTIVE	SUBMISSIVE	EMOTIONAL	ALL
Observer rating	H	2.17	1.04	2.41	1.87
	M	2.36	.81	2.17	1.78
	L	1.43	.87	1.58	1.30
Peer rating	H	2.06	1.11	1.75	1.64
	M	2.26	.77	1.87	1.64
	L	1.55	.87	1.34	1.25
Self-rating	H	2.81	2.34	2.91	2.69
	M	2.72	2.24	2.70	2.55
	L	2.79	2.34	2.55	2.56

* Questions were answered after each 20-minute role-playing session. Range of ratings was from 0–4.

on role-playing ability in the Submissive assigned role. This corresponds to the expectation that congruence of personality and assigned role should produce superior performance.

Still, in spite of the fact that Low Assertiveness persons are seen to play the Submissive assigned role best of the three by both peers and observers, these raters view this as the least enjoyable assigned role for the Low Assertiveness persons.

While the ratings by peers and observers are both high for role-playing ability and enjoyment for the High Assertiveness persons, these are not uniformly the highest ratings. A notion of congruency appears reasonable here, but obviously something else is operating. The Medium Assertiveness persons get the highest ratings in the Assertive assigned role, which suggests that they take that assigned role well and comfortably. If they take the Assertive assigned role well, it may be they take others well also. For this to be the case with the Submissive assigned role, they should simulate Low Assertiveness persons in that role. In terms of Total IPS (Table 2), they appear to do so. In other words, a possibility arises that a Medium rating on Assertiveness signifies persons who are as Assertive as the assigned role or moment requires, rather than usually, rarely, or half assertive. Such a person should enter these roles with relative ease—the versatile person. That this is the fact is at least partially supported in the qualitative profiles of IPS's (Table 2), where it is seen that Medium persons have the lowest tension rates generally (IPS 15). A question arises as to why the role-playing ability of the Medium persons is not higher for the peer and observer ratings of the Submissive assigned role. Here, speculatively, the interpretation of the rating task comes under scrutiny. The behavior of a Submissive person may contradict notions of competence in interpersonal relations, and thus behavior that simulates submission effectively may be negatively rated on more general grounds than role-playing ability. Effective simulation is indicated here, since the pattern of ratings for the Medium persons on the Submissive assigned role are similar to those for the Low persons. The interpretation suggested is that the Medium persons are being rated as though they were Low persons.

Interpretation of ratings in the Emotional assigned role for H, M, and L persons is not as direct, and only a general suggestion is made here. Assertiveness and Emotionality have a slight positive correlation as indicated previously. The ordering of ratings appears consistent with this for High and Low persons, with the Medium persons closer to the High than the Low. Since the notion of submissiveness implies withdrawal or inability to be assertive, and neither of these appears consistent with displaying emotionality, the ordering appears appropriate on this *ad hoc* basis. On the speculative side for the Medium persons, the ability to take the Emotional assigned role is as high as for the High persons, consistent with a notion of versatility. If meaning is attributed to the minor differences in higher ratings for the High persons, elaboration of the notion of versatility as associated with competence may be pursued. Competence is generally associated with rationality, and Emotionality is composed primarily of "irrational" aspects of behavior. Presumably, the versatile person would be less comfortable in the irrational role.

SUMMARY AND DISCUSSION

In this analysis attention has focused on the concomitants of characteristics of individuals in their rated ability, enjoyment, and performance in specified role-playing situations. Two role descriptions were designed to correspond to the assertiveness vs. non-assertiveness (submissiveness) dimension, and a third to emotionality. Persons were ordered on the basis of prior peer Assertiveness scores, and groups with the combination H, M, and L were systematically placed in each assigned role position of three fixed role-playing situations. After each of the three sessions, rating forms were completed by the participants and the observers, providing observer, peer, and self-ratings on role-playing ability and enjoyment. The interaction was scored on a revised set of observation categories (IPS's). Data were collected for two series involving the same subjects in non-overlapping groups. Analysis of the results appears to confirm a notion of facilitation in the situation of personality and assigned role congruency, but there is reason to suggest a need for attention to other factors. For example, favorable ratings may be related to societal approval of characteristics rather than to the experimental instructions of rating how well the assigned role-playing was done. When one plays an assigned role, he may be rated favorably because he is mistaken for someone with the favorable characteristics rather than because he has done a good job of role-playing.

Through the availability of other prior scores, the analysis was extended to examine findings for a classification of persons on a criterion of peer Emotionality scores. With this relatively independent analysis, additional support for facilitation of personality and assigned role congruency was found.

Additional re-analyses on the basis of two attitudinal scale scores (GZ 3 Ascendance and GZ 5 Emotional Stability) were presented as parallels to the analyses based on prior peer scores. Some power to reproduce the findings of peer Assertiveness is demonstrated for GZ 3 Ascendance. Differences that occur are not directly interpretable, and inevitably would appear to lead the investigator to a re-analysis of the development of the attitudinal scales. These types of difficulties were those anticipated and proposed to emphasize the appropriateness of utilizing peer (and observer) assessments as an important direct criterion basis for the classification of persons.

The common view of the relationship between personality and social structure includes two important propositions. (a) Personality types tend to gravitate to positions with consistent normative demands. (b) Occupancy of positions with given normative demands tends to alter the personality towards consistency with the normative demands. Stated in mundane language, an individual tends to do things consistent with his personality, and what he does tends to affect his personality. Concomitant with these propositions is a notion that when persons of given characteristics are placed in situations that make demands of them consistent with their characteristics, they will be able to satisfy the demands well and will do so with relatively little discomfort or with relatively more enjoyment. Implicitly, this notion would underlie the above two propositions. In this research we have not tested the notion of congruency of personality characteristics with role demands directly, but we have at least moved into the vicinity of such an exploration. It must be remarked that the concept of role is itself one that must be viewed as primitive and more subject to intuitive verbal gymnastics than to use in the study of personality and social structure in a formal sense (2). Of two obvious ways in which "role demands" could be manipulated, (a) by creating particular structures or (b) by instructing persons to assume them, we have chosen the latter. Within the scope of the types of positions identified (father, mother, son, policeman), the former is not subject to easy manipulation. To the extent that behavioral characteristics described are consistent with the position mentioned, the assigned roles should be interpretable, and the ability to assume them is of central concern to this research. While there is no doubt a level of detachment involved in role-playing (It's not for real!), there is also a level of ambiguity about the reality of structures created synthetically in the laboratory. These are limitations on the research in this area, but they are not total disqualifiers. Additional approaches should be taken in this study of personality and social structure, however, including longitudinal regression analyses of selective processes—particularly with emphasis on the comparison of persons of given characteristics who do and do not follow modal patterns in selection of roles.

REFERENCES

1. Borgatta, E. F. Rankings and self-assessments: Some behavioral characteristics. Replication Studies. *J. soc. Psychol.*, 1960, 52, 279–307.
2. Borgatta, E. F. Role and Reference Group Theory. In L. S. Kogan (Ed.), *Social science theory and social work research.* New York: National Association of Social Workers, 1960.
3. Borgatta, E. F. A systematic study of interaction process scores, peer and self assessments, personality and other variables. *Gen. Psychol. Monogr.* 1962, 65, 219–291.
4. Borgatta, E. F., Cottrell, L. S., Jr. Mann J. H. The spectrum of individual interaction characteristics: an inter-dimensional analysis. *Psychol. rep. monogr. sup. 4*, 1958, 4, 279–319.
5. Carter, L. F. Recording and evaluating the performance of individuals as members of small groups. *Personnel Psychol.*, 1954, 7, 477–484.

CHAPTER 6

GROUP INFLUENCE

Opinions and Social Pressure

SOLOMON E. ASCH

THAT social influences shape every person's practices, judgments and beliefs is a truism to which anyone will readily assent. A child masters his "native" dialect down to the finest nuances; a member of a tribe of cannibals accepts cannibalism as altogether fitting and proper. All the social sciences take their departure from the observation of the profound effects that groups exert on their members. For psychologists, group pressure upon the minds of individuals raises a host of questions they would like to investigate in detail.

How, and to what extent, do social forces constrain people's opinions and attitudes? This question is especially pertinent in our day. The same epoch that has witnessed the unprecedented technical extension of communication has also brought into existence the deliberate manipulation of opinion and the "engineering of consent." There are many good reasons why, as citizens and as scientists, we should be concerned with studying the ways in which human beings form their opinions and the role that social conditions play.

Studies of these questions began with the interest in hypnosis aroused by the French physician Jean Martin Charcot (a teacher of Sigmund Freud) toward the end of the 19th century. Charcot believed that only hysterical patients could be fully hypnotized, but this view was soon challenged by two other physicians, Hyppolyte Bernheim and A. A. Liébault, who demonstrated that they could put most people under the hypnotic spell. Bernheim proposed that hypnosis was but an extreme form of a normal psychological process which became known as "suggestibility." It was shown that monotonous reiteration of instructions could induce in normal persons in the waking state involuntary bodily changes such as swaying or rigidity of the arms, and sensations such as warmth and odor.

It was not long before social thinkers seized upon these discoveries as a basis for explaining numerous social phenomena, from the spread of opinion to the formation of crowds and the following of leaders. The sociologist Gabriel Tarde summed it all up in the aphorism: "Social man is a somnambulist."

When the new discipline of social psychology was born at the beginning of this century, its first experiments were essentially adaptations of the suggestion demonstration. The technique generally followed a simple plan. The subjects, usually college students, were asked to give their opinions or preferences concerning various matters; some time later they were again asked to state their choices, but now they were also informed of the opinions held by authorities or large groups of their peers on the same matters. (Often the alleged consensus was fictitious.) Most of these studies had substantially the same result: confronted with opinions contrary to their own, many subjects apparently shifted their judgments in the direction of the views of the majorities or the experts. The late psychologist Edward L. Thorndike reported that he had succeeded in modifying the esthetic preferences of adults by this procedure. Other psychologists reported that people's evaluations of the merit of a literary passage could be raised or lowered by ascribing the passage to different authors. Apparently the sheer weight of numbers or authority sufficed to change opinions, even when no arguments for the opinions themselves were provided.

Now the very ease of success in these experiments arouses suspicion. Did the subjects actually change their opinions, or were the experimental victories scored only on paper? On grounds of common sense, one must question whether opinions are generally as watery as these studies indicate. There is some reason to wonder whether it was not the investigators who, in their enthusiasm for a theory, were suggestible, and whether the ostensibly gullible subjects were not providing answers which they thought good subjects were expected to give.

The investigations were guided by certain underlying assumptions, which today are common currency and account for much that is thought and said about the operations of propaganda and public opinion. The assumptions are that people submit uncritically and painlessly to external manipulation by suggestion or prestige, and that any given idea or value can be "sold" or "unsold" without reference to its merits. We should be skeptical, however, of the supposition that the power of social pressure necessarily implies uncritical submission to it: independence and the capacity to rise above group passion are also open to human beings. Further, one may question on psychological grounds whether it is possible as a rule to change a person's judgment of a situation or an object without first changing his knowledge or assumptions about it.

In what follows I shall describe some experiments in an investigation of the effects of group pressure which was carried out recently with the help of a number of my associates. The tests not only demonstrate the operations of group pressure upon individuals but also illustrate a new kind of attack on the problem and some of the more subtle questions that it raises.

A group of seven to nine young men, all college students, are assembled in a classroom for a "psychological experiment" in visual judgment. The experimenter informs them that they will be comparing the lengths of lines. He shows two large white cards. On one is a single vertical black line—the standard whose length is to be matched. On the other card are three vertical lines of various lengths. The subjects are to choose the one that is of the same length as the line on the other card. One of the three actually is of the same length; the other two are substantially different, the difference ranging from three quarters of an inch to an inch and three quarters.

The experiment opens uneventfully. The subjects announce their answers in the order in which they have been seated in the room, and on the first round every person chooses the same matching line. Then a second set of cards is exposed; again the group is unanimous. The members appear ready to endure politely another boring experiment. On the third trial there is an unexpected disturbance. One person near the end of the group disagrees with all the others in his selection of the matching line. He looks surprised, indeed incredulous, about the disagreement. On the following trial he disagrees again, while the others remain unanimous in their choice. The dissenter becomes more and more worried and hesitant as the disagreement continues in succeeding trials; he may pause before announcing his answer and speak in a low voice, or he may smile in an embarrassed way.

What the dissenter does not know is that all the other members of the group were instructed by the experimenter beforehand to give incorrect answers in unanimity at certain points. The single individual who is not a party to this prearrangement is the focal subject of our experiment. He is placed in a position in which, while he is actually giving the correct answers, he finds himself unexpectedly in a minority of one, opposed by a unanimous and arbitrary majority with respect to a clear and simple fact. Upon him we have brought to bear two opposed forces: the evidence of his senses and the unanimous opinion of a group of his peers. Also, he must declare his judgments in public, before a majority which has also stated its position publicly.

The instructed majority occasionally reports correctly in order to reduce the possibility that the naive subject will suspect collusion against him. (In only a few cases did the subject actually show suspicion; when this happened, the experiment was stopped and the results were not counted.) There are 18 trials in each series, and on 12 of these the majority responds erroneously.

How do people respond to group pressure in this situation? I shall report first the statistical results of a series in which a total of 123 subjects from three institutions of higher learning (not including my own, Swarthmore College) were placed in the minority situation described above.

Two alternatives were open to the subject: he could act independently, repudiating the majority, or he could go along with the majority, repudiating the evidence of his senses. Of the 123 put to the test, a considerable percentage yielded to the majority. Whereas in ordinary circumstances individuals matching the lines will make mistakes less than 1 per cent of the time, under group pressure the minority subjects swung to acceptance of the misleading majority's wrong judgments in 36.8 per cent of the selections.

Of course individuals differed in response. At one extreme, about one quarter of the subjects were completely independent and never agreed with the erroneous judgments of the majority. At the other extreme, some individuals went with the majority nearly all the time. The performances of individuals in this experiment tend to be highly consistent. Those who strike out on the path of independence do not, as a rule, succumb to the majority even over an extended series of trials, while those who choose the path of compliance are unable to free themselves as the ordeal is prolonged.

The reasons for the startling individual differences have not yet been investigated in detail. At this point we can only report some tentative generalizations from talks with the subjects, each of whom was interviewed at the end of the experiment. Among the independent individuals were many who held fast because of staunch confidence in their own judgment. The most significant fact about them was not absence of responsiveness to the majority but a capacity to recover from doubt and to reestablish their equilibrium. Others who acted independently came to believe that the majority was correct in its answers, but they continued their dissent on the simple ground that it was their obligation to call the play as they saw it.

Among the extremely yielding persons we found a group who

quickly reached the conclusion: "I am wrong, they are right." Others yielded in order "not to spoil your results." Many of the individuals who went along suspected that the majority were "sheep" following the first responder, or that the majority were victims of an optical illusion; nevertheless, these suspicions failed to free them at the moment of decision. More disquieting were the reactions of subjects who construed their difference from the majority as a sign of some general deficiency in themselves, which at all costs they must hide. On this basis they desperately tried to merge with the majority, not realizing the longer-range consequences to themselves. All the yielding subjects underestimated the frequency with which they conformed.

Which aspect of the influence of a majority is more important—the size of the majority or its unanimity? The experiment was modified to examine this question. In one series the size of the opposition was varied from one to 15 persons. The results showed a clear trend. When a subject was confronted with only a single individual who contradicted his answers, he was swayed little: he continued to answer independently and correctly in nearly all trials. When the opposition was increased to two, the pressure became substantial: minority subjects now accepted the wrong answer 13.6 per cent of the time. Under the pressure of a majority of three, the subjects' errors jumped to 31.8 per cent. But further increases in the size of the majority apparently did not increase the weight of the pressure substantially. Clearly the size of the opposition is important only up to a point.

Disturbance of the majority's unanimity had a striking effect. In this experiment the subject was given the support of a truthful partner—either another individual who did not know of the prearranged agreement among the rest of the group, or a person who was instructed to give correct answers throughout.

The presence of a supporting partner depleted the majority of much of its power. Its pressure on the dissenting individual was reduced to one fourth: that is, subjects answered incorrectly only one fourth as often as under the pressure of a unanimous majority. The weakest persons did not yield as readily. Most interesting were the reactions to the partner. Generally the feeling toward him was one of warmth and closeness; he was credited with inspiring confidence. However, the subjects repudiated the suggestion that the partner decided them to be independent.

Was the partner's effect a consequence of his dissent, or was it related to his accuracy? We now introduced into the experimental group a person who was instructed to dissent from the majority but also to disagree with the subject. In some experiments the majority was always to choose the worst of the comparison lines and the instructed dissenter to pick the line that was closer to the length of the standard one; in others the majority was consistently intermediate and the dissenter most in error. In this manner we were able to study the relative influence of "compromising" and "extremist" dissenters.

Again the results are clear. When a moderate dissenter is present, the effect of the majority on the subject decreases by approximately one third, and extremes of yielding disappear. Moreover, most of the errors the subjects do make are moderate, rather than flagrant. In short, the dissenter largely controls the choice of errors. To this extent the subjects broke away from the majority even while bending to it.

On the other hand, when the dissenter always chose the line that was more flagrantly different from the standard, the results were of quite a different kind. The extremist dissenter produced a remarkable freeing of the subjects; their errors dropped to only 9 per cent. Furthermore, all the errors were of the moderate variety. We were able to conclude that dissent *per se* increased independence and moderated the errors that occurred, and that the direction of dissent exerted consistent effects.

In all the foregoing experiments each subject was observed only in a single setting. We now turned to studying the effects upon a given individual of a change in the situation to which he was exposed. The first experiment examined the consequences of losing or gaining a partner. The instructed partner began by answering correctly on the first six trials. With his support the subject usually resisted pressure from the majority: 18 of 27 subjects were completely independent. But after six trials the partner joined the majority. As soon as he did so, there was an abrupt rise in the subjects' errors. Their submission to the majority was just about as frequent as when the minority subject was opposed by a unanimous majority throughout.

It was surprising to find that the experience of having had a partner and of having braved the majority opposition with him had failed to strengthen the individuals' independence. Questioning at the conclusion of the experiment suggested that we had overlooked an important circumstance; namely, the strong specific effect of "desertion" by the partner to the other side. We therefore changed the conditions so that the partner would simply leave the group at the proper point. (To allay suspicion it was announced in advance that he had an appointment with the dean.) In this form of the experiment, the partner's effect outlasted his presence. The errors increased after his departure, but less markedly than after a partner switched to the majority.

In a variant of this procedure the trials began with the majority unanimously giving correct answers. Then they gradually broke away until on the sixth trial the naive subject was alone and the group unanimously against him. As long as the subject had anyone on his side, he was almost invariably independent, but as soon as he found himself alone, the tendency to conform to the majority rose abruptly.

As might be expected, an individual's resistance to group pressure in these experiments depends to a considerable degree on how wrong the majority is. We varied the discrepancy between the standard line and the other lines systematically, with the hope of reaching a point where the error of the majority would be so glaring that every subject would repudiate it and choose independently. In this we regretfully did not succeed. Even when the difference between the lines was seven inches, there were still some who yielded to the error of the majority.

The study provides clear answers to a few relatively simple questions, and it raises many others that await investigation. We would like to know the degree of consistency of persons in situations which differ in content and structure. If consistency of independence or conformity in behavior is shown to be a fact, how is it functionally related to qualities of character and personality? In what ways is independence related to sociological or cultural conditions? Are leaders more independent than other people, or are they adept at following their followers? These and many other questions may perhaps be answerable by investigations of the type described here.

Life in society requires consensus as an indispensable condition. But consensus, to be productive, requires that each individual contribute independently out of his experience and insight. When consensus comes under the dominance of conformity, the social process is polluted and the individual at the same time surrenders the powers on which his functioning as a feeling and thinking being depends. That we have found the tendency to conformity in our society so strong that reasonably intelligent and well-meaning young people are willing to call white black is a matter of concern. It raises questions about our ways of education and about the values that guide our conduct.

Yet anyone inclined to draw too pessimistic conclusions from this report would do well to remind himself that the capacities for independence are not to be underestimated. He may also draw some consolation from a further observation: those who participated in this challenging experiment agreed nearly without exception that independence was preferable to conformity.

Effects of Different Conditions of Acceptance upon Conformity to Group Norms

JAMES E. DITTES
and
HAROLD H. KELLEY

AMONG the variables influencing a person's conformity to a group's norms, two interrelated factors are likely to be important: (*a*) the extent to which he is attracted to or values his membership in the group; and (*b*) the extent to which he feels that other members are attracted to or value him. With respect to the first, it has been demonstrated that the more highly a person is attracted to a group, the more he conforms to the face-to-face pressures operating within it (1, 3) and the more he resists counternorm communications from outside it (6). The experiment reported here attempts to hold constant this first variable and to determine the effects on conformity of the second.

A relationship of *mutual dependence* is presupposed between the individual and group. Just as the individual is dependent on other members (a relationship emphasized in research on attraction to or valuation

FROM *Journal of Abnormal and Social Psychology*, 1956, 53, 100–107. Reprinted by permission of the authors and the American Psychological Association, Inc.

This experiment was conducted as part of a research program on communication and opinion change operating at Yale University on a Rockefeller Foundation grant and directed by Carl I. Hovland. The authors gratefully acknowledge the excellent cooperation of the members of the Yale Class of 1958 who served as subjects. Members of the 1954–55 senior seminar on the psychology of the small group provided expert assistance in the conduct of the experiment. The authors are also indebted to Arthur R. Cohen, Carl I. Hovland, and Ben Willerman for their suggestions on the manuscript.

of the group), they also, to some degree, depend upon him—his skills, knowledge, and general ability to contribute to group life. Through their behavior they can be expected to communicate the value they place on him (to be referred to as their *acceptance* of him) and their desire to have him continue as a member. The present research varies this information concerning a person's acceptance in a group and investigates the effects on his conformity to its norms.

The effect of either variable on conformity is probably mediated by various intervening acquired motives. We would assume that in our culture, conformity to group standards is generally learned as a means of satisfying many acquired motives, activation of which results, given appropriate conditions, in conformity behavior. The range of motives involved seems to include at least two fairly distinct clusters, one consisting of "approach" motives such as tendencies to help the group and to pattern one's self after admired persons, the other of anxiety-based motives such as desire to avoid social criticism and loss of membership.

It is probable that valuation of membership affects conformity through both kinds of motives, but that feelings of acceptance affect the person's sense of security about remaining in the group, which in turn affects primarily those motives based on anxiety. Assuming valuation constant, information communicated from fellow members that a person is little accepted by them increases his sense of insecurity, activating various acquired motives (to avoid social criticism, etc.), to which conformity behavior has been learned. Persons informed that they are well accepted in a group feel secure in their membership and have little anxiety-based motivation to conform.

In the present investigation, we are interested in two kinds of such information: (*a*) information about *how much* the person is accepted and (*b*) information about *how stable* the acceptance evaluations are. Either item would be expected to influence insecurity. Because of practical limitations, it was not possible to carry out a factorial design permitting evaluation of the separate effects and interaction of these two variables. It was decided that an investigation of their joint effects would provide a better initial test of the fruitfulness of our analysis than a study of either variable alone. Throughout the report, the label "acceptance" applies to both these components.

The hypothesis we propose to test is: Among persons who attach equal importance to their membership in a group, those who receive information that they are only minimally accepted by their colleagues and that this evaluation is subject to change, possibly becoming worse, conform more than persons who receive information that they are highly accepted and that this situation is stable.

A similar hypothesis was tested by Kelley and Shapiro (5) who found it supported by correlational evidence that nonconformity was associated with high actual popularity or acceptance. But the hypothesis was not supported by the experimental manipulations of fictitious information about acceptance. It was suggested that this relationship was obscured because valuation of membership was not held constant. They found that information that one is poorly accepted affects not only his feelings of acceptance but also his subsequent valuation of the group. As our analysis suggests, a decline in valuation should decrease the "approach" motives which prompt conformity (e.g., desire to aid the group) thus offsetting any increase in other conformity-prompting motives resulting from the insecurity derived from feeling poorly accepted.

The present experiment was designed to avoid this obscuring effect in two ways: (*a*) It was attempted, with partial success, to keep valuation uniform by motivating all *S*s so highly to participate in the group that their valuation of membership would remain constantly high throughout the experiment. (*b*) Several degrees of acceptance were introduced, instead of two, with the expectation that even if valuation varied significantly between the extreme conditions of acceptance, it might remain uniform between more similar conditions, particularly with the conditions of relatively high acceptance. In this case the hypothesis could still be tested by comparing the conformity among persons in those degrees of acceptance for which valuation remained relatively uniform.

METHOD

Subjects. One hundred and three volunteers from the Yale freshman class met in 18 five- and six-man groups. Members of each group had no prior acquaintance with one another.

Incentives to motivate Ss to value and participate in their group, and instructions about possible rejection. At the outset, each *S* agreed to work with his group in a contest against the other experimental groups. A cash prize and prestigeful recognition were offered as awards for the group best in efficiency, smoothness of working together, and soundness of decisions. These instructions carried the strong implication that unanimity in group decisions was highly desirable.

It was then announced that to guarantee an effectively working group, members would have the option of eliminating from their group any person who appeared detrimental to its success. For this purpose, subsequent tasks were to be interrupted periodically while each member anonymously rated each other one on this question:

How desirable is it that this person be kept in the group?

———extremely desirable

———very desirable

———somewhat desirable

———not very desirable, but he should be kept in

———he should be rejected from the group

It was made to appear likely that some *S*s would receive low ratings and that this would be unpleasant and penalizing for them: they would have to undergo the embarrassment of defending themselves in an open discussion of whether they should be rejected; rejection would carry the implication that the person was inadequate in his "social adaptability." (While the ratings were actually collected during the subsequent period, no *S* was ever discussed for rejection.)

Introduction of "delinquent gangs" problem and achievement of unanimous decision; interruptions to obtain ratings of others. In each group, an initial discussion concerned the relative worthiness of two gangs of juvenile delinquents, described in detailed simulated court records. A difference in the records insured that the same gang would be judged better in all groups, but this difference was slight enough that the decision could emerge only after considerable discussion. To heighten the tendency to conformity, the problem was described as being much like a jury's in that solution required the agreement of all. During the discussion, an observer kept a tally of each man's participation and whether his comments were for or against the gang ultimately favored by the group.

After general agreement was reached in free discussion, the norm was crystallized and registered by having the group rate the two gangs on several scales such that one gang was assigned labels such as "very deserving" and "fundamentally good"; and the other gang was characterized as "vicious," "malicious," etc. During this process *E* refused to record any rating until it was concurred in by every member. After this public agreement, *S*s privately rated the gangs on different scales, to provide a measure of their initial acceptance of the group's characterization of the two gangs.

The discussion of the gangs was interrupted three times to permit the members to rate one another as to the desirability of their remaining in the group. Each time, *E* quickly thumbed through the ratings, pretended that no *S* had received low enough ratings to warrant discussing his possible rejection, and "discarded" the ratings into a wastebasket.

Introduction of different conditions of acceptance. At the end of the "gangs" discussion, *E* suggested a rest period. While *S*s were relaxing, he casually inquired whether they'd be interested in seeing how they had been rated. Before anyone could object, *E* retrieved the slips from the wastebasket and distributed them. In this manner, each *S* was allowed to see privately what he thought to be the ratings made of him by the other members. These were in fact fictitious ratings prepared in advance and substituted for the originals in the wastebasket. So that *S*s would similarly interpret these ratings, *E* announced that he had noticed the average to be around "very desirable." In each group, one person found his ratings to be mostly higher than this average (*high* condition); two received ratings mostly at this average (*average* condition); two had ratings slightly below average (*low* condition); and one received ratings well below (*very low* condition). (In 5-man groups, only one of the intermediate conditions was represented by two persons.) Information about the probable stability of the ratings was provided by *E*'s statement, as though from experience with ratings in other groups, that the higher the rating the less likely it was to change; that low ratings were quite likely to change, possibly becoming higher or *even lower*. It was intended that as a result of this information, a person in the *high* condition would feel highly accepted, *and* that this was a stable situation. At the other extreme, a person in the *very low* condition was supposed to feel very little acceptance, *and* that his colleagues' evaluations might change, even becoming worse.

Before each session, the four conditions of acceptance were randomly assigned to positions around the discussion table. The 103 *S*s were distributed among the conditions as follows: 18 in *high,* 33 in *average,* 34 in *low,* and 18 in *very low.* The intermediate conditions were assigned more *S*s because greater variability of behavior was anticipated in them.

Additional information about the gangs, private judgments, and public discussion. After the fictitious ratings had been introduced and interpreted, the group proceeded to the second phase of the "gangs" problem. The purpose of this phase was to introduce pressure to deviate from the group consensus about the gangs and to determine each person's subsequent adherence to the norm, as indicated in his further private ratings of the gangs and in his opinions expressed in open discussion.

The pressure to deviate consisted of information suggesting that the unpreferred gang was superior to the previous evaluation, hinting at mitigating circumstances and desirable traits not clearly brought out in the original records. The *S*s privately evaluated the additional information by checking agreement or disagreement with evaluative statements that accompanied it. The tendency to discredit or "explain away" the new information was assumed to represent conformity with the group's original norm (these scores are reported as Gang Index 1). The *S*s also made additional ratings of the gangs after reading this information, one set anonymously and one set supposedly for public comparison (Gang Indices 2 and 3 respectively). To obtain an indication of each *S*'s speed of responding to the contradictory information, the observer noted the order in which *S*s finished making their evaluations and ratings.

Following the ratings, the group openly discussed the gangs for a short period during which were made observations comparable to those made during the initial discussion of the gangs.

Administration of number-judgment problem. A second situation for assessing conformity was next introduced, using a task requiring simple comparative judgments of numerosity—judging which of two squares contained more dots, the same problem used by Kelley and Shapiro (5). The problem was presented to *S*s working privately, in a series of eleven pairs of squares of decreasing difficulty, in which the correct answer was the same for the entire series. The *S*s were to share ideas and try to improve their group score by exchanging written messages between successive judgments. In fact, their messages were not delivered, but were intercepted and replaced by a standard set of messages which led each *S* to believe that all the other members of his group had decided that a given square, *A*, was the correct answer for the series. To heighten the pressure to conform to this consensus, the rule was imposed that the group would score points on any one of the eleven successive judgments only when the group was unanimously correct.

Pressure to deviate from the consensus was introduced by having the later pairs in the series provide increasingly clear evidence that the consensus was in error, that square *B* was the correct answer.

On each pair, *S* reported his "private opinion" (and degree of confidence in it) and also a "public vote" to be tallied toward the group score. These were summed over the last ten judgments (the ones made following receipt of messages indicating the group consensus), yielding Dot Index 1 for the private opinions (weighted by confidence) and Dot Index 2 for the public votes. It will be noted that these conformity indices may reflect two aspects of conformity; (*a*) initial acceptance of the apparent consensus and (*b*) continued adherence to it in the face of the contradictory evidence. Actually, there is little variability in conformity on the early judgments (the general level being high), so these indices reflect primarily the second aspect.

Subsequent measures. (*a*) The *S*s' perception of experimental conditions of acceptance were measured by a direct question immediately after they saw the ratings and at the end of the experiment, by recall of the ratings they had received. (*b*) Valuation of membership in the group: Immediately after receiving the ratings and also at the end of the experiment, *S*s answered short questionnaires containing items measuring their positive motivation to remain in their particular group, e.g., desire to be invited to further meetings, liking to work with the other members. (*c*) The *S*s' interpretations of conditions of acceptance: On a questionnaire given several months after the experiment, *S*s indicated how likely they considered it to be that they might be rejected, and the freedom they felt about expressing opinions contrary to the group's judgment.

Termination of experimental session. At the end of each session, the purpose and procedures of the experiment were disclosed and the *S*s were told that the ratings they had seen were fictitious. These disclosures were greeted with laughter, expressions of relief, and even a certain amount of disbelief. At no time did any *S* indicate that he had clearly doubted the genuineness of the ratings he had seen. Special care was taken to reinvolve as active and obviously accepted group members those *S*s who had been in the conditions of *low* and *very low* acceptance. The *S*s were requested to maintain secrecy during the remainder of the weeks scheduled for the experiment. Their excellent cooperation in this provides one of several indications of the favorable attitudes with which they left the experiment.

RESULTS

Direct Effects of Experimental Conditions

Perceived acceptance in group. The fictitious ratings clearly produced the intended differences among the experimental conditions in amount of perceived acceptance. The question, "From the point of view of the group, how desirable is it that you, yourself, be kept in?" ("extremely desirable" scored as 5 and "I should be rejected from the group" scored as 1), yielded average scores of 4.7, 3.8, 3.3, and 2.9, respectively for the *high*, *average*, *low*, and *very low* conditions. Analysis of variance reveals that the between-condition variance is significant at beyond the .001 level of confidence. Furthermore, at the end of the experiment, *S*s were able to recall their ratings accurately. The recalled ratings did not differ significantly from those actually received.

Perceived likelihood of being rejected. Several questions dealing with perceived likelihood of being asked to leave the group and with preoccupation about this possibility serve largely to differentiate the *very low* condition from the other three, the *very low* Ss viewing rejection as more likely. The *very low's* differ significantly ($p < .01$) from each of the other conditions which do not differ significantly among themselves. These questions were asked only in the questionnaire given some months after the experiment so the results must be viewed with some reservations.

Valuation of membership. The efforts to keep all Ss highly attracted to the group were only partially successful. The *high* and *average* conditions showed the highest and approximately equal levels of attraction while the levels for the *low* and *very low* conditions were markedly lower, especially the latter. This effect was the same whether measured immediately after the ratings were distributed or at the end of the experiment. The total valuation scores yielded a between-condition variance which is significant at beyond the .001 level of confidence. Table 1 indicates the different valuation scores and the statistical significance of the differences between adjacent conditions.

Because valuation of membership was kept uniform only for *high* and *average* conditions, major interest in the subsequent results will be in

TABLE 1

Valuation of Group Membership by Four Experimental Conditions of Acceptance

CONDITION OF ACCEPTANCE	HIGH		AVERAGE		LOW		VERY LOW
Average valuation of membership in group	40		39.5		37		35.5
Significance of difference between adjacent conditions		$p > .50$		$p < .0001$		$p < .0001$	

comparisons of these two conditions. In these, we may expect there to be little interaction of valuation with our two main variables, acceptance and conformity.

Effects on Participation

The Ss in the *very low* condition reduced their participation in the discussion of the delinquent gangs by about 50 per cent after seeing the ratings ($p < .01$ for the change from the prior amount of participation). In contrast, *average* acceptance tended to result in increased participation, the difference between before and after being significant at the .09 level of confidence. The amount of participation after the ratings were received, expressed as a percentage of the amount of prior participation, is as follows: 93 per cent, 131 per cent, 118 per cent, and 56 per cent, respectively for *high, average, low,* and *very low.*

Effects on Conformity

Conformity in responding to questionnaires. Average values of the conformity indices derived from the questionnaires used with the two tasks are presented in Table 2, high positive scores indicating high conformity, negative scores low conformity. The gang-judgment indices were adjusted to take account of individual differences in initial conformity to the group decisions and intergroup differences in conformity behavior.[1] The three separate gang indices were summed to give an over-all gang-judgment score. Also the five different measures were combined into an over-all conformity score by counting for each *S* the number of his scores on the five measures which were above the average of his experimental group. The average of these numbers for each experimental condition is presented in the last line of Table 2. Because the theoretical interest centers on the *high* and *average* conditions by virtue of their having the highest and approximately equal levels of valuation of membership, *p* values are given in Table 2 for differences between them. Since the two low conditions show the same tendency to be lower than the *average, p* values are also presented for the differences between their combined mean and that of the *average.*

In general, *S*s receiving ratings of *average* acceptability tended to show more conformity behavior than did *S*s receiving ratings of *high* acceptability. The results with *low* and *very low* conditions are less uniform, possibly for reasons connected with their rather low valuation of membership. They showed less conformity than the *average* and

1 The scores on initial acceptance of the group decisions on the gangs were obtained before the experimental manipulations of acceptance and, as might be expected, an analysis of them reveals no differences approaching significance among the *S*s who later found themselves in the different conditions. In order to eliminate these initial individual differences from the measures of subsequent conformity, each *S*'s score on initial acceptance was subtracted from each of the three later measures of opinion. Analysis of variance of each of these difference scores showed that the 18 experimental groups differed significantly in mean level of conformity and also in variability. These effects presumably reflect slightly different definitions of the norm and differing pressures to conform which developed during different experimental sessions. To eliminate these differences, on each measure of the gang judgment each *S* was given a standard score representing the amount of his conformity with reference to the mean and standard deviation of his particular experimental group. As noted in the text, the dot-judgment scores, based only on behavior occurring after the experimental manipulations, reflect both initial acceptance of the norms and resistance to contrary evidence, though largely the latter. It was not necessary to transform them to standard scores because they did not vary significantly among experimental sessions with regard either to means or variances.

TABLE 2

*Average Conformity Scores for the Four Experimental Conditions of Acceptance**

CONFORMITY INDEX	EXPERIMENTAL CONDITIONS OF ACCEPTANCE				p VALUES FOR	
	High	*Average*	*Low*	*Very low*	*High vs. Average*	*Average vs. Low and Very Low*
Gang judgments:						
1	−.22	.07	.10	−.09		
2	−.41	.32	−.10	.09	<.02	.10
3	−.31	.20	−.07	.04	<.10	
Over-all gang	−.92	.57	−.05	.02	<.05	
Dot judgments:						
1	39.0	43.4	33.2	36.4		.02
2	7.7	8.2	7.2	6.7		<.05
Over-all Conformity	2.5	3.2	2.5	2.6	.06	<.05

* Positive values indicate high conformity; negative values, low conformity. The significance of the difference between conditions on the over-all conformity index was tested with chi square, dividing those who were above their group mean on a majority of the five indices from the remainder. A t test was used to test the significance of the other differences noted.

more than the *high* condition on gang judgments, and less than either of of the other two on dot judgments.

The three indices of conformity on gang judgments were found to be significantly intercorrelated, as were the two indices on dot judgments. Significant correlations between gang and dot measures were found only for the *high* and *average* conditions and these had values of around .50. Despite this low degree of consistency between the two types of conformity behavior, Table 2 shows that the difference in conformity between *high* and *average* conditions of acceptance is consistent over the two somewhat different tasks.

A less direct indication of conformity gives results supporting those of Table 2. An observer noted the order in which the *S*s at each session completed the task of evaluating the additional information that suggested that the group's decision on the gangs was inaccurate. It might be assumed that persons oriented most strongly toward conforming would give less attention to the new information and make quick judgments simply on the basis of the previously established norm; and that persons less motivated to conform would give more conscientious attention to the information and hence complete the task more slowly. The average rank order of finishing the task is as follows: 4.2, 2.7, 3.8, and 3.1, for *high*, *average*, *low*, and *very low*, respectively. The condition of *average* acceptance was fastest, indicating, on the basis of the above assumptions, most conformity;

the *high* condition was slowest indicating least conformity. The difference between these two is significant at the .05 level of confidence using a chi-square analysis that divided Ss into slowest and fastest halves.

Conformity in open discussion. In Table 2, the measures intended to tap private opinions (Gang Index 1 and 2; Dot Index 1) and those supposed to reflect public expression (Gang Index 3 and Dot Index 2) reveal essentially similar trends over the four conditions of acceptance. However, as compared with the quasi-public nature of the latter measures, analysis of actual public expressions of opinion shows a somewhat different pattern of conformity from that noted in Table 2. (This finding suggests that the questionnaire results mainly reflect private conformity.) In the discussion of the gangs after the additional information had been read, there was a general decrease in the proportion of comments that expressed conformity to the group's earlier preference for one gang over the other. (Before the information, 88 per cent of the comments involving opinion were favorable to the group norm; afterward, only 49 per cent were so.) This decrease was less for the *very low* condition than for the others; i.e., in their actual public remarks, the *very lows* conformed more closely to the original norm than any of the other conditions. The scores[2] for the *high, average, low* and *very low* conditions, respectively, were: −.55, −.47, −.52, and −.23, with the greater negative number indicating the greater deviation from the norm. Chi-square analysis, dividing Ss at the over-all median into high and low changers, shows that the difference between *very low* and the other conditions taken together is significant at the .08 level. The difference between any other condition and the rest does not approach significance.

This result receives partial confirmation from responses to a question about how free the *S* would have felt to express an opinion contrary to the group opinion. *Very low* Ss report more hesitancy in this respect than do *High* Ss ($p = .07$) and the other conditions report intermediate degrees.

DISCUSSION

To simplify the reader's task of assimilating the results and trends reported above, they are summarized verbally in Table 3. We now consider the interpretation of these findings. In several respects, they are consistent with the hypothesized relationship between acceptance and conformity. However, the total pattern of results suggests that the relationship depends on more complex intervening variables than had been anticipated.

One set of data consistent with the hypothesis is provided by the

2 The score for each *S* represents the proportion of his total remarks in the later discussion which were pronorm, minus the proportion of his total remarks in the earlier discussion which were pronorm, plus the proportion of antinorm remarks in the earlier discussion, minus the proportion of antinorm remarks in the later discussion.

comparison of the *high* and *average* conditions. Since the relation between acceptance and conformity is likely to be obscured if valuation varies, as previously discussed, the hypothesis can be clearly tested only by comparing conditions having fairly similar levels of valuation—in this experiment, the *high* and *average* conditions. Between these two, higher conformity behavior was exhibited by the condition of lower and less stable acceptance. The available evidence does not indicate, however, any difference between *high* and *average* Ss in feelings of insecurity about their membership. If these groups actually do not differ in this respect, the higher conformity of the *average* Ss must be explained on some other basis than the one underlying our hypothesis: that they would be more motivated to avoid rejection. Their total pattern of behavior—high conformity on the questionnaires, rapid reactions to counternorm information, and heightened participation in the discussion after learning of their acceptance—is perhaps more suggestive of a desire to improve their social standing. The *S* in the *average* condition places considerable value upon the group, but at the same time, is not completely accepted in it. Since *E*'s comments indicate there is some possibility that his acceptance status may change, we might expect him to try to attain complete acceptance.

TABLE 3

Digest of the Results of the Four Experimental Conditions of Acceptance

VARIABLE	EXPERIMENTAL CONDITIONS OF ACCEPTANCE			
	High	*Average*	*Low*	*Very Low*
Perceived acceptance	High	Average	Low	Very Low
Perceived likelihood of being rejected				Higher than any other condition
Valuation of membership	Moderate	Moderate	Low	Very Low
Participation in group discussion		Highest		Lowest
Speed of reacting to counternorm information		Faster than any other condition		
Conformity in questionnaire responses (private?)	Low	High	Low	Low
Conformity in public statements				Higher than any other condition
Felt freedom to express deviant opinion	Highest			Lowest

Eager participation and uncritical conformity to the norms would presumably facilitate this improvement in status. That this conformity extends even to the expression of private opinions on the questionnaire is understandable if we consider that there may be a general tendency for upward-mobility-oriented persons to identify with and take over the values of higher status indviduals (7).

The behavior exhibited by the *very lows* is much more consistent with our initial notion of anxiety-motivated conformity. In general, and in accord with prior findings (4, 5), group membership loses its attractiveness for persons little valued by their colleagues.[3] Along with this loss goes a decline in tendency to accept the group's norm, at least in quasi-private settings. In the extreme case, however, where acceptance is so low that actual rejection is presumably an imminent possibility, anxiety about rejection is especially high and the result seems to be a pattern of guarded public behavior, i.e., the *very lows* withdrew from open participation in the discussion and showed the highest amount of conformity in the opinions they did publicly voice. Avoidance of rejection, which is presumably motivated by penalties particularly attached to rejection (embarrassment, suffering failure in front of the *E*), is of course a variable different from the positive motivation to participate in the group; so anxiety over rejection may have been high for the *very lows*, even though they had little positive motivation to stay in the group. (The questionnaire some months after the experiment indicated that the desire to be kept in the group and not be rejected had been as high for the *very lows* as for the other conditions, while at the same time, their estimate of the likelihood of this event had been higher.) Their public conformity, then, may reflect a relatively high motivation to avoid rejection. That they exhibit a high public conformity but little private acceptance is consistent with Festinger's hypothesis that this particular pattern of conformity results when the attractiveness of group membership is low, but people are constrained to stay in the group by external threats or barriers against leaving (2).

In brief, our results suggest two processes linking conditions of acceptance to conformity. For persons who value a group, are less than completely accepted in it, but have some possibility of achieving complete acceptance, conformity facilitates such a gain in acceptance. Their conformity is unquestioning and extends to private opinions as well as to public behavior. On the other hand, persons who are on the brink of unwelcome rejection manifest conformity only at the public level, presumably as a means of forestalling such rejection.

3 This raises interesting theoretical questions which cannot be discussed here: Is acceptance by others one of the prerequisites for desiring membership in a group? Why does valuation not decline with the change from *high* to *average* conditions, but drops sharply for the lower degrees of acceptance? Is this a level-of-aspiration effect, in which the motivation to stay in the group declines only as the possibility of success in this effort drops below some critical value?

The major variable in this experiment—security and degree of acceptance—is, from several points of view, an aspect of what is commonly called "status." We might therefore expect our results to shed some light on the problem of the relationship between status and conformity. In general, we doubt that this relationship is ever a simple one. Our results and interpretations suggest that to predict conformity from status, clarity is first needed as to the conditions under which conformity is to be observed, whether they involve surveillance by other members or relative privacy. Then, it must be asked whether the observed differences in status are associated with differences in (*a*) valuation of membership, (*b*) security in membership, and (*c*) motivation to improve one's acceptance. Under some conditions, as when low status is associated with relatively high insecurity about membership, it seems likely that status is inversely related to public conformity. But if there is a marked difference between high and low status persons in their valuation of membership, as a result of greater privileges and satisfactions being associated with higher status, status and conformity may be correlated positively.

Undoubtedly, a number of other factors also affect this relationship. For example, it is easy to imagine instances where special motives directed toward conformity would be operative for high status persons, but not for low status members. One such case would be that where the opinions of a high status member have carried inordinate weight in the setting of group standards so that they happen to coincide with his private preferences. What appears as conformity in his behavior may actually be motivated by private considerations that preceded the acceptance of his behavior as the norm. Another instance may be when special conformity demands are made of high status persons, for example, because of the special symbolic value their conformity may possess.

These considerations indicate that many factors affect the relation between status and conformity. In some instances, the relationship may be direct; in other, inverse; and in still others, perhaps, nonexistent. We believe the specific situations and results will be most intelligible when analyzed in terms of factors such as those suggested above.

SUMMARY

In experimental groups of *S*s, two different norms were developed: one concerning a social value judgment; the other, a simple perceptual judgment. The *S*s were experimentally made to feel different degrees of being accepted by the other members and were then given opportunities and incentives to deviate from the norms. Subsequent conformity, participation, and attitudes toward the group were studied in relation to the different conditions of acceptance.

The results point to two contrasting patterns of conformity evoked by different conditions of acceptance. The first appears to consist of a high degree of genuine adherence to the norms, as indicated by unquestioning conformity extending even to conditions of privacy, and a higher-than-average motivation to participate in group discussion. This pattern appeared for the experimental condition in which subjects enjoyed somewhat less than complete acceptance but probably saw the possibility of gaining this status. It is interpreted as based on strong positive attachment to the group and motivation to improve one's status therein.

The second pattern is marked by high conformity only under public conditions. It occurred for the experimental condition of lowest acceptance, in which *S*s saw total rejection as being a likely possibility. The interpretation is made that although *S*s in this condition have lost much of their positive motivation to conform to group standards (indicated by their very low valuation of membership and reflected in their low private conformity), they may nevertheless be concerned about the negative consequences accompanying rejection (at least, under the conditions represented in this experiment). Public conformity is seen as a way of forestalling this unpleasant eventuality.

REFERENCES

1. Back, K. W. Influence through social communication. *J. abnorm. soc. Psychol.*, 1951, 46, 9–23.
2. Festinger, L. An analysis of compliant behavior. In M. Sherif and M. O. Wilson (Eds.), *Group relations at the crossroads.* New York: Harper, 1953. Pp. 232–255.
3. Festinger, L., Schachter, S., & Back, K. *Social pressures in informal groups.* New York: Harper, 1950.
4. Jackson, J. Analysis of interpersonal relations in a formal organization. Unpublished doctor's dissertation, Univer. of Michigan, 1952. Reported in D. P. Cartwright and A. F. Zander (Eds.), *Group dynamics.* Evanston: Row, Peterson, 1953. P. 424.
5. Kelley, H. H., & Shapiro, M. M. An experiment on conformity to group norms where conformity is detrimental to group achievement. *Amer. sociol. Rev.*, 1954, 19, 667–677.
6. Kelley, H. H., & Volkart, E. H. The resistance to change of group-anchored attitudes. *Amer. sociol. Rev.*, 1952, 17, 453–465.
7. Lewin, K. Self-hatred among Jews. In *Resolving social conflicts.* New York: Harper, 1948. Pp. 186–200.

The Perpetuation of an Arbitrary Tradition Through Several Generations of a Laboratory Microculture

ROBERT C. JACOBS
and
DONALD T. CAMPBELL

ACCORDING to Sumner (12) "the mores can make anything right," and he went on to illustrate with a chapter on sacral harlotry and child sacrifice. According to Tarde (13) "imitation is the key to the social mystery," "society is imitation," "social man is a veritable somnambulist." Such quotations indicate the late 19th century awareness of the power of culture to perpetuate arbitrary beliefs. Less drastically expressed, some such perspective permeates present day social science, although tempered somewhat by functionalism in anthropology and sociology. In social psychology, for example, cultural tradition tends to be invoked primarily as an "explanation" for social evils, prejudice, resistance to ameliorative social change, and the like. The current emphasis upon conformity reinforces this view, in spite of Asch's (2) demurrer. Yet there are, no doubt, restraints upon a complete arbitrariness to culture, particularly with regard to beliefs that lie within people's direct range of observation. Thus arbitrary and erroneous superstitions about the shape of fishhooks probably would not long survive the systematic drift pressures resulting from continual minor variations some of which are in the direction of noticeably more effective form. Here lies the

FROM *Journal of Abnormal and Social Psychology*, 1961, 62, 649–658. Reprinted by permission of author and the American Psychological Association, Inc.

problem in the theory of culture for which a laboratory analogue was sought.

Since Sherif's (11) classic studies on the formation of "social norms" in laboratory groups, there have been sporadic efforts to bring the process of cultural transmission into the laboratory. While much small group research might be so interpreted, the present study was in particular inspired by Sherif's studies, by Rose and Felton's (10) "experimental histories of culture," and by the preliminary report of experiments on the evolution of "microcultures" by Gerard, Kluckhohn, and Rapoport (4). In the latter two studies and in the present one, there is an effort to demonstrate a perpetuation of "cultural" characteristics that transcends the replacement of individual persons. In the present study confederates have been employed to establish an extreme cultural norm, the inculcation and survival of which is then studied as the confederates are one by one taken out of the group, naive new members gradually introduced, who then unwittingly become the further transmitters of the belief to still newer entrants.

The specific culture trait and the ecology of the group relative to such traits should obviously affect the success in the indoctrination of each new generation, and the rate of erosion of the tradition by innovation. In the Rose and Felton (10) study, group interpretations of Rorschach cards were employed, a material offering considerable latitude for cultural arbitrariness and idiosyncrasy. In the Gerard, Kluckhohn, and Rapoport (4) study, the groups were continually faced with new instances of a very difficult puzzle series, and were continually confronted with evidences of the lack of perfection of their traditional solutions, a situation encouraging the evolution of more adaptive norms, and unfavorable to the perpetuation of pure superstition. For the present study, a task was sought which would allow as much latitude for cultural arbitrariness as the Rose and Felton situation, and which would, in addition, make possible the ready quantification of effects. The original Sherif (11) autokinetic movement situation was judged to provide this: if a person views a pinpoint of light in an otherwise totally blacked-out room, the light soon appears to move. The illusion is a strong one for most persons, and is apparent even to those who know the light to be stationary. As Sherif has shown, naive respondents are very suggestible as to the degree of movement seen, and laboratory group norms on the amount of movement are rapidly established without the respondents being aware of the fictitiousness of their judgments.

So labile is the autokinetic experience or at least the translation of it into judgments of linear extent, that one reading the reports of studies employing it might expect that an arbitrary group norm once established would be passed on indefinitely without diminution; that once well indoctrinated, the naive group members would become as rigid and reliable spokesmen for the norm as were the confederates who preceded them; that each new generation would unwittingly become a part of a self-perpetuating cultural conspiracy propagating superstition and falsehood.

But the autokinetic experience is not completely labile. The very fact that sophisticated observers under strong "suggestion" to see the light remain fixed still perceive movement, shows this. Haggard and Rose (6), in attempting to condition perceived movement on a right-left dimension, found for most respondents a strong rightward bias. In preliminaries to the present experiment, we learned that for our setting, respondents reporting alone produced mean individual judgments over 30 trials of from .64 to 6.67 inches, and with individual judgments rarely if ever approaching the arbitrary cultural norm of 15 to 16 inches which the confederates in our study provide. It is the presence of this potential natural norm that makes our inculcated cultural norm truly "arbitrary," and provides a counterpressure to the cultural tradition in its transmission across the experimental generations.

METHOD

Respondents

The 175 respondents who took part in this experiment were students, enrolled in introductory social sciences courses. They were unsophisticated concerning the autokinetic phenomenon and were unadvised as to the nature of the experiment previous to the time of serving in it. The respondents were assigned randomly to the six conditions involved. The number of respondents participating per group is shown in Table 1.

Materials, Apparatus, and Common Procedure

The experiment took place in a completely darkened, windowless, fan-ventilated room. The respondents were seated in a row 8 feet from a box designed to emit a small pinpoint of light. A 1 rpm induction motor was attached in series with the lamp, and a single switch controlled both. The motor was used solely as an auditory effect supporting the illusion of movement.

All respondents were blindfolded when brought into the experimental situation and were asked to put their blindfolds on whenever the door was opened to allow old respondents to leave and new ones to enter. This gave the respondents little if any knowledge of the size and arrangement of the experimental room. The individual respondents received the following instructions:

> This is a movement experiment. It is designed to test the students' visual perceptions with respect to space. In the next room is an apparatus that will project a small light. A few seconds after we begin the light will move. It may move in a wavy motion or pattern or it may follow a recognizable course. However, your specific task will pertain merely to judging the distance that the light moves from the time that it appears until it is turned off.

All judgments should be made in inches along a straight line connecting the starting point and the ending point on each trial.

Respondents going into group conditions received these additional instructions:

You are going to join a student (or number of students) who are already serving in this experiment. . . . You will be seated in the seat on the far left. To simplify recording procedure I will ask you to report your judgments beginning with the person on the far right and ending with you on the far left. When I stop you the person on the far right will leave, each of you inside will move right one seat, and a new person will be brought in.

Each trial was 5 seconds in length and after each block of 30 trials a ventilation fan was turned on by the experimenter. During this time in the group conditions, the "oldest" member of the group was taken out, other members moved to the right one seat, and a new member introduced. In the solitary conditions, respondents were told that ventilation took place as a health requirement. The ventilation period was timed to take approximately the same amount of time that was necessary to give instructions to a new respondent and bring him in in the other conditions.

Experimental Conditions

Table 1 shows the main feature of the six treatment conditions. (These have been given designations summarizing the group's construction. C and X stand for control and experimental. The first digit indicates the size of the group, while the second digit indicates the number of confederates present in the first generation.) There are two control conditions. In C-1-0 each respondent

TABLE 1

Experimental Paradigm

CONDITION	SIZE OF GROUP	NUMBER OF CONFEDERATES	TRIALS PER GENERATION	NUMBER OF GENERATIONS	GENERATIONS PER RESPONDENT	NUMBER OF REPLICATIONS	NUMBER OF NAIVE RESPONDENTS
C-1-0	1	0	30	—	4	24	24
C-3-0	3	0	30	10	3	3	30
X-2-1	2	1	30	9	2	3	27
X-3-2	3	2	30	10	3	3	30
X-4-3	4	3	30	11	4	3	33
X-3-1	3	1	30	9	3	3	29

judged the movement of the light in solitude for four periods (called generations for the group conditions) of 30 judgments each. In C-3-0 respondents were run in groups of three, replacing one each generation (or 30 trials), for a total of nine generations.

A major dimension of experimental variation was the number of "culture-bearing" confederates with which the first naive respondent found himself placed. In experimental groups X-2-1, X-3-2, and X-4-3, the initial generation consisted of a solitary naive respondent sitting to the left of one, two, or three confederates who gave their judgments before he did, and who had been instructed to give judgments between 15 and 16 inches. The experimental variation in number of confederates was expected to produce cultural traditions of increasing strength. Confederates were recruited from the same subject pool as were the naive respondents. All were pledged to secrecy, with apparent success.

Another mode of manipulating cultural strength was explored by adding X-3-1, a group of two naive respondents led by one confederate. Thus C-3-0, X-3-1, and X-3-2 provide a set of three-person groups of 0, 1, and 2 confederates in the first generation.

The confederates who were present in the starting condition were removed one at a time, after each round of 30 judgments. Thus the groups with more confederates present in the first generation likewise had some stooging present for more generations. The shifting of members one chair to the right each generation, plus the rule of responding in turn from right to left, insured that on each trial a confederate or the eldest member of the group spoke first.

Each of the groups was replicated three times, while 24 respondents were run in the solitary control condition. The conditions were given in a counterbalanced order insuring that the differences in respondent selection from one part of the term to the other were kept independent of treatments.

RESULTS

Control Treatments

Figure 1 shows the results for the two control conditions. It will be noted that for C-1-0 the mean of the 24 respondents starts at 3.80 and decreases steadily generation by generation to a value of 2.90. This decrease is highly significant statistically, being found in the individual records of 21 of the 24 respondents, for which, by a two-tailed sign test, $p < .0002$.

The three-person group control, C-3-0, shows very comparable mean levels, and likewise a general decline. The effect is not so clearly significant and is beclouded by the mutual influence that the group situation introduces. In the three replications, two groups declined, while one started abnormally low and increased. Comparing Generation 1 with the last generation with three persons present, Number 8, average judgment changes were 3.93–2.90, 6.72–2.03, and 1.72–2.49. Notice that in spite of the idiosyncratic norms of Generation 1, the three replications became more similar as the process of successive replacement went on. Of the 27 respondents present in more than one generation, 16 showed declines between their first and last generations.

In graphing C-3-0, the data have been averaged in a different fashion from the foregoing. To show the successive replacement and overlapping generational character, the careers of each successive replacement have been plotted separately. The plotted points represent the average of the three replications; that is, each plotted point represents the average judg-

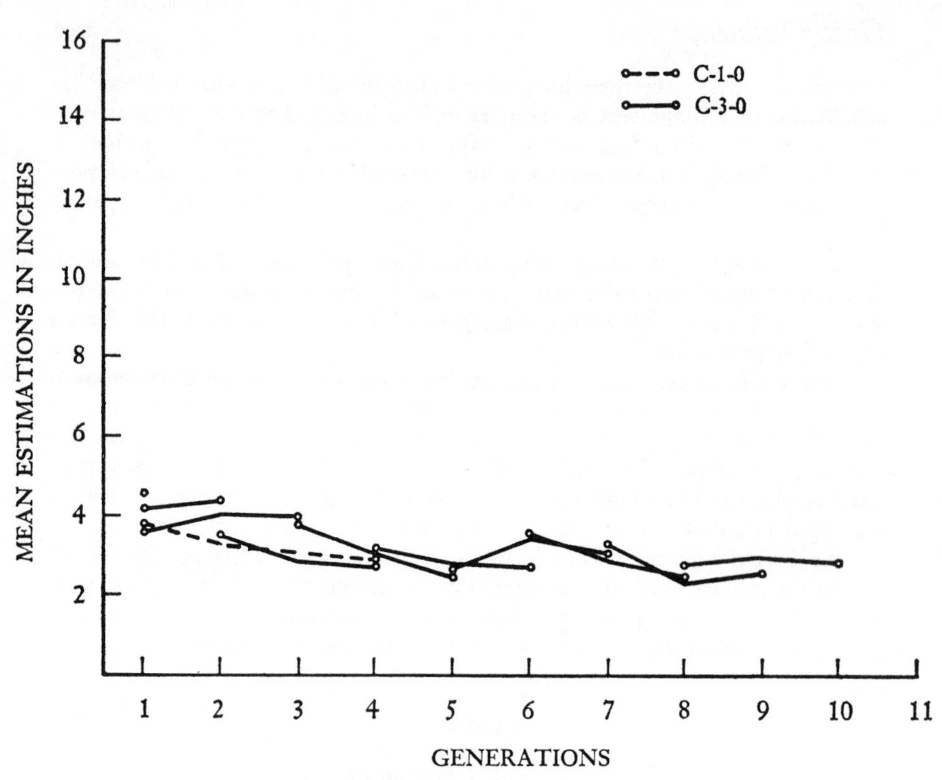

FIG. 1. Mean judgments of the control groups.

ment of three individual respondents, each taking the corresponding role in the three separate groups replicating this control treatment.

The two types of control established such similar reference standards that they cannot both be used conveniently as visual base lines in the graphing of the results of the experimental treatments. For this reason, in Figures 2, 3, and 4, only C-1-0 has been plotted. This plotting has been done in such a manner as to provide a parallel for each new starting generation in the experimental group. Thus in Figure 2, where each respondent stays only two generations, the first two generations of data from C-1-0 have been repeatedly plotted. In Figure 4, all four generations of C-1-0 are needed as a comparison base.

Transmission of Arbitrary Norms over Total Replacement of Indoctrinator

Figures 2, 3, 4, and 5 present the transmission results from X-2-1, X-3-2, X-4-3, and X-3-1. The first question that we ask of the data is whether or not the naive respondents, once indoctrinated by the confederates, have themselves transmitted any vestiges of the arbitrary cultural norm once the original indoctrinators have passed on. To test this, one can examine the judgments of the first generation of respondents to judge without any

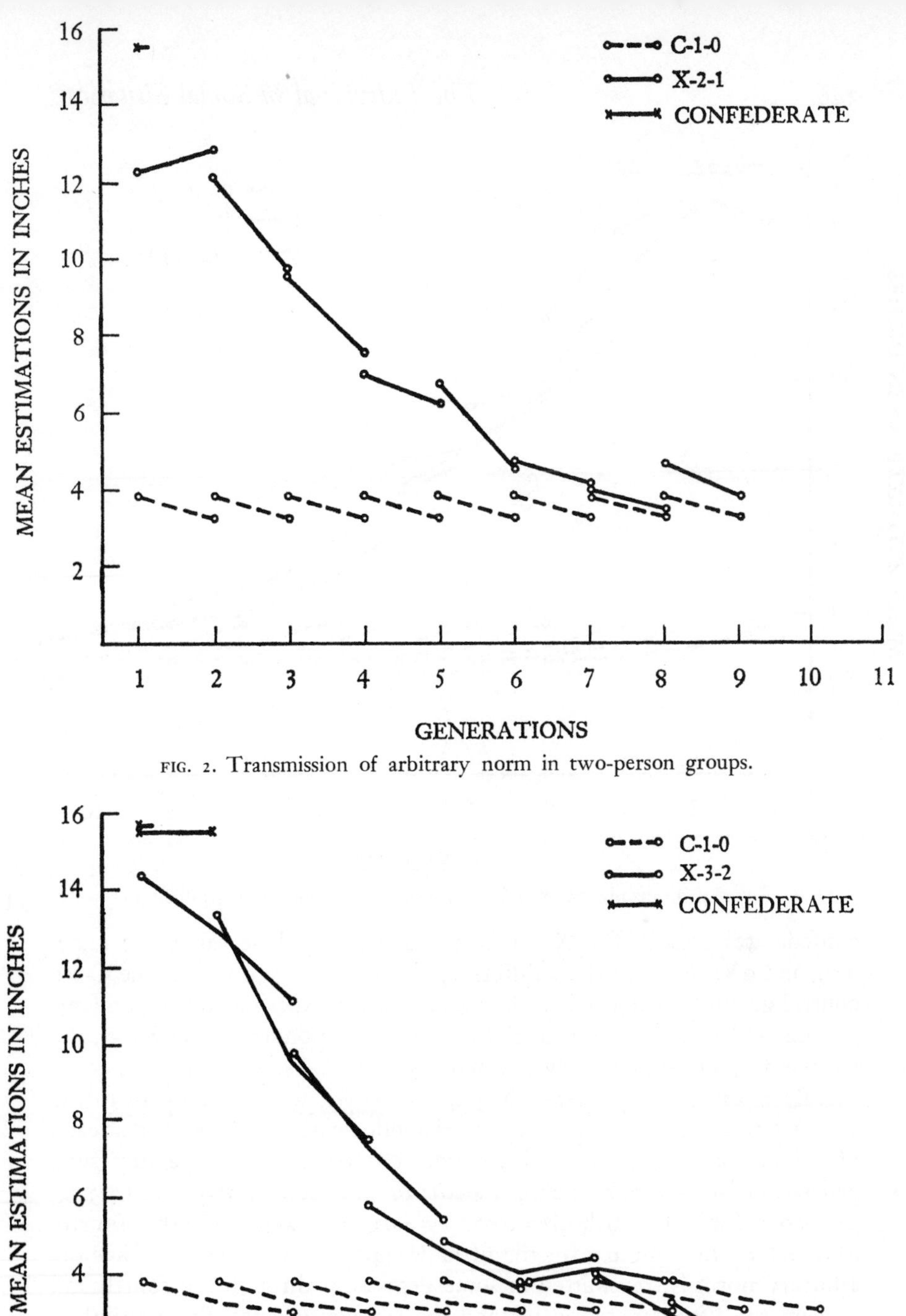

FIG. 2. Transmission of arbitrary norm in two-person groups.

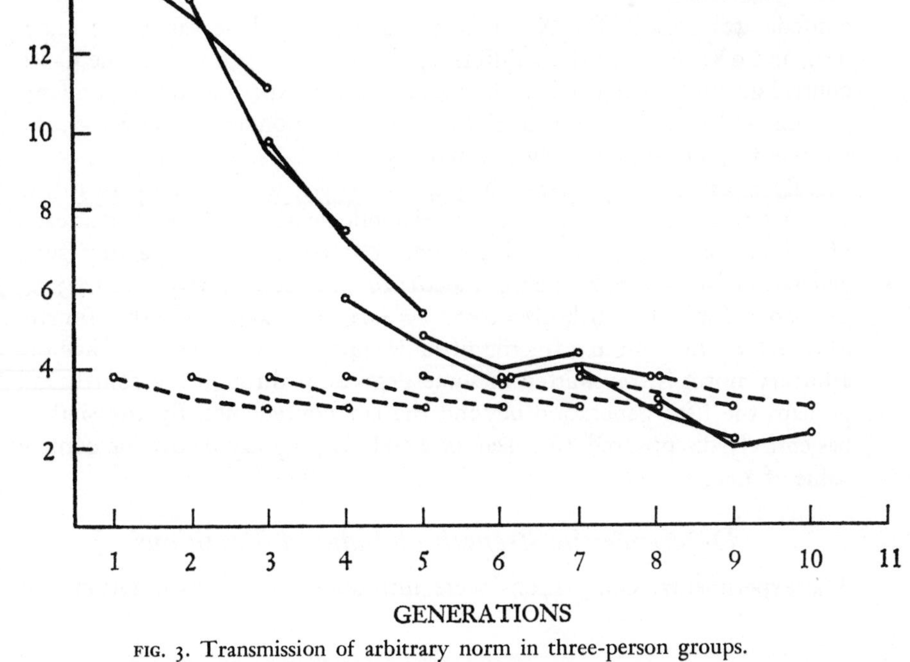

FIG. 3. Transmission of arbitrary norm in three-person groups.

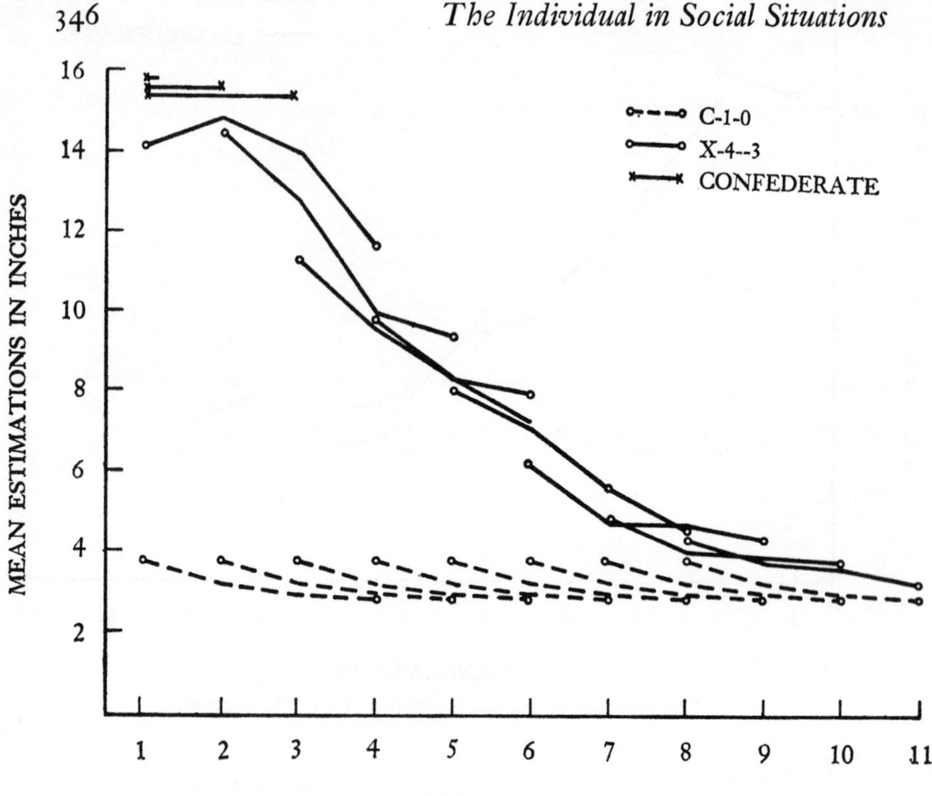

FIG. 4. Transmission of arbitrary norm in four-person groups.

confederates present. For X-2-1, X-3-2, and X-4-3 these values are 12.07, 9.79, and 9.82. Each of these differs significantly ($p<.01$) from the C-1-0 control group by t test, when the mean of the 3 experimental respondents is compared with the mean of the 24 control respondents. For X-3-1, the mean is 5.34, not significantly different from the C-1-0 value of 3.80.

By pooling groups X-2-1, X-3-2, and X-4-3, we can compare to the 24 C-1-0 respondents 9 experimental respondents newly introduced at each of several generations beyond the final confederate. For the first such generation, $M=10.57$, $t=7.25$, $p<.0001$; for the second, $M=7.80$, $t=3.74$, $p<.0001$; for the third, $M=6.06$, $t=4.02$, $p<.0001$; for the fourth, $M=5.08$, $t=2.04$, $p<.03$; for the fifth, $M=4.37$, $t=1.31$, $p<.10$. Thus the arbitrary norm is transmitted in some degree up through the fourth and perhaps the fifth generation beyond the last confederate. By the sixth it has entirely disappeared, the mean of 3.60 being slightly below the control value of 3.80.

Differences in Strength of Induced Traditions

The experimental comparisons were introduced in the expectation that

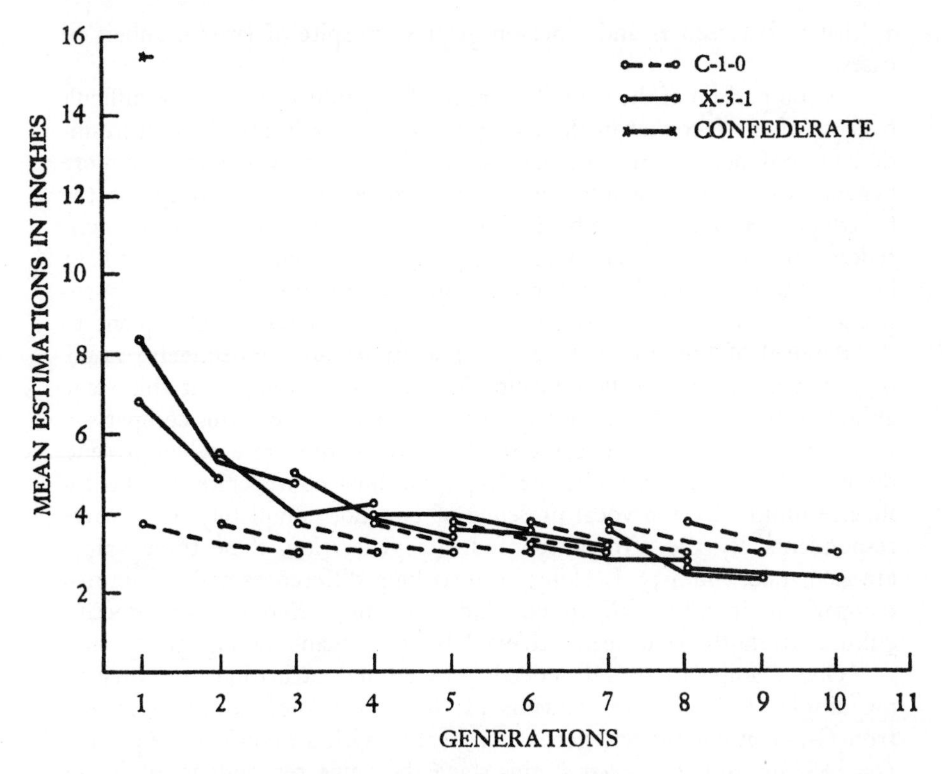

FIG. 5. Transmission of arbitrary norm in a three-person group initiated by one confederate and two naive respondents.

induced cultures of differing strengths and persistence would be produced. In fact, there was some expectation that the strongest conditions might produce an arbitrary culture which would persist without apparent diminution. No condition produced a culture of any such strength, and among the three experimental groups starting with one naive respondent, the number of confederates in the groups had little if any clear-cut effect. In the first generation, with all confederates present, the means for the naive respondents were, for X-2-1, X-3-2, and X-4-3, respectively, 12.23, 14.37, and 14.13. X-2-1 was expected to be lower than the others. The difference between 12.23 and 14.37 is significant ($t = 2.16$, $df = 4$, $p < .05$, one-tailed test). The absence of a difference between X-3-2 and X-4-3 is against our expectation. The literature on this point is confusing. Asch (1) finds almost no effect from a single confederate, whereas we, in X-2-1, and Goldberg (5) and Kidd (7) find strong effects from a single other. Asch finds the effect to increase strikingly when the confederates are increased to 2 and again to 3, whereas 4, 8, and 16 others have little or no greater influence than 3. Goldberg and Kidd find no significant gains between 1 and

3 (that is, between 2- and 4-person groups) in spite of large numbers of cases.

A comparison of the overall strength of the induced cultures is difficult because of the fact that in the larger groups not only are the culture-inducing confederates more numerous, but they are also retained for more generations. Thus it would seem unfair to compare all groups at the fourth generation from the beginning, since X-4-3 would have had a confederate in the immediately preceding generation, while X-2-1 would have been without a confederate for three generations. Perhaps more appropriate is a comparison of strength in the first generation subsequent to the removal of the last confederate. The values are, respectively, 12.09, 9.79, and 9.82. The smallest group, X-2-1, seems strongest at this stage although the differences do not approach significance. But this comparison is not exactly fair, either, because for X-2-1 the confederate, when present, dominated the culture, while for X-4-3 the final confederate had his influence diluted by the vocal presence of two not completely loyal naive respondents. By the fifth postconfederate generation, these three values are 4.69, 3.90, and 4.55. Lacking both striking differences and an optimal comparison, it seems fair to conclude that no differences in effective cultural strength have been achieved by thus manipulating group size.

One manipulation did indeed provide indoctrinations of varying magnitude. The naive respondents of X-3-1 were significantly different from C-1-0 only in the first generation, that is, with the confederate present ($t=3.88$, $p<.01$). But even at this stage the naive respondents of X-3-1 were significantly less indoctrinated than those of X-3-2 at Generation 2, when it likewise consisted of but one confederate and two naive persons ($t=4.69$, $p<.001$, 10 *df*). Thus manipulating the ratio of confederates to naive judges has little effect when achieved through adding more confederates, but has great effect when achieved through manipulating the number of naive respondents. As Asch (1) has noted, this adding of a "true partner" seems to have an effect disproportionally greater than would be expected from the simple fact of diluting the majority. This dimension has not been systemically explored, however. In the present setting it would be interesting to compare groups of varying size in which the naive-to-confederate ratio was held constant, as through a group consisting of two confederates and two naive respondents, to be compared with X-2-1, etc.

Judgments as a Compromise between Own and Other's Observations

The deterioration of the cultural norm occurs, in part, because each naive respondent makes judgments somewhat lower, somewhat closer to the natural norm, than do the confederates or elder citizens serving as his mentors. Of 36 naive respondents serving for the first time in X-2-1, X-3-2, and X-4-3 during the first four generations (where some significant strength to the cultural norm was still present) 34 made mean judgments lower than the average of their mentors (for which, $p <$ .0000001). This clear-cut fact we take as supporting the interpretation that each judgment represents a pooling of the person's own observations (the value for which we infer from the control group) with the reported observations of others. In the resulting compromise the person's own observations are not given much weight, but they are given some.

In the first generation of the experimental groups, the conditions are simple enough so that we can make some estimates of this relative weighting of own observations and other's reports. For the first naive respondent in X-2-1, the other's (confederate's) report averages 15.52. The own observation is inferred from C-1 to be 3.80. If the naive respondent weighted his own observation equally with the report of the confederate, his judgment would fall halfway between these values, at 9.66. Instead, the judgment is 12.23, much closer to the confederate's. Rather than regarding the confederate as an equally good observer as himself, the respondent has weighted the confederate's opinion 2.6 times as heavily as his own. The formula for the weighting ratio is $(12.23-3.80)/(15.52-12.23)$. Assuming each confederate to be equally weighted, and solving for the weight given a single confederate's opinion, we get values of 4.6 for X-3-2 and 2.5 for X-4-3. Since these ratios are based upon the performances of but three naive respondents each, they are quite unstable, and are provided here primarily for illustrative purposes. Similar computations for the later generations have been omitted because of the difficulty of taking into account the reciprocal effect of new respondents upon the older naive respondents acting as indoctrinators. The first generation situation is computable just because the confederates were unresponsive to the judgments of their fellows.

Whatever the weighting ratio, as long as some weight is given own observations, and as long as own observations deviate in a consistent direction from the cultural norm, the arbitrary culture is doomed to deterioration eventually, at least in the limited sanction system of this laboratory. While the question has not been stated in this form, the relative respect for own observations over the reports of others is much higher in less ambiguous situations, as Asch (1) has shown. It is easy to understand how the ambiguities of the autokinetic situation lead to lack of confidence in own opinion, but it is perhaps an indication of human trust that this same ambiguity does not lead to a proportional lack of confidence in the reports of others.

Forgetting and Reciprocal Influence

If the previous factor of compromise weighting were all that was involved, the deterioration in culture as graphed in Figures 2, 3, and 4 might have been of a stair-step fashion, with each new inductee starting lower than his indoctrinator, but once started, holding to his initial level through the several generations of his life in the group. As can be seen from the graphs, this is not the case. Instead, the respondent is less loyal to the old culture the longer he stays in the group. Of the 36 naive respondents introduced in the first four generations of X-2-1, X-3-2, and X-4-3, 31 made lower mean judgments on their last session than on their first (for which, $p < .00001$).

In the present design, three factors are confounded in generating this effect. While we have not extricated them, it seems well to mention them. The first factor is the autonomous decline noted previously in the control groups. In terms of absolute magnitude, this would seem to account for little of the total effect.

A second factor is forgetting. Were a respondent to judge with the leadership of a culture-bearing confederate, and then to judge in isolation for several sessions, he would in these later sessions be pooling his immediate visual impression of the stimulus with the remembered reports of the other in a previous session. As these memories dimmed, their weighting could be expected to diminish, and the relative weighting of own observation could be expected to increase. No doubt in the present situation forgetting of indoctrination provides some of the decline within the judgment series of a single respondent.

A third possible source of this within-respondents decline in loyalty to the arbitrary culture is the effect of the new group member upon his elders. Since judging was always from eldest to youngest on any given stimulus presentation, this would have to involve an influence carrying over from one turn to the next. We feel sure that some such influence was present, but its demonstration would require a separate experiment placing confederates in the final answering position.

DISCUSSION

In presenting these materials to our colleagues, we have found them most fascinated by the fact of the cultural transmission surviving total replacement of specific individuals, and by the fact of naive respondents becoming unwitting conspirators in perpetuating a cultural fraud. This demonstration was of course our main intent, and this outcome was inevitable if the conformity research upon which we built had any transfer validity. But while these results are highly significant statistically, they fall short of our expectations. The inculcated arbitrary norms turn out to be molded by innovation at a much more rapid rate than we had expected. We have hardly provided a laboratory paradigm for the examples of tenacious adherence to incredible superstition with which anthropologists and students of comparative religion provide us.

Of course, a relative weakness in strength is to be expected in a laboratory example. Mature individuals are undergoing transient indoctrination by unknown age-mates, as opposed to the natural setting of the teaching of the very young by tribal adults over a period of years. Fewer confederates are involved than in the tribal situation, although the effect of number upon degree of conformity is unclear in the laboratory. More important, there are no sanctions rewarding conformity or punishing innovation. Furthermore, it is even possible that the subject of judgment in our experiment is less ambiguous than the subject material of religious belief, for example. There is, after all, a fairly clear consensus among our naive solitary observers. In our situation, the spontaneous deviations from orthodoxy were all in the same direction, whereas for many arbitrary items of culture the deviations may lack such concerted direction.

Nonetheless, the outcome may well warn us against the assumption that a purely arbitrary cultural norm could be perpetuated indefinitely without other sources of support. Even if people weigh the opinions of their elders many times that of their own direct observations, the collective effect of their own observations probably soon erodes a *functionless* arbitrary belief. Where we observed tenacious bizarre cultural belief we must look to more than mere tradition, suggestibility, or conformity, to explain its retention. Latent functions (e.g., 8) at the personal or societal level must be present to counteract the pressures from continuous spontaneous innovation in a more natural direction. For example, Moore (9) and Aubert (3) have recently suggested such latent functions to superstitious magical lotteries used in the selection of hunting and fishing sites. As our understanding of the requisites of individual and social life further increases, we may expect to discover such latent functions for many if not all of those "meaningless" superstitions which stubbornly persist.

SUMMARY

In an autokinetic judgment situation in which solitary judgments of movement average 3.8 inches, confederates were used to establish arbitrary "cultural norms" of 15.5 inches. The transmission of this norm was studied as one at a time confederates and old members were removed from the group while new members were added. Significant remnants of the culture persisted for four or five generations beyond the last confederate. Gradually in each of the 12 experimental groups the arbitrary norm decayed and the group judgments drifted away from it back to the natural norm found in the control groups. The size of group had no clear effect upon the endurance of the norm established, although a group beginning with one confederate and two naive respondents was markedly weaker than the others and transmitted no culture beyond one generation.

Major effects are interpreted in terms of a judgment process in which each respondent weighs the reports of others and his own observations, achieving a compromise between them. Even with the respondents giving the reports of others from 2.5 to 4 times the weight of their own observations, slight "innovations" result which rapidly cumulate to erode the original arbitrary cultural norm. Details of the process and analogues to the cultural transmission of bizarre beliefs are discussed.

REFERENCES

1. Asch, S. E. Effects of group pressure upon the modification and distortion of judgments. In H. Guetzkow (Ed.), *Groups, leadership, and men.* Pittsburgh: Carnegie Press, 1951, Pp. 177–190.
2. Asch, S. E., *Social psychology*. New York: Prentice-Hall, 1952.
3. Aubert, V. Chance in social affairs. *Inquiry*, 1959, 2, 1–24.
4. Gerard, R. W., Kluckhohn, C., & Rapoport, A. Biological and cultural evolution: Some analogies and explorations. *Behav. Sci.*, 1956, 1, 6–34.
5. Goldberg, S. C. Three situational determinants of conformity to social norms. *J. abnorm. soc. Psychol.*, 1954, 49, 325–329.
6. Haggard, E. A., & Rose, E. Some effects of mental set and active participation in the conditioning of the autokinetic phenomenon. *J. exp. Psychol.*, 1944, 34, 45–59.
7. Kidd, J. S. Social influence phenomena in a task-oriented group. *J. abnorm. soc. Psychol.*, 1958, 56, 13–17.
8. Merton, R. K. *Social theory and social structure.* Glencoe. Ill.: Free Press, 1949.
9. Moore, O. K. Divination, a new perspective. *Amer. Anthropologist*, 1957, 59, 72.
10. Rose, E., & Felton, W. Experimental histories of culture, *Amer. sociol. Rev.* 1955, 20, 383–392.
11. Sherif, M. *The psychology of social norms.* New York: Harper, 1936.
12. Sumner, W. G. *Folkways.* Boston: Ginn, 1906.
13. Tarde, G. *The laws of imitation.* (Paris ed., 1890) New York: Holt, 1903.

PART III

THE *Group* AS A *System* OF *Social Interaction*

Introduction

WHEREAS *in the preceding part we were viewing the small group from the perspective of an individual facing in the present what to him is a social situation, we now broaden our perspective to take in the perspectives of all the individuals in the group and their reciprocal relations over a longer time span during which the effects of interaction have had a chance to work themselves out. We are now concerned with the processes by which the situation for each individual gets to be what it is, and how the ultimate effects of his action tend to make it remain stable or to change it.*

The individual may at first see the group as a collection of individuals, all different, or may view the group as a kind of undifferentiated entity, or in both ways at once. But as interaction proceeds, both views become more articulate and refined. One result of interaction is the mutal adjustment of individual perspectives toward a similarity in certain respects, and toward a knowledge of similarity. The content of this overlap in perspectives and expectations we can call the common culture of the group. Another result of interaction, however, is that the members of the group become more differentiated from each other, both as to who does what kind of thing overtly and when, and also as to the picture of the group that each individual carries in his mind. The individual now begins to see himself as having a particular position within a differentiated structure or system of positions.

The individual feels himself a part of the group and like all other parts in his orientation to the common culture, but at the same time, different from all other parts both because he has a particular position defined by the common culture, and also because he knows he has a life apart from the group—much or most of himself and his internal life is unknown to the others and is not part of the culture he holds in common with the other members of this particular group.

It is not to be supposed that any member of the group pre-visualizes in any detail what the common culture of the group will be. How it devel-

ops depends upon many situational factors that exist independently of their representation in the awareness of any of the individuals in the group. For example, the relations of the members in physical space, the size of the group, the constrictions on amount of time available are all important, as shown in Chapter 7, in determining the network of communication—who can interact with whom, how often, and how easily. These factors affect the way the common culture grows, what parts grow at what speed, and also, obviously, the degree of "commonness" that can be achieved, within sub-parts and within the whole. And then, conversely, the nature and content of the common culture reacts back to reinforce, maintain, or change the original constrictions in numerous ways.

Communications or interactions in real space and time are the only means by which the common culture can be built. The result is that the physical means for building the common culture always have an economic quality of scarcity relative to the ends sought. There are always problems of allocation and co-ordination, of balance between parts, and of balance in time. Some parts change before other parts change. Time taken for solution of one problem may result in lack of time for solution of some other. Problems of this sort, which may be called problems of equilibrium, are treated in Chapter 8. Many interesting characteristics of groups arise as more or less unforseen and sometimes unconscious attempts to solve problems of this order. In general, the perspective of the individual facing a social situation is not a perspective from which one most clearly sees these problems.

It is usually necessary to understand such problems from both individual and system perspectives. One needs to trace the problem to the individual focus to see how it affects the motivation of the individual. Most of the change that takes place in social organization and the building of the common culture comes about because some identifiable person or persons are unhappy with things the way they are. However, it is recognized, when one takes the system perspective, that it is not a sufficient explanation of why change takes place just to understand that someone wants it. On the one hand, one needs to know how it came about that the problem arose for him, and, on the other, one needs to know how it came about that the action he took solved or failed to solve the problem for him and for the other group members.

Many attempts by individuals fail to change the system because they do not affect enough other individuals at the same time, or because they affect other parts of the system in unforeseen ways. Sometimes actions which seem, from the perspective of the individual actor, to be headed straight toward a goal desirable to the whole group produce a net effect that is precisely the opposite of that intended. The net effects are the final results of the ways in which differentiated parts of a total system interact with each other.

Changes in group size (Chapter 9) and group composition (Chapter 10) will influence the relative amount of time the group must spend in solving tasks and social-emotional problems. However, the effects of differences in group size and group composition on the productivity of the group and on the morale of members are in turn related to the task and the general cultural setting. Groups that may be productive with one task in one situation may operate quite differently in another situation.

Specialization, or role differentiation within the group (Chapter 11), can best be understood when one is able to view it both from the individual and from the system perspective. It is intimately related to the solution of problems of equilibrium. In Chapter 12 leadership is seen as a unique type of specialization, in that it is paradoxically a specialization in generality. The leader is a person who is recognized as specialized in doing whatever has to be done. For this reason, it has been difficult to give leadership an adequate theoretical base, since it is necessary to have some fundamental notion of the problems of groups as systems which change a part at a time and go through cycles in time. The difficulty in defining what the leader does or in constructing a value theory of what he should do is certainly due in part to the fact that the leader is usually required to do different things at different times, according to the condition of the group and its common culture as a system. Our ability to specify what some of these important differences of condition are has improved in the past five or ten years, but one feels that we have only begun to be able to handle the problem empirically. On the one hand, a number of studies, particularly factor analyses, seem to be tending toward some kind of consistency in the specification of three or perhaps four very general factors that are typically associated with leadership, as Carter brings out in his paper. On the other hand, studies of leadership in groups of different kinds, where the norms and values of members are different, tend to come out with results that on the surface appear contradictory. An attempt to reconcile the apparent contradictions, for example, between the findings of Lewin and Lippitt, and those of Berkowitz and Torrance, is most helpful in broadening our perspective.

CHAPTER 7

COMMUNICATION NETWORK

The Distribution of Participation in Small Groups: An Exponential Approximation

FREDERICK F. STEPHAN

and

ELLIOT G. MISHLER

IN CONTEMPORARY sociological and social psychological theory and research an increasing amount of attention has been given to the functioning of small groups. Many attempts have been made to analyze the interaction that takes place in small group meetings and to discover general principles that appear to determine, or at least influence, the pattern of participation by the various members of the group. The research reported here is devoted to one of the basic aspects of small group research, namely the relative frequency of participation. Specifically, this

FROM *American Sociological Review,* 1952, 17, 598–608. Reprinted by permission of the authors and publisher.

study concerns the application of a relatively simple mathematical function that appears to express quite well the distribution of participation within a particular type of small discussion group.

In a recent paper (2) Bales suggested that a harmonic distribution might serve to approximate the relative frequency of acts of participation among members of small problem-solving groups. The results he obtained, however, indicated that this approximation is not close enough to be fully satisfactory and, for this reason, he concluded that a more complicated model may be necessary for greater precision (2, pp. 466–468).

The proven inadequacy of the harmonic model, however, does not necessitate the use of models of great complexity. A model of comparable simplicity is available which appears to provide a very good representation of data obtained from a variety of small discussion groups. It is a simple exponential model, that had previously been applied by one of the authors to another study of group participation. When it was applied to Bales' published data, it provided a good fit (6). This paper is primarily concerned with the general adequacy of this exponential model for representing other sets of participation data.

METHODOLOGY

The data presented here are drawn from a project (5) which is part of a general study of the educational process.[1] The findings are based on observations of a total of 81 separate meetings, held by 36 distinct groups, ranging in attendance from four to twelve participants.

The group meetings have certain formal characteristics in common which serve to distinguish them from the problem-solving groups that were studied by Bales. Since the generality of the model is the important consideration, it seems advisable to list these characteristics as specifically as possible. (A more abstract formulation of these conditions, as they affect the applicability of the model, is presented later in the discussion of results.) These common features are:

(*1*) *Social context of the meetings.* The weekly, 50-minute meetings are held at a prescribed time and place in connection with certain courses at Princeton University. The usual expectations, associated with college courses, governing attendance and the fulfillment of assigned work are thus operative here.

(*2*) *Composition of the group.* The members of the group are relatively homogeneous in regard to age, educational training, social background, etc. In addition, membership tends to be restricted to juniors and seniors, increasing the homogeneity within each group in terms of interest and special knowledge.

(*3*) *Role of the leader.* The leader of the group is an instructor in the course. He differs from the other members in his relationship to the group along those social dimensions which are involved in a student's orientation to-

1 The Study of Education at Princeton.

ward a teacher as compared with his orientation toward a fellow student. Although he receives his power ultimately from the outside structure, the leader has considerable freedom to do what he wants in the way he wants. In general, the norms hold that he should be friendly, sociable, and democratic.

(4) *Norms regarding student participation.* The meetings are conducted under the influence of strong traditional attitudes that emphasize discussion by the students and de-emphasize the dominance of the faculty leader in contrast to the usual patterns of lecture, class, and quiz section meetings. They are regarded as an especially valuable part of the education of students. It is expected (by both students and faculty) that all the students will participate actively during each meeting. The leader is expected to stimulate discussion (although specific devices to this end are not prescribed) or at least not to discourage the students from participating. Active participation is regarded as instrumental to the major goal of the meetings.

(5) *Goal of the meetings.* The institutionally defined objective of the meetings is an increase in the members' understanding of assigned course materials. There is a further goal, considered a function of the cumulative effect of many of these meetings in a variety of courses, of an improvement in the general analytical ability of students. It is understood that neither consensus nor action is to be taken as a specific end, although it is recognized that either may occasionally occur as by-products.

The 36 groups whose meetings were observed were a stratified random sample drawn to represent the more than 500 groups that met weekly in the Fall term of 1950. Two variables were used to stratify the population: the department of instruction and the time (day and hour) at which the group met. An additional restriction provided that no single leader (instructor) was represented more than once in the sample. It is assumed that there was no important systematic bias in the types of content discussed, styles of leadership exercised, or kinds of student members in the sample groups.

There are two important methodological differences between the procedure for recording participation and that developed by Bales (1). The basic unit of participation tallied by the observers is the word, sentence, or longer statement of an individual that follows such a participation by one member and continues until it is terminated by an appreciable pause or by the participation of another member. In other words, an individual's uninterrupted contribution is taken to be one participation. However, if there was a clear change of content during the course of a lengthy contribution, it was taken to be the beginning of a new unit of participation. If Bales' procedure had been used, these units of participation would have been divided into elementary "acts" each consisting of a simple sentence or equivalent meaningful expression. What is recorded here as one unit of participation would be recorded by Bales as many times as the number of "acts" it contained.

In the present study, the observers interrupted their recording of participation periodically to make other observations. They did this after each series of participations that totalled 50 units or covered a period of 15 minutes, whichever limit was reached first. This interruption of the recording lasted for less than five minutes, and was devoted to rating certain general aspects of group activity.[2] As soon as the ratings were completed the observers resumed the regular recording of participation. This sequence continued throughout the meeting. The participation records are, therefore, a sample rather than a full record of the meeting. Although systematic evidence was not collected, informal reports by the observers and certain other data indicate that this sampling procedure did not present a distorted picture of the distribution of the participation of members of the group during the entire period.

The differences between this approach and that of Bales have been cited in some detail. If results of both approaches can be described by the same simple model, these differences lend added significance to this finding.

Participation in the discussion groups was observed and recorded by 18 student observers. Each of them had a minimum of about 15 hours of experience in the development and use of the procedure before he started the regular observation of the sample groups. The reliability among observers was investigated by having pairs of observers record the same discussion meeting.*

PARTICIPATION DATA AND THE EXPONENTIAL FUNCTION

The data recorded by the observers were tabulated for each individual at a meeting and then the individuals were ranked according to the number of units of participation that were contributed by them. The tabulations for all meetings of the same size were then combined by adding the counts of units of participation for the members that had the same ranking. The result is given in column 3 of Table 1. Each individual was also ranked according to the number of units of participation that were directed to him. The tabulations of these units for all groups of the same size were combined according to this second ranking and appear in column 7 of Table 1.

Graphs of relative participation plotted against rank are similar to those reported by Bales (2) and are therefore omitted from the present paper. The decrease in rate from the leader to the highest ranking student becomes somewhat sharper as one goes from smaller to larger groups. It was found that the percentage distributions could be approximated by an exponential function,

$$p_i = ar^{i-1}, \qquad (1)$$

where p_i is the estimated percentage for students ranked i, r is the ratio of the percentage for any rank to the percentage for the next higher rank,

2 These ratings are related to the larger study noted above and will not be reported here. Cf. Mishler, (5).

* Discussion of reliability of observers has been omitted. (Eds.)

and *a* is the estimate for students ranked 1. The variation of *r* and *a* with the size of the group will be discussed later.

TABLE I

Distribution of Participation by and to Members of Small Discussion Groups *

(Data combined for all meetings of the same size, participations to the group omitted)

		Participations originated by the member				*Participations directed to the member*			
Size and number of meetings	*Rank of the member*	*Partici-pations*	*Per cent*	*Esti-mated percent-age*	*Differ-ence*	*Partici-pations*	*Per cent*	*Esti-mated percent-age*	*Differ-ence*
(1)	(2)	(3)	(4)	(5)	(6)	(7)	(8)	(9)	(10)
Six		*2951*		*36.9*		*2951*		*28.8*	
(17)	L	1261	42.8	44.8	+2.0	1402	47.5	47.5	0.0
	1	704	23.8	23.0	−0.8	471	15.9	16.2	+0.3
	2	455	15.4	14.3	−1.1	272	9.2	9.1	−0.1
	3	297	10.0	8.9	−1.1	162	5.5	5.1	−0.4
	4	175	5.9	5.6	−0.3	90	3.0	2.9	−0.1
	5	59	2.0	3.5	+1.5	39	1.3	1.6	+0.3
Seven		*1999*		*30.3*		*1999*		*21.9*	
(15)	L	912	45.6	45.8	+0.2	933	46.6	46.5	−0.1
	1	416	20.8	20.1	−0.7	287	14.5	14.1	−0.4
	2	245	12.2	13.2	+1.0	167	8.3	9.1	+0.8
	3	175	8.6	8.8	+0.2	118	5.9	5.8	−0.1
	4	119	5.9	5.8	−0.1	82	4.1	3.8	−0.3
	5	86	4.2	3.8	−0.4	55	2.6	2.4	−0.2
	6	46	2.4	2.5	+0.1	27	1.3	1.6	+0.3
Eight		*2042*		*31.9*		*2042*		*22.0*	
(14)	L	803	39.2	39.9	+0.7	946	46.3	46.0	−0.3
	1	434	21.2	21.3	+0.1	266	12.9	14.1	+1.2
	2	294	14.3	14.2	−0.1	218	10.6	9.0	−1.6
	3	184	8.9	9.5	+0.6	105	5.1	5.8	+0.7
	4	140	6.6	6.3	−0.3	87	4.1	3.7	−0.4
	5	98	4.8	4.2	−0.6	49	2.3	2.4	+0.1
	6	55	2.6	2.8	+0.2	32	1.5	1.5	0.0
	7	34	1.6	1.9	+0.3	17	0.7	1.0	+0.3

* a. The percentages for participations *to* within each size of meeting (columns 8 and 9) do not total 100. This is due to the fact, noted previously, that the percentage of participation *to* the group has been omitted.

b. The numbers in *italics* in columns 3 and 7 are the total number of participation units recorded. The totals in column 7 include participations directed *to* the group as a whole. These totals were the basis on which the percentages of total in columns 4 and 8 were calculated.

c. The numbers in *italics* in columns 5 and 9 are the percentages that would be estimated for the leader by extrapolation from the exponential model.

NOTE: Data for groups of 4, 9, 10, 11, and 12 are omitted. (Eds.)

In the fitting of his function, the percentages by and to the leaders and to the group were omitted from the distributions. There were several reasons for this step. First, they differed from the students in knowledge of the subjects under discussion, experience in discussion, etc. Second, they had different functions to perform in the meeting, a different role to play. Third, it was deemed a sufficient first step to find a function that fitted the student members' participation rates, without the addition of another function for the leaders' roles.

In order to give what was judged to be appropriate weight to the fit for large and for small percentages, the function was fitted to the data by minimizing the sum of squares of deviations of the logarithms of the estimated percentages from the logarithms of the observed percentages, each square being weighted by the observed percentage. That is, the quantity to be minimized was:

$$\Sigma\, p_i[\log p_i - \log(ar^{i-1})]^2$$

where p_i is the percentage observed for the members ranked i. It was not possible to establish a defensible probability model for maximum likelihood estimates or a more rational formulation of least squares procedure. The selection of this basis for fitting was to a degree arbitrary but it appears to be justified by the closeness of fit that was attained. It led to the following equations:

$$(2)\ \log a = \frac{CD-BE}{AC-B^2} \quad (3)\ \log r = \frac{AE-BD}{AC-B^2}$$

$$\text{where } A = \Sigma\, p_i,\ B = \Sigma\, ip_i,\ C = \Sigma\, i^2p_i,$$

$$D = \Sigma\, (p_i \log p_i),\ E = \Sigma\, (ip_i \log p_i)$$

These equations were solved for each distribution of percentages. Then estimates were computed from equation (*1*) and entered in columns 5 and 9 of Table 1.

To complete the estimates, a percentage was added for the leaders in each distribution that brings the total to 100 per cent. It may be compared with the figure above it, in italics, which is the percentage that would be estimated for the leader according to the exponential function, when he is assigned rank 0.

The percentages computed from the exponential function agree remarkably well with the actual percentages, except for the estimates for the leader. Considering participation *by* a member, 62 of the 72 differences in column 6 are less than one percentage point, positive or negative. For participation *to* a member, 59 differences are less than one percentage point, either way. There is a little evidence of systematic error, primarily a tendency toward negative errors in the middle rankings and positive errors for the very lowest ranks.

Table 2 presents the ratios (r in equation 1) that were used for computing the percentages and an approximation to them by two linear functions of the size of the meeting.

The ratios appear to increase with the size of the meeting in fairly close conformity to the linear functions. Thus, men of adjoining rank tend to have more nearly equal rates of participation as the size of the meeting increased.

The parameter, a, also changes in a fairly regular way with the size of the meeting. It can be represented by such an empirical function as $a_n = 234/(n + 4)$, for participations by the member, and $a_n = 157/(n + 4)$, for participations to the member.

DISCUSSION OF RESULTS

The findings presented above suggest that the simple exponential model may be applicable for describing the distribution of participation in other types of small groups. The problem now becomes one of discovering the conditions under which the model may be expected to remain applicable (i.e., of "explaining" this empirical law). Such an analysis should also be helpful in specifying those factors which influence the size of the ratio in

TABLE 2

Ratios r_n Used in Estimating Participations and Approximations by Linear Functions of the Size of the Meeting

SIZE OF MEETING, n, INCLUDING LEADER	PARTICIPATION BY A MEMBER *		PARTICIPATION TO A MEMBER †	
4	.589	(.590)	.566	(.582)
5	.611	(.607)	.638	(.596)
6	.623	(.624)	.563	(.610)
7	.661	(.641)	.643	(.624)
8	.667	(.658)	.640	(.638)
9	.668	(.676)	.656	(.652)
10	.694	(.693)	.667	(.666)
11	.710	(.710)	.682	(.680)
12	.727	(.727)	.686	(.694)

* Approximation using $r_n = .522 + .0172\ n$ is shown in parentheses.
† Approximation using $r_n = .526 + .0140\ n$ is shown in parentheses.

the exponential equation. A great deal of research may be necessary before this problem can be solved. As a step toward formulating hypotheses, the authors will set forth some of their thoughts about the essential conditions.

It would appear that, within the general context of a face-to-face group oriented toward some common problem or content, the fit of the model to the data may be a consequence of the following conditions:

1. There is a distribution of what might be labeled "verbal participation potential" among the participants present at a meeting. The genesis of this potential, i.e., whether it is a personality characteristic or situationally induced, is not relevant here although it would seem to be a fruitful

area for investigation. The inequality among the participants in this respect is the important factor rather than the reasons for this inequality. One qualification should be suggested, although it will not be elaborated in this paper. That is, that the differences among the participants should not be of such a nature as to divide them into two or more distinct groups characterized by markedly different systems of participation relationships. If this restriction does not hold, the variation involved in the distribution of participation may be more abrupt than the model can handle. The potential of a given member of the group may vary during the meeting and be affected by the influences to which he is subjected, but it is essentially a compounded resultant of individual factors. The data that are yielded by observation of participation reflect average differences in potential.

2. There is no systematic regulation of the "free competitive expression" of "verbal participation potentials." For example, neither the leader nor the group attempts to control the rates of participation by specifying when an individual may participate or by regulating the distribution of relevant information.
3. The members are relatively undifferentiated in regard to the roles they play in the discussion, except for the differentiation that results from the relative strength of their verbal participation potentials. There is no set of structured differentiated roles that has a major effect on the distribution of participation. In the groups described above there was always present, of course, a clearly differentiated leader role. This is not an exception to the general rule, however, since the leader's participation was calculated residually and not directly by the formulae. This device permits one to use the model in concrete instances where there is such a well-differentiated role.

It is believed that the groups from which the data were drawn fulfilled these conditions. The evidence is, however, inferential rather than direct. The controls which were exercised in drawing a sample, the manner in which the group discussions were conducted, and the processes of observing and tabulating the data operated to ensure that there was no systematic selection in terms of "verbal participation potential" or the possibilities for the "free expression" of this potential. The general norms for student behavior also served to mitigate against any well-defined role structure among the members.

The results presented in Table 2 suggest that under these conditions the size of the group is a major determinant of the ratio, r_n, in the exponential function that fits the participation relationships of the members.

In groups of a given size it might be expected that the ratio will vary with changes in some of the conditions noted above. For example, the effect of selecting members on the basis of factors closely associated with their verbal participation potentials is revealed by an experiment con-

3 The data on high and low participating groups are drawn from unpublished work by Bray (3).

ducted by the Study of Education.[3] Two groups were formed from students who had been observed in discussion groups during the preceding term. One of the groups consisted of individuals who had shown high rates of participation and the other of individuals who had shown low rates. This selection not only established a substantial difference between the two experimental groups in their average previous rate of participation, but it narrowed the range of verbal participation potential within each group. The results of applying the model to data drawn from two meetings of each of these groups are shown in Table 3.[4]

The exponential model is found to hold for these data also. Although one might have expected the homogeneity within each of the groups to have the same effect on the ratio, i.e., to increase it in both instances, it

TABLE 3

Participation by Individuals in High- and Low-Participator Groups

	MEETINGS OF HIGH-PARTICIPATOR GROUP			MEETINGS OF LOW-PARTICIPATOR GROUP		
RANK OF MEMBER	PER CENT OF TOTAL	ESTIMATED PERCENTAGE	DIFFERENCE	PER CENT OF TOTAL	ESTIMATED PERCENTAGE	DIFFERENCE
L	30.1	30.0	−0.1	42.3	40.3	−2.0
1	19.1	19.0	−0.1	28.3	26.7	−2.0
2	14.9	15.2	+0.3	12.9	15.1	+2.2
3	11.7	12.1	+0.4	8.9	8.6	−0.3
4	10.1	9.7	−0.4	4.0	4.9	+0.9
5	9.3	7.8	−1.5	3.6	2.8	−0.8
6	4.7	6.2	+1.5	0.0	1.6	+1.6
Ratio, r_7		.799			.567	

appears that there have been opposite effects. Members of adjacent ranks in high-participator groups seem to be more like each other; those in low-participator groups to be less like each other.

One source for this difference lies in the original selection of members. The members of the high-participator group were more homogeneous with regard to their previous rankings than were the members of the low-participator group. It was possible to recruit the former group from men who had been in the first to the fourth rank in their prior meetings; for the latter group it was necessary to select from men in a broader range of prior ranking that extended from the sixth to the fourteenth.

While the range of previous ranking was reduced for both groups by the process of selection, it was compressed to one-quarter of the original range for the high-participator group, while for the low-participator group it was compressed only one-half. This difference in the degree of

4 These meetings were chosen because they permitted comparison of meetings at which the size of the group was the same. Other meetings were observed at which the attendance was greater or less than seven. Some of them did not conform as closely as these to the exponential function, usually because of definite factors that tended to structure the discussion, such as assignment of reports to be presented by one or more members.

homogeneity in prior ranking is assumed to have produced a corresponding difference between the two groups in their range of verbal participation potentials and hence in their respective ratios, r, in the subsequent meetings. On this assumption the ratio for the low group should be roughly the square of the ratio for the high group and it is nearly so.

This explanation is by far the simplest one but does not sufficiently account for the fact that the low-participator ratio is also lower than that found in non-selected groups of the same size where one would normally expect to have even greater initial variation among the members. It may be that the nature of the participation pattern among those with low verbal participation potentials is such that a low ratio would result even though homogeneity were increased. It may be that here one finds some evidence that the fit of the exponential is defective beyond a certain degree of approximation. Further research is needed to separate out the effects of homogeneity from the effects of average strength of verbal participation potential, and to bring to light other factors that should be incorporated into the model.

One further illustration of the effect of various factors on the ratio in the exponential function is provided by a study of experimental groups at another university that compared two situations in which the behavior of the leader was markedly different.[5] For present purposes, the two styles of leader behavior might be described as active and passive. In the former instance the leader played a major role in the discussion through his own contributions. In the latter, the leader merely introduced the subject for discussion and permitted the group to function with a minimum of interference. The members within each group were heterogeneous in regard to a personality dimension usually labeled "ascendance-submission." That is, within each group the members represented a range of scores from high to low on personality tests considered to measure this variable. The groups under different leaders had similar membership in terms of this variable. They were not selected on any other variable. "Ascendance-submission" is not equivalent to "verbal participation potential," but it was found to have consistent though low correlations with actual participation.

In comparison to the groups in the last illustration, these groups appear to be relatively heterogeneous in regard to verbal participation potential and functioned under two different leader styles. Table 4 shows the results of applying the model to data drawn from three meetings of passive-leader groups and four meetings of active-leader groups.[6]

The ratios for the two styles of leadership are higher than the ratio

5 These data are drawn from an unpublished study in which the distribution of participation was an important but not primary focus. Cf. G. Mishler, (4).

6 The unit of participation counted in these groups differs from that used for the other groups reported in this paper. Briefly, a contribution could be assigned to from one to twelve separate problem-solving categories. Each assignment to a category constituted a unit of participation.

for the seven-man groups in Table 2 but differ very little between themselves. The different leadership styles did, of course, produce different effects. There was, quite obviously, a large difference between the proportions of total participation contributed by the members in each of the groups. The leadership styles did not differentially affect the participation relationships among the members. (Nor were these relationships significantly different from those holding among members in groups where leader styles were not altered in any systematic way.)

TABLE 4

Participation by Members of Discussion Groups Under Passive and Active Leadership

GROUP WITH PASSIVE LEADER				GROUP WITH ACTIVE LEADER			
RANK OF MEMBER	PER CENT OF TOTAL	ESTIMATED PERCENTAGE	DIFFERENCE	RANK OF MEMBER	PER CENT OF TOTAL	ESTIMATED PERCENTAGE	DIFFERENCE
1	34.3	33.0	−1.3	L	52.8	52.5	−0.3
2	23.3	22.9	−0.4	1	16.3	15.6	−0.7
3	14.3	15.9	+1.6	2	8.9	11.2	+2.3
4	9.9	11.1	+1.2	3	8.8	8.0	−0.8
L *	7.8	7.7	−0.1	4	6.8	5.7	−1.1
6	6.1	5.4	−0.7	5	4.4	4.1	−0.3
7	4.2	3.8	−0.4	6	2.0	2.9	+0.9
Ratio, r_7		.696				.717	

* In this instance, inasmuch as the leader did not have a role which differentiated him markedly from the other members, his participation was computed directly rather than residually.

To understand why a difference, which might have been expected, failed to appear, one may refer back to the previously listed conditions which were considered responsible for the fit of the model and for the derived ratios.

It would appear that in both the active- and passive-leader groups, the three required conditions were fulfilled. To the extent that the personality dimension of ascendance bears some relationship to participation (and as a minimum it may be said with assurance that heterogeneity in the former is not likely to produce homogeneity in the latter), the groups were heterogeneous in regard to verbal participation potential. Second, there were no clearly differentiated roles by which the members were distinguished from each other.

Third, although the active leader was indeed active, none of his activity was directed towards controlling "who" spoke during the time when he himself was not speaking. Although he controlled the content and contributed over half the total number of participations, he recognized whomever wanted to speak and neither attempted to stimulate nonparticipators nor ignore over-participators. There was, therefore, no systematic regulation of the "free competitive expression" of the "verbal participation potentials" present in the active-leader groups; and most certainly not in the passive-leader groups.

The last discussion raises an important point which should be borne in mind in research with different styles of leadership (whether autocratic *vs.* democratic, or directive *vs.* non-directive, etc.). The areas of group functioning to which the leader is to be systematically oriented (whether content, distribution of participation, etc.) must be specified if one is to understand the effects of alterations in leader styles. As has been pointed to above, marked differences in certain aspects of leadership behavior do not produce differences in the participation relationships of members when the leaders have not also been differentially oriented to the latter dimension.

Finally, it may be said that the usefulness of the model extends beyond its utility for describing the distribution of participation in small groups. Its fit in these cases is a function of certain theoretically postulated conditions. These conditions all refer essentially to groups which are unstructured, i.e., where a pattern of interaction is permitted to develop spontaneously.

Where the data do not fit or where the ratios are considerably different from what might be expected, this is a cue to search for the conditions which are responsible for these alterations. One cannot, with this model alone, develop a full theory of group functioning. The results of applying it, however, may stimulate work of this kind in other areas and so serve to further the development of a more complete and more adequate theory.

SUMMARY

A simple exponential model is fitted and is found to describe adequately the distribution of participation among the members of small groups. Where three conditions are fulfilled: a range of verbal participation potential among the members, no systematic interference with the "free competitive expression" of these potentials, and a lack of well-differentiated roles among the members—then the size of the group is found to be an important parameter affecting the size of the ratio in the basic equation. That is, as groups increase in size members of adjacent ranks become more like each other in their relative rates of participation.

The model is applied to other data where the conditions appear to vary from those required. Its fit in these cases is discussed along with suggestions for further research which develop out of these new applications.

REFERENCES

1. Bales, R. F. *Interaction process analysis*. Cambridge, Mass.: Addison-Wesley, 1950.
2. Bales, R. F., et al. Channels of communication in small groups. *Amer. sociol. Rev.*, 1951, 16, 461–468.

3. Bray, D. W. A comparison of precepts composed of low and high participating students. Study of Education, 1950. (Unpublished).
4. Mishler, E. G. Ascendant and submissive members and leaders: Their interaction in group discussion. Occasional Paper of the Conference Research Project. Univer. of Michigan, 1950.
5. Mishler, E. G. The Princeton preceptorial system. (In preparation).
6. Stephan, F. F. The relative rate of communication between members of small groups. *Amer. sociol. Rev.*, 1952, 17, 482–486.

Interaction of Individuals in Reconstituted Groups

EDGAR F. BORGATTA
and
ROBERT F. BALES

INTRODUCTION

THE RESULTS of this study indicate that it may be possible to use diagnostic sessions to estimate characteristic rates of particular individuals and from this information to predict certain aspects of performance of groups reconstituted from these individuals. Conversely, it may be possible to predict certain aspects of performance of the individual in a particular group if we have estimates of the characteristic performance of each of the individuals based on previous diagnostic sessions.

FROM *Sociometry*, 1953, 16, 302–320. Reprinted by permission of the authors and publisher.

This research was supported in part by the United States Air Force under contract number AF 33 (038)–12782 monitored by the Human Resources Research Institute, Maxwell Air Force Base, Alabama. Permission is granted for reproduction, translation, publication and disposal in whole and in part by or for the United States Government.

We are indebted to the research staff at Maxwell Air Force Base, which assisted in the collection of data.

We are also indebted to Richard Mann for his assistance in the devising of the arbitrary classification used in this paper, and to Jonathan Robbin for his constant attention to the accuracy of the data.

Evidence is presented that each individual who is a prospective member of a group can usefully be regarded as having a characteristic rate of interaction, and a characteristic upper bound, with a tendency to increase his rate to his upper bound, depending upon opportunity. The rate actually achieved by a given man in a group is an inverse function of the characteristic rates of his co-participators. The total rate achieved by a given group is in part a function of the summed characteristic rates of the participants. However, the total rate of a given group is also a function of the degree of differentiation of the characteristic rates of the individuals composing it.

For both groups and individuals, qualitative differences of performance are associated with differences in interaction rates. For individual persons, specialization on the side of task leadership is generally associated with high interaction rate. Persons with relatively lower rates tend to assume residual roles of supporting, modifying, qualifying, or rejecting. Persons with the lowest rates may be excluded or withdrawn, will tend to show high rates of tension, and may not contribute substantially either to the task or to the support of co-participators.

THE SAMPLE AND THE DATA

The data are obtained from observation of 166 sessions of three-man groups. One hundred twenty-six enlisted Air Force personnel were divided into fourteen batches of nine men each. Each batch of nine men was organized and reorganized into twelve three-man groups in such a way that each subject participated in four of the sessions and participated with each other subject in his batch only one time.[1] The design attempted to limit the contact of subjects with each other before the sessions. Subjects had equal experience at each stage of testing. Each session was 48 minutes long. The behavior observed was classed under two headings according to the type of task: *Actual Behavior* (24 minutes which included time spent getting acquainted, planning role playing sessions, and discussion) and *Role Playing Behavior* (24 minutes which consisted of role playing two scenes planned by the participants themselves). The social behavior of the participants (the interaction) was observed and classified according to Bales' categories of interaction process analysis.[2] The data will be treated as two sets of 166 sessions each.

1 Two sessions were lost in the scheduled 168 total since one subject went AWOL on a second day of testing.

2 Bales, (1). Briefly, the categories in this observation system may be identified as follows: Categories 1, 2 and 3, showing solidarity, tension release, and agreement; categories 4, 5 and 6, giving suggestion, opinion, and orientation; categories 7, 8 and 9, asking for orientation, opinion, and suggestion; and categories 10, 11 and 12, showing disagreement, tension, and antagonism. The first three and the last three categories are known as the positive and negative social-emotional categories, respectively. The central six categories are known as the task categories.

Greater detail on the characteristics of the sample and session organization will be found in two previous articles (2, 3). Problems of scoring reliability and consistency of subject behavior, and task and experience as factors in the interaction of these groups are considered in these articles. High scorer reliability and a reasonable range of consistency of subject behavior were reported. Interaction differences by task between *Actual Behavior* and *Role Playing Behavior* were manifest.

OBSERVATIONS OF INDIVIDUALS

Since we have four independent observations (sessions) in which each individual has participated, we have taken his average performance in these as the best available estimate of his characteristic interaction behavior.[3] On this basis of classification, and further, considering the ranking of the individual in his batch of nine, we have arbitrarily placed the subjects into five classes. The operations were as follows: A frequency distribution of the initiated behavior (total rates) of the 126 subjects was arbitrarily cut into three intervals. The arbitrary cuts were made on a basis that gave a relatively symmetric distribution of persons around the middle cell in both the Role Playing and the Actual Behavior. In the sessions of Actual Behavior 49 individuals were classed as High initiators, 34 Middle, and 43 Low. In the sessions of Role Playing Behavior, 40 were classed as High, 31 Middle, and 55 Low. It should be noted that the median initiator for the Role Playing set is lower in rate than the median initiator for the Actual Behavior set. The second point of reference used in the arbitrary classification is the cut nearest the mean score of the set. The third reference point in the classification is the ranking of the individual within his batch of nine persons.

The arbitrary definitions of the five classes are:

H The person is above the Middle initiators, and among the top four in the batch of nine persons from which he is drawn.

h The person is above the mean, and among the top five in the batch of nine from which he is drawn.

l The person is below the mean, and among the lowest five in the batch of nine from which he is drawn.

L The person is below the Middle initiators, and among the lowest four in the batch of nine from which he is drawn.

M The residual individuals are classed as M, which stands for mixture and is given a middle value.

Under these definitions we get the following distributions of persons. In the Actual Behavior set: H=46, h=19, M=4, l=15, L=42. In the Role Playing Behavior set: H=36, h=21, M=8, l=10, L=51. This distribution

3 Actually, there is a minor restriction of independence since a person's co-participators are chosen from his batch of nine persons rather than the total sample.

is approximately that which was desired, that is, one which would allow us to expect to find at least a few cases of groups composed of three participants at the same extreme.

Having a classification of individuals on the basis of an estimate of their characteristic behavior, we would like to know how well these estimates would predict the outcome of sessions of three-man groups composed of different combinations of these individuals, and further, the influence on the characteristic performance of the individual that participation with two other persons (of known characteristics) would have. To do this, the most rigorous research design would require that we again reconstitute our sample into three-man groups (again restricting contact before sessions) if we wish to maintain independence in our predictions in all possible ways. In our design, one would actually have used the first three sessions to predict the fourth, and thus satisfy the rigorous requirement at the cost of fewer cases. However, since we have not used information concerning the *rate of the group* in our derivation of types of persons and types of groups, we have not lost independence of prediction in this sense, and we decided to proceed with the larger available N of all sessions (166).

In analyzing the composition of groups we have made use of an arbitrary weighting of individuals according to their classification, i.e., H=4, h=3, M=2, l=1, L=0. This allows us, for example, to classify sessions according to the total weight of the participants (or mean weight). The distribution of sessions by types of groups, and by total weight, is given in Table 1.

TWO HYPOTHESES ON INTERACTION RATE OF THE GROUP

Two hypotheses were formulated before the analysis of the data. The first was that *the total interaction rate* (number of acts per unit time) *of the group is correlated with the total of the weights associated with the characteristic performance of the individuals composing the group.* This essentially states that individuals will tend to be relatively stable in their rate of participation, irrespective of the group they happen to be in from session to session. The weights have been indicated in Table 1, and these were correlated directly to the total interaction rates of the groups. The correlations (product moment) were .38 for the Role Playing Behavior set and .40 for Actual Behavior set. Both these results are significant at the .05 level with N=166, and we do not reject the hypothesis.

The second hypothesis stated that *the greater the differentiation of the group, the higher the interaction rate of the group.* Any definition of differentiation would be arbitrary, and the decision here was to use the amount of deviation from the maximally differentiated type, HML, as our

TABLE I

Distribution of Sessions by Characteristics of Participants. Role Playing and Actual Behavior, Arranged by Total Weight of Participants

TYPE OF GROUP	TOTAL WEIGHT OF PARTICIPANTS	NUMBER OF SESSIONS OBSERVED	
		ROLE PLAYING BEHAVIOR	ACTUAL BEHAVIOR
HHH	12	2	3
HHh	11	5	8
Hhh	10	5	4
HHM	10	4	3
hhh	9	1	—
HhM	9	3	3
HHl	9	5	10
HMM	8	1	—
hhM	8	—	—
Hhl	8	2	9
HHL	8	18	26
hMM	7	—	—
hhl	7	—	—
HhL	7	16	20
HMl	7	—	4
hMl	6	1	1
hhL	6	4	3
MMM	6	—	—
HML	6	11	2
Hll	6	1	2
hML	5	4	1
HlL	5	8	17
hll	5	1	—
MMl	5	—	—
HLL	4	24	17
hlL	4	13	8
Mll	4	—	—
MML	4	1	—
hLL	3	17	12
MlL	3	—	1
lll	3	—	—
MLL	2	5	1
llL	2	—	2
lLL	1	7	2
LLL	0	7	7
Total		166	166

measure of lack of differentiation.[4] The differentiation scores of the groups were correlated to the total interaction rates of the groups. The correlations were .14 for Role Playing and .22 for Actual Behavior. The correlation for Role Playing is just short of significance at the .05 level. We again do not reject the hypothesis.

4 This measure has an equivalent but reversed form which may be computed as follows: Find the minimum number of unit changes to reduce the group type to an undifferentiated form (e.g., to lll or MMM). To this number add 1 if the reduced form is lll or hhh, and add 2 if reduced form is MMM.

Since the measure of differentiation and the total weight assigned to the group type are independent, we may ask the question: How much of the variance in the total interaction rates of the groups may be accounted for just on the basis of these two measures? Again, using unit sized arbitrary weights with the base at zero (the simplest weighting), the total weight scores and the differentiation scores were added and correlated to the total interaction rates of the groups. The correlations were .39 for Role Playing Behavior set and .45 for Actual Behavior set, showing a small improvement in the prediction by using the two independent measures. The improvement could be greater with more sophisticated weighting, but here it is enough to demonstrate that these two factors alone will account for about 15 to 20 per cent of the variance.

The analysis is parallel in Role Playing and Actual Behavior, and the results are parallel. The Role Playing, however, apparently does not show the relationships tested as clearly as the Actual Behavior. The differences between these classifications are not significant. However, if such differences continued to occur, one area which would be suggested for further investigation is the influence of the roles participants assign to each other (or the roles assigned to them) on the interaction rate of the group. On an *a priori* basis, it might be expected that mis-matching of persons to roles would create tensions which would interfere with their ability to participate.

TWO HYPOTHESES ON INTERACTION RATES OF INDIVIDUALS

One of the crucial problems in the composition or reconstitution of groups (that is, assessment of individuals and assignment of them to new groups) is the effect that it will have on the particular individual to be placed with others of given characteristics. For example, group psychotherapists often face the problem of whether to compose groups of patients for homogeneity or heterogeneity on any of several characteristics. With regard to interaction rates, should low participators be put with low participators in order to minimize competition between them and raise their interaction rates? Or, should they be put in with high participators in order to stimulate them to greater activity? Conversely, should very high participators be put with very high participators to increase competition and lower their interaction rates? If they are put with low participators will it bore them into inactivity? Two hypotheses were advanced relevant to this problem: First, it was expected that *when all high interactors participate together, they depress each other's activity*. Second, it was expected that *when all low interactors participate together, they depress each other's activity*. The first hypothesis was based on reasoning concerning an upper limit for the group interaction rate, and the second hypothesis was based on the lack of stimulation and elicitation of response expected in such groups.

For each individual a weight has been assigned on the basis of his characteristic performance over the four sessions (H = 4, h = 3, etc., as described above). In a given session this individual participates with two co-participants. The weights designating the characteristic performance of each of these two individuals are added to find the "total weight of the co-participants."

For each of the five classifications of group members for both Role Playing and Actual Behavior, the total weight of the co-participants was correlated to the interaction rate of the group member. The coefficients are summarized in Table 2.[5]

TABLE 2

Coefficients of Correlation between the Interaction Rate of the Group Member and the Total Weight of His Co-participators

	r (PRODUCT MOMENT)	NUMBER OF CASES
Actual Behavior Group Member		
H	—.78	181
h	—.74	76
M	—.34	16
l	—.27	60
L	—.55	165
	Sum	498
Role Playing Behavior Group Member		
H	—.78	141
h	—.91	83
M	—.90	40
l	—.34	32
L	—.88	202
	Sum	498

The data confirm the first hypothesis, namely, that in sessions composed of all high participators, the group members depress each other's activity. The second hypothesis is emphatically rejected. In sessions composed of all low participators the group members do not depress each other's activity. The relation found, however, is an unusually stable one. Namely, *irrespective of the person's characteristic performance, and irrespective of the type of behavior (Role Playing or Actual), the rate of initiation of behavior of the group member will be an inverse function of the average characteristic interaction rate of his co-participants.*

5 Detailed tables showing the average raw and percentage profiles of initiated behavior for each type of person by each type of group, for Role Playing and Actual Behavior are not included for reasons of space.

The high coefficients of correlation and their replication indicates that a large amount of the variance is under control for prediction. While a number of explanations might be advanced for this extremely stable finding, the following seems to fit the data most reasonably.

For any group, given a set period of time, there exists an upper bound to the amount of interaction that can take place in the group and still preserve adequate communication, no matter how high the characteristic rates of the individuals may be. That individuals stay within such bounds may be viewed as a minimum condition of cooperation. The fact that the highest participators tend to depress each other may be due in part to this upper bound. This factor, however, does not explain why, when three characteristically low interactors are put together, they do not automatically rise to the mechanical upper bound. We infer, therefore, that the participation of a given individual is not infinitely elastic, that is, associated with his characteristic rate is an upper bound *for him* which appears to operate no matter how much opportunity he has to participate. We have already shown that a considerable part of the variance in the total interaction rates of groups may be accounted for by the simple addition of the characteristic rates of the constituent individuals. This could not be true unless such individual bounds existed. However, the inverse relation shown in Table 2 cannot be explained by either of these boundary conditions. It appears that no matter what the characteristic rates of the individuals may be, a competitive situation exists. This is to say that, in the absence of resistance, *the individual tends to his maximum rate.* The amount of resistance is determined by the characteristic rates of the coparticipants.

QUALITY OF INTERACTION ACCORDING TO RATE OF THE INDIVIDUAL

Since we know that the gross rate of interaction of the individual differs according to the rates of the other individuals who happen to be in the group with him, it is important to ask: What happens to the quality of the individual's participation when he is put in a group where his characteristic rate is depressed? What happens when he is in a group where he is allowed (or encouraged) to increase his participation? Or, in general, what is the typical quality of interaction for persons of different characteristic rates?

The categories in terms of which the observations were made give a qualitative breakdown as indicated in footnote 3. Table 3 shows the average raw rate of activity in each of the twelve categories for individuals of each type, H, h, M, l, and L, in the Actual Behavior sets. These rates are also given as percentages of the total rate. Table 4 shows the same breakdown for the Role Playing sets. The second half of each of these tables gives an

TABLE 3

Average Raw and Percentage Profiles of Initiated Behavior by Type of Person, Actual Behavior

All Cases (Regardless of Types of Co-participators):

TYPE OF PERSON	H	h	M	l	L
NO. OF CASES	181	76	16	60	165
CATEGORY					
1	2.4 (*2.0*)	2.5 (*2.5*)	2.6 (*2.6*)	2.5 (*2.8*)	1.9 (*2.7*)
2	6.1 (*5.0*)	5.8 (*5.8*)	6.6 (*6.7*)	7.8 (*8.6*)	4.7 (*6.7*)
3	9.3 (*7.7*)	9.3 (*9.3*)	13.9 (*14.0*)	9.0 (*9.9*)	7.9 (*11.3*)
4	7.3 (*6.0*)	6.2 (*6.2*)	5.6 (*5.6*)	5.3 (*5.8*)	3.8 (*5.4*)
5	35.6 (*29.4*)	25.7 (*25.5*)	26.3 (*26.5*)	24.8 (*27.3*)	16.8 (*24.0*)
6	44.0 (*36.4*)	35.0 (*34.7*)	30.6 (*30.8*)	27.3 (*29.9*)	21.4 (*30.5*)
7	7.4 (*6.2*)	7.6 (*7.5*)	7.1 (*7.1*)	6.4 (*7.0*)	5.2 (*7.4*)
8	2.4 (*2.0*)	2.0 (*2.0*)	2.2 (*2.2*)	1.3 (*1.5*)	1.4 (*2.0*)
9	0.9 (*0.7*)	0.8 (*0.8*)	0.7 (*0.7*)	0.5 (*0.5*)	0.6 (*0.9*)
10	1.1 (*1.0*)	1.1 (*1.0*)	0.6 (*0.6*)	0.8 (*0.9*)	0.5 (*0.8*)
11	4.3 (*3.5*)	4.6 (*4.6*)	3.0 (*3.0*)	5.3 (*5.8*)	5.8 (*8.3*)
12	0.1 (*0.1*)	0.2 (*0.2*)	0.1 (*0.1*)	0.1 (*0.1*)	0.1 (*0.1*)
Total	120.9 (*100.0*)	100.8 (*100.1*)	99.3 (*99.9*)	91.1 (*100.1*)	70.1 (*100.1*)

Those Cases where Average Weight of Co-participators is High:

TYPE OF PERSON	H	h	M	l	L
NO. OF CASES	58	28	10	28	69
CATEGORY					
1	2.7 (*2.3*)	2.2 (*2.6*)	2.6 (*2.7*)	3.1 (*3.6*)	1.9 (*3.0*)
2	7.1 (*6.1*)	5.9 (*6.9*)	7.6 (*7.9*)	8.6 (*9.9*)	4.3 (*6.8*)
3	9.7 (*8.4*)	8.3 (*9.7*)	14.9 (*15.5*)	8.0 (*9.2*)	7.2 (*11.4*)
4	6.6 (*5.7*)	5.1 (*6.0*)	5.1 (*5.3*)	5.4 (*6.2*)	3.2 (*5.0*)
5	35.2 (*30.3*)	20.6 (*24.1*)	26.3 (*27.4*)	24.3 (*27.9*)	16.3 (*25.7*)
6	39.1 (*33.7*)	29.6 (*34.6*)	26.7 (*27.8*)	24.1 (*27.7*)	19.3 (*30.4*)
7	8.0 (*6.9*)	6.9 (*8.1*)	6.7 (*7.0*)	6.7 (*7.7*)	4.7 (*7.4*)
8	2.1 (*1.8*)	1.6 (*1.9*)	1.9 (*2.0*)	1.1 (*1.3*)	1.3 (*2.1*)
9	0.7 (*0.6*)	0.6 (*0.7*)	0.5 (*0.5*)	0.6 (*0.7*)	0.5 (*0.8*)
10	1.1 (*0.9*)	1.2 (*1.4*)	0.9 (*0.9*)	0.9 (*1.0*)	0.4 (*0.6*)
11	3.6 (*3.1*)	3.6 (*4.2*)	2.8 (*2.9*)	4.1 (*4.7*)	4.3 (*6.8*)
12	0.1 (*0.1*)	0.0 (*0.0*)	0.1 (*0.1*)	0.1 (*0.1*)	0.0 (*0.0*)
Total	116.0 (*99.9*)	85.6 (*100.2*)	96.1 (*100.0*)	87.0 (*100.0*)	63.4 (*100.0*)

indication of "what happens when a man is put with high co-participators," (i.e., with two co-participators whose total weight is 5, 6, 7, or 8). (What happens when a man is put with low co-participators is, of course, just the reverse.)

Note first what happens to the total rates of participation. In general, under all conditions, the total rate declines as we go from High to Low. (This, of course, is expected from the original definition of types.) In every case, the total rate of a given type of man decreases when he is in a group with high co-participators. This is also expected from the findings in Table 2.

TABLE 4

Average Raw and Percentage Profiles of Initiated Behavior by Type of Person, Role Playing Behavior

All Cases (Regardless of Types of Co-participators):

TYPE OF PERSON	H	h	M	l	L
NO. OF CASES	141	83	32	40	202
CATEGORY					
1	0.8 (*0.7*)	0.6 (*0.6*)	0.5 (*0.6*)	0.8 (*0.8*)	0.5 (*0.8*)
2	2.2 (*1.7*)	1.7 (*1.7*)	2.6 (*2.9*)	1.8 (*2.0*)	2.0 (*3.1*)
3	9.8 (*7.8*)	10.6 (*10.7*)	13.5 (*14.9*)	10.7 (*11.8*)	8.6 (*13.0*)
4	3.8 (*3.1*)	2.3 (*2.3*)	2.8 (*3.1*)	2.8 (*3.0*)	1.9 (*2.9*)
5	53.8 (*42.9*)	38.9 (*39.1*)	34.9 (*38.6*)	38.9 (*42.7*)	27.0 (*41.1*)
6	39.5 (*31.5*)	31.6 (*31.8*)	23.6 (*26.1*)	25.4 (*27.8*)	16.0 (*24.3*)
7	5.5 (*4.4*)	4.0 (*4.0*)	5.9 (*6.5*)	3.4 (*3.7*)	3.0 (*4.6*)
8	6.3 (*5.0*)	6.1 (*6.1*)	3.8 (*4.2*)	4.6 (*5.0*)	3.4 (*5.2*)
9	0.2 (*0.1*)	0.4 (*0.4*)	0.3 (*0.3*)	0.2 (*0.2*)	0.1 (*0.2*)
10	1.8 (*1.4*)	1.3 (*1.4*)	1.3 (*1.4*)	0.9 (*0.9*)	0.8 (*1.3*)
11	0.8 (*0.6*)	1.5 (*1.5*)	1.2 (*1.3*)	1.5 (*1.6*)	1.9 (*2.9*)
12	0.8 (*0.7*)	0.5 (*0.6*)	0.1 (*0.1*)	0.3 (*0.4*)	0.3 (*0.5*)
Total	125.3 (*99.9*)	99.5 (*100.2*)	90.5 (*100.0*)	91.3 (*99.9*)	65.5 (*99.9*)

Those Cases Where Average Weight of Co-participators is High:

TYPE OF PERSON	H	h	M	l	L
NO. OF CASES	42	23	9	10	61
CATEGORY					
1	0.7 (*0.6*)	0.4 (*0.5*)	0.7 (*0.9*)	0.4 (*c.7*)	0.6 (*1.1*)
2	1.9 (*1.7*)	2.7 (*3.3*)	2.8 (*3.6*)	0.8 (*1.1*)	2.2 (*3.9*)
3	10.6 (*9.3*)	10.7 (*13.1*)	13.3 (*16.9*)	8.1 (*11.5*)	7.9 (*14.1*)
4	3.3 (*2.9*)	2.2 (*2.7*)	2.4 (*3.1*)	2.8 (*4.0*)	1.3 (*2.3*)
5	48.4 (*42.3*)	33.0 (*40.6*)	25.9 (*33.0*)	31.5 (*44.7*)	22.2 (*39.5*)
6	35.4 (*30.9*)	22.3 (*27.4*)	23.2 (*29.6*)	19.5 (*27.7*)	13.5 (*24.0*)
7	4.8 (*4.2*)	2.8 (*3.4*)	4.4 (*5.6*)	2.1 (*3.0*)	3.6 (*6.4*)
8	5.5 (*4.8*)	4.1 (*5.0*)	3.2 (*4.1*)	3.2 (*4.5*)	2.8 (*5.0*)
9	0.1 (*0.1*)	0.1 (*0.1*)	0.1 (*0.1*)	0.0 (*0.0*)	0.1 (*0.2*)
10	2.2 (*1.9*)	1.6 (*2.0*)	1.3 (*1.7*)	1.1 (*1.6*)	0.6 (*1.1*)
11	0.6 (*0.5*)	1.1 (*1.4*)	1.1 (*1.4*)	0.5 (*0.7*)	1.2 (*2.1*)
12	1.0 (*0.9*)	0.3 (*0.4*)	0.1 (*0.1*)	0.5 (*0.7*)	0.2 (*0.4*)
Total	114.5 (*100.1*)	81.2 (*99.9*)	78.5 (*100.1*)	70.5 (*100.2*)	56.2 (*100.1*)

If the quality of participation did not change according to changes in the total rate, we should expect the changes in each category to be proportional to those in the total rate. In other words, the rate in each category should decrease proportionately as we go from High to Low, and also as we compare the performance of a man under average conditions with his depressed performance when with high co-participants.

From an examination of the tables it may be seen that this is not the case. With minor exception, the task categories 4, 5, and 6 decrease more rapidly than expected. Low men are not only lower absolutely than High men in giving orientation, opinion, and suggestion, but they spend proportionately less of their own participation time in this type of activity. The other task categories asking for orientation, opinion, and suggestion, again with minor exception, decrease about as expected. Asking questions is about as characteristic of High men as of Low men, though possibly for different reasons.

One notable increase of rates occurs. Category 11, showing tension, actually *increases*, both absolutely and proportionately, as we go from High men to Low men. It might be suggested that this is an artifact of scoring, since "awkward pauses" and hesitations are scored in this category, and one might thus expect more scores in category 11 for Low persons. However, this cannot possibly be a simple relationship, since we find that while the total interaction rate of Role Playing is lower than that of Actual Behavior, the amount of tension shown is also consistently lower. Not only are the differences quite clear and consistent, but they are perfectly in line with the hypothesis very generally held, that tension is associated with reality pressures of the task and tends to be lowered in the non-threatening atmosphere of role playing.

This hypothesis, if sound, also serves to explain another curious thing about the rates of tension, namely, that when a man is put with high coparticipators, his rate of showing tension *does not increase*, as we might expect on the basis of a "competition" hypothesis. Rather his rate of showing tension decreases disproportionately fast. It may very well be that with two high co-participators in the group who can provide adequate resources for the solution of task problems, the anxiety associated with reality pressures is decreased. The data indicate that High men as well as Low men show lower tension rates when two high co-participators are present. This is consistent for *both* Actual Behavior and Role Playing. A hypothesis which rests on a notion of "shared confidence" rather than one which views tension simply as a result of "competition" and "getting crowded out of the discussion" seems to be necessary to explain this finding. It still remains true, however, that Low men show higher rates than High men, and so we are not able to dispense with the competition hypothesis. We conclude that both types of factors are operating. It may be quite important, in composing groups, to recognize that "sharing in the success of the group as a whole" may operate to offset the increased tension of the lower participators in the group resulting from their "unsuccessful competition" within the group. This way of looking at the problem is compatible with the notion that *differentiation of member rates* rather than uniformity *is associated with an over-all optimization of tension level.* (Earlier in this paper we have taken H M L as the maximally differentiated group and found that high differentiation is associated with high interaction rate.)

Although the absolute rates of disagreement and antagonism in the groups of this study are very low as compared to other groups that have been observed with the same method, there is some indication that these categories decrease more rapidly than expected by the hypothesis of decrease proportionate to total rate, as we do from High men to Low. Disagreement and antagonism are less inhibited types of negative reaction than is showing tension. Previous studies have tended to show that when tension is high, disagreement and antagonism tend to be low, and vice versa, as if they were alternate forms (passive and active) of the same general negative attitude. This inverse relationship among the variables may be seen in the comparisons of the Role Playing Behavior and Actual Behavior in Tables 3 and 4. It is perhaps worth noting that while the data are not unambiguous, there is an indication that in the Role Playing Behavior individuals tend to increase their rate of disagreement when put with high co-participators. This again would be consistent with the theory that in the role playing normal inhibitions are to some extent relaxed.

The changes in positive reactions as we go from High man to Low do not generally tend to decrease as fast as the proportionality hypothesis would require. Indeed, there is a strong suggestion that men in the middle positions (h, M, l) tend to be higher than either extreme. This is very possibly a result of the differentiation of roles which occurs when one person (in this case H) begins to specialize more heavily in the task categories. When this happens, a situation is created in which another person may specialize in endorsement and encouragement of the task efforts of the first man. These two, then, may form a complementary pair, distributing the major portion of the interaction between them. In a three-man group, if this happens, the third man may to some extent be excluded from the interaction. This interpretation of our findings is consistent with the earlier report by Mills concerning supportive behavior in three-man groups (4).

In the over-all picture of changes we find that decrease in total rate tends to be associated primarily with decrease in the task area, in particular, in giving orientation, opinion, and suggestion. If a man has a high characteristic rate and is granted the opportunity to go ahead, he is likely to do so by increasing his participation in the task areas. Since adequate integration of the group requires that task efforts receive response (supporting, modifying, qualifying, rejecting), the lower members tend to fall into the residual roles, and their rates in the social-emotional area tend to become proportionately higher than for the task specialist. Withdrawal, loss of involvement, or passivity, of course, are also residual roles and may result in a lowering of all rates for the person, including those in the social-emotional area, with the possible exception of showing tension. There is some evidence in our data that the Low man shows this tendency. The person who wishes to compose groups for special purposes may thus be able to control to some extent the *qualitative role* an individual may take, aside from his general tendencies, by placing him with other persons of higher or lower characteristic rates.

Conversely, if one knows that the placement of a given person relative to the others is likely to subject him to pressures to assume a given qualitative type of role, it may be desirable and possible to assess his aptitude or preference for this type of role ahead of time.

QUALITY OF INTERACTION ACCORDING TO RATE OF THE GROUP

In the last section we examined changes in the quality of participation of characteristically High men compared to Low under the hypothesis that changes in the categories would be proportional to changes in the total rate of interaction. It was found that the changes were not proportional. On the contrary, a *qualitative* differentiation of roles appeared. The qualitative differentiation that appeared, however, was the same in the Role Playing as in the Actual Behavior. There were absolute differences according to task, but aside from these, the qualitative differences from High men to Low were relatively constant over the tasks. Essentially, this may be interpreted to mean that there is a tendency for persons to fulfill the *same roles relative to each other* within the group if their relative total rates are the same, in spite of changes of task. There are probably tasks of such great divergence in character that this tendency will not be manifest. However, in the composing of groups, it is important to recognize the existence of this tendency since it implies that there are pressures for members to take different qualitative roles, other than those related to the technical demands of the task.

Another problem in composing groups is the quality of participation of groups with high interaction rate as compared to those with low interaction rate. Should one attempt to compose a group for a high total rate? If there are changes in quality of interaction from high groups to low groups, are they the same as those found from High men to Low? Tables 5 and 6 show the average rates in the qualitative categories of all groups, as compared to the twelve highest and the twelve lowest groups. Percentages of total rates are also shown. (All groups will serve as the reference point of change.) Again, if the quality of participation did not change, we would expect the changes in each category to be proportional to the changes in the total rate of the group.

It is seen that again the proportionality hypothesis does not fit the data. Perhaps the most notable departures from this hypothesis are in category 11, showing tension, category 9, asking for suggestion, category 4, giving suggestion. Each of these categories actually *shows an increase in the absolute rate* in the Role Playing Behavior as we view the trend from high groups to low groups. The same thing is found in the Actual Be-

TABLE 5

Average Raw and Percentage Profiles of Initiated Behavior for All Groups, and for the Twelve Highest and Twelve Lowest Groups, Actual Behavior

TYPE OF GROUP	HIGHEST	TOTAL	LOWEST
NO. OF CASES	12	166	12
CATEGORY			
1	9.7 (*2.7*)	6.8 (*2.3*)	4.7 (*2.3*)
2	25.6 (*7.1*)	17.3 (*6.0*)	6.6 (*3.2*)
3	39.3 (*10.8*)	27.0 (*9.3*)	13.8 (*6.7*)
4	20.8 (*5.8*)	16.9 (*5.8*)	14.3 (*7.0*)
5	104.3 (*28.8*)	79.2 (*27.3*)	45.6 (*22.3*)
6	116.3 (*32.1*)	98.0 (*33.8*)	63.7 (*31.2*)
7	22.5 (*6.2*)	19.7 (*6.8*)	16.7 (*8.2*)
8	7.6 (*2.1*)	5.6 (*1.9*)	3.1 (*1.5*)
9	1.3 (*0.3*)	2.2 (*0.7*)	2.3 (*1.1*)
10	3.6 (*1.0*)	2.6 (*0.9*)	1.0 (*0.8*)
11	11.1 (*3.1*)	14.7 (*5.1*)	31.9 (*15.6*)
12	0.3 (*0.1*)	0.3 (*0.1*)	0.2 (*0.1*)
Total	362.2 (*100.1*)	290.1 (*100.0*)	204.2 (*100.0*)

TABLE 6

Average Raw and Percentage Profiles of Initiated Behavior for All Groups, and for the Twelve Highest and Twelve Lowest Groups, Role Playing Behavior

TYPE OF GROUP	12	TOTAL	LOWEST
NO. OF CASES	HIGHEST	166	12
CATEGORY			
1	1.7 (*0.5*)	2.0 (*0.7*)	1.8 (*0.9*)
2	11.5 (*3.3*)	6.1 (*2.2*)	2.3 (*1.2*)
3	38.9 (*11.0*)	29.7 (*10.8*)	24.9 (*12.5*)
4	6.6 (*1.9*)	7.8 (*2.8*)	9.5 (*4.8*)
5	159.1 (*45.0*)	114.5 (*41.4*)	77.3 (*38.8*)
6	99.5 (*28.1*)	80.0 (*29.0*)	56.5 (*28.4*)
7	14.3 (*4.0*)	12.2 (*4.4*)	4.0 (*2.0*)
8	16.8 (*4.8*)	14.1 (*5.1*)	8.3 (*4.2*)
9	0.1 (*0.0*)	0.5 (*0.2*)	1.3 (*0.6*)
10	3.2 (*0.9*)	3.6 (*1.3*)	3.7 (*1.8*)
11	1.9 (*0.5*)	4.4 (*1.6*)	8.8 (*4.3*)
12	0.3 (*0.1*)	1.5 (*0.5*)	0.8 (*0.4*)
Total	353.8 (*100.1*)	276.5 (*100.0*)	198.9 (*99.9*)

havior, with the exception of category 4, giving suggestion, but even in this case the rate of decrease is slower than expected. If the rate of giving suggestion alone is considered, one might suppose that the low groups are more resourceful in dealing with the task than are the high groups. When the high rate of tension and asking for suggestion is considered, however, the indication is one of relative anxiety about the task and an inability to deal with it. In the Actual Behavior, categories 1, 2 and 3, showing solidarity, tension release, and agreement decrease at a rate faster than expected as we go from the high groups to the low. This fits with the picture of relative difficulty in arriving at a satisfactory solution of the task problem. In composing groups one may need to take care that the group has sufficient resources for dealing with its problem (particularly if he has put low interactors together with the hope of minimizing competition).

The task may make an important difference at this point, however. In the Role Playing Behavior we note that categories 1 and 3 decrease at a slower rate than expected. Further, category 10, showing disagreement, *increases in absolute rate* as we go from high groups to low groups. This does not change our interpretation of ineptness as associated with the low groups. It appears that in the Role Playing situation where a person may feel less threatened, as inability to cope with the task becomes evident, more random behavior occurs (more ill-considered suggestions), and is responded to in a less inhibited way, with rates in categories 3 and 10 (agreement and disagreement) proportionately higher than expected. Category 7, asking for orientation, apparently shows a difference in pattern between the Role Playing and the Actual Behavior, at least for the lowest groups. In the Actual Behavior the lowest groups are disproportionately high in asking for orientation, while in the Role Playing, they are disproportionately low. It seems reasonable to associate the high relative rate of asking for orientation with the greater reality pressures of the Actual Behavior for task solution. It may be noted that this relatively high rate of asking for orientation is not accompanied by a proportionately high rate of giving orientation, category 6. This is congruent with the notion that the lowest groups are low also in ability or resources for dealing with the factual and logical aspects of the Actual problem. The same types of pressures apparently do not exist as strongly in Role Playing.

The differences between the two tasks may be approached directly in terms of the profile of all groups taken together for each type of task. The absolute rate of interaction is lower in Role Playing. One possible interpretation of this difference is that the persons are generally more relaxed in the Role Playing, that is, under less pressure to get a specific decision made within a strict time limit. The qualitative differences are consistent with this notion. In the Role Playing there is less tension, more negative affect in categories 10 and 12, which suggests less inhibition. The Role Playing shows higher rates in asking for opinion and giving it, relative to questions and answers of orientation and suggestion, which again suggests a more affective and less guarded attitude. In the Actual Behavior the planning problem apparently tends to exert pressures toward more concrete specificity and emotional neutrality in remarks addressed to the task.

The Actual Behavior sets were not given over entirely to planning, however. Part of the task in these sets was "getting acquainted," so that they were actually mixtures of two tasks. This probably accounts partly for the fact that categories 1 and 2, showing solidarity and tension release, are higher for the Actual Behavior sets. Another factor is that the final period of Actual Behavior for each group was a permissive period of discussion of the two role playing sessions that had gone before, and a certain amount of joking and laughing occurred. Similarly, between the two role playing sessions, as tension built up, there were also occasional breaks of tension release in "kidding" concerning assignment of roles for the next session. In general, it may be remarked, high rates of joking and laughing cannot be taken at face value as signs of low tension. They should be considered in the context of the task and the rates in other categories, particularly category 11.

Finally, it is worth pointing out that the qualitative differences between high *groups* and low *groups* are not the same as the qualitative differences between High *men* and Low *men*. The differences between High men and Low men we attribute to their relative position with regard to each other in particular groups. The differences between high groups and low groups we attribute to the relation between the resources present in the group as a whole relative to the demands of the task. It is possible that resources of the group as a whole tend to be additive in relation to the task demands made on the group as a whole, but the evidence appears very strong that the qualitative tendencies of particular persons are not additive in the same sense. The constellation of positions within the group appears to be a complex interactive result of system formation.

SOME IMPLICATIONS FOR THE COMPOSITION OF GROUPS AND DEVELOPMENT OF LEADERSHIP

In composing groups, optimum composition presumably depends upon the ends one has in view. At least three types of purposes may be distinguished: (*1*) Accomplishment of an immediate task, with all other goals secondary, (*2*) accomplishment of a task or a series of tasks, extended over a period of time within which the development of a satisfactory social organization is a critical factor, and (*3*) training of personnel for improving individual performance in a given role.

For the realization of objective (*1*), technical ability in relation to the task at hand may call for selection of individuals according to this criterion alone. With regard to interaction rate, this might involve putting together all high participators with high technical ability. The risks of this procedure are that the social organization may be unstable and unsatisfactory for the participants.

Where a stable and satisfactory social organization is critical, as in objective (*2*), the optimum composition of the group, aside from technical requirements, would seem to call for a *gradient* of characteristic rates among the members, with personality characteristics which would incline them to take the roles likely to develop from their relative positions by activity rate. Thus, a mis-matched group might be one in which the person with the highest characteristic activity rate prefers specialization in the social-emotional area rather than the task area. Such a person, on the other hand, might be optimally located in a group where one other member had an activity rate at least as high or higher, and preference for the task area. In the first group the morale of the person might be as high as in the second, but the task performance of the first group might be unnecessarily low. We have found that there is a positive correlation between differentiation (existence of a gradient) and activity rate of the group. On the other hand, we have also noticed that the very lowest persons are likely to be excluded or withdrawn. This would suggest that one should not compose for a gradient so steep that the middle persons exclude the lowest even from the residual supportive roles. There is some indication that the lowest man inevitably suffers from his unfavorable location, but it is also indicated that this may be compensated for to some extent by his identification with the success of the group as a whole.

Finally, (*3*) when the major objective of composing the group is the training of individual personnel for improved performance in a specific role, particularly the task leadership role, one will probably wish to compose for a gradient much as in the case of (*2*) above, with special attention to the position of the individual to be trained. Presumably, practice in a given role is necessary for improved performance, and practice is available only if the person is properly located with reference to his co-participators. Simple rotation of personnel in a given group, where each is instructed (or admonished) to take the role of leader will probably not be as effective as the recomposition of the group in such a way that the person to be trained for task leadership is the person with the highest characteristic rate in the group. If only simple rotation is used, it may well be that what will occur is that the "natural" task leader will be more indirect in his leadership, i.e., the leadership becomes "hidden." Our findings indicate that this is true even though role playing is employed. Role playing as the group task may, however, aid in reducing reality pressures, lessening tension, lowering inhibitions, and promoting a more relaxed atmosphere in the group as a whole. This may be particularly valuable where the characteristic interaction rates of all the members of the group are on the low side. Role players, provided they are able to adjust the quality and rate of their interaction sensitively enough, may be used as co-participants for a given person, in lieu of actual reconstitution of groups.

REFERENCES

1. Bales, R. F. *Interaction process analysis*. Cambridge, Mass.: Addison-Wesley, 1950.
2. Borgatta, E. F., & Bales, R. F. Task and accumulation of experience as factors in the interaction of small groups. *Sociometry*, 1953, 16, 239–252.
3. Borgatta, E. F., & Bales, R. F. The consistency of subject behavior and the reliability of scoring in interaction process analysis. *Amer. sociol. Rev.*, 1953, 18, 566–569.
4. Mills, T. M. Power relations in three-person groups. *Amer. social. Rev.*, 1953, 18, 351–357.

Personality and Group Position

LEONARD BERKOWITZ

SOCIOLOGICAL and psychological theorizing have found a common meeting-ground in small group research. Laboratory investigations of social influence provide a fuller understanding of many social processes. Considerations of role and social system add to our knowledge of personality functioning (e.g., 3, 4), and the interaction of personality and social system in determining a given individual's behavior frequently can be demonstrated best in laboratory experimentation. The present paper describes an exploratory investigation of this interaction of personality and social systems and also illustrates a procedure through which additional research may be carried out under relatively controlled conditions.

Individuals with widely divergent personality characteristics frequently are assigned to common positions in on-going social structures. The usual outcome is that the initially different people are observed to behave in a strikingly similar fashion. Thus, McClelland writes, "The ability of people to transform themselves at least partly in accordance with the demands of a situation has long been observed by students of human nature and has an honorable place among the concepts used by social scientists" (3, p. 290). This similarity in position behavior frequently

FROM *Sociometry*, 1956, 19, 210–222. Reprinted by permission of the author and the American Sociological Association, Inc.
Thanks are due to Mrs. Marsel Heisel for her invaluable assistance in the collection and analyses of data, and to Dr. J. C. Gilchrist for his suggestions concerning the statistical analysis.

results from individual conformity to relatively similar role expectations. However, role expectations, no matter how strong, will not evoke a given response pattern if the individual assigned to the position does not have this pattern in his response repertoire.

The concept of "response hierarchy" appears to be useful here. Faced with similar group positions and, hence, similar situational requirements, individuals of different personality types will initially respond in a somewhat different fashion to the extent that the required response is located differently in the individuals' response hierarchies. In other words, the required response will probably occur sooner the higher response in the hierarchy. However, assuming that this required response *is* in the individual's repertoire and that there are no response inhibiting factors, it is likely that the required response eventually will occur. Over time, then, the individuals of different personality types will come to behave in a similar fashion.

The present exploratory investigation will attempt to demonstrate this change over time employing individuals markedly different in their characteristic level of ascendance. Four-man groups are utilized with one central position (a position that communicates directly with each member of the group) and three peripheral positions (who can communicate only with the central person). Individuals high or low in their characteristic level of ascendance are assigned either to a central or peripheral group position. The high ascendance subjects (Ss) in the central position, with its requirements for generally ascendant behavior, initially should behave differently from the low ascendance Ss. Ascendant responses are higher in the response hierarchies of the former. However, the low ascendance Ss then should gradually adapt to the position requirements so that by the last of the three trials given to the groups the high and low ascendant Ss should be similar behaviorally. Furthermore, to the extent that the central position does require ascendant behavior, the low ascendance central Ss should have the greatest change from Trial 1 to Trial 3 and they should change in the direction of the behavior exhibited by the high ascendance central Ss.

In addition, the present study will seek to determine whether the previously obtained relationship between the low job satisfaction and the occupation of peripheral positions (e.g., 2, 5) is similar for both the high and low ascendance Ss. High ascendance peripheral Ss may feel that their peripheral position imposes severe restrictions upon their communication opportunities and thus does not enable them to play so prominent a role in the group as they would wish. Low ascendance peripheral Ss, on the other hand, presumably do not have so strong a need to play a prominent role in the group and should be bothered less by the imposed communication restrictions. As a result we would expect the high ascendance Ss to be less satisfied with their positions than the low ascendance Ss.

METHOD

Selection of Subjects

Volunteers were recruited from introductory psychology classes and all completed the Guilford-Zimmerman Temperament Survey. Those scoring in either the upper or lower third of the range on the G-Z Ascendance scale (men and women were kept separate) were scheduled for further "screening." Groups of four men or four women were assembled consisting of two high ascendance and two low ascendance Ss. (Occasionally, however, one of the scheduled Ss did not keep his appointment and a three-person group had to be used.) Each group was given the task of assembling the framework of a small house, approximately 6 feet high and with a 4-foot-square base, from precut pieces of lumber, while two observers categorized the ongoing behavior. After 30 minutes—very few of the groups completed the task in this time—work was stopped and the Ss answered a brief sociometric questionnaire. The observers also rated each S on a number of scales.

An S was classified as being characteristically highly ascendant if he met the following criteria: (a) he had a G-Z Ascendance scale score in the upper third of the range for his sex, (b) both observers had rated him either highest or next highest in the observed group on their "attempted leadership" scale, (c) he had received the highest or next highest total ratings from the others in his group on the Subject Scale, "How frequently did each member attempt to influence your behavior?," and (d) he had the highest or next highest total amount of recorded participations (summed over both observers) in the given group. An S was classified as being characteristically low in ascendance if he had a G-Z Ascendance score in the lowest third of the range for his sex and a rank of 3 or 4 in his group on each of the remaining three measures. For the three-person groups the required ranks were 1 and 3 respectively.

The Experimental Session

The above screening process, together with the failure of some Ss to keep their appointments, resulted in the selection of 21 highly ascendant and 21 low ascendant Ss (10 men and 11 women in each category) out of the original pool of approximately two hundred volunteers. These Ss were employed in the major experimental session together with moderately ascendant Ss, Ss whose G-Z Ascendance scores had fallen in the middle third of the range. Four-person groups were assembled from this reduced pool, consisting of one highly ascendant, one less ascendant, and two moderately ascendant Ss. None of the Ss in a group had worked together previously.

The present group task was adapted from that employed by Shaw (5).

The apparatus consisted of a room partitioned into four cubicles radiating from a central point. Each cubicle was connected to every other cubicle by means of a slot through which message cards could be passed but which did not permit the Ss to see each other. Each cubicle was identified by a color: blue, red, green, or yellow. The message cards sent by a given position identified the sending position by its color and the designations were the color names.

The present communication network was a "star" pattern. Blue was the central person who could communicate directly to each of the other three positions. These other three positions were peripheral. Their communication slots were arranged so that the only communication possible for each was with Blue.

Each S maintained his position in the network over the three problem-solving trials given to his group. The first trial was stopped at the end of 20 minutes if the problem had not been completed by that time, while the time limit for each of the remaining two problems was 16 minutes. The problems were administered to the groups in a systematically rotated order. The following is an example of the type of problem used:

> A small company is moving from one office building to another. It must move four kinds of equipment: (1) chairs, (2) desks, (3), filing cabinets, and (4) typewriters. How many trucks are needed to make the move in one trip?

Each S was given two of the eight necessary items of information, and the items supplied to a given position were also continually changed from one group to the next.

Procedure

In half of the groups (High Ascend.-Center) a highly ascendant S was assigned to the central position, Blue, the low ascendance S to the peripheral position, Green, and the moderately ascendant Ss to the other peripheral positions, Red and Yellow. In the other groups (Low Ascend.-Center) the low ascendance person occupied the central position, while the high ascendance S occupied position Green.[1] The moderately ascendant Ss in this condition again were assigned to positions Red and Yellow.

After each S had been seated the E explained the task and then started the group on the first trial. An S would signal when he had obtained an

1 This design does not enable us to differentiate the "main effects" (in the analysis of variance sense) due to a given personality type's behavior over both the central and peripheral positions from the "interaction" of personality and position and from the effects upon a given personality type of the other type in the other position. The small number of Ss remaining after the screening process did not enable us to utilize a more satisfactory design. This small number of Ss, of course, also severely restricts the generality of the present findings. However, despite the inadequacies of the design, we believe the results are suggestive and that the present interpretations are entirely consistent with everyday observations.

answer satisfactory to him by raising his hand and the E noted the time at which each S gave this signal. These data are employed in the analyses of time to problem completion. When each S in the group indicated he had an answer or at the end of the time limit, whichever came first, the E collected the problem and information cards and the message cards received, distributed the problem and information for the new trial, and then started the group upon the new trial. When all three problems had been completed, the Ss filled out a brief sociometric questionnaire.

Every male group had at least one member reach an answer to the first problem that was satisfactory to him by the time limit. However, half of the female groups did not solve the first problem within this period. Because of this difference the data from the male and female groups were not combined, and the present analysis is restricted to the 10 male groups of 4 Ss each.

RESULTS

Time to problem solution

Table 1 presents the mean time to problem completion (in 10-second intervals) for each position in the different trials and conditions. Analyses of variance indicate that the significance differences were (all beyond the .01 level) among groups within a condition, among Ss within groups within conditions, and among groups within conditions and trials. However, the second order interaction of positions, conditions, and trials was still significant with the residual employed as the error term ($F=9.08$, $P=.001$). Also, as can be readily seen in the table, there were significant differences among trials ($F=92.89$, $P<.001$), with the time to solution decreasing from the first to third trials indicating a group "learning" effect.

A Duncan test (1) then was made to determine the significant differences involved in the second order interaction.[2] Trial I was significantly longer than the other trials for all the positions within both conditions. What is most striking in the first trial data is that Blue (the central position) in the High Ascend.-Center condition had a significantly shorter time to problem completion than all other positions in this condition, while Blue in the Low Ascend.-Center condition tended to have a longer time to problem solution than the peripheral positions in this condition. In this Low Ascend.-Center condition, however, only Green—the peripheral position occupied by the highly ascendant S—had a significantly shorter time to problem solution than the central person. Green, in turn, was significantly faster on Trial I than both Yellow and Blue in this condition, but not significantly faster than Red, although this last difference approached

2 Unless otherwise specified, all differences found to be statistically significant by means of the Duncan test are significant at the .05 level or less.

significance. There were no significant differences in the second and third trial data.

The highly ascendant Ss, whether in the center or periphery, perhaps because of a high degree of self-confidence, tended to complete their first problem and feel satisfied with their answers before the other group members. The low ascendance individuals in the central position, on the other hand, tended to have taken the longest of all the positions in this condition to indicate that they had reached a satisfactory solution to the first problem, perhaps because they were low in self-confidence. The Ss apparently first supplied their other group members with the relevant information they had received before deciding on a problem answer. They seem to have given information transmission a higher priority than their own problem solution. The high ascendance Ss in the center, on the other hand,

TABLE I

Mean Time to Problem Completion (in 10 second Intervals)

CONDITION	HIGH ASCEND.-CENTER				LOW ASCEND.-CENTER			
POSITION	*Blue*	*Green*	*Red*	*Yellow*	*Blue*	*Green*	*Red*	*Yellow*
TYPE	*High*	*Low*	*Mod.*	*Mod.*	*Low*	*High*	*Mod.*	*Mod.*
Trial I	70.8	93.8	97.2	98.0	88.4	71.2	80.8	84.8
Trial II	45.0	49.0	49.4	51.8	34.8	33.8	39.0	39.0
Trial III	38.4	33.4	44.2	39.2	37.4	35.0	38.0	37.0

may have minimized or at least delayed the information transmission aspect of their job in favor of their own problem solution.

These differences became minimal in the second and third trials. Two reasons may be advanced for this. First, the group members seem to have learned to use the communication network and time to solution was cut in half. As a result, the problem situation may have become easy enough for even the low ascendance Ss. With longer and more difficult problems the differences might have persisted. Second, each group member, regardless of personality, may have adapted to his position requirements sufficiently so that the first trial differences would not have emerged with even somewhat more difficult problems. According to this latter hypothesis, the low ascendance Ss in the center had learned to play a more active role in the group process than merely transmitting information, while the ascendant peripheral Ss had learned to take a less active role.

Communication Content

A rough check of this last possibility can be found in the analysis of the messages transmitted by each position. Because of the small frequencies involved, it was possible to utilize only two categories: (a) the transmission of any information in the particular message card, and (b) the transmission of any other communication (e.g., asking for information, proposing a solution to the problem, etc.). Information-seeking constituted the largest proportion of this second category. One message card could contain both categories, but only one of each category could be coded for each card. The two observers agreed on the categorization of 88 per cent of the messages sent by each position over the three trials for two randomly selected groups.

The frequencies in each category first were tabulated, and for each S we ascertained the proportion of all units transmitted by him which were informational. We assume here that the greater proportion of informational units the more passive the role played by the S. The nature of the present task is such that each position has to transmit information. The

TABLE 2

Per Cent of Units Which Were Informational Transmitted by Position (Arc Sine Transformation)

CONDITION	HIGH ASCEND.-CENTER		LOW ASCEND.-CENTER	
POSITION	*Blue*	*Green*	*Blue*	*Green*
TYPE	*High*	*Low*	*Low*	*High*
Trial I	45.4	62.0	51.6	35.0
Trial II	48.4	50.4	48.0	55.4
Trial III	47.2	65.0	36.8	55.2

individual demonstrates a more active role in the group process by communicating other kinds of content. These percentages then were subjected to the arc sine transformation.

The moderate ascendance peripheral positions, Red and Yellow, were not included in the present analysis. The small frequencies in the peripheral positions would mean that a very large part of the data would consist of relatively unreliable percentages if all four positions were to be included. The resulting means for positions Blue and Green are given in Table 2.

Two effects were significant by analysis of variance: positions within groups within conditions ($F = 8.13$, $P = .001$), and the second order interaction of conditions, positions, and trials ($F = 3.62$, $P = .05$). The Duncan test yielded differences consistent with the hypothesis of a change in the roles played by the high and low ascendance Ss in the Low Ascend.-Center condition.

In trial I, as can be seen in Table 2, the low ascendance Ss in the periphery tended to have a greater proportion of informational units than the central high ascendance Ss (significant between the .10 and .05 levels of confidence). The former, then, appear to be playing a more passive role than the latter. This expected difference supports the validity of the present interpretation of a high proportion of informational units. That this difference is probably personality-determined as well as position-determined is suggested by the trial I difference between the low ascendance and high ascendence Ss in this position. The former had a significantly greater proportion of informational units than the latter.

But, most important of all, the hypothesized changes had taken place in the Low Ascend.-Center condition by trial III so that the differences in this condition resemble the differences in the High Ascend.-Center condition. In both conditions during this last trial the central person had a smaller proportion of informational units than the peripheral person. (Both differences are significant between the .10 and .05 levels.) The low ascendance Ss in the center had become somewhat less passive (although there is no significant difference between trials 1 and 3), while the high ascendance Ss in the periphery had become more passive (difference between trials 1 and 3 significant betwen the .10 and .05 levels). Both the low ascendance Ss in the center and the high ascendance Ss in the periphery had changed their behavior with increased experience in their positions. Although it is not possible to determine the extent to which the change in one position was responsible for the other position's change, the trial III position behavior, at least for the present communication content, is largely determined by group position rather than personality alone.

Rates of Communication

The next analysis was to determine whether there were reliable differences in communication rates among the various positions. The number of message cards sent by each S in each trial was tabulated and this frequency was divided by the time taken by the slowest member of the group in that trial (in 10-second intervals). The mean communication rates are given in Table 3.

Analyses of variance of these data indicated that the following were the statistically significant effects (all at less than the .001 level of confidence). As expected, there were significant position differences ($F = 33.45$) over the two conditions with the central positions having the highest communication rates. There also were trial differences ($F = 38.07$). The communication rates increased in both conditions from the first to third trials. The interaction of positions and trials was also significant ($F = 19.32$), as was the second order interaction of conditions, positions, and trials ($F = 36.33$).

The Duncan test points to the differences going to make up these main effects and interactions. First, there were significant increases between trials I and II, and II and III in the communication rates of both the high and low ascendance Ss in the central position. These rates were similar for the high and low ascendance central Ss in the first two trials, but by the third trial the low ascendance Ss in this position had a significantly faster rate than the high ascendance central Ss. The reason for this difference is not clear. Furthermore, except for the high ascendance Ss in the periphery,

TABLE 3

Mean Number of Messages Sent Per 10-second Interval

CONDITION	HIGH ASCEND.-CENTER				LOW ASCEND.-CENTER			
POSITION	*Blue*	*Green*	*Red*	*Yellow*	*Blue*	*Green*	*Red*	*Yellow*
TYPE	*High*	*Low*	*Mod.*	*Mod.*	*Low*	*High*	*Mod.*	*Mod.*
Trial I	11.6	3.8	4.6	7.2	12.4	7.8	5.8	4.8
Trial II	17.2	3.4	5.4	5.4	15.4	10.0	5.8	7.8
Trial III	19.2	4.6	5.2	7.6	23.0	8.8	8.0	5.0

the communication rates in the peripheral positions tended to remain constant over the three trials. (There was a significant difference between trials I and II for the peripheral high ascendance Ss.) Assuming that the communications rate changes indicate some kind of learning, the learning—with the possible exception of the peripheral high ascendance Ss—was largely an effect of the central position.

Second, consistent differences between the high and low ascendance Ss emerged in the peripheral position with its weaker press of requirements. In each trial, the high ascendance Ss in the peripheral position had significantly faster communication rates than the low ascendance Ss in this position. Furthermore, the low ascendance peripheral Ss tended to have the lowest communication rates of all peripheral positions in their condition, while the high ascendance Ss tended to have the highest rates of communication in the periphery. These differences are constant for all three trials, but the low ascendant peripheral Ss have communication rates significantly lower than only Yellow's rates and only in trials I and II. (The differences with Red just fall short of significance in these trials.) The highly ascendant peripheral Ss in the Low Ascend.-Center condition had communication rates significantly faster than Yellow in all three trials, and significantly faster than Red in trial II. It would appear, then, that the differences in characteristic level of ascendance were most clearly related to differences in communication rate in the peripheral group positions.

Questionnaire Responses

The questionnaire responses were analyzed in order to determine whether there would be personality differences in the relationship between the position occupied by an individual and his "morale." The first question reads as follows: "How well did you like your job in the group?" The scores ranged from 6 (very much) to 1 (disliked very much). The means for each position in each condition are given in Table 4.

Analyses of variance of these data revealed only one significant effect: that for positions ($F = 10.25$, $P = .01$). (The number of degrees of freedom was halved in order to compensate for the between conditions heterogeneity of variance.) The Duncan test indicated that both central positions had significantly higher scores than the moderately ascendant peripheral positions, Red and Yellow, but they were not significantly higher than either the low ascendance peripheral position or the high ascendance peripheral position. Also, these latter peripheral positions were higher, but not significantly, than the two moderately ascendant peripheral positions.

TABLE 4

Position Means for Questionnaire Responses

CONDITION	HIGH ASCEND.-CENTER				LOW ASCEND.-CENTER			
POSITION	*Blue*	*Green*	*Red*	*Yellow*	*Blue*	*Green*	*Red*	*Yellow*
TYPE	*High*	*Low*	*Mod.*	*Mod.*	*Low*	*High*	*Mod.*	*Mod.*
QUESTION 1: "How well did you like your job?"								
MEANS	6.0	4.4	3.0	2.4	6.0	4.6	3.4	3.8
QUESTION 2: "To what extent did your position in this group permit you to participate as much as you would have wanted to participate?"								
MEANS	6.0	4.0	3.0	1.4	6.0	4.2	2.2	2.8

If, for the moment at least, we accept the ordering of the positions on their job satisfaction scores as being relatively reliable, the results, at first blush, are partly surprising. We had expected that the high ascendance Ss in the periphery would be very dissatisfied with their jobs because the communication restrictions upon this position would not enable them to become prominent in the group. The moderate satisfaction scores of the low ascendance peripheral Ss was expected; these Ss, it was thought, would not be as disturbed by the communication restrictions because of their lower needs to be prominent. However, the above results suggest that the high ascendance Ss in the periphery were just as satisfied with their jobs as the low ascendance Ss.

There is no reason to believe that these results (or any others) are an artifact of the Green position. Green was not adjacent to Blue's cubicle, and communication from Blue was not easier to Green than to any other peripheral position. A likelier possibility is that both types of Ss in the Green position did not feel that their communication was restricted to any significant extent. The low ascendance Ss would not feel restricted because they presumably would have little need for a high level of participation in the group, while the high ascendance Ss would not let the communication limitations interfere completely with their participation.

The responses to the next questionnaire item were analyzed in order to check this possibility. The item reads, "To what extent did your position in this group permit you to participate as much as you would have wanted to participate?" The scores range from 6 (Permitted me to participate as much as I wanted to) to 1 (Did not at all permit me to participate as much as I desired). The means are given in Table 4.

The analyses of variance, again halving the degrees of freedom because of the heterogeneity of variance, indicates that the only significant effect was for position ($F = 26.28$), $P < .01$). According to the Duncan test, the two central positions, as expected, had significantly higher scores than all other positions. They could participate as much as they wanted to. Both the high and low ascendance Ss in the periphery had higher scores than the moderately ascendant Ss, but the "highs" felt significantly less restricted than only Red, while the "lows" felt significantly less restricted than only Yellow. Thus, while the present results are not conclusive, they are consistent with the hypothesis that those either characteristically high or characteristically low in ascendance feel less restricted in a peripheral group position than those having a moderate level of ascendance.

SUMMARY AND CONCLUSIONS

On the basis of responses to the Guilford-Zimmerman Temperament Survey as well as their observed behavior in a mechanical assembly task, 10 male college students were classified as being characteristically high in ascendance, while another 10 were classified as characteristically low in ascendance. These Ss, together with Ss classified as being moderately ascendant, were assembled into four-man groups consisting of one S low in ascendance, one S high in ascendance, and two who were moderately ascendant. In one condition, High Ascend.-Center, the highly ascendant S was assigned the central position in a "star" communication network while the other three Ss were given the peripheral positions. In the other condition, Low Ascend.-Center, the low ascendance S was given the central position and the remaining Ss the three peripheral positions. Each group had to complete three problems, and measures were obtained for each of the three trials based on time to problem completion, the content of the messages sent by one position to another, and the communication rate. In addition, the Ss filled out a questionnaire indicating their satisfaction with their positions.

One of the areas investigated had to do with the question of differences in the behavior of the high and low ascendance Ss in the central group position. The results suggest that the behavioral differences between the two types of Ss in the central position that did emerge tended to exist only during the first trial. Under the high press of common situational requirements, both the high and low ascendance Ss behaved in a somewhat similar fashion by the third trial. Thus, in the first trial the high ascendance Ss in the center tended to complete their problems before the others in the group, while the low ascendance Ss in this position tended to complete their problems after the others in the group. However, by trial III the differences in the time to problem completion between these two types of Ss in the center tended to become minimal.

These changes have been hypothesized to be a result of a position adaptation, and there is additional evidence consistent with this interpretation. In the first trial the low ascendance Ss tended to play a more passive role in the group problem-solving process than the high ascendance central Ss, as indicated by their somewhat higher (but not significantly so) proportion of information giving units in their communications. They also had a significantly higher level of passivity than the high ascendance Ss in the peripheral position. However, there was a steady reduction in this level of passivity (i.e., an increase in the proportion of noninformation-giving units) so that by trial III the low ascendance Ss in the center were significantly more "active" than the high ascendance Ss in the periphery. This resembles the pattern that had remained consistent in the High Ascend.-Center condition.

These results, then, indicate that for the present central group positions the heavy press of situational requirements for these positions tends, over time, to count more in determining the individual's passivity level and time to problem solution than his characteristic level of ascendance. To what extent can these results be generalized? On one hand, we would expect that the greater problem complexity and the longer time spent in problem solving found in many "real-life" groups would facilitate the emergence of personality-determined differences in the behavior of the central group members. But, on the other hand, there frequently are traditions and expectations concerning the role behavior of those in the central positions, and it is likely that these would act to minimize the personality-determined differences.

The results tend to support the present theoretical interpretation of the interaction of personality and group positions. The high and low Ss differ primarily in that ascendant responses are higher in the response hierarchies of the former. When confronted with the central position and its requirements for ascendant behavior, these two types of Ss initially behave somewhat differently. The former initially are more likely to behave in an ascendant manner. However, ascendant responses *are* in the response hierarchies of even the low ascendance Ss and ascendant behavior tends to occur by trial III. Furthermore, the results also indicate that the central position does require ascendant behavior. The low ascendance Ss change toward the behavior of the high ascendance Ss.

The present results also suggest that when the behavioral differences between the high and low ascendance Ss persist over the three trials this is most likely to be the case in the peripheral group positions with their relatively low press of situational requirements. Thus, the high ascendance peripheral Ss have communication rates significantly faster than that for the low ascendance peripheral Ss over all three trials. However, there also was evidence of position adaptation changes in the behavior of those in the peripheral positions, particularly in the case of the high ascendance peripheral Ss. These Ss became more passive in their communications as they proceeded from trial I to trial III, as indicated by their significant increase in the proportion of information-giving communications. The high ascendance peripheral Ss resembled the low ascendance peripheral Ss on this measure of passivity by trial III.

The last set of results has to do with position differences in job satisfaction. As has been found by other investigators, the Ss in the central group position expressed the greatest degree of satisfaction with their jobs. The surprising result was that the high ascendance peripheral Ss were similar to the low ascendance perpiheral Ss in having somewhat greater job satisfaction than the moderately ascendant peripheral Ss. Further analyses of the questionnaire responses suggest that both the high and low ascendance peripheral Ss felt less restricted in their communication opportunities than the moderately ascendant peripheral Ss.

REFERENCES

1. Duncan, D. B. A significance test for differences between ranked treatments in an analysis of variance. *Virginia J. of Sci.*, 1951, 2, 171-189.
2. Leavitt, H. J. Some effects of certain communication patterns on group performance. *J. abnorm. soc. Psychol.*, 1951, 46, 38–50.
3. McClelland, D. C. *Personality*. New York: Dryden, 1951.
4. Parsons, T., & Shils, E. A. Personality as a system of action. In T. Parsons and E. A. Shils (Eds.), *Toward a general theory of action*. Cambridge, Mass.: Harvard Univer. Press, 1951, 110–158.
5. Shaw, M. E. Some effects of unequal distribution of information upon group performance in various communication nets. *J. abnorm. soc. Psychol.*, 1954, 49, 547–553.

Techniques for the Study of Group Structure and Behavior: Empirical Studies of the Effects of Structure in Small Groups

MURRAY GLANZER
and
ROBERT GLASER

AN EARLIER PAPER (8) reviewed techniques for analyzing the structure of groups that had been permitted to form their own pattern of interaction. This paper reviews laboratory studies in which experimenters imposed different structures on groups and measured the effect of the structures on performance.

The laboratory studies focus on communication structure. A communication structure is a set of positions with specified communications channels. Between any two positions, there may be a two-way channel, a one-way channel, or none at all. A channel is essentially the probability that a message can pass in a given direction between two positions. It may be defined more generally as the probability, p_{ab}, that a message can get from Position a to Position b. This is *not* the probability that a will try to send to b. It is, rather, the probability of his getting a message through if he tries to send one. In most of the structures studied, the channels are

FROM *Psychological Bulletin*, 1961, 58, 1–27. Reprinted by permission of authors and the American Psychological Association, Inc.

Prepared under Contract Nonr 2551(00), between the Office of Naval Research, Psychological Sciences Division, Personnel and Training Branch and the American Institute for Research, as part of a research project on team training and performance. The authors wish to thank Alex Bavelas, Harold Guetzkow, Robert L. Hall, John T. Lanzetta, Seymour Rosenberg, Marvin E. Shaw, and Gerald Shure, who read, and commented on, earlier drafts of the paper.

symmetric i.e., $p_{ab}=p_{ba}$ and the channels are either available or not, i.e., $p_{ab}=0$ or 1.

The studies are grouped in the following sections: The Initial Work, Variations and Further Analysis of the Basic Design, Testing the Limits of the Basic Design, Mathematical Analysis, Emphasis on Distribution of Functions in the Simulated Team, and Emphasis on Feedback and Learning.

THE INITIAL WORK

The area of communication structure was opened up 12 years ago by Bavelas (1) with a discussion of mathematical aspects of group structure. The paper is Lewinian in tone, using the terminology of boundary, region, etc. The Lewinian boundary, however, is translated into the link or channel. This translation is of major importance for all the work that follows. Bavelas then builds up a set of assumptions and definitions concerning a collection of cells. He defines cell boundary, region, open cell, closed cell, region boundary, chain, chain length, structure, cell distance, cell-region distance, etc., and considers the factors that cause each measure to vary, deriving theorems concerning the following: the limits of the values for the various distances and other measures, the relation between the distance measures and the spread of a change of state in the structure, and characteristics of pathways within the structure. Bavelas then shows how the various distances change as a function of structure types (e.g., organizations with varying degrees of horizontal coordination) and as a function of an increase in the number of levels in the organization. He also discusses the role of special positions such as liaison positions and possible applications of his approach.

The many provocative points raised in the paper were not directly followed by experimental work. Experimental work was set off by a second, much simpler paper (2), which differs markedly from the first. The Lewinian tone has disappeared. For example, regions within structures are not mentioned. Bavelas now discusses a few simpler concepts which readily generate experimental situations. Complex concepts such as inner and outer regions and chains of connecting cells do not appear again in the work in this area. The only concepts that survive from the first paper are those of links and distances. The focus of the discussion changes, moreover, from the larger *in situ* group, e.g., an industrial organization, to the small laboratory group.

In the second paper, Bavelas introduces the communication networks which were to become standard experimental arrangements. The channels of these networks are all two-way channels: a channel from *a* to *b* is also a channel from *b* to *a*. He also introduces the index of relative centrality to describe the structures. The index of the relative centrality (of Position *x*) is the ratio of the sum of the minimal distances of all positions to all others over the sum of the minimal distances of Position x to all others, or

$$C(x) = \frac{\sum_{x}\sum_{y} d_{xy}}{\sum_{y} d_{xy}}$$

where d_{xy} is the minimal distance between x and y. Many of the investigations of group structure published after this paper focus on this measure. In subsequent studies $C(x)$ is also summed over all positions, x, in the network to give net centrality.

The main question Bavelas now asks is the following: Is it possible that

> among several communication patterns, all logically adequate for the successful completion of a specified task, one gives significantly better performance than another (p. 726)?

In answer to this question, he describes experimental results obtained by S. L. Smith (unpublished report) and Leavitt (17) who use an experimental arrangement that is the model for the majority of the subsequent studies.

Five subjects were each given a list of symbols. Their task was to discover which symbol they all had in common. The physical setting was arranged so that some group members could send messages to each other, other group members could not. Smith's and Leavitt's subjects sat around a table partitioned into five sections with slots, some of which were open to allow notes to pass between sections. The pattern of open slots determined the communication pattern or structure. The subjects were free to use the open communication channels in any way they wished. They were not told the structure of the network.

The group's task required two main steps: distribution of individual information so that some or all members had all the necessary information, and determination of the common symbol. The task was completed when all subjects gave the answer. Smith imposed two communication structures: Circle and Chain (see Figure 1) and finds that structure affects group performance. The Chain is more efficient than the Circle. The performance ascribed to individuals is related to their positions. The central positions are most frequently seen as leaders.

Leavitt (17) used the same physical arrangement and problem as Smith did, but with four structures: Circle, Chain, Wheel, and Y (see Figure 1). His main positive findings are that the Wheel, Y, Chain, and Circle (most centralized to least centralized) rank in descending order (best to least) with respect to the following: (*a*) speed of development of organization for problem handling (the Wheel, Y, and Chain were, moreover, stable once they developed their organization. The Circle was inconsistent, i.e., problem solving procedure never became fixed); (*b*) agreement on who the group leaders were; and (*c*) satisfaction with the group. The ordering on these characteristics correlates perfectly with the ordering of the values of the net centrality index, $\Sigma_x C(x)$.

During the course of 15 trials, all the structures showed learning, reducing the time to complete trials. The networks did not, however, differ clearly from each other is speed or in learning rate. Leavitt asserts that the Circle used more messages and made more errors than the other networks. The interpretation of the data, however, is unclear since the analyses are based on a selection of the data, e.g., number of messages on successful trials.

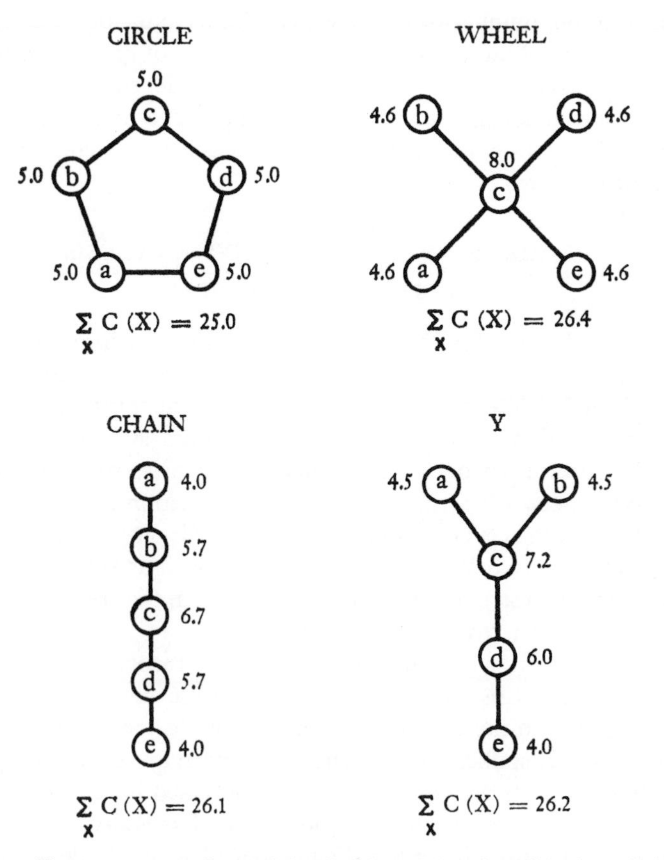

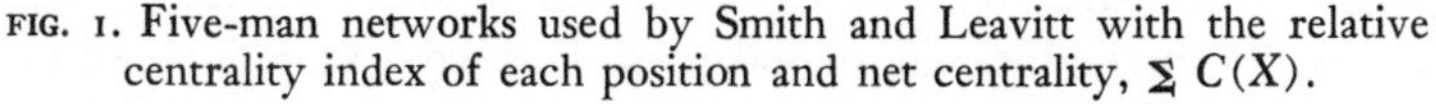
FIG. 1. Five-man networks used by Smith and Leavitt with the relative centrality index of each position and net centrality, $\sum_x C(X)$.

Leavitt, in analyzing the effects of position within a network finds that the most central position sends the most messages and the least central, the fewest. Subjects at the central position, moreover, enjoy their jobs more than those at peripheral positions. The relation of centrality to number of messages is to be expected, since the central positions had to serve as relays for messages from the peripheral members. Concerning the relation between position and morale, Leavitt (17) offers the following explanation:

> In our culture, in which needs for autonomy, recognition, and achievement are strong, it is to be expected that positions which limit independence of action (peripheral positions) would be unsatisfying (p. 48).

The dependent variables of the Smith and the Leavitt studies are the major concern of the subsequent network studies. The variables fall into four main classes: (*a*) efficiency—number of errors, correct completions, speed of solution, number of messages; (*b*) leadership—positions named as leader, agreement about leader; (*c*) morale—rating of group, rating of self; and (*d*) organization—consistency, type. These dependent variables and the two main independent variables, group structures and individual position within group structures, form the basic framework of the network studies.

VARIATIONS AND FURTHER ANALYSIS OF THE BASIC DESIGN

The work of Bavelas, Smith, and Leavitt proliferated into an abundance of network studies. The first of these was a study by Heise and Miller (13), introducing the following variations in the original procedures: (a) Communication took place over an intercom system. The subjects could, therefore, listen or speak simultaneously to as many of the other subjects as the network permitted. (*b*) Communication content was highly restricted. The subjects could only relay the words on a given list. (*c*) The communication network included one-way as well as two-way channels. The five three-man structures used are presented in Figure 2. (*d*) Intensity of noise was varied over the networks.

Using a task in which the subjects had to reconstruct a master list of words on the basis of incomplete lists, Heise and Miller find that: (*a*) As the signal-to-noise ratio in the intercom channels was lowered, the number of words spoken, errors, and the time required to complete the task increased for all networks. (*b*) With increased noise, the differences between networks became more pronounced. Generally, inefficiency of performance, measured by either the number of words spoken or the time required to finish the task, increased from Pattern 1 to 5 (in Figure 2). A second task, in which the subjects had to reconstruct a 25-word sentence based on parts given to each of them, gave similar results, except that Networks 2 and 3 were somewhat more efficient than Network 1 at the high noise levels. When, however, the subjects were given anagram problems in which communication between the subjects was not necessary, the results were as follows: intense noise decreased the number of words spoken; there was no systematic difference between the efficiency of the various nets.

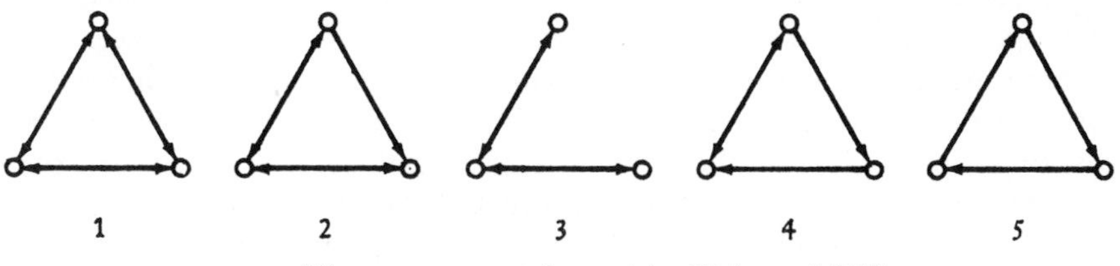

FIG. 2. Three-man networks used by Heise and Miller.

Aside from its introduction of a greater variety of channel arrangements, the main contribution of the study is probably that it demonstrates that no network is best in all situations. The efficiency of a structure depends on the characteristics of the task. Thus, in one of the first network studies, the complex interactions that will mar the apparent simplicity of the early findings appear.

Guetzkow and Simon (11) introduced the distinction between two classes of behavior in the network: direct problem solving behavior, such as relaying information and asking questions; and organizational behavior, such as assigning of roles and functions to team members. They hypothesize that communication restrictions affect only the ability of the group to organize; once the group is organized, however, the different structures are equally efficient in solving the problems. To test their hypothesis, they used three five-man networks: Circle, Wheel (see Figure 1), and All-Channel (see Figure 4). Under their variant of the network situation, a group member could send only coded problem information during trials, but could send any kind of message during the intertrial periods.

On the basis of the characteristics of the networks, Guetzkow and Simon predict that the Wheel should be highest in efficiency, the All-Channel intermediate, and the Circle lowest.

> The Wheel groups would have the least difficulty, for they have no channels to eliminate, no relays to establish, and already have one person occupying a dominant position in the net. The All-Channel groups would have the next grade of difficulty, since the elimination of excess channels and the evolution of one person as solution-former are both required, yet relays need not be established. The Circle groups should have the most difficulty, for they need both to establish relays and to evolve an asymmetrical arrangement among the positions. They also must do some eliminating of unneeded channels, although this last requirement is minimal (p. 240).

Their findings on speed of problem solution (which also agree with Leavitt's contention concerning the Wheel and the Circle) bear out this prediction.

They cite the following as evidence that the structures affect organizational efficiency: The interaction patterns were most stable (same channels consistently used) in the Wheel and least stable in the All-Channel; the greatest degree of differentiation of function is found in the Wheel, the least in the Circle. They show, furthermore, that if only the stable groups of each network are compared, then there are no longer differences in the speed in problem solution. They cite that finding as evidence that the communication restriction does not affect the problem solving directly.

Guetzkow and Dill (10) follow up this study with an investigation of what happens during the trial periods, in which communication was limited to exchange of coded information, and during the intertrial "organizing" periods. They reanalyze the Guetzkow-Simon data with respect to two factors—"local learning" (see Christie, Luce, & Macy, 1952, below) which occurs during the trials, and "planning mechanism" which functions during the intertrial period—and conclude that All-Channel shows the most planning activity while Wheel shows the least, presumably because its organization is dictated by the communication net. They furthermore note that the Circle network is handicapped in organizing itself during the intertrial period by the network restrictions, whereas the All-Channel structure does not seem to have this difficulty.

In order to explore this point, Guetzkow and Dill obtained new data by running groups of subjects under an alternating structure condition. During the task trials, the groups were run as Circles. During the intertrial periods, all communication restrictions were removed by opening the barred channels, giving an All-Channel net. These new experimental groups are called Circle–All-Channel. Guetzkow and Dill (10) hypothesize that

> task performance in a restricted net will be equal to that in an unrestricted net, if the restrictions are removed during the intertrial period so that a relay system may be organized (p. 191).

An analysis of task trial times failed to support the hypothesis. Circle–All-Channel groups do not differ in performance time from the Circle groups in the earlier experiment. All-Channel groups were, moreover, significantly faster than Circle–All-Channel groups. The main contribution of the two studies above is their suggestion concerning the ways in which communication structure impedes the group's attempts to organize itself for its work.

Goldberg (9) brings to the network study a new task, the unstructured group decision task, and a new dependent variable, influence (or, more precisely, "influenceability"). He hypothesizes that in group decisions, central positions in a network would be influenced less than peripheral positions. He placed subjects in the five-man Wheel, Y, and Chain and showed them a card bearing a number of dots. The subjects then communicated with each other and settled on an estimate of the number of dots. Influence, measured by the amount that a subject changed his initial estimate during the experimental session, is found to be negatively related to the centrality of the position only for the Y network. He finds, however, a positive relation between the centrality of a position and the number of leader nominations.

Trow (39) develops a point made by Leavitt (17, p. 49) into the hypothesis that centrality produces high morale and status not just because centrality implies greater access to communication channels, but because greater access to channels gives autonomy—ability to make independent decisions. Trow argues that though centrality and autonomy are usually correlated, they can be separated experimentally and that when they are separated, autonomy will be found to be the effective variable. He accomplished this separation by placing his subjects in apparent three-person chains and passing prepared notes to them to create the illusion of a group. Trow varied autonomy by giving some subjects a code book needed in planning the group's task and informing other subjects that someone else in the group had the code. He also gave the subjects a questionnaire to measure their need for autonomy.

The major findings are the following: autonomy produces a higher level of job satisfaction than does dependence; the effect of centrality upon satisfaction is not significant. The relation holds primarily for the high-need subjects. Trow concludes that "autonomy may be considered as mediating the observed relationship [found by Leavitt] between centrality and satisfaction" (p. 208). Predictions concerning a parallel effect of autonomy on self-ascribed status were not supported. Status was, however, affected by centrality.

The studies summarized in this section exemplify the major developments of the original theme: addition of new variables, e.g., noise, and analysis of the structural variables into psychological components.

TESTING THE LIMITS OF THE BASIC DESIGN

Shaw has systematically worked the area opened up by Bavelas, extending the investigations to include such variables as amount and distribution of information, problem complexity, and type of leadership. He has also suggested additional concepts: independence of positions (rather than centrality) and saturation.

Shaw (30) extended the network investigation to four-man groups (see Figure 3). The names he assigns to his networks raise an interesting question. Could not the four-man "Wheel" also be called a "Y"? The question has importance in comparing results for networks that differ in size. There is no empirical or rational basis for matching results from a

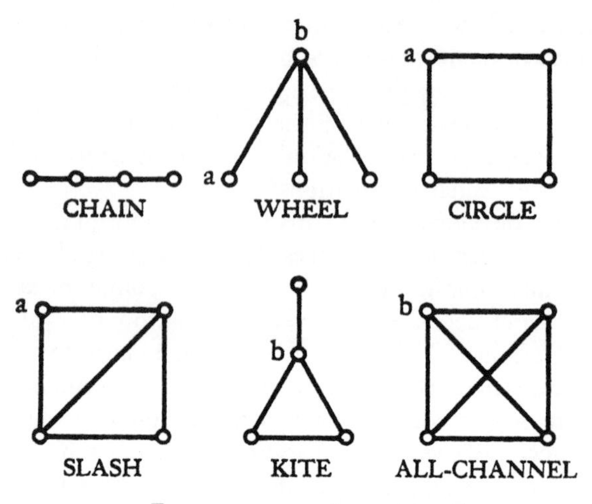

FIG. 3. Four-man networks used by Shaw.

four-man and five-man "Wheel." The only thing clear is that the number of distinct patterns decreases as the number of group members decreases. Therefore, although Chain, Wheel, and Y are distinct patterns for five-man groups, when the number of members is reduced by eliminating a peripheral member, only two of these three patterns remain: four-man Chain and Wheel-Y. If the number of members is reduced again, the two remaining networks coalesce into the simple three-man Chain. The difficulty caused by ignoring this characteristic will be pointed out later.

Shaw finds that the centrality of position is related, as in the Leavitt study, to number of messages sent, satisfaction, and frequency of nomination as leader. He proposes, however, an alternative to centrality, the related concept of independence, *I*, and constructs a measure of it. Shaw then plots mean number of messages, morale, recognition of leadership against *I* for his own and Leavitt's data. *I* appears to give plots that are more nearly monotonic than does centrality. The functions are, however, not only complicated, but also differ in form for presumably comparable Shaw and Leavitt data. For example, the equation relating morale to *I* is logarithmic for Leavitt's data and linear for Shaw's. The need for a concept like independence in explaining behavior within the networks had been expressed by Leavitt (17) and has received empirical support by Trow (39). Shaw's *I*, however, is an awkward and complex combination of variables. Since he gives no statistical evaluation of the improvement of *I*'s fit of the data over the fit yielded by centrality, it is difficult to judge whether *I*'s smoother curves compensate for its greater complexity. (The comparability of Leavitt's and of Shaw's data is of concern. Shaw told his subjects what the network structure was. Leavitt and the investigators following his procedures did not. Other aspects of the presumed comparability of data are discussed later on—e.g., 31).

The data Shaw considered above were drawn from a separately published study (32) aimed at testing the hypothesis that the distribution of information affects the behavior of networks. Since the more central positions usually have more information than the other team members during the major part of a trial, the effects of centrality and amount of information are ordinarily confounded. Shaw, therefore, varies the amounts of information initially given to positions within three networks. In this way, he separates to some extent the effects of the two variables.

He uses the three four-man communication patterns depicted in Figure 3: Circle, Wheel (or Y), and Slash. The groups solved arithmetic problems for which each team member held some of the necessary information. In some teams, all members had the same amount of information. In other teams, the information was unequally distributed with the positions marked *a* in Figure 3 receiving more information than the others.

He finds that central positions and the positions with the larger amount of initial information tended to solve the problems more quickly. There were no significant effects of networks or distribution of information conditions on network speed. Here, and in the following studies, Shaw centers much of his data analysis on the higher order interactions, e.g., network with information distribution with trials. Since his hypotheses and his conclusions are not at this level, attention will be given primarily to main effects.

The results on number of messages as related to network (Circle versus Wheel) and as related to position centrality agree with Leavitt's findings for five-man groups. In general, the Wheel required fewer items to reach a solution than the Slash or Circle and central positions sent more messages than peripheral positions. Shaw also finds that positions given more information sent more items than did the same positions under equal distribution of information.

What is the meaning of a relation between the number of messages—a measure used by Leavitt, Shaw, and the investigators who follow them—and position differences? Since the different positions have to send different minimum numbers of messages to complete a trial, it is not very enlightening to note that differences appear. In each five-man chain with each man holding one item of information, the end men have to send only one message in order to assure complete distribution of their information. The central man has to transmit five items. It is necessary to relate the number of messages sent by a position to the minimum for the position. Otherwise, it is as if an experimenter reported significant differences in the number of responses by two experimental groups when one group of subjects is requested to name two items each, the other requested to name only one.

Shaw does not find that differences in network affect the number of errors, although unequal distribution of information lowers the number of errors significantly. On the other hand, leadership, measured in terms of preference in a sociometric questionnaire, was related to centrality but not to information distribution. Similarly, group morale measures and individual morale or job satisfaction ratings were, as in the Leavitt study, related to centrality. They were not, however, related to information distribution.

Gilchrist, Shaw, and Walker (7) explored the effect of distribution of information further by giving additional information not only to peripheral, but also to central positions in the four-man wheel. Their three experimental conditions consisted of an equal distribution of information, an unequal distribution to the periphery (one peripheral subject receiving more information than the others), and an unequal distribution to the center (the center subject receiving more information). Distribution of information did not have any significant effect on overall group performance as seen in time scores, error scores, sociometric choices, number of message units, and leadership emergence. It did have an effect on behavior at individual positions. Increasing the initial information, in general, decreased the time scores and increased the number of messages transmitted, job satisfaction, and position status rating. The investigators' expectations concerning the order of the time scores are not met. The central position with additional information has a higher time score than the peripheral positions with additional information and also a higher time score than the central position under equal information distribution. Primarily to explain the latter result, they introduce the concept of saturation, defined as the input and output requirements which are imposed on positions within a group structure. The concept, a promising one which suggests that communication requirements may counteract the effects of centrality, is explored in a subsequent investigation (33).

Shaw (34) investigated the effect of another aspect of information distribution in communication networks: random versus systematic distribution. In solving an arithmetic problem consisting of four distinct steps, each member of a four-man group may have all the information items necessary to complete one of the steps. This is called systematic distribution. A random distribution is one in which each of the information items is assigned at random; a member, therefore, usually has to go to several sources (other members) for the information to complete one step of the problem. This type of experimental operation brings the network study close to the situations used by Lanzetta and Roby in their manipulation of "dispersion of information sources" (see below). Shaw predicts that systematic distribution will increase efficiency and job satisfaction and that the increase will be greater if the subjects are informed about the system of distribution and if the network permits freedom and action—e.g., All-Channel as compared with Wheel. Analysis of time to solution in the Wheel and All-Channel networks, in part, supports Shaw's predictions. Knowledge of distribution is not, however, significant as a main effect or in interaction with distribution of information. Networks, also, do not differ significantly on the time measures.

Another follow-up (31) of the distribution of information study by Shaw (32) attempts to reconcile an apparent discrepancy between his and Leavitt's (17) study. Leavitt found some evidence that the five-man Wheel network solves problems faster than the five-man Circle. Shaw's four-man Circles are somewhat faster than his four-man Wheels. The speed difference is, however, not statistically significant. Shaw suggests that the difference stems from the difference in the complexity of the problems used. This is essentially Heise and Miller's (13) point that different structures will be best for different tasks. Shaw's (31) main hypothesis is

> that a communication net in which all *S*s are in equal positions (the circle) will require less time to solve relatively complex problems but more time to solve relatively simple problems than will a communication net in which one *S* is placed in a central position (the wheel) (p. 211).

To test this hypothesis, Shaw gave simple (common letter) and complex (arithmetic) problems to the three-man Wheel and Circle (Networks 3 and 1, respectively, in Figure 2).

Two points should be noted concerning his structures: they are three-man groups not five-man groups, as in the Leavitt study, and not four-man groups, as in the other Shaw study; the question raised earlier concerning the naming of networks may be raised again. Why is the third pattern in Figure 2 called a "Wheel" rather than a "Chain"? With these points in mind, it seems unlikely that differences in the results of a study of five-man groups and a study of four-man groups can be resolved by a study of three-man groups. Resolution is especially unlikely since the Chain, which, according to Leavitt, tends to be slower than the Circle, and the Wheel, which tends to be faster than the Circle, reduce to a single network in the three-man group. Shaw identifies this network with the fast Wheel. It could just as well be identified with the slow Chain. In any case, Shaw's main hypothesis is that the interaction of problem complexity with network has an effect on solution time. The results tend to support his prediction, but are not statistically significant. Analysis of the number of items communicated and errors does not add any support to the hypothesis.

The problem complexity with net centrality interaction is pursued in one more study in which Shaw (35) manipulates complexity by the addition of irrelevant information to arithmetic problems given to the four-man All-Channel and Wheel. The evidence is again unclear. A significant effect of the interaction is found on the number of messages but not on time to solution.

Shaw (33) has better luck with a study of the effect of saturation and independence. He elaborates these concepts and through them arrives at the variables of the classic Lewin, Lippitt, and White study (18): autocratic versus democratic leadership. He assumes that the leader's style affects both saturation and independence: "autocratic" leaders decrease both the independence and saturation of the followers and "democratic" leaders increase both. Independence is assumed to improve performance and morale, with a greater effect on morale. Saturation is assumed to lower performance and morale, with a greater effect on performance. From these assumptions, Shaw derives the following predictions: autocratic leaders will promote better performance than democratic leaders, autocratic leaders will cause poorer morale, and differences between central and peripheral positions will be accentuated by autocratic leadership.

The two leadership conditions were used with the four-man Wheel, Kite, and All-Channel (see Figure 3) solving arithmetic problems. The subject at Position *b* in the network was assigned the role of leader and was instructed to be either "autocratic" or "democratic" in his handling of directions and suggestions. As Shaw predicted, the autocratic groups are higher in efficiency and lower in morale. Although analysis of data for individual positions confirms previous findings that the central positions solve the problems more quickly, send more messages, and have higher morale, it does not confirm Shaw's prediction that autocratic leadership will increase the difference on these measures between central and peripheral positions. It might be added that in the Lewin, Lippitt, and White study, autocratic and democratic leadership styles generated an analog of the Wheel and the All-Channel, respectively. Under autocratic leadership, for example, most of the group's communications were directed at the leader. Shaw's study, therefore, may be viewed as involving two types of manipulation of communication structure: direct manipulation through the elimination of channels and indirect manipulation through the effects of the leader's style.

In the preceding studies by Shaw and his associates, the groups worked two to four problems. The effect of prolonged experience was investigated by Shaw and Rothschild (36). Groups in the Wheel, Slash, and All-Channel structures (see Figure 3) solved two arithmetic problems a day for 10 days. The usual analyses are made of time scores, number of message units transmitted, and satisfaction ratings. The results, to some extent, agree with the results of previous studies (32, 33).

The merging, seen in the study on leadership style, of Shaw's network investigations with the more conventional social psychological tradition continues in a study by Shaw, Rothschild, and Strickland (37) in which they use unstructured group discussion tasks. Each member of the group starts with all the information required for a decision. The group members have to interact only to reach an agreement on the solution. The networks differ significantly in the time required to reach a decision. The Wheel requires the longest time and the All-Channel, the shortest. The finding agrees, to some extent, with Shaw and Rothschild's findings on the same networks solving arithmetic problems. Two other experiments reported in this article investigate the effect of the position within a network upon the ability of an individual to maintain nonconforming opinion. These experiments are similar to Goldberg's experiment (9). The results, in general, indicate that the amount of change that a subject is willing to make is a function of the amount of support and opposition he faces rather than any position characteristic. The data on the relation between position centrality and tendency to be influenced do not, however, permit clear interpretation. Goldberg, it may be recalled, finds no overall relation between centrality and tendency to be influenced.

In summary, Shaw and his associates have exhaustively worked the area opened by Bavelas and Leavitt. They have also introduced new concepts, e.g., independence and saturation, which are worth further examination. Their work forms a major body of data concerning the effect of structure on group behavior.

After a promising start, the approach has led to many conflicting results that resist any neat order. Perhaps more significant as a symptom of morbidity is the lack of new hypotheses. The lack is seen in the regression to nonstructural independent variables: leadership style, conformity pressure.

MATHEMATICAL ANALYSIS

Christie, Luce, and Macy and their associates have carried out an intensive program of investigation of behavior in group networks. They have emphasized "pure" structural characteristics and have subjected their data to detailed mathematical and logical analysis. The full range of their approaches to network behavior is set forth in two reports (5, 19). In the first report, they discuss the various aspects of network behavior extensively, and analyze data obtained in a series of experimental studies.

One of the studies was concerned with the effects of learning on performance in the networks in Figure 4. Christie (4) later published results for the five-man Circle, Chain, All-Channel, and Pinwheel.[1] The groups solved a series of 25 list reconstitution problems like those in the Heise-Miller (13) study. An "action quantization" restriction was imposed in order to simplify the data for analysis:

The subjects were required to send single-address messages at prescribed times,

1 This section draws both from results presented in the larger report (Christie et al, 1952) and from the separate report by Christie (1954).

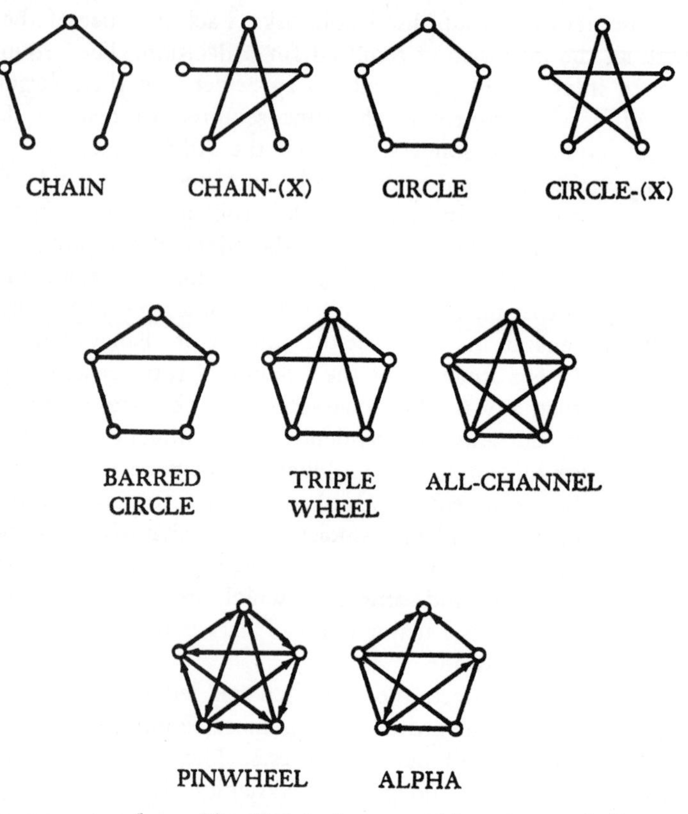

FIG. 4. Five-man networks used by Christie, Luce, and Macy. Arrows indicate one-way Channels. (The "Triple Wheel" is called "Wheel" by Christie et al.)

to include in their messages all problem information known to them at the time, and to write nothing other than problem information. . . . Thus, each message-sending action, hereinafter called an *act*, was a simultaneous sending by the whole group (p. 189).

In their data analyses, these investigators use the minimum number of acts in which it is possible for a network to complete its task as baselines. The minimum possible number of acts is an important consideration which has been neglected in other network studies. All networks in Figure 4 have minima of three acts except for the Chain with a minimum of five. Chain-(X) and Circle-(X) are topologically the same as Chain and Circle, respectively. They differ from Chain and Circle only in the physical arrangement of the positions. The investigators computed the distribution of the number of acts required for completion on the assumption that the group members distribute their information at random over their channels. It is not surprising that comparison of the theoretical with the observed number of solutions shows that the subjects do better than chance from the start. Clear differences in learning efficiency between networks are also demonstrated.

Christie (4) summarizes the results for four of the networks as follows:

Groups using the totally connected network [All-Channel] do somewhat better than random but show a negligible amount of learning. The groups in chain learn well, but their performance is good only with respect to the chain minimum of five acts per trial. The high minimum for this network makes its absolute performance poor in comparison to each of the other networks. The pinwheel network performs somewhat better than random, and its random distribution is a favorable one [i.e., the mode is close to the minimum]. Like totally connected it learns little, so that its final distribution is practically the same as that in totally connected. Circle is the one very different case; it achieves the best distribution [i. e., it frequently completes the task in the minimum possible] in the final block as a result of excellent learning (p. 193).

Christie, Luce, and Macy introduce the concept of "locally rational" behavior to explain the differences between networks on the basis of behavior at the individual positions. Locally rational behavior is the tendency to send successive messages to different stations so as to maximize the amount of new information received by neighboring positions. ". . . the behavior called for depends only on each subject's attending to conditions immediate to his own position, i.e., to whom he has sent and from whom he has received" (4, p. 195). The investigators used Monte Carlo runs on a computer in order to obtain the theoretical distribution of the number of acts to completion under both the equiprobable random behavior and the locally rational behavior model for each network. In a final summary of their work, Christie, Luce, and Macy (6) show that in successive trials, network performance (the distribution of number of acts) approaches more and more closely that of the locally rational model. It is not clear, however, whether this generalization holds for the All-Channel network.

In analyzing the learning of subjects within the various networks, they also pay attention to the importance of differences in the probability of various initial act patterns. For example, in the Circle a minimum solution is possible only with an initial pattern of two mutual interchanges and one unreciprocated message (e.g., *a* with *b*, *c* with *d*, and *e* to *a*). In the Chain, any initial pattern of acts can result in a minimal solution.

They find another stimulus for experimental work and analysis in information theory concepts. In a study on coding noise presented in the main technical report (5) and published separately by Macy, Christie, and Luce (20), they examine the effects of ambiguity of stimuli, interpreted as semantic noise. (Heise and Miller (13) studied the effect of acoustic noise in the communication channel.) They used the five-man Circle, Chain, Wheel, and Pinwheel (see Figures 1 and 4). Another variable, labeled "feedback," is introduced by giving some Wheel groups additional information concerning errors at the end of each trial.

The groups' task was to discover the color of a marble that all held in common. Fifteen problems with marbles of clearly identifiable color were followed by 15 trials with ambiguous stimuli—marbles of mixed, indistinct color. The authors state that the data on speed and number of messages agree with Leavitt's results. Their main findings on learning to handle the ambiguous stimuli do not give a simple picture. The Circle reduces its errors markedly over successive trials. The other structures do not. The explanation of these results may lie in Shaw's (31) hypothesis, as yet undemonstrated, that centralized structures are handicapped on complex problems. Introduction of additional feedback in the wheel network seems to improve performance somewhat.

They pursue their informational analysis with an estimate of "conditional receiver entropy" based on the number of different marbles called by the same name. They point out that the method by which the efficient networks reduce ambiguity seems to be by an increase in redundancy (computed in terms of the number of extra names given to a marble). The behavior of the networks is further analyzed qualitatively in terms of error feedback (the opportunity of the members to obtain the same information from at least two different sources) and the opportunity to correct errors (the presence of symmetric, i.e., two-way channels). The Pinwheel lacks the latter, while the Wheel, and to some extent the Chain (in its end members), lacks the former. The presence of both, the investigators argue, is necessary for optimal performance.

Christie et al. (5) try to carry out detailed analysis and derivation of every type of data generated by the original network studies. They try to derive the distribution of group latency data on the basis of assumptions concerning the individual latency distribution. They analyze the determinants of leader designation, using an index based on

> the relative frequency of use of a channel (on an equiprobable sending basis) and the mean input of the sending end of the channel as an estimate of the sending end's value to the receiving end (p. 179).

Their index fits the obtained values for two networks rather well.

They devote a similarly detailed analysis to the determinants of job satisfaction, following their general approach of using the individual position as a basis for prediction. An index called input potential which considers the input density for each position is found to be more highly correlated with job satisfaction than peripherality. The formula for input potential gives some idea of the level of the analysis.

$$g(I) = \frac{1}{\pi} \sin^{-1} \left\{ 2 \frac{e^{2I} - 1}{e^{2I} + 1} - 1 \right\} + \frac{1}{2} \quad [2]$$

where I is mean input.

In a subsequent report (19), they carry out the same types of analyses and also examine the additional problem of the effects of change of network structure, with subjects trained in one network and tested in another. The later work is even more complex, involving a multiplicity of approaches, and does not lend itself readily to summary. The general philosophy and major accomplishments of their research effort is summarized by Christie et al. (6).

The main tendency of the analysis by Christie, Luce, and Macy is away from functions involving overall measures of the group, e.g., network centrality, and toward the derivation of the behavior of the group from that of the individual positions. Their efforts may be considered to parallel Shaw's. Just as he carried the empirical work in the area as far as it can go, so do they carry the mathematical analysis to the limit. In both cases, it was desirable to have the job done. It seems unlikely now, however, that the payoff will be commensurate with the energy and ingenuity that was invested. This could, of course, be only discovered by the doing.

With the efforts of both Shaw and his associates and of Christie, Luce, and Macy carried as far as they can go, a new approach or new definition of the field seems necessary. The remaining sections of this paper will review some of the attempts at reanalyzing or redefining the area.

RETROSPECT AND PROSPECT

At this point, it is appropriate to look back at the problem as originally stated and its expression in experimental form.

Two main questions posed by Bavelas are the following: What effect does the structure of the group have upon its efficiency? What effect does position in the group have upon the subject's morale and job satisfaction? There is no simple answer to the first question. The effect of structure depends in part on the requirements of the task (13). Contrary to Leavitt's original generalization (17), in a number of studies the highly centralized structures are *less efficient* than other structures 20, 35, 37. The answer to the second question is somewhat clearer. Morale seems to be a function of centrality position. The psychological basis for this relationship, however, warrants further analysis. Explanations have been offered in terms of autonomy (39), independence (30), and input potential (5).

The unclear answer to the first question may arise from the peculiar experimental situation used to express it. The characteristics of the original Bavelas-Leavitt situation that recommend it are its apparent experimental simplicity and relevance to real-life situations. Does the situation actually have these characteristics? That the situation is not simple is evidenced by the introduction of techniques to simplify it further, e.g., action quantization. Even with the imposition of further restrictions, however, a precise analysis of the activity of the groups is unmanageably complex.

That the situation is far distant from most familiar real-life situations can be seen by reviewing the special characteristics of the laboratory networks. They are the following:

1. Interdiction of certain channels. This is the most obvious of the special characteristics of the laboratory networks. To some extent, this corresponds with conditions in natural groups. Some communication channels are frequently closed to members of groups. For example, a man may not be permitted to go over the head of his immediate supervisors in a work group, or he may be unwilling to make certain statements when another member is present.

2. Ignorance concerning other positions. This is probably both the effective and the really unique aspect of the communication restriction. The network members know very little about other positions and about behavior of any except adjacent positions. This is a condition that does not hold in small groups. The effect of this factor can, of course, be reduced to some extent by changes in the procedures of the network studies. In the Guetzkow-Simon (11) study, for example, this may have been done by having intertrial administrative discussions.

3. Necessity of each member. In almost all the network studies, each member is essential, because each member holds an essential piece of information and each member must present a solution to the problem. In some cases, one member may have more or less information but in almost all the studies the elimination of one member prevents success of the group. This is not generally true in real-life groups.

These special characteristics of the network studies would make generalization difficult even if the findings were unequivocal. The applicability of the findings of the network studies are in question because the characteristics of the structures employed in the studies are very different from other small groups. The following point, however, may be argued: If the network studies have any application, it will not be in the small group, but in a much larger unit such as an industrial corporation or an army. Characteristics analogous to those listed above are more clearly present in large groups. For example, departments of a company may not have direct communication channels; they often lack information concerning distant sections and all departments may be necessary for the company to function.

If the laboratory network cannot be viewed as a simplification of the general small group situation, can it be viewed as a laboratory simplification to permit testing of an explicit theory about group behavior? The answer, unfortunately, is no. At the present time, a theory concerning behavior in the network does not exist. This raises a major point. Perhaps the most surprising thing about the entire area is that despite the highly formal origins of these studies (1), the organized body of theory promised by the approach has not yet appeared.

Perhaps in response to considerations such as these, two attempts have been made to use a somewhat different approach to the study of the effects of group structure on behavior. One of these attempts is by Lanzetta and

Roby. Their main aim is to draw the experimental situation closer to a known type of group—the military work team. The other attempt is by Rosenberg and Hall. Their main objective is to simplify the experimental situation (two-person situations) and rephrase the problem so that available theory—learning theory—can be brought to bear on the problem. Both approaches assign new definitions to the term structure. For Lanzetta and Roby, team structure refers to the specialization and interrelation of jobs in a team. For Rosenberg and Hall, team structure refers to the degree to which the information that an individual receives about his performance is confounded by the performance of another team member.

EMPHASIS ON DISTRIBUTION OF FUNCTIONS IN THE SIMULATED TEAM

Lanzetta and Roby have directed one major attempt to examine, from a new viewpoint, the relation of group structure to performance. Their attempt is embodied in a series of studies in which they vary the ways that team members depend on each other for information. In a situation, quite unlike the Bavelas network, modeled after military teams, e.g., a bomber crew, they gave teams a series of very short problems in order to approximate a continuously changing environment. They vary communication structure not by interdicting channels as in the network studies, but by restricting relevant information or specific functions to a given position. Their team is like the All-Channel network but with each subject working on a separate problem and holding some information required by other team members. Despite these differences in experimental situation and in definition of structure, the basic concern remains the same: what factors in the organization of a group affect its performance?

An early study by Lanzetta and Roby (15) indicates both the development of their experimental situation and the type of practical situation from which it grew. In this study, they investigate the effect of two methods of work distribution (work structure) under two task load conditions on group performance. They model the experimental situation after an air defense center with two work structure conditions. In vertical structure, each group member had one of three tasks: tracking aircraft, identifying aircraft and keeping a record of the interceptors' fuel status, or deploying friendly planes. In horizontal structure, each group member performed all three functions for his own targets. Variations of the number of airplanes produced two different task load conditions. Of the main independent variables of the study—structural organization, load conditions, and their interaction—only load condition has a significant effect. The interpretation of this effect is, however, complicated by a significant interaction with sessions. The main outcome of the study was a methodological development rather than an empirical finding. It led to a simpler task with higher reliability for use in the subsequent studies.

This task, modeled after a bomber crew's task, was used in their next experimental study (14) to demonstrate the effect of relaying requirements upon group performance. Groups of three subjects sat, each in a separate booth that contained instrument reading displays, pairs of control switches, and instructions giving the correct switch settings for each possible pair of instrument readings. The instrument readings required to set a given control could be displayed in the booth containing the related control or they could be shown in one of the other booths. In the latter case, the subject receiving the information would have to relay it to its eventual user over the intercom system connecting the booths.

Roby and Lanzetta used four communication structures which differed in the degree to which the subjects had direct access to the information they needed. A significant difference in the number of errors appears between the communication conditions. Analysis indicates that more errors are made on a control if its two relevant items of information had to come from two sources rather than from one source. The results cannot be considered surprising. If a subject has to get the necessary information from someone else, who is also busy, he will not do as well on a highly speeded task as a subject who has his information immediately available. Furthermore, if he has to make two separate information requests in a brief (15-second) period, he will be more likely to fail than if he has to make only one request.

Lanzetta and Roby (14) next consider the effect of type of input presentation on efficiency in two communication structures employed in the previous study: a high dependence (or low autonomy) condition in which each member had to get all of the instrument readings necessary to operate his controls from other team members; and a low dependence condition in which a member had three out of the four necessary instrument readings available in his booth. They varied two aspects of the task input: task load (the time interval between successive presentations of instrument readings) and the predictability of the order of presentation to the three booths. They find again that high dependence gives rise to more errors, especially when the information has to be relayed from several different sources. For both structure conditions, errors increase as the rate of change of instrument readings increase, but predictability of the order of instrument changes has no significant effect.

These findings are further supported in another study in which Lanzetta and Roby (16) investigate learning and the details of communication behavior in their team situation. They vary dependence (relaying requirement), task load (speed of presentation of input), and operating procedure as determined by instructions to "volunteer" information or to "solicit" information.

In a later study, Roby and Lanzetta (24) consider the effect of "load balancing" or distribution of work. They used three structures that varied in relation between the number of instrument displays and the number of control switches for which the subject was responsible. In Structure I (equal observation load) a booth had either one, two, or three control switches, but it always had two displays. In Structure II (unequal load) a booth that had one control switch had one display; a booth with two control switches had two displays; etc. In Structure III (balanced load) a booth with one control switch had three displays; a booth with two control switches had two displays; etc. The experimental design is quite complicated and confounds the load balancing and dependence variables. The authors, however, conclude that "both load balancing and autonomy are influential but that the latter is more heavily weighted in this task" (p. 174).

The major accomplishment of Lanzetta and Roby is their introduction of controlled, experimentally manipulable tasks that capture more of the characteristics of real-life teams than do the earlier Circles and Wheels. They have also theorized extensively (21, 23, 25). The real payoff in their work will come, however, when theory and experimental work merge. Their theorizing consists of general statements that never arrive at the prediction or explanation of specific events. Without a theory to generate novel and testable predictions, the experiments usually establish the obvious, e.g., if a subject has to check with many people before he makes a response, he is not likely to complete the response in a short time period. Although Lanzetta and Roby have not completed the merger of theory and experiment, they have brought them several steps closer together.

EMPHASIS ON FEEDBACK AND LEARNING

Rosenberg and Hall have recently examined the effects of group structure from a different viewpoint than Lanzetta and Roby's. Rosenberg and Hall see the composition of information feedback to the individual members as a key aspect of structure. They concern themselves, therefore, with the relation of structure, defined in terms of information feedback, to performance. Figure 5 illustrates the basic structures they study. S^d is the stimulus which precedes a response, R is the response, and S^f is the feedback stimulus, i.e., the state of affairs in which the individual finds

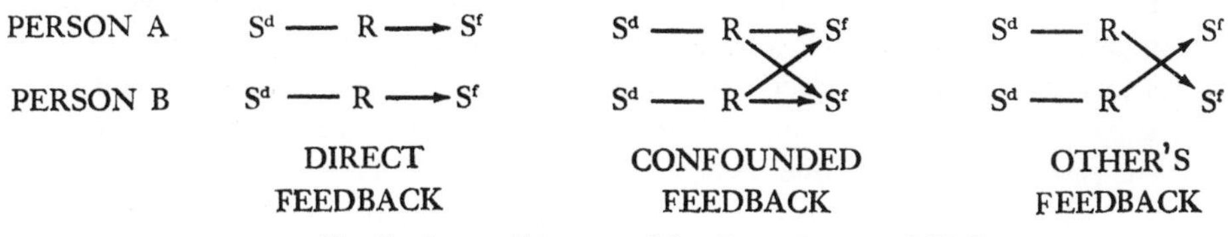

FIG. 5. Feedback conditions used by Rosenberg and Hall.

himself after performing the response. In the "direct" feedback condition the S^f reflects only the subject's own performance. With "confounded" feedback the response of one subject combines with that of another so that his feedback is a function of his teammate's performance as well as his own. With "other's" feedback the subject receives feedback solely from someone else's performance. In order to investigate the relation of these structures to performance, Rosenberg and Hall have carried out a series of studies using variations of an experimental situation similar to that of Sidowski, Wyckoff, and Tabory (38).

In their first study, Rosenberg and Hall (29) ran two-man groups under the three structures described above. The task was to learn to turn a knob a required number of turns. The amount of error (S^f value) was displayed to the subject after each trial. Under direct feedback, each subject had to learn to turn the knob four times. Under confounded feedback, the two team members had to attain a team average of four turns. They could reach this average by totaling eight turns distributed in any fashion between them. Under "other's" feedback, the subject had a perfect score displayed only if his partner turned the knob four times. The design of the study permitted the evaluation of both the effects of the subject's own feedback condition and his partner's feedback condition (which could be different) upon the subject's performance. The dependent variables were: individual accuracy, team or average accuracy, and role differentiation—a function of the absolute difference between the response magnitudes of the two team members.

The subjects learn most rapidly and to the highest level of proficiency under direct feedback. With confounded feedback the subject learns, but more slowly and to a lower level of proficiency. There is no improvement in individual accuracy under "other's" feedback. The partner's feedback condition has no significant effect on the subject's accuracy. With respect to team product, confounded feedback yields team accuracy (average performance) that is at least as good as that obtained with direct feedback. "Other's" feedback gave clearly inferior team performance. In the confounded feedback condition, one subject evidently learned to make two turns if his partner persisted in making six turns so that both subjects would have an average of four. Rosenberg and Hall label this compensatory difference between response magnitudes, role differentiation. They find that the confounded feedback conditions show more role differentiation than the direct feedback. The "other's" feedback condition, however, shows the greatest amount of all. Rosenberg (27) also considered the effect of switching subjects from a direct feedback situation to other structures. After the switch, the three structures show the same effects as above.

Hall (12), using similar apparatus, investigated two independent variables: type of pretraining, and the relative weights assigned to the responses of the team members during confounded feedback. He varied pretraining conditions by pretraining some subjects under direct feedback and others under the same confounded feedback conditions they received during later trials. The experimenter used two confounded feedback weightings—equal and unequal. In equal weighting, he fed back the mean of the two members' responses or

$$s^f = \tfrac{1}{2} R_1 + \tfrac{1}{2} R_2$$

as in the previous experiments. In the unequal weighting, he weighted the responses of one member three times as heavily as the other, i.e.:

$$s^f = \tfrac{3}{4} R_1 + \tfrac{1}{4} R_2$$

The dependent variables were team accuracy and role differentiation. The feedback weighting conditions do not have any significant effect on the dependent variables during either pretraining or training. In discussing the results, Hall emphasizes the compensatory behavior that occurs in the confounded feedback situation.

Zink (40) carried out a further study in this series using a more complex task and a different rule for determining feedback. Contrary at least to the reviewers' expectations, the results indicate greater role differentiation for the simple task than for the complex task. Rosenberg (26), later tried to produce role differentiation in Zink's complex task by pretraining the subjects under direct feedback. His hypothesis was that the subjects had not reached that level of proficiency in Zink's complex task to permit them to adjust to a partner's behavior. He is, however, unable to obtain differences in role differentiation between subjects given different amounts of direct feedback pretraining.

In a final set of three experiments, Rosenberg (28) systematically explored the effect of various combinations of feedback weights on team performance. He also varied the informational content of the feedback by letting some groups know only that an error had occurred and by informing other groups about both the occurrence and the direction of the error. On the basis of detailed consideration of the effects of feedback upon the response of the subjects in the various structures, Rosenberg makes predictions concerning the development of complementary or cooperative behavior. In general, he finds that more stable response patterns develop as the amount of information concerning the direction of errors increases. If both subjects have a feedback weight of .50 or more on their own response, then their combined responses tend to stabilize at some optimal value, i.e., one in which both members receive maximum reinforcement. The accuracy of the group product is therefore maximized.

With these experiments, this group has moved very far from the original network studies. In their earlier work (29), communication between the team members dropped out as an explicit independent variable.

In the last study, amount of reinforcement received replaces group accuracy as the dependent variable of primary interest. The work of Rosenberg and Hall has certain basic similarities to the work of Lanzetta and Roby. Here again the experimenters accomplish a very able reduction of the real-life team to laboratory proportions. The contribution with respect to methods is considerable. Here again, however, the work generates obvious results. The one study (28) with novel and systematically related results is one that has moved away almost completely from the variables of the early studies of group structure.

It is hoped that as the methods in the area are improved, theories which can tie together disparate findings and generate new predictions will develop. Rosenberg and Hall have done even more than help prepare the methodological groundwork for the phase of theorizing that is needed now. By reducing social interaction to feedback conditions, they have prepared the way for an attack with the armament of learning theory. (This has actually begun in work being carried out by Burke (3) and his associates.) Whether such an attack can be made without giving up the original objective of studying group structure remains to be seen.

SUMMARY AND CONCLUSIONS

Since the initial stimulus provided by Bavelas in 1948 there has been a considerable effort spent on the study of the effect of structure upon group and individual behavior. The main original questions posed were: What effect does the structure of the group have upon the efficiency of its behavior? What effect does position in the group have on morale and job satisfaction? There is no clear answer to the first question. The answer to the second question is that central positions in general are more satisfied with their tasks than peripheral positions.

Later investigators went beyond the first two questions to study other variables. Heise and Miller introduced a task complexity variable, the condition of communication interference (noise), and one-way channels. Guetzkow and his collaborators introduced the distinction between task behavior and organizational activity. Shaw continued the original trend of the experimental work and also investigated the effects of various types of distribution of information and task complexity. Christie, Luce, and Macy brought mathematics and information theory to bear on the communication networks. They presented the theory of "locally rational" behavior to explain learning in the networks and differences in performance between networks.

Neither straight empirical work nor the mathematically sophisticated analyses have approached the goal, implicit in Bavelas' original questions, of a rational system for arranging groups to maximize efficiency and satisfaction. The difficulties in building such a system may stem from the peculiar characteristics of the Bavelas network and the absence of a theory to order the data it generated.

In response to these difficulties, more recent investigators have reoriented the work on group structure. Lanzetta and Roby have redefined structure into terms of direct versus indirect accessibility of task information and distribution of task information. Under this type of definition they have constructed new types of groups and tasks. These investigators also have made some moves toward meeting the need for a theory in the area. Rosenberg and Hall have attempted to rephrase the problem and redesign the experimental setting so that learning theory can play the organizing role. To do this, they define structure in terms of the effect of one subject's responses on another subject's feedback (reinforcement) and have studied the effect of various feedback arrangements on group (dyad) and individual behavior.

At the present time, there is still a major need for a system to order the data already obtained and to direct further work on the effects of group structure. The difficulty in constructing this system may arise from the inappropriateness of either the experimental situations or the concepts that have been used. Attempts have been made to remedy both of these possible defects. The success of these attempts will determine whether this review is a prologue or an epitaph.

REFERENCES

1. Bavelas, A. A mathematical model for group structures. *Appl. Anthrop.*, 1948, 7, 16–30.
2. Bavelas, A. Communication patterns in task-oriented groups. *J. Acoust. Soc. Amer.*, 1950, 22, 725–730.
3. Burke, C. Applications of a linear model to two-person interactions. Paper read at Midwestern Psychological Association, Chicago, May 1959.
4. Christie, L. S. Organization and information handling in task groups. *J. Operat. Res. Soc. Amer.*, 1954, 2, 188–196.
5. Christie, L. S., Luce, R. S., & Macy, J., Jr. Communication and learning in task-oriented groups. *MIT Res. Lab. Electronics tech. Rep.*, 1952, No. 231.
6. Christie, L. S., Luce, R. D., & Macy, J., Jr. Information handling in organized groups. In J. F. McCloskey & J. M. Coppinger (Eds.), *Operations research for management.* Vol. II. *Case histories, methods, information handling.* Baltimore: Johns Hopkins Press, 1956. Pp. 417–537.
7. Gilchrist, J. C., Shaw, M. E., & Walker, L. C. Some effects of unequal distribution of information in a wheel group structure. *J. abnorm. soc. Psychol.*, 1954, 49, 554–556.
8. Glanzer, M., & Glaser, R. Techniques for the study of group structure and behavior: I. Analysis of structure. *Psychol. Bull.*, 1959, 56, 317–332.
9. Goldberg, S. C. Influence and leadership as a function of group structure. *J. abnorm. soc. Psychol*, 1955, 51, 119–122.
10. Guetzkow, H., & Dill, W. R. Factors in the organizational development of task-oriented groups. *Sociometry*, 1957, 20, 175–204.
11. Guetzkow, H., & Simon, H. A. The impact of certain communication nets upon organization and performance in task-oriented groups. *Mgmt. Sci.*, 1955, 1, 233–250.
12. Hall, R. L. Group performance under feedback that confounds responses of group members. *Sociometry*, 1957, 20, 297–305.

13. Heise, G. A., & Miller, G. A. Problem solving by small groups using various communication nets. *J. abnorm. soc. Psychol.*, 1951, 46, 327–335.
14. Lanzetta, J. T., & Roby, T. B. Effects of work-group structure and certain task variables on group performance. *J. abnorm. soc. Psychol.*, 1956, 53, 307–314. (a)
15. Lanzetta, J. T., & Roby, T. B. Group performance as a function of work-distribution patterns and task load. *Sociometry*, 1956, 19, 95–104. (b)
16. Lanzetta, J. T., & Roby, T. B. Group learning and communication as a function of task and structure "demands." *J. abnorm. soc. Psychol.*, 1957, 55, 121–131.
17. Leavitt, H. J. Some effects of certain communication patterns on group performance. *J. abnorm. soc. Psychol.*, 1951, 46, 38–50.
18. Lewin, K., Lippitt, R., & White, R. K. Patterns of aggressive behavior in experimentally created "social climates." *J. soc. Psychol.*, 1939, 10, 271–299.
19. Luce, R. D., Macy, J., Jr. Christie, L. S., & Hay, H. D. Information flow in task-oriented groups. *MIT Res. Lab. Electronics tech. Rep.*, 1953, No. 264.
20. Macy, J., Jr., Christie, L. S., & Luce, R. D. Coding noise in a task-oriented group. *J. abnorm. soc. Psychol.*, 1953, 48, 401–409.
21. Roby, T. B. On the measurement and description of groups. *Behav. Sci.*, 1957, 2, 119–127.
22. Roby, T. B., & Lanzetta, J. T. An investigation of task performance as a function of certain aspects of work-group structure. *USAF Personnel Train. Res. Cent. res. Rep.*, 1956, No. TN-56–74. (a)
23. Roby, T. B., & Lanzetta, J. T. Work group structure, communication, and group performance. *Sociometry*, 1956, 19, 105–113. (b)
24. Roby, T. B., & Lanzetta, J. T. Conflicting principles in man-machine system design. *J. appl. Psychol.*, 1957, 41, 170–178.
25. Roby, T. B., & Lanzetta, J. T. Considerations in the analysis of group tasks. *Psychol. Bull.*, 1958, 55, 88–101.
26. Rosenberg, S. A laboratory approach to interpersonal aspects of team performance. *Ergonomics*, 1959, 2, 335–348. (a)
27. Rosenberg, S. The maintenance of a learned response in controlled interpersonal conditions. *Sociometry*, 1959, 22, 124–138. (b)
28. Rosenberg, S. Cooperative behavior in dyads as a function of reinforcement parameters. *J. abnorm. soc. Psychol.*, 1960, 60, 318–333.
29. Rosenberg, S., & Hall, R. L. The effects of different social feedback conditions upon performance in dyadic teams. *J. abnorm. soc. Psychol.*, 1958, 57, 271–277.
30. Shaw, M. E. Group structure and the behavior of individuals in small groups. *J. Psychol.*, 1954, 38, 139–149. (a)
31. Shaw, M. E. Some effects of problem complexity upon problem solution efficiency in different communication nets. *J. exp. Psychol.*, 1954, 48, 211–217. (b)
32. Shaw, M. E. Some effects of unequal distribution of information upon group performance in various communication nets. *J. abnorm. soc. Psychol.*, 1954, 49, 547–553. (c)
33. Shaw, M. E. A comparison of two types of leadership in various communication nets. *J. abnorm. soc. Psychol.*, 1955, 50, 127–134.
34. Shaw, M. E. Random versus systematic distribution of information in communication nets. *J. Pers.*, 1956, 25, 59–69.
35. Shaw, M. E. Some effects of irrelevant information upon problem-solving by small groups. *J. soc. Psychol.*, 1958, 47, 33–37.
36. Shaw, M. E. & Rothschild, G. H. Some effects of prolonged experience in communication nets. *J. appl. Psychol.*, 1956, 40, 281–286.
37. Shaw, M. E., Rothschild, G. H., & Strickland, J. F. Decision processes in communication nets. *J. abnorm. soc. Psychol.*, 1957, 54, 323–330.
38. Sidowski, J. B., Wyckoff, L. B., & Tabory, L. The influence of reinforcement and punishment in a minimal social situation. *J. abnorm. soc. Psychol.*, 1956, 52, 115–119.
39. Trow, D. B. Autonomy and job satisfaction in task-oriented groups. *J. abnorm. soc. Psychol.*, 1957, 54, 204–209.
40. Zink, D. L. The development of role differentiation in dyads as a function of task complexity. *Amer. Psychologist*, 1957, 12, 371. (Abstract)

Seating Position and Small Group Interaction

A. PAUL HARE
and
ROBERT F. BALES

THE INTERACTION pattern of individuals in a small group can be predicted to a significant extent from the combination of information concerning their roles and their personalities (7). The importance of an individual's position in the communication network is perhaps the best documented aspect of role in experiments of the Leavitt type (9). Many experiments over the past ten years have replicated Leavitt's finding that an *explicit* communication network has a direct influence on the pattern and frequency of interaction. An early study by Steinzor (11) and more recent studies by Sommer (10) and Strodtbeck and Hook (13) have shown that communication networks are *implicit* in the seating arrangements of discussion groups and that these implicit networks also affect the interaction pattern. Steinzor found that individuals seated in a circle tended to talk more to group members opposite them than to those next to them. The studies by Sommer and by Strodtbeck and Hook both report that leaders are more likely to choose a position at the end of a rectangular table. Further, subjects who sit at the corners of a rectangular table tend to contribute least to the discussion. Thus we find that not only does seating position influence the amount of interaction a person will give and receive, but also persons who might be inclined to dominate the discussion choose the more "central" seats.

In the present study a further test of these generalizations as well as other hypotheses related to the relationships between personality, seating position, and interaction pattern is provided by the analysis of data from a series of studies of five-man laboratory discussion groups.

FROM *Sociometry*, 1963, 26, 480–486. Reprinted by permission of authors and the American Sociological Association, Inc.

EVIDENCE FROM FIVE-MAN LABORATORY GROUPS

For a number of years at Harvard, Bales and others have been observing small discussion groups in the laboratory. Most of these groups have been composed of five members seated on three sides of a rectanguar table with the side open toward the observation mirror. From the observer's position looking out of the mirror, man 1 was seated on the left side of the table nearest the door, men 2, 3, and 4 along the long side of the table opposite the mirror, and man 5 on the right side, farthest from the door. Members of one observation team had noted that subjects seated opposite each other appeared to talk to each other more than subjects seated next to each other and that subjects at the corners of the table seemed to be less active. This meant that subjects 1, 3, and 5 seemed to be doing most of the talking.

To test this assumption we turned first to some data from a study by Bales, Couch, and Kassebaum (1, 6, 8). They gave a large battery of personality tests to a sample of 60 Harvard undergraduates and then observed them in five-man groups over a series of five meetings with a variety of discussion tasks. Their research design had several complex features including the fact that one man from each group was switched to another group after the first three meetings. For this reason the combined data for the first three meetings only are used in the present test. In addition 2 of the subjects in 11 groups and all of the subjects in the 12th group were involved in another long-range clinical study. The interaction for each group session was recorded using the Bales categories for Interaction Process Analysis.

This study included a personality measure for Dominance which was essentially a prior paper and pencil measure of a subject's tendency to talk a lot in a group. Subjects who were high on Dominance showed a tendency to choose the high talking seats, 1, 3 and 5, (r approximately .30, significant at the .05 level). Subjects who were high on Dominance also tended to be talked to more by other group members. For each group member a correlation was computed between the amount he talked to each of the other four members and their Dominance scores. The mean correlation was .37.

In the Bales category system a record is made for each act of the person who is speaking and the person to whom he is speaking. Typically the person spoken to is "the group as a whole" (about thirty per cent of the time). The remaining acts are directed to particular individuals. For the 12 groups, a comparison of the five seating positions on average amount of "dyadic" interaction given and received seemed to indicate that subjects in seats 1, 3, and 5 both gave and received more interaction (See Table 1). However, an F Test did not indicate that these differences were significant.[1]

1 Since the behavior of the five men in each group is interrelated, the significance of the usual statistics should be viewed with caution. For some parts of the analysis

TABLE 1

Average Amount of Dyadic Interaction in 12 Laboratory Groups

MAN INITIATING INTERACTION	MAN RECEIVING INTERACTION					
	1	2	3	4	5	MEAN (SUM/4)
1	—	21	29	22	31	26
2	25	—	24	20	33	25
3	35	24	—	20	36	29
4	23	19	19	—	21	21
5	32	33	34	19	—	30
Mean (Sum/4)	28	24	27	20	30	—

Since the relation between seats seemed to exist more in the pattern of interaction directed to different seating positions than in the total amount initiated or received by subjects in any given seating position, a more explicit test of the seating hypothesis was formulated. By combining the hypothesis that some positions are more central in the communication network and the hypothesis, based on the work of Steinzor, that group members will talk more to persons who sit opposite them than to persons who sit next to them, one can first predict that a member in a given position for our particular table arrangement will talk most to members in seats 1, 3, and 5. Next, when two or more seats are equal in talking level, one can predict that a member will talk most to the person farthest away. Combining these two predictions, man 1, for example, would be expected to talk most to man 5, next to man 3, then man 4, and least to man 2. For Table 2 the highest rank is assigned the value 4 and the lowest rank the value 1 so that a high value will represent a high talking rate. The expected rank for each position is given in Table 2 together with the mean rank received for each position. The observed interaction rates received by each man from each man were ranked and the ranks summed for

TABLE 2

Expected Rank for Dyadic Interaction Initiated by Seating Position

MAN INITIATING INTERACTION	MAN RECEIVING INTERACTION				
	1	2	3	4	5
1	—	1*	3	2	4
2	2.5	—	2.5	1	4
3	3.5	1.5	—	1.5	3.5
4	4	1	2.5	—	2.5
5	4	2	3	1	—
Mean	3.50	1.37	2.75	1.37	3.50

* 4 is a high rank, 1 low.

it is clearly more appropriate to deal with the data as 12 groups of 5 rather than as 60 individuals.

each group. These 12 sets of sums were then correlated with the hypothetical patterns in Table 2. The mean correlation was .47, which is significant at the .01 level with a one-tail test, thus suggesting that dyadic interaction rates do follow the predicted pattern.

Since this particular pattern was "predicted" after the data had been collected it would be desirable to test the same hypothesis on a new set of data. Fortunately Bales was able to provide the interaction data for 31 five-man discussion groups, each observed for a single 40-minute session. Treating the data in the same way as before, we find that the average correlation between the predicted and observed interaction pattern is .23, which is significant at the .05 level using a one-tailed test. As a further test the actual interaction pattern was compared with a prediction based on the assumption that individuals would talk most to those most "opposite" them and in decreasing amounts to persons less "opposite." In this case man 1, for example, would be expected to talk most to man 5, less to 4, less to 3, and least to 2. Comparing the summed ranks over all five members of a group as before, the average correlation for the 12 groups is .13 and for the 31 groups is .14. Neither correlation is significant. Thus the central-member-plus-oppositeness hypothesis seems to be superior to the simple oppositeness hypothesis.

With a computer available it was possible to consider a further refinement in the test of these two hypotheses. The process of summing the ranked interaction data over the five group members may have obscured some differences between individuals. To test the prediction at the individual level, the pattern of interaction actually initiated by each member to each of the other four members was compared with each of the two alternate predictions. (The predicted ranking for man 3 is the same under either hypothesis.) For the twelve groups the grand mean correlation over an N of 60 was .47 for the central-member-plus-oppositeness hypothesis, and .15 for the oppositeness hypothesis. These are quite similar to the previous results. Since the data for the 12 groups were actually averages for three meetings of each group, we can go back and do the correlations meeting by meeting. This procedure yields an average based on 180 correlations. The average correlations are now .33 and .24. The difference between the two hypotheses is still apparent but not so striking.[2]

The data from the 31 groups do not supply a consistent picture. When the correlations for the individual data are computed, the mean for the 155 correlations under the first hypothesis is .27 and under the second .44, a reversal of the previous finding. Thus it does seem to make a difference whether the test is made for each individual in the group or for the sum of the rates for all members.

Cohen (5) also analyzed the same 31 groups. In addition to the "task"

2 If each of the 180 correlations were an "independent" estimate of the true correlation, both means would be significant at the .01 level using a one-tailed test.

session on which the present analysis was made, each group had a "social" session of about 13 minutes when they were asked to talk about anything they wished. Cohen found that during the social session individuals tended to talk more to the persons on either side of them, especially those in seats 2, 3, and 4. This pattern is different from either of those proposed above. It is, to use Bion's term, a "pairing" pattern.

There is additional evidence in the sample of 12 five-man groups that seating positions have differential importance. In 10 of the 11 groups in which, as noted above, there were two subjects who were participating in the more extensive "clinical" study, one of the two "clinical" subjects chose seat 5. In 9 of the 12 groups the subject in seat 5 was one of the two in the group who formed the highest-talking dyad. In general the "clinical" subjects seemed more active, perhaps because they were more "skilled" subjects, or perhaps because they felt they had a special status. Seat 5, it may also be noted, is the seat farthest into the room and most distant from the door.

In a study by Breer (3) using 20 groups in the same seating arrangement in a similar experiment, man 5 was the one who most often picked up the cards giving the answers to some predictions each group was making. In these groups the knowledge that a man held the cards contributed about as much to the prediction of how much he would talk in a given dyad as did a premeasure of Level of Dominance (both r's were about .30).

A questionnaire was designed to explore further the seating preferences of college-age subjects. The test contained diagrams of several different seating arrangements including one for the typical five-man laboratory group. This diagram was labeled "student committee" with an indication that there was no chairman. Subjects were asked which seat they would prefer, which avoid, and why. This test was given, together with a personality questionnaire which covered the same dimensions as the tests used in the Bales, Couch, Kassebaum study, to a sample of 86 men from Haverford and women from Bryn Mawr.[3] A replication was conducted later with another sample of 25 Haverford men and 3 Swarthmore women.

A significant correlation of .26 between Level of Anxiety and wishing to avoid seat one appeared in the first sample, indicating perhaps that subjects who had a high Level of Anxiety wished to avoid the High-Talking seats. However, this finding was not replicated in the second sample. In the larger sample, a comparison of actual frequencies of seating choices for men and women indicates that men prefer seats 1 and 5, while women prefer seats 2 and 4 (χ^2 significant at .02 level) (See Table 3).

An analysis of the reasons why subjects in the Haverford-Bryn Mawr sample choose the various seats, suggests that those who choose seats 2 and

3 The test was a short form of the "General Survey" used by Lindsey C. Churchill, Jr., (4), and based on the work of Couch (6).

TABLE 3

Seating Preference for Males and Females in Laboratory Group

SEAT	MALE	FEMALE	TOTAL
1 & 5	30	5	36
2 & 4	14	10	24
3	22	3	25
Total	66	18	84

4 do indeed wish to remain out of the discussion. A difference between those who choose seat 3 and those who choose seats 1 and 5 is also evident. Seat 3 seems to be the choice of a "social-emotional" type of leader who wishes to be in the center of things where he can see that all participate in the discussion. Seats 1 or 5 appear to be chosen by "individualists" who do not want to be hemmed in, wish to face the others so that they can make their points more easily, and perhaps become more "task" oriented leaders.

SUMMARY AND CONCLUSIONS

The analysis of several sets of data from five-man laboratory discussion groups tends to support a hypothesis related to the research of Steinzor and Strodtbeck and Hook that both centrality of seating position and distance in combination can be used to predict the interaction pattern. The apparent superiority of the combined hypothesis over a simple distance hypothesis depends somewhat on the level of data analysis.

Cohen's analysis of the data from a "social session" suggests that these findings will probably only hold in task-oriented groups where some pooling of information and a group decision are required. The pattern of interaction observed in the "social session" seems to reflect the "pairing" modality described by Bion (2) and later by Stock and Thelen (12). They have described three basic emotional states in groups: fight-flight, pairing, and dependency. Pairing is evident when group members wish to have more intimate conversation and turn away from the group to speak to the person next to them. This type of behavior is apparently the "expected" behavior for a social session whereas the subjects in a task session are expected to speak so that everyone can hear and often to direct their comments to the formal or informal leader.

Data from laboratory groups and questionnaires give evidence that personality variables are also related to seating choice and to interaction rate. In Breer's study, measures of both personality and centrality in the communication network provide independent predictions of interaction pattern. Although it would be desirable to demonstrate that an increase in predictability could be obtained by combining measures of personality and seating position, we have been unable, so far, to test this adequately, since in our data personality characteristics are not separable from choice of seating position.

REFERENCES

1. Bales, R. F., & Couch, A. S. *Interpersonal reactions contingent on personality characteristics of self and others.*
2. Bion, M. R. Experiences in groups: I–VII. *Hum. Relat.*, 1948–1951, 1–4.
3. Breer, P. E. Predicting interpersonal behavior from personality and role. Unpublished doctoral dissertation, Harvard Univer., 1960.
4. Churchill, L. C., Jr. Aggression in a small group setting. Unpublished doctoral dissertation, Harvard Univer., 1961.
5. Cohen, B. P. Seating position and interaction in five-man groups. Unpublished paper, Department of Social Relations, Harvard Univer., 1953.
6. Couch, A. S. Psychological determinants of interpersonal behavior. Unpublished doctoral dissertation, Harvard Univer., 1960.
7. Hare, A. P. *Handbook of small group research.* New York: Free Press, 1962.
8. Kassenbaum, G. G. Value orientations and interpersonal behavior: An experimental study. Unpublished doctoral dissertation, Harvard Univer., 1958.
9. Leavitt, H. J. Some effects of certain communication patterns on group performance. *J. abnorm. soc. Psychol.*, 1951, 46, 38–50.
10. Sommer, R. Leadership and group geography. *Sociometry*, 1961, 24, 99–110.
11. Steinzor, B. The spatial factor in face to face discussion groups. *J. abnorm. soc. Psychol.*, 1950, 45, 552–555.
12. Stock, Dorothy, & Thelen, H. A. *Emotional dynamics and group culture.* New York: New York Univer. Press, 1958.
13. Strodtbeck, F. L., & Hook, L. H. The social dimensions of a twelve-man jury table. *Sociometry*, 1961, 24, 397–415.

CHAPTER 8

INTERACTION AND EQUILIBRIUM

Some Effects of Feedback on Communication

HAROLD J. LEAVITT
and
RONALD A. H. MUELLER

INTRODUCTION

THE EXPERIMENTS reported here are concerned with the transmission of information from person *A* to person or persons *B*. Our problem deals with only one of the many relevant variables, the variable of feedback. The question becomes: how is the transmission of information from *A* to *B* influenced by the return of information from *B* to *A*? It is apparently taken for granted in industry, in the lecture hall, and in radio that it is both possible and efficient to transmit information from *A* to *B* without simultaneous feedback from *B* to *A*. On the other

FROM *Human Relations*, 1951, 4, 401–410. Reprinted by permission of the authors and publisher.

Readers familiar with the recent work of Professor Alex Bavelas and his group at M.I.T. will doubtless correctly recognize that many of the theoretical and experimental ideas in this research had their origins in that group. We are most grateful to Dr. Bavelas for both his direct and indirect help.

hand, the information theories of the cyberneticists and, to some extent, trial and error concepts in learning theory suggest that for *A* to hit successfully some target, *B*, requires that *A* be constantly informed of *A*'s own progress. The servomechanism needs a sensory system that is capable of transmitting cues about the errors of its own motor system. The human being learning some motor skill apparently utilizes the same process. But when the human being (*A*) seeks to transmit information to another human being (*B*), *A*'s own sensory system is hardly an adequate source of information *unless B* takes some action which will help *A* to keep informed of *A*'s own progress. If *A* were trying to hit *B* with a brick, *A*'s eyes combined with an inactive *B* would probably be adequate to permit *A* to hit his target after several trials. But if *A* seeks to hit *B* with information, he will probably be more successful if *B* helps to provide some cues which *A*'s own sensory system cannot pick up directly. In other words, where communication between *A* and *B* is the goal, feedback, in the form of verbal or expressive language, should make for greater effectiveness.

If we take the human memory mechanism into account, we need not require that there be *contemporaneous* feedback between *A* and *B*. It may not even be necessary that there be any feedback from B_2 if feedback from a similar B_1 has already occurred. The practice sessions of the past may have provided enough feedback to permit one to hit his present target accurately. Language, for example, may be thought of as a tool originally learned with feedback, but currently useful in a multitude of situations without simultaneous feedback to help us at least to get within range of our targets. But if the material to be communicated is relatively new and relatively precise, previously learned language may not be enough. Accurate transmission may require some additional contemporaneous feedback.

In addition to this hypothesis that contemporaneous feedback should increase the accuracy of transmission of information from *A* to *B*, is the hypothesis that the completion of the *AB* circuit produces other effects on the *AB* relationship. Feedback from both *A* and *B* can increase the certainty of *B* that he is getting the intended information, and the certainty of *A* that he is getting it across. This increase in certainty, assuming motivated participants, should have some effect on feelings of frustration or achievement and, hence, on the feelings of hostility or security that pervade the relationship.

Our purpose, then, in these experiments is to try to test these hypotheses; to try to determine experimentally the effects of feedback (or the absence of feedback) on certain kinds of *A* to *B* communications.

EXPERIMENT I

What Are the Effects of Progressive Levels of Feedback?

We chose as our material-to-be-communicated in these experiments a series of geometric patterns. The patterns were all composed of six equal rectangular elements, but the relationships of the elements to one another differed from pattern to pattern (see *Fig. IA* for sample pattern). *A*'s (the instructor's) job was to describe orally one of these abstract patterns

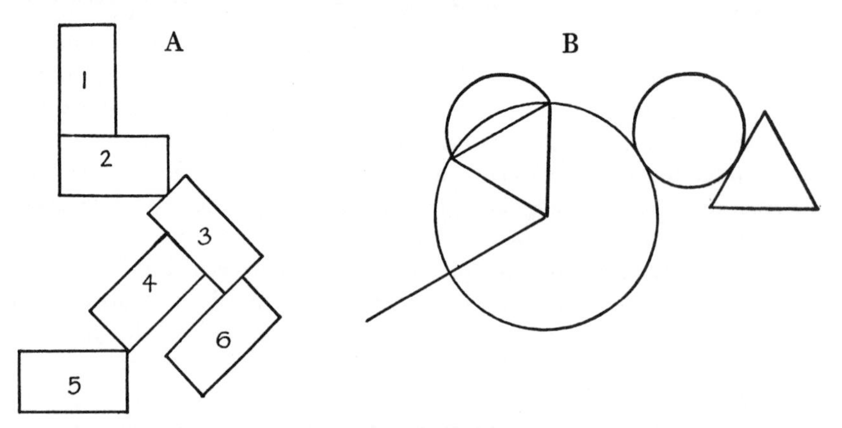

FIG. I. Sample Problems

A. Sample of problems used in Experiment I. B. Sample of problems used in Experiment II.

to the members of his class as accurately as possible, accuracy to be measured from the students' reproductions of the described (but unseen) patterns.

Two instructors were used, and four groups of students (total student N = 80), with each instructor describing four patterns to each student group. There were four conditions of feedback: 1. *Zero feedback* in which instructors sat behind a movable blackboard to describe the patterns. No questions or noises were permitted from the students. 2. The *visible audience* condition in which students and instructor could see one another but no speaking by students was allowed. 3. A *yes-no* condition in which the visible audience was permitted to say only yes or no in response to questions from the instructor. And 4. a *free feedback* situation in which students were permitted to ask questions, interrupt, etc.

With the use of a kind of Latin Square arrangement it was possible then to have each instructor use each condition of feedback in a different order. (See *Table 1*.)

Besides reproducing the test patterns, students were asked to estimate their confidence in the correctness of their answers and, after the last pattern, to indicate the feedback condition they found most comfortable. We also timed the description of each pattern.

All students were given the same instructions at the beginning of the class period. They were told that the experiment was a test of their ability to understand instructions, and that they were to work as rapidly and as accurately as possible. Both instructors had had some previous experience in describing similar patterns, and both had participated in the construction of the test patterns.

Students' papers were scored for accuracy on a scale from 0 to 6. A particular rectangular element was scored correct if it bore the correct relationship to the preceding element. The first element was scored correct if it was correctly oriented on the page.

TABLE I

Design of Experiment I

Pattern No.	*1 2 3 4*	*5 6 7 8*
Class 1:	zero V–A Y–N free (Instructor X)	zero V–A Y–N free (Instructor Y)
Class 2:	V–A Y–N free zero (Instructor Y)	V–A Y–N free zero (Instructor X)
Class 3:	Y–N free zero V–A (Instructor X)	Y–N free zero V–A (Instructor Y)
Class 4:	free zero V–A Y–N (Instructor Y)	free zero V–A Y–N (Instructor X)

Results

1. ACCURACY

The mean accuracy score for *all* patterns increased steadily from *zero* to *free feedback*. With *zero feedback* the mean was 4·7 out of a possible 6. The range of means for the eight different patterns given under this condition was 3·1 to 5·9. Under the *visible audience* condition the mean score was 5·3 with a range from 4·5 to 5·9. Under the *yes-no* condition the mean score was 5·5, the range 5·0 to 5·8. With *free feedback* the mean was 5·6 and the range 5·1 to 6·0.

2. CONFIDENCE LEVEL

Students' estimates of their own accuracy correlated closely with actual accuracy. For all patterns the mean confidence levels were: *zero feedback*, 4·6; *visible audience*, 5·3; *yes-no*, 5·6; *free feedback*, 5·5. No effects of experience could be detected. There was a tendency to favor one instructor for the *free feedback* situation and the other for all others. These differences were slight and may indicate a differential skill on the part of the instructors in handling the different feedback conditions.

3. TIME

The mean time required to give instructions under the four conditions were: *zero feedback*, 229 seconds; *visible audience*, 249 seconds; *yes-no*, 316 seconds; *free feedback*, 363 seconds. Any decrease in time with experience is once again obscured by differences in difficulty. No clear-cut differences between instructors were apparent.

4. OTHER OBSERVATIONS

Both instructors noticed some rather interesting behavior under certain conditions. When using *free feedback*, both found that on some occasions the students utilized their opportunities to speak by speaking aggressively and with hostility. There were comments like: "That's impossible"; "Are you purposely trying to foul us up?"; "You said left, it has to be right"; and so on. These comments even flowed on to students' papers, when they wrote beside their patterns such comments as: "The teacher made mistakes on this one, I didn't." These hostile reactions seemed to occur only when the *free feedback* condition *followed* other conditions. Both instructors noticed too that their *free feedback* experience stood them in good stead in the *zero feedback* situations. A student in the *free feedback* situation might say, "Oh, it looks like an L." In the next use of that pattern the instructors would find themselves saying, "It looks like an L."

Commentary

Although these data indicate that *free feedback* does yield more accurate results than the other conditions, some new questions arise. Can it not be argued that the *free feedback* method is more effective simply because it requires more time? Would the time required decrease if *free feedback* were used continuously? Does the *free feedback* method always put the teacher on the spot? Will he be attacked for his errors or lack of knowledge? Though free feedback may be helpful at first, is it of any use after the student and the teacher have had an opportunity to straighten out their language difficulties? Can the teacher improve just as much after a series of experiences without feedback as after a series with feedback? Can we show continuous improvement in the course of several trials without feedback?

EXPERIMENT II

Feedback vs. No Feedback

In an attempt to answer some of these questions we designed another series of experiments that seemed to permit the most efficient use of our limited supply of instructors and students. The purpose of these experiments was to compare the two extreme conditions, *free feedback* and *zero feedback*, over a longer series of trials.

Method

Using eight new geometric patterns, all made up of six elements (see *Fig. IB*), we selected ten instructors and ten separate groups of students, the groups ranging in size from six to twenty-four. Five of the instructors were members of the English Department at the Institute, one taught German, one economics, and three psychology. Four of the classes were speech classes, six were general psychology. For *three* pairs of instructors the procedure was as follows:

Instructor *A* faced class *A* with four patterns in sequence and *zero feedback*. Then instructor *B* faced class *A* with four new patterns in sequence and *free feedback*. Instructor *A* then faced class *B* with his original four patterns and *free feedback*. Then instructor *B* faced class *B* with his original four patterns and *zero feedback*. For the other two pairs of instructors the procedure was reversed, instructor *A* beginning with *free feedback*.

We again asked for confidence levels, from both the students and instructors.

Results

1. OVERALL

The results of this experiment bear out the trend of the first. The mean student accuracy score for all *zero feedback* trials was 5·2 of a possible 6; the mean with *feedback* was 5·9. These means represent the students of ten instructors. The ranges for individual instructors were, with *zero feedback*, 3·8 to 5·8; with *free feedback*, 5·6 to 6·0. This difference between these means is significant at the 1% level.

In students' confidence in their results, the data again correlate closely with accuracy. The mean for *zero feedback* is 5·0 with a range from 3·5 to 5·7, while for *free feedback* the mean is 5·8 and the range 5·4 to 6·0. These differences are also significant.

In terms of time required to describe each pattern, *free feedback* remains a more time-consuming process. The average time for *zero feedback* is 166 seconds with a range from 60 to 273. For *free feedback* the average time is 284 seconds with a range of 193 to 423. These differences too are significant.

Finally in our measure of teacher confidence, means were 4·5 with *zero feedback* and 5·0 with *free feedback*, with respective ranges of 2·5 to 5·5 and 4·5 to 5·8. In all cases instructors were *less* confident than their students.

In every case individual instructors changed in the same direction as the means. Every instructor got better results with feedback than without, and every instructor took longer with feedback than without.

2. EFFECTS OF EXPERIENCE

In *Figure II* are shown curves representing the changes in accuracy from pattern to pattern. Each instructor, you will recall, described four patterns in sequence under conditions of *zero feedback* and then *free feedback.*

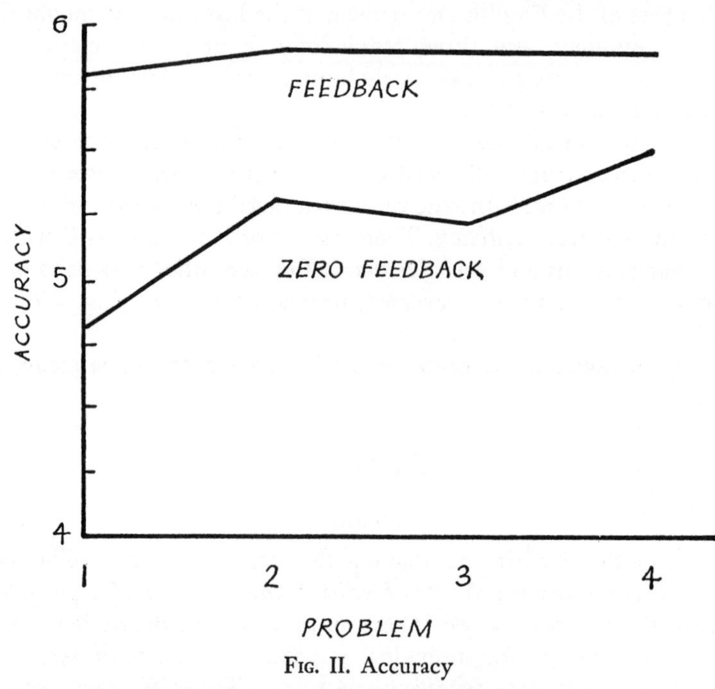

FIG. II. Accuracy

Each point represents the mean of 10 groups.

From these accuracy curves one can see that *free feedback* starts at almost the maximum level and stays there. *Zero feedback* changes in the direction of greater accuracy from trial to trial.

As far as time (*Fig. III*) is concerned, the reverse is true. *Zero feedback* remains more or less constant, while *free feedback* time *declines progressively*.

There is at least one other way of analyzing the data that provides some rather interesting results. Our experimental design supplied us with data for all combinations of (a) inexperienced (with these patterns) and experienced instructors, and (b) inexperienced and experienced classes, working (c) with and without feedback. The data broken down this way indicate that instructors' experience is the most significant factor present. Differences between experienced and inexperienced instructors are always greater than between experienced and inexperienced classes. This difference holds for *zero feedback* only, since with *free feedback* there are no perceptible differences among any of the different conditions.

3. OTHER OBSERVATIONS

One of our hypotheses in these experiments centered on the effects of feedback on the relationship between sender and receiver. We have no quantitative data that are relevant to this hypothesis, but we do have some

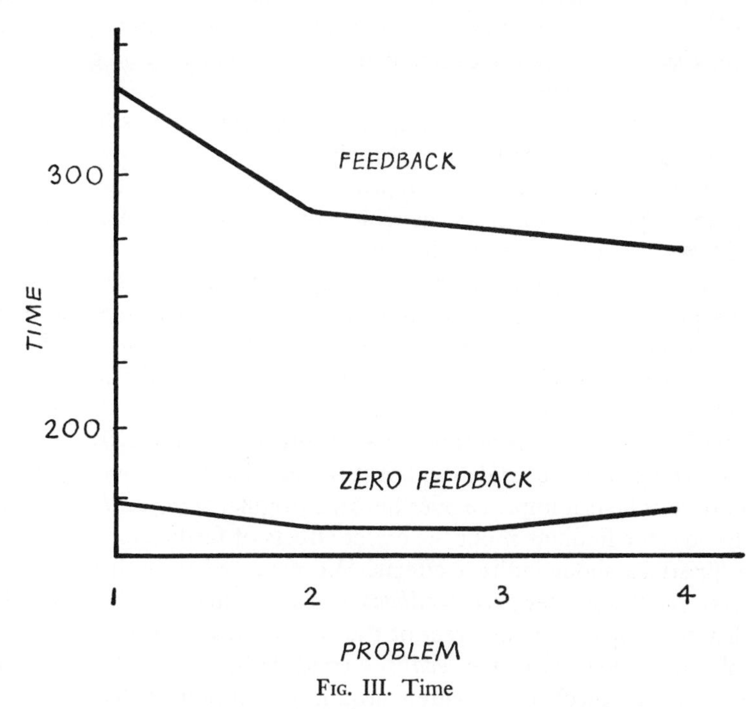

FIG. III. Time

Each point represents the mean of 10 groups.

observations that were astonishing in their consistency. These observations amounted to this. When an instructor faced a new class with *free feedback*, he got fairly rational feedback. That is, the students asked questions or asked for elaboration or repetition of a point. But when an instructor faced a class that had just been exposed to a *zero feedback* session, the instructor got an attack. The students asked lots of questions, but with barbs and implications about the instructor's (in)ability to do his job. The new instructor had innocently opened Pandora's box. This hostility did not last through more than one or two patterns, nor did it prevent the majority of students from expressing a preference for the *free feedback* method.

Commentary

In a sense these experiments demonstrate the obvious. When a receiver *B* is free to ask questions he can get a better understanding of what the sender *A* is trying to communicate. Moreover, with *free feedback* both the sender and the receiver can feel, correctly, more confident that they have respectively sent and received accurately. *Free feedback* requires more time, but there is some evidence that this time differential decreases with increased understanding between the sender and the receiver. Apparently the use of continuing *free feedback* could lead directly back into *zero feedback*, for once the common areas of misunderstanding have been clarified, contemporaneous feedback will no longer be necessary.

Apparently it is possible to improve communication skill with minimal feedback. The fourth *zero feedback* pattern is almost always more accurately sent than the first. This improvement can perhaps be thought of as a kind of personal feedback in which the instructor's own words are utilized to help him to increase his own effectiveness in the future. Much of it is no doubt empathetic, the instructor imagining himself in the receiver's place and correcting his sending as a consequence. Some of the improvement, however, may come from feedback which our experimental barriers failed to block out; feedback in the form of noises, sighs, shuffling of chairs. We do not know from these experiments whether or not an instructor using *zero feedback* could eventually reach the *free feedback* level of accuracy and confidence, but it is clear that under our experimental conditions he can improve over his own original *zero feedback* level.

Besides the findings about the direct effects of feedback, the data raise some questions about indirect effects. We observed in both experiments that *free feedback* after *zero feedback* is accompanied by hostility. This hostility was apparently an effect of the *zero feedback* experience. It lasts only through one or two *free feedback* trials. Why should this be so? We believe that the mechanism centers around the notion of "certainty." In our attempts to satisfy our needs we must be as certain as possible that we are successful. Uncertainty is frustrating. Without feedback uncertainty is prevalent.

In the same vein we noted that instructors' confidence is lower than students' confidence. We suggest that the instructor can be satisfied only by knowing that the receiver is getting the proper information. But the receiver can be satisfied by comparing his own work with the sender's directions. The receiver then has more information available against which to check his own progress toward his goal. Hence he can be more certain of his progress. But the sender is not sure of what the receiver is receiving. He can get *some* information with feedback, but almost none but his own empathy without feedback. Hence his certainty and confidence are low. These differential feelings of certainty, adequacy, and hostility seem to us to be the most significant differentials between our *free feedback* and *zero feedback* systems.

SUMMARY AND CONCLUSIONS

Since the scope of this research has been limited by the utilization of one kind of problem, one kind of sender-receiver situation, and a relatively short series of experiences, our conclusions must be severely circumscribed.

To summarize, we found that, within narrow limits: 1. a completion of the circuit between sender and receiver (feedback) increases the accuracy with which information is transmitted. 2. Feedback also increases receiver and sender confidence in what they have accomplished. 3. The cost of feedback is time. But the difference in time between *free feedback* and *zero feedback* appears to decrease. 4. A sender and a receiver can improve without what we have defined as feedback experience. 5. *Free feedback* experience improves subsequent *zero feedback* trials measurably. 6. Sender experience contributes more than receiver experience to improved accuracy of communication. 7. *Zero feedback* engenders some hostility in the receiver that becomes clearly perceptible when the situation *changes* from *zero* to *free feedback*. This hostility is short-lived, lasting through only one or two *free feedback* trials. 8. *Zero feedback* engenders doubt in the sender.

These findings support the hypothesis that *free feedback* is an aid to accuracy in interpersonal communication. *Free feedback* seems to permit the participants to learn a mutual language, which language once learned may obviate the necessity for further feedback.

The findings also support the hypothesis that the presence or absence of feedback affects the sender-receiver relationship. *Zero feedback* is accompanied by low confidence and hostility; *free feedback* is accompanied by high confidence and amity.

The Equilibrium Problem in Small Groups

ROBERT F. BALES

THE PURPOSE of this paper is to present certain empirical findings from the program of observation of small groups at the Harvard Laboratory of Social Relations and to discuss their relevance to the theory of equilibrium developed elsewhere.

METHOD

Some of these findings have been published previously, and the reader is referred to these earlier articles for details omitted here (1, 3, 4, 5). It will also be assumed that the reader is familiar with the method of observation, recording, and analysis used in the direct study of the interaction process as it takes place in our small laboratory groups (2). The observation categories are shown in Table 1. Certain aspects of their theoretical grounding in the general theory of action have been discussed earlier.

CONDITIONS OF OBSERVATION

A number of different types of groups have been observed, in natural as well as laboratory settings, and some of the generalizations to be discussed

ABRIDGED from T. Parsons, R. F. Bales, and E. A. Shils, *Working papers in the theory of action.* Glencoe, Ill.: Free Press, 1953. Pp. 111–161. Reprinted by permission of the author and publisher.

The research reported in this paper was facilitated by the Laboratory of Social Relations, Harvard University. The funds for the observation project now in progress are provided by the RAND Corporation, Santa Monica, California. I am indebted to Philip E. Slater, Research Assistant in the Laboratory of Social Relations, especially for work on the latter parts of this paper on problems of role specialization, and more generally for the many stimulating discussions we have had on the research as a whole. Similarly, I owe much to Christoph Heinicke, Social Science Research Council Fellow, for initial insights on the nature of the status struggle as it appears through the series of meetings of our groups. This phenomenon will be described in later papers.

were obtained before the present observational series was begun. For purposes of exposition, however, it will be simpler to confine the description of the conditions under which the generalizations hold best to the series of groups now under observation since these groups were specifically set up to epitomize the appropriate conditions.

Groups of sizes two through ten are under observation in the present series. Data for sizes three through six have been gathered. The groups are experimental discussion groups, each group meeting for four meetings. The subjects are all males, Harvard undergraduates, who are obtained through the Harvard employment service and typically do not know each other prior to the first meeting. In each of its four meetings, the group examines and discusses a "human relations case." A different case is used for each of the four meetings. Each case is a summary of facts, five pages in length, about a person in an administrative setting who is having some kind of difficulty with the men under him, and has some superior putting pressure on him to get some technically important job done. The summaries for a given case discussion are distributed separately to the subjects. After each member has read his summary the actual typed copy of the case is collected from each by the experimenter. The manner of presentation is such that the subjects are made specifically uncertain as to whether or not they possess exactly the same facts, but are assured that each does possess an accurate, though perhaps incomplete, factual summary.

The subjects are asked to consider themselves as members of the administrative staff of the central person in the case. He has asked them to meet and consider the case. He wishes an answer to two questions: (*1*) why are the persons in the case behaving as they do, and (*2*) what should he do about it. The members of the discussion group are asked to come to their decision in forty minutes. No leader is appointed. The host experimenter leaves the room. The discussion is observed through a one-way mirror and sound recorded. The interaction is observed and recorded in the categories shown on Table 1. After the meeting the members fill out a questionnaire asking certain questions about their reactions, their satisfaction, their relations to each other, and their opinions about their discussion group.

This particular concrete task has certain abstract characteristics which are important in eliciting a range of diversified behavior. The problems of *orientation*, *evaluation*, and *control* are each to a major degree unsolved at the beginning of observation. More specifically:

(a) With regard to *orientation*, members of the group have some degree of ignorance and uncertainty about the relevant facts, but individually possess facts relevant to decision. Their problem of arriving at a common cognitive orientation or definition of the situation must be solved, if at all, through interaction.

(b) With regard to problems of *evaluation*, the members of the group ordinarily possess somewhat different values or interests and the task is such that it involves several different values and interests as criteria by which the facts of the situation and the proposed course of action are to be judged. The problem of arriving at common value judgments necessary to a concrete plan must be solved, again, if at all, through interaction.

(c) With regard to problems of *control*, (that is, attempts of the members to influence directly the action of each other and arrive at a concrete plan) the acceptance of the task sets up in most instances a moderately strong pressure for group decision, with the expectation that the excellence of the decision can and will be evaluated by each of them as well as by the experimenter, so that the decision will affect their status. There are a number of possible alternative decisions or solutions, with uncertain degrees of potential frustration or satisfaction associated with various choices.

These abstract conditions, with emphasis varying according to circumstances, are met in very much this form and emphasis in a great many group conferences, work groups, committees, and the like. When group problems or tasks lack or greatly minimize any of the three abstract characteristics described above (a, b, c) we speak of them as being "truncated." When these three characteristics are all present and marked, we speak of the problem as "full-fledged." We have felt that full-fledged problems give us a better opportunity to explore the range and interconnections of various sorts of social behavior, and so have begun to develop empirical norms and a body of theory around this particular set of conditions as a standard diagnostic task. Once this baseline has been established, other sets of conditions expected to have different results can be described as modifications or accentuations or reversals of the laboratory conditions. The more we learn about the typical effects of the particular diagnostic *task* we employ, the more we are able to use discrepancies from our typical base-line patterns of observed interaction as diagnostic indicators of the *personalities, culture*, and *role organization* of the participants, since these are all sets of conditions which influence the way interaction actually goes.

Under each mode of analysis discussed below some of the main uniformities of behavior we have found will be compactly stated. Space does not permit the presentation of the evidence in detail. In general, the patterns described and illustrated can be understood to refer to approximate or average uniformities in aggregates of large numbers of group meetings under randomly varying external conditions, and in addition, they can be understood to hold more uniformly and in particular under the full-fledged conditions of the standard diagnostic task described above.

THE PROFILE OF ACTIVITY AND THE EQUILIBRIUM PROBLEM

One of the interesting characteristics of interaction is the distribution of total number of acts among the twelve categories, according to quality. A distribution of this kind in percentage rates based on the total is called a profile. An illustrative comparison of group profiles of two five-man groups working on the standard diagnostic task is shown in Table 1.

TABLE 1

Profile of a "Satisfied" and a "Dissatisfied" Group on Case Discussion Task

	MEETING PROFILES IN PERCENTAGE RATES			
TYPE OF ACT:	*Satisfied* *	*Dissatisfied* **	*Ave. of the two*	*Ave. rates by Sections*
1. Shows Solidarity	.7	.8	.7	
2. Shows Tension Release	7.9	6.8	7.3	25.0
3. Agrees	24.9	9.6	17.0	
4. Gives Suggestion	8.2	3.6	5.9	
5. Gives Opinion	26.7	30.5	28.7	56.7
6. Gives Orientation	22.4	21.9	22.1	
7. Asks for Orientation	1.7	5.7	3.8	
8. Asks for Opinion	1.7	2.2	2.0	6.9
9. Asks for Suggestion	.5	1.6	1.1	
10. Disagrees	4.0	12.4	8.3	
11. Shows Tension	1.0	2.6	1.8	11.4
12. Shows Antagonism	.3	2.2	1.3	
PERCENTAGE TOTAL	100.0	100.0	100.0	100.0
RAW SCORE TOTAL	719	767	1486	

* The highest of sixteen groups. The members rated their own satisfaction with their solution after the meeting at an average of 10.4 on a scale running from 0 to a highest possible rating of 12.

** The lowest of sixteen groups. Comparable satisfaction rating in this group was 2.6.

In the present illustration the "satisfied" group attained a higher rate of suggestions, more often followed by positive reactions and less often by negative reactions and questions than did the "dissatisfied" group.

The profiles produced by groups, however, are not completely and radically different from each other. The profile produced by the average of these two illustrative groups is more or less typical of averages of larger aggregates under laboratory standard conditions. Attempted Answers, that is, giving orientation, opinion, and suggestion, are always more numerous than their cognate Questions, that is, asking for orientation, opinion, or suggestion. Similarly, Positive Reactions, that is agreement, showing tension release, and solidarity, are usually more numerous than Negative Reactions, i.e., showing disagreement, tension, and antagonism. Intuitively one would feel that the process would surely be self-defeating and self-limiting if there were more questions than answers and more negative reactions than positive.

On the average, for groups we have examined, the relations of amounts by Sections are about as they are in the illustration. The relations between the amounts can be viewed as the final result of a repetitive series of cycles, each of which consists of: (*1*) an initial disturbance of the system (precipitated by the introduction of a new idea, or opinion, or suggestion into the group) followed by (*2*) a "dwindling series of feedbacks" and corrections as the disturbance is terminated, equilibrated, or assimilated by other parts or members of the system. Attempted Answers, or as one might call them for the moment, "Initial Acts," account for a little over half (or 57 percent) of the total activity, with Positive and Negative Reactions and Questions accounting for the other half, roughly.

Looking at the *Reaction* side alone, and assuming it to be 50 percent of the total, about half the reactions (or 25 percent of the total) are Positive and presumably terminate the disturbance introduced by the initial action. The other half of the time the Reaction fails to terminate the disturbance. Of this non-terminating portion again, about half (or 12 percent of the total) are Negative Reactions, which typically precipitate another Attempted Answer, thus beginning a repetition of the cycle. Of the remaining hypothetical 13 percent or so, about half (or 7 percent) are Questions, which also typically precipitate another Attempted Answer. If about 7 percent of Attempted Answers are in direct response to Questions, these might well be called "Reactions," thus leaving the relation of "Initial Acts" to "Reactions" about 50-50, as assumed above. One might say that quantitatively (as well as qualitatively, by definition) interaction is a process consisting of action followed by reaction. The balance of action with reaction is one of the equilibrium problems of the system.

ACT TO ACT TENDENCIES AND THE EQUILIBRIUM PROBLEM

A more detailed understanding of the equilibrating tendencies by which the characteristic profile arises may be obtained by examining the frequencies with which each type of activity tends to be followed by each other type. Two input-output matrices showing these act-to-act tendencies are presented in Tables 2 and 3. These particular matrices were obtained by tabulation from the interaction tapes of the total sixteen sessions of the four five-man groups of the present observation series. The total number of output acts occurring after each input type of act is considered as 100 percent, and the probabilities for each type of output act are derived by a percentage breakdown.

It will be noted that two matrices are presented, one called a Matrix of Proactive Tendencies, and the other a Matrix of Reactive Tendencies. A single matrix could be produced, of course, by omitting this distinction, but such a matrix would ignore the fact that the action "changes hands" at certain points, from one member to another. And this fact is crucial, since the equilibrium problem of social systems is not simply one of a certain "balance" in the relation of qualitatively different types of acts to each other, as shown by the profile. It is at the same time, and just as intrinsically, a problem of a certain balance in the way in which these activities are distributed between separate members. The distinction between "proaction" and "reaction," for the matrices presented, hinges on the member-to-member oscillation of activity. Very simply, an act which is a direct continuation by the *same* member who has produced the last act is called "proactive." An act which follows immediately the last act of *another* member is called "reactive."

The distinction is based on a suggestion by Murray:
"I . . . suggest . . . that the term *proaction*, in contrast to *reaction*, be used to designate an action that is not initiated by the confronting external situation but spontaneously from within. An action of this sort is likely to be part of a serial program, one that is guided by some directional force (aim) which is subsidiary to a more distally oriented aim. As a rule, a proaction is not merely homeostatic, in the sense that it serves to restore the organism to a previously enjoyed equilibrium or state of well-being. If successful, it results in the addition or production of something—another bit of physical construction, let us say, or more money in the bank, or greater social cohesion, or another chapter of a novel, or the statement of a new theory. The integrates of serials, of plans, strategies, and intended proactions directed toward distal goals constitute a large portion of the ego system, the *establishment* of personality which inhibits impulses and renounces courses of action that interfere with progress along the elected paths of life" (10, pp. 439–440).

The operational definition of the distinction for purposes of tabulating from interaction records does not correspond perfectly to Murray's theoretical distinction, but the basic idea is the same. In face to face interaction it is true by and large that the first act of a person following the last act of some other is "provoked" by the last act of the other as the "stimulus" and thus has a "reactive" quality. Conversely, it is sufficiently true that as a person continues talking his activity tends to change to a "proactive" quality, directed adaptively and instrumentally to the achievement of more distant aims. The activity is now *directed toward* the external confronting situation, including the situation external to the group as a whole, rather than immediately *initiated by* it, as in the "reactive case." It might be noted in passing that the term "initiation of action" is ambiguous, in that it is often defined empirically as the total of *all* types of activity "given out"

TABLE 2

Matrix of Proactive *Tendencies: Output Probabilities for a Given Input. 16 Meetings of 5-Man Groups*

CATEGORY OF PRIOR ACT (Input Type)	CATEGORY OF FOLLOWING ACT (Output)												TOTAL PERCENT
	1	2	3	4	5	6	7	8	9	10	11	12	
1 SHOWS SOLIDARITY, raises other's status, gives help, reward:	—	6.8	9.1	22.7	29.5	18.2	—	4.5	2.2	—	—	6.8	99.8
2 SHOWS TENSION RELEASE, jokes, laughs, shows satisfaction:	1.6	37.5	1.6	6.3	21.9	9.4	.8	1.6	2.3	3.1	3.9	10.2	100.2
3 AGREES, shows passive acceptance, understands, concurs:	3.0	4.6	6.6	9.7	41.6	22.1	2.8	2.1	.7	5.1	.8	.8	99.9
4 GIVES SUGGESTION, direction, implying autonomy for other:	2.6	4.8	1.6	55.6	19.3	9.6	1.0	2.6	.6	1.0	1.0	.3	100.0
5 GIVES OPINION, evaluation, analysis, expresses feeling, wish:	2.3	4.4	1.6	5.0	60.1	17.0	1.8	4.4	.7	.9	1.4	.3	99.9
6 GIVES ORIENTATION, information, repeats, clarifies, confirms:	.2	2.1	.2	3.4	22.6	61.4	4.7	2.8	1.3	.4	.8	.2	100.1
7 ASKS FOR ORIENTATION, information, repetition, confirmation:	1.1	1.1	1.1	6.5	19.4	38.7	21.5	7.5	1.1	1.1	1.1	—	100.2
8 ASKS FOR OPINION, evaluation, analysis, expression of feeling:	—	3.2	—	9.7	31.2	26.9	4.3	19.4	2.2	2.2	1.1	—	100.2
9 ASKS FOR SUGGESTION, direction, possible ways of action:	3.2	6.5	—	16.1	22.6	19.4	3.2	—	19.4	6.5	—	3.2	100.1
10 DISAGREES, shows passive rejection, formality, withholds help:	1.2	2.5	1.6	6.6	51.4	21.8	4.1	2.5	.8	1.6	5.3	.4	99.8
11 SHOWS TENSION, asks for help, withdraws "Out of Field":	—	4.2	2.1	8.3	45.8	35.4	—	2.1	—	—	2.1	—	100.0
12 SHOWS ANTAGONISM, deflates other's status, defends or asserts self:	5.9	27.5	—	5.9	19.6	7.8	5.9	2.0	—	—	3.9	21.6	100.1

TABLE 3

Matrix of Reactive *Tendencies: Output Probabilities for a Given Input. 16 Meetings of 5-Man Groups*

CATEGORY OF PRIOR ACT (Input Type)	CATEGORY OF FOLLOWING ACT (Output)												TOTAL PERCENT
	1	2	3	4	5	6	7	8	9	10	11	12	
1 SHOWS SOLIDARITY, raises other's status, gives help, reward:	28.4	11.9	3.0	13.4	14.9	11.9	4.5	4.5	—	3.0	1.5	3.0	100.0
2 SHOWS TENSION RELEASE, jokes, laughs, shows satisfaction:	.7	68.2	3.2	3.1	10.2	6.7	2.2	1.5	.3	1.7	.6	1.5	99.9
3 AGREES, shows passive acceptance, understands, concurs:	.6	2.7	15.9	8.5	40.8	21.4	2.3	3.0	.9	2.7	1.0	.2	100.0
4 GIVES SUGGESTION, direction, implying autonomy for other:	1.3	6.7	46.0	8.6	9.2	8.8	2.3	1.5	1.5	12.4	1.3	.4	100.0
5 GIVES OPINION, evaluation, analysis, expresses feeling, wish:	.6	4.3	48.9	2.2	19.2	6.3	2.3	2.8	.3	11.8	.6	.6	99.9
6 GIVES ORIENTATION, information, repeats, clarifies, confirms:	.6	5.8	35.0	3.6	15.2	24.0	5.6	1.3	.4	5.7	1.1	1.7	100.0
7 ASKS FOR ORIENTATION, information, repetition, confirmation:	—	1.0	5.6	.7	10.0	73.7	5.6	1.0	.3	1.6	—	.7	100.2
8 ASKS FOR OPINION, evaluation, analysis, expression of feeling:	1.5	5.4	9.2	2.4	45.9	13.2	10.7	3.0	.5	4.4	2.0	2.0	100.2
9 ASKS FOR SUGGESTION, direction, possible ways of action:	—	13.2	—	35.8	28.3	9.4	1.9	1.9	—	3.8	3.8	1.9	100.0
10 DISAGREES, shows passive rejection, formality, withholds help:	.3	6.6	12.4	5.2	25.0	13.5	3.6	2.0	.3	24.2	3.9	3.0	100.0
11 SHOWS TENSION, asks for help, withdraws "Out of Field":	4.1	7.2	5.2	2.1	39.2	22.7	2.1	4.1	—	4.1	9.3	—	100.1
12 SHOWS ANTAGONISM, deflates other's status, defends or asserts self:	1.0	18.1	4.8	3.8	12.4	11.4	1.0	3.8	—	5.7	1.9	36.2	100.1

by a specific individual, but usually carries the theoretical *connotation* of "proaction."

The Matrix of Proactive tendencies shows very clearly that when the same person continues talking, after having given an act of orientation, opinion, or suggestion, the probability is very high that he will continue with the same type of activity (probabilities of about .61, .60, and .55) presumably in a connected "serial program," to use Murray's term. When he does not continue with the same precise category of activity, the probability is still relatively high that he will carry on in one of the three types called Attempted Answers. If his preceding act was a Question of some type, and he continues himself instead of yielding the floor to some other, the highest probabilities are that he will either repeat or go directly ahead with an Attempted Answer. Indeed, the tendencies to continue proactively in the Attempted Answer area are very strong, even when the member has begun his participation with a Reaction to the other. As we all know, an act of agreement is often a way of "getting one's foot in the door" in order to go ahead and present one's own ideas. And similarly, when one has given a disagreement, he is very likely to go ahead and "tell why." In both of these cases, the tendency to present the argument in terms of "opinion" rather than "facts" is notable.

If the preceding Reaction was far over on the affective side, however, there are appreciable tendencies for the member to continue in the affective area. If one's former act was a display of antagonism, the present act is likely to be another, unless it passes over into tension release either of which is more probable than a direct return to the task area. Similarly, when the last act was one of tension release, the next act is likely to be *another* act of tension release, and the tendency to continue with an act of antagonism (possibly a joking one) is still appreciable. Once such a cycle of antagonism and tension release is set in motion, it appears to have a tendency to continue until presumably the major potential of implicit tension is "bled off" to a substantially lower level. Similar cycles also appear between showing solidarity and showing tension release, although they do not appear on this matrix because of our scoring convention (now changed) of scoring "jokes" in category two, as well as laughs. We now score the jokes themselves in either category one, or category twelve, according to whether the butt of the joke is outside the immediate group, or a member of it. This convention appears to us now to more satisfactorily represent affective dynamics of the process, but as a result of the change we obtain considerably more scores in category one than previously, and a few more in category twelve. The implication of the scoring change is simply that we now assume, on the basis of experience and intuition, that one of the reasons the number of acts in these two categories was formerly so low (of the order of one or two percent) is that in our particular type of groups, the management of positive and negative affect is typically accomplished in a "joking" rather than in a "serious" manner. Whether joking or serious, however, these cycles of affective activity, once started, have a tendency to "carry on," just as do the "serials" of instrumental-adaptive activity.

As we think of the matter, the instrumental-adaptive activity of the preceding participant tends to build up tensions in the present participant to some point where he enters the process and changes to activity of an expressive-integrative relevance, which tends to "bleed off" the tension to some point at which he changes the focus himself and continues again with instrumental-adaptive activity. *The problem of equilibrium is essentially the problem of establishing arrangements (or an "orbit of activity") whereby the system goes through a repetitive cycle, within which all of the disturbances created in one phase are reduced in some other.* The dilemma of all action systems is that no one disturbance can be reduced without creating another.

The individual personality is such an action system, and some of its cyclical tendencies can be seen in the Proactive Matrix. The combination of two or more personalities in interaction, however, is also an action system. Indeed, this is the level on which the systematic properties can be seen most fully articulated in overt observable behavior. The "switch-over" from reactive to proactive behavior can be seen in the individual person as he continues his participation, but the switch-over from proactive to reactive is most notable at those junctures in the process when the action changes hands. What happens to the quality of action when the action changes hands may be seen in the Matrix of Reactive Tendencies.

When the prior act of another member has been an Attempted Answer, the highest probabilities are that the present act will be a Positive Reaction, specifically an agreement, rather than a continuation in the task area, although there are appreciable tendencies for the reacting person to continue directly with further opinion or information. Probabilities of positive reactions (for these groups) far outweigh probabilities of negative reactions, and this is generally true, though occasionally we observe groups where it is not the case.

Theoretically, we tend to assume that a preponderance of positive reactions over negative is a *condition* of equilibrium or maintenance of the steady state of the system. The reasoning goes something like this: We assume that the instrumental-adaptive goals of the system involve the maintenance of a certain level of accomplishment output, and that this level *tends to fall* without the constant application of effort, energy, and activity applied successfully to the realities of the external situation. But the level of *accomplishment* can not be maintained for long without also maintaining the level of diffuse *satisfaction,* which depends upon the achievement of expressive-integrative goals. The full stable "orbit" will have to include tension release, gratification, and a feedback of positive sanctions to the person(s) performing the instrumental activities, in such a way as to "reinforce" them (in the learning theory sense), either in keeping them doing what they are doing, or in keeping them generalizing appropriately from their former accomplishments. Negative reactions tend to inhibit the behavior which preceded, but do not provide the basis for establishing a stable, positively defined orbit. Nor does generalization from negative reactions help appreciably in finding a positively defined orbit. It simply tends to cancel out or inhibit possible untried orbits, while the unstable "seeking" or "trial and error" fluctuation of the system continues.

Furthermore, each failure, and each negative reaction, tends to result *in its own right* in disturbance, and thus reduces the satisfaction levels directly. Assuming a quantitative equivalence of units of action observed (a shaky, but not inconceivable assumption), one might conclude that at least one positive reaction would be required for each negative reaction, simply to counteract the disturbances introduced by the negative reactions. On these assumptions, if positive reactions are only equal to negative reactions, the system barely manages to counteract the disturbances introduced by the "friction" of its own controlling apparatus, and the accomplishment and satisfaction levels will tend to sink because of lack of effort and instrumental activity applied constructively and successfully to the situation of the system. One concludes that the accomplishment and satisfaction levels can only be maintained in a steady state if an orbit is found in which positive reactions preponderate over negative. The degree to which they must do so in order to maintain steady levels will then depend upon such factors as levels of expectation or aspiration, the stringency of situational demands, and the abilities or resources of the actors in relation to aspirations and situational demands.

One obvious inference from this theoretical formulation is that the levels of satisfaction of members at the end of a problem-solving attempt will be a function of the degree to which positive reactions have outweighed negative reactions during the process. The two illustrative profiles given earlier demonstrate this relation. There are a considerable number of ways of constructing single indices from the balance of rates in the profiles which give reasonably good predictions of satisfaction. We do not yet know which of these is best in general. Several we have tried tend to yield correlations with average satisfaction at the end of meetings ranging from about .6 to .8.

Another possible inference is that the satisfaction ratings of individual members will tend to be a function of the preponderance of positive reactions received over negative reactions received by that member. We have not thoroughly explored this hypothesis as yet, but there are some indications that higher status members tend to receive higher relative proportions of positive reactions, and in general have higher satisfaction ratings.

The degree of satisfaction, we believe, as a working hypothesis, tends to be highest with the members of highest status, and to grade down as status grades down. On the basis of the theory, however, one should definitely not expect perfect correlations, either between total group profiles and average post-meeting satisfactions, or between positive reactions received by individual members and their individual post-meeting satisfactions. The reason is that starting levels are typically not known, and that other factors such as stringency of situational demands, abilities or resources of the members, and the content and stringency of levels of expectation or aspiration are believed to be involved also. Much work remains to be done in this direction.

On the Matrix of Reactive Tendencies it will be noted that the tendency to reply to an Attempted Answer of the other with a Positive or Negative Reaction increases from a prior act of giving orientation to one of giving opinion, to one of giving a suggestion. One might say that the "urgency" of giving a Positive or Negative Reaction increases as the proaction becomes more "directive" or "constricting." An act of giving orientation has only a probability of about .06 of provoking a disagreement. An act of opinion, however, has a probability of about .12 and an act of suggestion has a little higher probability. But an act of suggestion is a little less likely than an act of opinion to provoke an agreement. If one makes an index by representing the probability of disagreement as a percentage of the probability of agreement the index rises from .16 in response to an act of orientation, to .24 in response to an act of opinion, to .26 in response to an act of suggestion. The difference between the last two is very small, but in the expected direction. It should be pointed out that on the Proactive Matrix the probability that a member will follow a disagreement with an act of opinion is very high, .51. Consequently, the replies to opinion on the Reactive Matrix are often replies to an opinion which was in support of a still prior disagreement. If one took the trouble to segregate those cases where the acts of orientation, opinion, and suggestion are given without prior disagreement, it is likely that the differences between them would be greater.

The notions that proaction is likely to provoke reaction, that the probability of reaction increases as the process passes from problems of orientation, to evaluation, to control, and that the reaction will tend to swing to the negative side as the implications of the acts become more "directive" and "constrictive" are fundamental to the theory of equilibrium problems in small groups. The problem appears in many guises, and solutions are worked out in many directions, as will appear later in the discussion of the way in which participation tends to get distributed between members, the way in which quality of activity tends to move through a series of phases constituting a closed cycle in time, the way in which number of members affects the process, the way in which differentiated roles tend to appear, and the way in which the structure of roles tends to shift through a series of meetings.

On the Matrix of Reactive Tendencies the probabilities that a Question from the other will provoke a complementary or cognate Attempted Answer are seen to be very high. There is perhaps nothing very remarkable about this, but it does provide evidence of a kind of "reasonable continuity" in the process—the persistence of the system in an instrumental-adaptive direction of movement, once started, in spite of the fact that the action changes hands from one member to another. Questions provide a means of turning the process into the instrumental-adaptive direction of movement, with a low probability of provoking an affective reaction, and are an extremely effective way of turning the initiative over to the other.

Our impression is, however, that in our groups the number of questions which arise out of a self-conscious anticipatory attempt to guide the process in this way is comparatively small. They probably appear more often after strains arise out of earlier failures, as a result of disagreement, argument, and "backtracking" from premature attempts to proceed more "directively." Questions provide a "neutral way out"—a "patch up" procedure of last recourse when negative reactions are anticipated if one goes ahead himself. At least this way of looking at the process gives a reasonable explanation as to why the rates of Questions are in general so low (about half that of Negative Reactions). Questions constitute the last of the "dwindling series of feedbacks" mentioned earlier, and tend to be called into play only after more direct and obvious feedback controls have failed to equilibrate the system. Since they tend to prevent the asker from going ahead to give his own ideas, they provide little opportunity to raise one's status, but rather hand this opportunity over to the other. Thus, one might suppose, where competition is high (as it is generally in our initially leaderless groups) there will be a tendency to avoid them except as a last resort. Those who have a fixed high status, and those who have essentially accepted a low status, can "afford" to ask Questions, but not those who are in the thick of competition.

The tendency for antagonism to provoke antagonism is even more marked when the action changes hands (in the Reactive Matrix) than when the same person continues (in the Proactive Matrix). Similarly, in the Reactive Matrix, showing solidarity tends to provoke a like Reaction. Either type of marked affect tends to lead to tension release, and this type of activity, when once tripped off, is more likely to continue than any other type. "Laughter is contagious" as the saying goes. In the present context it is another instance of the tendency of the system, once started, to continue in a given direction of movement until checked by other factors. It is interpreted as a mechanism by which massive changes in the tension level take place in a short length of time, and typically appears only periodically, with intervening periods of tension build-up, as will be pointed out later in the discussion of phase movement.

The interpretation of the rate of tension release for given groups is a vexed problem. According to our present thinking, a "moderate rate" (around 7 or 8 percent) is associated with successful equilibration after normal hazards. Very low rates lead us to expect high residual tension, and very high rates lead us to look for extraordinary sources of tension. Levels of satisfaction as measured by post-meeting questions would appear to give us some entree to this problem, but the complex determinants of satisfaction have already been pointed out.

These problems of interpretation are general, however, not specific to certain types of acts or results of acts. The whole implication of an equilibrium theory as an interpretive device is that the determinants of any part of the process, or any result of it, are complex, and should be sought in some kind of complicated balance of the system as a whole, rather than in a maximization or minimization of supposedly isolated factors. The understanding of a *repeated* phenomenon in this type of approach lies in showing how it fits into a system, or constellation of interlocking systems, as one link in a closed, repetitive cycle of activities or orbit which constitutes the moving steady state of the system as its equilibrium is persistently disturbed and reestablished.

THE WHO-TO-WHOM MATRIX AND THE EQUILIBRIUM PROBLEM

A further unfolding of the equilibrium problem may be seen by a closer examination of the way in which participation tends to be distributed among members. The total number of different possible combinations of who is speaking and to whom for a given time period is called a "who-to-whom matrix." The scoring system recognizes acts addressed to the "group as a whole" as well as to specific individuals.

An aggregate matrix of a collection of 18 sessions of six-man groups (all types of activity) is presented in Table 4 as an illustration. The aggregate matrix is produced by rank ordering the members of each separate session according to the total amounts of participation given out, and then summing together all rank one men, all rank two men, all rank one men speaking to all rank two men, etc.

The pattern of distribution is different in detail under different conditions. For example, groups with no designated leader generally tend to have more equal participation than groups with designated leaders of higher status. However, in spite of these differences, the distribution of total amounts of participation of each member, as well as the pattern of who talks how much to whom, (and how, qualitatively) seems to be subject to system-influences, which tend to produce similarities from group to group, and some regular gradations by group size.

These generalizations may be illustrated in part by reference to Table 4. If the personnel are arrayed in rank order according to the total amount they speak ("basic initiating rank") we then find that they are spoken to in amounts proportionate to their rank order. Roughly speaking, each man receives back about half as much as he puts out in total. It will be remembered that something like half of all interaction is "reactive" and each man spends a certain portion of his time reacting to the initial acts of others. The amount of time spent reacting to specific other individuals rather than proacting to the group as a whole, however, differs according to the rank of the member. The profiles of participants tend to change systematically as we proceed downward in rank. High ranking men tend to have more proactive Attempted Answers in their profiles and to address more acts to the group as a whole than lower ranking men, while low ranking men have more "Reactions," both positive and negative, and address more of their acts to specific individuals. Quantitative differentiation in participation is accompanied by, or is symptomatic of, qualitative differentiation of roles of members. For example, the top man tends to give out more information and opinion to specific individuals than he receives, while, on the contrary, low men give out more agreement, disagreement, and requests for information than they receive.

TABLE 4

Aggregate Who-to-whom Matrix for 18 Sessions of Six-Man Groups, All Types of Activity*

RANK ORDER OF PERSON ORIGINATING ACT	SPEAKING TO INDIVIDUALS OF EACH RANK: 1	2	3	4	5	6	TOTAL TO INDIVIDUALS	TO GROUP AS A WHOLE	TOTAL INITIATED
1		1238	961	545	445	317	3506	5661	9167
2	1748		443	310	175	102	2778	1211	3989
3	1371	415		305	125	69	2285	742	3027
4	952	310	282		83	49	1676	676	2352
5	662	224	144	83		28	1141	443	1584
6	470	126	114	65	44		819	373	1192
Total Received	5203	2313	1944	1308	872	565	12205	9106	21311

* These groups were observed before the standard laboratory task was evolved. The general features of the standard task groups are similar.

If this is true one might expect quantity of participation to be related to the status hierarchy of the members. We typically find that the order produced by ranking individuals according to their "basic initiating rank" on total amounts of participation is fairly highly correlated with the order produced by their own ratings of each other as to "productivity," i.e., who has the best ideas, and who does the most to guide the discussion effectively. Similar findings are reported by Norfleet (11) and Bass (6) with correlations of about .95 in each case. Strodtbeck (13) finds in addition a fairly dependable connection between amount of activity given out and probability of winning in contested decisions, which is a kind of measure of power or influence. The empirical correlation between status in some generalized sense and amounts of participation given out and received seems to be pretty well established, but perfect correlation is definitely not to be expected in general.

Such approximate generalizations, once established, can typically be used to produce further valuable diagnostic information, as will be shown later. Any specific group, or some particular types of groups, may present exceptions, in one or more particulars, depending on the conditions operating. Exceptions to the empirical rule give the investigator the cue to look for exceptional conditions. For example, we have often found particular exceptions to the expected correlation between amount given out and amount received in cases where one of the members disagrees with the others persistently, and so tends to attract or receive a disproportionate amount of communication. Festinger and Thibaut (7) have produced this effect experimentally. We have found similar exceptions to the generalization when two highly interactive and agreeing members form a sub-group or coalition vis-a-vis a third neglected or rejected member.

Size of group is obviously an important condition affecting the distribution of activities. From present indications it appears that the top man in groups larger than five or so tends to speak considerably more to the group as a whole than to specific individuals in the group, as in Table 4. All other members tend to speak more to specific individuals (and particularly to the top man) than to the group as a whole. Each man tends to speak to each other man in an amount which is a probability function of both his own rank on outwardly directed remarks, and the rank of the other on the receiving of communication (8). As groups increase in size, a larger and larger proportion of the activity tends to be addressed to the top man, and a smaller and smaller proportion to other members. In turn, as size increases, the top man tends to address more and more of his remarks to the group as a whole, and to exceed by larger amounts his proportionate share. The communication pattern tends to "centralize," in other words, around a leader through whom most of the communication flows.

But if the situation is one in which *inter*action is expected by the participators, there would seem to be a top ceiling for the top man somewhere around 50 percent, apparently connected with the general tendency for interaction under such expectations to come to a system-closure, such that each "action" of one member, as it were, tends to be countered with a "reaction" from some other. Even if the top man is initiating most of the action, he still has to expect that he will receive a "feedback of reactions," both of a positive and negative sort, that will tend to equal the amount of action he initiates. It may very well be that the expectation of "equality" which is so often present in groups of our culture, refers rather to this over-all balance of action and reaction than to an equality of amounts of output of all members, which in practice, is never found.

Thus it can be seen that the differentiation between members as to specialized roles and status, is intimately related to the equilibrium problem. The tendency for the system, once started, to continue moving in the same direction until checked by opposing forces, is reflected in the tendency of given members to continue proacting until checked by other members. Negative Reactions appear to act as such a check, presumably through learning mechanisms. Their regular appearance should be viewed as a check on the widening of status differences, as well as a result of "objective mistakes" and task attempts which fail to appeal on other grounds. But if, as we have hypothesized, the system cannot maintain a steady state without a preponderance of positive reactions over negative, then in the equilibrated system more task attempts will be rewarded than punished, and they will be attempts by specific persons.

Here enters the crucial importance of "generalization" in the learning theory sense. Insofar as a given person "gets on the right track" and receives Positive Reactions from other members, he will be reinforced in his direction of movement, and will tend to keep on talking. He will "generalize" from the premises, logical and emotional, which underlay his original successful attempt. This is the "growing point" of the system of common symbols or group culture, as well as of role differentiation. And reciprocally, the other members will "generalize" from his earlier attempts, gratifying in some sense to them, to an expectation of further effective behavior on his part. The member begins to build a "specialized role." Insofar as the activity he performs is felt to be important in terms of the functional problems of the group, its goals and value norms, the "status" of the member will begin to rise. There will be a "generalization" from the specific *performance* of the person to a *qualitative ascribed* "position" in the group which bears a rank relation to other positions similarly developed. It is apparently in some such terms that one may understand the tendencies toward gross differentiation of amounts of participation given and received, the qualitative differences by rank, and above all, the emergence of a "top man" in larger groups, with an amount and quality of activity radically discontinuous with the more or less equal rank intervals between the other men. A system can not achieve a steady state without generalization, but the operation of generalization produces a differentiation of roles which introduces new strains. The price of accomplishment is differentiated status.

It should not be assumed, however, that once generalization in its various aspects has resulted in an ascribed status and role for a man, that his position is now stable. There are apparently a number of ways in which it may be undermined and subject to later shifts, two of which may be mentioned as likely. The first is that the effects of his role-specialized behavior, even if it does not change, put other members under ambivalent strains of some sort which gradually lead them to shift their perception of, attitudes toward, or behavior addressed to him. The second is that the psychological effects of holding a given position may result in gradual *changes* in his behavior (either by "overconfidence," "dissatisfaction" or in some other way) which finally "break through" stereotyped perceptions of his previously established role and become obvious to the other members, with a resulting shift in their attitudes toward him. In other words, the problem of equilibrium is relevant on the more macroscopic levels of role structure and in longer changes over time, as well as on the more microscopic levels we have so far discussed. The unfolding of the equilibrium problem on these levels will be discussed later in this paper. First, however, it may be useful to present, in a very tentative way, a sample of the type of statistical models we have been "playing with," which ignore these more macroscopic equilibrium problems of larger scale "social structure change."

A STATISTICAL MODEL FOR EXPLORING THE MATRIX EQUILIBRIUM PROBLEM

Some characteristics of the hypothetical learning process just described can be formalized slightly in terms of a statistical model. The model presented below is the fifth of a series of models which have been informally explored and discarded as their deficiencies forced to clearer awareness the sorts of assumptions which appear to be necessary to "reproduce" the characteristics of the average process as we have found it empirically. The present model has been barely explored as yet, and is by no means expected to be the last of the series. It is presented simply as another step in what is hoped to be the right direction. This model which we call T_5 (T for "temporary") takes the act-to-act tendencies represented by the Proactive and Reactive Matrices as given, makes certain additional assumptions about the effects of learning mechanisms and generalization as discussed above, and attempts to determine whether, if these givens and assumptions are true, the who-to-whom matrix we find for groups of each size will turn out to be the equilibrium state of the system.

No formal mathematics have been employed. The model is set up for easy "Monte Carlo" calculation. The results to be obtained are thus exceedingly "approximate." They have been quite adequate however, to show that previous models could not possibly be satisfactory, and this is all that is required for progress. To lighten the boredom we have typically employed an actual group of people, each of whom is given an identical set of Proactive and Reactive Matrices (thus erasing all "personality differences") and a table of random numbers. The process proceeds by a series of probability choices according to a set of "Rules of Order" administered by the experimenter. Still another person takes down the scores as they are determined by the probability choices, and these scores are later tabulated and analyzed just as we analyze actual scores. To forestall any misunderstanding it may be repeated: the group of people is in no sense necessary—the whole operation is defined by rules and probability choices and can be performed by a single statistical clerk. However, to do the calculation as a game gives an excellent setting for spotting specific deficiencies and artificialities of the model.

For use in the model, the probabilities in the Proactive and Reactive Matrices given earlier are translated into spans of random numbers, so that one can make a probability choice by drawing from a table of random numbers. For example, take the probabilities for what happens next following an act in Category 1 in the Proactive Matrix. The probabilities add to 1.000. Random numbers 001 to '000 are taken to represent this range. The probability that the output act will be in Category 1 is zero on the table, so no random number span is assigned. The probability that the output will be in Category 2 is .068, so the span of random numbers from 001 to 068 is taken to represent this probability. The probability of an output in Category 3 is .091, so the span of random numbers from 069 to 159 is taken to represent this probability, and so on.

Model T_5

The first two elements of the model are the two act-to-act matrices, represented in terms of random numbers, as explained:

The Matrix of Proactive Tendencies
(See Table 2)

The Matrix of Reactive Tendencies
(See Table 3)

The next two elements of the model are two tables which represent, not the *tendencies*, as above, but the *opportunities* arising out of the status order, and modified by a "learning" process, as explained in the Rules of Order.

The Table of Proactive Opportunities

This table contains a set of probabilities, one for each man, adding to 1. Initially each man's probability is $\frac{1}{N}$, where N = number of members in the group. However, Man 1 is designated for purposes of this model as "Leader," and he is given special treatment as indicated later. In the event a man's probability is to be increased, as under Step 8 in the Rules of Order, a suitable operator is applied which increases the probability of the given man and decreases the probability of each of the others, with the probabilities still adding to 1 after the operation.

Practically, the change will be accomplished in this Model T_5 by the following crude method. A set of numbered tags will be used, the numbers indicating the identification numbers of the members. Initially an equal number of tags (say 10) will be put in a hat for each man. When a probability choice is to be made, a tag will be drawn, and then returned. When a man's probability is to be increased, a single tag bearing his number will be added to those already in the hat.

Mathematically, this is a very awkward operator. However, with the present mechanical method the operation is very easily performed.

The Table of Reactive Opportunities

This table contains a set of probabilities, one for each man, adding to 1. Each man's probability will be set at $\frac{1}{N}$, where N = number of members in the group. These probabilities are not changed.

Practically, the probabilities will be represented by the assignment of an appropriate span of random numbers to each man, and the choices will be made from a random number table.

Following is the Table to be used for a six man group:

RANDOM NUMBERS:		MAN DESIGNATED:
001–167	=	1
168–333	=	2
334–500	=	3
501–667	=	4
668–833	=	5
834–1000	=	6

Rules of Order for T_5

PROACTION

1. A man is chosen from the table of *Proactive* Opportunities (it may be any man) and the Process goes to Step 2.
2. The quality of the man's proaction is chosen by probabilities from his Matrix of Proactive Tendencies, from the row of the preceding input act * and the Process goes to Step 3.

(* Note: If there was no preceding act—that is, if the present act is the first of the run—the present act is arbitrarily chosen as an act in Category 6.)

3. The proaction is delivered to a given target as follows:
   a. If the man *just received a Positive Reaction* (or if his present act is the first of a run) the present act is delivered to the *group as a whole*, and the Process goes to Step 4.
   b. If the man has *just given a Positive Reaction*, and he is now continuing, the present act is now delivered to the *group as a whole*, and the Process goes to Step 4.
   c. If the man has *just given an Attempted Answer, a Question, or a Negative Reaction to a specific individual or to the group as a whole*, the present act is now delivered to the same target, and the Process goes to Step 4.

CHOICE OF PROACTION OR REACTION

4. The number of a man is drawn by probabilities from the Table of *Proactive* Opportunities, and a decision is made as follows:
   a. If the number of the man is that of the man who *just spoke*,* he is allowed to *continue Proaction* and the Process returns to Step 2.
   (* Note: If the group as a whole delivered the last act (as in Category 2) any man drawn may be considered as having just spoken.)
   b. However, if the number is *different* from that of the man who just spoke, he is now required to *stop speaking* and another man is chosen to *continue with a Reaction*, as the Process goes on to Step 5.

REACTION

5. The man who just spoke is *excluded* from the *Table of Reactive Opportunities* and a *different* man is chosen from this Table by probabilities. The Process then goes to Step 6.

6. The quality of the man's Reaction is chosen from his Matrix of Reactive Tendencies, from the row of the preceding input act, and the Process goes to Step 7.

7. The reaction is delivered to a given target as follows:
   a. The act is delivered *to the man who just spoke*, and (unless the exception under "b" applies) the Process goes to Step 8.
   b. If the act under "a" is an act in Category 2 (Tension Release) each other man in the group is allowed to deliver an act in Category 2 to the same man, (but the receiver of these laughs does not deliver such an act to himself). The Process then goes on to Step 8.

REWARD AND PUNISHMENT

8. Depending upon the quality of the act, and who receives it, the Table of Proactive Opportunities may be changed as follows:
   a. If the "*Leader*' receives the act, *regardless of its quality*, he is "re-

warded" by an increase in his probability of speaking again in the Table of Proactive Opportunities, and the Process goes to Step 4.

b. If any other member receives the act, a change may be made or not, as follows:
   1. If he receives a *Positive Reaction,* he is rewarded, as above, and the Process goes to Step 4.
   2. If he receives a *Negative Reaction,* he is punished by a decrease in his probability of speaking again in the Table of Proactive Opportunities, and the Process goes to Step 4.
   3. If he receives a *Question or an Attempted Answer,* no change is made, and the Process goes to Step 4.

This particular model has not been in existence long enough at the point of this writing to provide data which might be presented. However, it includes one feature which previous models did not contain—the fact that one person is designated in the very beginning as "Leader." It also assumes that there will be no change in leadership, and indeed, that the equilibrium problems of role organization, once roles get specialized, are much simpler than we know them in fact to be. Some of these problems will be discussed later.

The "Leader" is rewarded by an increase in probability of speaking *each* time he speaks, regardless of the response. All other men are rewarded when they receive a positive response, and punished by a decrease in probability when they receive a negative response. All men are started equal, but with say 10 tokens each, so that one punishment does not extinguish the probability of speaking again.

The "rationalization" of the model, so far as it goes, is this: Any model generally similar to this one, so far as I can see, will only produce the aforementioned radical discontinuity between the top man and the others if the top man is somehow singled out for distinctive treatment. Otherwise he can not get so far ahead as he actually does. Of course the probabilities of speaking could be set on an empirical basis, but this would defeat the purpose of the model, except as a device for obtaining sampling distributions. It is hoped that there is some set of assumptions which will regulate the process in such a way that the empirical gradients will appear as an equilibrium state of the system. The problem is to discover some such set of assumptions.

One possible procedure is to employ further matrices which members use in speaking to the top man. This would involve constructing such matrices so that the probability of the top man receiving agreement (rather than disagreement) is enhanced, or even set to the point where disagreement is not received. However, empirically we know that the top man *does* receive disagreement—in fact he receives, absolutely, more than any other member, just as he receives absolutely more agreement. His ratio of agreement to disagreement may, however, be somewhat higher than other members.

This will come about automatically, however, I think, for the rest of the members on the gradient, if not the leader, by the working of the model. That is, a man obtains the opportunity to go ahead by receiving agreement. Those who go ahead will have higher totals of amounts given out—or vice versa, those who are found with higher amounts given out will also be found to have received more agreement, since that is the mechanism by which they got ahead. All will be held down by disagreement however, to some extent, with the exception of the top man. He will receive the full probability of agreement in the model, whereas the others will all have been held down.

The reward of the top man each time he speaks can be given some rationalization in various ways. One can assume that the leader is the man who is speaking as the expression of a self-consistent set of norms, and is internally rewarded by the "knowledge that he is right," no matter what response comes from others. For the same reason, he can receive disagreement and antagonism without abandoning his self-initiating and self-rewarding tendencies. If his status is the highest in the group, and he is the source of authority, it is as if he "can do no wrong" and disagreements from other members are taken simply as signals that they are confused, in error, or deviant. It is then the leader's job to "remain steadfast," and to correct the deviance by his own consistent attitude and administration of rewards and punishments. So long as his status is the highest in the group, his positive and negative responses function as rewards and punishments to the other members, but not vice-versa.

The original sources of such a position might be assumed to be various. They might proceed from some initial positive affective reactions of the members to the leader. The leader in this case is the major target of positive affect in the group—the "sociometric star." They might proceed from the identification of the leader with a set of norms or a coherent symbol system, where both the leader and the members identify with the symbol system and the leader is identified by the members as the "true spokesman and interpreter" of the symbol system. Both of these sources would involve a kind of "generalization" of response. In the first case affective responses of liking are organized by generalization so that the leader is persistently "liked" in spite of variability of his behavior. In the second case affective responses of evaluation and of agreement with verbal or symbolic propositions are generalized in such a way that new propositions appropriately linked with (or "deduced from") the existing symbol set are also felt to compel agreement.

There is a third case, perhaps, where one might say that whatever will tend to "insulate" a given man from the ordinary influences men have on each other by reward and punishment will tend to produce an

"Archimedean Point" for change and readjustment of the system around the unyielding and stable element. The psychotic or semi-psychotic personality, or the rigidly neurotic one can thus be seen to answer the formal requirements perhaps as well as the former cases. By extension one might say that if one wishes to move a system as a leader, he must be able to "take it"—i.e., take disagreement and antagonism, without reacting in the usual way. The refusal of the therapist to assume a full reciprocity of relation with the patient is a case that is formally similar, in this "immovable" quality. The therapist often differs from other leaders and influencers of behavior, however, in that he takes a "passive" immovable role rather than an "active" one, as in the case of the charismatic leader.

The preliminary character of this speculation is obvious. In fact, it clearly overlooks the complications introduced by the fact that the role of "Leader" in the sense of the man with "the best ideas" or who "does most to guide the discussion" tends *not* to be the sociometric star, as will appear later in this paper. This model, T_5, is simply not complicated enough to handle this problem. Perhaps it will suggest, however, the way in which an effort toward more formal models can play a part in clarifying the assumptions involved in the type of equilibrium theory toward which we are aiming, and give some inkling as to how they may be handled formally as they get too complicated for intuitive grasp.

PHASE MOVEMENT AND THE PROBLEM OF EQUILIBRIUM

Changes in quality of activity as groups move through time in attempting to solve their problems may be called phase patterns. The pattern of phases differs in detail under different conditions. However, these changes in quality seem to be subject to system-influences which produce similarities from group to group. An increase of task-oriented activities in the early parts of a meeting, that is, Questions and Attempted Answers, seems to constitute a disturbance of a system equilibrium which is later redressed by an increase in social-emotional activities, that is, both Positive and Negative Reactions.

Part of our observations prior to the development of the standard diagnostic task were kept by time sequence. Each available meeting was divided into three equal parts, and the amount of each type of activity in each part of each meeting was determined. The meetings were divided into two kinds: those which were dealing with full-fledged problems (essentially problems of analysis and planning with the goal of group decision as described for the standard diagnostic task), and those dealing with more truncated or specialized types of problems. Those groups dealing with full-fledged problems tended to show a typical phase movement through the meeting: the process tended to move qualitatively from a *relative* emphasis on attempts to solve problems of *orientation* ("what is it") to attempts to solve problems of *evaluation* ("how do we feel about it") and subsequently to attempts to solve problems of *control* ("what shall we do about it"). Concurrent with these transitions, the relative frequencies of both *negative reactions* (disagreement, tension, and antagonism), and *positive reactions* (agreement, tension release, and showing solidarity), tend

CHART I

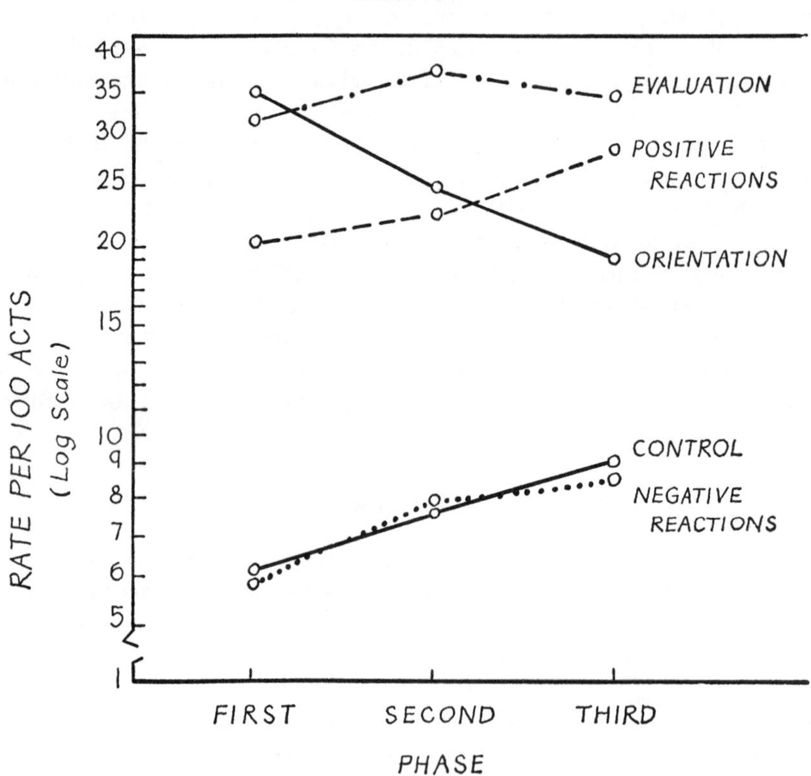

to increase. Chart 1 presents the summary data for all group sessions examined in the phase study.

The underlying theory as to why the phase movement just described is characteristic of full-fledged conditions is again a system-equilibrium rationale. An individual may be cognitively oriented to a situation and speak of it to others in cognitive terms without committing himself, or the other when he agrees, either to evaluation of it, or an attempt to control it. But in speaking to the other in evaluative terms he attempts to commit both himself and the other to some assumed previous orientation, and further, if he suggests a way to control the situation by joint cooperative action, he assumes both previous orientation and evaluation. When the problems of arriving at a common orientation and evaluation of the situation have not been substantially solved by the group members, attempts at control will meet with resistance on the part of the others and frustration on the part of the person attempting to exercise the control. Probably generally, unless there are contrary cultural, personality, or group organizational factors, the interacting persons tend to avoid or retreat from this frustration-producing type of interaction by "back-tracking" toward orientation and evaluative analysis until the prior problems are solved.

In addition to their task problems, the members of any cooperating group have problems of their social and emotional relationships to each other to solve and keep solved. Efforts to solve problems of orientation, evaluation, and control as involved in the task tend to lead to differentiation of the roles of the participants, both as to the functions they perform and their gross amounts of participation. Some major features of this differentiation have already been described in the presentation of findings about the matrix. Both qualitative and quantitative types of differentiation tend to carry status implications which may threaten or disturb the existing order or balance of status relations among members. Disagreement and an attempt to change existing ideas and values instrumentally may be necessary in the effort to solve the task problem but may lead, nevertheless, to personalized anxieties or antagonisms and impair the basic solidarity of the group.

This impairment, or the threat of it, we may assume, tends to grow more marked as the group passes from emphasis on the less demanding and more easily resolved problems of cognitive orientation on to problems of evaluation, and still more acute as it passes on to its heaviest emphasis on problems of control. It will be recalled that this notion appeared earlier in the examination of act-to-act tendencies. This assumption seems to be a more generalized way of stating the findings of certain other studies. For example, Lippitt (9) found negative reactions to autocratic control or leadership in boys' clubs under certain conditions, while Rogers (12) and his associates tend to find a minimization of negative reactions on the part of clients when the counselor confines himself to nondirective (or, in our categories, orienting rather than evaluating or controlling) types of activity. The present assumption may be regarded as a generalization of this connection between degree of control and negative reactions, so that it is viewed as applying to different points in the process of the same group, not simply to differences between groups. Thus, a series of changes in the social-emotional relationships of the members tend to be set in motion by pressures arising initially from the demands of the external task or outer situation. These social-emotional problems tend to be expressed in overt interaction as they grow more acute—hence the increasing rate of negative reactions.

However, at the extreme end of the final period, assuming that the members' attempts at control over the outer situation and over each other are successful and a final decision is reached, the rates in Categories 1, 2, and 3 also rise to their peak. In other words, one might expect the successfully recovering group to confirm its agreement and to release the tensions built up in its prior task-efforts, repairing the damage done to its state of consensus and social integration. We note joking and laughter so frequently at the end of meetings that they might almost be taken as a signal that the group has completed what it considers to be a task effort, and is ready for disbandment or a new problem. This last-minute activity completes a cycle of operations involving a successful solution both of the task problems and social-emotional problems confronting the group. The apparent incongruity of predicting a peak for both negative and positive reactions in the third phase is thus explained. Negative reactions tend to give way to positive reactions in the final part of the crudely defined third phase.

CHANGES IN ROLE STRUCTURE AND THE EQUILIBRIUM PROBLEM

We now consider a series of role changes which take place on "the next rung up" the ladder of microscopic-to-macroscopic contexts in which the general theory of action systems can be applied. Changes in quality of act from one act to the next are on a very microscopic level as to time span involved. Changes in rates of acts of various types through the course of a single meeting are on a more macroscopic level. As we have seen, very much the same sort of general system theory can be applied to both, with proper allowance for changes in conditions which will surely be characteristic of any shift up or down on the microscopic-macroscopic ladder. We now proceed up another rung of the ladder to consider changes that take place from meeting to meeting in a time span of four meetings. And for the present analysis, we shift from a primary emphasis on consideration of interaction rates to a consideration of more "generalized" or partially "structured" roles as reflected in post-meeting ratings and choices of members by each other. Much more detailed treatment of changes within the four meeting time span, using interaction rates as well as post-meeting measures will be given in later publications.

The essential rationale for the ratings and choices we ask members to make at the end of meetings is rooted back in the four types of system problems, the "dimensions" along which system change takes place—the instrumental, adaptive, integrative, and expressive. For present purposes we link the instrumental and adaptive dimensions together to obtain one "pole" of specialization: the instrumental-adaptive pole. On the other side we link the integrative and expressive dimensions together to obtain the integrative-expressive pole.

Toward the instrumental-adaptive pole we distinguish two types of roles: The first is a role emphasizing specifically task-oriented achievement addressed to the problems of the external situation confronting the group. In terms of the type of task we give our groups, this role appears to be fairly well defined operationally by answers to the question: "Who contributed the best ideas for solving the problem? Please rank the members in order. . . . Include yourself." The second type of instrumental-adaptive role we distinguish is one which emphasizes regulation or management of the group process in the service of task oriented achievement—a role approximating that of "chairman" or perhaps in a more general sense that of "executive," (as contrasted with that of "technical specialist" which is the first type of role above). We attempt to get at the second type of role by the question: "Who did the most to guide the discussion and keep it moving effectively? Please rank the members in order. . . . Include yourself."

Toward the integrative-expressive pole we also distinguish two subtypes of roles, but this time according to a "positive-negative" distinction rather than according to an "external-internal" distinction as above. The questions we ask here are fairly orthodox sociometric choice questions—essentially "Who do you like in rank order" and "Who do you dislike in rank order," although we ask them in a somewhat more complicated way that would take unnecessarily long to describe here. Detailed description of scoring methods will also be omitted—by inverting ranks it is possible to obtain high scores for top ranking men and low scores for low ranking men. This is done for greater intuitive ease in grasping the meaning of the data. I shall refer to high ranking men as "receiving the most votes," sacrificing accuracy a bit to convenience.

Now, according to the line of thought embodied in the sample statistical model for reproducing the matrix, and its "rationalization," one might make the following sorts of inferences: Since a man may receive agreement for advancing ideas which appeal to other members, or for making neutral suggestions with procedural content rather than task content, or simply because people like him emotionally, and since agreement tends to encourage a man to go ahead and talk more, we might suppose that such men would tend to have high rates of participation. Conversely, since disagreement tends to discourage a man from talking, and since disagreement is often a manifestation of dislike, we might suppose that dislikes would tend to center around men with low rates of participation. And since the model makes no assumptions about the incompatibilities of these various roles (excepting the incompatibility of Liking and Disliking) we might suppose that the same man—"The Leader"—might receive the most votes on all three roles—Best Ideas, Guidance, and Best Liked, and that another man—"The Scapegoat"—at the bottom of the heap might receive the fewest votes on all three of these virtuous roles, but the most on Dislikes. The simplest assumption is that the votes on each of these roles will grade according to Basic Initiating Rank—the rank on total amounts of participation given out. Such a group we might call a "simply organized group," meaning that no matter what criterion of status were chosen, it would place the men in the same rank order of relative status. Now those who are acutely aware of the lack of such perfect integration of various criteria of status in larger social systems will be likely to suspect that small groups will not be so "simply organized" either. Nevertheless, we had evidence of some appreciable degree of positive correlation of these various status criteria with Basic Initiating Rank, and the hypothesis of the "simply organized group" was adopted as a working hypothesis for the first ordering and examination of the data.

Our first major insight with regard to what we now regard as a basic problem of role structure was obtained from a tabulation of data from twelve meetings of five-man groups (twelve instead of sixteen because of absences in four meetings). No distinction was made as to which meetings in the series of four were represented. The identity of men was not preserved from meeting to meeting. We simply took each meeting, listed the men in rank order of total amounts of participation given out, and recorded "the number of votes received" on each role. Then the data for all rank one men on total acts initiated were pooled, and so for all rank two men, and so on for the five. The fact that Joe Smith might have been rank one man in the first meeting, rank two man in the second, and so on, was ignored. The data are represented in Chart 2.

First it may be noted that there is a general gradation of votes on Best Ideas and Guidance by Basic Initiating Rank as expected by the working hypothesis. Second, note that these two curves are very close together and move in the same way, indicating the relative lack of segregation of these roles from each other. But there is a departure from the prediction of the working hypothesis: on both curves the second man is unaccountably low.

But a more serious departure from the prediction is in terms of the curve on Likes. There the top man is unaccountably low, and the second man is highest in the group—by an insignificant margin, but still enough to give birth to the idea: can there be any connection between the fact that the second man, who is unaccountably low on Best Ideas and Guidance, is also Best Liked? Can it be that he is avoiding too heavy participation in the instrumental-adaptive area? Can it be that the man who is participating most heavily and is receiving the most votes on Best Ideas and Guidance is provoking dislikes and losing likes? Here we note the Dislike curve. Contrary to the prediction of the working hypothesis, the top man receives *most* Dislikes, and they grade down by rank—until we come to the bottom man, and here the curve shows an upturn. The upturn is consistent with the scapegoat hypothesis.[1] Looking again at the Like curve, we note that although the second man is receiving more likes than the top man, actually both are depressed in terms of an expectation of an evenly graded curve. The new hypothesis is strengthened: there must be something about high participation and specialization in the technical and executive directions which tends to provoke hostility.

CHART 2

"Total Number of Votes Received" on each of four roles, pooled for men of each basic initiating rank as of each meeting. (Data from twelve assorted meetings of four five-man groups.)

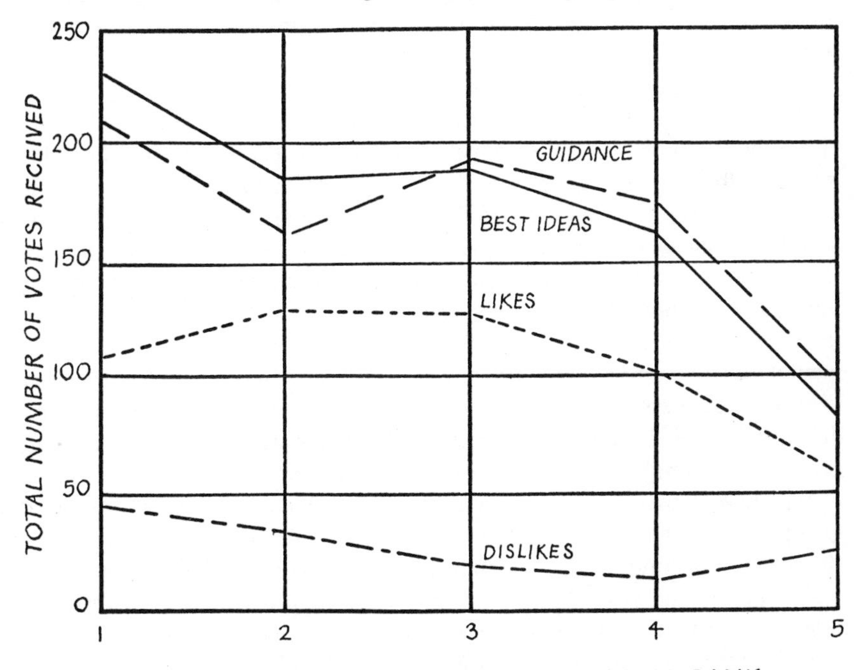

Here I think it can be seen that we are dealing with the same equilibrium problem encountered before in attempting to understand the uniformities of the profile, the matrix, and the phase movement. Movement in the instrumental-adaptive direction tends to upset the equilibrium of the system, and recovery mechanisms must be worked out if the system is to turn full cycle and regain equilibrium. The more "directive" and "constricting" the quality of activity, the more likely it is to arouse negative reactions. If a man begins to specialize noticeably in this direction, the

[1] Similar curves are found in 3 and 4-man groups. The 6-man groups introduce a special complication at a level of subtlety which is inappropriate to these preliminary generalizations.

negative reactions tend to be centered on him. The displacement of hostilities on a scapegoat at the bottom of the status structure is one mechanism, apparently, by which the ambivalent attitudes toward the instrumental-adaptive specialist—the "top man"—can be diverted and drained off. The centering of positive affect on a secondary man is another mechanism by which the solidarity of the group—its integration as a collectivity of persons—can be re-established. Such a man can be warm, receptive, responsive, and rewarding, can "conciliate" and "bind up the wounds," without diverting the movement of the system too far from the kind of movement in the instrumental-adaptive direction which is also felt to be necessary. He can do this because he does not assume the "responsibility" for the movement of the system in these directions, but leaves this to the technical or executive specialist.

But suppose the best liked man is not willing to do this? Suppose that his perceptions of the likes of others "goes to his head" and encourages him to begin to "take over" from the technical or executive specialist? He is in a position to command considerable support, and the "top man" is in a vulnerable position because of the latent or overt hostility centered on him. Or suppose, on the other hand, that the top man is emotionally unable to stand the hostility, or is unable to tolerate the fact that not he, but another, is best liked? The top man is under strains, we might suppose, to try to "undercut" his nearest rival. Here are the seeds of a fundamental status struggle, exceedingly damaging, in potentiality, both for the instrumental-adaptive achievement of the group, and for its affective integration. This, as I see it now, is the core of the status struggle we see our groups go through in the course of their four meetings. The first meeting is typically rather cautious and tentative, and such "simply organized groups" as we do find, tend to be found at the end of this meeting. With the second meeting, the role structure which has crystallized, if at all, in the first meeting, is challenged in a status struggle which may result in either confirmation of the first structure, or an exchange of status positions between the top two or three men. If the original structure "holds up," the group may begin to "level out," and the status struggle slacks off. If a new man comes to the top, the *new* structure is challenged in the third meeting. Some groups apparently arrive at a fairly stable differentiated structure, others never do. Things go "from bad to worse," with a last meeting that breaks records for disagreement, antagonism, tension, perhaps tension release, and other signs of serious strains and an inability to achieve an equilibrated role structure. However, the stable structure is never, in our data, a "simply organized" one. It is rather one in which differentiated roles have appeared, in which one specialist "undoes" the disturbance to equilibrium created by another, and in turn is dependent upon another to remove the strains he himself creates—the total constellation of specialists being one which allows or aids the system to establish a full orbit in its dimensions of necessary movement.

Furthermore, there are probably "typical" solutions which tend to be found with considerable frequency, and may in older and more permanent types of groups, give rise to cultural arrangements and supporting symbol constellations including explicit ritual. Three constellations which are exceedingly ubiquitous, in a cross-cultural sense, come to mind as possibly significant in this connection. They are incest taboos, totem taboos and rituals, and scapegoat patterns. In the experimental small-group setting, of course, nothing concretely resembling these exceedingly complicated and elaborate cultural complexes appears, but certain functional equivalents may be possible.

There is some reason to believe that one possible arrangement by which the status struggle between the top instrumental-adaptive leader and the best liked man can be prevented or stabilized is the formation of a kind of "coalition" between them, such that the two tacitly agree, as it were, not to undercut each other, which is to say, not to be "seduced" into attempting to form a coalition with lower status members in order to displace each other. If such a coalition can be formed, it becomes quite difficult for lower status members to revolt, unseat the top men, or develop the norms of the group in any different direction.

Does this bear any resemblance, in functional terms, to the incest taboo as a cognate mechanism in the nuclear family? Is the incest taboo, at least in certain of its aspects, a kind of coalition between the father (in some family systems comparable to the senior technical and executive specialist) and the mother (similarly often the first major target of positive affect)? Such a coalition could be a powerful mechanism for forcing the socialization of the child, by putting him in a position where he must accept the authority and values of the father in order to obtain gratification, rather than allowing him to retain and overdevelop an affectively gratifying relation to the mother which would leave him insufficient incentive to acquire the skills, values, and other characteristics of the adult role. It may well be, I think, that the ubiquity of the incest taboo as it applies in the nuclear family, is simply another case of the much more general equilibrium problem.

Similarly with totem taboos and rituals. This is not the place for an adequate attempt to examine the problem, but the killing of the totem on certain ritual occasions is certainly suggestive of a ritual display of aggression against the principal authority figures, and the eating of the totem can be viewed as an "undoing"—a reacceptance of the target of aggression after all. In some cases, as Frazier documents at length, the king himself is killed—the king becomes the scapegoat. In many other cases, as we know, some low status person or group is victimized. These facts are well known, and on one level, fairly well understood. The only new emphasis here, if any, is the suggestion that these patterns, culturally elaborated and various in form, can be viewed as particular cases of mechanisms relevant to the much more general problem of equilibrium, which has cognates on every level, from the most microscopic to the most macroscopic.

REFERENCES

1. Bales, R. F. A set of categories for the analysis of small group interaction. *Amer. sociol. Rev.*, 1950, 15, 257–263.
2. Bales, R. F. *Interaction process analysis: A method for the study of small groups.* Cambridge, Mass.: Addison-Wesley, 1950.
3. Bales, R. F. Some statistical problems of small group research. *J. Amer. statist. Assn.*, 1951, 46, 311–322.
4. Bales, R. F., & Strodtbeck, F. L. Phases in group problem solving. *J. abnorm. soc. Psychol.*, 1951, 46, 485–495.
5. Bales, R. F., Strodtbeck, F. L., Mills, T. M., & Roseborough, Mary E. Channels of communication in small groups. *Amer. sociol. Rev.*, 1951, 16, 461–468.
6. Bass, B. H. An analysis of leaderless group discussion. *J. appl. Psychol.*, 1949, 33, 527–533.
7. Festinger, L., & Thibaut, J. Interpersonal communication in small groups. In L. Festinger, et al., *Theory and experiment in social communication.* Ann Arbor: Research Center for Group Dynamics, Univer. of Michigan, 1950. Pp. 37–49.
8. Keller, J. B. Comment on "Channels of communication in small groups." *Amer. sociol. Rev.*, 1951, 16, 842–843.
9. Lippitt, R. An experimental study of authoritarian and democratic group atmospheres. *Stud. Topolog. Vector Psychol., Univer. Ia. Stud. Child Welf.*, 1950, 16, No. 1.
10. Murray, H. A. Toward a classification of interactions. In T. Parsons, & E. A. Shils (Eds.), *Toward a general theory of action.* Cambridge, Mass.: Harvard Univer. Press, 1951. Pp. 434–464.
11. Norfleet, Barbara. Interpersonal relations and group productivity. *J. soc. Issues*, 1948, 4 (2), 66–69.
12. Rogers, C. R. Counselling and psychotherapy: New concepts in practice. Boston: Houghton Mifflin, 1942.
13. Strodtbeck, F. L. Husband-wife interaction over revealed differences. *Amer. sociol. Rev.*, 1951, 16, 468–473.

Task and Interaction Process: Some Characteristics of Therapeutic Group Discussion

GEORGE A. TALLAND

BALES' (1) *interaction process analysis* furnishes a valuable technique for analyzing and also for constructing models of small group functioning. Records based on problem-solving discussions in the laboratory have suggested to Bales (2) certain significant empirical uniformities in group interaction which, for heuristic purposes, he treats as a closed system. To the extent that such situational variables as membership composition, motivation, expectancies, task set and conditions of performance differ from those in the laboratory debate, predictions can be made about the areas and directions in which the process of interaction will deviate from Bales' model in other types of group discussion.

Psychotherapy groups, for instance, differ from experimental problem-solving groups in several clearly marked respects. They meet in order to discover problems rather than to solve one neatly formulated for their attention; they neither have to reach a solution nor must they finally close a case unresolved at the end of a meeting. Insofar as the psychotherapeutic technique stresses spontaneity, the discussion is allowed a free course, wheras in the laboratory its trend is implicitly determined by the task even in the absence of directive chairmanship. Finally, discussing a hypothetical or didactic case and a transient acquaintance do not lead to deep emotional involvements that occur when patients grapple with their own

ABRIDGED from *Journal of Abnormal and Social Psychology*, 1955, 50, 105–109. Reprinted by permission of the author and the American Psychological Association, Inc.

The author wishes to express his appreciation of the valuable help and constructive criticism he received from Dr. R. F. Bales of Harvard University in this research which was carried out at the University of London Institute of Psychiatry, Maudsley Hospital.

and each other's personal problems, baring their inmost thoughts and experiences week after week in intimate fellowship. Consequently the process of interaction would be expected to differ in the two situations, and more particularly in such dynamic aspects of the model as the phase sequence of acts indicated by and the equilibrium properties of the interaction system inferred from observations made in laboratory debates.

By analyzing the proportionate shares within the total interaction of acts registered as informative, evaluative or control, Bales and Strodtbeck (3) traced a consistent shift of emphasis in the course of a typical problem-solving discussion. Dividing meetings into three phases, orientation reached its peak in the first, evaluation in the second, control in the third. Since these groups are instructed to reach some solution by the end of a meeting and since each member enters with some piece of information on the case, which he may believe to be different from and complementary to his fellow members' information, the phase sequence is logically indicated. In therapy groups the pressure of time is much milder and the problems, so far from being clearly formulated at the outset, are expected to emerge as the discussion proceeds; the meeting, however, is unlikely to conclude with a solution or control of these problems. The probability of the problem solving phase sequence occurring here is therefore, no higher than that of any other or of no phase sequence whatever.

Bales' (2) other dynamic principle of the interaction process conceives of the group discussion as progressing by cycles, each of which begins with the introduction and ends with the resolution of a disturbance. His empirical findings closely correspond to the theoretical model which, here again, is logically dictated by the situation. If problem-solving groups are to succeed within the time available for discussion, they must indeed proceed in this manner; they cannot leave unresolved a conflict over a relevant issue and they cannot well afford to discuss irrelevances. In problem-solving debates the aim is to resolve a disturbance initially introduced by the experimenter; in therapy groups the very purpose of the discussion is to maintain disturbance at a level throughout, and to bring it back to that level if it has flagged. The patient must talk or listen to talk about disturbing personal problems; in order to benefit by group therapy he must be emotionally involved in it. If, as it periodically happens, the discussion drops below the required degree of affective involvement and consequent disturbance, the therapist regards this event as a manifestation of resistance, and not as a state of equilibrium to be maintained. In these groups therefore, the sequel to an initial act is not necessarily nor preferably an equilibrating response. Disturbances are introduced all the time to provide the groups with tasks and are generated spontaneously through personal interaction. Therapy groups are not unique in this respect; many political, committee or board meetings start with little more than a formal agenda, and would soon peter out if some disturbance were not introduced into them by personal interaction, or do come to a premature end for the lack of it.

SUBJECTS: PROCEDURE

As part of a research on psychotherapy groups, interaction process analysis was applied to four groups, of 6 to 8 members excluding the therapist, during the first eight weeks of therapy. Observations made over a total of 18 meetings, each lasting 90 minutes, were analyzed for the purposes of the present report. The groups met once weekly at the Maudsley Hospital, London, and were conducted by psychiatrists according to the principles of *group analytic psychotherapy* (4, 6). Their members were outpatients suffering from psychoneuroses; they were between 23 and 45 years of age, of high average or higher intelligence, the men in most instances clerical workers, the women with few exceptions not occupied outside their homes.

Records of interaction were kept according to Bales' (1) method, but only of verbal acts. Although all observations were made while the meeting was in progress, those registering tension and tension release were not thought to be sufficiently reliable, and these categories were therefore entirely omitted. The very scarce antagonistic acts were bracketed with disagreements. For the analysis of phase sequences the interaction records were divided into three equal time sections, each representing a thirty minute phase of a meeting. In the final analysis the corresponding phases of the 18 meetings were summated, as were the records of entire meetings, according to a classification of acts (3) into orientation, evaluation, control, positive and negative reactions, and further also attempted answers and questions. Each of these categories was tested for the presence of a consistent phase sequence by chi square, using frequency data.[1] The null hypothesis was formulated in two versions: (a) that in a given category the absolute frequencies of acts vary from phase to phase only within the limits of chance; (b) that the phase to phase variation of frequencies expressed as proportions of the total acts per phase, is within the limits of chance at the one per cent level of confidence. It was thought necessary to apply the test in both these versions, because the meetings were divided into phases by the clock and not by parcelling out the total of acts into three equal shares.

The prediction that in psychotherapy groups discussion does not tend

1 Bales and Strodtbeck (3) used rankings of phases in preference to frequency values, and tested goodness of fit to prediction by the number of transpositions required. This method may give undue importance to numerically small differences, and moreover in the final analysis allows equal weight to all the categories, however small or large their share in the total interaction. In the present study this method would have had the additional disadvantage of providing no information beyond the finding that one particular phase sequence does not apply.

towards equilibrium was tested by fitting the category profile based on observed data to that of Bales' theoretical model.

RESULTS

Average frequencies of acts per phase in therapy groups are given in Table 1 according to the combined categories used by Bales and Strodtbeck.

It is quite apparent that positive reactions, attempted answers and questions keep on a level throughout, and indeed the observed frequencies fit an equal threefold division more closely than could happen by chance once in a hundred instances, testing either version of the null hypothesis.

TABLE 1

Phase Movement of Categories

	MEAN FREQUENCIES PER PHASE		
	I	II	III
Positive reactions	15.56	16.89	15.33
Control (suggestions)	6.44	10.72	8.33
Evaluation (opinions)	45.11	54.73	59.50
Orientation	170.46	159.68	159.57
Negative reactions	3.56	5.50	5.78
Attempted answers	199.79	203.12	204.95
Questions	22.22	22.00	22.45

The upward trend of negative reactions and the steep rise of control acts from the first to the second phase, followed by a partial relapse, deviate significantly from a distribution of equal frequencies, once again testing either statement of the null hypothesis. The steady increase of opinions and the initial decline of orientation to a level maintained through the second and third phases, are significantly different as deviations from the null hypothesis, in form (a) at the 2 per cent, in form (b) at the 1 per cent level of confidence.

Although trends indicated by distributions of frequencies summated over 18 meetings are of some interest, much significance should not be attached to these results. They are not typical of single meetings in the sense of being modal. Indeed, the meeting to meeting variability is so high that, even choosing the criterion of ranking phases, not a single occasion could be shown as exemplifying the phase pattern typical of the summated records in each of the categories. Bales and Strodtbeck's method of counting the transpositions required to bring rankings of phases on actual frequencies in line with the norm, necessitates at least three steps in every instance. Since the norm derived from the summated data allows for a maximum of two transpositions in one category (orientation) and three each in another three categories, each of the 18 meetings observed deviates in its phase pattern from the norm to an extent which is beyond chance, even at the five per cent level of confidence.

Whilst the theory of phase movement was derived from the analysis of actual sequences, the equilibrium principles of group interaction are based on hypothetical sequential patterns. Bales' (2) theoretical model assumes that, in a group which maintains equilibrium, half the total acts are

TABLE 2

Category Profiles

CATEGORIES	PERCENTAGE RATES OF ACTS					
	THEORETICAL * EQUILIBRIUM		LABORATORY GROUPS		THERAPY GROUPS	
		REACT.		REACT.		REACT.
Showing solidarity	3.8		3.42		2.0	
Showing tension-release	7.7		5.97		—	
Agreement	15.2		16.54		4.8	
		26.7		25.93		6.8
Giving suggestion	7.6		7.94		3.5	
Giving opinion	30.4		30.06		20.2	
Giving orientation	15.3		17.89		59.2	
		6.7		6.97		8.5
Asking for orientation	3.8		3.53		5.5	
Asking for opinion	1.9		2.39		2.3	
Asking for suggestion	1.0		1.05		0.7	
		6.7		6.97		8.5
Disagreement	7.6		7.78		1.8	
Showing tension	3.8		2.66		—	
Showing antagonism	1.9		.73		—	
		13.3		10.67		1.8
Total	100.0		99.96		100.0	
		53.4		50.54		25.6

* The theoretical values postulated for interaction tending towards equilibrium and the percentage rates of categories in problem-solving groups are based on records as yet unpublished by Dr. Bales. The latter represents averages of 96 meetings, each lasting 40 minutes.

reactive, and half of these in turn close a cycle while the remaining half start new cycles. Empirical data are so interpreted as to class all positive and negative reactions by definition as reactive, and the former also as closing a cycle. Questions and an equal number of attempted answers, i.e., those given in direct reply to questions, are also regarded as reactive. Taking this principle of classification, the category profile observed in Bales' laboratory groups closely fits the model; that characteristic of therapy group discussion, however, does not. The two category profiles expressed in percentage rates are compared in Table 2.

The most striking difference between the two profiles is the overwhelmingly large share taken up by orientational acts in therapy groups. This finding is, of course, entirely in agreement with the nature of the task this group performs, and has in itself no decisive bearing on the problem of equilibrium. Taking all the acts which according to Bales' model are reactive, the total amounts to little over a quarter of the entire interaction. The omission of nonverbal acts may account for some of the discrepancy between the profiles of the two types of group, though this would not alter the balance in favor of new disturbances as against equilibrating responses, since in psychotherapeutic discussion acts indicating tension outweigh those of tension-release. Interaction analysis thus confirms the theoretical argument that termination of disturbance occurs far less frequently in therapy than in problem-solving groups. Whether we accept the value of 6.8 as the percentage of positive reactions, or correct it for the omission of records of tension-release, it falls far below a quarter of total interaction. It is also worth noting that most acts of solidarity are expressions of identification and are typically followed (in 69 per cent of all instances) by acts of orientation, i.e., some elaboration of the information on which identification is based, and would therefore carry on the disturbance or start a new one. Also 41 per cent of all agreements are followed by negative responses, questions or opinions, and cannot therefore be considered as acts resolving a disturbance. In fact, analysing actual sequences of acts, it appears that only 61 per cent of all positive reactions, i.e., 3¼ per cent of the total interaction and about half the opinions, i.e., those followed by positive responses or orientation, are likely to close a cycle. This would allow for little over 13 per cent of the total as acts terminating a disturbance.

SUMMARY

The weekly discussions of four therapy groups were recorded by the method of *interaction process analysis*. It was predicted that, though structuring similar to that found in problem-solving groups would take place, the dynamic pattern of the process would be characteristically different in these groups, in accordance with their different task and conditions of discussion. More particularly, the research tested the hypotheses that (*1*) the control-oriented phase sequence of interaction does not apply to therapeutic group discussion, and (*2*) there is no tendency to establish equilibrium in successive cycles.

Analysis of quantified records confirms the predictions that in therapy groups there is no consistent progress from orientation through evaluation to control within single meetings, and that there is a tendency to keep disturbance at a certain level.

REFERENCES

1. Bales, R. F. *Interaction process analysis: a method for the study of small groups.* Cambridge, Mass.: Addison-Wesley Press, 1950.
2. Bales, R. F. The equilibrium problem in small groups. In T. Parsons, R. F. Bales, &

E. A. Shils, *Working papers in the theory of action.* Glencoe, Ill.: The Free Press, 1953. Pp. 111–161.
3. Bales, R. F., & Strodtbeck, F. L. Phases in group problem solving. *J abnorm. soc. Psychol.*, 1951, 46, 485–495.
4. Foulkes, S. H. *Introduction to group-analytic psychotherapy.* London: Wm. Heinemann Medical Books, 1948.
5. Talland, G. A. The working system of psychotherapy groups. *Group Psychother.*, 1954, 7, 67–80.
6. Taylor, F. K. The therapeutic factors in group-analytical treatment. *J. ment. Sci.*, 1950, 96, 967–997.

Interaction Process Analysis of the Mediation of Labor-Management Disputes

HENRY A. LANDSBERGER

A RECENT review (9) of studies of small groups concluded with the statement that the investigation of this field is flourishing and that promising research techniques are now available with which further studies could be conducted. Inspection of the research reviewed reveals, however, that most of the investigations have of necessity been confined to groups composed of college students. Subjects were often assembled only for the purpose of the experiment and the tasks facing them were frequently

FROM *Journal of Abnormal and Social Psychology*, 1955, 51, 552-558. Reprinted by permission of author and the American Psychological Association, Inc.
This article is based on a dissertation submitted in partial fulfillment of the requirements for the degree of Doctor of Philosophy at Cornell University. The writer wishes to express his appreciation to the members of his committee: W. F. Whyte, Chairman, and W. W. Lambert and U. Bronfenbrenner, members. He also wishes to thank Philip J. McCarthy for suggestions in connection with statistical work. Warmest thanks are also due Professor R. F. Bales for precious time spent in training the author in Interaction Process Analysis, as well as in discussion of its theoretical background, and to Dr. Anna G. Douglas, who made these case recordings available to me.
The initial stages of this study were financed through Contract No. 401 (04) by the Office of Naval Research. Later stages were financed by the New York State School of Industrial and Labor Relations. The help of both institutions is gratefully acknowledged.

somewhat artificial. This compounding of artificiality leaves open the question of how far the results obtained, and the methods employed, are transferable to groups in other settings. The research reported in this article is intended to contribute toward answering this question, and the groups utilized differ in almost every respect from student groups in laboratories. Each of the groups studied consisted of: (*a*) a labor mediator, (*b*) employers and their lawyers or other adjunct personnel, and (*c*) labor-union officials who were accompanied by the employees they represented in six of the twelve cases. The labor mediator's function was to assist the two parties in reaching an agreement after bipartite negotiations between them had previously broken down.

Our aim was also to help to determine whether previous findings and established techniques from the social sciences could be utilized to shed fresh, practical light on various important substantive problems which have long been under discussion in the mediation field and in the whole field of collective bargaining of which mediation is a part. With one exception (7) no empirical study of the collective bargaining process appears to have been made which employs quantitative methods based on theories from the behavioral sciences.

DATA AND SETTING

The data utilized consisted of the transcribed recordings of 12 mediation cases. The 12 cases analyzed do not constitute a random sample. They do, however, appear to be representative of the small type of case (involving enterprises with less than 25 employees) that constitutes almost half of this agency's case load. When compared with the agency's annual statistics, the cases are representative in terms of type of industry, whether a strike threat was or was not involved or whether a strike was actually in progress, the type of settlement reached, etc.

Each of the 12 cases analyzed was settled or adjourned sine die at the end of only one meeting—the one recorded. This is fortunate from an analytical point of view, because it makes these meetings comparable to the single, complete group meetings customarily utilized in psychological experiments. It is accounted for by the fact that neither the owner-employers nor the employees involved in these small cases are in a position to stand the costs of a strike, or even of prolonged negotiations.

Mediation is practiced both by a Federal agency established for this purpose—the Federal Mediation and Conciliation Service—and by agencies established by a few individual states. Each mediator—at least in the state agency here studied—has his own office much as does a counselor, and it is chiefly in these rooms that the mediation process takes place. The mediator, it should be noted, differs from an arbitrator. The latter typically hears a case much as does a judge, and thereafter makes a formal award. The mediator does not make an award; he clarifies, persuades, and suggests as seems appropriate. Because cases vary, so does the behavior of the mediator (6) and depending on the nature of the case and his personality, he may say very little in one instance, dominate the proceedings in another. Resort to mediation as far as the state agency here studied is concerned, is generally not on the motion of the agency but at the request of one of the parties—usually at the union's request.

METHOD OF ANALYSIS

Interaction Process Analysis

Interaction Process Analysis (2) was selected as the most satisfactory method for classifying verbal behavior in these small face-to-face groups. It has the advantage of permitting statistical treatment to be given to such behavior while yet retaining its grosser meaning. Moreover, results obtained with the method so far (1, 3, 4) were presented by the originator of the method with the avowed purpose of providing a series of quantitative base lines, discrepancies from which were to serve as "indicators of the personalities, culture and role organization of the participants, since these are sets of conditions which influence the way interaction actually goes" (5, p. 8). Making such a comparison was the purpose of the research reported here; hence the availability of such base-line data made the selection of this particular method even more logical.

No reliability check was made on the author's scoring of the sessions, chiefly because of limitations of time, resources, and persons who could be trained in the method in order to enable such a check to be made. However, the author received training in the method over a period of a week directly from R. F. Bales, from whose laboratory interscorer reliability of between .75 and .95 is reported (4, p. 150). In view of this fact, and in view of the fact that an investigator without such training in the method achieved satisfactory reliability (8, p. 68), it seems justifiable to assume that the reliability of the scoring in this study is adequate.

Ranking of Cases by Success

The 12 cases were ranked for "success" on the basis of how far the issues with which the parties had embarked on the mediation session were settled at the end of the session.

The full description of the cases presented elsewhere (6) makes it clear that while doubt may exist as between cases with closely similar ranks, substantial and unmistakable differences exist between the most successful cases, those in the middle, and the unsuccessful ones. These rankings were made after the cases had been scored, but before crucial data had been computed from these scores and cases compared with respect to such data and the ranking.

THE PHASE MOVEMENT IN A NONLABORATORY SITUATION

The application to our 12 mediation cases of base-line data and hypotheses, which Bales and Strodtbeck termed "the phase movement" (3), constituted the first step in testing whether the results of Interaction Process Analysis and its related theories had any meaning in situations other than the laboratory.

The "phase movement," or rather the hypothesis that such a movement occurs, consists of the following five predictions:

a. that the percentage which the two orientation categories (giving and asking for information) form of all interactions will progressively decrease from a peak at the beginning of a group meeting;

b. that the percentage which the two evaluation (opinion) categories form of all interactions will be at a peak during the middle of a group meeting and lowest at the beginning;

c. that the two suggestion categories will increase progressively toward a peak at the end;

d. that the sum of the three positive social-emotional categories will increase progressively to reach a peak at the end;

e. that the sum of the three negative social-emotional categories will likewise rise progressively to reach its highest point during the final phase of the meeting.

Bales and Strodtbeck reasoned that such sequences followed both the logic of, and the emotional reactions of individuals to, the process of successful problem solving. Thus the authors reasoned that despite ultimate relief (high final positive social-emotional interaction) at the solution of a problem, heightened tension would accompany the actual decision-making, commitment-requiring, process (heightened final negative interactions). The authors also felt, however, that tendencies toward this type of phase movement might be found in all groups—even those not solving a problem, or not even faced with a specific problem. Bales and Strodtbeck therefore considered the possibility that "certain conditions . . . more or less inherent in the nature of the process of interaction or communication . . . exert a constant biasing effect," (3, p. 493) so as to make the "phase movement" tend to appear.

To test whether the phase movement was in fact related to successful problem solving outside of a laboratory situation, we validated the appearance of the movement against the cases ranked in terms of success of outcome (Table 1, last column). Each of the 12 cases was inspected for the extent to which it deviated from the hypothesized phase movement. The number of transpositions required to convert the actual movement in the case into the hypothesized one was then calculated (See Table 1) in accordance with the method suggested by Bales and Strodtbeck (3, pp. 491–492).

TABLE 1

Hypothesized and Actual Phase Movement, and Number of Transpositions Required to Establish the Hypothesized Phase Movement for the Twelve Cases, for the Five types of Acts, Together with Rank of Case for Success of Outcome

CASE	HYPOTHESIZED PHASE MOVEMENT	TYPE OF ACT: ORIENTATION HML	EVALUATION LHM	SUGGESTION[a] LMH	NEGATIVE LMH	POSITIVE LMH	TOTAL TRANSPOSITIONS REQUIRED	RANK OF CASE FOR SUCCESS OF OUTCOME
A1	Transpositions required	1	0	1	2	0	4	11
	Actual movement	(HLM)		(LHM)	(MHL)			
A2	Transpositions required	0	1	0	1	0	2[b]	2
	Actual movement		(HLM)		(LHM)			
A3	Transpositions required	1	3	0	0	2	6	8
	Actual movement	(HLM)	(MHL)			(MHL)		
A4	Transpositions required	1	1	1	2	0	5	5
	Actual movement	(HLM)	(LHM)	(MLH)	(MHL)			
B1	Transpositions required	1	2	1½	1	2	7½[c]	10
	Actual movement	(MHL)	(MLH)	(——)	(LHM)	(HLM)		
B2	Transpositions required	0	1	½	0	0	1½[bc]	4
	Actual movement		(LMH)	(– – H)				
B3	Transpositions required	0	0	0	1	0	1[b]	1
	Actual movement				(LHM)			
B4	Transpositions required	2	3	1½	2	0	8½[c]	6
	Actual movement	(MLH)	(MHL)	(– H –)	(MHL)			
C1	Transpositions required	1	0	1	2	0	4	12
	Actual movement	(HLM)		(LHM)	(MHL)			
C2	Transpositions required	0	1	1½	0	0	2½[bc]	9
	Actual movement		(LMH)	(– H –)				
C3	Transpositions required	0	0	0	1	0	1[b]	3
	Actual movement				(LHM)			
D1	Transpositions required	0	1	0	1	2	4	7
	Actual movement		(LMH)		(LHM)	(HLM)		

[a] In cases where no suggestions were made in the entire case, or in any one of three parts of the sessions, the number of transpositions to be expected by chance was taken as the actual sequence.
[b] Significant congruence with phase movement, at or beyond the .05 level.
[c] When combining the 12 independent tests, totals containing halves were increased to the next whole number (e.g., 7½ became 8).

The cases were ranked according to the number of transpositions required (See Table 1, next to last column). It was then reasoned that if conformity to the phase movement was indicative of the successful solution of problems, then the ranking of cases according to number of transpositions required should correlate with the ranking of our cases in terms of success of outcome. This rank correlation was computed and a rho of .58 (significant beyond the .05 level) obtained. We deduce that for our sample the phase movement was to some extent a valid index of the successful solution of the dispute with which the parties came to mediation.

As an example of new light that may be thrown on the mediation process by this otherwise rather microscopic method, we may examine the deviations from the phase movement which occurred. In the three least successful cases: (*a*) suggestions were not highest at the end, (*b*) nor was negative activity at its highest in these cases, while (*c*) in two of the three least successful cases, positive activity did attain a peak, and (*d*) the evaluation (opinion) categories fell off toward the end. We interpret this as possibly indicating that the parties had rather amicably agreed to continue their disagreement at least for the time being, and that they therefore refrained at the end from making suggestions or offering opinions which would only have been acrimoniously rejected.

Second, the general tendency of the negative categories to decline toward the end should be noted. It may indicate that these mediation sessions serve a catharsis function for the parties in successful and unsuccessful cases alike.

THE PREVALENCE OF THE PHASE MOVEMENT AND ITS MEANING

The method suggested by Bales and Strodtbeck (3, Table 4, p. 492) for calculating whether a series of meetings, taken as a whole, conformed to the phase movement was then applied to our data. Table 2 presents the parallel calculations.

The sum 74.71 given in the lower right of Table 2 is chi square and the appropriate number of degrees of freedom is $2n$, in this case 24. Since the .05 value for chi square with 24 *df* is 43.00, it is legitimate to reject the null hypothesis that the distribution of phase sequences is random.

The interpretation of this result is made more difficult by the existence of the two alternative causes for it that were described above. The more interesting of the two is the first one: to take the prevalence of the phase movement throughout our cases as indicating that they were by and large successfully resolved, relative differences between them notwithstanding. Such an interpretation would follow from the assumption that the phase movement occurs only when specific problems are successfully solved.

TABLE 2

Combination of Independent Tests of Phase Hypothesis

TRANSPOSITION (*a*)	$2 \log. \frac{1}{p}$ (*b*)	FREQUENCY (*c*)	$b \times c$ (*d*)
0	17.9176	0	0
1	13.1218	2	26.24
2	9.6958	2	19.39
3	7.0765	1	7.08
4	5.0389	3	15.11
5	3.4608	1	3.46
6	2.2633	1	2.26
7	1.3863	0	0.00
8	0.7787	1	0.78
9	0.3897	1	0.39
10–15		0	0.00
Total		12	74.71

This interpretation would imply that many minor and rather subtle issues may have been resolved in the course of even a so-called "unsuccessful" mediation session. While insufficient for overt agreement on, e.g. a new contract, sufficient progress may have been made in these "unsuccessful" meetings to permit precisely that "temporary agreement to disagree" that we noted in the previous section.

A high level of success in resolving disputes would be in accord with two items of knowledge which we possess independent of our interaction data. First, the agency from which these cases were drawn is known to have a high rate of success and is very highly regarded by experts in the field. Second, the mediation of labor disputes from small companies is likely to be frequently successful, both because the negotiators can make decisions on the spot, and because each side lives so close to the economic margin that the cost of prolonged strife—and even of prolonged negotiating—becomes prohibitive. The phase movement might lend itself, therefore, to measure differences in success both as between one agency and another, and between one type of case and another, once its validity as an index of success has been further substantiated.

The second, alternative cause for our finding the phase movement as hypothesized by Bales and Strodtbeck would be that it is intrinsic to group interaction. If one wishes to maintain this explanation (and we cannot exclude either it or the alternative to it), then the present study would certainly constitute a substantial confirmation. For the groups here studied differ profoundly from the groups reported on by Bales and Strodtbeck, however much the latter groups may have differed from each other. In each of the following respects, mediation groups differ from those utilized by Bales, made up largely of students previously unacquainted with each other.

1. The mediation groups consisted of adults whose roles are culturally defined in terms such that one role differs greatly from the other.

2. The parties (employer, employees, and union officials) in each mediation group had developed expectations of each other over time, and these, of course, differed from group to group.

3. The mediation groups seemed frequently to convene not only in order to deal with specific problems, but also for the purpose of ventilating their pent-up annoyance with each other. They often met, in part at least, explicitly to engage in that type of expressive behavior which would preclude the appearance of the phase movement if the latter occurred only in groups intent upon solving specific problems (see 3, p. 487).

4. The members of the mediation groups dealt with problems of very great personal significance to each of them, on the resolution of which they were deeply divided.

The conclusion which may be drawn from the above two sections is as follows: the tendency toward the production of the phase movement may or may not be an inevitable concomitant of any group interaction. But certainly the *magnitude* of its appearance is related to the resolution of specific problems in the course of such group interaction (Alternative 1).

THE SUCCESS OF THE MEDIATION SESSION AND THE PARTIES' RELATIONSHIP

Bales and Strodtbeck, in the article already cited (3), went further than merely to postulate an association between the phase movement on the one hand and successful problem solving on the other. They hypothesized also that a group could not be successful in solving a problem unless the relationship of group members to each other was sufficiently strong and positive to make ultimate agreement a desirable goal, and temporary tension bearable but at the same time something to reduce.

To test this hypothesis, with its interesting implications for collective bargaining, we selected the parties' interactions during the first part of the mediation session as an index of the relationship of group members to each other. The parties' interactions with each other were considered to be the most crucial (as compared with activity directed toward, or coming from the mediator, or intraparty activity). Interaction at the beginning, rather than at any other period, was used because interparty interactions at that time were most likely to be representative of the parties' state of mind prior to coming to mediation, and least influenced by the progress of the session or the activities of the mediator. The results of rank correlations between initial interparty relationship and success of outcome is given in Table 3. This table also contains correlations between success of outcome and interparty interaction during other phases of the mediation session, and for the session as a whole.

Inspection of the table shows that, among the positive social-emotional categories, success is correlated significantly with support, not at the beginning but only at the end of the session. This association is very likely attributable to the parties' relief over having achieved agreement. Otherwise, however, correlations for the positive categories seem to fluctuate around zero.

TABLE 3

Rank Correlations Between Success of Outcome and Percentages of Interparty Emotional Interaction for Beginning and other Parts of Mediation Session

INTERACTION CATEGORY	BEGINNING OF SESSION	MIDDLE OF SESSION	END OF SESSION	SESSION AS A WHOLE
1—Support	+.07	−.28	+.63*	−.10
3—Agreement	−.29	+.30	+.25	+.07
10—Disagreement	−.27	−.38	−.55*	−.55*
12—Hostility	−.58*	−.38	−.26	−.50

* Significant beyond the 5% level.

The negative categories, however, show a more consistent trend. First, we may note the high correlation between factual disagreement at the end of the session, and lack of success at the end of the session. This indicates that the rate of activity in the disagreement category may actually be a valid measure of broader interparty disagreement on the issues in dispute.

The most important figure, however, seems to be the significant correlation between initial interparty hostility (as an index of the parties' relationship) and final success. This association is the one for which we were looking. It indicates that the parties' prior state of mind—as thus measured—does indeed bear a relationship to the outcome of the mediation session.

It is open to speculation whether the initial hostility is symptomatic of a generally poor interparty relationship that makes settlement of specific issues more difficult, or whether intense but temporary disagreement (prior to mediation) over specific issues is the cause both of hostility and of ultimate failure. The figures in Table 3 seem to indicate that the former explanation is somewhat more likely. For if disagreement over specific issues rather than generalized hostility were the cause of failure, then the former would be more closely related to failure than the latter. This, however, is not the case: disagreement is negatively correlated with success only to the extent of −.27, while hostility is correlated to the significant degree of −.58. As the difference between these two correlation coefficients is not significant, our conclusion must be highly tentative.

INVESTIGATING THE QUALITY OF THE PARTIES' RELATIONSHIP TO EACH OTHER

If greater or lesser hostility between the parties is correlated with less or greater success, and if we have previously found that the disputes here studied may be regarded as generally successfully resolved, can we now find indications that the relationship between the parties is "generally" good?

TABLE 4

Comparison of Bales' Percentage Rates and Suggested Limits for Four Social Emotional Categories, with Average Percentage Rates and Ranges Obtained for Interparty Interaction in the 12 Mediation Cases*

INTERACTION CATEGORY	PERCENTAGES		BALES SUGGESTED LIMITS		RANGES FOR MEDIATION CASES	
	Bales	*Mediation Cases*	*Low*	*High*	*Low*	*High*
Support	1.0	3.2	0.0	5.0	0.6	5.8
Agreement	12.2	8.9	6.0	20.0	3.4	19.9
Disagreement	6.6	15.8	3.0	13.0	7.5	35.4
Hostility	2.4	13.5	0.0	7.0	3.6	39.6

* From R. F. Bales, A set of categories for the analysis of small group interaction, *Amer. sociol. Rev.*, 1950, 15, 257–263. Limits were established by Bales by the use of binomial confidence limits as given in Snedocor, *Statistical methods*, 1946, p. 4. P="percentage of total" and $n=100$. The actual variance of Bales' sample was not used, because it was known to be heterogeneous. See p. 262 of his reference cited above.

The data for making a judgment on this point consist of a comparison between the base-line group profile published by Bales (1), with the typical profile of a mediation session. The crucial figures are again likely to be the relationship of the parties to each other rather than the interactions which occur within each side, or between the sides and the mediator. Also, our interest at this point is in the nature of the average relationship between the parties summed over all cases. To measure this average relationship, we once again utilize only interactions in the four crucial social-emotional categories, omitting interparty interaction in the task area categories. The comparison is presented in Table 4.

The table shows, as is only to be expected, that interaction between the parties in a mediation session is substantially more hostile and characterized by somewhat more disagreement than is the case for the types of student groups from which the base-line data were obtained. The significant result, however, is that interaction between the disputants in the

"Support" category is not only not lower, but is actually more than three times as high as the average suggested by Bales (3.2 as compared with 1.0). The high hostility, together with the relative high rate of support, may indicate that the relationship between the parties in these cases is a strong emotional one with very definite positive as well as negative elements. It is not—as it may be in other types of disputes—an affectively neutral or purely negative relationship. Both a qualitative, clinical interpretation of the cases and a priori reasoning would support such an interpretation. The participants in these cases were not specialist staff representatives of each side who meet only once a year and otherwise have no contact with each other. In these small disputes, the owner-employers themselves were present, and knew and were known both by their employees (also frequently present) and by union officials. Despite the very real resentment that one side felt toward the other over several or even all aspects of their relationship, there was at the same time frequently a good deal of equally real warmth shown.

This finding may have some bearing on the interpretation of the previously found result that the phase movement seems to be present throughout our group of cases. The interpretation that this phenomenon may be due to a generally high level of success is reinforced by our finding that one of the preconditions to success—a sufficiently strong relationship—does indeed seem to exist. This in no way precludes the alternative explanation: it only establishes the possibility of this one being true also.

SUMMARY

Interaction Process Analysis was applied to 12 recorded labor-management mediation cases. This was done with the purpose of exploring (*a*) whether findings obtained in somewhat artificial student groups could be replicated in this very different type of group, and (*b*) whether utilization of the method could be of some help in answering questions of real practical significance in the collective bargaining field.

It was found that the extent to which a mediation session went through a hypothesized phase movement was of some validity in indicating the extent to which specific items in dispute between the parties were resolved.

Secondly, it was found that ultimate success of the session could be partially predicted from the parties' state of mind when they embarked upon the session: the more hostile their expressed feelings, the less likelihood of success.

Thirdly, it was found that the phase movement occurred generally in our cases, not only in the most successful cases. A possible explanation for this is that the phase movement occurs in the course of any group interaction. However, the alternative explanation—that it occurs only if groups disband after successfully solving their problem—is in this instance also a possible one. Our reason for thinking so is that one of the preconditions of successful problem solving in small groups—a generally good relationship between the disputants—was found to be present in these cases.

REFERENCES

1. Bales, R. F. A set of categories for the analysis of small group interaction. *Amer. social. Rev.*, 1950, 15, 257–263.
2. Bales, R. F. *Interaction process analysis.* Boston: Addison Wesley Press, 1950.
3. Bales, R. F., & Strodtbeck, F. L. Phases in group problem-solving. *J. abnorm. soc. Psychol.*, 1951, 46, 485–495.
4. Bales, R. F. Some uniformities of behavior in small social systems. In G. E. Swanson, T. M. Newcomb, and E. L. Hartley (Eds.), *Readings in social psychology.* New York: Holt, 1952, 146–159.
5. Bales, R. F. Some uniformities of behavior in small social systems. Unpublished manuscript, Dept. of Social Relations, Harvard Univer., 1952.
6. Landsberger, H. A. A study of mediation through an analysis of the background of disputes and the activities of the mediators. Unpublished doctor's dissertation, Cornell Univer., 1954.
7. Osterberg, W. A method for the study of bargaining conferences. *Personnel Psychol.*, 1950, 3, 169–178.
8. Pease, Damaris. The relationship between homogeneity of growth pattern and social interaction in preadolescence. Unpublished doctor's dissertation, Cornell Univer., 1953.
9. Roseborough, Mary E. Experimental studies of small groups. *Psychol. Bull.*, 1953, 50, 275–303.

CHAPTER 9

GROUP SIZE

Size of Group as a Factor in the Interaction Profile

ROBERT F. BALES
and
EDGAR F. BORGATTA

THIS is a report of the effects of group size on the kind of social interaction of members within the group. The report has two major purposes. The first purpose is to analyze certain observed variations in social interaction by group size in order to develop and systematize a set of substantive hypotheses about the effects of group size. Group size has been a focus of interest in the social sciences for a very long time, and the present study draws on earlier theory and research for many of the basic hypotheses advanced.[1]

This report is the first of several on a study of group size. The research was facilitated by the Laboratory of Social Relations, Harvard University. The planning and execution of the larger study was done by a team of researchers, who have consulted and advised on the present report. The team includes Philip E. Slater, Arthur S. Couch, Bernard P. Cohen, Nathan Altshuler, Richard D. Mann, and in the early stages, Christoph M. Heinicke. We are grateful to Hugh Williams and Jonathan Robbin for work on the extensive computation required for this report.

1 Citations to the relevant literature are common in later small groups reports and are thus omitted here.

The second purpose is to present basic data from which interaction norms for further diagnostic and experimental purposes can easily be prepared. A series of groups of sizes two through seven were observed using Bales' method of interaction process analysis (1).[2] According to this method every observed act of verbal and non-verbal communication between members is classified into one of twelve categories, which in turn combine into four major types. *Questions* consist of asking for orientation, opinion, and suggestion (categories 7, 8, and 9). *Problem Solving Attempts* consist of giving orientation, opinion, and suggestion (categories 6, 5, and 4). *Positive Reactions* consist of showing agreement, tension release, and solidarity (categories 3, 2, and 1). *Negative Reactions* consist of showing disagreement, tension, and antagonism (categories 10, 11, and 12). The person who performs the act, and the person(s) to whom it is addressed are also recorded. A number of studies have been completed using this method and there is a need for norms in a standard test situation in order to extend its usefulness as a diagnostic device.

THE SAMPLE AND THE DESIGN

The members of the groups were all male students drawn from the university employment office and paid for their time. No special attempt was made to compose groups of given characteristics, except that the requirement was made that members should not know each other previous to the first meeting. Pairs who were previously acquainted were put in separate groups. Persons who said they could not continue for the full four sessions were rejected. A number of groups were lost nevertheless, because of unavoidable drop outs. New groups were run to replace the broken groups. Groups of each size, two through seven, were observed. Each group of persons met for four sessions, each session with the identical membership. There were four groups of each size. The total number of persons participating was thus 108, and the total number of sessions from which data are drawn was 96.[3]

THE TASK OF THE GROUPS

The task of each session was the discussion of a human relations case, a five page presentation of facts about a problem facing an administrator in his organization. Members were given copies of the case separately, to

2 Bales was the only observer present through the entire series, which required more than two years to complete. A second observer was nearly always present, and data on reliability will be the subject of one of the reports of the series. In order to avoid the introduction of variability due to change in scorers, Bales' observations alone were used for this study.

3 At a late stage of analysis, it was found that the coded information was improperly entered for one six man group. As necessary, the data for the six man groups are reduced in this presentation.

read ahead of time, and were told that although each was given accurate information, we intended to leave them uncertain as to whether they each had exactly the same range of facts. The cases were collected after they had been read by the members individually, to prevent direct comparison of typed copies, although members were allowed to take notes. The task defined for each session was to assemble the information, to discuss why the people involved were behaving as they did, and to decide what should be recommended as action for the solution to the problem presented. Four quite similar cases were used to provide each group with a different but comparable task each session.[4] For each group size, a Latin square design was utilized to randomize any possible effect on developmental trends in the groups because of the particular human relations cases used. The groups were asked to time themselves to 40 minutes, and to dictate the group solution for the sound record in the final one or two minutes of the meeting. There was some variation in the time taken, since the groups were not arbitrarily stopped at the 40 minute limit.

TRANSFORMATION OF THE DATA

The data consist originally of a raw number of acts recorded in each of the twelve categories, called a raw profile, per member, per session. Profiles for sessions and groups are obtained by adding the appropriate raw member profiles. For the analysis, any raw profile to be examined, whether of an individual or a group, is then converted to a percentage profile by finding the percentage of the total number of acts in the profile that is contained in each of the twelve categories. This operation thus standardizes all profiles for time differences and for differences in the total number of acts contained in the profile. Certain effects which might be called artifacts result from this procedure, as will be pointed out in the analysis.

Time rates would be preferable for certain purposes, but since we desired to study variability as well as means, of categories, individuals, groups, and sessions, percentage rates have a certain advantage. Time rates for most of the categories do not give normal distributions. Percentage rates, however, can be converted to distributions that are approximately normal, by the arcsine transformation. The square root of each percentage rate is transformed to its corresponding arcsine angle.[5] The distribution

4 Copies of the four cases and complete instructions to subjects will be provided to persons who may wish to use them as tasks for various experimental or diagnostic purposes. The task and instructions were prepared in such a way as to provide a basic situation for which norms could be constructed, and within which a large number of experimental variations could be introduced.

5 This procedure is described simply in Snedecor (7). In our analysis the transformation was done by using the first five steps of the approximation series. The degree of accuracy obtained is sufficient for our purposes.

of these angles has asymptotic normal properties. These properties are desirable for the comparisons we wish to make, since the effects of skewness on estimates of variability are minimized as the distribution approaches normality. Preliminary examination indicates that without the transformation, the means of the time rate distributions in certain of the categories place severe restrictions on the variance. With the transformation this restriction is at least reduced, since the mean and variance of the normal distribution are independent.

The numbers in all the tables thus represent the arcsine equivalents of the original percentage rates. Those who wish to prepare norms in easily used form can do so by transforming the arcsine numbers back to percentage rates. Cutting points above and below the mean can be obtained by finding the standard deviation indicated in the proper table, adding the desired number of standard deviation units to the arcsine mean, above and below, and then transforming these numbers back to percentage equivalents.

THREE KINDS OF EFFECTS OF SIZE

In speculating about the possible effects of group size on interaction patterns, at least three kinds of effects might be expected. First, there may be some effects which vary directly with size. For example, if there is an absolute time limit for a meeting, it is obvious that the talking time available for each person decreases as the group size increases. Second, there may be some effects which are uniquely associated with a group of a given size. For example, in a group of size two it is impossible to form a majority except by unanimity. Third, there may be effects which are associated with the way a group can be divided into sub-groups. It has often been said that it is wise to appoint a committee with an odd number of members so that a division of the group into two equal and opposed subgroups is impossible. Thus, there may be some effects associated with groups of odd and even numbers of members.

Each of the tables which follows shows rates of interaction for groups of sizes two through seven. Each table will be examined first for trends by size, then for any indication of a unique size, and finally for effects of odd and even number of members. Hypotheses suggested by the data will be stated. Differences which are found significant will be indicated by asterisks as explained in a footnote.[6] In general, the level of significance

6 Tests of significance were computed only for the statements which are followed in the text by the number of the category involved. All statements of this kind, however, were tested. Absence of asterisks thus means that a test has been made but the relationship does not satisfy the .05 significance requirements. One or more asterisks indicates significance at the .05 level on some relevant comparison. The comparison

will be .05 on a two tailed test. Our discussion, however, will not be confined only to those differences which are found significant. Since our object is to develop an integrated set of hypotheses, and the number of groups of each size studied is relatively small, we wish to take advantage of every lead provided by the data, even though the effect may be slight. While some of the hypotheses might reasonably be accepted on the basis of the interaction data alone, additional evidence will be brought to bear in later reports which will include other kinds of measurements as well.

TABLE I

Mean Profile of N Individuals, by Group Size

GROUP SIZE	2	3	4	5	6	7
N	8	12	16	20	18	28
CATEGORY						
1	9.2	9.1	10.3	9.7	11.2	10.5
2	11.2	11.4	12.8	14.2	18.4	16.6
3	27.2	27.0	22.3	23.1	21.6	21.3
4	14.3	13.5	13.7	15.9	18.4	19.2
5	31.7	34.0	35.0	32.0	32.1	31.2
6	25.3	23.3	23.7	26.6	24.1	25.7
7	12.0	10.2	10.5	10.2	10.2	10.1
8	9.8	8.5	8.2	8.5	7.4	7.1
9	5.2	5.9	5.0	6.4	4.6	5.9
10	10.2	15.6	19.9	14.5	17.7	16.4
11	12.4	8.6	10.0	9.1	6.3	6.6
12	1.0	3.5	5.2	3.3	3.9	3.8

Note: The profile of each individual is the sum over four sessions of his raw profile in each session, converted to a percentage profile and transformed to arcsine equivalents.

TRENDS ACCORDING TO SIZE

The mean profile of initiated behavior for individuals by group size is indicated in Table 1. When the size of the group increases, showing tension release * (category 2) and giving suggestion * (category 4) show emphatic increases. Showing solidarity (category 1) appears to increase somewhat with group size, and if groups of size two are excluded from consideration, giving information * (category 6) also appears to increase. Showing tension * (category 11) shows an emphatic decrease with increase in group

made varies by the proposition to be tested. The number of asterisks indicates the type of comparison, as follows:

* Size 3 compared to size 7
** Smaller sizes compared with larger sizes
*** Size 2 compared to size 3
**** Sizes 4 and 6 compared with sizes 3, 5, and 7
***** Size 2 compared to sizes 4 and 6
****** A given size compared with all other sizes

size, and decreases are also visible in showing agreement * (category 3) and asking for opinion ** (category 8). Again, if groups of size two are disregarded, giving opinion ** (category 5) shows a decrease when the group size increases.

Most of the trends observed appear to be results of two gross factors. The first is that the relative talking time available per member decreases as size increases. The second is that each person is confronted with an absolutely larger number of persons as size increases. Each is under pressure to maintain a more or less adequate relationship with each other. Thus as size increases, each member has more relationships to maintain, and less time to do so. Some time might be gained by increasing rates of activity; however, the requirements of effective communication place limits on this source of gain. In a previous study we have shown that members of three man groups adjust their activity rates to each other as if there were an upper limit to the total activity rate for the group as a whole (4).

The relative lack of time in which to build an argument may account for the increase in giving suggestion, and also the decrease in both asking for and giving opinion. Giving suggestion is a more direct response to the demands of the task than is giving opinion. When time is at a premium members may feel under pressure to take the most direct approach, and suggestions may be made without taking time to justify them with opinions or to ask others for their opinions. It may also be that the larger group represents a more formidable sanctioning system than the smaller one, and as a result evaluative statements may be inhibited. This might also account for the relative increase in giving orientation since one may state the facts in his possession with less fear of disapproval. The relative increase in giving orientation may also be due in part to a "round robin" procedure of stating facts which results in considerable repetition of detail. Similarly, giving suggestion may increase as a result of the emergence of repetitive patterns built around the necessities of coordinating the activities of more persons. If true, the larger groups should show more procedural suggestions, as distinguished from content suggestions.

The requirement that persons greet each other pleasantly and make some attempt to establish their solidarity presumably applies about equally strongly to all groups in our sample. Since the number of relationships increases very rapidly with the size of the group, the proportion of time devoted to this business might be expected to be greater as size increases. It may be pressure of this kind that results in the trend toward increase in showing solidarity in the larger groups.

A general result of the time pressure and the larger number of persons is that the number of persons who participate at absolutely low rates will be increased. Those who participate minimally tend to be forced more and more toward types of behavior which can be performed simultaneously with others and thus do not compete for time. Simply listening, of course, is the prime example, but this is not scored directly. The other two main types of activity which can be performed without time competition are showing tension (by withdrawal, nervous mannerisms, or awkward pauses that occur for the group as a whole) and showing tension release (primarily through laughter of the group as a whole).

According to the scoring system used, activities such as awkward pauses or laughter which involve the group as a whole are credited separately to each individual. Thus, when the raw profiles of low participators are converted to percentage profiles, these types of activities are apt to show up as particularly prominent. In Table 1 it is seen that showing tension release does indeed show a marked increase by size, which is probably due to the presence of more minimal participators. However, the increase is not as large as would be expected if this were the only factor operating. Apparently there is a counter factor which results in fewer occasions of general laughter in the larger groups.

By the same reasoning one would expect showing tension to increase as the size of the group increases, but, in fact, there is a marked decrease. This may be due partly to the fact that the observer is too busy to note the signs of tension which do occur, but probably this is not the whole explanation. It is suggested, rather, that the increased number of persons has two effects which may tend to minimize certain types of tension. First, in the larger groups the role requirements for task completion and adequate group maintenance may be allocated over a larger range of persons, so that there is more likelihood that the necessary roles will be performed by some persons without difficulty. Second, and this is really the other side of the coin, the larger size group permits relative anonymity for persons who might be prone to show tension if forced into greater involvement.

The drop in rate of showing agreement is possibly related to the increase in time pressure. Just listening may be a form of tacit agreement. If the responsibility of the formal show of agreement falls to the more active members of the group, again, the minimal participators, especially in the larger groups, will residually have little agreement scored. For the larger groups, which have more minimal participators, this may result in low rates of showing agreement on the mean profiles.

UNIQUE ASPECTS OF TWO MAN GROUPS

Inspection of Table 1 for the possibility that any given size may show unique characteristics strongly suggests that size two is unique. The mean profile for groups of this size has a notably high rate of showing tension *** (category 11), and at the same time low rates of showing disagreement *** (category 10) and antagonism *** (category 12). Asking for orientation *** (category 7) is uniquely high, and although giving orientation (category 6) is not uniquely high, it is somewhat higher than would be expected from extrapolating the trend for the remaining group sizes. Similarly, giving opinion (category 5) although not uniquely low, is lower than would be expected from extrapolation. Asking for opinion (category 8), on the other hand, is uniquely high. Giving suggestion (category 4) is somewhat on the high side in the sense that it deviates from an otherwise perfectly clear and consistent trend seen in the remaining group sizes.

Most, if not all, of the unique features of the interaction profile of the two person group may be associated with one major feature which distinguishes it from groups of all other sizes. This is the fact that in a group of two it is impossible to form a majority except by unanimity. Either person in the diad possesses power to influence the decision by withdrawal or veto. Neither person is able to influence the other by bringing a majority to bear against him. In this sense there is no public opinion or group sanction to which either can appeal. Similarly, there is no good office, mediator, or arbitrator for the differences. Consequently, each person is under pressure to behave in such a way that the other will not withdraw and will continue to cooperate even though he may have to yield a point at a given time. Essentially, this is the problem of allowing the co-participant to "save face" when he does yield a point. The dominant person is thus under pressure to avoid the implication of superiority, and to persuade the other by gentle and self-effacing means.

The low rates of showing disagreement and antagonism and the high rates of asking for information and opinion are reasonably associated with the necessity of a gentle, persuasive approach. The high rate of showing tension is probably associated both with the delicate balance the dominant person tries to maintain and with the tendency to withdraw used as a power device by the less dominant person. The concentration on giving orientation and relative avoidance of giving opinion may be a device used for the neutralizing of the evaluative implications of what is said or suggested, by sticking to that which is most self evident and incontrovertable. The relatively high rate of giving suggestion, if indeed the rate is high, may reflect the development of procedural suggestions to handle the high tension. It is of some interest that there is high rate of asking for opinion and that this is not accompanied by a correspondingly high rate of giving opinion. This suggests, again, the hesitancy to respond in terms which are evaluative.

DIFFERENCES IN GROUPS OF ODD AND EVEN NUMBER OF MEMBERS

In the presence of trends which are appreciable and vary directly with group size, complicated by the unique character of size two, any effects which are due to odd and even number of members are likely to be masked to some extent. If the effects are systematic and distributed with some strength, however, they may be discernible in terms of peaks and troughs. Such regular effects appear in Table 1 as follows: excluding size two, groups with even numbers of members (sizes 4 and 6) are high in showing disagreement **** (category 10) and antagonism **** (category 12), and are low in asking for suggestions **** (category 9). The data also suggest that the even groups may be higher in showing solidarity (category 1), and possibly lower in showing agreement (category 3).

The unique character of the two man group may be viewed as the result of the restriction that the group may subdivide in only one way. Groups of larger sizes may also have special characteristics due to the ways in which they may subdivide, but obviously, all sizes above two may subdivide in a number of ways which increases very rapidly as size increases. Groups of even numbers, however, can divide into two equal parts, in which case there is no majority. In such splits each person has an ally and may maintain the hope of achieving a majority. Consequently, there is not the same stringent pressure to avoid overt conflict as in the two man group.

It may be, thus, that even numbered groups will persist in deadlock whereas odd numbered groups will more easily break into a majority and a minority and so arrive at a decision sooner. The observed differences between groups of odd and even number of members (excluding the special case of size two) are consistent with this theory. The disagreement and antagonism are presumably the overt manifestation of the conflict, and the relative lack of asking for suggestion and showing agreement are consistent with a state of conflict. There is no obvious reason why showing solidarity should be higher for the groups of even number.[7]

VARIABILITY OF GIVEN INDIVIDUALS OVER SESSIONS

For each individual the standard deviation over the four sessions in which he participated was computed. The mean standard deviation for individuals, by size of group, is presented in Table 2.

Examination of this table indicates that, essentially, all categories show a tendency toward greater variability for each individual's performance as the size of the group increases.** This allows for at least two interpretations. The first and most obvious is that the larger groups partition scores among a greater number of persons, and thus the estimates of

7 One hypothesis is that the members within a faction may show more solidarity to each other in the face of an external threat. However, this is a very tenuous ad hoc hypothesis. In contrast, the hypothesis that groups of even size would show less agreement and more disagreement and antagonism was stated in a theoretical memorandum prepared in advance of the research. This prediction, however, did not recognize size two as a special case.

one session are less reliable than for smaller sizes. This is particularly true for the low interactors in the large group, where a relatively small number of acts shifting for a category may make a considerable shift in the percentage profile.

A second possibility is that there may be more shifting of roles in the larger groups, due to the larger number of persons among whom roles

TABLE 2

How the Profile of an Individual Varies over Successive Sessions: The Mean for N Individuals of the Standard Deviation of Each Individual over Four Sessions, by Group Size

GROUP SIZE	2	3	4	5	6	7	
NUMBER OF INDIVIDUALS OR OF STANDARD DEVIATIONS	8	12	16	20	18	28	MEAN
CATEGORY							
1	2.5	2.8	3.4	4.0	5.6	4.1	3.7
2	2.5	2.9	3.0	3.8	5.8	7.3	4.2
3	2.3	2.9	2.9	2.6	3.8	3.7	3.0
4	2.6	2.5	3.7	3.4	3.7	4.9	3.5
5	2.4	2.9	3.2	2.6	3.6	4.0	3.1
6	2.3	2.4	3.6	3.1	4.1	4.6	3.4
7	2.3	2.1	3.4	2.7	2.5	3.3	2.7
8	1.6	2.3	2.2	2.7	3.5	3.6	2.7
9	1.6	1.7	2.7	2.8	3.0	3.6	2.6
10	1.6	3.4	3.0	2.7	3.3	3.5	2.9
11	2.4	2.2	4.3	3.7	3.2	3.7	3.3
12	.5	2.5	3.0	2.3	2.3	2.2	2.1
MEAN	2.0	2.5	3.2	3.0	3.7	4.0	

Note: The standard deviations are based on the four profiles of each individual which have been converted to percentage profiles and transformed to arcsine equivalents.

may be allocated. If particular profiles are associated with particular roles for which there is some evidence (2, 3, 6), the greater variety of roles a person may hold would contribute to the greater variability of performance.

Probably both these factors are operating. A preliminary check of the data indicates that at least the first can be demonstrated to be a significant factor. The proportion of responses in category five (or six) is known to be highly correlated (usually about .80) with the total interaction rate. If persons are chosen for their interaction level by the proportion of acts in category five (or six), then examination of the standard deviations indicates that persons with high proportions of category five (or six) have less variability in the other categories. Thus, high variability is associated with persons of lower interaction rate, those who have fewer scores in each category. The larger groups will have relatively more low participators than the smaller.

The two man groups appear to have uniquely low variances in showing disagreement *** (category 10) and showing antagonism *** (category 12). While the low variance of showing antagonism may be accounted for by the fact that the mean is extremely low and may place an automatic restriction on the variance, this will not account for the low variance in showing disagreement. The low variability here indicates that the constraint on overt negative reactions characteristic of the two man groups operates consistently through sessions.

The odd and even effect above size two is not marked, but there is some indication that the mean variability of the even groups is slightly higher than might be expected. This would only be inconsistent with the interpretation that even size groups are prone to conflict if there is the expectation that conflict is continuous over sessions. If the amount of conflict changes from session to session according to changes in task or session order, we would expect the variability in individual profiles as shown.

VARIABILITY AMONG INDIVIDUALS

The standard deviations of profiles among all individuals of a group size are given in Table 3. The profile for a given individual is based on the sum of his four single session profiles.

Trends in this table are not clearly marked. The apparent reason for this is that the odd and even effect is so prominent. Making allowance for size two and the odd and even differences, consistency of trends is observable. The variability among individuals in showing tension release (category 2) and giving suggestion ** (category 4) increases with increasing size, while showing agreement (category 3), disagreement (category 10), showing tension ** (category 11) decrease.

The increase of variability among members in showing tension release is probably accounted for by the fact that when laughter occurs for the group as a whole, each individual is credited for an act in that category. When the raw profiles are converted to percentage profiles, this affects the profile of the low participators more than that of high participators. Thus, since the range of total interaction rates of participation in the large groups is larger, the members will diverge more from each other with the increase in size.

The increasing variability among members in giving suggestion does not have a parallel explanation. It is probably due to an actual increase in the degree to which certain members rather than others specialize in this activity. Giving suggestion is probably the most characteristic behavior of the person who specializes in the solution of the task problem and is associated with the subject's own attribution of leadership. This change by size, thus appears to be some evidence that as size increases, the probability of a clear cut differentiation between leader(s) and followers increases.

The decreasing difference between the percentage profiles of different individuals in showing agreement, disagreement, and tension indicates perhaps that these are types of activity in which specialization does not tend to take place as the size increases. On the contrary, this seems to

TABLE 3

How the Profiles of Different Individuals Vary from Each Other: The Standard Deviation of Individual Profiles, by Group Size

GROUP SIZE	2	3	4	5	6	7	
NUMBER OF INDIVIDUALS	8	12	16	20	18	28	MEAN
CATEGORY							
1	3.9	3.5	2.5	3.4	2.7	3.7	3.3
2	3.6	4.8	2.4	6.6	3.9	6.7	5.0
3	9.5	5.3	2.9	4.7	2.6	4.3	4.4
4	3.1	2.0	2.6	2.7	3.5	3.1	2.9
5	6.4	4.7	2.5	4.7	1.6	4.5	3.9
6	2.1	3.8	1.1	5.7	1.9	3.6	3.2
7	3.1	2.1	2.3	1.8	2.4	2.4	2.3
8	3.5	2.1	2.7	2.2	1.7	3.0	2.5
9	1.2	1.5	2.6	1.6	1.4	1.9	1.8
10	3.7	4.6	2.5	3.8	1.6	3.7	3.3
11	3.4	3.9	3.3	3.0	2.8	2.9	3.1
12	1.7	3.6	2.2	3.4	3.5	3.6	3.2
MEAN	3.8	3.5	2.5	3.6	2.5	3.6	

Note: The profile of each individual is the sum over four sessions of his raw profile in each session, converted to a percentage profile and transformed to arcsine equivalents.

point to the fact that as the groups grow larger, the participation of members in these categories is a function of their general participation. Some people agree, disagree, and show tension more than others, of course, but not disproportionately more in relation to their total interaction. It may very well be that in the larger groups the relative anonymity and lack of pressure to participate unless one wishes to do so, underlies all three of these decreasing trends. One does not need overtly to agree or disagree unless he is specifically addressed or wishes to enter the conversation. Similarly one can escape more or less successfully into anonymity and relative non-participation without remaining in the focus of a tense situation.

Groups of size two appear to be unique in the amount of variability among individuals. Every category except asking for suggestion and showing antagonism shows higher variability than one might expect, particularly when compared to other even groups.***** The mean variability is higher than for any other size. The hypothesis which would account for the low variability in showing antagonism has already been stated earlier. The high variability of the other categories suggests that in two man groups there is a very strong tendency for the roles of the two individuals to become differentiated from each other, presumably in a complementary way. The plainest clue, perhaps, is the high variability in giving opinion and showing agreement. Presumably one person tends to give most of the opinion, and the other tends to give most of the agreement. More generally, probably, one person tends to gravitate toward a more active initiating role, while the other tends to be more passive and spends more of his time reacting. In this respect, at least, there is a certain similarity between size two and the larger sizes with their tendency to differentiation into a leader(s) and followers structure.

The most striking feature of Table 3 is the difference between odd and even size groups. Excluding size two it is seen that the profiles of individuals tend in general to be more like each other in the groups of even size than in the groups of odd size. The tendency toward similarity (low variability) appears particularly in all types of positive reactions, showing solidarity,**** tension release,**** and agreement **** (categories 1, 2 and 3), in giving opinion **** and orientation **** in the task area (categories 5 and 6), and in showing disagreement **** (category 10). Giving suggestion (category 4) is the only type of activity in which the differences between persons appear more marked in the even groups.

The combination of categories in which variability among individuals is low is congruent with the hypothesis of more occasions in the groups of even size when the members split into two equal parts, in conflict with each other, and unable to break the deadlock. Protracted argument tends to increase the rates of disagreement and giving opinion, and to decrease the rates of positive reactions, at least during the period of the conflict. The more general the conflict, the more equal the participation rates of members may become, and the more similar they become in their concentration on disagreement and opinion. The only fact that does not fit into this picture is that the effect of similarity through competition does not appear in the category of giving suggestion. If anything, the converse is true. This effect may be connected in some way with the emergence of a specialized mediator or arbitrator who tries desperately, after a long period of deadlock or in the final few minutes of a session, to force a final formulation of the decision for the experimenter, even though it is not basically acceptable to the members. This hypothesis, however, is tenuous.

VARIABILITY OF GIVEN GROUPS OVER SUCCESSIVE SESSIONS

The average standard deviation of a group over four sessions is shown for groups of each size in Table 4. Only a few trends are discernable. The mean variability of all categories shows a minor upward trend with group size. Showing solidarity ** (category 1) increases slightly, and showing tension release ** (category 2) increases more prominently.

TABLE 4

How the Profile of a Group Varies over Successive Sessions: The Mean for Four Groups of the Standard Deviation of Each Group over Four Sessions, by Group Size

GROUP SIZE	2	3	4	5	6	7	
NUMBER OF GROUPS	4	4	4	4	3	4	MEAN
CATEGORY							
1	2.1	2.3	2.5	1.9	2.9	2.9	2.5
2	2.1	2.5	2.8	2.7	5.1	5.6	3.5
3	1.5	2.3	2.0	2.0	2.0	2.2	2.0
4	2.1	1.6	3.3	1.0	2.7	2.4	2.2
5	1.9	2.0	1.7	1.2	2.3	2.7	2.0
6	1.3	1.8	2.3	1.7	2.4	2.3	2.0
7	1.6	1.1	1.9	1.4	3.3	1.2	1.8
8	1.1	1.0	1.3	1.2	.9	.7	1.0
9	1.3	1.0	1.8	.6	.8	1.2	1.1
10	1.3	2.6	2.0	1.4	2.0	2.1	1.9
11	1.7	1.2	2.9	2.8	.8	1.3	1.8
12	.4	2.7	2.4	2.0	2.2	1.5	1.9
MEAN	1.5	1.8	2.2	1.7	2.3	2.2	2.0

Note: The standard deviations are based on the four profiles of each group, which have been converted to percentage profiles and transformed to arcsine equivalents.

The larger variability between sessions in the larger groups in showing solidarity is probably related to the necessity of getting acquainted. Greetings, introductions, and friendly social remarks are generally scored as showing solidarity. The problem of getting acquainted is presumably greatest in the first session, and since a greater proportion of time may be spent in this activity, this would produce variability by session for all groups. In the larger groups there are more people to get acquainted initially, and thus the variability between sessions due to this effect would be expected to be greater among the larger groups.

Showing tension release has been demonstrated to increase through successive sessions (2, 3, 4, 5, 6), and thus variability by session is especially characteristic of this category. It should be noted that the mean variability of this category is the highest of all categories taken over all groups. Since laughter of the group as a whole is credited to each member individually, a general laugh in the larger groups will produce a more marked change in the rate for the category than in the smaller groups. And since this category of activity tends to increase through successive sessions, the variability by sessions will be more marked in groups of larger sizes.

As to effects connected with a unique size, size two evidences the low variance expected in showing disagreement (category 10), and particularly in showing antagonism ****** (category 12). Of more interest, in view of previous theory and research, is that size three shows a uniquely high variance over sessions in these same two categories. Size three has often been thought to be peculiarly "unstable" in some sense or other, connected with the fact that in case of disagreement of two members, the third has it within his own power to form a majority by combining with one other, whereas in case of the agreement of two, the third is left almost powerless, whether he agrees or disagrees. Formation of a majority is particularly damaging to the unity of the whole group, since whenever it appears it tends to isolate one member who is left with no support. Whether this member then elects to give in, or to fight it out against an alliance which has already solidified, probably depends upon the relative dominance of the member in terms of status and personality.

Thus, the amount of disagreement in the group profile for the period of a given coalition could be markedly influenced by the propensity of the isolated member to handle his difficulty in an active or a passive manner. If any given coalition persisted over sessions with little or no disagreement to give the isolated member a chance to combine with one and isolate the other, the session to session variance would be expected to be small. But it is not small—rather, it is uniquely large. The inference that appears most plausible, then, is that the coalitions tend to be fragile, changing from session to session, and that the amount of disagreement and antagonism in a given session varies according to whether a coalition forms, and if so, whether the isolated member is active or passive. If this were the case, variability of sessions would be the result for showing disagreement and antagonism (categories 10 and 12) in the three man groups.

The effects of odd and even sizes are seen most clearly in the mean variability for each size, without regard to particular categories. Sizes four and six (the even sizes excluding the special case of size two) show higher variability over sessions than odd sizes. The categories which contribute most to this variance are giving suggestion **** (category 4), giving orientation (category 6), and asking for orientation **** (category 7). One possible explanation is that during actual periods of conflict, the rates in these categories tend to fall, as more time is taken up with disagreement and giving opinion. Suggestions are rejected and are not allowed to build up as the argument regresses to opinion and counter opinion. Matters of factual information are neglected because the heat of the argument interferes with the degree of objectivity or emotional neutrality required to make facts seem effective and important. There may be a growth curve over sessions, however, in the degree to which these types of activity are utilized in an attempt to get around disagreement by procedural suggestions and concentration on facts. Or this may happen periodically. In either case, variability between sessions would be the result, only providing these activities are low for certain sessions.

VARIABILITY AMONG GROUPS

The variability of the profiles of different groups is represented in Table 5 by the standard deviation of the four groups of each size, averaged through the sequence of four sessions.

Showing tension release ** (category 2), giving opinion ** (category 5), and giving orientation ** (category 6) show fairly clear increasing

TABLE 5

How the Profiles of Different Groups Vary from Each Other: The Mean for Four Sessions of the Standard Deviation of Each Session over Four Groups, by Group Size

GROUP SIZE	2	3	4	5	6	7	
NUMBER OF SESSION ORDERS FOR WHICH A S.D. WAS COMPUTED AND ON WHICH THE MEAN IS BASED	4	4	4	4	3	4	MEAN
CATEGORY							
1	4.2	3.2	2.9	2.9	3.2	3.0	3.2
2	3.3	4.3	3.4	6.0	5.0	5.0	4.5
3	2.9	2.9	2.7	3.4	3.3	1.9	2.9
4	2.6	2.3	3.4	1.4	4.4	2.3	2.7
5	2.4	2.3	2.9	3.8	5.1	4.8	3.6
6	1.5	2.3	2.2	4.5	4.5	3.0	3.0
7	1.3	1.5	1.9	1.2	2.3	1.2	1.6
8	2.5	1.6	1.2	1.5	2.1	1.2	1.7
9	1.8	1.6	1.6	.8	1.5	.9	1.4
10	3.6	3.5	2.3	2.7	3.4	2.2	3.0
11	3.5	1.3	3.3	2.3	2.3	.8	2.3
12	1.6	3.1	2.7	2.8	3.0	3.5	2.8
MEAN	2.6	2.5	2.5	2.8	3.4	2.5	2.7

Note: The standard deviations are based on the group profiles of the four separate groups on a given session, e.g., four separate groups on their first session. Each raw group profile was converted to a percentage profile and transformed to the arcsine equivalent.

trends by size. The reason for the greater variability between larger groups in showing tension release is probably the same as indicated previously—namely, that general laughter produces a number of scores equal to the number of persons in the group, thus affecting the profiles of larger groups in a more marked manner than in smaller groups. Whatever variability there is between groups, then, is emphasized progressively more as the number of members increases. The greater variability of the larger groups in giving orientation is probably the effect of the more or less mechanical procedure adopted by some (but not other) groups of "going around" the whole circle of members in the reporting of the facts of the case given to them. Whenever this device is adopted, it tends to increase the rate of the group as a whole in the category of giving information, in a degree which is proportionate to the number of members. Insofar as members fail to stick strictly to giving information on the "round robin" and include an admixture of opinion, this procedure would also increase the variability between groups in a more marked way for larger groups in giving opinion.

So far as effects of unique sizes are concerned, neither size two nor size three show evidence of unusual variability among groups, except for the low variability for two man groups of showing antagonism ****** (category 12), with which we have already dealt. Size seven, however, shows uniquely low variability among groups in showing agreement ****** (category 3), showing tension ****** (category 11), and showing disagreement (category 10). Showing disagreement, however, is not so clearly defined as the others, and is included because of the consistency of the argument that follows. These are the same three categories, it will be recalled, on which individuals showed decreasing variability with group size. The hypothesis advanced earlier was that these are categories in which specialization by role tends not to occur in the larger groups, and participation in these categories tends to be a function of the total rate of the participant. If this is the case, then the group rates in these categories would tend to be functions of the group total rates. It will also be remembered from Table 1 that the rates of agreement and showing tension show a decreasing trend by group size, and there is some indication that showing disagreement as well may be undergoing a general decrease from an earlier high point. It may be that these categories are approaching a minimum operating rate no longer associated with role specializations. While data are not available it is possible that with further increase in size, others of the categories might also tend toward such an operating minimum, and so reduce the variability among groups. This might be the case with asking for suggestions (category 9). It is noticed that the mean variability for size seven is lower than the two preceding sizes, and as low as that of any other size. This may be the point at which such a trend begins to become visible.

Effects of odd and even size are not marked in this table, except for giving suggestion **** (category 4) and asking for orientation **** (category 7), which are high in the even groups. The variability of these two categories was also high over sessions, as shown in the previous table. The hypothesis advanced there, was that these are types of activity which tend to decline during periods of conflict, and this hypothesis holds with equal plausibility as an explanation of the variability between groups. Conflict is not supposed to be a feature of every group of even size. The hypothesis is rather that even size simply increases the probability of longer periods spent in deadlock if deadlocks occur. This should increase the variability among groups.

VARIABILITY OVER SESSIONS COMPARED TO VARIABILITY AMONG GROUPS

Finally, we call attention to a finding which bears on the question of whether groups of these sizes and short duration develop and maintain structural features through time which distinguish one group from another. A positive answer is inferred directly from the fact that the mean variability over all categories and sizes of groups is substantially lower over sessions than among groups.

REFERENCES

1. Bales, R. F. *Interaction process analysis: A method for the study of small groups.* Cambridge, Mass.: Addison-Wesley, 1950.
2. Bales, R. F. The equilibrium problem in small groups. In T. Parsons, R. F. Bales, & E. A. Shils, *Working papers in the theory of action.* Glencoe, Ill.: Free Press, 1953. Pp. 111–161.
3. Bales, R. F., & Slater, P. E. Role differentiation in small groups. In T. Parsons, R. F. Bales, *et al., Family, socialization, and interaction process.* Glencoe, Ill.: Free Press, 1955.
4. Borgatta, E. F., & Bales, R. F. Interaction of individuals in reconstituted groups. *Sociometry*, 1953, 16, 302–320.
5. Heinicke, C. M., & Bales, R. F. Developmental trends in the structure of small groups. *Sociometry*, 1953, 16, 7–38.
6. Mann, R. D. The relation of informal status to role behavior in small discussion groups. Unpublished honors thesis, Harvard College, 1954.
7. Snedecor, G. W. *Statistical methods.* (4th Ed.) Ames, Ia.: Iowa State College Press, 1946.

Twenty Questions: Efficiency in Problem Solving as a Function of Size of Group

DONALD W. TAYLOR and WILLIAM L. FAUST

TWENTY QUESTIONS, popular as a parlor game in earlier years and now popular as a program on both radio and television, involves a type of problem solving that is of considerable interest psychologically.[1] To start the game, the participants are told only whether the object they are to attempt to identify is animal, vegetable, or mineral. In searching for the object which is the solution to the problem, they ask a series of questions, each of which can be answered "Yes" or "No." To find the solution most economically, they must use a high order of conceptualization, gradually increasing the specificity of the concepts employed until they arrive at the particular object.

The game is of psychological interest first of all because it appears to involve a type of problem solving more similar to much problem solving in everyday life than that ordinarily studied in psychological experiments. The solution is obtained not by a series of rigorous well-defined steps. Rather one starts with a general, somewhat vague problem. Questions are asked and information obtained. Upon the basis of this information, new questions are formulated. This procedure continues until the problem is

FROM *Journal of Experimental Psychology*, 1952, 44, 360–368. Reprinted by permission of the authors and the American Psychological Association, Inc.

This experiment was carried out under Project NR 192–018 supported by Contract N6 onr-25125 between the Office of Naval Research and Stanford University. The first author designed the experiment, supervised the analysis of the data, and prepared the present report. The second author conducted the experiment and carried out the analysis of the data. Work on the contract is under the direction of the first author.

1 The idea of using "Twenty Questions" in experimental studies of problem solving is not new. As was discovered after the present study was partly completed, Lindley (3) suggested the use of the game for this purpose in an article published in 1897.

solved. This type of problem solving is also of interest because it seems more similar to much of the problem solving in scientific research than does that involved in problems susceptible of rigorous, deductive mathematical or logical solution.

The use of the game in psychological experiments is recommended by several other considerations: It is quite interesting to college undergraduates; motivation is easily sustained for a period of several days. A very large number of problems of this kind are available. The same problems can be used with children and with adults. The same problems are appropriate for use with individuals and with groups of varying size.

The present experiment, the first in a series planned using the game, was designed to answer three questions: (*a*) How rapidly is the skill involved in the game learned? (*b*) How does efficiency in solving this type of problem vary as a function of the size of the group participating? (*c*) Does improvement in individual performance occur more rapidly with individual practice or with practice as a member of a group?

The second of these three questions is perhaps the most interesting. For many kinds of work, it seems quite reasonable that if a particular job must be completed in a shorter time, the number of people in the group working on it should be increased. It is not clear that increasing the size of a group engaged in solving a problem will necessarily reduce the time required for its solution. Indeed, it appears likely that in some cases it will actually increase the time required. Shaw (4) has presented data which indicate that the performance of groups of four is superior to that of individuals. However, further experimentation with larger samples, varying size groups, and different types of problems is needed to determine adequately the relation between group size and efficiency in problem solving.

PROCEDURE

A total of 105 students from the elementary course in psychology served as *S*s. The *S*s were assigned by chance to work in solving the problems either alone, in pairs, or as a member of a group of four. There were 15 individual *S*s, 15 groups of two, and 15 groups of four. Each individual or group was given four problems a day for four successive days. On the fifth day, all *S*s worked alone, each being given four problems.

From a longer list of objects originally constructed, 60 were selected for use as problem topics. Included were 20 animal, 20 vegetable, and 20 mineral objects. Excluded were objects which did not clearly fit in only one of the three categories; e.g., hammer was not included because, with a handle of wood and a head of metal, it would be classed as both vegetable and mineral. Also excluded were objects which could not be expected to be familiar to almost every college student. Examples of objects included are: newspaper, Bop Hope, scissors, camel, dime, rubber band.

With four problems a day for five days, a total of only 20 problems was needed for presentation to any particular *S* or group. However, to minimize the possibility that an *S* would have any knowledge of what problem object to expect, it was decided to use a total of 60 different objects. This precaution seemed desirable although the instructions to be given all *S*s specifically requested that they not discuss the problems with other students. It should be added that no evidence was obtained during the course of the experiment to indicate that any *S* had previously heard mentioned a problem object he was to be given.

Since the nature of the learning curve was of interest, it was necessary to control the order of presentation of the problems in such a way that those given on any one day would be equal in difficulty to those given on any other day. In the absence of any measure of the difficulty of the individual problems, the following procedure was employed: The 20 animal objects were listed in chance order, as were the 20 vegetable and the 20 mineral objects. To obtain a group of four for use the first day, the first item was taken from each of the three lists together with the next item from one of the three chosen by chance. Similarly, to obtain four objects for use the second day, the next item was taken from each of the three lists; the fourth item was then obtained by taking the next in order on one of the two lists from which the extra item had not been taken the first day. This procedure was repeated to provide four problems for the third, fourth, and fifth days. A second and a third set of four problems for each of five days were obtained by continuing the same procedure. Next the three lists of 20 were individually reshuffled and the entire procedure repeated to obtain a fourth, fifth, and sixth set.

In the experiment, the first, seventh, and thirteenth individual, pair, or group of four *S*s received the first set of problems. The second, eighth, and fourteenth received the second set, and so on. As a result of this procedure, the order and the frequency of appearance of the problems were the same for individual *S*s as for groups of two or of four.

All *S*s were told that both the number of questions and the time required to reach solution would be recorded, but it was emphasized that number of questions was the more important score. In presenting each problem, *E* stated simply whether the object sought was animal, vegetable, or mineral. Time was measured by means of a stopwatch. A special data sheet was used for groups of two and of four to record which *S* asked each question. To each question, *E* replied "Yes," "No," "Partly," "Sometimes," or "Not in the usual sense of the word." If the question could not be answered in one of these ways or was unclear, *S* was asked to restate it.

The instructions given to groups of two or of four made clear that they might talk freely to each other, reviewing answers to previous questions or suggesting possible questions to ask. It was emphasized that they were not to compete against each other, but were to cooperate as a group to get the answer; they were told that the efficiency of their group would be compared with that of other groups.

As the name of the game indicates, *S*s are traditionally allowed 20 questions in which to obtain the solution. Pretesting showed, however, that with naive *S*s this limit results in a rather large proportion of failures. Accordingly, to simplify the analysis of the data to be obtained, the number of questions permitted

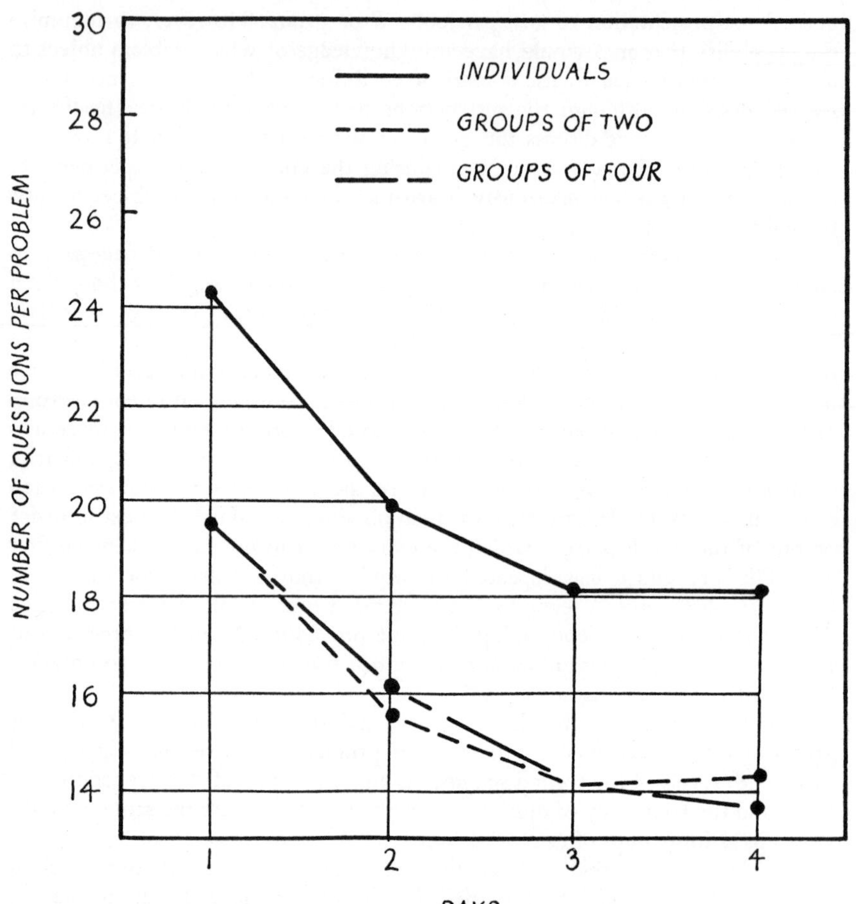

FIG. 1. Number of questions per problem as a function of days of practice and of size of group

was increased to 30. Examination of the distributions of scores obtained suggests that, at least after the first day, the performance of individuals or groups of *S*s who do not reach solution in 30 questions is qualitatively different from that of those who do. The *E*'s impression is that in most cases of failure there was established an incorrect set which was unchanging even in the face of answers irreconcilable with it; it seemed that in such cases the *S*s might easily have asked 50 or 60 questions without solving the problem.

RESULTS

Rate of Learning

The first question the experiment was designed to answer concerned the speed of learning of the skill involved. The data in Fig. 1 show that there is rapid improvement in the performance of both individuals and groups. By the fourth day the curves appear already to be flattening out. The score for an individual or single group for one day was the median of the number of questions required to solve each of the four problems on that day.

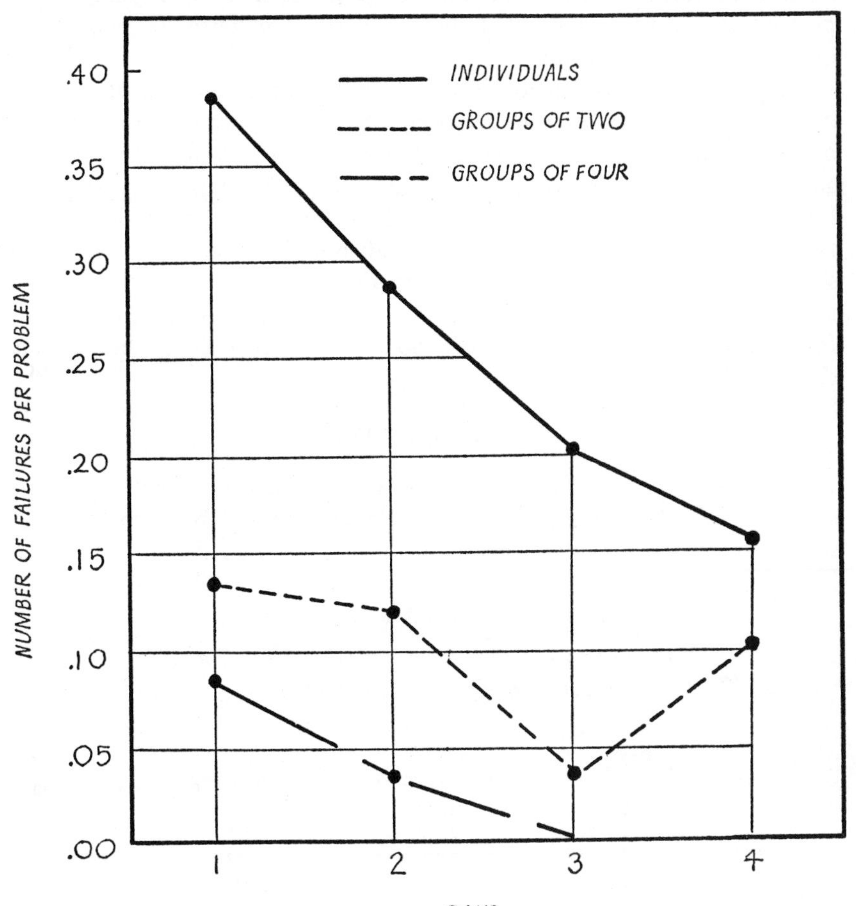

FIG. 2. Number of failures per problem as a function of days of practice and of size of group

The median was used instead of the mean because there were some failures. Each point plotted in Fig. 1 is the mean of these median scores on one day for 15 individuals, or for 15 groups of two or of four. In those few cases where an individual or group failed two or more problems on a single day, the median was obtained by treating the failures as though solution had been reached in 31 questions; the number of such cases was too small to affect the results appreciably; after the first day there were no such cases except among individual *S*s and even there they were rare.

The mean number of failures per problem on each day by individuals or groups is shown in Fig. 2. Thus, for example, on the first day the mean number of failures per problem among the 15 groups of four was .08; in other words, about one-twelfth of the problems were failed. The improvement in performance over four days in terms of number of failures per problem is consistent with that shown in Fig. 1 in terms of number of questions per problem solved.

Figure 3 shows the decrease over four days in the amount of time required per problem. The time required, of course, is somewhat dependent on the number of questions asked, although not entirely so. The score for an individual or single group for one day was the median time required for solution of the four problems. In those few cases where there were two or more failures in one day, the median of the four times was taken simply as obtained; this procedure underestimates somewhat the median time that would have been required to solve all four problems, but as before the number of such cases was too small to affect the general results appreciably.

Size of Group

The second and major question with which the experiment was concerned involved the relation between efficiency in problem solving and size of group. As is evident in Fig. 1, there was no significant difference

TABLE 1

Values of t for Differences between Mean Scores: Number of Questions Per Problem

DAY	INDIVIDUALS VERSUS GROUPS OF TWO	INDIVIDUALS VERSUS GROUPS OF FOUR
1	2.67	2.18
2	2.86	1.96
3	2.30	2.22
4	2.11	2.45
All 4	2.64	2.62

between groups of two and groups of four in terms of the number of questions required to reach solution. The performance of individuals working alone, however, was consistently inferior to that of either size group. The t technique was used to test the difference on each day between the mean score of the 15 individuals and the mean score of the 15 pairs of Ss, and also that of the 15 groups of four. The values of t obtained are presented in Table 1. With 28 df, a t of 2.05 is required for significance at the .05 level and of 2.76 at the .01 level. All of the differences but one are significant at or beyond the .05 level.

A score for all four days was obtained for each individual or single group by taking the median number of questions required to solve the 16 problems. In terms of the means of these scores, the performance both of groups of two and of four is significantly better (.02 level) than that of individuals working alone (see Table 1).

That there were differences as a function of group size in terms of number of failures to reach solution is suggested by Fig. 2. Because of the fact that, as would be expected, the distributions of failure scores were not normal, t could not be used to test the significance of these differences. Instead a test described by Festinger (2) was employed. The mean number of failures per problem, all four days included, was for individuals, .26;

TABLE 2

Values of t for Differences between Mean Scores: Time Per Problem

DAY	INDIVIDUALS VERSUS GROUPS OF TWO	INDIVIDUALS VERSUS GROUPS OF FOUR	GROUPS OF TWO VERSUS GROUPS OF FOUR
1	.85	1.14	.12
2	1.01	2.36	.93
3	2.20	2.22	.06
4	2.15	3.49	1.90
All 4	2.39	3.27	1.18

for pairs, .10; for groups of four, .03. The values of d obtained indicate that the difference between individuals and groups of four is significant at well beyond the .01 level; the difference between individuals and pairs and the difference between pairs and groups of four are both significant at about the .02 level.

Differences in mean time to solution among individuals, groups of two, and groups of four may be seen in Fig. 3. Fortunately, the distributions of the median times, of which the individual points plotted in Fig. 3 are the means, were such as to make the use of t appropriate in testing the significance of differences between means. Table 2 presents the values of t obtained for the various comparisons. As in the case of number of questions required, none of the differences between groups of two and of four is significant. Differences between individuals and groups of two on the third and fourth days are significant at the .05 level; differences between individuals and groups of four on all except the first day are significant at the same level or beyond.

A score for all four days was obtained for each individual or single group by taking the median time required for the 16 problems. The means of these scores were 5.06 for individuals, 3.70 for groups of two, and 3.15 for groups of four. The values of t given in Table 2 show that the difference between the first and second mean is significant at the .05 level, and between the first and third mean at the .01 level.

Group performance was superior to individual performance in terms of elapsed time to solution. However, if, instead, an analysis is made in

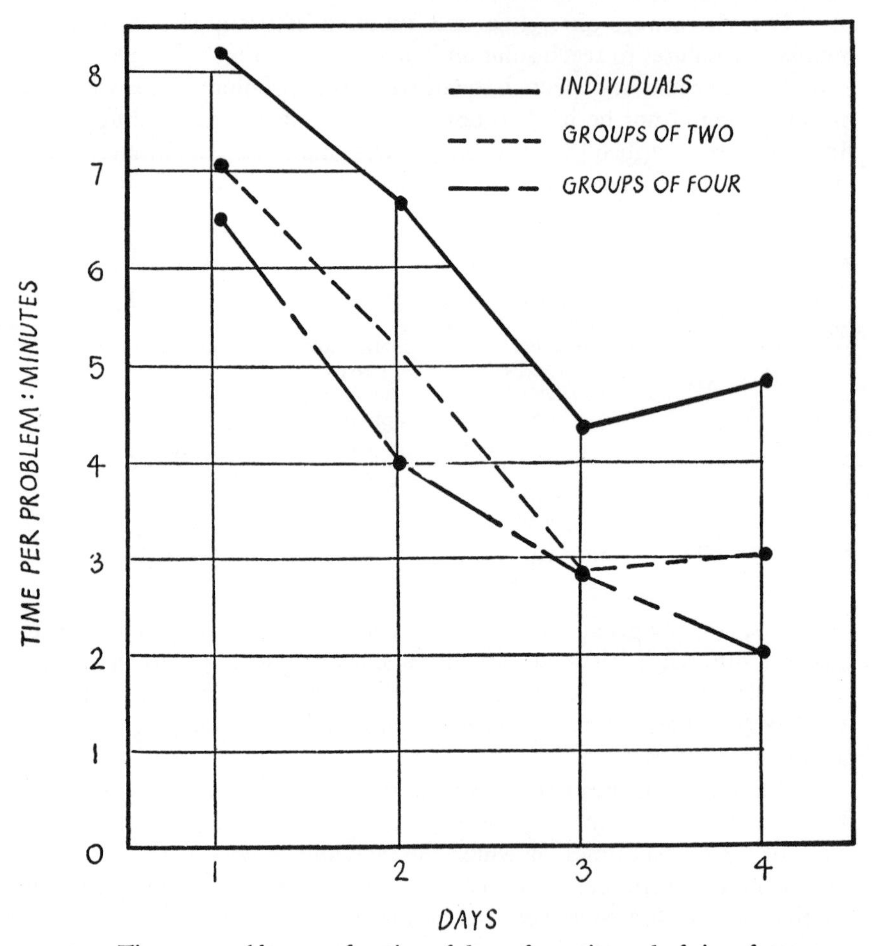

FIG. 3. Time per problem as a function of days of practice and of size of group

terms of number of man-minutes required for solution, the nature of the results obtained changes sharply. The number of man-minutes for a problem will, of course, be equal to the elapsed time multiplied by the number of persons in the group. In terms of man-minutes, the mean of the scores for all four days was 5.06 for individuals, 7.40 for groups of two, and 12.60 for groups of four. Since the variances for these three means were clearly not homogeneous, the use of t was not appropriate for testing the significance of the obtained differences. Instead, t' was employed (1). Both the difference between individuals and groups of two and the difference between groups of two and groups of four are significant at the .02 level. The difference between individuals and groups of four is significant at the .001 level. Clearly, in terms of man-minutes, the performance of individuals was superior to that of groups of two or of four; in addition, the performance of groups of two was superior to that of groups of four.

A supplementary question of some interest is whether the member of a group of two or of four getting the correct answer asked significantly more questions than the other member or members of the group. An analysis for all four days combined showed that for groups of two, the individual getting the correct answer asked an average of 1.55 questions more than the individual who failed to get the answer. A t of 5.04 with 14 *df* shows this to be significantly different from zero at the .001 level. However, it may be plausibly argued that in making this comparison, the final question which identified the correct object should be excluded. Before asking it, the individual had correctly formulated the answer. If the final answer is excluded, the difference is reduced from 1.55 to .55. This yields a t of 1.74 and is not significantly different from zero.

A similar analysis was done for groups of four. When the final question is included, the mean difference between the number of questions asked by the individual getting the answer and the average number asked by the other three members was 1.53. With a t of 6.50, this is significantly different from zero at the .001 level. Excluding the final question reduces the mean difference to .53. However, with a t of 2.25, this is still significantly different from zero at the .05 level. There appears to be some tendency for the member of a group of four getting the correct answer to ask more questions, even excluding the final question, than do other members of the group.

Individual Versus Group Practice

The third question which the experiment was intended to answer was whether improvement in individual performance occurs more rapidly with individual practice or with practice as a member of a group. To answer this question, all *S*s worked alone on the fifth day. As before, the score for each individual was the median number of questions required to solve the four problems. The mean of these scores for the 15 *S*s who had previously worked alone was 20.8;[2] for the 30 who had worked in pairs, 19.3; and for the 60 who had been members of groups of four, 19.1. None of the differences among these means is significant. Nor were any of the dif-

2 Comparison of this mean for the fifth day with that for the fourth day (20.8 versus 18.1) shown in Fig. 1 may raise the question: Why should the performance on the fifth day be inferior to that on the fourth day in view of the fact that the conditions under which these 15 individuals worked were the same on both days? However, the difference between these two means is not significant ($t = 1.04$).

ferences significant among the corresponding means on the fifth day for number of failures or for time scores. Learning went on as well in groups of two or of four as in individual practice.

DISCUSSION

The results obtained show that there is rapid learning of the skill involved in the game. The question now arises as to just what it is that is learned. To determine this, a qualitative analysis of the kinds of questions asked on successive days will be necessary. In a second experiment, now in progress, a complete record of all questions asked is being made in order that such an analysis can be carried out.

Group performances were superior to individual performance in terms of number of questions, number of failures, and elapsed time per problem; but the performance of groups of four was not superior to that of groups of two, except in terms of the number of failures to reach solution. Whether one could confidently have predicted such group superiority is questionable: Individual members of the group might have failed to make effective use of the information yielded by questions asked by other members; if this had been the case, the number of questions required by a group would have been larger, rather than smaller, than that required by an individual.

The fact that there were negligible differences between groups of two and of four either in number of questions or in elapsed time strongly suggests that the optimum size group is not larger than four. Proof of this will require further experimentation with other size groups. Additional experiments are also needed to determine whether the optimum size group is similar for other types of problems.

The question may be raised as to why there was a significant difference between groups of two and of four in number of failures to reach solution, this in spite of the fact that there were negligible differences in number of questions or elapsed time. A possible explanation is that increasing the number of participants from two to four reduces the probability of a persisting wrong set resulting in complete failure. For an individual, a wrong set once established may make it impossible to solve the problem. The probability that a wrong set would be established simultaneously for all participants would be smaller for a group of four than for a group of two.

Although group performances were superior to individual performance in terms of elapsed time to solution, the performance of individuals was superior to that of either size group in terms of number of man-minutes required for solution. The practical implications of this fact should not be overlooked. It appears probable that there are many kinds of problems which a group will solve more quickly than an individual. If elapsed time in hours, weeks, or months is the primary consideration, then such problems should be undertaken by groups. However, it appears equally probable that few of those same problems will be solved more efficiently in terms of man-minutes or man-hours by groups than by individuals. If a group of two is to solve a problem more efficiently than an individual in these latter terms, it must solve it in less than half the elapsed time required by the individual. Similarly, a group of four to be more efficient must solve the problem in less than one-fourth the elapsed time required by the individual. The importance of this point appears to be frequently overlooked.

What it is that accounts for the superiority of group as compared to individual performance in terms of number of questions or elapsed time remains to be determined. The suggestion may be made that the superiority of the group is due to the performance of the best member of the group. If one were to pick the most able individual from each of 15 groups of four, it would be expected that the performance of these 15 individuals would be superior to that of 15 individuals chosen by random sampling. The mean number of questions required by groups of four on the fourth day was 13.6. The mean of the best individual performances on the fifth day by former members of each of the 15 groups of four was 14.8, not significantly different from 13.6. This fact would seem to support the suggestion just made. However, this comparison is not fully valid. Which former member of a group of four had the best performance on the fifth day very probably depended partly on ability and to a considerable extent on chance. Selecting the best individual performance from each of the 15 groups thus capitalizes on chance in a way that reduces the mean obtained; it may yet be true that the mean performance of the 15 groups would be superior to that of the best individuals in each of the 15 groups.

That the superior performance of the group is not simply a function of the performance of the best member of the group is suggested by another consideration. If this were the case, then the larger the group, the better on the average should be the performance of the best member on the basis of sampling alone; hence the larger the group, the better should be the performance. The negligible differences obtained between groups of two and of four fail to confirm this expectation.

It may be expected that other factors such as broader range of relevant information, greater flexibility in approach, etc., are at least partly responsible for the superiority of group over individual performance. What these factors are and how they operate to produce an optimum size for a group can be determined only by additional experimentation.

An interesting supplementary question is whether the member of a group who obtains the right answer does so largely because he asks more questions than the other members of the group. The data obtained show that the number of questions asked by the member of a group of two obtaining the correct answer does not differ significantly from the number asked by the other member. A difference significant at the .05 level was found between the number asked by the member of a group of four obtaining the correct answer and the mean number asked by the other three members. However, this significant difference was only a matter of .53 questions per problem. It seems doubtful that getting the right answer is primarily due to the asking of more questions either in groups of two or of four.

The results obtained on the fifth day showed that learning resulting in improvement in individual performance occurred as rapidly with individual practice as with practice as a member of a group of two or of four. This fact, of course, should not be taken to mean that improvement is qualitatively the same under the different conditions. It may or may not be.

SUMMARY AND CONCLUSIONS

The game of "Twenty Questions" was employed in an experiment on problem solving. A total of 105 *S*s were assigned by chance to solve such problems working either alone, in pairs, or in groups of four. There were 15 individual *S*s, 15 groups of two, and 15 groups of four. Each individual or group was given four problems a day for four successive days. On the fifth day, all *S*s worked alone, each being given four problems.

Both the number of questions and the time required to solve each problem were recorded. Problems not solved in 30 questions were counted as failures.

1. In terms of number of questions, rapid improvement occurred in the performance both of individuals and of groups. By the fourth day, the curves appeared to be flattening out. Similar results were obtained in terms both of number of failures and of time per problem.

2. Group performances were superior to individual performance in terms of number of questions, number of failures, and elapsed time per problem; but the performance of groups of four was not superior to that of groups of two, except in terms of the number of failures to reach solution.

3. In terms of man-minutes required for solution, the performance of individuals was superior to that of groups; the performance of groups of two was superior to that of groups of four.

4. Improvement in individual performance occurred as rapidly with individual practice as with practice as a member of a group.

REFERENCES

1. Cochran, W. G., & Cox, G. M. *Experimental designs.* New York: Wiley, 1950.
2. Festinger, L. The significance of difference between means without reference to the frequency distribution function. *Psychometrika,* 1946, 11, 97–105.

3. Lindley, E. H. A study of puzzles with special reference ot the psychology of mental adaptation. *Amer. J. Psychol.*, 1897, 8, 431–493.
4. Shaw, M. E. A comparison of individuals and small groups in the rational solution of complex problems. *Amer. J. Psychol.*, 1932, 54, 491–504.

Effects of Group Size

EDWIN J. THOMAS
and
CLINTON F. FINK

THIS REPORT is an effort to formulate generalizations about the effects of group size from a critical review of past research and an analysis of methods and problems relating to this subject. It is focused mainly on studies of face-to-face groups ranging in size from 2–20 members, in which behavior was studied directly by observations, questionnaires, or interviews. Because of their relevance a few studies are included that depart in some respect from these criteria. While making no claim to comprehensiveness, we have included all studies that we could locate through 1960 meeting the above standards. In earlier reviews of research relating to small groups there were sections on group size, but no thorough review has been written. Studies of the size of families, organizations, cities, and societies are only generally relevant in this context and therefore have been excluded (see (8) for a review of studies relating to organizational size).

The studies discussed here do not represent an integrated attack upon a single problem or set of problems. Instead, they deal with a wide range of dependent variables and are concerned with establishing empirical relationships rather than with testing the implications of some general theory. To order the findings meaningfully, we have found it convenient to discuss them as specific topics under one of two major categories: (*a*) effects on the group as a whole, which include group performance, the distribution of participation, the nature of interaction, and group organ-

FROM *Psychological Bulletin*, 1963, 60, 371–384. Reprinted by permission of the authors and the American Psychological Association, Inc.
This article reports portions of a research project financed by a grant from the Horace H. Rackham School of Graduate Studies of the University of Michigan.

ization; and (*b*) effects on member behavior, including individual performance, conformity and consensus, and member satisfaction.

EFFECTS FOR THE GROUP AS A WHOLE

Group Performance

Ten experimental studies dealt with the effects of group size on group performance in problem solving or judgmental tasks. These findings are summarized according to four main classes of dependent variables: quality of performance, speed, efficiency, and productivity.

The quality of group problem solving was examined in four studies with mixed results. Taylor and Faust (41) found that in playing the game Twenty Questions, four-man groups correctly solved more problems than did two-man groups. Similarly, Fox, Lorge, Weltz, and Herrold (14) found that the quality of solutions to complex human-relations problems was significantly greater for groups of 12 and 13 than for groups of 6, 7, and 8. In contrast, Lorge and Solomon (29, 30) discovered no relationship between group size (2–5 members in the first study and 3, 4, 6, and 7 members in the second) and the proportion of groups which arrived at the correct solution to the Tartaglia problem.

The quality of group judgments based on collective decisions also showed mixed relationships to group size. South (36) found no difference between three-person and six-person groups in their ability to judge emotional expressions from photographs, but he did find that the six-person groups were better (i.e., agreed more with expert opinion) at judging the quality of English compositions. Ziller (46) presented groups of two to six Air Force officers with two types of task: he found a positive relationship between group size and the quality of the group's judgment concerning the importance of certain facts for making military decisions; however, there was a curvilinear relationship between size and the accuracy of the group's judgment of the number of dots on a card with four- and five-man groups doing less well than two-, three-, and six-man groups. Perlmutter's study (34) involved group memory rather than judgment: he found that three-person groups had somewhat better immediate recall for a story (The War of the Ghosts) than did two-person groups, but the difference was not statistically significant.

Speed of group performance was observed in three of the above studies (34, 36, 41) as well as in the study by Kidd (25). In each case, speed was measured in terms of the amount of time required for the group to complete the task. Group size did not influence speed in the case of four problem solving tasks or the memory task. However, in the two judgmental tasks used by South, three-person groups were faster than six-person groups. South suggested that the judgmental tasks required the group to reach a compromise; to the extent that more discussion is needed in order to reconcile a wider variety of initial opinions, this would account for the fact that the larger groups took longer to reach a decision.

The efficiency with which the group solves a problem was considered in connection with two tasks we have designated as "concept attainment" tasks. According to Taylor and Faust, two-person groups were more efficient than four-person groups since they expended fewer man minutes of "labor." However, this is not really a new finding, since it is mathematically implied by the fact that there was no difference in speed as a function of size. Another meaning of problem solving efficiency involves the amount of intellectual effort expended, which in this case is measured by the number of questions asked by the group before they reached a solution. This measure of efficiency failed to differentiate between two- and four-person groups in the Taylor and Faust study, but South found that six-person groups were more efficient than three-person groups.

Group productivity, defined as the number of correct units produced in a given time period, was examined in three experiments. Comparing groups of Sizes 3–10 Watson (45) found a correlation of .65 between size and the number of different correct words created in an anagrams task. With a similar task, unscrambling sentences, Kidd found no differences in productivity between groups of two, four, and six. Gibb (16) briefly reported a comparison between individuals and groups of Sizes 2, 3, 6, 12, 24, 48, and 96 and reported that the number of suggested solutions to a complex problem increased as a negatively accelerated function of group size.

Considering the group performance findings as a whole, it appears that both quality of performance and group productivity were positively correlated with group size under some conditions, and under no conditions were smaller groups superior. In contrast, measures of speed showed no difference or else favored the smaller groups. The heterogeneity of tasks and of measurement procedures prevent more precise generalizations.

Distribution of Participation

Four studies were focused on the relative degree of participation of each member. In one of the earliest investigations in this area Dawe (10) kept a record of the number of remarks made by each child in kindergarten classes ranging in size from 14 to 46. The total number of remarks decreased with increasing size, but not to a statistically significant degree. While an increase in the size of the group was accompanied by an increase in the total number of children who spoke ($r=.82$), there was a decrease in the proportion of the group who spoke ($r=-.58$). Dawe reported also that the members who were seated toward the front of the room tended to speak more often than those seated further back, indicating that a spatial factor may be one determinant of the relationship between size and participation.

Using Bales' categories, Bales, Strodtbeck, Mills, and Roseborough (3) observed interaction in leaderless discussion groups ranging in size from three to eight members. As size increased there was an increase in the relative discrepancy between the percentage of participation for the person ranked first and that for the person ranked second and a reduction in the difference between the percentage of participation for the person ranked second and for all those with less participation. The authors attempted to fit a harmonic function to these curves, but with no success. Later Stephan (38) was able to fit an exponential curve more successfully to the same data.

Stephan and Mishler (39) conducted an experiment to assess the generality of their exponential model beyond the type of group and method of gathering data used in the study by Bales et al. (3). The unit of participation was all the verbal behavior exhibited by an individual between the time the previous speaker finished and the next began—a much larger unit than was used in the earlier study. In groups ranging in size from 4 to 12 members, they obtained results essentially the same as those of Bales et al.

The relationship between group size and the distribution of acts was analyzed by Miller (33) for groups of Sizes 3–10, 12, 14, 16, 18, and 20. Although Miller used the same unit of participation as Stephan and Mishler, the task was different: the game Twenty Questions. As in Dawe's study, it was found that the average number of participations per member decreased as size increased ($r = -.80$). This of course is what would be expected when the length of the discussion period and the rate of participation are both held constant: as the group increases in size there is less opportunity for any individual to speak. However, this reduction in opportunity to speak did not seem to be accompanied by decreasing participation of the members not ranked highest, for there was found a small, nonsignificant negative correlation between group size and the number of persons who deviated from their expected percentage of participation based on equal distribution. Thus Miller's study casts doubt on the generality of the findings of Bales et al. and Stephan and Mishler and of the models developed to depict the results.

Nature of Interaction

Four additional studies provided information about the qualitative characteristics of group interaction. To study the "interaction profile" of the acts in the 12 categories of Bales' scheme, Bales and Borgatta (2) observed discussion groups ranging in size from two to seven. The raw number of acts in each category was made a percentage of the total number of acts in the 12 categories and then converted by an arc-sine transformation. Analysis indicated that as size increased, there was an increase in the categories of showing tension release and giving suggestions; and a decrease in categories of showing tension, showing agreement, and asking for opinion. In addition, two-person groups appeared to have certain unique properties, namely, a high rate in the category of showing tension coupled with low rates in the categories of showing disagreement and showing antagonism. An odd-even effect was also apparent: groups of four and six showed higher rates than did groups of three, five, and seven in the categories of showing disagreement and showing antagonism, but lower rates in the category of asking for suggestions. These findings must be interpreted as representing *relative* increases or decreases in an interaction category. Bales and Borgatta offer intriguing speculations to interpret the trends, but it is difficult to draw conclusions about what the *critical changes* may be as size increases from two to seven because a relative increase in one category may come about due to either an absolute increase for the category or an absolute decrease for all other categories, or both.

Bales and Borgatta also analyzed variability over four sessions for individuals and groups. They found increased variability for each individual's performance as size increased. The authors claimed that scores may have been less reliable in the larger groups because of partitioning scores among a greater number of persons. Another interpretation given by these researchers is that there may have been more shifting of roles in larger groups because there were more persons to perform role functions. Trends of variability among individuals, of given groups over successive sessions and among groups, revealed no clear-cut size effects.

Slater (35) used Bales' categories with groups ranging from two to seven and concluded that there were inhibiting forces in the smallest groups which prevented the expression of dissatisfaction and disagreement. Scores on an Inhibition Index (the ratio of the number of acts in four agreement categories to the number of acts in five disagreement categories) were significantly higher in groups of two, three, and four than in groups of five, six, and seven. Slater's explanation was that the consequences of alienating a single member may have been more severe in the smaller than in the larger groups.

A study by Berkowitz (5) of groups of 3, 4, 6, 7, 9, and 10 members revealed that there was more disagreement in solving logical problems in the larger groups than in the smaller groups—a finding consistent with those of Slater and Bales and Borgatta.

Bass and Norton (4) observed leaderless discussion groups of 2, 4, 6, 8, and 12 members in which each member was rated on nine aspects of leadership behavior. As group size increased, the average leadership rating assigned to group members decreased significantly—group size accounting for 83% of the variance. There was also a nonsignificant tendency for the within-group variance of ratings to increase with size. The authors concluded that opportunity to adopt leadership functions decreased directly with an increase in group size.

Tentatively it would appear that smaller groups inhibit expression of disagreements and dissatisfactions more than larger groups and give each individual more opportunity to interact and to exhibit leadership behavior. The possibility that there are unique, odd-even and near-linear size effects on the nature of interaction, as Bales and Borgatta suggest, should be pursued further, possibly using different methods from the ones employed by these researchers.

Group Organization

The last set of studies related to effects on the group as a whole concerns group organization. In Berkowitz's study of the social organization of problem solving groups, 20 variables were found to be significantly affected by group size and most of these were reduced by a cluster analysis to two relatively independent sets of variables. The first cluster was called group cohesion, consisting mainly of sociometric variables such as the number of friendship choices. The components of this cluster were negatively related to size. The second cluster consisted of variables reflecting organization and division of labor. The variables in this cluster and their relationship to size follow: as size increased, there was decreasing contribution of the least active member, higher member variation of interaction, higher variation in the number of rules for solving the problem suggested by members and subsequently adopted by the group, increasing number of leaders, higher variation of rules suggested by each man, increasing number of votes required to reach decisions, increasing suggestions conveyed by those who did not originally make the suggestion, and higher specialization in the use of rules to solve the problems.

In a study of factors affecting consensus in decision making groups, Hare (19) found a greater tendency for groups of 12 than for groups of 5 to break into factions or cliques. This trend was not significant, however, and was based on the reports of group members. Probably more reliable are the findings of Miller who observed directly the frequency with which two or more members of a group talked or whispered among themselves rather than to the group as a whole. A significant correlation of .77 was found between the number of members (3–10, 12, 14, 16, 18, and 20) and the number of cliques. Also, Miller found that this increase in cliques was associated with a decrease in group cohesiveness; a Cohesiveness Index correlated −.52 with group size and −.60 with the number of cliques.

After familiarizing subjects with the concept of the primary group, Fisher (13) asked them to describe the primary groups to which they belonged and rank them for intimacy. Within the size range of 2–12 members, smaller groups were ranked as significantly more intimate.

Taken together, these studies indicate that as size increases there will be decreasing group cohesiveness and increasing organization and division of labor in the group, along with the development of cliques and possibly of factions.

EFFECTS OF MEMBER BEHAVIOR

Individual Performance

The effect of group size on individual performance has been considered primarily in connection with practical problems. In education, for example, there is a long history of concern with class size as a possible influence on classroom learning. We will not attempt to review this literature here, since it has been covered by Hudelson (20), Von Borgersrode (44), Goodlad (18), and McKeachie (31). Hudelson reported on 59 controlled experiments of the effects of class size, 46 of which favored large over small classes. In Von Borgersrode's review 73 studies were appraised, 19 of which were classified as semicontrolled and 24 as controlled, his conclusion was that "On the whole the statistical findings definitely favor the large classes at every level of instruction except kindergarten" (p. 199). In his review of the effects of lecture size at the college level, McKeachie noted that more recent studies have not been as complimentary to large lectures as were the earlier studies done during the 1920s. Nevertheless, he concluded that large lectures were not generally inferior. Lorge et al. (27) made reference in their review of together-alone studies to some of the literature on classroom learning and concluded that there was probably an interaction between class size, teaching methods, and study methods as determinants of educational effectiveness. But even so, the consensus of the reviewers was that large classes are either superior to small classes or at least not inferior.

A second area of practical concern is the productivity of individual workers as a function of the size of work groups. Marriot (32) found that the amount produced by male workers in a British factory, as measured by average piecework earnings per man, declined significantly as the size of the work group increased from 10 to 50 members. In contrast, Gekoski (15) found a nonsignificant positive relation between individual productivity and size of work group (4–19 members) among female clerical workers in an American insurance company. Because these studies differed simultaneously along several dimensions, we have no basis for speculation as to the specific conditions which determine whether group size will be positively or negatively correlated with individual productivity.

Two experiments dealt with the individual's improvement in problem solving as a result of his interacting in groups of varying size. Taylor and Faust (41) found that practice in playing Twenty Questions enhanced the individual's ability to solve such problems, but it did not matter whether the practice was obtained alone, as a member of a two-person group, or as a member of a four-person group. By contrast, positive results were reported by Utterback and Fotheringham (43) in regard to the quality of solutions to human relations problems. Individual answers were recorded both before and after a discussion in groups of 3, 6, 9, or 12 members. Improvement in quality of the individual's solutions was significantly greater for the larger groups. However, there was also a significant interaction between group size and the manner in which the discussion was led: when the moderator intervened a great deal ("full moderation"), individual improvement was greatest for 12-person groups; but when the moderator intervened very little ("partial moderation"), individual improvement was greatest for 3-person groups. Thus group size sometimes is related to individual problem solving, but the direction of the relationship is highly dependent on group conditions other than size.

Conformity and Consensus

In his famous experiment on yielding to a group of peers who, unknown to the naive subject, had been instructed to report unanimous but incorrect judgments of the length of visually presented lines, Asch (1) manipulated the size of the unanimous opposition. He found that as the number of confederates increased from 1 to 3, the amount of yielding to their unanimous judgment increased significantly; but there was no further increase in conformity as the confederates increased in number to 4, 8, or 16. In two related studies, Goldberg (17) and Kidd (25) failed to find any effect of group size even though their manipulations of group pressure did succeed in producing a significant amount of conformity. Goldberg's subjects, in groups of 2 or 4, made individual judgments of the intelligence of persons from their photographs; while Kidd's subjects, in groups of 2, 4, or 6 made individual judgments of flicker frequency. In both experiments, each individual made a second judgment after being exposed to false feedback concerning the group's average first judgment. Conformity, as measured by shifting toward the bogus group average, occurred in all groups, but the amount of yielding was not related to group size in either experiment. In contrast, Kishida (26) found a significant size effect using groups of 5, 10, and 30 Japanese university students. Subjects responded individually to an opinion questionnaire, then received true feedback as to the majority opinion, and finally responded a second time to the questionnaire. Although there was a shift toward conformity in all groups, magnitude of opinion change showed a curvilinear relationship to group size, being greatest in 10-person groups and least in 5-person groups. The results of these four studies indicate that the magnitude of the group's influence on the individual is a function of group size under some conditions, but differences in task and procedure again preclude specification of the relevant conditions.

A second set of findings involved measurement of the individual's opinion both before and after group discussion of a problem. Half of Kishida's (26) groups discussed the opinion items and arrived at a group decision. Analysis of the individual postdiscussion responses indicated that shift toward the group opinion bore the same curvilinear relationship to group size under discussion conditions as in the condition involving feedback of the majority opinion. A negative effect of group size was found by Hare (19) with groups of 5 and 12 Boy Scouts, with two measures showing that consensus increased more in the smaller groups. Finally, Utterback and Fotheringham (43) reported a significant interaction between group size and the amount of intervention by the discussion moderator. Increase in consensus was greatest in 12-person groups under full moderation, but greatest in 3-person groups under partial moderation. However, there was no main effect of group size in this study. These findings lend further weight to the conclusion that group size is an important factor in determining the amount of yielding to conformity pressures.

Member Satisfaction

Questionnaire measures of members' subjective reactions to the group were included in four of the studies cited above. Both Hare (19) and Slater (35) found that members of larger groups were significantly less satisfied with the amount of time available for discussion, with their opportunity to participate, and with the group meeting or its decision. In addition, Slater found that his subjects considered five members to be optimum (i.e., neither too large nor too small) for the task of discussing a human relations problem. In contrast to the others, Ziller (46) found no clear relationship between group size and members' satisfaction with their own part in the discussion, and Miller (33) found no relationship between group size and three measures of satisfaction. With this exception, the general trend of the findings indicates that the smaller the group, the more likely it is that the individual will be satisfied with the discussion and with his own part in it. McKeachie's (31) review of studies on discussion groups at the college level also indicated that larger groups were less satisfying to both students and instructors. It must be remembered, however, that the studies referred to here all dealt with discussion groups attempting to solve particular problems, and that the generalization may not apply to other types of groups.

CONCLUSIONS

On the basis of this review it is apparent that group size has significant effects on aspects of individual and group performance, on the nature of interaction and distribution of participation of group members, on group organization, on conformity and consensus, and on member satisfaction. This appraisal suggests that the variable of group size should be included in theories of group behavior, distinguishing where possible between the effects that result from the interaction of group size with other independent variables and the effects arising from intervening variables that are dependably and nondependably associated with size.

It is concluded furthermore that future research on group size should proceed systematically, making every effort (*a*) to vary size in complete sequence over a suitably large range; (*b*) to conceptualize, identify, and measure relevant intervening variables; (*c*) to determine in advance whether these variables should be expected axiomatically to be correlated with size or would be only contingent variables; and (*d*) to use multivariate designs, where appropriate, in which group size and significant intervening variables are both manipulated experimentally.

REFERENCES

1. Asch, E. E. Effects of group pressure upon the modification and distortion of judgments. In D. Cartwright & A. Zander (Eds.), *Group dynamics.* Evanston, Ill.: Row, Peterson, 1953, Pp. 151–163.
2. Bales, R. F., & Borgatta, E. F. Size of group as a factor in the interaction profile. In A. P. Hare, E. F. Borgatta, & R. F. Bales (Eds.), *Small groups.* New York: Knopf, 1955. Pp. 396–413.
3. Bales, R. F., Strodtbeck, F., Mills, T., & Roseborough, Mary E. Channels of communication in small groups. *Amer. sociol. Rev.,* 1951, 16, 461–468.
4. Bass, B. M., & Norton, F. T. Group size and leaderless discussions. *J. appl. Psychol.,* 1951, 35, 397–400.
5. Berkowitz, M. I. An experimental study of the relation between group size and social organization. Unpublished doctoral dissertation, Yale University, 1958.
6. Borgatta, E. F., & Cottrell, L. S., Jr. Directions for research in group behavior. *Amer. J. Sociol.,* 1957, 63, 42–48.
7. Bossard, J. H. S. The law of family interaction. *Amer. J. Sociol.,* 1944, 50, 289–293.
8. Caplow, T. Organizational size. *Admin. sci. Quart.,* 1957, 1, 484–506.
9. Caplow, T. Further developments of a theory of coalitions in the triad. *Amer. J. Sociol.,* 1959, 64, 488–493.
10. Dawe, Helen C. The influence of size of kindergarten group upon performance. *Child Develpm.,* 1934, 5, 295–303.
11. Ekman, G. The four effects of cooperation. *J. soc. Psychol.,* 1955, 41, 149–163.
12. Eysenck, H. J. The validity of judgments as a function of the number of judges. *J. exp. Psychol.,* 1939, 25, 650–654.
13. Fisher, P. H. An analysis of the primary group. *Sociometry,* 1953, 16, 272–276.
14. Fox, D., Lorge, I., Weltz, P., & Herrold, K. Comparison of decisions written by large and small groups. *Amer. Psychologist,* 1953, 8, 351. (Abstract)
15. Gekoski, N. The relationship of group characteristics to productivity. Unpublished doctoral dissertation, Ohio State University, 1952.
16. Gibb, J. R. Effects of group size and threat reduction on creativity in a problem-solving situation. *Amer. Psychologist,* 1951, 6, 324. (Abstract)

17. Goldberg, S. C. Three situational determinants of conformity to social norms. *J. abnorm. soc. Psychol.*, 1954, 49, 325–329.
18. Goodlad, I. I. Classroom organization. In C. W. Harris (Ed.), *Encyclopedia of educational research.* New York: Macmillan, 1960. Pp. 221–225.
19. Hare, A. P. Interaction and consensus in different sized groups. *Amer. sociol. Rev.*, 1952, 17, 261–267.
20. Hudelson, E. *Class size at the college level.* Minneapolis: Univer. Minnesota Press, 1928.
21. Indik, B. P. Organization size and member participation. Unpublished doctoral dissertation, University of Michigan, 1961.
22. Jennings, Helen H. Sociometric choice process in personality and group formation. In J. L. Moreno (Ed.), *The sociometry reader.* Glencoe, Ill.: Free Press, 1960. Pp. 87–113.
23. Kelley, H. H., & Thibaut, J. W. Experimental studies of group problem solving and process. In G. Lindzey (Ed.), *Handbook of social psychology.* Cambridge, Mass.: Addison-Wesley, 1954. Pp. 735–785.
24. Kephart, W. M. A quantitative analysis of intragroup relationships. *Amer. J. Sociol.*, 1950, 60, 544–549.
25. Kidd, J. S. Social influence phenomena in a task-oriented group situation. *J. abnorm. soc. Psychol.*, 1958, 56, 13–17.
26. Kishida, M. A study of the effects of group norm upon the change of opinions. *Jap. J. Psychol.*, 1956, 27, 172–173. (Abstract)
27. Lorge, I., Fox, D., Davitz, J., & Brenner, M. A survey of studies contrasting the quality of group performance and individual performance. *Psychol. Bull.*, 1958, 55, 337–370.
28. Lorge, I., & Solomon, H. Two models of group behavior in the solution of Eureka-type problems. *Psychometrika,* 1955, 20, 139–149.
29. Lorge, I., & Solomon, H. Individual performance and group performance in problem solving related to group size and previous exposure to the problem. *J. Psychol.*, 1959, 48, 107–114.
30. Lorge, I., & Solomon, H. Group and individual performance in problem solving related to previous exposure to problem, level of aspiration, and group size. *Behav. Sci.*, 1960, 5, 28–39.
31. McKeachie, W. J. Research on teaching at the college and university level. In N. Gage (Ed.), *Handbook of research on teaching.* Chicago, Ill.: Rand McNally, 1963. Pp. 1118–1172.
32. Marriot, R. Size of working group and output. *Occup. Psychol.*, 1949, 26, 47–57.
33. Miller, N. E., Jr. The effect of group size on decision-making discussions. Unpublished doctoral dissertation, University of Michigan, 1951.
34. Perlmutter, H. V. Group memory of meaningful material. *J. Psychol.*, 1953, 35, 361–370.
35. Slater, P. E. Contrasting correlates of group size. *Sociometry*, 1958, 21, 129–139.
36. South, E. B. Some psychological aspects of committee work. *J. appl. Psychol.*, 1927, 11, 348–368.
37. Steiner, J. D., & Rajaratnam, N. A model for the comparison of individual and group performance scores. *Behav. Sci.*, 1961, 6, 142–148.
38. Stephan, F. F. The relative rate of communication between members of small groups. *Amer. sociol. Rev.*, 1952, 17, 482–486.
39. Stephan, F. F., & Mishler, E. G. The distribution of participation in small groups: An exponential approximation. *Amer. sociol. Rev.*, 1952, 17, 598–608.
40. Taylor, D. W. Problem solving by groups. In, *Proceedings of the XIV International Congress of Psychology: 1954.* Amsterdam: North Holland Publishing, 1954.
41. Taylor, D. W., & Faust, W. L. Twenty questions: Efficiency in problem-solving as a function of size of group. *J. exp. Psychol.*, 1952, 44, 360–368.
42. Thomas, E. J., & Fink, C. F. Models of group problem solving. *J. abnorm. soc. Psychol.*, 1961, 63, 53–63.
43. Utterback, W. E., & Fotheringham, W. C. Experimental studies of motivated group discussion. *Speech Monogr.*, 1958, 25, 268–277.

44. Von Borgersrode, F. Class size. In W. S. Monroe (Ed.), *Encyclopedia of educational research.* New York: Macmillan, 1941. Pp. 197–200.
45. Watson, G. B. Do groups think more efficiently than individuals? *J. abnorm. soc. Psychol.*, 1928, 23, 328–336.
46. Ziller, R. C. Group size: A determinant of the quality and stability of group decisions. *Sociometry*, 1957, 20, 165–173.

CHAPTER 10

GROUP COMPOSITION, COALITIONS, AND SUBGROUPS

On the Dimensions of Group Behavior

EDGAR F. BORGATTA,
LEONARD S. COTTRELL, JR.,
and
HENRY J. MEYER

SOCIAL PSYCHOLOGY is in a phase of renewed interest in the systematic study of the properties of social groups.[1] It is especially important at this point that investigators take time to clarify the nature of the problem, to identify the more promising lines of attack, and to avoid certain sterile types of effort which have sometimes been made. This paper is oriented to the preliminary task of clarifying and structuring the problem. The position taken here is that it is necessary to further progress in the scientific study of social groups that we achieve a clear and systematic identification of the essential dimensions in terms of which any social interactional field can be described.

FROM *Sociometry*, 1956, 19, 222–240. Reprinted by permission of the authors and the American Sociological Association, Inc.

---

1 The problem of the classification of groups has historically been dealt with in sociology proper. For a review of relevant sociological literature on this topic see (16).

When it becomes possible to arrange all social collectivities on a meaningful set of orthogonal (independent) dimensions, the definition of group and the discrimination of group from not-group become arbitrary matters of convenience and not issues of critical debate. As a preliminary to any other objectives, this should save time and energy otherwise wasted searching for the best definition of *a group* by trying to fit alleged groups in some definition. Similarly, this should circumvent the problem of developing valid criteria for determining when a collectivity is a group and when it is not.

Further, a successful outcome of the approach proposed here would provide a basis for a meaningful typology of collectivities or interactional fields which would have wide general utility. In addition to this positive gain, the discipline could be spared fruitless controversy as to the merits and validity of various ad hoc taxonomies. In this connection an incidental gain would be the ease of settling the question as to whether or not laboratory experimental groups are "real" groups. Even modest progress in the direction suggested would ensure that research efforts in comparative study of groups and in relating specifiable characteristics of process and product to specific characteristics of the group would be more likely to yield significant generalizations. Experimentation can certainly be designed and conducted with more clarity and specificity when the significant dimensions to be controlled and manipulated are identifiable and measurable. It is not too much to expect that a knowledge of the dimensions of natural groups will free and stimulate scientific imagination to hypothecate concerning configurations of dimensions not found in nature and to test such hypotheses experimentally.

Without doubt few investigators would disagree with the importance of the strategy here proposed. Its desirability is implicit in many formulations and explicit in some, but development along these lines as an actuality has generally been placed in the future. For example, in 1941 one of the present authors urged the necessity for the kind of development we are proposing here but his suggestion was not followed up (10). The practical question is, of course, whether the necessary technology and theoretical sophistication are available at this time to implement such a strategy. It is true that studies pointed in this direction are few and for the most part unsatisfactory. Two in particular mark substantial progress in the desired direction of systematization on an empirical basis. We shall discuss them in some detail and, in so doing, indicate some next steps.

In considering studies bearing on our problem it is useful to recall the experience of psychology in attempting description and classifications of personality characteristics. Of particular interest and relevance is the fact that the many descriptive and taxonomic efforts have given way to efforts to identify and measure dimensions in terms of which any personality may be described. This shift was greatly facilitated by the development of factor analytic procedures. Excellent reviews of factor studies of personality have been published by French (11, 12) and Cattell (3, 6, 7). These reviews, while differing in their form and approach, do contain a number of useful lessons and stimulating suggestions for investigators interested in exploring the dimensions of groups. Some of the more salient of these we shall indicate in our following discussion.

The first of the pioneering studies in the dimensions of groups we shall discuss is that by John K. Hemphill and Charles M. Westie, the results of which were published in 1950 under the title "The Measurement of Group Dimensions" (13).

Hemphill and Westie

The task to which Hemphill and Westie directed themselves was to choose a limited number of variables for systematic group description which were (a) meaningful within a sociological or psychological framework, (b) capable of expression in simple linear measures, (c) molar rather than molecular, and (d) relatively independent (orthogonal). Fourteen characteristics were, on the basis of examination of available descriptive and theoretical materials of others, judged to satisfy the criteria:

1. *Autonomy* is the degree to which a group functions independently of other groups.
2. *Control* is the degree to which a group regulates the behavior of group members.
3. *Flexibility* is the degree to which a group's activities are marked by informal procedures rather than by adherence to rigidly structured procedures.
4. *Hedonic Tone* is the degree to which group participation is accompanied by a general feeling of pleasantness or agreeableness.
5. *Homogeneity* is the degree to which members of a group possess similar characteristics.
6. *Intimacy* is the degree to which members of a group are familiar with the personal details of one another's lives.
7. *Participation* is the degree to which members of a group apply time and effort to group activities.
8. *Permeability* is the degree to which a group permits ready access to membership.
9. *Polarization* is the degree to which a group is oriented and works toward a single goal which is clear and specific to all members.
10. *Potency* is the degree to which a group has significance for its members.
11. *Size* is the number of members of the group.
12. *Stability* is the degree to which a group persists over a period of time with essentially the same characteristics.

13. *Stratification* is the degree to which a group orders its members into status hierarchies.

14. *Viscidity* is the degree to which members of the group function as a unit.

College students were asked a series of open-ended questions descriptive of groups, and from these responses 1100 descriptive items were constructed. Then, five judges screened the items and classified them according to their relevance to the 14 proposed dimensions. The result was a reduction of the number of items to 355. The number of items falling in each category ranged from 9 in Hedonic Tone to 47 in Permeability. (Size of group, of course, had only one question.) Following, 200 subjects (college students) gave descriptions involving 35 different groups in terms of the 355 items. Campus groups comprised most of the list described and the groups ranged in size from 6 to 27,000. Corrected estimates of split-half reliability of the dimensions based on 100 respondents ranged from .59 to .87. An internal consistency check based on responses from all 200 subjects was done by correlating with each dimension score: (a) the constituent items, (b) items previously judged relevant but not satisfying the arbitrary conditions for inclusion, and (c) five randomly selected from other scales. The median correlations with the dimensions by items so chosen were respectively .36, .15, and .12. Descriptions of the same groups by different respondents were compared and substantial agreement was noted.

TABLE I

*Intercorrelations among Fourteen Group Dimension Scores**

	1	2	3	4	5	6	7	8	9	10	11	12	13
1. Autonomy													
2. Control	−.06												
3. Flexibility	.29	−.29											
4. Hedonic tone	.16	−.37	−.16										
5. Homogeneity	.12	.10	−.02	.40									
6. Intimacy	.12	.19	−.21	.38	.31								
7. Participation	−.25	−.12	−.25	.38	.12	.21							
8. Permeability	.46	−.29	.07	.19	−.02	.10	−.53						
9. Polarization	.03	−.02	−.31	.40	.28	.19	.49	−.10					
10. Potency	−.34	.03	−.46	.25	.07	.28	.69	−.51	.34				
11. Size	.03	.19	−.46	.07	−.16	.10	−.10	.19	−.16	−.02			
12. Stability	.00	−.19	.25	.19	.25	−.02	.00	−.06	.28	−.16	−.54		
13. Stratification	−.40	.21	−.10	−.49	−.31	−.12	.29	−.51	−.16	.34	.10	−.12	
14. Viscidity	.19	−.46	−.02	.81	.38	.03	.38	.16	.38	.19	−.16	.21	−.46

* The probability of securing a correlation value of .29 or larger by chance is .01. This table corresponds to Table 5 in (13).

The scores of the 35 groups on each dimension were intercorrelated using tetrachoric coefficients. Their results are shown in Table 1.

With respect to these results the authors commented that "While the majority of the intercorrelations among dimension scores are small enough to meet the criterion of independent dimensions, others were considered high enough to demand further attention." Following the analysis described above, the authors made some revisions of the scales to reduce overlap among the measures but reported that there was probably a substantial overlap among such dimensions as Viscidity and Hedonic Tone, or Participation and Potency. The intercorrelations among the revised scales were not reported.

While we could not do a factor analysis on the revised scale scores, it is of interest to note that a complete centroid analysis of the matrix given in Table 1 showed it to contain four relatively substantial factors which jointly accounted for 58.4 per cent of the total variance of the dimensions. The communalities (h^2) ranged from .30 to .91, suggesting that that even the most independent scale appreciably overlaps other scales in the matrix. The rotated factor matrix is shown as Table 2 and the four factors separately listed with variables on which loadings of $|.40|$ or greater occur. Tentative descriptive names, even though awkward, are attached to them.

Since the number of items per scale used by Hemphill and Westie is

TABLE 2

Rotated Factor Matrix

	1	2	3	4	h^2
1. Autonomy	23	−51	20	09	36
2. Control	−55	12	49	−23	61
3. Flexibility	−08	−38	−19	56	50
4. Hedonic tone	91	07	25	−13	91
5. Homogeneity	29	03	58	12	44
6. Intimacy	23	10	46	−15	30
7. Participation	34	81	−05	14	79
8. Permeability	27	−72	−02	−18	62
9. Polarization	40	36	31	15	41
10. Potency	20	80	05	−17	71
11. Size	−05	−10	−05	−81	67
12. Stability	15	00	15	63	44
13. Stratification	−44	54	−28	−06	59
14. Viscidity	90	04	−00	09	82
					$\bar{x}=58.4$

already large and the corrected reliabilities reported for the scales account, in a simple average (sum of squared reliabilities), for about 57 per cent of the variation, the hypothesis that the 14 scales are orthogonal cannot be supported. However, a comparison of the reported reliabilities with the factor loadings will indicate that the estimate of reliabilities may be low and, concomitantly, that the four extracted factors leave considerable room for several unique factors.[2] We conclude, therefore, that in the original matrix of items there are more than four factors, but the existence of 14 orthogonal scales is not demonstrated. Thus, the concepts for scale construction, while they may have had meaningfulness in a "sociological or psychological framework," also may have forced the empirical data to fit them rather than modifying themselves to fit the data.

But we are not so much concerned with this possible shortcoming of the Hemphill and Westie study as we are with indicating its value in providing leads to further productive effort.[3] Certain things should be considered in future investigations.

1. The attempt by Hemphill and Westie to apply their definition of a group was probably a mistake.[4] At this stage the most inclusive definition should be used. The authors themselves suggest difficulty with their definition and indicate that some conception of degree of "groupness" might better be employed rather than a group—not-group dichotomy.

2. Distinguishing between groups and other collectivities is of no utility at this stage. The essential problem is to identify basic dimensions in terms of which any interactive situation may be described. Meaningful classifications may emerge later but these will be identified by particular score configurations or profiles.

3. The Hemphill and Westie study contributes an important corrective to the tendency occasionally found to "throw everything in the hopper" of factor analysis with the apparent expectation that meaningful structures will somehow result. The work of these authors suggests the desirability of a much more systematic approach to sampling a universe of items descriptive of collective behavior. *The problem is on the one hand to avoid a primitive empiricism and on the other to avoid being limited by confining theoretical frames.* Probably a good compromise could be to range widely for theoretical formulations and to extract as many implied

2 In some cases the h^2 is low while the reliability is high, indicating the independence of the variable. On the other hand, the relationship reported between Hedonic Tone and Viscidity is either too high, or the reliabilities reported are too low, or both. This is seen when the correction for attenuation is made and the corrected statistic accounts for more than 100 per cent of the variance.

3 Shortly before this paper went to press the recent publication by Hemphill (14) was brought to our attention. In this monograph Hemphill reviews five applications of the Group Dimensions Description Questionnaire, which was based on the Hemphill and Westie study (13). This questionnaire is available through the Educational Testing Service, 20 Nassau Street, Princeton, New Jersey. In one of the studies reviewed a factor analysis of the group dimensions is reported, and in this case the three rotated factors retained account for 49 per cent of the total variance. The factor structure indicated is quite different from that reported here. This difference may be accounted for in part on the basis of changes in the items, but it may also be related to the sensitivity of the measures to sampling variation.

4 The authors accept a rather confining definition of a social group, taken from Smith (15), as ". . . a unit consisting of a plural number of separate organisms (agents) who have collective perception of their unity and who have the ability and tendency to act and/or are acting in a unitary manner toward their environment."

FACTOR 1*

Task Focused Agreeable Cooperativeness vs. Disagreeable Control

	LOADING
4. Hedonic tone	.91
14. Viscidity	.90
2. Lack of control	(−).55
13. Lack of stratification	(−).44
9. Polarization	.40

* The sign in parenthesis is the one which occurs in the factor table.

FACTOR 2

Responsible Membership Commitment vs. Self-Structured Commitment

	LOADING
7. Participation	.81
10. Potency	.80
8. Lack of permeability	(−).72
13. Stratification	.54
1. Lack of autonomy	(−).51

FACTOR 3

(Peer) Primary Groupness vs. Secondary

	LOADING
5. Homogeneity	.58
2. Control	.49
6. Intimacy	.46

FACTOR 4

Size: Small Informal vs. Large Formal

	LOADING
11. Small size	(−).81
12. Stability	.63
3. Flexibility	.56

descriptive items as possible from each. As an additional means of ensuring coverage the list thus constructed could be checked against the lexicon of adjectives referring to social entities to see whether or not experience embodied in the language indicates other items or dimensions.

4. The Hemphill and Westie procedure supplemented by factor analytic procedures to locate the dimensions (rather than assuming them) constitutes a promising pattern of attack on the problem.

5. Other studies should also be conducted, both for replication and extension of generality of findings. Some possibilities are:

a. Replication of the Hemphill and Westie study of campus groups with the effort to ensure inclusion of all the more formalized groupings and a large sample of the informal groupings, friendships, ephemeral mass groups, etc.

b. The selection of special readily identifiable classes of aggregates such as the family and covering as wide a range of kinds of relationships as possible within that category.

c. The study of diadic friendship pairs.

d. The study of the range of group-life situations of individuals in routine living experience.

With a little reflection the reader can, of course, greatly extend this list of suggestions stimulated by the approach made by Hemphill and Westie. We can now turn to the second of the pilot studies which we wish to discuss.

Cattell

The work of Cattell in the classification of both persons and groups is well known, and he has been a leading exponent of factor analytic approaches to the classification problem. He has provided a number of well-formulated statements of the requirements for the classification of groups (4, 5), but here we shall consider only a part of the theoretical position he takes.

For the classification of groups to be maximally effective, Cattell suggests that the measures used should constitute an array which is "very catholic and highly varied." By indicating that one should be aware of the "degrees of homogeneity of population" on which a classification study is done, Cattell also points to the need for replication and for overlapping studies. However, in this light his definition of a group is not entirely clear. A group is ". . . an aggregate of organisms in which the existence of all is utilized for the satisfaction of some needs of each." Using this definition, an aggregate would need to be examined in each case to see if "some needs of each" are satisfied before it is called a group, a requirement which might make the definition more difficult to utilize than others. However, if "satisfaction of some needs of each" is defined to include potential satisfaction, the definition may be made as inclusive as one wants. As with Hemphill and Westie, the end product of Cattell's research is profile classification so that the problem of defining a group is not crucial unless the definition is restrictive.

Central to Cattell's work is a distinction in the classes of variables which are to be considered. He identifies three panels as exhaustive: (5)

> These three panels exhaust all the kinds of observation, i.e., all the data, measurable or qualitative, which can be collected with regard to a group as the reference point. The first panel is quite simple: population variables or dimensions are merely *means (or other statistical parameters) of the measured characteristics of the component individuals*, such as the mean I.Q., mean stature, etc., of the component members. These are clearly distinct from the characteristics of the group *as a group*, which arise by interaction, for they can be measured in the individuals before they become a group. By structural variables or dimensions we mean the descriptions of the internal behavior of the group, such as the status gradients, the clique relations as revealed by sociometry, the reciprocal role relations, the form of leadership structure, and, in organized groups, what Stogdill has called "the sociometry of working relations in formal organizations." These are inferred from observations on the internal interactions, processes, and procedures of the group and they are often quite high level abstractions involving such complex concepts as status and leadership

structure. The third category comprises the true syntality variables, which represent the *performances* of the group *acting as a whole* and commonly through its executive, e.g., its decision in a committee-like situation, its constructive performance on a building task or its acts of aggression or assistance towards other groups.

The only difficulties so far found with these three panels lies (a) in finding a place among them for the concept of cultural tradition and (b) in distinguishing sufficiently sharply between structural and syntality variables. In regard to the first it must be said that the culture pattern lies in all three panels: it exists in the personality of the individuals and therefore in the mean population characteristics, it expresses itself in the structure adopted by the group and therefore ultimately in the group behavior, i.e., in the group syntality. Thus the culture pattern is a different order of abstraction from the other three.

The second difficulty—that of drawing a clear and functional division between structure and syntality variables or dimensions—is solved if we bear in mind that the former are always statements of relations among (the behavior of) group members. Outstanding among structure variables are those statements which are about the relation between the behavior of one person—the leader—and the behavior of the rest. Only statements about relations which include all members of the group constitute adequate descriptive parameters of structure. On the other hand observations of internal interaction of the whole group which do not involve relations are not in the structure panel but in the syntality panel. For example, the total number of words spoken per hour within the group is a characteristic of syntality, not structure, as also would be the ratio of criticisms to suggestions for the group as a whole. But a sociometric study of communication which showed that the group had four subgroups within it would be a statement about structure. Structure variables are in general of a higher order of abstraction than syntality variables; but structure and syntality variables are equally attributes of and statements about the group, while population measures have to do only with the people in the group.

A further difference of structure and syntality is that the former can be manipulated in experiments as the "independent variable" by introducing rules affecting the manner of internal interaction, e.g., the absoluteness of leadership. Further, less essential differences are that syntality variables can often be inferred without seeing the group as a whole: one may observe the construction job before and after the group's visit, to determine its productivity, or speak to its ambassador to determine its attitude toward another group. But to determine a structure variable, such as the social distance between classes, or the lines of hierarchical communication, one must observe internal interaction.

The relationships that exist among the data from these three panels of observation and systematization await the verdict of empirical investigation, but it is nevertheless possible to explore a priori certain major probabilities. The primary relation to be expected is that the population measures, which are a mere mean of the population level on such personality factors as general intelligence, schizothymia, surgency, and desurgency, when properly combined with statements regarding the structure of a group, should enable one to predict the syntality, that is to say the performance, of the group, in any one of a number of fields. Except where structure is imposed artificially by an experimenter or from the past by tradition, the personality measures, in conjunction with the environmental circumstances, should theoretically enable us to predict both the emergent structure and the syntality (group performance) measures that follow from it. But there will also be circular and feedback influences. For example, the success with which a group tackles a certain job, i.e., its measure on a syntality dimension or trait, is in turn likely to influence the way in which the group organizes itself. And the way in which a group organizes itself may again influence the mean level of the group's possession of certain individual personality traits.

While Cattell is obviously aware of a number of difficulties in distinguishing the three panels, there are additional ambiguities which are not easily dismissed and which need to be emphasized. For example, the performance of persons in a group might be accounted for by population measures. If the characteristic performance of persons indicated by such a variable (used by Cattell, Saunders, and Stice) as "dynamometer sustained pull," to select one illustration, correlated substantially with group performance and both correlated the same way with a given factor structure, it would be difficult to describe the group performance as a "syntality variable." At minimum, it would suggest that the characteristic of the group is to be accounted for in part by the population measure. As a further example, if it should turn out that the total amount of talking a group does is a function of the mean amount of talking done by members of the group characteristically as persons (i.e., in all group situations), it would be difficult to call the amount of group talking a syntal "emergent."

It is fruitful to regard the distinctions made by Cattell among population, structural, and syntality variables as suggestive rather than final. The suggestion serves to remind the researcher of the need for an *inclusive set of measures* on group behavior, and it also points to the possibility of "explaining" syntality characteristics through the structural and population panels. However, these emphases need to be further considered and extended, and this should be the natural product of additional systematic empirical exploration of group data. Here we may introduce a few additional refinements and questions.

1. Let us define a syntality characteristic simply as one associated with the aggregate which cannot be accounted for through parallel measures taken on the individual members of the aggregate. Thus, if we consider such a measure as the total amount of talking which is done in an aggregate in a given period of time as a variable, the syntality component is that which remains in the consistent performance of the aggregate once the total amount of talking which would have been expected on the basis of the mean performances of the individual members has been accounted for. Such a measure would presumably have both syntality and population components. In dealing with syntality characteristics, thus, the researcher

should always take cognizance of the possibility that the measure associated with the aggregate may be (at least in part) *directly* "explainable" in terms of the parallel measure taken in terms of the characteristic performance of the individual members. To restate the issue, there is a characteristic performance of the aggregate as such, and there are characteristic performances (presumably over-all situations) of individuals, and the distinction between these two measures must be kept clear.

It should be evident, however, that the measures to which we have alluded presume a parallel in the individual. For these measures we may suggest that the aggregate (among other things) defines the situation for any individual, and so may be viewed as accounting in part for the variation of the performance of the individual from aggregate to aggregate (situation to situation). In this and the previous statements we may recognize the intimacy and complete interdependence of the study of personality characteristics with that of syntality characteristics.

2. It is possible to understand the behavior of the aggregate in terms of individual measures which are not parallel. Here, however, we must at least provisionally think of the situation as one of emergence, i.e., certain characteristics associated with individuals result in certain *other* characteristics associated with aggregates. Once the "invariant" relationships between characteristics of the members and those of the aggregate are established, they may be used as any other invariants are in science, within their limits of error. It may be possible at some time to go beyond the invariant sequences found for "explanations" by breaking the variables up into more rudimentary measures, but we shall not concern ourselves with this additional reduction.

3. Measures on the *arrangement* of members of the aggregate may be considered to have counterparts in the members in certain circumstances. As a simple example, if the variance of amount of talking of the members of the aggregate is the measure, the direct counterpart is the variance of the members' characteristic rates (presumably over all groups). Similarly, the implicitly more complex measure of "democracy" in an aggregate has as its counterpart the mean characteristic action of the members in this regard, or possibly the mean characteristic perception of "how a group should run." Manifestly, qualitatively different arrangements which fall into a class definition, such as families, may have counterparts in arrangements of persons without the family definition.

4. The problem of the counterpart in the individual members of the characteristic of the group-as-a-whole should not be dismissed easily because measures are said to be unitary in regard to the group. For example, a "group decision" may be defined in terms of a vote. This may be considered a group product which is unitary because there is only one decision. However, votes may be taken in many different ways, and the parallel questions to individuals in regard to the vote may be phrased in

as many ways. The group product which is said to be unitary should be examined for its counterpart.

5. One of the implicit assumptions which has favored the study of development of structure in ad hoc groups is that development decelerates with time, the greatest learning among members in regard to each other occurring at the earliest time. With reference to the developing group, the difference between the aggregate at one point in time and at another point in time needs to be considered in terms of syntality. If a given product (such as talking rate) is measured at one point in time, and again at another point in time, the same measure is, by definition, another product (another variable). This is an important issue to consider, for the coming together of several persons in an aggregate may lead to the swift development of a number of group products—as swiftly as the communication of certain gross characteristics occurs among people, and the emergence may be much as one thinks of a chemical combination. On the other hand, there may be other products which are more closely analogous to processes such as growth or maturation. Both these kinds of products need to be considered as syntality characteristics.

6. Consideration of this last point requires us to note the reflected consequence of aggregate performance on population characteristics, and to emphasize the circularity of the personality-syntality dichotomy. Participation in aggregates has noticeable effects on the behavior of individuals. These changes in individuals as products of aggregate participation need to be considered as syntality variables.

We may summarize as follows: (a) There are measures which are associated with products of individual members and there are those associated with the aggregate itself. Aggregate measures which are based on the characteristic performances of the individual members (presumably taken over all relevant situations) may be considered *population* variables. Aggregate measures, to the extent that they cannot be accounted for as population variables (in direct parallel measures), may be considered *syntality* variables. Population and syntality variables are thus relatively defined. Further, changes in population variables attributable to social interaction should be regarded as syntality variables. (b) Syntality characteristics may arise swiftly in aggregates, as with chemical compounding, or may arise in processes analogous to growth, maturation, aging, etc. (c) Measures of aggregates may describe the arrangements of persons, and these variables, along with others, may not be capable of simple quantitative ordering. Where such difficulties arise in ordering, the discreteness of the qualitative categories must be considered, and studies replicated for each category. The situation is not different from the examination of uniqueness of characteristics of aggregates of different size. For example, the jump from size two to size three implicates many discrete differences; in size two there is only one way of having a majority, there is no mediator possible, etc.

Cattell, Saunders, and Stice

The research by Cattell, Saunders, and Stice (8), which was more comprehensive than the earlier Cattell and Wispe (9) study, is briefly reviewed here. This study, extensive and ingenious, involved a sample of 80 groups of 10 men each, with 93 measures in the factor analysis. Fifteen factors were extracted from the matrix, and, recognizing the problem of interpretation, the descriptions of the factors were cautiously stated. The factor names are listed below. We have additional comments, derived from the published paper, where it appeared appropriate.

Factor 1. *Vigorous unquestioned purposefulness vs. self-conscious unadaptedness.* This factor appears characterized on one pole by high feeling of being accepted in the group, of working toward a common goal, and by high performance and liking of coordinated vigorous action in well-defined tasks.

Factor 2. *Immediate high synergy vs. low motivation.* On one pole this factor is characterized by apparent high motivation, cohesiveness, and acceptance of a high degree of leadership.

Factor 3. *Democratic, explicit procedure-orientation vs. horde urgency.*

Factor 4. *Schizothyme rigidity vs. conformity to circumstances.* Schizothyme rigidity is here characterized by an apparent unadaptable and unrealistic aspiration level with rigidity in planning.

Factor 5. *High intrinsic synergy vs. low intrinsic synergy.* One pole of this factor is characterized by a high level of immediate enjoyment of the group life itself, by a high level of gregarious satisfactions.

Factor 6. *Intelligent role interaction vs. low morale 1.* One pole of this factor is characterized by a propensity for intellectual problems, mutual understanding and adaptability, and apparent acceptance of role differentiation.

Factor 7. *Democratic "savoir faire" vs. lack of self-possession.* This factor orders democratic organization on one pole and individual control on the other.

Factor 8. *High verbal interaction.*

Factor 9. *Recklessness.* Groups high in recklessness performed certain tasks (voting) quickly and concentrated resources on a few alternatives.

Factor 10. *Group elation vs. group phlegm.* One pole is characterized by high we-feeling, high freedom of group atmosphere, high motivation, and apparent slow considered questioning with quick arrival at solutions.

Factor 11. *Homogeneity of emotional maturity.* Homogeneity here is associated with optimistic aspiration and improvement in a task.

Factor 12. *Disregard of group vs. acceptance of group goals.* Disregard of group here refers to preference for impersonal activities, to dawdling and horseplay, with an apparent rejection of the group as a means to one's ends.

Factor 13. *Frustrating temperamental heterogeneity vs. morale from homogeneity.* Heterogeneity in certain personality characteristics appears associated with inability to agree on goals and how to achieve them.

Factor 14. *Diffidence in internal communications.* Low verbal interaction appears associated with quick performance on manual activities, though with little planning and inferior results.

Factor 15. *Anarchy* (Not clearly defined).

Full appreciation of the meaning of the factors can only be achieved through careful consideration of the original paper, and the reader is advised to make this worthwhile investment of time. We note that the authors are cognizant of limitations of the study which deals with one somewhat narrowly defined class of groups, namely groups of 10 persons each brought together for test purposes and for which motivation of performance as groups on tasks was provided by competitive awards ($100). We emphasize here, in the context of considering the problem of classification as a general one, several kinds of interpretative limitations.

A first limitation of the study in terms of generalizations to other populations is the limitation of size to 10 persons in each aggregate. To illustrate, compared to a group of two, in a group which is as large as 10, it is possible for fine subdivision of roles among the members, and consequently for the members to seek anonymity or the particular roles in which they are more comfortable. In a group of two there is only one way in which a majority decision may be accomplished, while in a group of 10 there are many. In a group of three, a majority decision is either unanimous, or with one person (isolated) in a minority, while in a group of 10 it is possible for minorities to exist without isolation. These and additional considerations (1) suggest that generalizations about classifications of groups of 10 persons should not be hastily extended without replication in groups of other sizes.

A second limitation of the study is the difficulty of interpretation of the kinds of measures which were used. One can hardly criticize the selection for inclusion without proposing substitute items, and full recognition should be given to the ability to muster as wide a variety of tasks and measures as occurs in this study. On the other hand, the wide variety of measures may not be so easily or clearly interpreted as one might ideally desire when viewed in a factor structure. Let us examine the problem. The first factor presented by Cattell, Saunders, and Stice is descriptively called Vigorous unquestioned purposefulness vs. self-conscious unadaptedness. Fifteen variables are listed having a range in loadings from $|.32|$ to $|.69|$. Among the 11 highest loadings there are 7 which are population means on the *16 Personality Factor Test.* (Adventurous cyclothymia, Deliberate will control, Positive character integration, Dominance, Polished fastidiousness, Calm trustfulness, and Lack of nervous tension.) Now, since these appear to dominate the factor definition, we might suggest that they could be used to define the factor. How, then, would one identify the meaning of this factor except in terms of either the sample distribution or the suggestion that the tests are in fact fairly strongly interrelated in individuals? The latter is a likely reason for the high covariation. In addition to the seven population means, among the top 11 variables are: (a) *Dynamometer,* jerking pull: Total pull; (b) *Discussion:* Dislike for group judgment situation; (c) *Discussion:* Preference for dynamometer situation; and (d) Felt acceptance by other group members. The four final loadings were: Wide range of independent self-sufficiency; Subject rating, commonness of purpose; Observer rating, many "principal" leaders; and Subject rating, members do feel free to participate. Assuming that the population variable means reflect contamination of tests, it is difficult to ascribe meaning to the factor in terms of (a), (b), (c), and (d). Looking over the entire range of variables, one can see the logic of identification of the factor, but this does not alter the difficulty of interpretation. The convenience of utilizing personality tests in which the characteristics have been measured in terms of orthogonal categories is emphatic here! If the personality tests were orthogonal, distributions of population variables would be expected to be random, and the occurrence of relationship among the tests could be interpreted as related to the syntality characteristics.

Whatever the limitations one sees in Cattell's work, it is apparent that the direction of experimental observation has been motivated. One may question the kinds of tasks set for the groups of 10, particularly since group behavior is not always or possibly even not often one which is testing performance of a group as a group. One may question the selection of subjects. One may question the size of group. And there are a number of other limitations which may be indicated; but these should be regarded as suggestions for replication studies rather than criticisms of the research.

Additional Studies

We have not discussed the Cattell and Wispe study (9) since we regard it as preliminary. However, one additional recent study may be mentioned in this connection (2). In this study 166 three-man groups were observed, each participating for a single short session of 48 minutes, half the time in a situation designated as actual behavior and the other half in a situation designated as role playing. Seven factors were extracted as follows:

Factor 1. *Tension-neutral activity.* Members operate under tension but respond in patterns of emotionally neutral activity.

Factor 2. *Involvement activity.* Activity indicates emotional involvement with relative absence of tension.

Factor 3. *Group identification.*

Factor 4. *Leader-structure.* Groups high on this factor appear to have clear allocation of roles, a sense of direction, and unambiguous leadership.

Factor 5. *Discussional involvement.* Members get involved in much discussion at an intellectual rather than emotional level.

Factor 6. *Task interest.* Preoccupation with task is accompanied by corresponding lack of interest in other group activities.

Factor 7. *Maturity of members.* Groups more mature in age and military grade show less tension and antagonism, more agreement or acknowledgement.

DISCUSSION

Our general review of empirical approaches to the study of groups indicates a paucity of work in the area. If we attempt to examine the possible overlap of the studies presented, as indicated in Table 3, we note the completely tenuous status of any generalization from one study to another. The differences in factor names are not only characteristic of the differences in variables used, but also a reflection of the early stage of experimentation with groups. The situation is analogous to that in personality research which produced many factor names which are now in process of being narrowed down. Because classification of groups is recognizable at this early stage, it is valuable to emphasize some of the lessons learned in the personality area.

The most obvious lesson, already apparent in our Table 3, is the value of using marker variables, that is, variables which are identical in manifest definition and can thus be used to tie one analysis to another. The extraordinary need for this becomes apparent in the review by French (12) in the personality area. Although he reduces the number of factor names from 450 to about 50 which appear to occur in two or more studies, there is little question that considerable overlap remains. His screening procedure was one of careful examination of the psychological meaning of the factors and the contents of the items. A second and consequent lesson may be read as follows: It is difficult to reduce the number of variables to a stable set with factor analytic procedures. These convenient tools, however, are the most powerful currently available. One may therefore anticipate that classifications which do not have the assistance of arbitrary tools which can reduce empirical data to manageable proportions will not be so firmly grounded. This does not mean that such classifications are not of use, but only that they should be considered provisional and awaiting rigorous testing. This is by no means to set aside thought and judgment in the design of research. Because the tools are available the strategic step would seem to be the direct accumulation of empirical data which may become the basis for classifications from which revision of the theory in the area may take place.

A third lesson is so universal in science that it can always be usefully repeated. Studies must be replicated, and replication should be oriented to the testing of generality of findings as well as their stability.

We may conclude with a few additional comments. The generality of any classification is limited by definitional bounds. In general, when persons have talked about the classification of groups they have not always meant the same things. Sociologists, for example, have frequently implied in their definition the restriction to "natural" groups of persistent duration and have emphasized ad hoc categories of a qualitative phenotypical

TABLE 3

Possible Convergences of Empirically Derived Group Classifications

CATTELL, SAUNDERS, AND STICE	HEMPHILL AND WESTIE	BORGATTA AND COTTRELL
1. Vigorous unquestioned purposefulness*	9. Polarization	6. Task interest
2. Immediate high synergy	7. Participation, 10. Potency, and 13. Stratification	4. Leader-structure
3. Democratic explicit procedure orientation vs. horde urgency	3. Flexibility	1. Tension-neutral activity
4. Schizothyme rigidity		
5. High intrinsic synergy	14. Viscidity, and 4. Hedonic tone	3. Group identification
6. Intelligent role interaction vs. low morale 1.*		5. Discussional involvement
7. Democratic "savoir faire" vs. lack of self-possession	2. Control	2. Involvement activity
8. High verbal interaction		
9. Recklessness		
10. Group elation		
11. Homogeneity of emotional maturity		
12. Disregard of group*		7. Maturity of members
13. Frustrating temperamental heterogeneity	5. Homogeneity	
14. Diffidence in internal communications		
15. Anarchy		
	1. Autonomy†	
	6. Intimacy†	
	8. Permeability†	
	11. Size†	
	12. Stability†	

* Apparent overlap to the Cattell and Wispe study is reported.

† These are essentially held constant by the laboratory conditions of research in the other two studies.

sort. On the other hand, the emphasis implicit in this review follows in the wake of formal sociology. Here we might more appropriately suggest that we are dealing with the classification of "interaction fields" or "interaction situations," or with "aggregate behavior." It is important to recognize the assumption of definitional limits. Particularly at this early stage of empirical exploration, it is suggested that the most inclusive definition of the "group" is the most appropriate. The study of *relevant stable factors* for the classification of behavior of persons in aggregates should in the end be inclusive of all aggregates.

It is our conviction that the tools are developed, the shortcomings of theory and research are evident, and the opportunity now exists for replicating and cumulative research.

REFERENCES

1. Bales, R. F., & Borgatta, E. F. Size of group as a factor in the interaction profile. In A. P. Hare, E. F. Borgatta, and R. F. Bales, *Small groups*, New York: A. A. Knopf, 1955.
2. Borgatta, E. F., & Cottrell, Jr., L. S. On the classification of groups. *Sociometry*, 1955, 18, 665–678.
3. Cattell, R. B. *Description and measurement of personality*. New York: World Book, 1946.
4. Cattell, R. B. Concepts and methods in the measurement of group syntality. *Psychol. Rev.*, 1948, 55, 48–63.
5. Cattell, R. B. New concepts for measuring leadership, in terms of group syntality. *Hum. Relat.*, 1951, 4, 161–184.
6. Cattell, R. B. The chief invariant psychological and psycho-physical functional unities found by p-technique. *J. clin. Psychol.*, 1955, 11, 319–343.
7. Cattell, R. B. The principal replicated factors discovered in objective personality tests. *J. abnorm. soc. Psychol.*, 1955, 50, 291–314.
8. Cattell, R. B., Saunders, D. R., & Stice, G. F. The dimensions of syntality in small groups. *Hum. Relat.*, 1953, 6, 331–356.
9. Cattell, R. B., & Wispe, L. G. The dimensions of syntality in small groups. *J. soc. Psychol.*, 1948, 28, 57–78.
10. Cottrell, L. S. The case-study method in prediction. *Sociometry*, 1941, 4, 358–370.
11. French, J. W. *The description of aptitude and achievement tests in terms of rotated factors*, Psychometric Monogr., No. 5, 1951.
12. French, J. W. *The description of personality measurements in terms of rotated factors*, Princeton, New Jersey: Educational Testing Service, 1953.
13. Hemphill, J. K., & Westie, C. M. The measurement of group dimensions. *Jour. Psychol.*, 1950, 29, 325–342.
14. Hemphill, J. K. *Group dimensions: A manual for their measurement*, Research Monograph 87, Bureau of Business Research, Ohio State University, 1956.
15. Smith, M. Social situation, social behavior, social groups. *Psychol. Rev.*, 1945, 52, 224–229.
16. Wilson, L. The sociography of groups. In G. Gurvitch and W. Moore, *20th Century Sociology*, New York: Philosophical Library, 1945.

The Harvard Compatibility Experiment

WILLIAM C. SCHUTZ

DESIGN AND PROCEDURE

The Postulate of Compatibility Evidence

INVITATIONS were sent to every tenth freshman at Harvard (selected from an alphabetical list) to participate in an experiment to be conducted over a six-week period. When about one hundred accepted, they were called together and given the FIRO–1 and a few other questionnaires. On the basis of the results of the FIRO–1 and a consideration of the students' mathematics and verbal scores on the Scholastic Achievement Test, twelve groups were formed. Four groups followed the patterns described previously (75), Compatible Pattern O; four followed the Incompatible Pattern, and four followed a new pattern, a compatible group based on the fact that all members were underpersonal. This last will be called Compatible Pattern U. Triads of groups (one from each compatibility type) were matched on intelligence as well as possible within the limitations of composition requirements (Table 7–9).

The fundamental basis for compatibility in this experiment—as well as in the Washington experiment—would in the present theoretical formulation be best approximated by affection interchange compatibility (xK^A). All compatible group members for pattern O were overpersonal; all members of Compatible Pattern U were underpersonal; some members of the incompatible groups were overpersonal and some underpersonal. The other need areas were not systematically controlled, except that the two key figures in the compatible groups, the focal person (*FP*) and the main supporting member (*MS*), were designed to have high control originator compatibility (oK^C). The rationale behind the composition pattern beyond the interpersonal orientations (the *FP* and the *MS*) has been discussed in the previous publication and will be briefly summarized at this point.

TABLE 7–9

Composition Patterns for Three Types of Groups

VARIABLES (FIRO-1 NAMES)					
	COMPATIBLE GROUP MEMBERS (TYPE O)				
	FP_o	MS_o	M_o	M_o	M_o
Personalness (Affection)	H	H	H	H	H
Dependence (Control)	L,M	M,H	L,M	L,M	L,M
Assertiveness (Inclusion)	H	L,M	L,M	L,M	L,M
Intelligence	H	H	L,M	L,M	L,M
	COMPATIBLE GROUP MEMBERS (TYPE U)				
	FP_u	MS_u	M_u	M_u	M_u
Personalness	L	L	L	L	L
Dependence	L,M	M,H	M,H	M,H	M,H
Assertiveness	H	L,M	L,M	L,M	L,M
Intelligence	H	H	L,M	L,M	L,M
	INCOMPATIBLE GROUP MEMBERS				
	FP_o	MS_o	FP_u	MS_u	M_n
Personalness	H	H	L	L	M
Dependence	L,M	L,M	H	H	M
Assertiveness	H	L,M	H	L,M	L
Intelligence	H	L,M	H	L,M	L,M

Overpersonal Subgroup (FP_o + MS_o)

Underpersonal Subgroup (FP_u + MS_u)

Antagonistic Subgroups

Key:

FP = focal person		*H* = roughly, highest quartile
MS = main supporting member	*o* = overpersonal	*M* = roughly, second or third quartile
M = member	*u* = underpersonal	
	n = neutral	*L* = roughly, lowest quartile

It was found in the Washington experiment that a stable group structure for a five-man group seems to require not one, but two, key figures. These have been called the Focal Person (*FP*) and the Main Supporting Member (*MS*). The role of the focal person is to initiate the personal atmosphere (high affection interchange) of the group, and the *MS* to support the *FP* and, with him, to form the core of the group. For the incompatible groups two pairs of *FP–MS*'s are put in the same group.

These pairs differ in that one pair wishes an atmosphere with much personalness, whereas the other desires little personalness—hence the affection interchange incompatibility.

It should be emphasized that the designation of focal person is a predictive act of the experimenter when he composes the groups on the basis of their FIRO scores, without the knowledge of the group members. As far as the group is concerned, there are five members at initially equal status levels, and the experimenter treats them that way at all times.

Each of these twelve groups were brought to the group laboratory of the Harvard Social Relations Department and run through fourteen meetings over a period of six weeks. There were four one-hour meetings a day at 4:00, 5:00, 7:30, and 8:30 P.M., Monday through Friday; and at 10:00 and 11:00 A.M. and at 1:00 and 2:00 P.M., Saturday. Each group met twice a week at the same time (except Saturday), three days apart (such as Monday at 5:00 P.M. and Thursday at 5:00 P.M.).

Each group was given exactly the same sequence of tasks (shown in Table 7–10).

Productivity differences between groups were measured by comparison of the objective productivity scores received on each task. The intercept contests in the eleventh to fourteenth meetings were games played between two teams of different compatibility types such that each team played approximately the same number of contests against groups of differing compatibility types.

TABLE 7–10

Schedule of Activities of Groups in the Harvard Experiment

MEETING	TASK
1	Indoctrination: discussion (Name): discussion (Prison)
2	Building task (Toy); discussion (Cheat)
3	Intercept task
4	Intercept task; discussion (Child)
5	Free behavior, no task, standings announced, each group told "all groups are close, you are among lower ones"
6	Discussion (Groups); concept task
7	Building tasks (2)
8	Intercept tasks; discussion (Traffic)
9	Group projective; concept task
10	Building task; intercept task
11–14	Intercept contests (pairs of groups)

The discussion tasks were administered in a standard fashion. The experimenter read aloud a short (three-paragraph) description of a situation involving a difficult decision (typically based on authority vs. friendship, or something similarly related to the interpersonal areas). Each subject then wrote down what he would do in that situation and the reasons for his decision. The group was later allowed from fifteen to thirty minutes to discuss the problem and come to a "group decision," a purposely ambiguous phrase not specifying unanimity, majority, or any other procedure for decision making. Then the group was asked to appoint one of its members to be the spokesman and present the group's decision. The experimenter returned on the group's signal and, before hearing the group's decision, first had the subjects write their own individual post-discussion decision. This assignment fulfilled the conditions of a standard attitude change study.

A typical meeting proceeded as follows. The members of the group arrived about five minutes before the hour and went directly to the laboratory room (they had all been given a tour of the observation room at the first meeting, so they were fully aware of the observers). The recording apparatus (Gray Audiograph) was turned on in the observation room. The experimenter watched through a one-way mirror for several minutes, allowing the group time for free discussion. The members were under the impression that they were simply waiting for the session to begin. Generally about five minutes was allowed unless there was some especially important interaction occurring.

The experimenter then entered the experimental room, greeted the group, and presented the day's activity. He attempted to be distantly friendly with all groups, trying not to encourage or discourage any single group. After he was assured that the instructions were understood, the experimenter left the room, to return only when summoned at the end of an activity. The experimenter attempted to be with the group only when necessary, allowing maximal opportunity for unfettered group interaction. After the group's activity was finished, he returned to the room and completed the hour's work. Usually he then left, allowing a few more minutes for free behavior; later he returned and dismissed the group.

All experimental tasks were new to the subjects. There was no indication that any subject had special knowledge that would assist him in the solution of the tasks. The previous acquaintance of the subjects with one another varied; on the whole, the members of any one of the five-man groups were typically unacquainted. No group ever met *as a group* prior to the experiment.

Virtually no restraints were placed on the groups regarding seating arrangements or communication. With regard to leadership, the experimenter never designated a particular member as any type of leader. In some tasks the experimenter named certain *roles* (for example, coordinator, recorder) which had to be filled by men chosen by the group itself. The group could always oust the man they chose from any role at any time. (The term "oustable" shall be used for this type of role.)

Motivation to perform optimally was engendered in the subjects by (1) a talk to all subjects on the importance of the experiment to various industrial, governmental, military, and research activities; (2) a statement at the outset of the experiment that the experimenters wanted only participants who would appear promptly at *every* meeting and participate fully; (3) a reward of $25 to the "best" group, and several $10 prizes for the "best" individual performances, (4) payment of $1 per hour of meeting for each subject.

There was one further condition that is relevant to the conduct of this experiment and others like it. A special problem arose with regard to attendance at meetings. The design required sixty subjects (twelve groups of five men) to attend, on time, fourteen tightly scheduled meetings each, covering a period of six weeks. Since group composition was the key variable, it was not feasible to replace men after the groups had been formed. If any member dropped out, his whole group would have to be eliminated, because otherwise the design would be upset. To meet this problem it was decided to take the chance of losing all our volunteers at the outset, in the hope that if they stayed under the drastic conditions then imposed, they could be relied upon. The subjects were told that they would be paid only at the end of the experiment—that if they missed any *one* meeting *they would not be paid anything*, no matter how many meetings they had already attended. (This threat was, of course, not carried out). This condition resulted in the situation that attendance at each meeting made attendance at the following meeting more imperative. It emphasized to the subjects the great importance of attendance, which was strongly stressed and forthrightly explained on several occasions. Prior to the beginning of the experiment all the subjects were told the conditions, and given a chance to leave if they wished.

This technique, fortunately, was highly successful. After the first week, during which four or five meetings were rescheduled, there were only about five meetings that had to be rescheduled because one member forgot to appear. Since there were 141 meetings altogether, this record was most gratifying. In other words, of 705 instances where a man could have forgotten to attend, he actually forgot only about 10 times, less than 2 per cent. It seems safe to say that this type of long-run experiment, depending on repeated appearances of the same subjects, is quite feasible.

TASKS

Game (Intercept). This task of Game (Intercept) is . . . a modified chess-type game which requires that the entire group come to a decision within thirty seconds. One man was chosen oustable coordinator by the group and had complete authority and responsibility for making the decisions.

Concept. This is the task used by Bruner for individual concept formation studies. It was adapted to the group situation and administered similarly to the intercept task, except that (1) there were *two* oustable coordinators with equal authority, and (2) there was a penalty for total time rather than for a time limit for individual moves. This served to introduce a new type of decision, that between taking a chance by acting quickly and not taking a chance but being more cautious and deliberate.

Toy. The group was assigned the task of building a specified structure as fast as possible. The materials used are sold commercially under the name "Toy." The task was a division-of-labor type requiring the coordination of several different jobs.

QUESTIONNAIRES

Throughout the course of the experiment several questionnaires were administered. Following is the list of questionnaires and their abbreviations:

1. Slater, *Parental Role Preference Questionnaire* (PRP)
2. Blum, *Blacky Projective Test* (B)
3. Blum, *Defense Preference Inquiry* (DPI)
4. Schutz, *Fundamental Interpersonal Relations Orientation* (FIRO–1)
5. *California F–scale* (Authoritarianism) (A)
6. Edwards, *Personal Preference Schedule* (PPS)
7. La Forge and Suczek, *Interpersonal Checklist* (IPC)
8. Guilford, *R* (*Rhathymia*) *and C* (*Cyclothymia*) *Scales*
9. Bales and Couch, *Value Profile* (VP)

These questionnaires were administered intermittently over the entire fourteen meetings so that the required work would be spread over a reasonable period.

OBSERVATION

Each meeting was observed by from two to five observers, all graduate students in the Department of Social Relations. No observer knew which groups were composed according to which compatibility pattern. The primary observational data were a series of ratings made once or twice a meeting. When there were two activities in one meeting, for example, a discussion and an objective task, two ratings were made at that meeting; otherwise only one rating was made. The ratings were for a variety of roles commonly noted in group meetings, such as discussion guider, influencer, and promoter of personal feelings (see Appendix C). The observer was first asked to decide whether or not any members of the group clearly fulfilled the description of the role, and then he was asked to rank all five group members with respect to this role. The weighted sum of all rankings for all meetings was computed for each role for each group member. These ratings were standardized and used as the behavioral data. An on-going category system was used to record the behavior only for a few meetings which involved special projects.

SOCIOMETRICS

In order to obtain the most comparable data the subjects were given a rating sheet almost identical to that used by the observers. These were filled out at both the fifth and tenth meetings. In addition, the subjects filled out regular sociometric questions regarding "like," "work with," and "influences."

RESULTS

Productivity. Since all the tasks were of different types, it was difficult to combine scores to obtain an over-all productivity measure. It was therefore decided to rank all twelve groups on each task and use the sums of these ranks for the total productivity score. This procedure minimized the effect of scoring differences between tasks.

There were four objective tasks: Toy, Concept, Game, and Game Contest. Where there was more than one concurrence of the same task (as in Toy and Concept), the ranks were averaged to give a final rank for that task. Thus the final rank was based on one rank for each task. (See Table 7–11.)

With the use of the Mann-Whitney U-test the difference in ranks between the combined compatibles and the incompatibles is significant beyond the .02 level.

TABLE 7–11

Ranks on Productivity for All Groups on All Tasks

GROUPS	TOY	CONCEPT	GAME	CONTEST	FINAL TOTAL	FINAL RANK
OVERPERSONAL COMPATIBLE GROUPS						
NO. 1	3	8	7	10	28	9
2	1	1	11	1	14	1
3	7.5	4	2	4	17.5	2
4	10	10	1	6.5	27.5	8
				TOTAL	87	20
UNDERPERSONAL COMPATIBLE GROUPS						
NO. 5	6	6	4	2	18	3
6	2	7	10	3	22	4
7	10	5	5	6.5	26.5	7
8	7.5	2.5	2	11	23	5
				TOTAL	89.5	19
INCOMPATIBLE GROUPS						
NO. 9	10	11.5	8	6.5	36	11
10	12	11.5	9	9	41.5	12
11	4.5	9	6	6.5	26	6
12	4.5	2.5	12	12	31	10
				TOTAL	134.5	39

There is virtually no difference in productivity between the overpersonal compatibles (*OP–K*'s) and the underpersonal compatibles (*UP–K*'s). The *UP–K*'s have one final rank less, while the *OP–K*'s have two and one-half total ranks less. Neither difference is significant. The ideal result of the final ranking would have placed the incompatibles ($\overline{K}$'s) in ranks 9, 10, 11, and 12, and shown the first eight ranks distributed among the compatible groups. Actually, this outcome occurred with the exception of $\overline{K}$ group 11 and *OP–K* Group 1, who ideally should have interchanged ranks 6 and 9.

A Theory of Coalition Formation

WILLIAM A. GAMSON

MANY NOVELISTS as well as political scientists have been fascinated by the intrigues that mark political life. When these intrigues involve not only individuals but also nations we have the stuff of history. This paper deals in a general way with a subject that has been treated specifically by historians and journalists for centuries.

In every historian's description of a revolution, in every political biographer's description of the ascent of his subject, there is a more or less explicit account of the coalitions and alliances which furthered the final outcome. Few areas exhibit less external uniformity. "Politics makes strange bed fellows" we say to express our bewilderment at some new coalition which belies our expectations from past knowledge of the participants.

There are three separate streams of work which have been concerned with the theme. The sociological tributary flows primarily from Simmel

FROM *American Sociological Review,* 1961, 26, 373–382. Reprinted by permission of author and the American Sociological Association, Inc.

The author is indebted to Dorwin Cartwright of the Research Center for Group Dynamics and Anatol Rapoport of the Mental Health Research Institute for their critical comments and suggestions. This paper was completed under a grant from the Social Science Research Council.

(12), and has focused, in particular, on the relatively simple and manageable three-person group. The triadic relationship has been explored in a series of experimental and theoretical papers by Mills, Strodtbeck, Caplow, and Vinacke and Arkoff (8, 13, 1, 14).

A second tradition has grown entirely since the end of the Second World War following the publication of von Neumann and Morgenstern's *Theory of Games and Economic Behavior* in 1944 (15). Articles by Shapley and Shubick and by Luce and Rogow on *a priori* power distributions, the von Neumann-Morgenstern "solution" to n-person games and the notion of psi-stability are relevant examples (10, 7). Both the small group and the mathematical literature will be discussed in detail following the presentation of the theory.[1]

The third body of work comes from historians and journalists and is primarily descriptive. Not only do these accounts capture much of the drama of coalition formation, but they also serve as a valuable reference point for a theory with descriptive rather than strictly normative ambitions. The accounts of the French National Assembly by Lerner and Aron (4) and by Leites (3) and descriptions of the rise of Hitler and Stalin highlight the dimensions of a theory of coalitions.

Coalitions are temporary, means-oriented alliances among individuals or groups which differ in goals. There is generally little value consensus in a coalition and the stability of a coalition requires *tacit neutrality* of the coalition on matters which go beyond the immediate prerogatives. This makes the pursuit of power itself, i.e., control over future decisions, an ideal basis for coalition formation since it is an instrument for the achievement of widely ranging and even incompatible goals. Two members may realize their mutual goal antagonisms but such decisions lie in the future and the present alliance may make both better able to achieve a wide range of goals not all of which will be incompatible. Power is the currency of politics.

THE THEORY

Some Definitions. A *decision* is a selection among alternatives. When there are several participants, the selection of any given alternative will distribute rewards among them in a particular fashion. The reward which accrues to any participant or group of participants from a decision is the *payoff*. The payoff may include influence on future decisions.

In any decision, there exists a weight associated with each participant involved such that some critical quantity of these weights is necessary for the decision to be made. We shall call these weights *resources*. They vary with the situation, from military force and industrial capacity in a

1 The fine book by Luce and Raiffa (6) contains excellent summaries of work in the theory of games of relevance to social scientists.

war to votes in a parliamentary situation to verbal and logical ability in a court of law. One may be able to influence the decision more than his resources would warrant through his strategic position. In fact, this "influence of position" is a primary focus of the theory. The *rules of the game* provide the manner in which the decision may be made; this includes specification of the resources which are relevant to the decision.

A *social unit* is any individual or group which for the duration of the decision follows the same coalition strategy. It might be a state delegation to a political convention, a voting bloc in the United Nations, or an association of retail stores. A *coalition* is the joint use of resources by two or more social units. Once formed, a coalition will frequently meet the definition of a social unit from the period of formation until the decision has been made. A *winning coalition* is one with sufficient resources to control the decision. The *decision point* is the minimum proportion of resources necessary to control the decision.

Conditions of the Theory. A full-fledged coalition situation is one in which the following conditions are present:

1. There is a decision to be made and there are more than two social units attempting to maximize their share of the payoffs.
2. No single alternative will maximize the payoff to all participants.
3. No participant has dictatorial powers, i.e., no one has initial resources sufficient to control the decision by himself.
4. No participant has veto power, i.e., no member *must* be included in every winning coalition.

The first two of these conditions imply that each of the participants has some stake in the outcome—we are not dealing with a null game—and the situation is competitive. Together with condition three, we are assured that a full-fledged coalition situation is an essential game.[2] The portion of condition one which states that more than two social units are involved can easily be derived from the last two conditions. In a one-man group, the participant has dictatorial powers and, in any dyad, either one member is a dictator or each possesses a veto power.

While the first three conditions merely remove trivial situations from consideration, condition four places much more severe limits on the generality of the theory. Many interesting situations involving *blocking* coalitions are excluded by this condition for reasons which will become apparent shortly.

However, if the decision point is 50 per cent or less, condition three implies condition four. Then, condition four would be violated if and only if some member controlled more than 50 per cent of the resources; but if

2 An *inessential* game, write Luce and Raiffa (6, p. 185) is one in which "no coalition of players is more effective than the several players of the coalition operating alone. . . . For every disjoint R and S, $V(R \cup S) = V(R) + V(S)$. . . . Any game which is not *inessential* is called *essential*." We will call a game strictly essential if the players operating alone always get zero payoff.

this were true, then this member would be a dictator and condition three would be violated.

Parameters of the Theory. To predict who will join with whom in any specific instance, the model requires information on the following:

1. *The initial distribution of resources.* We must know, of course, what the relevant resources are for any given decision and, at some starting point, how much of these resources each participant controls.

2. *The payoff for each coalition.* Every alternative coalition is a partition of the players into classes, and for every such partition we must know the total rewards for each class. In Game Theory, the *characteristic function* of a game is calculated by computing the payoff to any subset of players on the assumption that the complementary set of players will form a coalition. In short, it is postulated that the players assume that every game will reduce to a two-person game. This sometimes gives an unrealistically conservative value for a coalition.

We shall include partitions into more than two classes of players in calculating the payoffs. The same subset may receive one payoff when the complementary set is partitioned in one manner and an entirely different payoff when it is partitioned in a second way. To illustrate, a coalition may be losing and have an estimated payoff of zero if we assume that its opponents will combine but it may be winning on the contrary assumption.

The function which we require appears more complicated than the characteristic function. However, since the theory specifies that only one coalition wins and the payoff to all non-members is zero, in practice we need know only the payoff associated with each possible winning coalition.[3]

Since the rewards will frequently include anticipations of future events, the payoff must reflect differences in the probability of achieving future rewards. To illustrate, the payoff for a coalition at a political convention should reflect the various probabilities that the coalition's candidate will be elected. The payoff for a coalition would be the *expected value* of future decisions—the total payoff from such decisions multiplied by the probability of the coalition's achieving them.

3. *Non-utilitarian strategy preferences.* We must have a rank ordering (with ties allowed) of each participant's inclination to join with every other player *exclusive of that player's control of the resources.* The sources of this non-utilitarian preference will vary depending on the situation: in a small committee, the primary source would probably be interpersonal attraction. In a political convention, we would expect the relative similarity of others' ideology and beliefs to be the principal determinant.

4. *The effective decision point.* The rules of the game will frequently

3 Thus, the complete payoff function for any particular game maps every possible coalition into some single value—zero if the coalition is losing and some positive but variable value if the coalition is winning.

specify an amount of resources *formally* necessary to control the decision. Yet an amount of resources less than the formal amount may be sufficient to control the decision for all practical purposes. This may occur through considerations which prevent a potentially winning opposition from uniting or through a "bandwagon effect."

For example, in a political convention when a candidate reaches a certain number of votes, close to but still short of a majority, the opposition will "stampede." The decision point in which we are interested is the *effective* rather than the *formal* decision point, although there will be many situations in which these are identical.

If we know the payoff for each coalition, then we can logically deduce the effective decision point. However, in practice the construction of the payoff matrix is dependent on our prior knowledge of this value. In other words, to specify the complete payoff function we must know both whether a coalition has sufficient resources to be winning and how much it will receive. Since separate information is required, we have handled this as an additional constant, but it is not a genuinely independent one.

Additional Definitions and Assumptions: A minimal winning coalition is a winning coalition such that the defection of any member will make the coalition no longer winning. The *cheapest winning coalition* is that minimal winning coalition with total resources closest to the decision point. A *payoff class* is a set of payoffs of which the lowest is no more than K per cent less than the highest. The value of K is something which must be determined empirically for a given coalition situation. It specifies, in effect, how large a difference in payoff there must be to make a difference.

The theory applies to full-fledged coalition situations in which we assume the following to be true:

Assumption One: The participants have the same (but not necessarily perfect) information about the initial distribution of resources and the payoff to any coalition.

Assumption Two: Participants do not distinguish between payoffs in the same payoff class.

Assumption Three: Every participant has a rank ordering of non-utilitarian preferences for joining with the other players.

These assumptions and the conditions of the full-fledged coalition situation define the class of games to which the theory is applicable. We can now state the empirical hypotheses of the theory, starting with the general hypothesis:

Any participant will expect others to demand from a coalition a share of the payoff proportional to the amount of resources which they contribute to a coalition.

Any participant, A, estimates the *payoff to himself* from a prospective coalition as a product of the *total payoff* to that coalition and A's expected share of that total. The total payoff is known to A and the general hypothesis specifies the share which A will expect to give to others. Thus, A can assign to any prospective coalition a personal payoff value—his proportion of the resources in the coalition multiplied by the total payoff for that coalition.

These values can be assigned to payoff classes of which A will prefer the highest. He does not recognize payoff differences between coalition strategies (prospective coalitions) in the same payoff class. Within any class, he will pursue that coalition strategy whose members have the highest mean rank on his scale of non-utilitarian preferences.

When a player must choose among alternative coalition strategies where the total payoff to a winning coalition is constant, he will maximize his payoff by maximizing his share. The theory states that he will do this by maximizing the ratio of his resources to the total resources of the coalition. Since his resources will be the same regardless of which coalition he joins, the lower the total resources, the greater will be his share. Thus, where the total payoff is held constant, he will favor the *cheapest winning coalition.*

As an illustrative example, let us say that A has 30 per cent of the resources, B has 19 per cent, C has 30 per cent, and D has 21 per cent where the decision point is 51 per cent. For A, the minimal winning coalitions which he must consider are AC and AD. In the former, he will expect 1/2 of the payoff, while in the latter he expects to get approximately 3/5. If they differ in payoff as well, 1/2 of payoff AC may be higher than 3/5 of payoff AD. If these two figures are in the same payoff class, then he will choose to join with the one which he ranks higher on non-utilitarian strategy preference.

Finally, a coalition will form if and only if there are *reciprocal strategy choices* between two participants. To illustrate, let us assume that X's desired coalition in some three-person game is XY, that Y's is XY or YZ, and that Z's favored coalition is XZ. Only X and Y have *reciprocal strategy choices,* i.e., require the other in their *preferred coalition,* and, thus, the coalition XY is predicted by the theory.

The model envisions the process of coalition formation as a step-by-step process where the participants join two at a time. Once a coalition has been formed, the situation becomes a new one—that is, there is a fresh distribution of resources—and, in the new coalition situation, the original strategies may or may not be appropriate. *If a coalition which forms was predicted by the theory, then each player's original strategy will remain the same.* Thus, if W's preferred coalition was WXY in some game, then if X and Y join, W will still *necessarily* prefer the strategy WXY. If, however, a coalition forms which is an "error" in terms of the theory, the strategy requirements for some players *may* change. Thus, if player W planned to join with X and Y but Y and Z joined, W might now prefer the group YZ to X.

TABLE 1

Predicted Coalitions in Triads of Varying Initial Strength

TYPE NO.	DISTRIBUTION OF RESOURCES	PREDICTED COALITION	
		CAPLOW	GAMSON
1	$A=B=C$	any	any
2	$A>B, B=C, A<(B+C)$	BC	BC
3	$A<B, B=C$	AB or AC	AB or AC
4	$A>(B+C), B=C$	none	none
5	$A>B>C, A<(B+C)$	BC or AC	BC
6	$A>B>C, A>(B+C)$	none	none
7	$A>B>C, A=(B+C)$	AB or AC	Inapplicable
8	$A=(B+C), B=C$	AB or AC	Inapplicable

We can now explain why we have excluded games in which some member possesses veto power, i.e., in which condition four of the full-fledged coalition situation is violated. The bargaining situation which is essential for the general hypothesis to be correct is one in which every participant has alternatives. Where one member has veto power, there is no alternative to his inclusion; he could no longer be expected to demand only a proportional share of the payoff.

COALITIONS IN THE TRIAD

Caplow has published two papers on a theory of coalitions in the triad including an evaluation of the experimental evidence (1, 2). He specified eight types of coalition situations based on the initial distribution of resources. Table 1 reproduces the eight types with Caplow's predicted coalition for the continuous situation.

To make our theory applicable to the Caplow situations, we must assume (1) that all winning coalitions have the same payoff, (2) that there are no differences in nonutilitarian strategy preferences, and (3) that the decision point is a simple majority of the resources. It is clear, then, that the prediction from our model will be simply the *cheapest winning coalition* in the applicable situations.

Four of the eight types in Table 1 do not meet the conditions for a full-fledged coalition situation. Type Four and Six represent a dictator situation, and Caplow's prediction for these *inessential* games is also that no coalition will form. Types Seven and Eight fail to meet our fourth condition that no member have veto power for in each of these A must be included in any winning coalition.

In Type One, any coalition will have the same total resources and thus, under the previous assumptions that other things are equal, any coalition would have equal probability. In Type Two, B and C will form a winning coalition, and since A is greater than either B or C, the coalition BC must be cheaper than either AB or AC. Therefore, our prediction for Type Two agrees with Caplow's.

In Type Three, where A's position is ideal for the role of *tertius gaudens*, the coalitions AB and AC are equal in strength and both are cheaper than the coalition BC. Once again, our prediction corresponds to Caplow's.

Type Five is the only situation in which the two theories differ in their consequences. Caplow finds the following assumptions equally plausible (2): "The 'chooser' in a triad seeks the maximum advantage or minimum disadvantage of strength relative to his coalition partner" or, "The 'chooser' in a triad seeks to maximize the strength of the coalition in relation to the excluded member." He reasons that the weak man, C, in a Type Five situation, would be sought as a coalition partner by both of the others and could choose on either basis.

Our theory clearly implies the first of these two assumptions. C will prefer the coalition BC to the coalition AC because he expects that the stronger A will demand a larger share of the payoff in accordance with his superior resources. The coalition BC is, of course, the cheapest coalition.

Caplow has discussed several experimental studies of triads with the conclusion that they lend some support to his analysis although designed with other purposes in mind. For example, Mills discovered that a subject who was the "odd man" (A) in a Type Three situation tended very slightly to make more efforts to disrupt the coalition between the equals than the subject placed in A's role in a Type Two situation (8). Caplow concludes that "we would expect less resistance to the 'inevitable' coalition of BC in Type Two than to the improbable, and, therefore, unstable coalition of BC in Type Three." (1)

The most crucial and significant evidence on coalitions in the triad comes from Vinacke and Arkoff who, stimulated by Caplow's first paper, designed an experiment to test the first six of his situations (14). This experiment is certainly a test of our theory as well, given the earlier predictions of Table 1. Furthermore, in testing the Type Five situation, it provides a comparison at the only point where our predictions differ.

The experimenters had subjects play a parchesi game in which each player's moves were weighted by a numbered counter which he drew from a hopper at the beginning of the game. The weights on these counters represented the six different initial distributions of resources specified by Caplow's theory. Table 2 gives the weights for each situation. Thirty triads played each game three times with the order arranged to vary systematically the position of the situation in each series.

Vinacke and Arkoff suggested a "game theory" prediction for each of these situations as well, which we shall call the Strict Rationality Theory. They reason that the strictly rational player must realize in a situation such as Type Five that any pair will win, and that if he fails to form a coalition, he can expect his opponents to do so. This reasoning will hold whether one has a weight of two, three, or four, and there is no reason to expect, on rational grounds, that any coalition will form with greater frequency than any other. In fact, this reasoning holds for the first three types as well. In the non-essential types four and six, there is nothing to be gained by forming a coalition and the prediction is that none will take place.

TABLE 2

Vinacke and Arkoff Design for Experimental Test of Six Caplow Situations

TYPE NO.	DESCRIPTION	WEIGHTS A	WEIGHTS B	WEIGHTS C
1	A=B=C	1	1	1
2	A>B, B=C, A<(B+C)	3	2	2
3	A<B, B=C	1	2	2
4	A>(B+C), B=C	3	1	1
5	A>B>C, A<(B+C)	4	3	2
6	A>B>C, A>(B+C)	4	2	1

This experiment, then, gives us a chance to compare its results with three different theoretical predictions—Caplow's, Strict Rationality, and our own. In Table 3 we compare these predictions with the actual results of the experiment.

TABLE 3

Results of Vinacke-Arkoff Experiment with Three Theoretical Predictions

PREDICTED	1 A=B=C	2 A>B, B=C, A<(B+C)	3 A<B, B=C	4 A>(B+C), B=C	5 A>B>C, A<(B+C)	6 A>B>C, A>(B+C)
Caplow	any	BC	AB or AC	none	AC or BC	none
Strict rationality[a]	any	any	any	none	any	none
Gamson	any	BC	AB or AC	none	BC	none
Actual						
AB	33	13	24	11	9	9
AC	17	12	40	10	20	13
BC	*30*	*64*	*15*	7	*59*	*8*
Total	80	89	79	28	88	30
No coalition	10	1	11	62	2	60
Probability[b]	NS	.01	.01	NS	.01	NS

[a] These are also the predictions made by Caplow for the "episodic" situation.
[b] From Vinacke and Arkoff: Chi Square with two degrees of freedom.

In situations one, four, and six, where there are no differences between theories, each is supported. Coalitions do not usually occur in the latter two situations, and in situation one, they seem to occur approximately at random.

In situations two and three, the results provide negative evidence for the strict rationality predictions and positive evidence for the other two theories. Apparently, the ability to perceive the necessity for a coalition in these situations is more difficult from certain positions than from others. "It is harder," Vinacke and Arkoff write, "for an initially stronger member to reach the conclusion that the relative strengths are irrelevant than for the other one or two to arrive at this interpretation. In effect, the weaker members can immediately understand the necessity for forming a coalition, whereas the stronger member must go through more complex reasoning to do so."

Situation five is perhaps the most crucial since each theory makes a different prediction for the outcome. While Caplow predicts that either of the coalitions AC or BC are equally likely, the cheapest coalition BC actually takes place three times as frequently as the alternative!

This confirmation is interpreted by Vinacke and Arkoff in a manner which echoes the general hypothesis of our theory: ". . . the weakest member was found to be most often a member of the winning coalition; furthermore, his share of the winnings was larger than his strength might seem to warrant mainly because there was competition for him, *because the other players saw him as weaker, hence more readily to be induced into partnership*." (14) [Emphasis mine.]

Willerman draws similar conclusions from his study of coalitions in a fraternity council (16). ". . . Distribution of control within the coalition was isomorphic with the relative status and resources of the members outside of the coalition. However, there seem to be occasions when the strategic position of a member gives him power out of proportion to his rank order of status or resources."

There is apparently some basis for the assumption that the size of the demands which a participant will make reflects the proportion of resources which he controls—or, at least, will affect what others will *expect* him to demand. In a situation where participants meet with each other sequentially rather than simultaneously, these expectations of others' bargaining demands become even more crucial.

In short, the small group studies of coalitions in the triad uniformly support the theory presented here. While Caplow's predictions are in most cases consistent with the predictions from our theory under the special case where payoffs and non-utilitarian strategy preferences are held constant, in one crucial difference, the results of Vinacke and Arkoff support the prediction made here.

MATHEMATICAL LITERATURE

The mathematical theory of games of strategy as it presently exists is a rich source of ideas, but it can only provide orientations in situations of the type with which we are concerned here. This is true for several reasons. The most powerful mathematical developments of the theory are in the area of two-person, zero-sum games. The theory of games involving many players is, to quote Abraham Kaplan, "in a very unsatisfactory state." (11)

We do not object to the theory of games on the grounds that its assumptions are "unrealistic." They are, at least, clearly stated and we may substitute more plausible ones if we can find some which are workable. Luce and Raiffa write: ". . . it is crucial that social scientists recognize that game theory is not *descriptive* but rather (conditionally) *normative*. It states neither how people do behave nor how they should behave in an absolute sense, but how they should behave if they wish to achieve certain ends." (6) Our own object is descriptive but a normative theory often provides a useful starting point for a descriptive theory.

One attempt to handle the problem of the n-person game is the von Neumann-Morgenstern "solution" theory.[4] A *solution* generally consists of a *set of imputations* (an imputation is an n-tuple giving the payoff to each player and satisfying certain conditions) having the following two properties: (1) no imputation in the set *dominates* any other imputation, and (2) every imputation not in the set is dominated by one in the set.[5]

I shall illustrate this with a solution to the three-man game: (1/2, 1/2, 0), (1/2, 0, 1/2), (0, 1/2, 1/2). No imputation among the three dominates another since only one player could improve his position by switching from one to another. Any particular imputation in the solution such as (0, 1/2, 1/2) is dominated by imputations outside of the set—for example, (1/6, 2/3, 1/6), but this, and in fact any imputation outside of the solution set, is dominated by a member of the solution (in this case by 1/2, 0, 1/2).

Luce and Raiffa argue that a "solution must be interpreted as a description of a set of possible payments, any of which might arise if the players choose strategies and form collusive arrangements as they 'should.' " This would seem to offer some promise for our purposes in spite of the fact that the emphasis is on distribution of payoffs. An imputation where some values are positive and others are zero defines an implicit coalition between the positive entries.

Unfortunately, we are not given a single imputation as a solution but rather a set of these, and furthermore, a set in which all possible coalitions are allowed. As if this difficulty were not sufficient, the solution to the

4 This is discussed in relatively non-technical fashion in Luce and Raiffa (6). In a sense, we are proposing in this paper a new definition of solution for certain classes of n-person essential games, but because of the specific meaning of "solution" in the von Neumann-Morgenstern sense, we have refrained from using the word.

5 For a formal definition of imputation and domination, see Luce and Raiffa (6, pp. 193 and 201).

three-man game given above is not the only solution; in fact, there is an infinity of solutions. "In their theory," write Luce and Raiffa, ". . . freedom to cooperate leads to vast numbers of 'solutions' with no criteria to select among them. They are forced . . . to the *ad hoc* assumption that in practice there exist social standards which determine *the* solution which actually occurs, but no attempt is made to exhibit a theory of these standards."

There has been an attempt by Vickrey (6) to narrow down the number of solutions to be considered. "Roughly, a solution is called *strong* if the sequence—(1) an imputation in the solution, (2) a change to a non-conforming imputation, and (3) a return to an imputation in the solution—*always* means that at least one of the players participating in the original deviation ultimately suffers a net loss. Thus, a strong solution has an inherent stability not possessed by other solutions, and so it might be expected to occur rather than one of the weaker solutions."

It turns out, encouragingly, that the *only* strong solution for the three-person game is the symmetric one given earlier: (1/2, 1/2, 0), (1/2, 0, 1/2), (0, 1/2, 1/2). Since none of these imputations dominates any other, again extra-theoretical reasons will determine which imputation in the set is chosen.

Vinacke and Arkoff (14) present data on the division of spoils made by their subjects which allow us to examine the frequency with which the strong solution did occur. In the Type One situation where all players had an equal share of the resources originally, the final imputation was a member of the solution set 60 per cent of the time, but in the Type Three situation ($A<B$, $B=C$) only 39 per cent of the time. Many of these may have occurred on those occasions (19 per cent) in which the two strong, equally powerful members joined.

We may tentatively conclude that where the initial distribution of resources *differs* among the three members of the triad, not only are the various imputations in a solution set *not* equally probable, but the tendency to divide the rewards symmetrically is considerably less than when participants have equal power.

A second mathematical concept, that of psi-stability, would seem to be more appropriate for our purposes since here a game is described by both an imputation and a coalition structure. The basis of this notion, which has been developed by Luce (5) is that a pair—an imputation and a given coalition structure—is stable when no *admissible* change in the coalition structure is immediately profitable.

An important addition here is the recognition that from any given coalition structure, every possible coalition is not admissible. The concept of non-utilitarian strategy preferences developed earlier is, in part, an attempt to define the admissible changes between any two stages of the process of coalition formation.

The implications of psi-stability for the theory presented here are less important than one might hope. First, we are concerned primarily with the process of coalition formation rather than coalition stability. Although problems of stability can frequently be translated into the terms of the theory, essentially the game is over when a winning coalition has been formed for a particular decision, and the next decision involves a new game.[6] Secondly, psi-stable pairs, like solutions, are not generally unique and the problem of how to select just *one* still exists.

A full-fledged coalition situation is a strictly essential game and it is not difficult to see that any losing coalition will be psi-unstable. However, in the full-fledged triadic situation, any two-man coalition will meet the conditions of psi-stability regardless of the initial distribution of resources. If our aim is uniqueness, we are no better off here than under solution theory. Attempts by Milnor (6) to describe n-person games in terms of "reasonable outcomes" involve the same type of difficulties ascribed to solution and psi-stability theory.

Shapley (9) gives a method for evaluating the worth of an n-person game for any player that should help us to determine the relative bargaining positions of the several players in a game. He lists three *apparently* weak conditions and then shows that these uniquely determine an evaluation function. Ultimately, he arrives at an explicit formula for calculating the value for a player, *i*. "It amounts," to quote Luce and Raiffa, "to a weighted sum of the incremental additions made by *i* to all the coalitions of which he is a member." In the full-fledged triadic situation, the values are 1/3 for each player. This suggests the symmetric solution.

In an article by Shapley and Shubik (10), the authors attempt to apply the Shapley value to certain "simple" games (in a *simple* game, every coalition has as its payoff either one or zero, i.e. it is either winning or losing). They argue that the value gives an *a priori* estimation of relative power in many committee or parliamentary situations. An individual's power is given by the index, P/N, where N is the total number of permutations among the players and P is the number of permutations in which his resources are *pivotal* in turning a losing coalition into a winning one. Luce and Rogow (7) applied this to an analysis of coalitions between the President and the parties in the two houses of Congress.

The calculations involved in the Shapley-Shubik power index are relatively simple to make, especially when the N is small. In the triad, there are 3! or six permutations, and in the full-fledged coalition situation each person will be pivotal twice, giving rise to the earlier figure of 1/3.

Suppose, however, we did not assume that resources are used as a bloc. Instead of asking which person is pivotal in the permutation, we

6 This is not a criticism of Luce since coalition stability is obviously an important problem in its own right. Eventually, a satisfactory theory of coalitions should be able to handle both coalition formation and stability.

might ask which resource unit is pivotal. Referring back to Table 3, we can see that for the Type One situation, the Shapley value remains as 1/3. However, for Type Two, there are 7! permutations instead of 3!. Any given resource unit will be pivotal in 6! ways since the other six units can be permuted that many ways while it remains fixed in the pivotal spot. It follows that A's three resource units will be pivotal 3 x 6! times while B and C will have the pivotal unit in 2 x 6! ways each. The resultant Shapley values are 3/7, 2/7, 2/7 respectively or exactly proportional to the share of resources.

Finally, suppose we make the assumption that within any coalition, a player can expect to share in the payoff proportionately to his Shapley value. It then follows that one will maximize his share in a simple game if he can maximize his power relative to the other members of his winning coalition. In short, we are led to predict that the cheapest coalition will form!

It is certainly possible to question the assumptions by which we used the Shapley value to yield the predictions of our theory. Why should the resource rather than the player be considered the unit and why should the Shapley value determine the proportion of payoff within a coalition? Certainly these are not Shapley's assumptions and his analysis strongly suggests the symmetric solution to the triadic situation, but it is interesting to note that we can reach the same theoretical predictions by this slightly different pathway.

SUMMARY

We have presented a theory of coalition formation to apply to a full-fledged coalition situation defined by four conditions. It is intended to apply where several parties are competitively attempting to determine a decision and in which no participant has either dictatorial or veto powers. The theory requires information on the initial distribution of resources, the payoff for each coalition, the non-utilitarian strategy preferences, and the effective decision point. Three additional assumptions further defined the situation to which the model applies.

Our general hypothesis stated that participants will expect others to demand from a coalition a share of the payoff which is proportional to the amount of resources which they are contributing to it. Each participant will estimate the value of any coalition strategy as the total payoff to a coalition multiplied by his share. He estimates this latter figure by the ratio of his resources to the total resources of the coalition. Every player will pursue strategies in the highest payoff class, but among alternative strategies in the same class, he will choose that one which maximizes his non-utilitarian strategy preference.

A coalition will form between two players if and only if there are reciprocal choices of coalition strategy between them. Thus, the model envisions the process of coalition formation as a step-by-step process until by successive pairing, the decision point has been reached.

The theory was compared with Caplow's predictions for coalitions in the triad and we found that in the special case where payoffs and non-utilitarian strategy preferences are constant, the two theories make identical predictions with one exception. In an experimental test by Vinacke and Arkoff, the results supported Caplow's and our own theory where they were opposed to the predictions of a strict rationality theory. At the one point where Caplow's theory differed from the one presented here, Vinacke and Arkoff's evidence supported the latter.

In examining the mathematical literature, we found that the von Neumann-Morgenstern solution theory was inadequate for our purposes because of its profusion of solutions for many games. An attempt by Vickrey to limit these somewhat by defining a *strong* solution still left the crucial difficulty of determining which member of a set of imputations would actually occur. The concept of psi-stability also left the unique specification of a coalition to extra-theoretical determination.

Finally, we explored the Shapley value and showed that it still suggests the equal probability of coalitions despite initial differences in resources. However, by the addition of two not unreasonable assumptions, it will lead to the same predictions as the theory presented here.

REFERENCES

1. Caplow, T. A theory of coalitions in the triad. *Amer. sociol. Rev.*, 1956, 19, 23–29.
2. Caplow, T. Further development of a theory of coalitions in the triad. *Amer. J. Sociol.*, 1959, 64, 488–493.
3. Leites, N. On the game of politics in France. Santa Monica, Calif.: Rand Corp., unedited advance copy, 1958.
4. Lerner, D., & Aron, R. *France defeats EDC.* New York: Frederick A. Praeger, 1957.
5. Luce, R. D. A definition of stability for n-person games. *Annals of Math.*, 1954, 59, 357–366.
6. Luce, R. D., & Raiffa. *Games and decisions.* New York: Wiley, 1957.
7. Luce, R. D., & Rogow, A. A. A game theoretical analysis of congressional power distributions for a stable two-party system. *Behav. Sci.*, 1956, 1, 83–96.
8. Mills, T. M. Coalition patterns in three person groups. *Amer. sociol. Rev.*, 1954, 19, 657–667.
9. Shapley, L. S. A value for n-person games. *Annals of Math. Stud.*, 1953, 28, 307–317.
10. Shapley, L. S., & Shubik, M. Method for evaluating the distribution of power in a committee system. *Amer. polit. sci. Rev.*, 1954, 48, 787–792.
11. Shubik, M. *Readings in game theory and political behavior,* Garden City, N.Y.: Doubleday, 1954.
12. Simmel, G. Significance of numbers for social life. In A. P. Hare, E. F. Borgatta, and R. F. Bales (Eds.), *Small groups.* New York: Knopf, 1955.
13. Strodtbeck, F. L. Family as a three person group. *Amer. sociol. Rev.*, 1954, 19, 23–29.
14. Vinacke, W. E., & Arkoff, A. Experimental study of coalitions in the triad. *Amer. sociol. Rev.*, 1957, 22, 406–415.

15. von Neumann, J., & Morgenstern, O. *Theory of games and economic behavior.* (2nd Ed.) Princeton, N.J.: Princeton Univer. Press, 1953.
16. Willerman, B. A final report: research on cohesive and disruptive tendencies in coalition type groups. Unpublished manuscript, Univer. of Minnesota, 1957. (Mimeo.)

Coalitions in the Triad: Critique and Experiment

HAROLD H. KELLEY
and
A. JOHN ARROWOOD

VINACKE AND ARKOFF (4) have presented an experiment which tests some of Caplow's hypotheses (2) about how the relative power of three persons affects the formation of pair coalitions. The situation studied is one in which each person is trying to obtain for himself as much of some valuable but scarce commodity as he can. The three individuals differ in ways relevant to their ability to gain a share of the rewards (referred to as "power"). This work has been especially interesting because of the paradoxical result that with certain distributions of power among the three individuals, in Caplow's words, "the triadic situation often favors the weaker over the strong." Under certain conditions the stronger of the three is at a disadvantage and actually receives the smallest share of the available rewards.

The purpose of the present research is to state with greater precision than heretofore the conditions under which this phenomenon prevails and to test experimentally some of the limits of these conditions. In order to do so, it is necessary to clarify certain ambiguities in the concept of power as used in the Vinacke and Arkoff experiment. This clarification is accomplished through use of the analysis of power provided by Thibaut and Kelley (3).

The problem can best be illustrated by a brief description of the

FROM *Sociometry*, 1960, 23, 231–244. Reprinted by permission of authors and the American Sociological Association, Inc.

Vinacke and Arkoff procedure. Three subjects play a game in which each moves his counter along the spaces of a game board. The first one to reach the goal receives a prize of 100 points. On successive trials, the experimenter rolls a single die and each player advances a number of spaces determined by the product of two numbers: (a) the number of pips turned up on the die and (b) a "weight," ranging from 1 to 4, which was randomly assigned him at the beginning of the game. For example, in one game player A may have weight 4, player B, weight 2, and player C, weight 1. Since all players start at the same point on the board and move each time the die is cast, the person assigned the largest weight automatically wins. A further rule, however, enables any pair of players to form a coalition by combining their weights at any time during the game. When they do so, they are given a single counter placed at a position equal to the sum of the distances the two have attained at that time. On subsequent rolls, they advance according to the sum of their two weights. The formation of a coalition is acknowledged by the experimenter only when the two players have agreed upon how they will divide the 100 point prize, should they receive it; and, once formed, a coalition is indissoluble for the remainder of that game. Thus, the individual or coalition that can mobilize the largest weight automatically wins that game and there is really no need for going through the motions of rolling the die.

The weight each player receives is said to constitute his *power*, but consider this point more closely. In what sense does a player with a weight of 4 have more power than a player with a weight of 2? In the game where the three weights are 4, 2 and 1, the player with the 4 weight has power in the sense that he is able, regardless of the actions of the other two players, to induce his "environment" (the game) to give him the prize. However, in the game with weights 4, 3 and 2, the player with 4 weight can exercise this control over the environment only if the other two players fail to form a coalition. Since any pair can mobilize more weight than the remaining person, each pair has the same amount of power over the third person as does any other pair. The variability in 4's outcomes is as much under the control of the joint actions of the other two players as is the variability in either 2 or 3's outcomes. Hence, as Vinacke and Arkoff point out, the initial weights in the 4–3–2 game are irrelevant with respect to the power a person has in the three-way bargaining situation.

In view of this logical analysis of the objective interdependency relations among the three players, Vinacke and Arkoff's results from the 4–3–2 and similar games are unexpected: The three players treat the weight 4 as if it does yield greater power. As his price for entering a coalition, player 4 apparently asks for a lion's share of the prize, because he typically receives more than 50 of the 100 points when he is in a coalition. Furthermore, players 2 and 3 tend to form the majority of the coalitions, presumably because each one can make a better deal with the other than he can with 4. From the point of view of rational analysis, then, the subjects act inappropriately, attributing to 4 a power that he does not in fact possess. The irony of the situation is that this erroneous belief about 4's advantage, which he usually shares, works to his disadvantage in the long run because of his exclusion from coalitions.

The first of the experiments reported below has the purpose of showing that Vinacke and Arkoff's data are, in a sense, spurious. They reflect a misunderstanding of the experimental situation that is not intrinsic to it, but results from the complexity of their total procedure. Confronted with the complexity, subjects erroneously equate initial weights with real power. (Our reasons for believing this erroneous assumption to be a reasonable one, considering the circumstances, are given in the Discussion.) The experimental hypothesis is that with a simpler procedure, subjects will acquire an adequate understanding of the true power relations and act more in accord with a rational analysis of the situation than the Vinacke and Arkoff data would suggest.

The second experiment has the purpose of testing Caplow's hypothesis under conditions where the power differences among the three persons are real rather than illusory. We expect the resulting bias in coalition formation (predominantly between the weaker members) to persist even though subjects are permitted thoroughly to familiarize themselves with the situation. (The limiting conditions under which the Caplow effect can be expected to appear are also described.)

EXPERIMENT I

In the Vinacke and Arkoff procedure, the relationship between weights and power is quite complicated. Each trio of subjects is required to play a series of games in which six different sets of weights are used. In the games played with a given set of values, a player need not have the same weight twice. With some sets of weights (such as 4–2–1) initial weight is relevant to power, and with others (such as 4–3–2) it is not.

In the present experiment, in order to simplify the subjects' task, only one set of weights was used (4–3–2) and each triad was given a lengthy series of trials, each player keeping the same weight throughout. It was expected that, with repeated experience in the single situation, the subjects' analyses of it would come to correspond with the analysis presented above, and their coalition formation and bargaining behavior would be increasingly consistent with an understanding that all players in the game have the same power.

Procedure

Ninety male students, volunteers from an introductory (sophomore) psychology class, served as subjects in thirty experimental triads. There is no reason to believe that the subjects were notably different from Vinacke and Arkoff's. Data were gathered first from 20 triads and, later, from ten additional triads. The first series were given a variable number of trials (10 to 70 trials, 26 on the average), and in the second series all groups completed 20 trials.

With the exceptions noted above, the experimental procedure followed that of Vinacke and Arkoff as closely as was possible from the available statements of their procedure. A major difference is that, whereas they gave very brief introductory instructions and relied on informal answers to questions to clarify the procedure, we gave rather full formal instructions and tried to minimize the necessity for subjects to ask questions. The subjects were given an individualistic orientation, it being emphasized that each was to accumulate as many points for himself as possible, attempting to maximize his outcomes without regard to those of any other players.

Results

In Table 1 are presented the frequencies of occurrence of the various coalitions. Data from our first and last three trials are presented for com-

TABLE 1

Frequency of Occurrence of Various Coalitions in the Three Experiments

	Vinacke and Arkoff's Three Trials		Experiment I First 3 Trials		Experiment I Last 3 Trials			Experiment II First 3 Trials		Experiment II Last 3 Trials	
COALITIONS	N	%	N	%	N	%	(COALITIONS)	N	%	N	%
2–3	59	66	41	46	37	41	(0–2)	24	53	29	64
2–4	20	22	24	27	26	29	(0–4)	12	27	13	29
3–4	9	10	21	23	27	30	(2–4)	9	20	3	7
No coalition	2	2	4	4	0	..		0	..	0	..
Totals	90	100	90	100	90	100		45	100	45	100

Vinacke and Arkoff: $X^2_{n=88,\ 2df} = 47.07$, $p < .001$

Experiment I, Last 3 Trials: $X^2_{n=90,\ 2df} = 2.47$, $.20 < p < .30$

Experiment II, Last 3 Trials: $X^2_{n=45,\ 2df} = 22.93$, $p < .001$

Vinacke and Arkoff vs. Experiment I: $X^2_{n=86,\ 2df} = 8.12$, $.01 < p < .02$

Experiment I vs. Experiment II: $X^2_{n=45,\ 2df} = 8.40$, $.01 < p < .02$

parison with those from Vinacke and Arkoff's three trials in the 4–3–2 condition. They calculated a Chi-square for the 88 instances of coalition formation (excluding the two instances of "no coalition") to determine the likelihood of the departure of the observed distribution from a theoretical distribution in which the three possible coalitions occur equally often. This procedure is not strictly justified, inasmuch as each group of subjects provides three instances of coalition formation, hence the various entries are not independent. However, we present similar Chi-squares in order to provide some basis for comparing the two sets of results.

It appears that the present procedure yields a distribution of coalitions which, although biassed in a manner similar to Vinacke and Arkoff's, is closer to the chance distribution than is theirs. The divergence from the earlier experiment appears even on the first three trials. A comparison of our first three with theirs yields a Chi-square of 8.48, $p = .02$. (The distribution of first coalitions formed in each triad resembles their distribution most closely, the percentages, in order, being 63, 20, and 17.) These results suggest that, either because of the concentrated experience with the single situation, or perhaps because of greater clarity in the experimental instructions, a number of subjects became aware of the objective power relationships rather early in the game.

From the first to the last trials there is not a significant change in the incidence of the three coalitions, hence we cannot be sure that further experience increased their understanding of the situation. However, this result must be interpreted in the light of the rather limited degree to which the occurrence of the early coalitions departed from chance. To the extent that subjects achieved an understanding of their relationships very early, further improvement in this respect was limited. Upon examination of the data on a trial-by-trial basis, it is clear that the learning is very rapid, so that after the first three or four trials there is little more than chance exclusion of 4 from coalitions.

In Vinacke and Arkoff's experiment, associated with the tendency for 2 and 3 to be reluctant about forming coalitions with 4, was the tendency for him to receive more than half of the 100 point prize when he did manage to enter a coalition. This effect appears in the early trials of the present experiment and declines, though not significantly so, during its course. During the first three trials, player 4 was a member of a coalition in 26 triads and in 17 of these he managed to come out with more than 50 per cent of the rewards. During the last three trials of the experiment, this was true in only 10 of 29 possible instances. Of the 25 groups in which person 4 was in coalitions during both the first and last three trials, his share of the coalition reward declined in 13 instances, increased in six instances and did not change in the remaining six. Omitting the last six, the difference between the number of decreases and increases yields a p-value of .168 by the Sign test.

There are, then, two behavioral manifestations of the players' perception that 4 has the most power: (a) He is excluded from coalitions and, (b) when he is included in coalitions, he receives more than half the points.

When early and later trials are compared, the extent to which 4's frequency of being included increases and the extent to which his percentage winnings per trial decrease provide two indicators of downgrading in the perception of his power. A comparison of the first and last three trials of the experiment reveals that in 18 triads the 4 man was downgraded on both of these indicators or downgraded on one with no change on the other; in six triads, he was upgraded on both indicators or upgraded on one with no change on the other; and in six triads, he did not change on either indicator or was upgraded on one and downgraded on the other. When the last six are omitted from the analysis, the Sign test indicates there was significantly more downgrading than upgrading ($p = .026$).

On the questionnaire at the end of the experiment all subjects were asked the following open-ended question: "Many subjects believe that 4 is more to be feared, has greater potential, etc. Did you at any time think that this was the case?" All but 14 of the 90 subjects admitted that they at some time had held this belief. This estimate of the extent of the belief, if it errs at all, is probably an underestimate because of the general realization at the end of the experiment of the incorrectness of this view. Most of those admitting to this belief reported having it "at first" or on the first one or two trials. Subjects with the three different weights were equally susceptible to this belief.

The next question asked when the subject realized that no position has any more power than any other and that nobody is justified in asking for more than half the 100 points. Forty-three of the 90 claimed to have realized this before or during the first three trials. Another 33 did not localize their insight so sharply in time. Only 13 admitted they had never realized this. On the basis of their answers to other questions about power relations, preferred position, position likely to win, and ease of bargaining with various positions, another nine subjects were added to the latter category of those who had failed to attain a correct understanding of the situation by the end of the experiment.

In brief, the self-report data suggest that, while some 85 per cent of our subjects believed at some time during the experiment (largely, in the early stages) that the 4 weight carries greatest power, only 25 per cent held this belief at the end of the experiment. As far as we could judge from their answers to questions asked after the experiment, the other 75 per cent had achieved a correct understanding of the power relations and apparently most of them did so during the actual trials of the experiment.

One may ask to what extent this change in belief about power relations reflects the subjects' direct experience with the game, as opposed to their being taught by the small number of their colleagues who had analyzed the situation correctly from the start. To answer this question, a comparison was made between those groups in which, from the sound recordings of the discussion, there appeared to have been some possibility of "teaching," and the remaining groups. There were no differences between the two sets of data either in the amount of learning that took place or in the coalitions formed. Hence, explicit teaching seems not to account for the observed effects.

A final open-ended question asked: "Why do you think that many subjects would believe that 4 is more to be feared, has greater potential, etc.? What is there in the situation that leads to this belief?" The most frequent response, given by 34 of the 90 subjects, dealt with the fact that 4 would win invariably if no coalitions were formed. Another 13 merely stated, without further amplification, that 4 was the largest number. Nine subjects mentioned the multiplicative aspect of the game, pointing out that multiples of 4 are larger than multiples of 2 or 3. Apparently, the 56 responses in these three categories either discount or overlook the possibility of coalition formation. A fourth category of response deals with 4's "psychological" or "cultural" power. Seventeen of the 90 suggested that it was natural to react to 4's higher weight in the light of their previous experience in games that higher numbers are generally better ones and in everyday life that quantity often has the upper hand. This answer is silent concerning the possibility of coalitions but highlights the stereotype that "more" is "better."

It is difficult to evaluate the validity of these post-experiment explanations for the earlier misinterpretation. Because the misperception of 4's power is largely corrected by the end of the experiment, subjects may be somewhat reluctant or even unable to discuss the real basis for their mistaken views. Hence the reasons given by the 22 players who seem never to have realized the true nature of the power situation may be especially valuable indications of the source of the error. Seven of the 22 seemed to believe that coalitions including 4 were somehow more sure of obtaining the prize than were other coalitions or that 4 was the only player capable of bargaining and that the other players had either to accept his terms or receive nothing. We believe it noteworthy that it is only among these 22 players that we find the assertion (made by another seven of them) that a high-weight player is justified in demanding a majority share of the coalition reward because he *contributes more* to the coalition. One might guess that this interpretation figures more prominently in the early reaction to the situation than the overall figures would indicate. The comments about 4's larger number and the multiplicative aspects of the game may well be oblique references to earlier beliefs (which now appear to the subjects as totally unjustified) that the higher weight player makes a greater contribution to coalition success.

EXPERIMENT II

Under the Vinacke and Arkoff procedure, the alternative to being in a coalition on any given trial has the same value (zero) for each player regardless of his weight. Hence, 4's outcomes are as much subject to control through the joint actions of the other two players as are either 2 or 3's outcomes. It is in this sense that 4 has no more power than they. In the present experiment, real power differences are created by giving the three subjects differential ability to obtain rewards from the game, an ability that can not be attenuated by the actions of the other two persons. This is done by giving each person a specific alternative level of outcomes which he receives if he fails to gain membership in a coalition or if, once in a coalition, he and his partner fail to reach agreement on a division of the spoils. (The bargaining involved in the division of the prize *follows* rather than precedes the choice of coalition partners.) The person with a higher alternative value has high power in the sense that (a) he is less dependent upon getting into a coalition, and (b), during the bargaining following coalition formation, he can hold out for a larger share because he has less to lose if no agreement is reached. The long run effects of the latter, demanding a preponderant share of the reward, are of rather little concern to him because of the first fact. At the same time, factor (b) makes him less desirable than a weaker person as a coalition partner. Hence, we would expect that the poorer a player's alternative, the greater the likelihood of his being included in a pair coalition. Of course, this will be true only when the size of prize given a coalition does *not* increase in proportion to the power of its members. (In the present case, as in the Vinacke and Arkoff procedure, the prize is the same for all coalitions.) It is under these circumstances that Caplow's statement is relevant—that "the weakest member of the triad has a definite advantage, being sure to be included in whatever coalition is formed."

Procedure

Forty-five male students, volunteers from an introductory (sophomore) psychology class, served as subjects in 15 experimental triads. The task was presented as a simple business game in which each player was a corporation chairman, controlling a certain share of the market each month. Each player's object was to accumulate as many points for himself as possible, not to compete but to attempt to maximize his own outcomes without regard to how this might affect the outcomes of the other players. Each subject was randomly assigned a weight—either 4, 2, or 0—which represented the number of points he could earn on each trial if he chose to play the game independently. Any pair of subjects, however, had the option of forming a coalition which was then given one minute to decide in what manner to divide a ten-point prize between them. Coalitions were formed by a series of written choices. At the beginning of each trial, each subject privately indicated the number of the other player with whom he would most like to form a coalition. Reciprocated choices became coalition partners, thereby having the opportunity to attempt to decide how they wanted to divide the ten points between them. The third man, the player *not* in the coalition, was paid off immediately with the number of points equal to his weight or alternative and did not enter into the bargaining for that trial. (If there happened to be no reciprocated choices on a given trial, the subjects were requested to consider the problem again and indicate their choices once more. This procedure was continued until a reciprocated choice appeared. This was necessary on only 43 of the 300 trials. Most of the instances of non-reciprocation were found early in the game.) If the two members of the coalition reached some mutually satisfactory division of the ten points during the minute allotted for bargaining, they then received that number of points as their scores for that trial. If, however, they did not agree before the time limit, they forfeited the ten points and each received the number of points equal to their weights or alternatives. A time limit was placed on the bargaining so that the weaker player could not gain power by stalling and controlling time. Each subject retained the same weight throughout the game, and each triad completed 20 trials.

Although the weights employed in the present study differ from those used in the Vinacke-Arkoff experiment, they are comparable in at least two ways: first, if no coalitions are formed, or if no agreement is reached in the coalitions which are formed, the high-weight man will always win; and, second, the coalition is always assured a chance at a larger number of points than is any independent player. For certain analyses, then, we shall consider the present 0–2, 0–4, and 2–4 coalitions as equivalent, respectively, to the 2–3, 2–4, and 3–4 coalitions in the previous experiment.

Results

Table 1 presents the frequencies of occurrence of the various coalitions. Data from the first and last three trials of Experiment II may be compared with those from Vinacke and Arkoff and Experiment I. The relative incidence of the various coalitions for the first three trials of Experiment II does not differ significantly from that of Experiment I. The difference between the two distributions for the last three trials of each experiment is significant at the .01 level with a Chi-square of 10.72. The difference between the two distributions for Experiment II is not significant (Chi-square $= 3.48$, $p < .20$).

It appears, then, that the present procedure yields a distribution of coalitions which, although departing initially from the Vinacke-Arkoff distribution, does not do so as markedly as does the distribution from Experiment I and comes to approximate the Vinacke-Arkoff distribution far more closely as the trials progress.

The data also suggest that this is not merely an illusory effect which disappears with repeated experience in the situation. Table 2 presents the mean frequencies per triad of the various coalitions, and the significance levels for these differences. The 0–2 coalition occurs significantly more frequently than do either of the other possible pairs, both over the whole series of 20 trials and in both the first and second halves of the experiment; but only over the entire series of trials does the difference between the relative incidence of the 0–4 and 0–2 coalitions approach significance. Moreover, the average frequency of 0–2 coalitions tends to increase from the first to the second half of the experiment, while that of the 2–4 coalitions tends to decrease during the same period (in both instances $.05 < p < .10$, using the ordinary t-test for differences).

TABLE 2

*Mean Frequency of Occurrence of Various Coalitions Overall and by Halves of Experiment II with Comparisons**

MEAN FREQUENCY PER TRIAD	OVERALL	FIRST HALF OF TRIALS	SECOND HALF OF TRIALS
0–2	12.33	5.67	6.67
0–4	5.20	2.80	2.40
2–4	2.47	1.53	.93
	20 trials	10 trials	10 trials
MEAN DIFFERENCE PER TRIAD			
0–2 > 0–4	7.13 $t = 10.62$ $p < .02$	2.87 $t = 8.28$ $p < .02$	4.27 $t = 9.19$ $p < .02$
0–2 > 2–4	9.87 $t = 14.68$ $p < .02$	4.13 $t = 11.94$ $p < .02$	5.73 $t = 12.35$ $p < .02$
0–4 > 2–4	2.73 $t = 4.07$ $.02 < p < .10$	1.27 $t = 3.66$ p=NS	1.47 $t = 3.16$ p=NS

* The t values in this table were calculated using the Tukey method for multiple comparisons.

Another way of looking at the evidence is in terms of partnership choice data. Each of the positions predominantly chose the lower alternative man as a partner—i.e., 0 chose 2 66 per cent of the time, 2 chose 0 77 per cent of the time, and 4 chose 0 60 per cent of the time. Sign tests show that the results differ significantly from those expected by chance (equally frequent choice of the other two players) at beyond the .05 level in all three cases.

The previous experiments revealed an initial tendency for the 4 man to ask for and receive the majority of points from those coalitions which he did manage to enter. Over the entire series of 20 trials in the present experiment, there was a similar tendency for both 4 and 2 to receive more points than 0 in the 4–0 and 2–0 coalitions respectively (significant at better than the .02 level by the Tukey method for multiple comparisons). The slight tendency for 4 to receive more points than 2 from 2–4 coalitions proved non-significant. The over-all results are duplicated in the first half of the trials for each triad, but largely disappear during the second half—the only significant result remaining in the 4–0 coalition. As expected, on the average 4 received significantly more points per coalition from 0 than he did from 2, as did 2 from 0 over 4. The 0 man was slightly better rewarded by 2 than by 4, and especially during the second half of the game ($.05 < p < .10$). A comparison of first and second half scores reveals that 0's scores per coalition increase significantly ($p < .01$) while 4's scores per coalition decrease slightly ($.05 < p < .10$).

In a questionnaire administered at the end of the experiment the subjects were asked to indicate the following: which weight they would choose as a permanent partner; in general, which weight they believed each of the players should form coalitions with; which weight had the most power; which are the easiest and hardest weights with which to bargain; which weight would win in the long run; and which member, if either, of any coalition is justified in asking for a majority of the points. Their answers reflect the coalition formation and bargaining behavior discussed above. Only five of the 45 subjects, for example, failed to pick the available lower alternative player as a permanent coalition partner. The question: "Which of the three players has the most power?" was asked twice—once early in the questionnaire and once again at the end. At the first asking, four subjects responded that 0 had the most power, three picked 2, 36 chose 4, and two said that there were no power differences. At the later asking, 13 of the subjects who had previously singled out 4 as having power changed their answers to 2. The open-ended explanations accompanying these changes indicate a growing awareness of 2's ability to entire 0 into a coalition although still noting that, *if selected*, 4's higher weight becomes important. In general, however, subjects continue to view power as residing in a higher alternative.

DISCUSSION AND SUMMARY

It appears that Vinacke and Arkoff's procedure does initially give player 4 an illusory kind of power. In Experiment I, most of the subjects are initially subject to this misperception but apparently achieve a more correct understanding in a few trials. These results are in accord with our general contention that the phenomenon reported by Vinacke and Arkoff is limited to instances where the complexity of the learning task is so great in relation to the amount of contact and experience subjects have with it that they are not able properly to analyze it. In consequence, we witness actions that are "irrational" with respect to the analysis the experimenter makes at his leisure. However, these actions are not necessarily irrational when viewed in the light of the understanding subjects are able to achieve under the pressures of time and task complexity. Incomplete understanding is not to be confused with irrationality.

There are at least two possible interpretations of the initial erroneous attribution of power to player 4. The first is that the initial attribution of power to 4 reflects a general pessimism about the dependability of co-operative action. Logically, player 4 is more powerful *unless* the others join forces against him. Until one knows that joint action will be instituted dependably, attributing superior power to him is not wholly unwarranted. This interpretation is suggested by the most commonly given explanation for the attribution: 4 has more power because he would win if no coalitions were formed. The declining tendency to attribute power to 4 may reflect a growing confidence that in this situation, at least, cooperative action against him is to be taken for granted.

Another possible interpretation is that our subjects have learned to use a person's potentialities in a field of independent actors as an indication of his ability to contribute to cooperative efforts. This is explicitly suggested by the comments that he makes a larger contribution to any coalition he enters and is consistent with other more general explanations provided by the subjects. In view of their likely experiences with these matters, this conclusion is a highly reasonable one. It is probably true that in everyday situations a person's effectiveness, when everyone is acting for himself, is rather closely related to how much he can add to any joint effort. Thus, the common misperception in the Vinacke and Arkoff situation may reflect a positive correlation in the social environment of the typical subject. The reader may note the similarity of this interpretation to Brunswik's explanation (1) of, for example, the size-weight illusion as reflecting a correlation between size and weight over the universe of objects the person has experienced in his physical environment. In Brunswik's terms, we are suggesting that a person's effectiveness as an individual has "ecological validity" as a cue from which to predict his ability to contribute to joint efforts, and thus enjoys considerable "impression value" or "response-eliciting power." This is the case in the Vinacke and Arkoff situation. In Experiment I, subjects initially utilize this cue extensively, but later learn that it is inappropriate in this situation and, hence, its subsequent degree of utilization declines.

The procedure of Experiment II, in contrast to that of Vinacke and Arkoff, appears to create large and lasting power differences among the members of the triad. Given differentially good alternatives to being in a coalition or, more important, to acquiescing to a coalition partner's demands, the predicted pattern of coalition formation emerges, and the weakest member of the triad is in the most favored position when it comes to joining pair coalitions. The score and self-report data, however, suggest certain minor trends worth brief consideration. We have noted a tendency for o's average score per coalition to increase and 4's to decrease. This finding may be taken as an indication that during the course of the trials some o's are beginning to capitalize on their status as preferred coalition partners by asking for a larger share of the prize and some 4's are recognizing that they must be more generous in dividing the prize if they are to be allowed to enter further coalitions. We have also noted some changes in subjects' perceptions of the most powerful player and in the reasons accompanying their answers. Mention of 2's great ability to entice o into coalitions suggests that some subjects are becoming aware of the truth of Caplow's hypothesis. These findings raise the interesting side problem of how a high-power individual in a situation with limited communication possibilities would go about establishing trust. Once excluded from coalitions, the high-weight man would probably tend to remain excluded, since unless he could enter a coalition there would be no way for him to demonstrate to the others that he would not use his power against them.

It must be noted that in general 4 tends to accumulate the most points during the game—93 on the average as compared with 86 for 2 and 66 for o. However, this is probably an artifact of the relative sizes of the alternatives and the prize to be divided. By making the coalition reward larger in relation to the largest weight, one could create a situation in which the highest alternative player would, by reason of his exclusion from coalitions, end up with the smallest accumulated score. However, as the coalition prize becomes larger, the differential power implications of any given set of weights becomes less important.

One might also manipulate the weights and coalition prize in such a manner that the highest alternative player would emerge as the most preferred partner. This is an important point because it indicates the boundary conditions for the phenomena observed in Experiment II. For example, different sizes of rewards might be given to different coalitions. If the various rewards were proportional to the weights of the persons comprising the various coalitions, one would expect no difference in the relative incidence of the three possible types of coalition or even a bias in favor of coalitions including the high-power person. The latter effect would be expected, for example, if the 2–4 coalition received a prize of 12 points, the o–4 coalition, 8 points, and the o–2 coalition, 4 points. This would reproduce the situation where the more effective a person is as an independent actor, the more effective is the joint effort to which he contributes. It is not unreasonable to believe that, in many natural situations, joint effectiveness is a direct function (and perhaps even a multiplicative one) of individual effectiveness. In these cases, if the above analysis is correct, coalitions would appear largely among persons of high power. On the other hand, the Caplow effect will appear when coalition effectiveness bears no relation (or a negative one) to the effectiveness of the component members.

REFERENCES

1. Brunswik, E. *Systematic and representative designs of psychological experiments.* Berkeley: Univer. of California Press, 1949.
2. Caplow, T. A theory of coalitions in the triad. *Amer. sociol. Rev.*, 1956, 21, 489–493.
3. Thibaut, J. W., & Kelley, H. H. *The social psychology of groups.* New York: Wiley and Sons, Inc., 1959, Chapters 7 and 11.
4. Vinacke, W. E., & Arkoff, A. An experimental study of coalitions in the triad. *Amer. sociol. Rev.*, 1957, 22, 406–414.

CHAPTER 11 ROLE DIFFERENTIATION

Husband-Wife Interaction over Revealed Differences

FRED L. STRODTBECK

IN THE course of a series of pilot studies of power, or influence, in small group situations a procedure has been developed, called the revealed difference technique, which has shown promise in a first application to husband-wife interaction. In the attempt to validate the results obtained by this technique, use has been made of similar groups in different cultures. The following paper is organized in a form to emphasize how this methodological innovation and the technique itself grew from successive sequences in which pilot findings led to further research operations.

BACKGROUND

During 1948–49 a series of groups were observed engaged in decision-making. An effort was made to determine some of the correlates of dif-

FROM *American Sociological Review*, 1951, 16, 468–473. Reprinted by permission of the author and publisher.

Data for this paper were collected under the auspices of the Comparative Study of Values Project being conducted by the Social Relations Laboratory, Harvard University, with the assistance of the Rockefeller Foundation and the Peabody Museum.

ferential ability to persuade others in accordance with the actor's desires. In one instance, four mathematics students were requested to recommend jointly the best of three possible solutions to particular problems. While these students were in the process of developing consensus they were asked to record privately the alternative they personally favored. Thus, the experimenter was provided with a continuous means of relating a type of private opinion to public behavior. The experimentation indicated that the ultimate decision could be most accurately predicted by simply weighting the privately pre-determined opinion of each participant by the total time he had spoken during the experimental interaction. This finding was duplicated in various groups who worked at the task of jointly selecting the best move in a chess problem. This simple answer did little, however, to recapture the subtlety and complexity of social interaction as it is generally understood.

We recognized that we had up to this time worked with *ad hoc* groups which had no group structure at the beginning of the observation period and no expectation of participating with one another at a later time. The problems they had considered were delimited and specific; the nature of their arguments and responses was highly structured. On the basis of this analysis, we were led to consider experimentation with groups whose members approached the opposite extreme of broad common interests, daily contact, and permanence—so-called primary groups.

Among the various types of primary groups that might profitably be studied, husband-wife dyads were selected because of the ease of replication of these units. Each couple was asked to pick three reference families with whom they were well acquainted. The husband and wife were then separated and requested to designate which of the three reference families most satisfactorily fulfilled a series of 26 conditions such as: Which family has the happiest children? Which family is the most religious? Which family is most ambitious? After both husband and wife had individually marked their choices they were requested to reconcile their differences and indicate a final "best" choice from the standpoint of their family. For the first ten couples studied, this pooling took place with the experimenter out of the room and under conditions such that the couple did not know they were being observed or having their voices recorded. Their lack of knowledge of the observation was ascertained after the session, at which time their permission to use the material in a scientific inquiry was obtained.[1] The anticipated experimental difficulties—(a) producing "polite" interaction because of the intrusion of the experimenter, and (b) structuring the task to such a degree that the mode of interaction would be highly determined—were judged to have been satisfactorily avoided.

1 Ursula Marsh, Donald Michael, Theodore M. Mills, and Herbert Shepard were joint participants in this phase of the research.

Omitting, for present purposes, a discussion of the content of the recorded protocols, it was found that women won 47 of the contested decisions and men, 36. In six of the eight cases in which there was a difference both in number of decisions-won and in talking-time, the spouse who talked most won the majority of the decisions. At this time there was no basis for appraising whether the women had won slightly more decisions because they had known more about the types of information under discussion, or whether the decision winning represented, as we had hoped, the operation of structured power relations in an area in which both participants were equally informed. The observed margin by which the women exceeded the men was not significant—a result which might have been much more valuable if we had predicted it in terms of independent knowledge of the equalitarian characteristics of the married veteran couples used in the sample. In short, further application was necessary to determine whether the technique was a valid method of indicating in any more general sense the balance of power between participants.

A field study was designed to throw further light on this problem. Three communities were selected which presumably differed in terms of the degree to which the wife was favored by the cultural phrasing of power. The communities were at the same time sufficiently small to increase greatly the probability that both spouses would be adequately, if not equally, informed concerning the behavior of the reference couples. The technique as described above was applied to ten couples from each of these cultures. It was proposed that the conformity of the experimental results with the a priori cultural expectations be taken as a crude measure of the validity with which the technique reflected power differences.

DESCRIPTION OF CULTURES

The cultures which were selected for study are geographically adjacent communities in the Arizona–New Mexico area. Briefly described, the groups are Navaho Indians; dry farmers from Texas who have recently homesteaded in the area; and early settlers who utilize a dam operated under the supervision of the Mormon church. These communities will be described in detail in forthcoming publications of the Comparative Study of Values Project.[2] For present purposes the communities will be designated Navaho, Texan, and Mormon. A brief recapitulation of power attributes of the culturally legitimized role of women in each culture is presented below.

The young Navaho man, who marries a girl from a moderately successful family, typically leaves his own family and resides with the girl's

2 Clyde Kluckhohn gives a brief description of the Navaho studies which are now considered a part of this project in the introduction to *Gregorio, the Hand Trembler* (5).

family and works under her father's direction until he has established himself as a responsible person. When this change of residence is made, the man leaves his sheep with his own family of orientation and his work activities result in little immediate increase in his own holdings. The children are considered a part of the wife's consanguine group, and marriages are generally unstable. Both men and women own sheep, but the women do the processing of wool into rugs and blankets. This assures the women a regular income throughout the year. The man has greater earning power when he performs wage work, but the wage work opportunities are scarce and seasonal. The man is considered the head of the household, but the relative economic independence of the wife and her close integration with her own consanguine group effectively limit his exercise of power. All but one of the ten Navaho couples studied maintained Navaho religious practices, the one exception was a recent convert to a fundamentalist church now proselytizing in the area.

The Texan group is composed of migrants who came from Eastern Texas during the drought and depression of the early 1930's. With minor exceptions the households are farms on contiguous sections headed by persons who as young adults made the earlier move, or by their older children who have more recently married. Due to the short growing season and lack of rainfall, the cultivation of pinto beans has developed into the major cash crop. The ten couples who participated in this study were members of the ranking Presbyterian clique in the community.[3]

The ten couples selected for study in the Mormon village were chosen from the most active participants in the affairs of the local church. Religious teachings which exercise a pervasive effect upon local social organization specifically stress the role of the husband as the head of the family. The position of the church is stated in different ways in quotations similar to the following:

> There must be a presiding authority in the family. The father is the head, or president, or spokesman of the family. This arrangement is of divine origin. It also conforms to the physical and physiological laws under which humanity lives. A home, as viewed by the Church, is composed of a family group, so organized as to be presided over by the father, under the authority and in the spirit of the priesthood conferred upon him (8, p. 81).
>
> This patriarchal order has its divine spirit and purpose, and those who disregard it under one pretext or another are out of harmony with the spirit of God's laws as they are ordained for recognition in the home. It is not merely a question of who is perhaps best qualified. Neither is it wholly a question of who is living the most worthy life. It is a question largely of law and order, and its importance is seen often from the fact that authority remains and is respected long after a man is really unworthy to exercise it (7, p. 359).

3 A forthcoming publication by Evon Z. Vogt will describe the social organization of this community in detail.

Corresponding prescriptions for the wife's role emphasize that she should above all else be a mother, for "motherhood is the noblest, most soul-satisfying of all earthly experiences." Mormonism has a this-worldly orientation, divine grace is attained through effort, and the symbol of progress is the advancement the man makes in the priesthood and in extending his flocks and fields. The woman is not eligible for membership in the priesthood and her status is coupled with that of her husband both in her present life and in the next, by the regular Temple marriage. From the incomplete evidence now available, Mormon women of this community do not appear to have important land-holdings nor independent sources of income, and accounts of women's participation in church activities confirm the correspondence of women's current attitudes with the church writings quoted above. The historic emphasis by Brigham Young and others on woman's education and political participation was always hedged by the general reservation that motherhood should not be interfered with—the women of the community in question strongly emphasize this reservation.

In Navaho mythology and folklore the actions imputed to women contrast sharply with the emphasis of Mormon theology. For the Navaho the women become major charismatic figures.[4] Marriage customs are also consistent with this conception of the Navaho woman as an active and demanding person. On the morning after a Navaho wedding the groom runs a foot race with his bride. The cultural interpretation is that "the one who wins will become rich" (6, p. 141). This practice is quite different from the familiar custom in which the bride is passively carried over the threshold, and it is also a commentary on the independence of the economic fortunes of Navaho marriage-mates.

In summary, the favored position of the Navaho woman in contrast to the Mormon woman was judged in terms of economic, religious, and kinship considerations to be quite unequivocal. Between Texan and Mormon women there is less difference, but in terms of holding church office and the present possession of productive land and semi-professional jobs, the women in the Texan community appear to be more favored than the Mormon women. On the basis of this analysis it was predicted that Navaho women would win the highest percentage of the decisions and the Mormon women the smallest.

4 These include Changing Woman, Spider Woman and Salt Woman. Blessing Way, the most frequently repeated ceremonial, stresses that each of the four poles of the hogan represent still different female divinities. Kluckhohn and Leighton comment that this practice "speaks volumes for the high place of women in the traditional conceptions" (4, p. 56).

EXPERIMENTAL PROCEDURE

The area under study had no electrification, and since it was impractical to attempt to bring the subjects to an observation room, the field sessions of the experimental procedure were recorded by portable sound equipment powered from a truck. Although the subjects were separated from the experimenter and other persons, they knew that their voices were being recorded. The task was explained to the Navahos by an interpreter. An appropriate picture was presented for each question and underneath the illustration there were pockets representing the three reference couples. The Navaho would place his marker in the pocket which represented the couple of his choice. In those instances in which there had been a difference between the choice of the man and wife, the illustration was presented again to the two of them with their markers in separate pockets. They were requested to combine their markers in the position which best represented their joint opinion. Some questions were changed somewhat by translation into Navaho; for example, the question, "Which family is the most religious?" became "Which family follows the 'Navaho Way' best?" It was not felt that these changes would significantly modify the results here presented. These recordings were transcribed and, in the case of the Navaho, translated into English.

TABLE 1

Decisions Won, by Spouse and Culture

CULTURE	NUMBER OF COUPLES	DECISIONS WON BY: HUSBAND	WIFE
Navaho	10	34	46
Texan	10	39	33
Mormon	10	42	29

The written protocols were analyzed to determine the number of acts used by each participant and the distribution of these acts in terms of interaction process categories.[5] This information plus knowledge of the number of decisions won by each participant provides the basis for the analysis presented below.

FINDINGS

We present in Table 1 the sum of the decisions won by the husbands and wives in each of the three cultures. The appropriate null hypothesis is compounded of two elements: (a) the proposition that the Mormon

5 For a description of the categories used see Bales, (1).

wives win an equal or greater number of decisions than their husbands (p=.007); and (b) the proposition that Navaho husbands win an equal or greater number of decisions than their wives (p=.16). Since the combined probability associated with these two propositions is less than .01, we reject the null hypothesis and conclude that we were able to predict the balance of decision-winning from our study of the comparative social and cultural organization of the groups from which our sample was drawn.

Having to this limited degree established the validity of the technique, we are encouraged to inquire further into elements of behavior in the small group situation which are linked with decision-winning. Our earlier experience had indicated a very strong relationship between decision-winning, or leadership, and talking-time in *ad hoc* groups of four persons.[6] In the present instance two-person primary groups are involved. From a broader study of the rank characteristics of participants in groups ranging in size from two to ten persons it is known that differentiation in speaking-time in two-person groups is relatively less than it is in larger groups, hence it is probable that the relation between speaking-time and decision-winning is less clearly defined in two-person than in larger groups (2). There was no compelling rationale for predicting the effects of the primary relationships upon "speaking and decision-winning." By combining the ten cases observed at Cambridge with the thirty cases from the field and eliminating the six cases in which the decisions were split evenly, we obtain the thirty-four cases compared in Table 2. The null hypothesis of independence between talking most and winning may be rejected at the .05 but not the .01 level.

TABLE 2

Decisions Won and Talking-Time for 34 Married Couples

SPOUSE WHO TALKED MOST	SPOUSE WHO WON MOST	
	HUSBAND	WIFE
Husband	14	5
Wife	5	10

To approach a more systematic description of the interaction characteristics of the spouse who talks most, we have selected the 24 cases in which there was a significant difference between the number of acts originated by the husband and the wife. We find that the most talking spouse tended more frequently to *ask questions*, carry out *opinion and analysis*, and make *rewarding remarks*. As Simmel suggested, in a dyad there can be no coalitions—the speaker does not have alternative audiences, so the

6 Bass reports a correlation of .93 between the time a participant in an eight-man group spent talking and the votes he received from observers for having demonstrated leadership (3).

"threat of withdrawal" is generally a more compelling adjustmental device in two-person than in larger groups. While we do not as yet have norms by group size for category usage on a common task, the unexpected finding in the present study that the most active participant is significantly high in question-asking gives us further insight into how withdrawal is anticipated and prevented. The finding that the frequency of opinion and analysis acts is higher for the most talking person is in agreement with Bales' notion that acts of this type have a central generative function which results in their being heavily represented in the profile of the most talking person in groups of any size.

The categories which discriminate the profile of the least talking participants are, in order of magnitude, the following: simple *acts of agreement*, *aggressive acts* designed to deflate the other actor's status, and simple *disagreements*. Taken together, these characteristics suggest the passive agreeing person who from time to time becomes frustrated and aggresses.

Concerning cultural differences in category usage, the Navahos gave *opinion*, *evaluation*, and *analysis* acts during the solution of their differences only one-half as frequently as the Mormon and the Texan group. As a result they required on the average fewer acts per decision (8 in contrast with 30 for the other groups) and the reasoning and persuasion in their protocols seemed extremely sketchy. They did not emphasize the arguments that might bear upon the issue, they tended to reiterate their choices and implore the other person to "go with them;" "go together," or simply consent. This is in marked contrast with the other couples who appeared to feel that they had to give a reasoned argument to show that they were logically convinced, even when they were giving in to the other person. It is a matter for further research to determine if other "traditional" people show a similar tendency to minimize analysis in social problem solving.

For the Texans it was a rational exercise, sometimes directly commented upon, to see that the decisions came out even, the standard deviation between spouses in decisions won was only 1.3. The Mormons were less concerned with equality, the comparable figure is 2.1, and among the Navaho there were marked differences between spouses, the standard deviation being 5.1.

SUMMARY

The essence of the revealed difference technique here described consists of: (a) requesting subjects who have shared experiences to make individual evaluations of them; and then, (b) requesting the subjects to reconcile any differences in interpretations which may have occurred. It has been shown that the disposition of these reconciled decisions is related both to power elements in the larger social and cultural organization and amount of participation in the small group situation. It is believed that other couples as well as parent-child, foreman-worker, and similar relationships may be profitably studied with the technique, since it appears not only to reveal the balance of power, but also to produce a sample of interaction in which modes and techniques of influence can be studied by methods of content and process analysis.

REFERENCES

1. Bales, R. F. The analysis of small group interaction. *Amer. sociol. Rev.*, 1950, 15, 257–264.
2. Bales, R. F., Strodtbeck, F. L., Mills, T. M., & Roseborough, Mary E. Channels of communication in small groups. *Amer. sociol. Rev.*, 1951, 16, 461–468.
3. Bass, B. M. An analysis of leaderless group discussion. *J. appl. Psychol.*, 1949, 33, 527–533.
4. Kluckhohn, & Leighton. *The Navaho.* Cambridge, Mass.: Harvard Univer. Press, 1947.
5. Leighton, A. H., & Leighton, D. C. *Gregorio, the hand trembler.* Papers to the Peabody Museum, Cambridge, Mass., 1949.
6. Reichard, Gladys A. *Social life of the Navaho Indians.* New York: Columbia Univer. Press, 1928.
7. Smith, J. F. *Gospel doctrine.* Salt Lake City, 1929.
8. Widtsoe, J. A. *Priesthood and church government.* Salt Lake City, 1939.

Some Consequences of Power Differences on Decision Making in Permanent and Temporary Three-Man Groups

E. PAUL TORRANCE

MOST of the sociological and social psychological studies of the consequences of power differences on decision making have been concerned either with communities, large organizations, temporary groups, or artificially created groups without histories of interaction. The present study deals with decision making in permanent groups with uniform, well-established, and clear-cut hierarchical structures. A number of studies suggested that the consequences may be due as much to patterns of behavior developed as a result of interaction as to power itself. For this reason, a second aspect of the study is concerned with a comparison of the decision making behavior of permanent groups with that of similarly constituted temporary groups.

SUBJECTS

It was found that B-26 combat crews are particularly well suited for the purposes of the study. A B-26 crew is composed of three men: a pilot, a navigator and a gunner. The pilot as the aircraft commander has final authority to make crew decisions regardless of differences in rank. The navigator is a commissioned officer and may even outrank the pilot; he makes many decisions and as a commissioned officer may exercise certain power over the gunner, an enlisted man. He may be overruled by the pilot and

FROM *Research Studies, State College of Washington*, 1954, 22, 130–140. Reprinted by permission of the author and publisher.

in many ways occupies a status inferior to that of the pilot. The gunner is definitely the "low man on the totem pole." He is an enlisted man and has relatively little power over the two officers.

The permanent crews had been together for several months and had reached the final stage of their crew training before entering combat. The temporary groups were drawn from the same type of personnel. They were only regrouped so that no man was on a crew with a member of his regular crew. For each set of three crews, the following pattern was followed in the regrouping.

CREW A: Pilot 1, Navigator 2, Gunner 3
CREW B: Pilot 2, Navigator 3, Gunner 1
CREW C: Pilot 3, Navigator 1, Gunner 2

EXPERIMENTAL DESIGN

Each of the 62 permanent and 32 temporary crews was administered four decision-making problems varying in nature and difficulty. Both individual and group decisions were required. A crew description and decision making questionnaire were administered the permanent crews. The procedures used in reaching the decisions were also studied, using the Bales categories (1).

The first problem was the Maier Horse-Trading Problem (5):

"A man bought a horse for $60 and sold it for $70. Then he bought it back for $80 and sold it for $90. How much money does he make in the horse trading business?"

Each individual was first asked to write on a slip of paper his solution without conferring with anyone. Crew members were then asked to confer to reach a crew decision.

The second problem required the subjects to estimate the number of dots on a 16″ x 21″ card with 3155 black dots scattered evenly but not geometrically over a white background. The card was exposed for 15 seconds and then each subject was asked to write his individual estimate on a slip of paper. They were then asked to confer to decide upon the best estimate. Finally, each man was asked to write on a slip of paper the number of dots he personally *really* thought there were.

The sketch of the conference group in the Michigan Group Projection Sketches (4) was used in the third problem. The subjects were instructed to write within a five-minute limit a story about the picture. They were asked to write what they thought was going on in the picture, what had been going on, and what the outcome would be. After the individual stories had been collected, the subjects were asked to agree upon and write within a ten-minute limit a crew story about the same sketch.

The fourth problem was a survival situation in which the crew had been downed in enemy territory. After two days, one of the members of the crew had been slowing down the attempts to reach safe territory, estimated to be about 40 miles away. He had developed severe blisters on his feet and felt that he was nearing exhaustion. He does not believe that he can continue and urges the other two men to go ahead without him. The crew was instructed to designate one member to act as the man who insists on giving up, and to make its decision as it would in an actual situation.

After the four decision-making problems, a very brief questionnaire regarding their reactions to the fourth decision-making situation was administered, along with a question concerning their attitude toward being transferred to another crew.

ANALYSIS OF DATA AND RESULTS

Horse-Trading Problem

Only about three different answers are possible on the Horse-Trading Problem: $0, $10, and $20. If any member of the group has the correct answer, the solution is so simple and obvious that his answer is usually accepted, if it is really considered by the group. This makes it very easy to determine influence and failure to influence. For example, in one crew, the pilot's answer was $0, the navigator's was $20 and the gunner's was $10. The crew correctly decided upon $20. It may thus be assumed that the navigator influenced the decision. If the crew had decided upon $0, it might have been assumed that the pilot influenced the crew to accept an incorrect answer while the navigator failed to influence the crew to accept a correct answer.

In the permanent crews, 31 percent of the pilots, 50 percent of the navigators and 29 percent of the gunners had the correct answer. As shown in Table 1, the pilots are most successful and the gunners least successful in influencing the crew to accept their correct solutions. Only 6 percent of the pilots, compared with 20 percent of the navigators and 37 percent of the gunners, failed to influence the crew to accept their solutions when they had the correct answer (differences all significant at the 5 percent level of confidence).

When temporary crews were compared with permanent crews, it is found that the temporary crews had a higher percentage of correct answers than did the permanent crews (78.2 percent against 60.4 percent with the difference significant at the 10 percent level of confidence). Some understanding of the dynamics emerges when failure to influence is analyzed by crew position as shown in Table 1. In the temporary crews, the effects of status differences seems to have been diminished and all members less frequently fail to influence when they have the correct answer

TABLE 1

Percentage of failures to influence to accept correct answer on horse-trading problem in permanent vs. temporary crews

	CREWS	
	PERMANENT (N = 62)	TEMPORARY (N = 32)
Pilots	6.0	0.0
Navigators	20.0	10.5
Gunners	37.0	12.5

(significant at better than the 10 percent level of confidence).

These findings support the contention of Heinicke and Bales (3) that in groups with a history of development, the opinions and suggestions of high status members tend to be accepted and these individuals no longer have to do much to win their point. It further supports their contention that the high status individual responds favorably most often to members of the group close to him in prestige while suggestions of members of less importance are often passed over.

The Dot Test

Success or failure in influencing the group estimate on the Dot Test is less easy to trace than in the Horse-Trading Problem. It can be traced with reasonable certainty, however. In one crew, the pilot's estimate was 800, the navigator's was 2,000, the gunner's was 8,000 and the crew's was 2,500. It seems fairly reasonable to argue that the navigator exerted the greatest influence. Following the principle illustrated by this example, the results shown in Table 2 were obtained. There is a tendency for the gunner, the least powerful member of the crew, to exert the least influence on the crew's decision. When he had the best answer, he failed 64 percent of the time to exert a dominant influence, compared with 46 and 50 percent for the navigators and pilots respectively (difference significant at the 10 percent level of confidence). Only 11.3 percent of the gunners as compared with 21 and 14.5 percent of the pilots and navigators respectively influ-

TABLE 2

Consequences of Power Differences on Influence of Crew Decision on Dot Test

	PERCENTAGES	
POSITION	TIMES HAD BEST ANSWER BUT FAILED TO INFLUENCE	TIMES INFLUENCED DECISION WITH POOR ANSWER
Pilots	50.0	21.0
Navigators	46.1	14.5
Gunners	64.0	11.3

enced the decision when they had poor answers (differences not statistically significant).

When permanent crews are compared with the temporary crews, essentially the same effect is found.

Evidence presented by the writer in a previous study (6) indicates that a very important aspect of decision making is the degree to which the members accept the decisions made by the crew. Greater acceptance of crew decisions characterized the more effective crews in survival training and in combat. In the present study, a measure of acceptance of the crew's decision was obtained by computing the difference between the crew's estimate and the individual's estimate made after the crew decision. The results in Table 3 show a consistent, though not statistically significant (except in the case of pilots vs. gunners), effect of power differences

TABLE 3

Mean deviancy scores between crew estimates and individual estimates after the crew decision

	CREWS	
	PERMANENT	TEMPORARY
Pilots	686.20	444.63
Navigators	888.03	825.16
Gunners	1151.90	946.93
Crews	908.71	738.91

on the degree to which the decision was accepted. These results suggest the possibility that individuals low in status tend to resist accepting the group's decisions, possibly as a consequence of their not participating more fully in the decision-making process and in not having their ideas considered more adequately.

When the acceptance scores of the permanent crews are compared with those of the temporary crews, it is found that essentially the same picture occurs. A consistent, though not statistically significant, trend occurs for the members of temporary crews to accept more fully the crew decisions.

Conference Group Story

Since individuals wrote their stories about the conference group sketch before the crew story, it is possible to develop an index of influence for each person. In each case, the five most salient aspects of each story were identified and then the individual stories were checked for the presence of these same five aspects. If all five aspects are common to the crew and individual stories, a score of "5" was assigned; if four aspects are common, a score of "4" was given, etc. If four or five aspects were common, it was considered that the individual exerted a strong influence on the crew's decision. If three elements were common, the individual was considered to have exerted "some influence." Less than three common aspects was considered as evidence of little or no influence.

The results, shown in Table 4, indicate that the members of perma-

TABLE 4

Consequences of Power Differences on Influence on Decision Concerning Story about Conference Group

	PERCENTAGES		
DEGREE OF INFLUENCE	PILOTS	NAVIGATORS	GUNNERS
Strong influence	58.7	37.7	0
Some influence	23.4	26.9	23.2
Little or no influence	17.0	34.6	78.6

nent crews influenced the crew's decision according to the power structure (differences significant at better than the 5 percent level of confidence).

Permanent and temporary crews were compared on the basis of the percentages of those who exerted little or no influence, or failed to influence. Results, presented in Table 5, indicate that the same trend holds in temporary as in permanent crews. A striking fact is that there is a consistent tendency for fewer in all positions to fail to influence the decision (difference for gunners significant at the 5 percent level of confidence).

Differences in perceptions of group functioning as measured by content analyses of the conference stories are too complex to be discussed in this paper, but one aspect of this analysis supports the hypothesis that the low status member of the group does not feel free to disagree and therefore withholds his ideas. Only 46 percent of the gunners, compared with 70 percent of the navigators and 72 percent of the pilots perceive disagreement in the conference group (difference significant at the 5 percent level of confidence). In the temporary groups, the gunners perceived as much disagreement as did the other members of the crew.

TABLE 5

Percentage of failure to influence conference group story decision in permanent vs. temporary B–26 crews

	CREWS	
	PERMANENT (N = 62)	TEMPORARY (N = 32)
Pilots	17.0	9.4
Navigators	34.6	25.0
Gunners	76.9	53.1

Survival Problem

In the survival problem, influence was studied through participation analysis and the questionnaire administered after the crew decision. Both amount and type of participation were considered. Amount of participation was computed by adding the number of interactions credited to each individual. The navigators contributed 40.7 percent of the total participations in contrast to 34.1 and 25.2 percent for pilots and gunners respectively (differences significant at the one percent level of confidence).

The interaction seems to be most clearly represented by the percentage in each position who interacted one or more times in each category. The results, presented in Table 6, indicate that certain types of interaction tend to characterize the occupants of each position. From these data, the pilots appear to show more solidarity; do less joking and laughing; give more suggestions, opinions, evaluations, and information; do more asking

TABLE 6

Consequences of Status Differences on Participant Roles in Crew Decision in Survival Problem

	PERCENTAGE PARTICIPATING IN CATEGORY		
CATEGORY	PILOTS	NAVIGATORS	GUNNERS
1. SHOWS SOLIDARITY, raises other's status, gives help, reward	29.6	17.2	12.0
2. SHOWS TENSION RELEASE, jokes, laughs, shows satisfaction	37.0	41.4	48.0
3. AGREES, shows passive acceptance, understands, concurs, complies	48.1	44.8	48.0
4. GIVES SUGGESTIONS, directions, implying autonomy for other	92.5	82.7	44.0
5. GIVES OPINION, evaluation, analysis, expresses feeling, wish	96.3	82.7	76.0
6. GIVES ORIENTATION, information, repetition, confirmation	81.5	72.4	56.0
7. ASKS FOR ORIENTATION, information, repetition, confirmation	25.9	20.7	40.0
8. ASKS FOR OPINION, evaluation, analysis, expression of feeling	33.3	44.8	24.0
9. ASKS FOR SUGGESTIONS, direction, possible ways of action	25.9	13.8	8.0
10. DISAGREES, shows passive rejection, formality, withholds help	25.9	41.4	24.0
11. SHOWS TENSION, asks for help, withdraws out of field	3.7	10.3	16.0
12. SHOWS ANTAGONISM, deflates other's status, defends or asserts self	0.0	3.7	3.7

for suggestions and less withdrawing from the field. The navigators tend to do less agreeing, more disagreeing, less asking for information, and more asking for opinions. The gunners manifest less show of solidarity, do more joking and laughing, offer fewer suggestions and opinions, give less orientation and information, do more asking for orientation and information, do less asking for suggestions, and show more tension and withdrawal from the field.

Responses to the decision-making questionnaire are summarized in Table 7. According to self reports, the pilots and gunners make less effort to influence the crew's decision than the navigators (significant at the one percent level of confidence). Very few of them, however, feel that they influenced the decision greatly (difference in percentages between pilots and navigators significant at the one percent level of confidence). None of the gunners felt that they had greatly influenced the decision. Probably as a result, fewer of the gunners and navigators completely agreed with the decision (difference significant at the one percent level of confidence).

The subjects were also asked how they felt about being transferred to another crew. Of the navigators, 28.1 percent, compared with 8.3 of the pilots and 10.5 percent of the gunners, stated that it would not matter greatly if they were transferred (difference between navigators and pilots and gunners combined, significant at the one percent level of confidence). This is another indication of the navigator's relatively poor identification

TABLE 7

Consequences of Power Differences on Decision-making Behavior According to Individual Declarations

ATTITUDE OF BEHAVIOR	PERCENTAGE		
	PILOTS	NAVIGATORS	GUNNERS
Made little effort to influence decision	43.8	28.1	55.3
Had most influence on decision	41.7	8.8	0.0
Complete agreement with decision	77.1	59.6	52.6
Complete satisfaction with decision	89.6	86.0	84.2

with the crew. The gunners, on the other hand, seem to be better satisfied with their roles, even though they make little effort to influence crew decisions. It might be inferred that their status needs are not as great as those of the navigators.

Unfortunately, the temporary crews cannot be compared with the permanent crews on the aspects just discussed because of incompleteness of data. They can, however, be compared in regard to the characteristics of the decisions submitted. The results of the categorization of decisions, presented in Table 8, indicate that the temporary groups more frequently make sequential decisions which require testing and revision. The meaning of this becomes clearer when it is noted that more of the permanent crews decided to keep the ailing crew member with them in spite of all circumstances. They simply did not even entertain the notion that this might not be possible. Their decisions were therefore presented as final and not needing future revision in harmony with reality events. Of the permanent crews, 93.7 percent manifested much concern for keeping the

TABLE 8

Comparison of Type of Decision Made in Survival Problem by Permanent vs. Temporary Crews

CHARACTERISTIC OF DECISION	PERCENTAGES PERMANENT N = 48	PERCENTAGES TEMPORARY N = 32	*t*-RATIO	LEVEL OF CONFIDENCE
Sequential decision	43.8	75.0	3.03	$<$.01
Decision to keep crew together in spite of everything	70.8	56.2	1.33	$<$.20
Concern for keeping crew together, if possible	93.7	71.8	2.27	$<$.05
Administration of first aid (physical)	50.0	31.3	1.71	$<$.10
Administration of first aid (psychological)	35.4	28.1	0.68	.50

crew together, whereas only 71.8 percent of the temporary crews showed such a concern. The permanent crews also tended to mention provision for first aid and attempts to bolster the ailing member's morale. This finding might be accepted in support of Cartwright and Zander's (2, p. 74) hypothesis that willingness to endure pain or frustration for the group is a possible indication of the group's cohesiveness. This, of course, does not answer questions concerning the quality of the decisions. This willingness to endure pain or frustration for the group may in some instances be taken too far and result in blindness to the realities of the situation. This, in fact, is the major reason for difficulties in developing adequate criteria for assessing the quality of the decisions. It is, nonetheless, important to recognize the operation of the phenomena which have just been described.

SUMMARY

In this paper, an attempt has been made to study some of the consequences of power differences on decision making in permanent groups with well-defined power structures and to compare these effects with those obtained in similarly constituted temporary groups. B-26 combat crews were chosen for study.

Each of 62 permanent crews and 32 temporary crews were administered four decision-making problems of varying nature and difficulty: Horse-Trading Problem, Dot Test, Conference Group Projection Sketch, and a survival problem. Both individual and group decisions were elicited.

An attempt was made to study the "influence" and "failure to influence" of each group member. On all four problems, influence was directly and clearly in accord with the power structure of the group. In general, the effects were somewhat lessened in the temporary crews. On the Horse-Trading Problem, this resulted in a greater percentage of correct crew decisions in the temporary groups. In the Dot Test, evidence was found to indicate that the less powerful members of the crew do not accept the crew's decision as completely as does the more powerful member. The perceptions of the Conference Group Picture suggest that the least powerful member of the group does not feel free to disagree with the more powerful members. Interaction analysis reveals that certain types of interaction tend to characterize occupants of each position. Navigators make more effort to influence the decision but feel that they have little influence on the decision and do not agree with it completely. The gunners make little attempt to influence the decision, recognize the fact that they influence the decision very little, and tend not to accept it completely. In the survival problem, the permanent crews show much concern for keeping the crew together at any sacrifice while the temporary crews are more willing to leave the ailing member behind. The former are also more concerned about giving the ailing member physical and psychological first aid. Solutions of temporary groups are less absolute and final and provide more frequently for sequential decisions.

REFERENCES

1. Bales, R. F., & Strodtbeck, F. L. Phases in group problem solving. *J. abnorm. soc. Psychol.*, 1951, 46, 485–495.
2. Cartwright, D., & Zander, A. F. *Group dynamics research and theory*. Evanston, Ill.: Row, Peterson, 1953.
3. Heinicke, C., & Bales, R. F. Developmental trends in the structure of small groups. *Sociometry*, 1953, 16, 7–38.
4. Henry, W. E., & Guetzkow, H. Group projection sketches for the study of small groups. *J. soc. Psychol.*, 1951, 33, 77–102.
5. Maier, N. R. F., & Solem, A. R. The contribution of a discussion leader to the quality of group thinking: The effective use of minority opinions. *Hum. Relat.*, 1952, 5, 277–288.
6. Torrance, E. P. *Crew performance in a test situation as a predictor of field and combat performance*. HFORL Report No. 33. Washington, D.C.: HFORL, Bolling Air Force Base, 1953.

Role Differentiation in Small Groups

PHILIP E. SLATER

SMALL group research provides a most fruitful meeting-ground for psychological and sociological thinking. Few fields of study lend themselves so easily to this dual perspective. The concept of "role" holds a potentially strategic position in this rapprochement, but its rather indiscriminate use has thus far seemed to create as much confusion as enlightenment in the small group area.

We might define a role as a more or less coherent and unified system of items of interpersonal behavior. With even this minimal definition it becomes apparent that role performance in the small group situation will have both consequences which are important to the functioning of the group in which the role is performed, and personal consequences of importance to the individual who performs it. Similarly, an individual may be motivated to perform a role both by specific inducements offered by the group, and by more general needs operating within the individual himself.

The rather general failure to consider simultaneously both of these aspects of role performance has constituted a very real stumbling-block in small group research. This paper will attempt to illustrate the way in which consideration of both psychological and sociological factors may aid in the interpretation of tendencies for members of small experimental groups to behave in systematically differentiated ways. Our research in this area [1] has been centered around five problems:

1. To what extent do group members distinguish between different

FROM *American Sociological Review,* 1955, 20, 300–310. Reprinted by permission of the author and publisher.

This research was carried out under the direction and guidance of Robert F. Bales. The larger project of which this study was a part was facilitated by the Laboratory of Social Relations, Harvard University. Funds were supplied by the RAND Corporation, Santa Monica, California.

1 The theoretical assumptions underlying this research are discussed elsewhere (2, 3).

kinds of favorable evaluations of their fellow group members, or, conversely, to what degree do they tend to rank fellow members similarly on criteria assumed to be different? A consistent tendency for subjects to rate one man high on one criterion and another man high on a second criterion would constitute prima facie evidence for the existence of a set of differentiated roles, at least in the minds of the subjects themselves.

2. What effect do repeated interactions have upon such discriminations? Since randomly composed laboratory groups are rather ephemeral organizations, it might be assumed necessary for some time to elapse before even a crude protoype of the elaborate kind of differentiation found in permanent groups would appear.

3. How do individuals differentiated by their fellow group members differ in their behavior? How can we characterize this behavior, and how do these characterizations relate to the criteria upon which the individuals were rated?

4. How do such individuals respond to each other? Do differentiated "specialists" cooperate or compete with each other?

5. What is the relationship of personality factors to role differentiation? Are there factors which predispose an individual to assume a particular role? What is the effect upon the group as a whole of variations in the motivations of various "specialists"?

PROCEDURE

The sample consisted of 20 groups of from three to seven men each, with four groups of each size. Each group met four times, so that a total of 80 meetings was studied. The groups were composed of paid male undergraduates at Harvard who knew each other only casually, if at all, prior to the first meeting. They were told that we were engaged in the study of group discussion and decision-making, and that we would observe them through a one-way mirror. Each subject was given a five-page factual summary of an administrative problem which they were asked to solve as a group, assuming the role of administrative staff to the central authority in the case under discussion. They were given 40 minutes to discuss the case and decide (a) why the persons involved in the case were behaving as they did, and (b) what the central authority should do about it. A new case was used for each meeting. The subjects' remarks during the discussion were classified according to Bales' set of interaction categories (1). Following each session the subjects filled out a questionnaire which included the following questions:

(a) Who contributed the best ideas for solving the problem? Please rank the members in order. *Include yourself.*

(b) Who did the most to guide the discussion and keep it moving effectively? Please rank the members in order. *Include yourself.*

(c) How well did you personally like each of the other members? Rate each member on a scale from 0 to 7, where zero means "I feel perfectly neutral toward him," and seven means "I like him very much." [2]

At the end of the fourth session an additional question was asked:

(d) Considering all the sessions, which member of the group would you say stood out most definitely as a leader in the discussion? How would you rank the others? *Include yourself.*

These questions, along with the Bales interaction scores, constituted the major source of data for this study.

Prior to analysis of the data, each of the 20 groups was assigned to one of two classes, according to whether the members showed high or low agreement on their responses to questions (a) and (b) above. This procedure was followed on the basis of findings by Heinicke and Bales that these two types of groups showed different developmental characteristics (6). It was felt that role differentiation might take different forms in groups with varying degrees of agreement on status ratings.

The measure used to represent agreement on status ratings is based on Kendall's "Coefficient of Concordance" (8, 10) which he calls "W." It is obtained from a matrix of rankings, each individual (placed in vertical order on a series of rows) ranking each individual (placed in horizontal order on a series of columns). In Kendall's formula:

$$W = \frac{12\,S}{m^2\,(n^3 - n)}$$

where S equals the sum of the squares of the deviations of the column totals from the grand mean, and n equals the number of individuals ranked by m observers. In our rankings $n = m$, since everyone in the group ranks everyone, including himself. When agreement is perfect, W is equal to one; when there is no agreement, W is equal to zero.

W indices obtained from the rankings made on questions (a) and (b) were averaged, and the resulting mean called the "Index of Status Consensus." When the average Index of a group over all four meetings was .500 or above the group was classified as a "High" group. When the Index was below .500 the group was classified as a "Low" group.

SPECIALIZATION AS PERCEIVED BY SUBJECTS

Subjects in this sample may be ranked in five different ways for each session. From the interaction scores it was possible to rank order the men according to who talked the most, and who *received* the most interaction. From the post-meeting questions it was possible to rank order the men on the perceived quality of their ideas, their perceived ability to guide the

2 A different form of question was used for some of the earlier groups, but both forms were reduced to rank orders for the present study.

discussion, and their personal popularity. Our interest in role differentiation stemmed from the relationships of these rank orders to each other.

A simple method of seeking out tendencies toward specialization consists of counting the number of times a man with top rank on any one of these five measures holds top rank on none of the other measures. Such a man might be considered a "specialist," and if such "specialists" are found in one characteristic more often than in the others, this characteristic might be considered a specialized one.

Table 1 indicates that there are more cases in which the Best-liked man holds top ranking in only that one characteristic than cases of any

TABLE 1

*Number of Sessions * Out of a Possible 80 in Which a Given Person Holds Top Position in One and Only One Rank Order Out of Five Possible Rank Orders.*

Talking	T	11.0
Receiving	R	10.5
Ideas	I	12.0
Guidance	G	11.6
Liking	L	30.4
TOTAL		75.5

* The decimals arise from ties in rankings.

other sort of isolated prominence. The difference between this characteristic and the other four is significant at the .001 level, using a Chi-square test. Popularity is apparently a relatively specialized achievement.

Further information may be obtained by proceeding in the obverse manner and asking rather, how often does the same person in a particular group hold top position on two characteristics? Table 2 shows, for each pair of characteristics, the percentage of cases in which such coincidence occurs.

Table 2 indicates that for both High and Low status-consensus groups, Popularity is least often associated with other characteristics. The difference is significant at the .01 level in both cases, using a Chi-square test. Marked differences between High and Low groups appear, however, when we examine the table further. The two participation measures, Talking and Receiving, are significantly less often associated with Ideas in the Low groups than in the High (.01 level), and Ideas and Guidance are significantly less often associated with Liking (.01 level). In other words, in the High groups high participation (Talking and Receiving) is associated with high rated task ability (Ideas and Guidance), but neither is strongly associated with Popularity. In the Low groups the association of high rated task ability with popularity is even lower (less in fact than chance expectancy), while the association of high participation with high rated task ability tends to break down.

Note that Talking and Receiving are strongly associated in both High and Low groups, as are Ideas and Guidance. This fact perhaps justifies the groupings made above, which will be used throughout this section wherever they seem to be appropriate.

These techniques for determining the amount of specialization among these various characteristics are not entirely satisfactory, since they deal only with the top man on each rank order. To meet this problem, mean

TABLE 2

Percentage of Total Number of Sessions (80) in Which the Same Person Holds Top Position in Two Rank Orders at the Same Time.

HIGH STATUS-CONSENSUS GROUPS

	T	R	I	G	L
Talking T		51.3	63.3	36.5	20.5
Receiving R			53.3	39.0	34.3
Ideas I				56.3	32.0
Guidance G					45.5
Liking L					

LOW STATUS-CONSENSUS GROUPS

	T	R	I	G	L
Talking T		52.5	43.7	40.0	32.0
Receiving R			28.7	42.5	37.0
Ideas I				50.0	16.5
Guidance G					20.0
Liking L					

rank order correlations [3] between all pairs of characteristics were computed, and are shown on Table 3.

First, as we might expect from Tables 1 and 2, the correlations between Liking and the other four characteristics are the lowest correlations in both the High and Low group matrices. Second, the tendency for amount of participation and rated task ability to be highly correlated in the High groups and poorly correlated in the Low groups is even more sharply outlined in Table 3 than in Table 2.[4]

3 The use of rank order correlations here involves serious statistical problems, due to the small sizes of our groups. Clearly a *rho* drawn from a three-man group means very little, and *rhos* from even the larger sizes are not too reliable. In dealing with this problem two different techniques were used: (a) Median values were computed; (b) Means based on the raw *rhos* of all but the three-man groups were computed. While these methods yielded identical results, neither is entirely satisfactory, and we suggest that the reader accept these findings with reserve.

4 All of the correlations in the Low groups are in fact lower than those in the High groups, a result which is not surprising in view of the fact that low agreement between

Differences between the correlations in Table 3 were tested in the following manner: the 10 correlations in each matrix were divided into three sets, with the Talking-Receiving and Ideas-Guidance correlations in the first set, the four correlations between the participation measures and the rated task ability measures in the second set, and the four correlations between Liking and the other measures in the third set. The three sets were then tested against each other by means of sign tests. Note that in the first set the correlations are high in both High and Low groups, in

TABLE 3

Intercorrelations between Talking, Receiving, and Ratings on Ideas, Guidance, and Liking. Mean Rank Order Correlations of 64 Sessions (Size 3 Excluded).

HIGH STATUS-CONSENSUS GROUPS

		T	R	I	G	L
Talking	T		.88	.80	.75	.38
Receiving	R			.74	.74	.46
Ideas	I				.83	.41
Guidance	G					.49
Liking	L					

LOW STATUS-CONSENSUS GROUPS

		T	R	I	G	L
Talking	T		.69	.48	.51	.10
Receiving	R			.44	.52	.16
Ideas	I				.71	.14
Guidance	G					.27
Liking	L					

the second set they are high in the High groups and relatively low in the Low groups, while in the third set they are relatively low in both.

In the High groups there was no significant difference between the first two sets. The first set was significantly higher than the third set, at the .01 level, and the second set was significantly higher than the third at the .05 level. In the Low groups the first set was significantly higher than the second and the second significantly higher than the third, both at the .01 level.

raters is equivalent to low reliability of measures, which would tend to produce lower correlations in the Low groups. All of the differences between High and Low groups in Table 3 are significant at the .05 level or better, with the exception of the Talking-Receiving correlations (which are not based on ratings), the Ideas-Guidance correlations, and the Guidance-Liking correlations. It is notable, however, that Ideas and Guidance are very highly correlated even in the Low groups, and this fact, along with the existence of several High group-Low group differences which are not based upon ratings, suggests that unreliability of Low group measures plays little part in the creation of qualitative differences between High and Low groups.

Popularity, then, again appears to be the most specialized characteristic, regardless of the degree of status-consensus in the group. In Low status consensus groups, however, the tendency for Liking to separate itself from other characteristics is stronger, and seconded by the dissociation of rated task ability from amount of participation.

In summary, role differentiation in the High groups seems to be bipartite, with an active "task specialist" and a Best-liked man. In the Low groups it tends to be tripartite (as well as more extreme), with an active participator who is neither well-liked nor highly rated on task ability, a more passive task specialist who is not well-liked, and a popular individual who is neither active nor highly rated on task ability.

CHANGES OVER TIME

Common sense and sociological folklore would lead us to expect that any tendency toward role specialization in these groups would increase over time, as the group became more highly "organized" or "structured." This expectation is fulfilled. Table 4 shows the number of times in each meeting

TABLE 4

*Percentage of Cases in Which the Same Man Holds Top Position on Like Ranking and Idea Ranking at the Same Time, by Sessions.**

SESSIONS			
1	2	3	4
56.5	12.0	20.0	8.5

* The trends for High and Low groups are identical.

in which the top man on Ideas is also Best-liked. Table 5 shows the number of times in each meeting in the Low groups in which the top man on either participation measure is also top man on either task ability rating. The trend in Table 4 is significant at the .01 level, the trend in Table 5 at the .05 level, using Chi-square tests.[5]

The selection of Ideas rather than Guidance as the task ability measure in Table 4 is based upon the fact that it is in general less highly correlated with Liking, and thus in some sense "purer." Guidance and Liking do tend to correlate less with the passage of time, but the trend is more gradual, as we might expect.

ROLE DIFFERENTIATION AND LEADERSHIP

At the end of the fourth session, after differentiation has become well-developed, our subjects are asked to rank each other on the most general-

5 Computations using mean *rhos*, in the manner of Table 3, yield similar results.

ized of criteria, leadership. What is the relationship of this ranking to the five more specialized ones?

This relationship may be determined by finding the top man on each measure for all four sessions taken together, and then computing the percentage of cases in which top rank on leadership coincided with top rank on each of the five other measures. The results were as follows: Guidance 80 per cent, Receiving 65 per cent, Ideas 59 per cent, Talking 55 per cent, and Liking 25 per cent.[6] A Chi-square test showed Liking to coincide significantly less often (at the .01 level) with leadership than the other four characteristics. The Best-liked man is in fact chosen leader no more often than would be expected by chance.[7]

TABLE 5

*Percentage of Cases in Low Status-consensus Groups in Which the Same Man Holds Top Position on a Participation Measure (Talking or Receiving) and a Task Ability Measure (Ideas or Guidance) at the Same Time *, by Sessions.*

SESSIONS			
1	2	3	4
55.0	28.7	41.3	30.0

* Using the mean of the four possible combinations.

Yet, strangely enough, leadership is most *strongly* associated with those measures which are in turn most strongly correlated with popularity, namely, Receiving and Guidance (see Tables 2 and 3). This fact seems less strange if we consider the generalized character of Leadership. Subjects choosing a leader must take into account a wider range of abilities and virtues than in deciding who has the best ideas or whom they like best. The chosen leader of a group is perhaps the man who has the highest hypothetical *combined* rating on all possible characteristics related to the group's purposes and needs. The man so chosen is not likely to be *dis*-liked, nor to have unacceptable Ideas nor to be unable or unwilling to participate in the discussion. Hence those measures which are themselves more general, that is, related to a wider range of abilities, will correlate more highly with leadership. Tables 2 and 3 suggest that Guidance and Receiving are more general in this sense than their counterparts, Ideas and Talking.

6 There were no important differences between High and Low groups.

7 Computations using mean rank order correlations between Leadership and the five other characteristics yield the same results.

BEHAVIORAL DIFFERENCES BETWEEN IDEA MEN AND BEST-LIKED MEN

Thus far we have dealt with the differentiation of task ability and popularity primarily as perceived by the subjects. We might now ask, is this trend a reflection of actual behavioral differences between the perceived "specialists," or have our subjects merely been gripped by some sort of sociological delusion while making their ratings? What, for example, does a Best-liked man *do*?

TABLE 6

Composite Profiles in Percentages of 44 Top Men on Idea Ranking and 44 Top Men on Like Ranking for the Same Sessions.

	INTERACTION CATEGORY	INITIATED		RECEIVED	
		IDEA MEN	BEST-LIKED MEN	IDEA MEN	BEST-LIKED MEN
AREA A: *Positive Reactions*	1. Shows Solidarity	3.68	4.41	2.57	3.15
	2. Shows Tension Release	5.15	6.98	7.95	9.20
	3. Shows Agreement	14.42	16.83	23.29	18.27
AREA B: *Problem Solving Attempts*	4. Gives Suggestion	8.97	6.81	7.01	7.22
	5. Gives Opinion	32.74	28.69	25.52	31.09
	6. Gives Orientation	18.54	17.91	14.06	14.54
AREA C: *Questions*	7. Asks Orientation	3.04	3.71	3.62	2.80
	8. Asks Opinion	1.84	2.94	1.94	1.74
	9. Asks Suggestion	.93	1.33	.85	.84
AREA D: *Negative Reactions*	10. Shows Disagreement	8.04	7.60	10.65	9.35
	11. Shows Tension Increase	1.92	2.16	1.59	1.35
	12. Shows Antagonism	.73	.63	.95	.45

In order to compare the Bales' interaction profiles of Idea men and Best-liked men, the following procedure was followed: (a) All sessions in which the Best-liked man also held top rank on Ideas were eliminated. (b) All sessions in which ties for top rank occurred in either ranking were eliminated. The raw profiles of the remaining 44 matched pairs of Idea men and Best-liked men were added together, and percentage profiles computed, as shown in Table 6.[8]

The most salient general difference in Table 6 is the tendency for the Idea man to initiate interaction more heavily in Area B (Problem Solving Attempts) and the Best-liked man in Area A (Positive reactions). The Idea man also seems to disagree somewhat more, and show a little more antagonism, while the Best-liked man asks more questions and shows more tension. On the Receiving end, the situation is largely reversed, with the Idea man receiving more agreement, questions, and negative reactions,

8 Although some suggestive variations in these differences appear when the sample is divided into High and Low group pairs, the major outlines are the same.

while the Best-liked man receives more problem solving attempts, and more solidarity and tension release. The general picture is thus one of specialization and complementarity, with the Idea man concentrating on the task and playing a more aggressive role, while the Best-liked man concentrates more on social-emotional problems, giving rewards and playing a more passive role.

The problem of testing the significance of these differences is a vexed one, in view of the interdependence of the categories. Several different techniques have been utilized, the most satisfactory of which has been the use of category indices based upon the raw profiles of each man.[9] If, for example, we wish to test the apparent tendency for Idea men to interact more in Area B and Best-liked men in Area A, we simply divide the number of scores each man has in Area A by his score in Area B, and compare the resulting indices of the two types of men. Best-liked men should and do have significantly higher indices than Idea men (at the .01 level, using a sign test).

Another index may be constructed by simply placing in the numerator all categories in which the Best-liked man initiated more interaction and in the denominator all categories in which the Idea man initiated more. The same procedure may be followed for the Receiving profiles. On both of these indices the Best-liked man is significantly higher (at the .01 level).

The principal drawback of these indices is that they fail to show us which categories are most crucial in differentiating Idea from Best-liked men. Unfortunately, there is no satisfactory solution to this problem, in view of the statistical difficulties mentioned above. Comparing raw scores in each category would be fruitless, since the Idea men have a somewhat higher total rate of participation and will therefore tend to show larger scores in every category. Percentage profiles for each man may be computed, and percentage scores in each category compared, but this exacerbates problems of interdependence and distribution. In order to give some clue, however, to the relative importance of the various categories in differentiating Idea men from Best-liked men, sign tests were performed on individual percentage profiles, category by category, for interaction initiated by each type of man. These showed categories 2, 3, 4, 5, 8, and 11 as the strongest differentiating categories.[10] Grouping categories by area, however, produces differences stronger than those generated by any of

9 Such a technique gives equal weight to each man, contrary to the composite profiles in Table 6, which, since they lump together all acts of all men, give greater weight to those men whose total rate of participation is higher. As a result, some differences which seem negligible in Table 6 are actually very consistent, and vice versa.

10 A study by Richard Mann (9), performed on a different sample, showed almost identical results for a slightly different type of comparison. Mann used not top men, but all men, comparing those who had higher ratings on task ability than on Liking with those who had higher Liking ratings than task ratings.

the component categories, with the single exception of Area D. In other words, Area A differentiates Idea men from Best-liked men better than Categories 1, 2, and 3 taken individually, Area B better than categories 4, 5, and 6 taken individually, and Area C better than categories 7, 8, and 9 taken individually. In Area D, grouping does not seem meaningful, since the three categories do not tend in the same direction. The tendency for the Idea men to initiate more in categories 10 and 12, however, is so weak that it may almost be discounted.

These findings indicate that qualitative differentiation in the subjects' ratings of each other is accompanied by qualitative differentiation in the overt behavior of the subjects rated, such that Idea men tend to specialize in active problem-solving attempts, and Best-liked men in more reactive, less task-oriented behavior. The apparent complementarity of these two patterns suggests that a large share of the group's interaction may take place directly between the two "specialists." Since both are by definition highly valued in one way or another by the group, a high rate of interaction between them would be an indication that this relationship constitutes some sort of focal point in the group, and that the welfare of the group may be to some extent dependent upon the strength of this relationship. It would, therefore, be useful to know whether or not the two men interact more with each other than with other members.

Table 7 shows the extent to which this interaction preference existed. The tendency seems sufficiently marked, especially in the High groups, to justify the conclusion that the relationship is quantitatively important, though not always dominant in the group. Since the total amount of participation of the Best-liked man averages no more than the average for all men, the findings in Table 7 suggest that his interaction is concentrated around the Idea man to a greater extent than that of the other group members. In other words, although there may be men in the group who interact in general more heavily than the Best-liked man, they do not engage the Idea man in interaction to the same degree.

Some evidence also exists indicating that the relationship between the two "specialists" tends on the whole to be the most positive in the group, especially in the High groups. Comparing the ratings each subject gave to each other subject on the question "How well did you personally like each of the other members?", we find that:

(a) The Best-liked man tends to give the Idea man a rating higher than the average of the other group member ratings of the Idea man. This difference is significant at the .01 level, using a sign test.

(b) The Best-liked man gives the Idea man a rating higher than his mean rating of other group members (significant at the .05 level).

(c) The Idea man gives the Best-liked man a rating higher than the average of the other member ratings of the Best-liked man in the High groups (significant at the .05 level) but not in the Low.

(d) The Idea man gives the Best-liked man a rating higher than his mean rating of other group members (significant at the .01 level).

We thus have the rather interesting picture of a respected task-oriented group member who is at best only moderately well-liked, receiving strong support from a perhaps more socially-oriented member who is the most popular man in the group, and with whom the task-oriented

TABLE 7

Interaction between Top Ranking Men on Ideas (I) and Top Ranking Men on Being Liked (L).

CHARACTERISTIC OF INTERACTION OBSERVED	PERCENTAGE OF CASES IN WHICH CHARACTERISTIC OCCURRED		SIGNIFICANCE LEVEL FOR HIGH AND LOW GROUPS COMBINED
	HIGH GROUPS	LOW GROUPS	
I interacted with L more than he did with any other number.	44.7	48.0 *	**
I interacted with L more than any other member interacted with L.	52.6 *	50.0 *	***
L interacted with I more than he did with any other member	73.7 ***	52.0 **	***
L interacted with I more than any other member interacted with I.	57.9 *	30.0	*
Percentage expected by chance	28.9	26.0	

Level of significance:
No asterisk: not significant
*: .05
**: .01
***: .001

member forms a close and active relationship. Qualitative differentiation seems to be associated, then, with cooperation. Quantitative differentiation, i.e., differentiation along any single status dimension, may well be associated with more competitive responses.

PERSONALITY FACTORS IN DIFFERENTIATION

The data from which this study was drawn includes little material which bears directly upon an analysis of personality characteristics. An indirect source of material, however, appears in the subjects' ratings of each other on the question, "How well did you like each of the other members?" Many subjects tend to give all other members the same rating on this question. Since these subjects also tend to rate highly, they are saying, in effect, "I like everyone." Such undifferentiated ratings constitute about one-fifth of all the ratings in the sample, but they are not by any means divided equally among different types of subjects. Best-liked men are the most frequent non-differentiating members, Idea men the least frequent. The difference between them is significant at the .05 level, using a Chi-square test. Top Guidance, Talking, and Receiving men fail to differentiate about as often as the sample as a whole.

There is also a striking difference between High and Low status-consensus groups on the distribution of undifferentiated ratings. In the High groups, subjects who refuse to differentiate their ratings tend to be persons with low status, i.e., persons who do not hold top rank on any of the five characteristics mentioned above. In the Low groups, non-differentiating persons tend to be high status persons. This tendency is significant at the .01 level, using a Chi-square test.

TABLE 8

Mean Scores on 30-Item F-Scale for Top Men on Five Characteristics and Leader, in High and Low Groups.

	HIGH GROUPS	LOW GROUPS	ALL GROUPS
Leader	76.2	85.2	80.7
No. 1 Guidance	88.7	79.2	83.9
" 1 Receiving	83.3	94.2	88.7
" 1 Talking	74.9	103.8	89.3
" 1 Ideas	82.3	101.2	91.7
" 1 Liking	91.1	99.9	95.5

The meaning of this tendency to make undifferentiated ratings will perhaps become more clear if we examine its relationship to the only direct measure of personality characteristics available, i.e., subject scores on the California F-Scale. A 30 item F-Scale was given to 62 of the 100 subjects in the sample, with differentiating raters receiving a mean F-score of 85, and non-differentiating raters a mean score of 103. The difference is significant at the .001 level, using a standard t-test.

High F-scores would thus be expected to distribute themselves much as do the undifferentiated Liking ratings. Mean F-scores of all top-ranking men in High and Low groups are shown in Table 8, and three types of differences are immediately apparent. First, top men in High groups generally have lower F-scores than top men in Low groups. This tendency is significant (at the .01 level) only in the case of Talking and Ideas, however. Second, Idea men have significantly lower scores than Best-liked men (.05 level) in the High groups, though not in the Low. Third, there is a tendency for top men on what have been described as more generalized characteristics, namely, Leadership, Guidance, and Receiving, to have lower F-scores than top men on the more specialized characteristics, Talking, Ideas, and Liking. This difference is significant at the .05 level.

Both relatively high F-scores and undifferentiated ratings may be interpreted as reflecting a tendency toward a rigid and oversimplified approach to interpersonal relations. Fine perceptual discriminations, or flexible and situationally-determined behavior, are perhaps not to be expected from subjects falling into this category.[11] Their behavior will be determined rather by chronic, compulsive responses to inner needs, such as the need to be accepted and loved, the need to deny negative feelings toward members of one's own group, and so forth.

When we recall that Low groups are more sharply specialized than High groups, and that the Best-liked role is the most specialized of all our measures, it becomes clear that the common factor in all these findings is a strong relationship between this personal rigidity and specialization. The sharper the role differentiation in the group, or the more specialized the role played by the individual, the greater the rigidity in the personality or personalities involved.

DISCUSSION

According to Barnard (4), the survival of any organization depends upon its ability to solve two problems: the achievement of the purposes for which the organization was formed, and the satisfaction of the more immediate needs of the members of the organization. On the small group level, Bales (1, p. 10) makes a related distinction between the problems of the group involving goal achievement and adaptation to external demands, and problems involving internal integration and the expression of emotional tensions. The first group of problems he calls Adaptive-Instrumental problems, the solution of which demands activity in the Task area. The second he calls Integrative-Expressive problems, the solution of which demands activity in the social-emotional area. Bales goes on to emphasize the difficulties inherent in attempting to solve both groups of problems at the same time.

Similar difficulties arise when the same *individual* attempts to take an active lead in solving these problems simultaneously. In large organizations, e.g., the solution of Integrative-Expressive problems is in large part left to the leaders of informal groups, the importance of which Barnard and others have emphasized (4, pp. 223–224; 7, pp. 48 ff.).

We have found that the most fundamental type of role differentiation in small experimental groups is the divorcing of task functions from social-emotional functions. Presumably, the ideal leader of a small group would be sufficiently skillful and flexible to alternate these types of behavior in such a way as to handle both problems, and maximize his status on all possible dimensions. He would be able to make both an active, striv-

11 An inference which might also be made on the basis of the high negative correlation between F-score and intelligence.

ing response to the task and a sympathetic response to the individual needs of group members. He would be a high participator, well-liked, rated high on task ability, and eventually chosen leader.

Such individuals are rare. They appear occasionally in High status-consensus groups, almost never in Low. It is possible that the absence in the Low groups of anyone approaching this ideal type is responsible for their low status-consensus. Where a group must choose between individuals who are in different ways one-sided and limited in their capabilities, agreement on ratings will be difficult to attain.

There are at least two kinds of reasons for the rarity of such men. First, there are sociological factors, revolving around the non-compatibility of the task and social-emotional roles. Adaptation to pressures from outside the group, such as are created by a task which must be performed, involves, by definition, change. The individual who presses toward solution of a task inadvertently forces those around him to make continual minor adjustments in their behavior, and to continually re-examine their ideas and values, in the light of these external demands. The individual who concerns himself with internal social-emotional problems, on the other hand, is supportive in his responses to the ideas and behavior of those around him, and continually reaffirms their dominant values. The orientation of the task specialist is thus more technological, that of the social-emotional specialist more traditionalistic. It is presumably the latter type of behavior which seems more appealing to members called upon to indicate whom they personally like best.

This is not to say that the task specialist will actually be disliked, but rather that his task emphasis will tend to arouse some negative feelings—feelings which may not be expressed, and which will never outweigh his value to the group in the minds of its members. Such feelings merely neutralize any strong positive feelings other members may hold toward him. Only in the Low groups are task specialists actually *un*popular, and this phenomenon is perhaps expressive of the rigidity with which Low group task specialists perform their role.

The second set of reasons may be called psychological. These have to do with the individual's predisposition to assume a particular role. Men who are Best-liked, e.g., may "have to be liked," and may achieve prominence in this role because of the ingratiating skills they have acquired during their lives in bringing this desired situation about. Avoidance of conflict and controversy may be a felt necessity for this type of person—hence, his behavior will show nothing that could be a source of disharmony. He will avoid even the thought that he might like some of his fellow members better than others. His rate of interaction will be average—not too high, not too low. He will in fact retire into the conventional safety of the "average Joe." He may even avoid the performance of task functions altogether, because of the personal threats which task activity might hold for him. Instead, he will express the group's feelings and questions, and place its stamp of approval upon what has already come to pass.

The task specialist, on the other hand, may assume this role only because of an unwillingness or inability to respond to the needs of others. A compulsive concentration on an abstract problem will serve as an intellectual shield against the ambiguity of human feelings. Needs to express hostility may be channeled into aggressive and dogmatic problem-solving attempts.

When these motives determine the assumption of a specialized role in a group, the outlook for this group would seem to be poor. The F-score data suggests that such motives may in fact determine the behavior of specialists in Low status-consensus groups.

It is even possible that the presence, in a group, of individuals with motives of this sort *creates* low status-consensus. The difficulty of choosing between inadequate specialists has already been mentioned. Furthermore, it seems reasonable to expect that rigidity in the personality structure will be associated with rigidity in the value structure of the individual concerned. The F-scale is in fact founded on this assumption. Such absolutistic value systems, rigidly held and zealously defended, will impede the formation of any kind of consensus, particularly consensus on the relative emphasis the group should place upon task and social-emotional activities.

The way in which this kind of consensus in turn determines the degree of consensus on a particular rating may be illustrated by considering again the process of choosing a leader. It was suggested above that the man chosen as leader is that individual who is felt to possess those qualities which best serve to satisfy *both* the task and social-emotional problems of the group. Since different groups emphasize task and social-emotional problems in varying proportions, the attribution of leadership will depend not only upon the choice of one person over another but also upon the differential stress placed upon these group problems by the group. The group problems might thus be conceived as factors, with weights assigned to them by the group according to some elementary kind of value consensus. One group, e.g., might attribute leadership on the basis say, of .7 task ability, .3 likeability; another might reverse the weights.[12] The fact that Liking coincides so seldom with Leadership suggests that in our sample social-emotional skills are not highly valued, and are given a low weight. This may be due to the heavy task demands placed upon the group by the experimental situation, or to the emphasis placed upon task ability and achievement by our culture.

In any case, Leadership will be attributed to that member who has the highest combined rating on these and perhaps other factors. But if

12 This discussion of leadership as a fused role is founded on suggestions by Arthur Couch. A factor analysis of leadership variables by Couch and Carter (5) produced factors closely related to those discussed here.

implicit agreement on weights is lacking, each rater will be making a qualitatively different evaluation, and Leadership consensus becomes almost impossible.

Similarly, in making more specialized evaluations, a rater must decide what a specialist is supposed to do before deciding how well he does it. If there is no agreement in a group about what a given role should include, then roles will be performed in accordance with individual norms, and evaluated in terms of personal criteria. Agreement on role definitions is thus hindered by rigid value systems at the very time when the inflexibility characteristic of specialists operating under these conditions makes this agreement all the more imperative.

In this discussion we have isolated three types of role structure:

1. The rare case in which a single leader performs all functions and differentiation does not occur. This is a High group phenomenon.

2. The case in which moderate specialization arises simply because the specialists lack the exceptional talent necessary to counteract the sociological pressures toward differentiation. Choice of role is undoubtedly determined by personality factors as well as situational factors, but such preferences will not be immutable. This is the more common case in High groups.

3. The case in which extreme specialization is brought about by psychological as well as sociological pressures. Specialization is sharp and disruptive, due to the fact that it springs from an overdetermined response to inner needs rather than a flexible response to the needs of others, or to the demands of an ever-changing task situation. Specialists perform in a particular role because they "have to" rather than because it is useful or desirable. This is a Low group phenomenon.

Thus while differentiation occurs in both High and Low status-consensus groups, it seems to occur for different reasons. It is only the depth and breadth of the differentiation which will supply an immediate clue as to which kinds of reasons are operating. One final example of this duality of meaning is the highest participator, who has not been considered in much of the foregoing analysis.

It will be recalled that in High groups, the highest participator usually receives the highest rating on task ability. Approval and acceptance of his ideas perhaps encourages him to participate more heavily, and also generates his high rating. In Low groups, the highest participator is far less often rated highly. He apparently does not adjust his amount of participation to the approval and acceptance he receives, but persists in interacting despite their absence. His participation time is determined by his own aggressiveness, by insensitivity rather than responsiveness to feedback from others. In keeping with the motivations of other Low group specialists, he talks, not because it is helpful to the group for him to do so, but because he has to.

In short, Low group specialists are going through many of the same motions as High group specialists, but their needs and purposes differ. It would seem likely that double entendres of this sort constitute a major factor in obscuring the complexity of small group relationships.

REFERENCES

1. Bales, R. F. *Interaction process analysis: A method for the study of small groups.* Cambridge, Mass.: Addison-Wesley, 1949.
2. Bales, R. F. The equilibrium problem in small groups. In T. Parsons, R. F. Bales, & E. A. Shils, *Working papers in the theory of action.* Glencoe, Ill.: Free Press, 1953. Pp. 111–161.
3. Bales, R. F., & Slater, P. E. Role differentiation in small groups. In T. Parsons, R. F. Bales, et al., *Family, socialization, and interaction process.* Glencoe, Ill.: Free Press, 1955.
4. Barnard, C. I. *The functions of the executive.* Cambridge, Mass.: Harvard Univer., 1938.
5. Carter, L. F. Leadership and small group behavior. In M. Sherif, & M. O. Wilson (Eds.), *Group relations at the crossroads.* New York: Harper, 1953, Pp. 257–284.
6. Heinicke, C., & Bales, R. F. Developmental trends in the structure of small groups. *Sociometry*, 1953, 16, 7–38.
7. Homans, G. C. *The human group.* New York: Harcourt Brace, 1950.
8. Kendall, M. G. *Rank correlation methods.* London, 1948.
9. Mann, R. D. The relation of informal status to role behavior in small discussion groups. (Unpublished honors thesis, Harvard Univer., 1954.)
10. Taylor, F. K. Quantitative evaluation of psychosocial phenomena in small groups. *J. ment. Sci.*, 1951, 97, 690–717.

Sex Role Differentiation in Jury Deliberations

FRED L. STRODTBECK
and
RICHARD D. MANN

THE EMPIRICAL approach to the study of role behavior which has grown from the application of Bales interaction process categories in different situations is now approaching the phase of development in which the original findings generate new problems (1, 2, 5). The instance being considered in the present paper relates to the carry-over of interaction role specializations from primary groups to a type of *ad hoc* problem solving group—a 12 person jury deliberation.

The subjects in the jury experiments—unlike the students, military personnel and patients on whom so much small group research has been done—were markedly differentiated in age and socio-economic status. In addition, although male and female college students and patients have been subjects in some previous small group research, the men and women drawn as jurors are fully established in their sex and occupational roles. Thus, if conventional structural variables like age and socio-economic status and sex are important determinants of interaction roles in groups, then a subject population of the type provided by the jurors should be maximally favorable to the identification of the relationships involved.

In the search for structural correlates of interaction roles there are effects like age in the adult range for which there are no clear *a priori* expectations; for others, the socio-economic status, expectations growing from empirical studies are available; and for sex role, both empirical and theoretical expectations exist. In general, however, research directed to-

FROM *Sociometry*, 1956, 19, 3–11. Reprinted by permission of authors and the American Sociological Association, Inc.

A report of the experimental jury investigation conducted as part of the Law and Behavioral Science Project with funds granted by the Ford Foundation at the Law School, The University of Chicago.

ward the relation of small group performance and conventional structural variables is not extensive (3, p. 351).

In the present instance, age and socio-economic status may be quickly treated. Age does not appear to be an important determinant of interaction role for the persons 21 to 65 involved in the jury deliberations. There is some evidence that middle-aged women and young and old men are more active, but these trends do not emerge clearly. Strodtbeck's prior cross-cultural family study (8) and an unpublished work by Caudill suggested that higher status persons would participate more heavily in the group discussion. This has been confirmed (10). Activity level, which is believed to be the most important determinant of status in the small group, has been retained as a classification in the present analysis. This offers an approximate means of assessing the contribution of socio-economic status to the differentiation observed in the present data.

Only for sex role differences were there qualitative expectations which might be tested in terms of interaction process categories. Consider the following:

a) Slater (7) has found in small *ad hoc* discussion groups that the member designated by other members as having contributed most to getting the job done is characterized by an interaction profile which is different from the man designated as "best-liked" in the following ways: the task specialist gives a *higher* percentage of his acts in 4) Gives Suggestion, 5) Gives Opinion, and 8) Asks for Opinion, while giving a *lower* percentage of his acts in 2) Shows Tension Release, 3) Shows Agreement, and 11) Shows Tension. These findings have been supported in a study by Mann (4).

b) Strodtbeck (8, 9) has demonstrated that in both father-mother-son and in husband-wife interaction there is a task and social-emotional specialization and, further, that it is the husband or father who preponderantly plays the task role and the mother-wife who plays the social-emotional role.

c) In Parsons, Bales, and Shils (6), the authors suggest two points which exist as a part of their theory and relation a) and b) above. First, task and social-emotional specialization, equated roughly with concentrations of activity in Attempted Answers (categories 4, 5 and 6) and Positive Reactions (categories 1, 2, and 3) is described as arising in all groups (see also 7, p. 306). Therefore, this differentiation may be expected in jury deliberations as well as in groups working on the type of task employed by Slater. Second, the authors state their thesis that the instrumental leadership of the father and the social-emotional specialization of the mother is a pervasive pattern with important implications for such matters as: the effective socialization of the child; the stability of the nuclear family; and the channeling of latent personality patterns of males and females. Task and social-emotional differentiation becomes the central theme of the later book, *Family, Socialization and Interaction Process* (5).

Taken together, the above points suggest the hypothesis that sex role differentiation in the jury will arise, and will result in men more frequently being task, and women, social-emotional specialists. Our objective is to test this hypothesis on a particular set of deliberations.

SOURCE OF DATA

The data employed arises from mock jury deliberations conducted in connection with the Law and Behavioral Science research of the Law School, University of Chicago. The participants in these deliberations are jurors drawn by lot from the regular jury pools of the Chicago and St. Louis courts. The jurors listen to a recorded trial, deliberate, and return their verdict—all under the customary discipline of bailiffs of the court. The deliberations are recorded with two microphones to facilitate binaural identification of individual participants. The recordings are fully transcribed and these protocols are in turn scored in terms of interaction process categories. The scoring is done by an assistant who listens again to the recording and has available the indications of nonverbal gestures made by the original observer. The level of inter-scorer reliability is checked before the scoring begins and rechecked periodically while scoring is in process.

The 12 protocols utilized in the present paper were the final 12 in a set of 30 in which the jurors considered an auto negligence case. Seventeen of the 144 jurors originated less than 5 acts each and have been dropped from the tabulations. For each of the remaining jurors, the acts originated by category have been expressed as a percentage of their total acts originated. In this form the standard deviation of each category is highly correlated with the percentage of acts in that category (rho is 0.90). For computational purposes, the percentages have been transformed to log $(x+1)$; the rank correlation between the mean and standard deviation is reduced to rho equals -0.05 after the transformation.

ANALYSIS

Initial inspection of the data reveals that men originate significantly more acts than women in each socio-economic status level, but category usage and socio-economic status themselves do not seem to be closely related save for the fact that higher status persons originate more acts. The reader is reminded that by expressing the frequency of acts in each category as a percentage of each person's own total, the reflection of the actual number of acts originated has been removed. It is, however, indicated that persons who have been high or low participators be tagged and followed separately in the remainder of the analysis.

The reason for tagging activity level can be made clear by use of a set of 17 comparable deliberations (the first 18 in the series excluding one hung jury). For these deliberations the interaction profile by participation rank was prepared. In Table 1, this result is presented. In order for the interaction profiles to be based upon nearly equal frequencies, adjacent ranks have been collapsed. The trend with decreased activity may be read by comparing the values from left to right. These data are not transformed; each cell entry is a percentage of the base number of acts shown at the bottom of each column.

In Table 1, the rank one participants are high in 4) Gives Suggestion and 6) Gives Orientation but not in 5) Gives Opinion. The lower ranks, in terms of participation, are high on 2) Shows Tension Release and 3) Shows Agreement, but it is the intermediate participation ranks which are highest in 1) Shows Solidarity. The close, but not perfect, correspondence

TABLE 1

Interaction Profile by Participation Rank

CATEGORIES	RANK				TOTAL
	High 1	*2 & 3*	*4, 5, & 6*	*Low 7 thru 12*	
A. *Positive Reactions*					
1. Shows solidarity	.87	1.34	1.26	1.14	1.16
2. Shows tension release	1.64	2.54	3.32	4.60	2.96
3. Agrees	14.38	16.67	18.61	22.49	17.86
B. *Attempted Answers*					
4. Gives suggestion	5.05	4.79	3.27	2.66	4.01
5. Gives opinion	21.23	26.36	27.90	29.32	26.13
6. Gives orientation	46.50	38.11	36.49	31.46	38.32
C. *Questions*					
7. Asks for orientation	4.49	5.12	4.57	4.51	4.69
8. Asks for opinion	3.70	1.83	1.11	1.01	1.93
9. Asks for suggestion	.44	.10	.10	.13	.19
D. *Negative Reactions*					
10. Disagrees	1.29	2.43	2.30	1.87	2.00
11. Shows tension	.33	.42	.90	.71	.59
12. Shows antagonism	.07	.29	.16	.11	.17
Total	99.99	100.00	99.99	100.01	100.01
Base Frequencies	5411	6177	5777	4656	22021

between high activity and emphasis upon Attempted Answers and low activity and Positive Reactions suggest that *both* sex and activity may be determinants of task and social-emotional specialization and hence should be viewed as joint effects in the analysis.

One further consideration arises concerning the perceived appropriateness of behavior by persons of each sex and activity level. In each of the juries, the participants were asked to indicate four fellow jurors whom they felt "really helped the group arrive at its decision." This question was phrased in such a way as to permit the respondent to nominate fellow participants for either task or social-emotional contributions. A classification based upon the number of choices received has been retained in the analysis.

In summary, the classificatory designations are:

Sex:	M	male
	F	female
Activity:	A	active, originated more than the median 80 acts.
	I	inactive, originated less than 80 acts.
Choice:	C	chosen, received more than the median 2 votes.
	U	underchosen, received less than 2 votes.

The 127 individuals are distributed as follows:

MAC	32	FAC	8
MAU	13	FAU	10
MIC	16	FIC	8
MIU	25	FIU	15

For a particular category, the acts of the 127 persons can be distributed into a 2 x 2 x 2 factorial pattern. The authors are indebted to Lee H. Hook and John Nadler for adapting generalized formulae for the analysis of variance into a form that would accommodate the unequal frequencies in the cells. It is to be noted that the multinominal character of the full set of Bales' categories causes findings reported for different individual categories to be highly dependent. The reader should understand category by category comparisons to be the equivalent of viewing interrelated data from different perspectives. The comparisons are not independent.

RESULTS

In Table 2, percentage profiles for 127 jurors split into inactive and active males, inactive and active females are presented. The data in this form show women to exceed men in the three Positive Reactions categories and to be exceeded by men in the three Attempted Answers categories. This finding strongly confirms the hypothesis that there is a continuance in jury deliberations of sex role specialization observed in adult family behavior.

The results of the factorial analyses are presented in Table 3. To conserve space, several conventions have been adopted which require explanation. Since all of the analyses of variance were identical, the detailed breakdown of the degrees of freedom is shown on the left. The order of the two factors involved in instances which were significantly different, and the significance level, are given in the appropriate cells. In the actual

TABLE 2

Interaction Profile By Sex and Activity

CATEGORIES	MALE *Inactive*	MALE *Active*	FEMALE *Inactive*	FEMALE *Active*
A. *Positive Reactions*				
1. Shows solidarity	1.14	1.03	1.39	1.45
2. Shows tension release	1.75	1.50	8.49	2.91
3. Agrees	10.50	8.26	16.98	20.59
B. *Attempted Answers*				
4. Gives suggestion	3.50	3.54	2.31	1.52
5. Gives opinion	25.44	19.42	22.07	18.07
6. Gives orientation	41.59	48.49	35.96	34.95
C. *Questions*				
7. Asks for orientation	4.85	5.09	6.33	6.76
8. Asks for opinion	1.08	2.65	.77	1.26
9. Asks for suggestion	.00	.08	.00	.03
D. *Negative Reactions*				
10. Disagrees	6.46	4.99	3.70	.77
11. Shows tension	1.82	2.61	1.54	9.31
12. Shows antagonism	1.88	2.36	.46	2.36
Total	100.01	100.02	100.00	99.98
Base frequencies	1486	12413	648	3093
Jurors	41	45	23	18

TABLE 3

Significance Tests for Activity, Sex and Choice Effects

SOURCE OF VARIATION	D.F.	POSITIVE REACTIONS (1, 2 & 3)	ATTEMPTED ANSWERS (4)	ATTEMPTED ANSWERS (5)	ATTEMPTED ANSWERS (6)	QUESTIONS (7, 8 & 9)	NEGATIVE REACTIONS (10, 11 & 12)
Activity	1	—	—	—	A>I*	A>I‡	A>I‡
Sex	1	F>M‡	—	M>F†	M>F*	—	—
Choice	1	—	C>U†	—	—	—	—
Interactions	4	—	—	—	—	—	—
Deviations	119						

* F greater than .05.
† F greater than .01.
‡ F greater than .001.

computations, each degree of freedom was isolated. Since none of the interactions were significant, they have been pooled for this table. In addition, each category was analyzed separately before being combined into the major areas shown in the table. There was an appreciable number of persons with no acts in category 1) Shows Solidarity and 2) Shows Tension Release. While some discrimination has been lost by grouping the three Positive Reactions together, categories with inconsistent trends were not pooled. Similar compressions were made for *Questions* and *Negative Reactions.* In the Attempted Answers categories, the trends for 5) Gives Opinion and 6) Gives Orientation were not identical, and these categories have been analyzed separately. Category 4) Gives Suggestion has a low mean frequency and would have been pooled with adjacent categories if the inconsistent trends had not been present. As a result, it was necessary to check with non-parametric methods the significance tests reported for category 4.

Concerning the substantive information in Table 3, consider the first row of the table. It may be seen that more active persons, A, exceed less active persons, I, in three ways. They have a greater frequency of acts in category 6) Gives Orientation. In Table 1, it may be noted that almost 50% of the acts of the most-speaking person (most frequently, the jury foreman) are directed to non-interpretative orientation remarks. This effect persists after the correction by sex role and choices received involved in the analysis have been made. In addition, more active persons are higher in Negative Reactions—this could not have been anticipated from Table 1, but it is consistent with the conception of the more active person as assuming more responsibility to curb and control activities of others in the meeting.

The finding that more active persons are significantly high in Questions raises an interesting point. Is this the function of the necessity for consensus in the jury, or does it relate to the increased need to use questions to keep low participating members from withdrawing in a group as large as twelve? Comparisons with profiles from 12-man groups engaged on other tasks would be helpful here.

With regard to the male-female differences reported in the second line of Table 3, the apparent trends by sex groups in Positive Reactions forecast by Table 2 have been confirmed—females are significantly higher than males. For the task component as reflected by Attempted Answers, the two larger categories 5) Gives Opinion and 6) Gives Orientation are significantly differentiated by sex—males are higher than females. For category 4) Gives Suggestion, which has a mean incidence rate of less than 2%, the difference is consistent in direction, male being higher than female, but not clearly significant.

Differences in the number of choices received from fellow jurors do not seem to be related to relative category usage, save in one instance. Persons making more suggestions appear to have received more choices.

In the analyses by individual categories, there was just a suspicion of evidence that 2) Shows Tension Release (i.e., laughing and joking) increased the choices received by males but reduced the choices received by females. This interaction disappears in the composite calculation.

A similar effect occurs in Questions; asking questions increases choices received by men but reduces choices received by women. This interaction effect, which approaches the .06 level, is not shown in Table 3 in which an .05 probability criterion is used. These fragmentary clues involving interaction effects may deserve attention in later research, but for present purposes there is no conclusive evidence that male-female reversal of typical roles results in higher choices received, nor are there other interactions which result in significant effects.

DISCUSSION

To recast our findings slightly, the data suggests that men *pro-act*, that is, they initiate relatively long bursts of acts directed at the solution of the task problem, and women tend more to *react* to the contributions of others. These important differences, which may be read from the interaction profiles, coexist with similarities arising from the information-exchanging, consensus-seeking nature of the deliberation problem. By and large, the jurors' interaction profiles are quite similar. In the face of this similarity the direction of attention of the differences associated with sex roles should not be permitted to obscure the determinative influences of the problem situation.

Concerning the problem-situation, one might be inclined to believe that women were generally less competent than men to discuss the issues of negligence and damages involved in the deliberation. This line of reasoning suggests that social-emotional specialization is a substitute for task competence. While this cannot be proven or disproven with our data, it may be of value to note the category usage of less active men. If one assumes less active men were less competent than more active men, then less active men should also have been higher on social-emotional emphasis. There is little evidence for this in Table 2. Both the active and the less active men are clearly distinguished from the women. Thus, the exact role of competence for the problem is not clear, but it is strongly doubted that it accounts for a substantial portion of the profile differences here observed.

It should perhaps be stressed that the acts involved in the task and social-emotional distinction are included in the repertoire of all persons. When taken in isolation, these acts do not suggest male or female behavior; it is only in the statistical analysis of aggregates of acts that the sex-typed connotation emerges. Among the various subjects, there are many individual instances in which men are more social-emotional than women, and vice versa. The twelve juries reported upon contained from one to six women; however, in the aggregate profiles there were no discernible trends associated with the increased number of women in the group.

Parsons has noted that occupations like teacher, social worker, secretary and nurse, which have a high representation of women, involve large expressive and supportive components, like those associated with the wife-mother role (see 5, p. 15 fn.). Direct appraisal of the implied hypothesis that women seek jobs outside the nuclear family similar to their job in the nuclear family is difficult. It involves both a disentangling of historical and cultural factors and an empirical study of the quality of relationships in the jobs in question. While this has not been done, the hypothesis is of interest as illustrative of a type of reasoning which might plausibly be applied to the interaction differences found in the present data.

For the small system of social relations involved in a deliberation, the interaction profile is in many ways analogous to an occupation in the larger social system. People select, or drift into, their behavior in the group much as they do their occupation. Training and aptitude requirements foreclose some roles (or "jobs"), but among the remainder there is a latitude for selection. Insofar as the effects of the differential socialization of boys and girls and their subsequent sex-typed associations have been lasting, it may be reasoned that a latent personality basis has been formed for interaction role selection. As a result, from among the allowable interaction roles in the deliberation, a task emphasis tends to be selected by men and a social-emotional emphasis by women.

Each juror, or more generally, each person, has the ability to play a variety of roles which almost always exceeds the number elicited by the situation in which he operates. Each problem-situation is potentially solvable by a range of role assignments. Each group will tolerate a variety of role combinations. But finally, and this is perhaps the appropriate perspective for viewing the present findings, there are traces of continuity notwithstanding the latitude arising from individual, situational, and group sources. Our data indicates that the structural differentiation of sex role, relating as it does to the nuclear family experience, constitutes a slight, but persistent continuity and that over the range from family problem solving to jury deliberations, sex-typed differentiation in interaction role can be reliably demonstrated.

REFERENCES

1. Bales, R. F. *Interaction process analysis.* Cambridge, Massachusetts: Addison-Wesley, 1950.
2. Hare, P., Borgatta, E. F., & Bales, R. F. *Small groups: Studies in social interaction.* New York: Alfred A. Knopf, 1955.
3. Katz, D. Special Review: Handbook of social psychology. *Psychol. Bull.*, 1955, 52, 346–353.
4. Mann, R. D. The relation of informal status to role behavior in small discussion groups. (Unpublished honors thesis, Harvard Univer., 1954.)
5. Parsons, T., & Bales, R. F. *Family, socialization and interaction process.* Glencoe, Illinois: The Free Press, 1955.
6. Parsons, T., Bales, R. F., & Shils, E. A. *Working papers in the theory of action.* Glencoe, Illinois: The Free Press, 1953.
7. Slater, P. E. Role differentiation in small groups. *Amer. sociol. Rev.*, 1955, 20, 300–310.
8. Strodtbeck, F. L. Husband-wife interaction over revealed differences. *Amer. sociol. Rev.*, 1951, 18, 141–145.
9. Strodtbeck, F. L. *Family interaction, ethnicity, and achievement.* In McClelland, D. C. (Ed.), *Talent and society.* New York: Van Nostrand, 1958.
10. Strodtbeck, F. L., & James, R. M. Social process in jury deliberations. Unpublished paper presented at the Annual Meeting of the Sociological Society, 1955.

Compositional Effects, Role Systems, and the Survival of Small Discussion Groups

JAMES A. DAVIS

SURVEY analysts have recently become intrigued with a phenomenon called variously contextual analysis, structural effects, social climates, or compositional effects. The general idea is that similar individuals can be shown to behave differently when they are members of different kinds of groups. More narrowly, such analyses treat individuals characterized by the presence or absence of a given property and their behavior in groups which vary in the proportion of members who possess the property, for example, the behavior of whites and Negroes living in areas which vary in their racial composition or the behavior of promoted and nonpromoted soldiers in outfits which vary in promotion rates. Technically, such analyses require multivariate tables in which individual-level characteristics are held constant and aggregate-level differences between groups are allowed to vary. A fuller discussion of the idea and technical problems of analysis is given in the introduction to this symposium, and the particular technique in our analysis is described in another publication.[1]

Most of the reported studies of this type treat values as the contextual variable and stress the effect on voting, morale, opinions, etc., of the values which predominate in a person's social milieu. Thus, Berelson, Lazarsfeld, and McPhee report influences of the political climate of Elmira, New

FROM *Public Opinion Quarterly*, 1961, 25, 574–584. Reprinted by permission of the author and publisher.

1 This is one of several reports from a National Opinion Research Center study of the Great Books program, under a grant from the Fund for Adult Education. A more detailed analysis of the data reported in this article appears in Davis, Gebhard, Huson, and Spaeth (6). The author is indebted to Ursula Gebhard, Carolyn Huson, and Herbert Hamilton for analyses and suggestions which contributed to this article.

York; Levin in this journal reports the influences of political climates in Illinois towns; Coleman treats value climates within high schools; Blau analyzes the influence of occupational norms on white-collar workers; and Lazarsfeld and Thielens infer influences from political climates among college professors (2, 3, 4, 7, 8).

At a very abstract level, the implicit design for such studies consists of taking a number of groups with similar social structures and demonstrating effects associated with the density of endorsement of a given cultural or subcultural value. In this report we shall vary the problem a little, by seeing what happens in groups with similar value climates, when the density of certain social structures varies. That is, we shall look at the effects of the proportion of members possessing a given role or social relationship in a number of small discussion groups in the Great Books program.

THE GREAT BOOKS PROGRAM

One of the more interesting phenomena in American cultural life is the Great Books program, one of the most successful organizations for the liberal education of educated adults. The program itself consists of some 2,000 discussion groups in the United States, and a few in Canada and Europe. Each group meets every other week from September to June, and at each meeting the members discuss specific selections that they have read before the meetings. The readings are either complete works or excerpts from such writers as Aristotle, Virgil, St. Francis, Melville, Shakespeare, Hume, Darwin, and Aeschylus. The readings are organized into blocks of one year each, and, in theory, groups proceed from the first-year readings through the second, third, and so on, in a never-ending progression.

From the viewpoint of the social scientist, the groups are as interesting as the books they read. They vary in size, around an average of eleven, and in sponsorship—most are affiliated with public libraries, but some are sponsored by churches and business firms and some are unsponsored. The participants tend to be upper-middle-class professional men and wives of businessmen. They have high education (84 per cent have some college training) and they are concentrated in the thirties and early forties in terms of age. They split 50-50 between Republicans and Democrats; 62 per cent are Protestants. The participants are very active in community organizations, and, interestingly, they are *less* upwardly mobile than comparable people in the general population. Thus, the program is not a self-help movement but an outlet for intellectual and social motivations among a population with high educational achievement.

To a social scientist, however, the most striking characteristic of the groups is the things they don't have. The leaders are not professional teachers but volunteers who receive no pay. Members pay no tuition and receive no diplomas, promotions, or merit badges. In fact, no one can complete the program, as additional readings are always available, currently up to the fourteenth year. The national Great Books Foundation makes up the curriculum and sells the readings, although purchase of the readings is not required, but the foundation has little or no contact with a given group.

The upshot of all this is that there are very few institutionalized pressures for a member to continue, since he has invested no money and has no diploma as a reward. Although it is dangerous to compare "live" groups with laboratory ones, Great Books come pretty close to being "pure" discussion groups in which very few variables other than the books, the members' characteristics, and the discussion process can affect the results.

THE STUDY

In December 1957 NORC interviewers attended the meetings of 172 Great Books groups, sampled on a national basis. Members had not been informed before the meeting that they were going to participate in the research that night. Each member of the sampled groups was asked to fill out a rather lengthy self-administered questionnaire, netting us 1,909 completed schedules.

A year later an additional grant from the Fund for Adult Education, our sponsors, enabled us to determine the continuation status of all the groups and 92 per cent of the respondents in our original sample.

It turned out that 64 per cent of the members had continued with the same group, 3 per cent had transferred to other groups, and 33 per cent had left the program. In terms of groups, 3 per cent kept all their members; 60 per cent lost some, but less than half, of their members; 20 per cent lost a majority of their members; and 17 per cent were defunct.

The aim of our research was to find out what variables explained attrition and differences in attrition among these groups. In particular, we wanted to know how much of the process could be explained by individual characteristics of the members, and how much by characteristics of the groups themselves.

Role structures and drop-out. Detailed analyses of these data turned up some dozen and a half variables that influence program retention, but the most important of these is the role structure of the discussion group. That roles are important for groups can hardly come as a surprise to sociologists, but the precise nature of the relationship turns out to be one which is rather unexpected.

Through a large number of sociological writings runs an implicit or explicit thread which we can call the functional hypothesis. Bales (1), for example, writes:

A basic assumption here is that what we call the "social structure" of groups can be understood primarily as a system of solutions to the functional problems of interaction which become institutionalized in order to reduce the tensions growing out of uncertainty and unpredictability in the actions of others (pp. 15-16).

It seemed to us that if role structures arise to meet functional needs and if small groups have similar needs, then groups with different role structures might show differences in survival rates, since loss of members is a reasonable index of inability to meet needs.

In order to assess role structures, it is necessary to begin by assessing roles. Our procedures were as follows. In the questionnaire, five discussion roles were listed:

1. Providing "fuel" for the discussion by introducing ideas and opinions for the rest of the group to discuss (Fuel)
2. Getting the discussion to the point by getting terms defined and pointing out logical problems (Clarification)
3. Pulling the threads of the discussion together and getting different viewpoints reconciled (Threads)
4. Making tactful comments to heal any hurt feelings which might arise in the discussion (Tact)
5. Joking and kidding, finding the potentially humorous implications in the discussion (Joking)

Role 1, "Fuel," is a "proactive" task role; roles 2 and 3, "Clarification" and "Threads," are "reactive" task roles; and roles 4 and 5, "Tact" and "Joking," are socio-emotional roles.

Each respondent was asked to rate himself on activity in these areas and then to list the other members of his group who "tend to perform this role frequently." The associations between self-ratings and designations by others indicated fair agreement. (Q coefficients for the associations run from .51 on Fuel to .73 on Joking.)

Granted then that the groups have these roles, what do we mean when we talk about role structure? It seems to us that by role structure we mean role differentiation and that a set of roles has a structure to the degree that they are not randomly related to each other, that playing a given role affects the probability of playing another role. If this convention is satisfactory, role structure can be assessed by the intercorrelations of roles. In Table 1, we see Q coefficients for the associations between our roles, using as our dichotomy two or more mentions by other members versus zero or one.

What kind of role structure does Table 1 suggest? First, since all the relationships are positive, Great Books groups apparently do not have a highly differentiated role system. If we had taken roles such as mother,

TABLE 1

Interrelations of Roles (Yule's Q)

ROLE	JOKING	FUEL	CLARIFICATION	THREADS	TACT
Joking		.68	.45	.51	.16
Fuel	.68		.83	.84	.55
Clarification	.45	.83		.88	.60
Threads	.51	.84	.88		.72
Tact	.16	.55	.60	.72	

father, son, daughter, we would have gotten a matrix of strong negative correlations, but here people who play one role also tend to play another. This, of course, suggests some general dimension of role activity per se underlying the data.

On the other hand, the associations are not 1.00, and the pattern of relationships suggests that the system is not unidimensional. Without subjecting the data to sophisticated analytical techniques that are unsuited to these measures, we can assume that there is some qualitative differentiation of role performance along with a general tendency for persons active in one role to be active in others.

Because the associations are moderate, we can expect that some roles and combinations of roles will be present in some groups and not in others. This enables us to see whether the presence or absence of specific roles is related to the success or failure of a group. Thus, if joking serves to express the tensions of the members, and if the expression of tension helps maintain the social system, then groups with jokers should have greater retention. The reasoning involves two steps, so negative findings would be difficult to interpret. If, for instance, the presence or absence of a joker is not related to retention, it could be because either (1) joking is not necessary for the expression of tension or (2) expression of tension is not necessary for membership retention, or both.[2] Our test of the functionalist hypothesis will be pretty weak but, because it is seldom tested at all, it will be worth a try.

Table 2 arrays members according to characteristics of the role systems of their groups. The rows refer to members in groups characterized by the presence or absence of members playing specific roles, the columns refer to members in groups characterized by various proportions of the group named as playing any one or more of the five roles. Thus, the group context is varied simultaneously in terms of role quality and role quantity.

There are no consistent differences among the drop-out rates in the different rows of Table 2. We do not have enough cases to examine all combinations of all five roles simultaneously, but every combination we

2 It could also be that our measures do not tap the right functions or measure them unreliably. All the conclusions in this paper should carry the implicit qualification, "roles, as we have measured them."

have examined gives results much like Table 2: the presence or absence of a given role has no consistent effect on drop-out when role volume is controlled. At the same time, although there are exceptions and a number of cells with too few cases to percentage, in most of the comparisons drop-out is inverse to role volume. Thus, in groups with both types of task roles drop-out declines from 49 to 36 to 23 per cent as the proportion of members playing some role increases.

TABLE 2

Role Differentiation, Role Volume, and Drop-out: Percentage Dropping Out of Their Discussion Group between 1957 and 1958

DIFFERENTIATION		PER CENT NAMED AS ACTIVE: LESS THAN 20	20–49	50 OR MORE
a. Task roles:				
*Fuel**	*Clarification or Threads*†			
+	+	49 (102)	36 (616)	23 (514)
+	–	58 (89)	15 (20)	(0)
–	+	37 (79)	30 (56)	37 (16)
–	–	55 (232)	(6)	(0)
b. Socio-emotional roles:				
*Joking**	*Tact**			
+	+	67 (39)	35 (349)	24 (423)
+	–	48 (136)	28 (171)	25 (64)
–	+	69 (35)	16 (73)	13 (37)
–	–	49 (292)	58 (105)	(6)

* + means one or more members were named as playing that role; – means none.
† + means one or more people were named as playing one role or the other or both; – means none were named for either.

Table 2 suggests that there is a relationship between roles and survival of small discussion groups, but the relationship is not due to variation in role content, but rather to variation in role volume.

Role volume and drop-out. Let us then pursue the volume idea a little. To begin with, we are curious whether it is a true contextual effect, or whether it is a reversed ecological correlation fallacy. Groups with many members named as active role players do very well in terms of holding their members, but we do not know—from that—whether role volume creates a favorable group climate or whether individuals who play roles tend to stick with Great Books and the success of the high-volume groups is due merely to the fact that they have lots of people who are good risks. An answer to this problem is to examine the loss rates for role players and non-role players in groups which vary in the proportion of role players.

The accompanying chart gives the results. Each respondent is classified according to whether he is named as a role player or not, and also in terms of the proportion of his group who are named as role players. Two kinds of effects are apparent. At each level of volume, active members (role players) have lower drop-out rates than inactive members. This is an individual-level effect. At the same time, drop-out rates for both actives and inactives decline with the proportion active in a group. This is a group-level or compositional effect, since the group characteristic shows a difference when the individual characteristic is held constant.

DISCUSSION ACTIVITY AND DROP-OUT

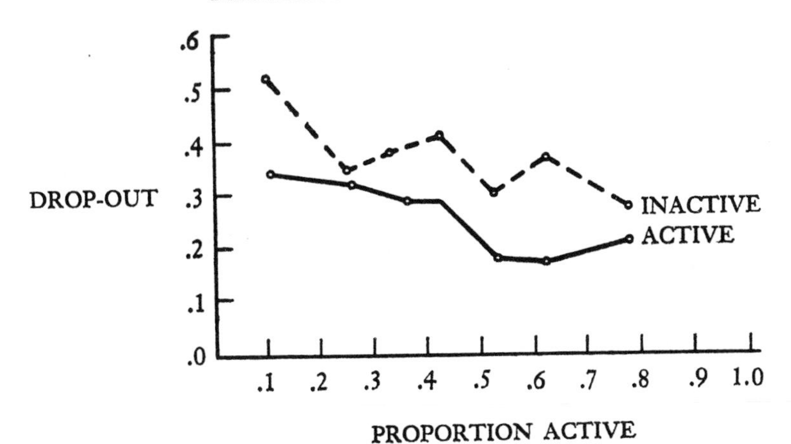

NOTE: The N's for this chart were:

MEMBERS	*0–.19*	*.2–.29*	*.3–.39*	*.4–.49*	*.5–.59*	*.6–.69*	*.7–1.00*
	PROPORTION ACTIVE IN THE DISCUSSION						
Active:							
Drop-out	16	14	31	31	25	18	22
Stay	31	30	74	77	108	82	80
Total	47	44	105	108	133	100	102
Inactive:							
Drop-out	241	56	72	56	35	21	8
Stay	214	69	108	80	78	36	17
Total	455	125	180	136	113	57	25

Both effects are fairly important. The individual-level difference averages about 12 per cent but at the same time active members in low-volume groups have higher drop-out rates than inactive members in high-volume groups.

Outside contacts and drop-out. We began by asking whether sociologists are correct in claiming that roles are important for the survival of small social systems. We found that Great Books groups do have roles, in the sense that members' claims about their role performance are in accordance with their group's perception. Next we found that there is a role structure, although not a highly differentiated one. Then we found that, while *content* of the role structure had little to do with membership retention, the *volume* of role performance goes with higher membership retention in a way that cannot be explained by individual-level risks. Thus, roles in these groups seem to affect their survival by creating climates of activity and participation, rather than by the content of their contribution.

What are the sources of these role climates? Why do some groups have many active participants and some very few? Interestingly, group size and age have very little to do with it, but to a degree role volume is a function of another climate, the climate of interpersonal relationships outside the group discussions.

Each respondent was asked, "How many members of your group (excluding your spouse) do you see regularly outside the group discussion?" When respondents are divided into those who see one or more vs. those who see none, and groups are arrayed in terms of the proportion with one or more outside contacts, we can see the relationship between outside contacts and role volume, at the group level and at the individual level. Groups are divided into those with 50 per cent or more college graduates and those with less than half college graduates. Table 3 gives the results.

TABLE 3

Outside Contacts, Activity, Educational Composition, and Role Volume: Percentage Named as Active in Discussion Roles

PER CENT COLLEGE GRADUATES	INDIVIDUAL CONTACTS	PER CENT WITH ONE OR MORE OUTSIDE CONTACTS	
		LESS THAN 60	60 OR MORE
50 or more	Yes	31 (277)	45 (506)
	No	28 (368)	43 (123)
	Total	30 (645)	45 (629)
Less than 50	Yes	37 (118)	31 (164)
	No	40 (158)	38 (50)
	Total	39 (276)	33 (214)

Table 3 gives us the percentage named as active role players for individuals with and without extragroup contacts, in four types of groups: high education, high contacts; high education, low contacts; low education, high contacts; and low education, low contacts. We can begin with the groups with a majority of college graduates. We see that regardless of whether the individual himself has social relationships with the members outside of the meetings, role activity is greater where the proportion with such relationships is higher. There is very little individual-level difference. Thus, among highly educated groups there appears to be a climate effect such that high volumes of outside interaction produce high volumes of role participation in the discussion. This stands to reason, as we would expect role relationships developed outside the program to carry over into Great Books.

When, however, we consider the less educated groups, the climate effect reverses. Among individuals with and without outside contacts, role activity is, if anything, lower in groups with high outside interaction, and there is some tendency for the active role players to be people with no outside contacts, whereas among the highly educated groups the actives, if anything, had more contacts.

With cross-sectional survey data it is impossible to draw firm conclusions about these relationships. However, one line of interpretation is as follows: Among highly educated people, the cultural climate of extragroup interaction is probably more intellectual and leads to a set of interpersonal relationships that are highly consonant with group discussion of intellectual matters. Among the less educated (remembering, however, that in our sample the less educated are typically part college rather than high school graduates or less), however, the outside culture is probably less intellectual and the role patterns which exist are less transferable to active group discussion of ideas. Thus, depending on the value climate of the extragroup social relationships, they either facilitate or inhibit role volume in the discussions.

The net result is that there is a relationship between outside contacts and role volume, but the relationship varies with the educational level of the group. Table 4 shows these differences.

TABLE 4

Outside Contacts, Role Volume, and Education: Q Association between Outside Contacts and Role Activity (Group Level)

PER CENT COLLEGE GRADUATES IN GROUP	Q	NUMBER OF GROUPS
70 or more	.76	58
50–69	.43	68
40–49	−.38	20
0–39	−.33	26

Since most Great Books groups are composed of a majority of college graduates, over-all outside contacts are associated with lower drop-out rates. Common sense suggests that people who are knit together by high outside contacts would be more cohesive. Perhaps, then, people who see each other a lot stick together, and the high rate of role performance is merely a side effect.

In order to check this hypothesis, let us consider the simultaneous effects on group retention of role volume and outside contacts, controlling for educational level. Table 5 suggests that the effect of role volume is not spurious. Regardless of educational level and volume of outside interaction, groups with higher role volume keep more of their members. Outside contacts, however, show different effects in the two educational levels. Among the highly educated groups, high outside contacts go with high membership retention. Among the less educated, however, high outside contacts go with greater loss of members, a reversal similar to the one we saw in the relationship between outside contacts and role volume.

TABLE 5

Role Volume, Outside Contacts, Educational Composition, and Drop-out: Percentage Dropping Out

PER CENT COLLEGE GRADUATES	PER CENT WITH OUTSIDE CONTACTS	PER CENT ACTIVE ROLE PERFORMERS		
		40 OR MORE	0–39	TOTAL
50 or more	60 or more	21 (414)	31 (214)	24 (628)
	Less than 60	34 (164)	42 (462)	40 (626)
Less than 50	60 or more	39 (59)	67 (136)	58 (195)
	Less than 60	32 (137)	41 (143)	37 (28)

CONCLUSION

Now, let us see whether we can piece all of this together.

We began by wondering whether role structures were related to membership retention in Great Books discussion groups. Applying ideas from laboratory studies of small groups, we asked whether the *kind* of role played in the group affected the group's ability to keep its members. It turned out that role quality is unimportant but that role quantity is a major factor. Our analysis showed not only that active role participants are more likely to stay with the program but that, for both active and nonactive members, retention increases with the volume of role performance in the group. In short, it appears that heavy participation in the discussions creates a climate favorable for group survival.

Further analysis suggested a second climatic or contextual factor, and that is the volume of interaction outside the discussion meetings. This climate appears more catalytic than anything else, and it has two different effects: (1) Among groups with high education, high rates of outside contact lead to greater role volume and also contribute independently to membership retention. (2) Among groups with lower educational levels, high rates of outside interaction inhibit role volume and also contribute independently to membership loss. Thus, among highly educated people the climate of outside interaction is a double benefit to the group, and for less educated people the climate of outside interaction is a double drawback.

We began with a theory which essentially assumes that the process of interaction in small groups is determined by the content of the immediate interpersonal relationships and the problems they present. We have ended, however, with a rather different conception of role processes in these—admittedly rather different—groups. Great Books groups appear heavily affected, not by role quality, but by the quantitative climate of role participation. This in turn is heavily influenced by the content of interpersonal relations outside of the immediate situation. As contrasted with laboratory groups, these natural groups appear strongly affected by their degreee of fit or abrasion with role patterns and cultural values in the larger social world.

REFERENCES

1. Bales, R. F. *Interaction process analysis.* Cambridge, Mass.: Addison-Wesley, 1950.
2. Berelson, B. R., Lazarsfeld, P. F., & McPhee, W. N. *Voting: A study of opinion formation in a presidential campaign.* Chicago: Univer. of Chicago Press, 1954.
3. Blau, P. Structural effects. *Amer. sociol. Rev.*, 1960, 25, 178–193.
4. Coleman, J. S. The adolescent subculture and academic achievement. *Amer. J. Sociol.*, 1960, 65, 337–347.
5. Davis, J. A., Spaeth, J. L., & Huson, Carolyn. A technique for analyzing the effects of group composition. *Amer. sociol. Rev.*, 1961, 26, 215–225.
6. Davis, J. A., Gebhard, Ruth U., Huson, Carolyn, & Spaeth, J. L. *Great books and small groups.* Glencoe, Ill.: Free Press, 1961.
7. Lazarsfeld, P. F., & Thielens, W. *The academic mind.* Glencoe, Ill.: Free Press, 1958.
8. Levin, M. L. Social climates and political socialization. *Pub. op. Quart.*, 1961, 25, 596–606.

CHAPTER 12
LEADERSHIP

An Experimental Approach to the Study of Autocracy and Democracy: A Preliminary Note

KURT LEWIN and RONALD LIPPITT

IF ONE hopes to investigate experimentally such fundamental socio-psychological problems as: group ideology; conflicts between and within groups; types of their spontaneous substructuring; the stability of various spontaneous group structures versus structures created by external authority; minority problems; renegade, scapegoat, double loyalty conflicts—one has to create a setup where group life might be studied under rather free but well defined conditions. Instead of utilizing the groups in schools, clubs, factories, one should create groups experimentally because only in this way the factors influencing group life will not be left to chance but will be in the hands of the experimenter.

However, one should break away from the rather narrow aspect of studying the effect of the group influence on the individual (e.g., the effect of various groups on the suggestibility of the individual) as the main problem; one should consider not only one effect of a given social situation

FROM *Sociometry*, 1938, 1, 292–300. Reprinted by permission of Mrs. Gertrude W. Lewin and the publisher.

(e.g., the influence on productivity). Rather one should try to approach an experimental procedure: (a) where group life can proceed freely; (b) where the total group behavior, its structure and development can be registered. Any specific problem such as group ideology should be approached in the experimental setup and in the analysis of the data as a part of this greater whole.

Such data might always be analyzed with a double frame of reference, that of the individual group member and of the group as a dynamic unity.

The main interest of the present preliminary study is to develop from this point of view techniques to investigate "democracy" and "autocracy" as group atmospheres.

Two experimental mask-making clubs of ten and eleven year old children were selected from a group of eager volunteers of the fifth and sixth grades of the University Elementary School. A preliminary sociometric survey, following Moreno's technique, was made of the affinities and rejections existing in the two classrooms. With a sociogram of each group at hand the groups were selected (one from each schoolroom) from the available volunteers so that the groups would be as nearly equated as possible on the number and potency of friendship and rejection relationships, and on general popularity and leadership characteristics of the members. Instead of choosing a clique of close friends five children were chosen in each case who had expressed little relationship with each other, either in the school situation or in playing together in non-school groupings. It was believed that any inter-personal relations that developed during the life of the club could then be more closely correlated to the common life space of the new group membership.

In a ten minute preliminary meeting with each group the leader made it clear that the aim of the club would be to make theatrical masks (a new activity for all of the children); that the masks would belong to the group as a whole; and that one mask would be made at a time rather than each individual making one by himself. Two half-hour meetings a week were held with each group, the same experimenter being the leader in both clubs.

It is methodologically meaningless in studying democracy and autocracy experimentally to be guided mainly by the question: What is "the" prototype of democracy and which is the "true" autocracy. One should realize from the start that there are many varieties of such atmospheres. The experimental approach can only try to attack one case at a time. What type of democracy should be chosen should be less guided by the tendency to copy some historically given case than by the attempt to realize those types of group atmospheres which promise the best insight into the underlying dynamics and laws. Only the insight into these laws, and not the search for a prototype, will enable us to answer the question of what are the common properties and individual differences of autocracies and democracies.

With such a point of view the experimenter attempted to differentiate the atmospheres of the two groups chiefly in the following ways:

AUTHORITARIAN	DEMOCRATIC
1. All determination of policy by the strongest person (leader).	*1. All policies a matter of group determination, encouraged and drawn out by the leader.*
2. Techniques and steps of attaining the goal (completed mask) dictated by the authority, one at a time, so that future direction was always uncertain to a large degree.	*2. Activity perspective given by an explanation of the general steps of the process (clay mould, plaster paris, papier mache, etc.) during discussion at first meeting. Where technical advice was needed the leader tried to point out 2 or 3 alternative procedures from which choice could be made.*
3. The authority usually structured autocratically the activities of each member—the task and whom to work with.	*3. The members were free to work with whomever they chose and the division of tasks was left up to the group.*
4. The dominator criticized and praised individual's activities and remained aloof from group participation. He was always impersonal rather than outwardly hostile or friendly (a necessary concession in method).	*4. The leader attempted to be a group member in spirit but not in the actual work. He gave criticism and praise, generally in regard to the group as a whole.*

It is obvious that with voluntary group participation, and with the cooperation of the school system radically autocratic methods would not be utilized. A congenial extra-group relationship was maintained with all of the children during the entire course of the experimental sessions. The attempt was to make the authoritarian atmosphere as much more autocratic than the schoolroom as the democratic one was freer than the schoolroom.

During the series of twelve meetings for each group four trained observers made observational records, synchronized in minute units, of a varied nature. These techniques are here described very briefly:

1. A quantitative running account of the social interactions of the five children and leader, in terms of symbols for ascendant, submissive, and objective (fact-minded) approaches and responses, including a category of purposeful refusal to respond to a social approach.

2. A quantitative group structure analysis minute by minute with running comments to give a record of: activity subgroupings (e.g. three

of the children are busy mixing plaster of paris, one is tearing up paper towels for papier mache, and the fifth is working on the clay mould. This would be a 3-1-1 group structure with three subgroups. One individual may be a subgroup.); the activity goal of each subgroup; whether the subgroup was initiated by the leader or spontaneously formed by the children; and ratings on the degree of interest and unity of each subgroup.

3. Running comments and ratings indicating shifts of interest from minute to minute for each member (from complete involvement in the club activity to "out-of-the-field" preoccupations).

4. A stenographic record of conversation.

5. To the observers' records outlined above was added a post-meeting writeup by the leader of his impressions gathered from the more intimate contacts with the children.

Laid side by side these records give a rather complete minute by minute, meeting by meeting picture of the ongoing life of the group. A wide variety of quantitative and qualitative analyses are possible. Below are listed a few upon which we have already made some progress:

1. The total volume of social interactions broken down into ascendant, submissive, objective, and ignoring behavior.

2. The volume and types of social interactions between subgroups as compared to those within subgroups.

3. Analysis in terms of individual activity curves of these same data.

4. The stability of group structure and of specific subgroupings under varied conditions.

5. The influence on unity and stability of structure of leader-initiated and spontaneous subgroupings.

6. Analysis of stenographic records in terms of such categories as hostility; attention demands, resistant behavior, hostile and objective criticism, expression of competition and cooperation, amount of dependence on authority, expressions of "I-centeredness" (ego-centrism) versus "we-centeredness" (group spirit), etc.

7. Analysis of gradients of activity such as increase of hostility, and volume of total activity.

8. Changes of interest in terms of such related factors as group stability, outbreak of hostility, and standards of production.

The first purpose of this technique of observation is to record as fully and insightfully as possible the total behavior of the group. This is a distinct break away from the usual procedure of recording only certain symptoms which are determined in advance. It is an attempt to apply the same "total behavior" methodology in social psychology which has proven fruitful in a number of investigations into individual psychology (i.e. Dembo's study on anger, Karsten's of psychological satiation, and that of Dembo and Barker on frustration), and which is a logical procedure for the "field theoretical" approach in social psychology.

The second point we wish to stress is that exact quantitative records become valueless if one loses sight of the meaning which the single action had within the total setting. It is therefore most important to have some complete characterization of the atmosphere as a whole. The necessary quantitative analysis (choice of items, classification of items, and statistical combinations) should always be made in view of these larger wholes.

The comprehensiveness of these data makes it possible to follow up with re-analysis new clues which arise from time to time as to behavioral relationships. It is our belief at the present time that this "total behavior" technique, combining strands of all degrees of quantitativeness and qualitativeness offers the most hopeful methodology yet developed for the experimental study of group life. The possibility of focusing numerous strands of evidence upon one or two focal points corrects to some extent for the necessity of working with such a number of variables as the social situation presents.

An interesting set of problems has arisen in the statistical analysis of social interactions which has led to the development of an embryo "mathematics of group life." It became obvious that before statements could be made about the relative amount of interactions between members of in-groups under various circumstances or between members of out-groups, it was necessary to take into account the possibilities of in- and out-group communication in each type of group structure. For example, it is clear that if all members were working on isolated individual bits of activity there could be no in-group relationships for no subgroup would have more than one member. If all five children were united in one activity unity there would be no possibility of interactions with an out-group member. In case the total group were divided into two subgroups these possibilities are different in case the two subgroups contain 4 and 1 children, or 3 and 2 children.

It is necessary then to compute the possibilities of in- and out-group communication for each possible group structure. In case the total group contains 5 individuals the following 7 group structures are possible:

5, 4-1, 3-2, 3-1-1, 2-2-1, 2-1-1-1, 1-1-1-1-1

The formula for computing in-group interaction possibilities (*ip*) and out-group interaction possibilities (*op*) for any given group structure may be stated simply:

$$ip = a\,(a-1) + b\,(b-1) + \cdots r\,(r-1)$$
$$op = m\,(m-1) - ip$$

where $a, b, \ldots r$ are the number of members in the various subgroups coexisting in a particular group structure and where m is the total number of members in the group.

In our case we find the following interaction possibilities:

Possible group structures

	5	4-1	3-2	3-1-1	2-2-1	2-1-1-1	1-1-1-1-1
ip	20	12	8	6	4	2	0
op	0	8	12	14	16	18	20

Weighting these possibilities by the time that each group structure existed we get an index with which to measure the relative in-group, out-group, and total social interactions in the authoritarian and democratic atmospheres. We can use the following formula for the total in-group interaction possibilities (Σip) during a given period of group life:

$$\Sigma ip = ip(A) \cdot t(A) + ip(B) \cdot t(B) + \cdots + ip(L) \cdot t(L)$$

where $A, B, \ldots\ldots, L$ are the various types of group structure which came up during that period; $t(A), t(B), \ldots t(L)$ the duration of each group structure; $ip(A), ip(B), \ldots ip(L)$ their in-group interaction possibilities.

The total out-group possibilities (Σop) is:

$$\Sigma op = op(A) \cdot t(A) + op(B) \cdot t(B) + \cdots + op(L) \cdot t(L)$$

The total social interaction possibilities (Σsp) is:

$$\Sigma sp = \Sigma ip + \Sigma op$$

Ex: If, during a certain club meeting the structure was 4-1 for 5 minutes, 3-1-1 for 10 minutes, and 2-1-1-1 for 10 minutes the formulation of the index would demand this computation:

$$\Sigma ip = 12 \times 5 + 6 \times 10 + 2 \times 10 = 140$$
$$\Sigma op = 8 \times 5 + 14 \times 10 + 18 \times 10 = 360$$
$$\Sigma sp = 140 + 360 = 500$$

The computation of these interaction possibilities seems an essential step in the experimental treatment of group relationships. It makes possible also the correction for missing members now and then over a series of club meetings.

There is little space in this note for an adequate exposition of the analyses which have been completed on the lives of these two experimental clubs. In summary form the findings indicate that:

1. A higher state of tension existed in the atmosphere of the autocratic group. A number of findings focus on this point: (a) a much higher volume of social interactions (55% more) in spite of the fact that the ongoing activity demanded less communication than in the democratic group; (b) a less stable group structure was maintained; (c) more ascendance and less submissiveness and objectivity of members toward each other; (d) the development of two scapegoats during 12 meetings; (e) about 30 times as much hostility expressed between members as in the democratic group.

2. More cooperative endeavor emerged in the democratic group;

(a) a much higher incidence of offering and asking for cooperation; (b) many more occurrences of praise and expressions of friendliness.

3. More expression of an objective attitude in the democratic group: (a) many more constructive suggestions offered; (b) more give and take of objective criticism without personal involvement.

4. Constructiveness was higher in the democratic group: (a) superiority of the group products; (b) more careless and unfinished work in the autocratic group; (c) greater incidence of constructive suggestions in the democratic group.

5. The feeling of "we'ness" was greater in democracy, and that of "I'ness" was greater in the authoritarian group as shown by test situations and by analysis of the stenographic records.

6. The group structure was more stable and tended to maintain a higher degree of unity in the democratic group. When the authority withdrew his influence on the situation the group structure tended toward disorganization in the autocratic group.

7. Twice in the autocratic group a situation arose where the group combined its aggression against one individual, making him a scapegoat. In both cases the scapegoat quit the group. No such lack of harmony existed in the democratic group.

8. The feeling for group property and group goals was much better developed in the democratic group as shown by test situations and the stenographic accounts.

9. Following the one exchange of group members which was made there was a decrease in dominating behavior for the child transferred to the democratic group and an increase in like behavior for the child changed to the authoritarian group.

It seems necessary to reiterate that a number of these specific results, which will be tabulated more fully when further analysis is completed, may be due to the particular types of autocratic and democratic atmospheres developed in these groups. For instance there would probably not be such an overt expression of hostility in most cases of authoritarian group atmosphere, for it would be suppressed. This "steam valve" of free expression was purposely left open however in this investigation because it was hoped it would prove a good measuring stick for the record of tension when it existed. This seems to have been the case. The thoughtful establishment of such test areas seems at the present to be a very fruitful procedure. Only further research, some of which is already under way, with a variety of groups and leaders will make possible a more assured statement as to the common factors in these dynamic relationships. These new experiments indicate, for example, that the dynamic differences between free and authoritarian atmospheres present quite a different picture in case the freedom of the group swings from democratic group determination to anarchic individualism.

A more sociological survey of the atmospheres of the other groups (e.g. family, school) in which the children have membership-character will also need to be made for clues as to the influence of overlapping group memberships upon the development of the experimental group ideology. New methods of experimental manipulation are also being developed as we become more oriented to the nature of the task.

A Further Investigation of the Criteria of Leadership

LAUNOR F. CARTER, WILLIAM HAYTHORN,
and
MARGARET HOWELL

IN A PREVIOUS paper Carter and Nixon (1) have reported the results of a study of the relationship between four criteria of leadership ability for three different tasks. From their work with high school students they drew two major conclusions: first, that leadership in certain intellectual and clerical situations tends to be independent of leadership performance in mechanical assembly tasks; second, that there was not a high relationship between assessments of leadership based on leaderless-group situations, on supervisor's ratings, on student nominations, and on participation in extracurricular activity.

Since these results were based on high school students observed for only a relatively short period of time a new experiment was designed to determine if the above conclusions would be supported when based on a different group of subjects studied more intensively. The scope of the work was expanded by increasing the number and diversity of the work-tasks used in the leaderless-group technique and by increasing the number

ABRIDGED FROM *Journal of Abnormal and Social Psychology*, 1950, 45, 350–358. Reprinted by permission of the authors and the American Psychological Association, Inc.

The work described in this paper was done under a contract between the U.S. Navy, Office of Naval Research and the University of Rochester.

of criteria used. In the current work assessments were obtained from use of the leaderless group technique, from nominations, from faculty members, from the subject's friends and from an evaluation of their past leadership activities. The results of this more intensive investigation will be reported by discussing each of the different criteria separately and then considering the interrelations between the criteria.

THE LEADERLESS GROUP WORK-TASK CRITERION

The basic method common throughout the use of the leaderless-group technique is the setting up of miniature work-tasks similar to actual problems to be faced later in real life by the members of the group. Several individuals are introduced into these situations without an appointed leader and careful note is made of the group interaction and leadership behavior of those involved. It is hoped that those demonstrating leadership behavior in such "artificial" miniature situations will later perform similarly when faced with real leadership problems. More extensive accounts of the methods used in a variety of situations can be found in 1, 3, 4, and 6.

Work-Tasks and Observation Technique

In the present study six different types of work-tasks were used. A short description of each follows:

THE REASONING TASKS. Each subject was handed a card containing four "given statements" for a syllogistic reasoning problem. The group as a whole received a paper containing statements which were to be marked true, false, or indeterminate, in terms of the given statements. The subjects were allowed to tell each other their given statements but could not show the cards to one another. Group agreement was required.

THE INTELLECTUAL CONSTRUCTION TASKS. The group was given a diagram of a field or court, such as a basketball court. Some dimensions were given and others had to be determined from known relationships. The group plotted the court on the floor with string and scotch tape.

THE CLERICAL TASKS. The subjects were asked to sort a large number of cards by several breakdowns. The requirements were such that considerable coordination between different sortings of the cards was required.

THE DISCUSSION TASKS. Group discussion was required in the acceptance or rejection of some questions, such as: "Resolved: the recent election of Harry Truman as President will help continue the present high level of national prosperity." A written conclusion was to be composed.

THE MOTOR COOPERATION TASK. The motor cooperation task involved the use of the spiral-ball apparatus devised by French (2). By tipping the apparatus the subjects tried to roll the ball to the top of the spiral. The closest cooperation and coordination between the subjects was required to accomplish this purely motor task.

THE MECHANICAL ASSEMBLY TASKS. The subjects were furnished with a very general diagram of the object they were to assemble. They built such things as bridges, backstops, goal posts, etc., using bolts and pre-cut and pre-drilled lumber.

SUMMARY AND CONCLUSIONS

Five different criteria of leadership ability were investigated. These five criteria included use of the leaderless-group technique, the nominating method, ratings by faculty members, ratings by friends, and the assessment of leadership in previous extracurricular and out-of-school activities.

The reliability of ratings made by observers from the leaderless-group situations was quite high. There was some indication that as the number of people observed increased, the reliability of the ratings decreased. The coefficients of attenuation between a session involving groups of four subjects and later sessions involving these same subjects averaged .65.

The correlations between the leadership ratings given the subjects on six different kinds of tasks were computed. Almost all of the coefficients were positive, indicating a certain generality of leadership performance from task to task. At the same time there were noticeable groupings of relationships between certain tasks. By the use of factor analysis it was indicated that there were two different kinds of tasks apparently calling for different leadership abilities. These two factors were called an "intellectual leadership" factor and a "doing things with one's hands leadership" factor.

On two occasions the subjects nominated from their members the men they thought would be the best and the poorest leaders. These nominations were quite reliable. The nominations were made with regard to six different tasks. Again the intercorrelations between the tasks were positive; factor analysis revealed essentially the same pattern of leadership factors as was determined from the ratings made by the observers in the leaderless-group sessions.

The ratings by faculty members and by friends proved to be quite unreliable. In contrast, the reliability obtained from high school faculty members' ratings, using the same technique, had been fairly high in a previous study. The difference in reliability appears to be due to the fact that in the high school study all of the subjects were rated by the same judges whereas in the college study a large number of different judges was required to obtain the ratings. The subjects' past leadership performance was assessed from their activities and positions of leadership in clubs, social groups, extracurricular activities, etc.

Intercorrelations between these five criteria of leadership tended to be quite low. The average correlation between the leaderless-group ratings and the nomination scores, our two most reliable criteria, was .39. These results would tend to indicate that the generality of studies of leadership is limited by the nature of the particular criterion used.

The results of this study correspond closely with that of a previous study using high school subjects.

REFERENCES

1. Carter, L. F., & Nixon, M. An investigation of the relationship between four criteria of leadership ability for three different tasks. *J. Psychol.*, 1949, 27, 245–261.
2. French, J. R. P. Organized and unorganized groups under fear and frustration. In *Studies in topological and vector psychology.* Iowa City: Univer. Iowa Press, 1944.
3. Gellhorn, W., & Brody, W. Selecting supervisory mediators through trial by combat. *Publ. Admin. Rev.*, 1948, 8, 259–267.
4. Taft, R. Use of the "group situation observation" method in the selection of trainee executives. *J. appl. Psychol.*, 1948, 32, 581–587.
5. Williams, S. B., & Leavitt, H. J. Group opinion as a predictor of military leadership. *J. consult. Psychol.*, 1947, 11, 283–292.
6. Office of Strategic Services Assessment Staff. *Assessment of men.* New York: Rinehart, 1948.

The Sociometry of Leadership in Temporary Groups

CECIL A. GIBB

INTRODUCTION

LEADERSHIP is such a common phenomenon of experience and is so frequently spoken of that there is ordinarily little conscious awareness of the variety of social relationships the term embraces. A moment's thought, however, reveals the diversity of leaders and of leader-follower relations in the culture. Few words in the English dictionary have a greater variety of meanings than does the verb "to lead."

In its dictionary sense, however, leadership is usually defined, in what might be called a social-dynamic sense, as "the exercise of authority and influence." But there is almost general agreement in the psychological lit-

FROM *Sociometry*, 1950, 13, 226–243. Reprinted by permission of the author and publisher.

erature of the last few years that the exercise of authority and influence varies qualitatively as the group-dynamic relations between the influencer and the influenced vary from rigid to more free structuration. Cowley (2) drew attention to such a distinction by differentiating headmen from leaders. Pigors (12) differentiated between these two forms of social influence by defining as domination that "process of social control in which accepted superiors assume a position of command and demand obedience from those who acknowledge themselves as inferiors in the social scale, and in which, by the forcible assumption of authority and the accumulation of prestige, a person (through a hierarchy of functionaries) regulates the activities of others for purposes of his own choosing." Many observational studies have confirmed the need for this kind of distinction with consequent restriction of the definition of leadership. Anderson (1), studying the social behavior of young children, distinguished dominative from integrative modes of behavior. The former involved the use of commands, threats and attacks on the personal status of the individual; while the latter entailed explaining the situation to the other person, and by means of this, getting voluntary cooperation. Steward and Scott (14), observing the behavior of a herd of goats, reported that there was no more than chance correlation between leadership and dominance. They suggested, in fact, that these two phenomena are the result of two separate learning processes which are not associated. They pointed out also that their results agreed with similar experiments done on human subjects (e.g., Anderson) and that it was therefore possible to conclude, tentatively at least, that the lack of correlation between dominance and leadership is a general phenomenon independent of cultural factors.

In the more restricted sense required by this differentiation leadership is best defined, by Pigors, as "a concept applied to the personality-environment relation to describe the situation when one, or at most a very few, personalities are so placed in the environment that his or their will, feeling, and insight direct and control others in the pursuit of a common cause (12)." Leadership is, then, to be understood as rather more than taking initiative, planning and organizing, as more than a positional relationship. Leadership implies a particular dynamic relationship between the leader and his followers. The chief characteristics of this relationship are: (a) an influence hierarchy; (b) integrative cooperative behavior; (c) mutual interaction and stimulation; and (d) the absence of a fixed social structure which maintains an individual's status in this hierarchy after he has ceased to perform the functions upon which the status originally rested.

One further distinction, employed in this report, is that between the leader of a group and that person who may be called (following R. B. Cattell) its socio-center. The latter term is used to fit the general terminology of Moreno (11) from whose work it derives. Jennings (7, 9), in particular, has done a great deal of very significant work in the field of leadership using the techniques of sociometric choice. By this method, however, the most chosen individual or the person who has highest "choice-status" is, by definition, a leader. It will, of course, sometimes be the case that this "leader" will also meet the criteria of the definition of leadership advocated above. But there is no reason why this should always be so. Thus it seems desirable to call this most chosen person a socio-center and to leave open to investigation the relation between the roles of socio-center and leader. A further advantage of this terminology is that socio-center and "isolate" are more logical opposites than are Jennings' leader and isolate. The terms leader and follower may then be counterposed in such a way that both represent distinct but related social roles. The isolate is not necessarily, of course, a follower, any more than the socio-center is necessarily a leader. It is one of the objects of this report to examine the relation between sociometric choice-status and leadership in temporary groups of men.

Before this may be done, however, there is a further concept, introduced by Jennings (9), which requires exposition and testing. This is the distinction between socio-groups and psyche-groups. Socio-groups are defined (9) as those "where sociometric structure is based on a criterion which is *collective* in nature." Thus sociometric choice based upon the criterion of wishing to work in a common unit defines a socio-group. On the other hand psyche-groups are those "where sociometric structure is based on a strictly private criterion which is totally personal in nature." Associating or indicating a desire to associate in leisure time is such a criterion. Further, it is suggested by Jennings (9) that "the tele between persons in respect to collaborating with one another in socio-groups may be called sociotele," and "the tele between persons in respect to associating with one another in psyche-groups may be called psychetele, since it is founded upon response towards associating or not associating with others in a purely personal matter, and concerns no situation common to all the members." Jennings has contended that there is very little overlap between these two groups, that there are few common choices by any individual on psychetelic and sociotelic bases. This contention has been submitted to a preliminary experimental test in temporary groups.

THE PRESENT INVESTIGATION

In the course of a comprehensive study of group behavior and of the emergence of leaders in small temporary groups of men (5) [1] an investigation has been made of the degree of overlap between socio-groups and psyche-groups and of the extent of correlation between sociocentral and leadership status. For the purpose of the larger study small aggregations

[1] Conducted under the general direction of Raymond B. Cattell at the University of Illinois and with the cooperation of Glen F. Stice.

of ten men were brought together in a particular way, under certain controlled conditions. These individuals were motivated generally to cooperate by the offer of financial rewards and by their needs to fulfill requirements of study courses, as part of which participation in this program was required. Men were allocated to aggregations, as nearly as possible, on the basis of their being unknown to one another, but with no other criterion of selection. Each aggregation was directed to a variety of activities so chosen that they found interaction expedient or essential and so formed a group. Ten such groups were established among male students of psychology classes at the University of Illinois and twenty among male candidates of the Air Force Officer Candidate School at Lackland Air Force Base.[2]

Each of these groups met in three three-hour sessions. This was necessary in order to have the group in existence long enough for leadership to emerge and for the members to become aware of the group as a functioning unit. It was necessary that each session be of sufficient duration to permit participation in a number of different activities and that there be a sufficient number of sessions to permit variation of the leadership structure. The design was such that in the first session leadership was left unstructured completely. It was a "leaderless" session, and the only leadership present was that which occurred spontaneously in the group. Where the group did not, of its own accord, reach the conclusion that a leader would help in planning the second session, it was suggested to them, at the end of session one, that they might select a leader for session two. When they reported for the second session an opportunity was given to reconsider this leader-choice and to elect another leader if they cared to do so. Whether this offer of change was accepted or not, another similar opportunity was offered about halfway through session two. Again, at the conclusion of this session the group was offered a change of leader in that it was asked to select a leader for session three. At the beginning of the third session a reminder was given concerning this choice and the person so chosen was then directly addressed and told that he was the leader and that he could use that office as he saw fit. Throughout session three the experimenter dealt directly with this leader in a way that had been carefully avoided up to that time.

Within this structural framework each session was planned to include a varied program of activities so that situations would occur characterized variously by demands upon: (i) cognitive abilities; (ii) social skills; (iii) special interests; (iv) group cohesion; (v) previous leadership experience, etc. Detailed descriptions of these activities and of the many measures

2 The writer wishes to express his thanks to instructors and students at the University of Illinois and to Officers and Candidates of the Air Force O.C.S., whose cooperation made possible this research. Thanks are due, too, to those members of the 3309 Research and Development Squadron who assisted, and to senior administrative officers whose approval was a prerequisite to the program.

made of: (a) personal characteristics of members; (b) inter-member relationship patterns; (c) physical equipment; and (d) the behavior of the group as a group need not be given here.

Both to gather information to be used in a study of syntality correlates of leadership (5) and to explore the foundations of some of the findings of Jennings (8, 9) a number of sociometric questions were put to participants of this program as each separate activity was completed and at the end of each session. Thus among some fifteen questions to be answered after each session were placed one (sociotele) which asked each participant to indicate those members of the group he would like to have remain in the group for future repetitions of the particular activity, or for other similar activities, and also to indicate (by circling a number) those members he would prefer to have allocated to another group; and another (psychetele) by which participants were asked: "If you were to choose personal friends from among this group which members would you choose?"

With the object of casting some light on problems already raised implicitly in what has been said above, two other questions of the general sociometric type were put to participants. After each session participants were asked a question designed to discover their judgments of behavior influencing the group. This question was: "Some groups are so closely knit that the removal of any one person changes its complexion. For which persons, if any, in this group, would this be the case?" Further, in the second and third sessions, during which they were more or less aware of leadership, at the conclusion of the construction situation participants were asked whom they would judge to have been leaders in this situation. This activity of constructing a wooden model was chosen as the vehicle for this question because it was known to involve several difficulties, was expected to afford a good opportunity for leadership to occur, and since it was an active participation task, rather than a verbal one, it was anticipated to be one in which leadership could be relatively reliably judged both by independent observers and by participants. While this latter expectation was realized the former was not. This situation did not reveal a great deal of leadership but what was revealed was reliably rated. Thus, while it did not turn out to be the best situation for this question, it was not the worst choice for the purpose. Experience with student groups, however, led to a slight re-wording of this question and its re-location at the end of the final session.

DISCUSSION OF RESULTS

(i) Socio-group and Psyche-group

One test of Jennings' claim that there are, in a group, few common choices based upon social, common criteria and purely private criteria, may be made by examining the extent of overlap of socio-centers based upon the sociotelic and psychetelic questions quoted in the previous section. Upon examination of the distribution of choices based upon each question, it was found that their shapes suggested the normal curve and that six or more choices in each group of ten men would conveniently define a socio-center. Since the assumption of normality seemed justified and the criterion choice score determining a socio-center was so chosen as to divide the distributions near their medians, the tetrachoric correlation coefficient has been chosen as an adequate index of the relation between any pair of choices.

TABLE I

*Reliability Coefficients * for Sociometric Questions*

	SESSIONS COMPARED			
	20 OFFICER CANDIDATE GROUPS			10 STUDENT GROUPS
QUESTION	I–II	I–III	II–III	II–III
A. Sociotelic–Future working together	.45	.50	.66	.78
B.14. Psychetelic–Personal friends	0 †	0 †	.80	.78
B.6. Influence	.77	.64	.83	.78

* Tetrachoric coefficients with sectioning at the median.
† This question was not asked in session I since time had scarcely been sufficient to form judgments concerning the friend potentialities of members.

First, as an indication of the reliability of the sociometric test, choices indicated on the sociotelic and the psychetelic questions respectively, were compared from one session to another. In particular sessions two and three were chosen for this purpose on the assumption that by this time members had some knowledge of one another. (See Table 1.)

For the sociotelic question the tetrachoric correlation coefficient between sessions two and three was 0.78 ± .09 [3] for the ten student groups and 0.66 ± .075 for the twenty O. C. S. groups. Similarly choices made in response to the psychetelic question, concerning choice of personal friends, in the two sessions were corrected and the coefficients were 0.78 ± .09 for the student groups and 0.80 ± .06 for the O. C. S. groups.

Tetrachoric intercorrelation of choices for the psychetelic and sociotelic questions could not be calculated for session two with student groups since no persons were chosen on a psychetele basis who had not been chosen on a sociotele basis. In this session with the criterion mentioned, there were 75 socio-centers on a sociotele basis. There were but 34 socio-centers on a psychetele basis and every one of these was included among the sociotelic socio-centers. Using the notion of common elements (10) a

3 The figure given thus in each case is the standard error of the appropriate tetrachoric coefficient when both dichotomies are at the medians. Since some variation from median sectioning does occur this figure is approximate only.

coefficient may be estimated at 0.67. This situation was almost duplicated in the third session with student groups where there were 60 sociotelic socio-centers and 44 psychetelic socio-centers of which 38 were common. This situation gave a tetrachoric correlation coefficient of 0.70 ± .10. With the O. C. S. groups in session two r_{tet} for these two sets of socio-centers was again 0.70 ± .07 and in session three r_{tet} was 0.81 ± .05.

These two sets of data confirm Jennings' (9) claim that "the structures built by sociotele are in general larger in size (quantitatively 'take in' more individuals) than the structures built by psychetele." On the other hand, since the correlations between sociotele and psychetele choices are comparable with the "reliability" coefficients of the sociometric tests, it must be concluded that Jennings' claim of "very little overlap" is not confirmed.

The significance for this comparison of the temporary nature of the present groups is not known. It would be a reasonable guess that as individuals came to know each other in more detail there might be less overlap between sociotelic and psychetelic structures. But it is interesting that within the narrow confines of this study the degree of overlap *increased* between the second and third sessions, from 45 per cent to 50 per cent for students and from 50 per cent to 66 per cent for officer candidates.

In attempting any interpretation of these findings it must be remembered that these were relatively small homogeneous groups observed over the period of group formation. As group self-consciousness increased and the group members perceived the group as achieving something, positive group feeling increased and this may well be a common factor in determining both sociotele and psychetele choices. Further, preparedness to accept an individual as a personal friend on short acquaintance is different from the actual designation of friends after longer association. But it is difficult to assess the force of accidental situational factors and of opportunity in the long-term choice of friends, and consequently it is not possible to choose between these criteria in the determination of the overlap between socio-group and psyche-group. On the face of the evidence here presented, in temporary, traditionless groups, at least, there is considerable overlap between sociotele and psychetele choices. It would still be true as Jennings (9) contends that "the psychetele pattern of a social atom cannot be predicted from its sociotele pattern," though it might be anticipated that such prediction would be a possibility if the sociometric test could be modified to respond more sensitively to differences in degree of feeling.

(ii) Leadership and Sociometric Choice-Status

The primary concern of this study, however, is with the sociometric conception of leadership. Jennings (8) claims to have shown that prominence and choice status in the socio-group are a "reflection of demonstrated capacities to affect favorably the social milieu of the group." Choice status in the psyche-group is apparently less closely associated with behavior influencing the group but represents rather "capacities to 'accept' the milieu of the group" (9). In either case "leadership" and choice-status are indentified and the inverse of leadership is isolation. Jennings says those persons who are much chosen are leaders because they "count," because they "set the tone for the group in large measure." Some of them, she says, "may function chiefly as steadiers or moral support for the others, some may lead in ideas and activities, and some may be wanted on account of a special aptitude." And again (9) she writes, "While the varieties of styles of leadership (and of isolation) are many, nevertheless a number of characteristics of leader individuals stand out as common attributes. The social milieu is 'improved' from the point of view of the membership through the efforts of each other. Each widens the area of social participation for others (and indirectly his own social space) by his unique contribution to this milieu. Each leader seems to sense spontaneously when to censure and when to praise and apparently is intellectually and emotionally 'uncomfortable' when others are 'left out,' and acts to foster tolerance on the part of one member towards another." A footnote recognizes that other patterns of behavior are also found among leaders.

The point here is that, on this purely verbal level, Jennings' description appears to characterize leaders as defined in this paper as well as she claims it describes leaders by sociometric choice, i.e. socio-centers. As the writer interprets Jennings, she first meant that the much chosen individual, the socio-center, affected the group milieu because, by virtue of her choice position, she provided telic linkages with other group members. If one can think of direct and indirect influencing behavior, this would be relatively indirect. But Jennings also ascribes direct influencing to these socio-centers and thus suggests an hypothesis of some identity between them and leaders as rated by external observers using the definition of this paper. One may hypothesize also some identity between socio-centers derived from the sociotelic and psychetelic questions already examined and those derived from additional questions which imply influence and leadership criteria.

(A) LEADERSHIP RATINGS COMPARED WITH SOCIOTELIC AND PSYCHETELIC CHOICE

The first of these hypotheses has been examined by comparing sociotelic and psychetelic sociocentrality with leadership ratings for the sessions as a whole. These criterion ratings have been obtained by regarding as leaders only those group members who were "chosen" for leadership in a majority of situations in all sessions by both of the non-participant observers. Estimates of the reliability of these ratings have been made in two ways.

First, inter-observer correlations have been calculated session by session for each group. These have been found to be 0.92, 0.77, 0.74 for the student groups in successive sessions, and 0.60, 0.60 and 0.68 for the O. C. S. groups in corresponding sessions. Second, for O. C. S. groups observer identifications over the whole period have been correlated and a coefficient of 0.80 has been obtained. This latter figure is the best available estimate of the inter-observer consistency which constitutes "reliability" for this criterion rating. Again tetrachoric correlation has been used since the assumptions of normality of the traits are quite well met here.

TABLE 2

*Correlations * between Sociometric Choices and Leadership Ratings*

QUESTION	20 OFFICER CANDIDATE GROUPS SESSION			10 STUDENT GROUPS SESSION	
	I	II	III	II	III
A. Sociotelic—Future working together	.44	.40	.59	.20	.36
B.14. Psychetelic—Personal friends	0	.46	.45	.32	.41
B.6. Influence	.77	.80	.77	.88	.86
B.15. Leaders as judged by participants	0	0	.80	0	.75 †

* Tetrachoric coefficients.
† Construction situation only.

The correlations are as set out in Table 2. Between rating as a leader and sociotelic choice r_{tet} is found to be 0.20 ± .16 in session two and 0.36 ± .15 in session three for student groups; while for O. C. S. groups the corresponding values are 0.40 ± .10 and 0.59 ± .08. The suggestion, inherent here, that the coefficient tends to rise between the second and third sessions, may have very considerable significance for Jennings' contentions. While, at this stage of mutual knowledge, there is little similarity between sociotelic choices and leader ratings, it may be that the two become more alike as group members become more familiar with each other.

Correlations between psychetelic choice and leader ratings are found to be 0.32 ± .15 and 0.41 ± .14 for student groups in sessions two and three respectively. Again, the corresponding coefficients for the officer candidates are 0.46 ± .09 and 0.45 ± .09 respectively. The suggestion of increasing correspondence just noted for sociotelic choice is not present here for psychetele. Whether sociometric choices or ratings of leadership by non-participating observers most nearly indicate "true" leadership cannot be told; but it must be recognized that they are not, in this study at least, representing the same things.

(B) LEADERSHIP RATINGS COMPARED WITH SOCIOMETRIC "INFLUENCE" CHOICES

Further light on these facts is obtained from participants' responses to the "influence" question included in this investigation. As indicated earlier participants were asked a question designed to get at judgments of behavior influencing the group "milieu." This question was: "Some groups are so closely knit that the removal of any one person changes its complexion. For which persons, if any, in this group would this be the case?" After an examination of the distribution of identifications ("choices") on this question the socio-center criterion score was set at five choices or more rather than five plus, as it had been for the more directly sociometric questions. The nature of this question was evidently such as to encourage fewer identifications than did the two questions discussed above, in spite of the fact that an individual was himself available for identification on this question in a way that he could not normally be for the other questions.

The tetrachoric correlations between identifications on this milieu-influencing criterion and leadership ratings are, for student subjects 0.88 ± .06 in session two and 0.86 ± .06 in session three. Officer candidates yield coefficients of 0.80 ± .05 for session two and 0.77 ± .06 for session three. These coefficients are considerably and statistically significantly different from the values, given in sub-section (A) above, of the correlations between leadership ratings and sociotelic and psychetelic choices. This fact suggests that participants in a group do recognize and can identify those members who primarily determine group behavior and group atmosphere but they do not necessarily choose these persons to be members either of a socio-group or of a psyche-group.

(C) "INFLUENCE" IDENTIFICATIONS VERSUS SOCIOTELIC AND PSYCHETELIC CHOICES

Identifications based on the "influence" question have been correlated (tetrachoric) with sociotelic and psychetelic choices. For student data this analysis was made for the third session only. It is found that r_{tet} for the sociotelic choices and "influence" is 0.53 ± .13 and that for the psychetelic choices is 0.30 ± .15. For O. C. S. groups a more complete analysis was made and there tetrachoric coefficients for the sociotelic choices and influence identifications are 0.38 ± .10, 0.46 ± .09 and 0.65 ± .075 respectively for the three sessions. For psychetelic choices and influence identifications the coefficients are 0.54 ± .09 and 0.64 ± .075 for sessions two and three respectively. (See Table 3.)

The implication of these data would seem to be that in the minds of group members in a program of this nature socio-centers whether based upon sociotele or psychetele are not identified with those persons who are recognized as "counting" and as most affecting the group "milieu." Since in sub-section (B) above some evidence has been presented to suggest that participants responding to this "influence" question do identify "leaders" as they are identified by non-participating observers, the evidence of this section indicates that *socio-centers are not necessarily leaders.* Certainly these two concepts are not coincident.

On the other hand, the consistent tendency for these coefficients to increase as the period of association increases does suggest that there may be a tendency towards Jennings' notion that in a larger, well-established group, the sociotelic and psychetelic questions identify leaders well enough. This hypothesis gives rise to the question whether there may be found some systematic shift over these three sessions. (Do the leaders become the socio-centers or do the socio-centers become the leaders?) The

TABLE 3

Correlations between Sociotelic and Psychetelic Choices and Other Forms of Leader Identification

Identification	SOCIOTELIC QUESTION SESSION			PSYCHETELIC QUESTION SESSION		
A. STUDENT GROUPS	I	II	III	I	II	III
Observer ratings of leadership (overall)		.20	.36		.32	.41
"Influence" question			.53			.30
"Leaders" in construction			.25			.36
B. O.C.S. GROUPS						
Observer ratings of leadership (overall)	.44	.40	.59	*	.46	.45
"Influence" question in appropriate session	.38	.46	.65	*	.54	.64
Leaders in session III			.59			.65

data have been examined from this point of view and it is found that the tetrachoric "reliability" coefficients of the three questions concerned are as given in Table 1; and the respective correlations with leadership ratings are as given in Table 2.

These data suggest somewhat greater consistency for the "influence" question and indicate that this question identifies leaders earlier and more consistently than either sociotelic or psychetelic questions. One implication of the figures might be that the people who "count" by their influencing the group milieu tend to be chosen more readily as work companions (sociotele) when their influence is recognized and when the group settles down to working together in a more matter-of-fact way. Examining the several choices and identifications group by group suggests that the increasing coincidence is due largely to a general shrinkage of the number of socio-centers on sociotelic and psychetelic criteria, in which the "influencing" persons tended to retain their choice-status better than others. There is nothing here to suggest why this should have occurred, though one might hazard a guess that participants may have become increasingly aware of the experimental interest in leadership in the study and may have endeavored to make their own records "look better" by choosing only those whom they expected the observers would also choose on quite different criteria. In other words, there is a possibility that choices became less genuine. "Reliability" coefficients, however, offer no support to this hypothesis.

(D) LEADERSHIP JUDGMENTS OF PARTICIPANTS AND OBSERVERS

As already indicated, participants in the student groups were asked, at the conclusion of the construction situation in both the second and third sessions, whom they would judge to have been leaders in this situation.

The analysis of data derived from this question must begin by noting that in some 30 per cent of cases the respondents replied that there was no leadership. This may be contrasted with the fact that the observers never agreed that there was no leadership in the construction situation. However, when the remaining participants' recognition of leadership is correlated with observer ratings the coefficient obtained is 0.75 ± .10. Further the correlation in the third session between choices on this question and those on the sociotelic question was 0.25 ± .16 and with those on the psychetelic question was 0.36 ± .15. Considering the brevity of this one situation these figures are consistent with the finding (see Table 2) that these sociometric choices are correlated with the leadership ratings of observers, in the same situation, 0.36 and 0.41 respectively.

O. C. S. groups were asked, at the end of the third session, to identify the leaders for the whole session. Bearing in mind the leadership design of this session, which was to have one leader throughout, it is necessary to comment here that this never occurred in practice. Though there was this designation of an official leader, and thus, of the elements of an "official" influence structure, this was quickly forgotten in the course of the group's activities, and leadership was determined by the relation between group needs and individual ability, as much in this session as in either sessions one or two (cf. 4, 13). The distribution of "choices" on this question was such that five or more "choices" were taken as indicative of leader selection by participants. The corresponding criterion among the ratings was agreement between the two observers. With these criteria and for this session observers' identifications of leaders varied from two to seven in any one group, while participants identifications ranged between three and six. The tetrachoric correlation between the two sets of identifications is 0.80 ± .05.

For these groups, and for this third session, the correlation between the sociotelic question and the identification of leaders was 0.59 ± .11; and for the psychetelic question r_{tet} was 0.65 ± .10. In this case the comparison of these coefficients with the corresponding correlations with observer ratings, reveals that for sociotele the results are identical. For psychetele the association with participants' leader identifications is considerably closer than that with observer ratings.

In Table 3 have been drawn together the coefficients of correlation between the sociotelic and psychetelic questions and all the other identifications made in this study. Viewed in contrast with the last two rows of Table 2, this would suggest that "leadership" is not identified in the minds of participants with either socio-group choice or psyche-group choice and further question is cast upon this common sociometric identification. When asked simply to indicate leaders, without being given any definition of leadership for the purpose, participants did so with a fair degree of validity—.80 if observers' ratings can be regarded as a criterion of leadership. This would, in fact, tend to reinforce any argument that observers' ratings may be regarded as such a criterion and that socio-centers are not necessarily leaders.

(E) "STATUS-SCORES" AND LEADERSHIP RATINGS

Recently French and Eng (3) defined "status-scores" in terms of the number of choices received minus the number of rejections received on a sociometric test. Using these scores French and Eng found a number of significant correlations with leadership behavior. Since data was readily at hand in part of the present study to examine this status-score against a different, and rather more stable, criterion of observer ratings, this was done for student groups, for status-scores derived from the sociotelic question.

The distributions of status-scores, for both leaders and non-leaders, approximate normal, so that again tetrachoric correlation has been used as an estimate of the relation. The coefficient obtained has a value of 0.44 ± .14 which compares well with results reported by French and Eng for socio-group scores with such categories of behavior as dominance, generosity, fairness, purpose, etc. The present finding, however, but slightly favors these "status-scores" over the more usual "choices." The size of the correlation coefficient is still so small as to indicate that "status-scores" and leadership ratings have little variance in common.

(iii) The Value of First Impressions

(A) "FIRST IMPRESSION" AND PSYCHETELIC CHOICE

As indicated above sociometric questions were also asked after each specific situation was completed. The first situation of the first session was usually construction, but sometimes it was a situation known as "group judgment" in which the group was asked by discussion to derive answers to several questions of fact. In either case the situation took no more than fifteen minutes to complete, and these were, of course, the first fifteen minutes of acquaintance. At this stage participants were asked to indicate the two members of the group they liked most because of the kind of persons they appeared to be and also the two liked least. Since participants were, in general, previously unknown to one another, the responses to this question at this time must therefore have represented first, or very early, impressions. Consequently it has been of some interest to correlate these responses with the indication of willingness to choose friends within the group, made at the conclusion of the third session, that is after some ten hours of formal association, probably longer when casual meetings coming to the group and leaving the building are considered.

The relation between the two sets of responses has been estimated by tabulating friend choices and not-friend choices against most liked, not mentioned and least liked. Both of these distributions may be conceived as really normal. Therefore a tetrachoric correlation coefficient may be regarded as a more appropriate summarizing statement of the relation than a contingency coefficient would be. Thus the "not-mentioned" category has been thrown first to one side, then to the other, and two tetrachoric coefficients found.

For the 10 student groups these two coefficients agreed very closely, the one being 0.30 and the other 0.28. Since the number of judgments upon which this calculation is based is approximately 900, this is a highly significant value and is consistent with the value of $P < .001$ obtained by the chi square test.

The 20 O. C. S. groups give tetrachoric coefficients of 0.31 and 0.45 (average $r_{tet} = .38$) for the correlation between first impression and choice of friends. This again is highly significant.

The significance of these values does not mean, of course, that this correlation coefficient is high. It cannot be said that first impression is a close function of final willingness to choose friends or vice versa, but there is a considerable relation between them.

(B) "FIRST IMPRESSION" AND LEADERSHIP RATINGS

It is to be expected that these first impressions would bear less relation to leadership ratings than to friend choice since the latter was made by the same individuals on much the same criterion. Nevertheless, it was thought worthwhile to investigate the correlation between first impression and leadership rating. The procedure was exactly as for the previous comparison.

Chi square was again significant at or beyond the .001 level. Again, tetrachoric correlation has been used putting scores of the "not-mentioned" category first with "most liked" and then with "least liked." For student groups in the first case the coefficient given was 0.20 and in the second case 0.10. Regarding the mean of these as a summarizing coefficient the value is 0.15 which is significant at the .01 level. Corresponding values of the coefficient for O.C.S. groups were 0.10 and 0.25 respectively. The summarizing value in this instance is thus 0.17 which is again statistically significant.

These results indicate that there is no close relation between ultimate leadership in a small temporary group and making a favorable impression very early in the group's association. On the other hand, the correlation is significantly positive and thus suggests that something of leadership has already emerged when a first impression is recorded.

SUMMARY AND CONCLUSIONS

Small temporary traditionless groups, each of ten men, have been formed for the purposes of experimentation with factors associated with emerging leadership. Ten such groups were composed of male students at the University of Illinois and twenty of male O.C.S. cadets at Lackland Air Force Base. Among the many aspects of group and group-member behavior which has been observed and assessed by non-participant observers, ratings were made of the leadership behavior of each participant. These ratings have been based upon a definition of leadership as an inter-individual relation of influence, voluntarily accepted by the influenced person, in which leader and follower mutually stimulate one another and in which the relationship is not maintained beyond its mutual usefulness by a rigid social structure.

At the same time participants have completed a number of sociometric "tests" in which both sociotelic and psychetelic choices have been called for, among others specifically introduced here. Relations among these sociometric tests and between them and leadership ratings have been examined. Centrally, the relations between the sociometric definition of "leader," (or what has here been called "socio-center") and the "influence" definition employed in the observer ratings, and in two of the introduced sociometric devices, have been examined.

Both sociotelic and psychetelic types of sociometric test have a session two-session three reliability coefficient in the range 0.72 to 0.78, the psychetelic choices being rather more consistent. The introduced "influence" question had a reliability of approximately 0.80. Intercorrelation between sociotelic and psychetelic choices was approximately 0.70.

The correlation between sociotelic choice and leadership ratings is shown in Table 2 from which it may be seen that a value of approximately 0.45 will represent this relation. Similarly the correlation between psychetelic choice and leadership ratings may be said to be approximately 0.42. The implication is that these two concepts, while overlapping, are not identical.

When participants were asked a sociometric question which implied the "influence" criterion, correlation with observer ratings of leadership was approximately 0.80. And when participants were asked directly whom they regarded as having been leaders, the correlation with observer ratings was again 0.80. But this same question correlated only 0.25 and 0.36 with sociotelic and psychetelic choices respectively, for student groups; and 0.59 and 0.65 respectively for O.C.S. groups. Despite these slightly higher values for O.C.S. groups it seems safe to conclude that sociotelic and psychetelic choices are not identified in the minds of participants with leadership.

The correlation between leadership ratings and socio-group "status-scores," as defined by French and Eng, was examined in ten groups, and found to be 0.44. The indication is that these two have little variance in common and that these status-scores are not superior to sociotelic choices in their correlation with leader identification by external observers.

Another form of sociometric question has been used to study the value of first or early impressions. It was found that correlations between first impression and final willingness to choose as friends, and between first impression and leadership ratings, are so low as to indicate that there is no close relation between these. But the fact that these coefficients were significantly positive may suggest that something of the value one individual has in the eyes of another, which must partially determine his leadership status, is already evident at the stage of a first impression.

In drawing conclusions from this study, it must be remembered that these were temporary, artificial and traditionless groups; and that this quality alone may be sufficient to explain what differences there are between these findings and those of the sociometrists, particularly Jennings. Nevertheless, there can be little doubt but that real groups have been formed here and that data derived from them may have real significance in understanding the dynamics of more well-established groups. In a sense this has been a group embryological study which can illuminate the dynamics of formed groups much as embryology contributes to the study of anatomy and physiology.

Some of the sociometric findings are clearly confirmed. For example, it is clear that structures built by sociotele are more inclusive than those built by psychetele. On the other hand, the sociometric concept of leadership as roughly identical with sociocentrality is brought under fire. The evidence suggests that leadership defined in terms of influencing behavior cannot be measured by sociometric tests using either sociotelic or psychetelic criteria. The fact that participants (for whom leadership was not defined) identify "leaders" in a closely similar way to observers (for whom leadership was defined as a voluntary influencing relationship) indicates that this definition does no violence to common sense and that, in fact, this is the relation which is generally conceived as that of leadership. Further, the lower correlations between these identifications and the sociotelic and psychetelic choices is indication enough that, in the minds of these participants, they were not choosing leaders in making those choices.

An additional fact is that participants in responding to a question, in which the influence criterion is implied, but not stated and in which the notion of leadership is not introduced, did identify leaders much as did external observers. The implication of this fact is that the sociometric technique is applicable to the identification of leaders but that sociotele and psychetele are not adequate criteria.

Finally, and in summary, it may be said that participants in such groups as these understand the relation of leadership and that if adequately questioned they can identify leaders in the group with both reliability and validity.

REFERENCES

1. Anderson, H. H. Domination and integration in the social behavior of young children in an experimental play situation. *Genet. Psychol. Monogr.* 1937, 19, 343–408.
2. Cowley, W. H. Three distinctions in the study of leaders. *J. abnorm. soc. Psychol.* 1928, 23, 144–157.
3. French, R. L., & Eng. Value categories differentiating leaders and isolates in adolescent boys' groups. Paper read at Midwestern Branch of A. P. A. meetings in Chicago, 1949.
4. Gibb, C. A. Principles and traits of leadership. *J. abnorm. soc. Psychol.* 1947, 42, 267–284.
5. Gibb, C. A. The emergence of leadership in small temporary groups of men. *Ph.D. Thesis Univer. of Illinois*, 1949.
6. Guetzkow, H. *University of Michigan Conference Research Report.* April 1948.
7. Jennings, Helen H. *Leadership and isolation.* (1st Ed.) New York: Longmans, Green, 1943.
8. Jennings, Helen H. Leadership and sociometric choice. In Newcomb & Hartley (Eds). *Readings in social psychology.* New York: Holt, 1943.
9. Jennings, Helen H. Sociometry of leadership. Beacon House, 1947. *Sociometry Monogr.* No. 14.
10. McNemar, Q. *Psychological statistics.* New York: Wiley, 1949.
11. Moreno, J. L. *Who shall survive?* Washington, D.C.: Nervous & Mental Disease Publishing Co., 1934.
12. Pigors, P. *Leadership or domination.* London: Harrap, 1935.
13. Sherif, F. *An Outline of social psychology.* New York: Harper, 1948.
14. Stewart, J. C. & Scott, J. P. Lack of correlation between leadership and dominance in a herd of goats. *J. comp. physiol. Psychol.* 1947, 40, 255–264.

Sharing Leadership in Small, Decision-Making Groups

LEONARD BERKOWITZ

SOCIAL scientists engaged in research in the area of leadership have approached the exceedingly complex problems in this area from many different directions. The personalities of the leaders (2) and of the followers (12) have been investigated, as have the behavioral characteristics of elected or sociometrically chosen leaders (8) and of institutionalized or designated leaders (13). But despite the approach used, as Katz indicates (9), the present trend is to emphasize the relational aspects between the leader and his group. The characteristics of the leader, whether personality-wise or behavioral, become significant only in terms of the leader's group. A leader's behavior, thus, may or may not satisfy the needs of the group, and a group member's behavior may or may not be in conformity with the traditions of his group.

In this sense, training in "democratic" leadership may not benefit the leaders of certain groups, particularly if those groups have learned to expect and adjust to, or even require, more "authoritarian" leadership practices. "Democratic" leadership may affect the group adversely (for example, in terms of criteria such as satisfaction with the group meeting) because it is not in keeping with the group's needs and expectations. The present study does not test the efficacy of "democratic" groups as contrasted with "authoritarian" groups. However, one aspect of "democracy"

FROM *Journal of Abnormal and Social Psychology*, 1953, 48, 231–238. Reprinted by permission of the author and the American Psychological Association, Inc.

This study is part of a larger series of investigations undertaken by the Conference Research project at the University of Michigan. Thanks are due to the project staff, and to Drs. R. W. Heyns and H. Guetzkow in particular, without whom this study would not have been possible, and to Dr. Daniel Katz and the members of my doctoral committee for their helpful suggestions. An overview of some of the general findings of the project is presented elsewhere (11). The full data upon which this report is based are to be found in the author's dissertation, Some Effects of Leadership Sharing in Small, Decision-Making Conference Groups, 1951, University of Michigan Library, and in the reports of the Conference Research project (1).

in groups may be described in terms of leadership sharing. We may define a "democratic" group as one in which many members may influence the group in the course of its goal setting and goal achievement. French has pointed out (5) that many conditions may intervene to affect the relationship between group "democracy" and criteria of group effectiveness. One such condition may have to do with the expectations of the groups.

Very broadly, then, this is the problem with which we are presently concerned. What happens when the functions of the institutionalized or designated leader are shared by others in the group?

METHOD

The present study is based on the methodology and many of the hypotheses developed by the Conference Research project. The most extensive study undertaken by the project was a field observation of 72 conferences in government and industry. The present report is concerned with a small part of the data collected in the course of this study.

The Data

Of the 72 conference groups in the sample, 42 were industrial in nature, i.e., they were conference groups in organizations devoted to manufacturing. Fourteen were business groups from organizations engaged in retailing, banking, newspaper publishing, and hotel enterprises. The remaining 16 came from federal and local governmental organizations. The size of the groups ranged from 5 to 17 members with a mean of 9 members, and the duration of the conferences was from 16 to 191 minutes. Many of these groups, furthermore, were composed of members having high status in their organizations. Of particular relevance to the present study is the chairman's status relative to the mean status of the group as measured by distance on the organizational chart from the head of the organization. Only 9 of the chairmen are at or below the mean level of the group; the great majority of the 72 chairmen are thus above the mean of the group in organizational status. Lastly, the sample of conferences was restricted to those primarily decision-making in nature.

Methods of Data Collection

Three observers, each with a specific area of interest, were present at all the meetings. The independent measures used in the present study were largely obtained from the records of one of these observers. The task of this individual, the "problem-solving coder," was to code the remarks of the participants according to the problem-solving category system developed by Heyns (7). In essence, the observer noted every participation—the total speech of an individual from the time he started to speak until the next person spoke—breaking each down into the categories it included.

Upon the completion of the meeting, each conference member was given a five-item questionnaire attempting to assess his satisfaction with various aspects of the meeting. Some of these ratings, all highly intercorrelated, were later averaged to form a measure of the group's satisfaction with the conference. After these ratings were collected–but before they were examined–the observers left the meeting room and immediately made a series of 54 ratings describing the interactions among the conference participants. The final source of data came from interviews with the participants within 48 hours after the meeting. Among other things, the data gathered at this time had to do with the members' perceptions concerning the interactions within the group.

The Measures

In general, the functions or behaviors going to make up the role of the conference chairmen are behaviors either directly influencing the group to follow him or behaviors facilitating this influence. Previous exploratory work carried out by the project led to the development of hypotheses as to what some of these behaviors might be, and measures of these were used as the independent variables in the present study. The meaning of these variables is twofold. In a sense they are two sides of the same coin. The variables have to do with the extent to which conference leadership is shared by members other than the designated leader, the chairman. When the chairman is said to be firmly in control over the group's procedure, it is also implied that there are few other group members attempting to influence the course of the meeting. Again, the greater the proportion of solution proposing contributed by the other conference members the smaller the proportion of all the solution proposing accounted for by the chairman. The independent variables are as follows:

1. *Leader Control of Process*–postmeeting observer rating. This item refers to the leader's control over the *manner* in which the group went about handling its problems, and not the content of the problems.

2. *Leader Permissiveness in Content*–postmeeting observer rating. This measure is a rating of the designated leader's restrictiveness in the area of the *content* of the group's problems.

3. *Functional Differentiation of the Leader*–postmeeting observer rating. This has to do with whether or not the conference chairman behaved differently from the other group members by performing somewhat unique functions. A separate analysis has revealed that there were generally two or more behavioral leaders among the group members when the chairman was rated low on this item. Thus, the more the designated leader was differentiated from the others, the more the leadership functions were centered in him alone.

4. *Percentage of Member Participation*–observer tally made during the meeting. This is the percentage of all the participation in the group that was accounted for by the members other than the chairman.

5. *Percentage of Functional Units to the Leader*–observer tally made during the meeting. Within each participation a group member may perform several different functions: he may propose a solution to the group's problems (solution proposing), develop and enlarge upon the solution (development giving), and seek further comments from the others (development seeking). Furthermore, each of these functional units may be directed to a different member.

This, then, is the proportion of the total number of functional units contributed by the group members which were directed to the chairman.

The following 3 variables have to do with the functional units or categories within the participations. In computing the following scores we used the proportion of all the units within any one category that were accounted for by the members other than the chairman.

6. *Percentage of Goal Setting by Members.*
7. *Percentage of Solution Proposing by Members.*
8. *Percentage of Summarizing by Members.*

Three of the dependent measures used in the Conference Research field study are employed here. They are designed to assess some of the more important outcomes of conferences: the cohesiveness of the group, the members' satisfaction with their meeting, and the productivity of the meeting.

1. *Cohesiveness.* The series of experiments carried out by the Research Center for Group Dynamics (3, 4) have demonstrated the theoretical importance of this construct. The present definition is the sum of five highly interrelated observer ratings of the attractiveness of the group situation, e.g., the pleasantness of the group atmosphere, the degree of personal liking, etc.

2. *Satisfaction with the Conference.* This is a mean of five highly interrelated ratings made by the conference participants at the conclusion of their meeting or shortly thereafter. These include: satisfaction with the decisions arrived at, satisfaction with the leader, satisfaction with the group's process, etc.

3. *Productivity.* The operational definition of productivity is the proportion of agenda items completed of those brought up for consideration. This information was obtained from the tallies made by one of the observers in the course of the meeting.

RESULTS

Relationships Over All Groups in the Sample

Table 1 reveals the correlations between the measures of leadership sharing and the three criteria. The results with the group's satisfaction with its meeting are fairly clean cut. The more the chairman is the sole major behavioral leader the more satisfied the group with its conference. This can be seen in the following correlations. Satisfaction increases: the more the chairman controls the group's process, the more functionally differentiated he is, and the greater the proportion of functional units addressed to him. Satisfaction also increased the less the members participate relative to all the participating done in the group, and the less they do of all the solution proposing done in the group.

But although the conference groups in the present sample tend to be less satisfied when leadership is shared—when others besides the chairman perform leadership functions—it appears that productivity does not suffer. The indices of leadership sharing bear no relation to the proportion of agenda items completed of those considered.

The only leadership measure significantly related to the ratings of cohesiveness was the rating of the leader's permissiveness in the area of the content of the group's problems. The more permissive the leader the higher the rating of group cohesiveness. Just as good a case may be made for saying that permissiveness produces cohesiveness as for saying that cohesiveness gives rise to permissiveness. It is likely that both are correct, that allowing the group freedom to express opinions can both result from and enhance the attractiveness of the group situation.

TABLE I

Correlations between Criteria and Measures of Leadership Sharing for All 72 Groups

MEASURE	COHESIVENESS	SATISFACTION WITH CONFERENCE	PRODUCTIVITY
Leader control of procedure	.04	.29 *	—.09
Leader permissiveness in content	.57 **	—.04	.05
Functional differentiation of leader	.15	.33 **	—.04
% Participation by members	—.17	—.38 **	—.20
% Functional units to leader	.10	.31 **	.13
% Goal setting by members	—.02	—.23	.06
% Solution proposing by members	.01	—.30 **	—.15
% Summarizing by members	—.24	—.18	—.03

* Significant at the 5% level of confidence.
** Significant at the 1% level of confidence.

The Effects of Situational Factors

It is not possible to go into all of the additional "breakdowns" carried out to test the effects of situational conditions upon the above relationships. For example, they suggested that there are "negative reactions"—lowered cohesiveness and satisfaction—to leadership sharing in both more and less permissively led groups.

Although there is more sharing of the leadership functions in the more permissive situations, the chairman's control of process, the extent to which he is functionally differentiated from the others in the group and the percentage of units addressed to him tend to be positively correlated (statistically significant or almost so) with cohesiveness and member satisfaction in both the more permissively led and the less permissively led groups. Similarly, the proportion of all the participations in the group accounted for by members is related to decreased cohesiveness and satisfaction under both types of conditions. This is shown in Table 2.

It should be pointed out that though the results indicate that the present groups want behavioral control by the socially recognized conference

TABLE 2

Correlations between Criteria and Measures of Leadership Sharing for Groups Contrasted on the Chairman's Permissiveness in the Content of the Group's Problems

MEASURE	*N*		COHESIVENESS		SATIS. WITH CONF.		PRODUCTIVITY	
	HI PERM.	LO PERM.	HI PERM.	LO PERM.	HI PERM.	LO PERM.	HI PERM.	LO PERM.
Leader control of process	39	33	.38 *	.21	.44 **	.18	.08	—.22
Functional differentiation of leader	39	33	.37 *	.24	.49 **	.18	.14	—.18
% Participation by members	39	33	—.43 **	—.29	—.35 *	—.46 **	—.23	—.25
% Functional units to leader	39	33	.27	.22	.27	.37 *	.15	.17
% Goal setting by members	37	32	—.14	—.16	—.14	—.38 *	.12	—.05
% Solution proposing by members	39	33	—.39 *	.02	—.18	—.47 **	—.17	—.23
% Summarizing by members	30	23	—.06	—.30	.03	—.38	.11	—.14

* Significant at the 5% level of confidence. ** Significant at the 1% level of confidence.

leader, they do not indicate that they want substantive control over what should or should not be said.

An attempt was made to determine whether the negative effects of sharing could be attributed to those groups having an opposing relationship with the chairman. That is, is the lessened satisfaction due to the fact that the sharing may be done in opposition to the chairman?

The 72 groups in the study were subdivided into three categories. (*a*) Those groups having no consistent leadership sharers, as indicated by a high rating on the continuum of functional differentiation of the chairman. There is evidence indicating that there were more emergent leaders the lower the rating of designated leader differentiation. (*b*) Those groups having a somewhat lower rating on the differentiation of the chairman scale, but who appeared to be in a positive, supporting relationship with the chairman. These are termed the *positive-sharing* groups. (*c*) Those groups having consistent leadership sharers, but who were in less of a supporting relationship with the chairman. These groups are termed the *negative-sharing* groups.

The positive-sharing groups were differentiated from the negative-sharing groups on the basis of the ratio of supporting to supporting-plus-opposing interchanges with the chairman. It was reasoned that this proportion of supporting remarks to and from the chairman could serve as an indication of the extent of the group's supporting relationship with the chairman. Those groups having a higher proportion of supporting interchanges are more likely to be in a positive, supporting relationship with the chairman.

Several conclusions may be drawn from the correlations shown in Table 3. We can organize them in terms of the relationships with the criteria. But what seems to be generally indicated by the results is that there is little evidence that the type of relationship with the chairman is of primary significance in determining the correlation between the measures of sharing and the criteria.

1. Cohesiveness.

a. The leader's permissiveness in the content of the group's problems is positively related to the rating of group cohesion in the less supporting, negative-sharing group as well as in the more supporting, no-sharing and positive-sharing groups.

b. Despite the general supporting relationship with the chairman in the positive-sharing groups, the group attractiveness tends to decrease the more the members participate relative to the chairman and the less they address their remarks to the chairman.

2. Satisfaction with the conference.

a. The greater the proportion of the total number of participations accounted for by the members other than the chairman, and the less clearly the chairman is the major behavioral leader by being functionally

TABLE 3

Correlations between the Criteria and Measures of Leadership Sharing for the Three Kinds of Sharing Groups

MEASURE	KIND OF GROUP	COHESIVENESS	SATISFACTION WITH THE CONFERENCE	PRODUCTIVITY
Leader control of process	o sharing	.02	.12	—.13
	+ sharing	—.10	.32	.17
	— sharing	.31	.22	—.10
Leader permissiveness in content	o sharing	.64 **	.03	.11
	+ sharing	.43	—.12	.02
	— sharing	.59 **	.01	—.06
Functional differentiation of leader	o sharing	—.36	.13	—.08
	+ sharing	.29	.54 *	.41
	— sharing	.52 *	.20	—.06
% Participation by members	o sharing	—.14	—.15	—.15
	+ sharing	—.54 **	—.47 *	—.42
	— sharing	—.24	—.59 **	—.33
% Functional Units to leader	o sharing	—.13	.12	.01
	+ sharing	.50 *	.31	.30
	— sharing	.22	.58 **	.52 *
% Goal setting by members	o sharing	.14	—.05	—.32
	+ sharing	—.25	—.15	.24
	— sharing	—.13	—.31	—.18
% Solution proposing by members	o sharing	.03	—.45 *	—.35
	+ sharing	—.32	—.04	—.09
	— sharing	.12	—.25	—.31
% Summarizing by members	o sharing	—.22	—.36	—.09
	+ sharing	.02	—.16	—.15
	— sharing	—.48 *	—.02	—.23

* Significant at the 5% level of confidence.
** Significant at the 1% level of confidence.

differentiated from the rest of the group the less the group's satisfaction in the more supporting positive-sharing groups.

In general, then, the indications are that cohesiveness and member satisfaction may be lessened by leadership sharing even though the group is in a supporting relationship with its designated leader, the chairman.

Correlations with the Sharing Measures in Groups Contrasted on the Urgency of Their Problems

Unlike the correlations in the groups contrasted on the permissiveness of the leader, and the relationship between the group and its leader, there is evidence that the urgency of the group's problems may affect the reactions to the sharing of leadership. The groups in the present sample were "broken down" into groups with more and less urgent problems, depending upon the mean of the members' ratings on this scale. Judging from the correlations (not given here) with the urgency scale, we might characterize the groups with urgent problems as being more motivated, and with this motivation focused on the reaching of definite problem decisions. There is also a tendency for these groups to have greater interdependence among the members.

The correlations shown in Table 4 fairly clearly indicate differences in relationships with the sharing measures in the more and less urgent situations. For one thing, the results suggest that the designated leader's control over the group and his being functionally differentiated from the rest of the group are related to group cohesiveness and satisfaction only when the problems confronting the group are not pressing ones. These correlations are significantly different from the *r*'s in the more urgent situations. The percentage of all the participations accounted for by the members is negatively related to cohesiveness and satisfaction in only the less urgent situations, but the differences in correlation are not significant.

It is also interesting to note that the relationships with the percentage of all the solution proposing accounted for by the members vary depending upon the urgency of the group's problems. This measure is *negatively* related to cohesiveness and member satisfaction in the less urgent situations, but *positively* related to cohesiveness in the more urgent situations. This difference is statistically significant. Last, the chairman's permissiveness is positively related to the cohesiveness of the group only in the more urgent situations. This difference in correlations is also statistically significant.

DISCUSSION

Over all groups in the present population and in several different situations, leadership sharing is associated with lessened group cohesion and lessened satisfaction with the conference. Although we have no direct evidence on this matter, these results would appear to suggest that the present groups have an expectation maintaining that the designated leader, the chairman, is to be the major behavioral leader in the group. Group members performing leadership functions are then reacted to negatively if their behavior is seen as challenging the position of the chairman as the group's major behavioral leader. This hypothesis does not deny that there may be other causes for negative reactions to the sharing of leadership functions; members perform these functions when they attempt to influence the group, and the group may not agree that the influence attempt is in the proper direction. However, if there is the tradition we have hypothesized, it will tend to act like any social norm and nonconformists will be rejected.

Other investigations undertaken by the Conference Research project lend some support to this *post hoc* hypothesis. One of these was an interview study of executives in 75 business and governmental organizations; the other was an experiment carried out at the University of Michigan. One of the conclusions from the interviews was stated as follows: "Most

TABLE 4

Correlations between the Criteria and Measures of Leadership Sharing in Groups Contrasted on the Urgency of Their Problems

MEASURE	*N*		COHESIVENESS		SATIS. WITH CONF.		PRODUCTIVITY	
	HI URG	LO URG	HI URG	LO URG	HI URG	LO URG	HI URG	LO URG
Leader control of process	35	37	—.27	.34	—.04	.59 **	—.17	—.23
Leader permissiveness in content	35	37	.79 **†	.26	.12	—.19	.17	.05
Functional differentiation of leader	35	37	.02	.32	.06	.68 **†	—.16	.09
% Participation by members	35	37	—.01	—.34 *	—.26	—.51 **	—.05	—.30
% Functional units to leader	35	37	.06	.15	.31	.32	.09	.17
% Goal setting by members	33	36	—.00	—.02	—.02	—.22	.02	.11
% Solution proposing by members	35	37	.30	—.37 *†	—.17	—.39 *	—.00	—.18
% Summarizing by members	27	27	—.26	—.23	—.18	—.36	—.20	.11

* Significant at the 5% level of confidence.
** Significant at the 1% level of confidence.
† Correlation significantly different from other correlations at the 1% level of confidence.

of the executives felt that what occurs in a conference is primarily the responsibility of the leader. When asked what they thought were the important factors in obtaining a successful conference, 86 per cent of their replies were in terms of factors which ordinarily are controlled by the leader before the conference begins" (10, p. 16). Few executives considered motivational factors. "The paucity of comment on this score clearly reflects the executive's conception of conferences as serving only his administrative needs" (10, p. 16). We may readily infer from this that the present population of groups can be characterized as having customary leader control and leader dominance.

Results from the experiment mentioned above also suggest a fairly widespread tradition concerning the role of the conference chairman. If there is such a tradition, one that has the properties of a group norm, we might predict that violators of the tradition would tend to be rejected by the group. There is evidence on this point in the experiment conducted by Heyns (6).

Heyns set up two divergent leadership styles: "positive" and "negative" leadership. The "positive" leader performed functions related to group maintenance and goal attainment while the "negative" leader not only failed to perform these functions, but attempted "to create the impression that one part of the group was working at cross purposes with other parts." The obtained correlations suggest, in part, that when the designated leader does perform leading functions, performance of these behaviors by members other than the leader tends to result in these members being rated by the group less acceptable both as a person and as a participant. However, when the leader is inactive and nonhelpful, "responsibility for behaviors which are accepted as leader behaviors tends to make one perceive unity and feel accepted both as a person and as a participant" (6, p. 115). In other words, those members who acted like leaders when the designated leader performed his functions tended to be rejected, while they were not rejected when the designated leader failed to perform the functions associated with his role.

In the two populations considered, then, college students in experimental situations and executives in business, government, and industry, the groups behaved *as if* they wanted the designated leader to be the sole major behavioral leader. In somewhat different terms, they may have expected a role differentiation with the chairman's role being clearly differentiated from the members' roles. The conditions under which the field study and experiment were conducted suggest a possible limiting condition for this expectation. In both cases the designated leaders were clearly of a higher status level than the majority of the group members. (The departmental chairman was the leader of the experimental groups.) Desire to maintain this hierarchical structure—not to have rivalry with the high status leader—may thus account for the present results.

The evidence reported in this paper also suggests two types of conditions that may affect the group's reactions to violations of this expectancy. In the Heyns' experiment there are indications that the hypothesized group tradition becomes less important when the designated leader does not perform the functions associated with his role. The members who attempt to fill the "gap" left by the chairman are not rejected by the group.

This expectancy may also be less important when there are urgent problems confronting the group, according to the results of the field study presented above. It will be recalled that cohesiveness and satisfaction tend to decrease the less differentiated the chairman is from the other group members, the more the members participate relative to the chairman, and the less the chairman controls the group's process—but only when the group's problems are not too urgent. On the other hand, there are positive relationships with the permissiveness of the leader and the percentage of all the solution proposing done by the members when the group's problems are relatively urgent. The group's motivation to reach a problem solution as quickly as possible thus appears to be stronger than its motivation to conform to the expectancies concerning role differentiation. Not only does leadership sharing fail to lessen cohesiveness and member satisfaction in the more urgent conditions, but the leader's permissiveness and the proposing of solutions by the members tends to make for more attractive group situations.

The present results point up the necessity of considering the relational aspects of leadership. In the present case, the effects of leadership sharing cannot be fully understood without taking into consideration the relationship between this sharing and the expectancies and motivations of the group.

SUMMARY

Seventy-two groups of small decision-making conferences in business, industry, and government were studied by a team of observers. The conference participants filled out a brief questionnaire upon the completion of the meeting and were later interviewed. Correlational analysis was applied to the data obtained from the observers and the conference participants. The following hypotheses were developed to explain the results:

1. There is a general expectation in the present population of groups maintaining that the socially designated leader, the chairman, should be the sole major behavioral leader. In other words, there appears to be an expectancy of role differentiation between the designated leader and the group members with each performing somewhat unique functions.

a. Leadership sharing by members other than the designated leader tends to be related to a decrease in group cohesiveness and satisfaction with the meeting over the entire sample of groups, and in groups with more and less permissive leaders.

b. These results also hold in groups contrasted on whether the leadership sharing is generally supporting or less supporting of the chairman.

2. Leadership sharing is not generally reacted to negatively in groups with urgent problems. It may be that the group's motivation to reach an adequate problem solution as quickly as possible lessens the importance of the hypothesized group tradition.

Some other investigations undertaken by the Conference Research project are cited to support the hypothesis of an expectancy of role differentiation in the present population.

REFERENCES

1. Conference Research project. Dittoed reports, University of Michigan, 1948–1951.
2. Cowley, W. H. Traits of face-to-face leaders. *J. abnorm. soc. Psychol.*, 1931, 5, 304–313.
3. Festinger, L., *et al. Theory and experiment in social communication.* Ann Arbor, Michigan: Univer. of Michigan Press, 1950.
4. French, J. R. P., Jr. Organized and unorganized groups under fear and frustration. *On authority and frustration: Studies in topological and vector phychology.* III. Iowa City: State Univer. of Iowa, 1944.
5. French, R. L. Leadership and the authoritarian-democratic dimension. Paper read at Amer. Psychol. Ass., State College, Pa., September, 1950.
6. Heyns, R. W. Effects of variation in leadership on participant behavior in discussion groups. Unpublished doctoral dissertation, Univer. of Michigan, 1948.
7. Heyns, R. W. Functional analysis of group problem-solving. Dittoed report Conference Research, Univer. of Michigan, 1948.
8. Jennings, H. In T. M. Newcomb and E. L. Hartley (Eds.), *Readings in social psychology*. New York: 1947. Pp. 407–412.
9. Katz, D. Social psychology and group processes. In C. P. Stone (Ed.), *Annual review of psychology*. Vol. II. Stanford: Annual Reviews, 1951. Pp. 137–142.
10. Kriesberg, M. Executives evaluate administrative conferences. *Advanced Management*, March, 1950, 15–17.
11. Marquis, D. G., Guetzkow, H., Heyns, R. W. A social psychological study of the decision-making conference. In H. Guetzkow (Ed.), *Groups, leadership and men*. Pittsburgh: Carnegie Press, 1951. Pp. 55–67.
12. Sanford, F. H. *Authoritarianism and leadership*. Philadelphia: Institute for Research in Human Relations, 1950.
13. Shartle, C. L. Leadership and executive performance. *Personnel*, March, 1949, 370–380.

Small Group Discussions with Participatory and Supervisory Leadership

A. PAUL HARE

THE PURPOSE of this research was to repeat with a different age-group an experiment by Preston and Heintz (2) which showed that participatory leadership was more effective than supervisory leadership as a technique in producing change of opinion in small discussion groups of college students.[1]

METHOD

A number of troops of Boy Scouts in a summer camp were told a story about a camping trip which would require each boy to travel alone through unknown country. They were then asked to rank 10 items of camping equipment in the order of their importance for such a trip. Next the troops were divided into groups of a leader and five followers for a 20-minute discussion period during which each leader recorded his group's decision concerning the importance of the items of camping equipment. Just before the discussions the leaders were taken aside and given instructions for participatory or supervisory leadership. After the discussions each individual ranked the equipment again and recorded his reactions to the discussion and to the leader on a questionnaire.

In addition to computing the rank-order correlations used by Preston and

FROM *Journal of Abnormal and Social Psychology*, 1953, 48, 273–275. Reprinted by permission of the author and the American Psychological Association, Inc.

Abstracted from Hare, A. P. A study of interaction and consensus in different sized discussion groups. Unpublished doctor's dissertation, University of Chicago, 1951. Pp. 144–168.

1 The writer is indebted to Professor Preston for suggesting this research and for providing material and advice in the early stages of the experiment.

Heintz, within each group the average correlation of all rank orders, r_{av}, was computed before and after discussion (3, pp. 372–375).

The questionnaire was modified so that instead of reporting on influence, satisfaction, etc., the Scouts were asked to report good and bad things about the leadership and to describe what they would have done if they had been the leader.

Subjects

The subjects (*S*s) were Boy Scouts who attended a Philadelphia Scout Camp during the summer of 1949. Since the Scouts usually came to camp with their home troops the members of all but one of the discussion groups knew each other the year round. The average age of the followers was 13 years. The leaders, boys from the same troop who had had some leadership experience, averaged 14 years.

A Nonrandom Factor in the Sample

For each group led by a supervisory leader there was not always another group from the same troop led by a participatory leader. As a result, 6 pairs of the groups in the sample were matched and 3 were unmatched; that is, they came from different troops. When the amount of change in opinion ($\bar{r}_{av}$ before–$\bar{r}_{av}$ after) was compared for the matched and unmatched groups a significant difference was found,[2] indicating a greater similarity in the amount of change in consensus when the supervisory and participatory groups come from the same Scout troops than when they come from different troops.

TABLE 1

Average Correlation of All Rank Orders for Followers before and after Discussion

LEADER TYPE	NUMBER OF GROUPS	$\bar{r}_{av}$ BEFORE	$\bar{r}_{av}$ AFTER	*Diff*	*t*	*p*
Supervisory	9	.28	.65	.37	4.18	$<.01$
Participatory	9	.27	.81	.54 *	3.85	$<.01$

* This value for the difference between the $\bar{r}_{av}$ before and after discussion is similar to that obtained in an experiment by the *E* (1) in another camp using participatory groups of the same size.

RESULTS

A comparison of the means of the average correlation of all rank orders ($\bar{r}_{av}$) before and after discussion indicates that there is a significant change in the amount of agreement in each type of group as a result of the discussion (Table 1). Furthermore, the amount of change in the participatory groups (.54) is greater than the amount of change in the supervisory

2 In this experiment a result is considered significant if it has a probability of $<.10$ of occurring by chance.

groups (.37), although the difference is not significant, having a probability of >.30 of occurring by chance.

The resemblance between the initial and group ranking, $\bar{r}'_{12}$ (Table 2), is higher in every case than that reported by Preston and Heintz, suggesting that there is more initial agreement among Boy Scouts concerning camping equipment than among college students concerning the desirability of presidential candidates.

The average correlation of the group and final ranking, $\bar{r}'_{23}$, is also higher in every case than the corresponding correlation obtained by Preston and Heintz with the participatory followers showing significantly more agreement with the group ranking than the supervisory followers.

TABLE 2

Rank Correlations as a Function of Leadership Techniques and the Role of the Individual

SUBJECTS	N	$\bar{r}'_{12}$	$\bar{r}'_{23}$	$\bar{r}'_{13}$
Leaders				
Supervisory	9	.50	.80	.72
Participatory	9	.77	.98	.78
Followers				
Supervisory	36	.55	.86	.61
Participatory	36	.56	.96	.60

The participatory leaders have a significantly higher correlation for r'_{12} than do either the supervisory leaders or participatory followers, which, when combined with a high r'_{23} and r'_{13}, suggests that they influenced the group decision. This result, which is not obtained by Preston and Heintz, is, however, consistent with the way the discussions were conducted. Most of the Boy Scouts participating in this experiment were very interested in the subject for discussion. (In some cases the arguments touched off by the "camping game" continued for several days.) For this reason, the participatory leaders were generally anxious to give their views as well as to insure an equal chance for everyone else. On the other hand, the supervisory leaders who were specifically told to stay out of the discussion had little chance to influence the group. They tend to have the least agreement with the group ranking after discussion as well as a high degree of consistency between their initial and final rankings.

The data in Table 3 supplement those given in Table 1 by providing another measure of the change in opinion which results from the two types of leadership. In every case the difference between the $\bar{r}'_{13}$ and $\bar{r}'_{23}$ is negative, indicating that the correlation between the initial and final rankings is smaller than the correlation between the group and final rankings. The difference is significant for all but the supervisory leaders. This suggests that each of the other three types of group members tends to be influenced more by the group ranking than by his initial ranking. Participatory leaders and followers show relatively more agreement with the group ranking than do the supervisory leaders and followers. Both the r_{av} and the r' data tend to substantiate the finding of Preston and Heintz that group activity under participatory leadership is more productive of change of opinion.

TABLE 3

Correlation between Group and Final Rankings Compared with Correlation between Initial and Final Rankings

SUBJECTS	$\bar{r}'_{13}-\bar{r}'_{23}$ *	t	df	p
Leaders				
Supervisory	−.20	−.52	16	>.50
Participatory	−.95	−3.93	16	<.01
Followers				
Supervisory	−.52	−3.93	70	<.01
Participatory	−.96	−6.55	70	<.01

* Differences are the equivalents of differences in z functions.

Questionnaire Responses

A summary of the responses to the questionnaire given after the final ranking indicates that participatory *S*s are generally better satisfied with the decision made by their group than are the supervisory *S*s. The differences between leaders and followers of each type, while not significant, are consistent with the findings of Preston and Heintz.

On the three 160-mm. linear rating scales all subgroups rate their group discussions as generally friendly and enjoyable, as interested in the task, and as efficient and productive. Although Preston and Heintz report statistically significant differences in the responses in the direction of more enjoyable, interesting, and efficient discussion in the participatory groups, a series of t tests reveals no significant differences in the present experiment. The fact that differences are not reported may be due to a tendency for 13-year-old boys to withhold unfavorable comments about their peers from an adult experimenter. This same tendency toward a positive report is evident in the responses to open-end questions included to provide some descriptive data about the effects of the two types of leadership style. No matter what the leader style, the boys tried to say something good about it.

SUMMARY

When 13-year-old boys were used as *S*s in an experiment which compared the effects of supervisory and participatory leadership on group judgment in discussion groups of five members, the results generally substantiated the findings of a similar experiment using college-age *S*s. The data indicated that participatory leadership was more effective than supervisory leadership as a technique for changing opinion. In addition, the participatory leader generally had more influence on the group, a result not obtained with college *S*s. Although participatory *S*s were generally better satisfied with the results of the group decision than were the supervisory *S*s, the differences were not statistically significant.

REFERENCES

1. Hare, A. P. A study of interaction and consensus in different sized groups. *Amer. sociol. Rev.*, 1952, 17, 261–267.
2. Preston, M. G., & Heintz, R. K. Effects of participatory vs. supervisory leadership on group judgment. *J. abnorm. soc. Psychol.*, 1949, 44, 345–355.
3. Woodworth, R. S. *Experimental psychology*. New York: Henry Holt, 1938.

Methods of Conducting Critiques of Group Problem-Solving Performance

E. PAUL TORRANCE

THE PURPOSE of this study is to evaluate the relative effectiveness of four alternative methods for conducting brief critiques of a short problem-solving exercise designed to assist groups (air crews) to function more effectively as groups.

In many training situations, both military and civilian, it is necessary to conduct brief on-the-spot critiques of a group's performance. Instructors of the Advanced Strategic Air Command Survival School, the scene of the present study, are faced with this problem many times during the course of the field training of each crew they instruct. In all of these

FROM *Journal of Applied Psychology*, 1953, 37, 394–398. Reprinted by permission of the author and the American Psychological Association, Inc.

situations, there is the problem of how much guidance by the instructor or expert produces the best results. Can a crew effectively criticize itself and improve its problem-solving performance, or is the assistance of the expert necessary? When the expert conducts the critique, should he be the evaluator or should he keep the locus of evaluation within the crew?

THEORETICAL CONSIDERATIONS

Much has been written in the areas of counseling and guidance and industrial training about techniques applied to the individual to bring about proper evaluation and improved adjustment or performance. One set of considerations deals with the locus of evaluation. One group, of which Rogers is the chief spokesman, holds that only when the locus of evaluation is in the individual does real growth and development take place (20). According to this theory, an evaluation by an expert or an evaluation resulting from a test would remove the locus of evaluation from the individual and would not result in development and growth. Essentially the same theory is represented in the work of Cantor (1, 2), Maier (14), Lippitt (12), French (4), Katzell (10), Haas (5), and others.

If one were to apply this theory to the problem of critiques, the superior method would be expected to be one in which the leader assumes a non-evaluative role and stimulates the group to evaluate its performance and discover improved methods.

A second set of considerations centers about the role of group decision in changing behavior. Recent findings in industrial research and nutritive education research (6, 8, 11) indicate that group discussion as such results in very little change in behavior, while group decision as a component of group discussion brings about considerable change. In these experiments, scientifically developed information was given by the expert as it was needed but the decision was left to the group. Haire (6) points out, however, that group decision does not work with passive or apathetic groups, although its use almost always stimulates a desire for participation and eventually changes the apathy.

A number of experiments have explored situations and leadership techniques which set up resistance or retard growth, and others which win acceptance or stimulate growth. The problems of resistance have been treated by Zander (22), Torrance (20) and Coch and French (3). All emphasize the importance of respecting the individuals or groups involved. A variety of methods are discussed by Maier (14, 15, 16), Cantor (1, 2), Haas (5), Haire (6), Lippitt (12), and Rogers (18). There seems to be agreement that improved performance does not result merely through reading or hearing lectures. More active participation methods, such as through discussion and role playing procedures, are required.

The skill of the leader must also be considered as a factor. A series of experiments conducted by Maier (17, p. 170) showed that "a leader, if skilled and possessing ideas, can conduct a discussion so as to obtain a quality of problem-solving that surpasses that of a group working with a less skilled leader and without creative ideas. Further, he can obtain a higher degree of acceptance than a less skilled person."

Maier concludes, however, that "even an unskilled leader can achieve good quality solutions and a high degree of acceptance" using democratic leadership. In another experiment (16), he demonstrated the superiority of the permissive discussion leader over the self-critique discussion with an observer present. Maier maintains that the major part of the difference was due to the relatively greater influence exerted by individuals with minority opinions in the "leader" groups than in the "observer" groups. "A discussion leader can function to up-grade the group's thinking by permitting an individual with a minority opinion time for discussion" (16, p. 287).

METHOD AND PROCEDURE

Subjects

The subjects of the experiment were 57 combat air crews undergoing training at the Strategic Air Command's Advanced Survival School at Stead Air Force Base, Nevada. Most of these crews were B-29 (11 men) crews, but a few B-50 (10 men) and B-36 (usually about 15 men) crews were also included. Most of the crews had been functioning as crews for about four months, although some had been together for two or more years.

Problem-Solving Exercises

Two of the Intellectual Talents Tests (401-B and 701-X) developed by the Human Resources Research Laboratories were used. Both tests are thought to tap common-sense judgment and are alike in that each presents the examinee with problem-situations too complex for solution by any step-by-step logical reasoning process and requires the examinee to select the most essential or most critical of the many elements presented in the problem-situation. The problem-situations are rather commonplace and can be solved on the basis of knowledge gained from background experiences common in most persons' lives. Differences in the 401-B and the 701-X are that the 701-X consists of a larger number of shorter problems and permits an unlimited number of choices.

Experimental Procedures

The crews were tested in tents measuring 16 feet by 32 feet on the first day of their training. Each crew was first given an orientation regarding the nature and purpose of the test. Following this, each member of the crew was asked to make an estimate of his crew's performance. The first problem-solving test was then administered, after which a post-test estimate of crew performance was obtained from each crew member.

Following this, a critique of the first problem-solving performance was conducted by one of the following methods:

1. Unstructured non-authoritarian or crew-centered critique: The crew was asked to evaluate and discuss its own performance. Discussion was centered on both the decision as to method and the way it was reached, as well as the way the decision was executed. The experimenter tried to stimulate discussion and encourage crew members to evaluate their performance, but the experimenter did not evaluate their performance. The experimenter accepted questions but referred them back to the crew. The attitude of the experimenter was definitely non-authoritarian. Techniques used were similar to those described by Cantor (1, 2), Maier (14), and Rogers (19).

2. Directive or expert critique: The experimenter diagnosed the performance of the crew according to a set of 13 rating scales (listed later), pointed out ineffective procedures, and suggested ways of improvement. He stated that through research, certain characteristics have been found to differentiate between crews which operate effectively and those which do not. The analysis included both the way the group went about making its decision and what they decided, as well as how they worked together to carry out the decision.

The experimenter took a very active role, assuming the role of the "expert." He tried, however, to give his advice in the most tactful way possible. He, nonetheless, gave definite evaluations and advice. The experimenter accepted questions and answered them as an "expert."

3. No critique: The experimenter went ahead and administered the California F-Scale which required about 15 minutes, before administering the second problem-solving test.

4. Self-critique: Time was allotted for a critique and the experimenter left the tent, returning after 15 minutes.

5. Structured non-authoritarian or crew-centered critique: The experimenter used the set of rating scales as a guide in getting the crew to evaluate itself and discover more effective ways of performing. The locus of evaluation was still within the crew, however.

Following the 15 minute critique period, the second problem-solving test, the 701-X, was administered. The rules were the same as for the first problem except that the time limit was ten minutes.

Observations and Ratings

After each of the two problem-solving tests, the experimenters completed a set of five-point rating scales following a set of descriptive scales on each of the following characteristics: (*1*) Organization of manpower; (*2*) Selective use of personnel; (*3*) Supervision; (*4*) Participation in decision-making; (*5*) Acceptance of suggestions or criticisms; (*6*) Consideration of available time; (7) Checking work; (*8*) Leadership function; (*9*) Survey of the situation; (*10*) Understanding instructions; (*11*) Group atmosphere; (*12*) Speed of reaction to the problem situation; and (*13*) Officer-airmen relations.

RESULTS

A problem-solving score was computed for each crew on both of the problem-solving tests, using the scoring formulae already in use for these tests. A performance rating was also computed for each crew on both of the problem-solving situations by adding the thirteen ratings made by the examiner. In order to hold constant scores and ratings for the first problem-solving test and to determine if the variance in scores and ratings is due to the method of conducting the critique, analyses of co-variance were then carried out both for ratings and for scores. Using the ratings, the variance for critique methods was found to be statistically significant at the one per cent level of confidence ($F = 4.968$). Using problem-solving scores, however, the variance was not statistically significant at less than the five per cent level of confidence ($F = 1.957$). Because of the small number of crews critiqued by each experimenter by each method, it was not possible to compute the interaction of experimenter and critique method.

Crews participating in the unstructured non-authoritarian critique were combined with those participating in the self-critique and crews participating in the expert critique were combined with those participating in the structured non-authoritarian critique in order to study the effect of structure vs. non-structure in critiques. Analysis of co-variance revealed that the variance due to structure is significant at the five per cent level both for ratings ($F = 5.664$) and for scores ($F = 5.124$). Analysis of co-variance also showed that the variance due to different experimenters is not statistically significant ($F = 0.429$) for ratings and for scores.

In order to study relative improvement in performance which might be attributable to differences in methods of conducting critiques, each crew was ranked in order from one to fifty-seven on each of the four variables (score on 401-B, score on 701-X, ratings on 401-B performance, ratings on 701-X performance). Crews were then divided equally into a most improvement category and a least improvement category on ratings and on scores. Table 1 shows the percentage falling into each category according to method of conducting the critique for both ratings and scores.

The *t*-test of significance of differences in percentage reveals the superiority of the expert critique over the non-authoritarian critique (significant at the .001 level of confidence), no critique (significant at the .01 level), and the self-critique (significant at the .02 level). The differences in percentages between the expert critique and the structured non-authoritarian critique are not statistically significant. The latter tends to be more frequently followed by improvement than are the unstructured non-authoritarian critique (significant at the .01 level of confidence), no critique (significant at about the .10 level of confidence), and the self-critique (not statistically significant).

The situation in regard to improvement on problem-solving scores is about the same as for ratings, except that the superiority of the expert critique is not as clear. The *t*-test of significance of the difference in percentage shows that the expert and structured non-authoritarian methods are superior to the unstructured non-authoritarian, the self-critique and no critique at about the .02 level of confidence. The unstructured non-

TABLE 1

Comparison of Effectiveness of Methods of Conducting Critiques

BASIS OF COMPARISON	EXPERT CRITIQUE (11 *crews*)	STRUCTURED NON-AUTHORITARIAN CRITIQUE (11 *crews*)	SELF-CRITIQUE (12 *crews*)	UNSTRUCTURED NON-AUTHORITARIAN CRITIQUE (11 *crews*)	NO CRITIQUE (12 *crews*)
Percentage showing "most improvement" in standing on scores	73	73	33	36	33
Percentage showing "most improvement" in standing on ratings	91	64	50	9	33

authoritarian method and the self-critique appear to have no superiority over no critique.

DISCUSSION

The fact that the structured non-authoritarian is superior to the unstructured non-authoritarian method and that the expert method is not superior to the structured non-authoritarian method would suggest that the locus of evaluation is not important in the type of critique studied in this experiment. Of course, it may be that even though the "expert" makes evaluations, the crew still makes its own evaluations and does not surrender its evaluative function to the expert as readily as some might suppose. A close examination of crews subjected to the expert method and making little improvement indicates that some of the evaluations given by the "expert" were definitely rejected by the crew. The crucial thing may be the giving of evaluations that can be accepted rather than the giving or not giving of evaluations.

The issue of group decisions does not become crucial in this experiment since in every case the decision was left to the crew, although that decision may have been made by one person, usually the aircraft commander. In using the unstructured non-authoritarian, however, it was observed by almost all of the experimenters that a crew would recognize and discuss improved solutions and even appear to give general approval to these solutions. Yet, when the time came to decide how to organize for the second problem, the Aircraft Commander would simply say,

"We'll do it the same way we did the other one." This may explain why this method is not more effective than no critique of any kind.

In regard to the overcoming of resistance, the less structured methods are least effective. It must be mentioned, however, that some of the crews which made the most outstanding improvement were crews using the self-critique. The difficulty is that not all crews are able to look objectively at their performance and discover more effective ways of working together. Most crews seem to require enough structure or guidance to assure that their evaluations and considerations will be concerned with the salient elements. This does not in any way deny the importance of the participation and involvement of the group. It does, however, emphasize the importance of the "expert" and the nature of the role he must play in order to be effective where single trial, immediate performance is concerned.

Although the variation due to experimenter differences was not significant, differences in the success of experimenters were observed. For example, 70 per cent of the crews critiqued by two of the experimenters were in the "most improvement" category while only 25 per cent of the crews of another experimenter were in this category (significantly different at about the 5 per cent level of confidence). The least well trained experimenter differed very little from the best trained experimenters.

The results would appear to have important implications for training of many types, especially training of the on-the-job variety in industry, education, and the military services. Although there are a number of questions which need to be subjected to further study, the results of this study seem to point the way to using structured critiques where decisions are still left to the group, where final evaluation is left to the group, but where the trainer can help guide the evaluative process. This study also suggests several directions for further research which are being pursued through a series of additional studies now under way. These studies are concerned with the role of the expert, the decision-making techniques of the group's usual leader, spread of learning within the group, and transfer of learning to more different situations.

SUMMARY

A total of 57 combat air crews undergoing survival training were divided randomly into four experimental groups and one control group. Each experimental group was administered a problem-solving test, critiqued according to one of four methods, and then administered a second problem-solving test. The control group was given no critique between the two problem-solving tests.

Crews obtained scores on both of the problem-solving tests and ratings of manner of performance on both of the tests.

Analysis of co-variance indicates statistically significant variances in ratings due to method of conducting critiques. Analysis of co-variance indicates statistically significant variance in both scores and ratings due to structuring the critique but no statistically significant variance due to experimenters.

Crews critiqued according to the more highly structured methods are more frequently followed by "greater improvement" than are crews critiqued according to the less highly structured methods. Crews participating in the unstructured non-authoritarian and the self-critique do not perform significantly better than crews receiving no critique.

REFERENCES

1. Cantor, N. *The dynamics of learning.* Buffalo, N.Y.: Foster and Stewart, 1946.
2. Cantor, N. *Learning through discussion.* Buffalo, N.Y.: Human Relations for Industry, 1951.
3. Coch, L., & French, J. R. P. Overcoming resistance to change. *Hum. Relat.*, 1948, 1, 512–532.
4. French, J. R. P. Field experiments: changing group productivity. In J. G. Miller (Ed.), *Experiments in social process.* New York: McGraw-Hill, 1950.
5. Haas, R. B. Action counseling and process analysis; a psychodramatic approach. *Psychodrama Monogr.*, 1948, No. 25.
6. Haire, M. Some problems of industrial training. *J. soc. Issues*, 1948, 4, 41–47.
7. Hendry, C. E., Lippitt, R., & Zander, A. Reality practice as educational method. *Psychodrama Monogr.*, 1947, No. 9.
8. Hendry, C. E. *A decade of group work.* New York: Association Press, 1948.
9. Human Resources Research Laboratories. *Intellectual Talents Tests 701-X and 401-B.* Washington, D.C.: HRRL, Bolling Air Force Base.
10. Katzell, R. A. Testing a training program in human relations. *Personnel Psychol.*, 1948, 1, 319–329.
11. Lewin, K. Group decision and social change. In T. M. Newcomb, & E. L. Hartley (Eds.) *Readings in social psychology.* New York: Holt, 1947.
12. Lippitt R. An experimental study of the effect of democratic and authoritarian atmospheres. *Univer. Iowa Stud. Child Welf.*, 1940, 16, 43–195.
13. Lippitt, R. *Training in community relations.* New York: Harper, 1949.
14. Maier, N. R. F. *Principles of human relations.* New York: Wiley, 1952.
15. Maier, N. R. F., & Zerfoss, L. F. MRP: a technique for training large groups of supervisors and its potential use in social research. *Hum. Relat.*, 1952, 5, 177–186.
16. Maier, N. R. F., & Solem, A. R. The contribution of a discussion leader to the quality of group thinking: the effective use of minority opinions. *Hum. Relat.*, 1952, 5, 277–288.
17. Maier, N. R. F. The quality of group decisions as influenced by the discussion leader. *Hum. Relat.*, 1950, 3, 155–174.
18. Rogers, C. R. *Client-centered therapy.* Boston: Houghton Mifflin, 1951.
19. Rogers, C. R. Divergent trends in methods of improving adjustment. *Harvard Educ. Rev.*, 1948, 38, 209–219.
20. Torrance, E. P. The phenomenon of resistance in learning. *J. abnorm. soc. Psychol.*, 1950, 45, 592–597.
21. Torrance, E. P., & Levi, M. *Crew performance in a test situation as a predictor of performance in the field.* Stead Air Force Base, Nevada: HRRL Detachment No. 3, 1952.
22. Zander, A. Resistance to change—its analysis and prevention. *Advanc. Mgmt.*, 1950, 15, 9–11.

Some Findings Relevant to the Great Man Theory of Leadership

EDGAR F. BORGATTA, ARTHUR S. COUCH,
and
ROBERT F. BALES

INTRODUCTION

A CENTRAL area of research and theory in social psychological science, particularly in group dynamics and small group research, is that of "leadership." The interest apparently lies in the expectation that the "effectiveness" of group performance is determined in large part by the leadership structure of the group. Effective performance is usually defined by the joint occurrence of high task accomplishment and high satisfaction of members of the group.

There are at least six types of thinking about the optimum leadership structure of the group for effective performance. (*1*) The most effective group is the one which has the most adequate all-around leader ("great man"). (*2*) The most effective group is the one in which all members have been chosen according to ability for the specific task. (*3*) The most effective group is the one in which members are selected on the basis of their sociometric choices of each other as co-workers. (*4*) The most effective group is the one in which the various qualities of task ability and social ability are distributed among the members to allow or encourage role differentiation and division of labor. (*5*) The most effective group is one in which members are similar in values or some critical area of values.

FROM *American Sociological Review*, 1954, 19, 755–759. Reprinted by permission of the authors and publisher.

This research, carried out at the Harvard Laboratory of Social Relations, was supported in part by the United States Air Force under Contract A33 (038)-12782 monitored by the Human Resources Research Institute. Permission is granted for reproduction, translation, publication and disposal in whole and in part by or for the United States Government. We are grateful to Hugh Williams for assistance in computations.

(*6*) The most effective group is the one in which members are selected primarily on the basis of compatibility of personality characteristics, such as authoritarianism, major mechanisms of defense, ascendance-submission, etc.

Our concern here is in exploring some aspects of the first principle which we arbitrarily call the "great man theory of leadership." This is probably the oldest of the six theories and one which has received attention throughout the centuries. Such attention is understandable when one considers that history is frequently written from the reference point of "great men." It is equally understandable in terms of the implicit ease with which manipulation is possible if the organizational performance is determined by the single person in the top position. Much psychological research, assuming the great man theory, has been oriented to the problems of selecting persons who are best fitted for a top position of leadership. However, tests of the great man theory which involve the performance of groups rather than the consistency of the leader's behavior are relatively absent in the literature.

PROCEDURE

The data to be presented, bearing on the great man theory, are based on 166 sessions of three man groups.[1] The subjects (N = 126) were male enlisted Air Force personnel assigned to the research project on temporary duty. They were recruited from different organizations, and acquaintance was minimal. The purpose of the testing was represented to the subjects as being the observation of how small groups work together, and presumably, this observation was to take place when they did some role playing. However, they were also observed in periods during which they planned the role playing session and periods of informal participation. It is this data which is analyzed in this experiment. Each of these 166 sessions was 24 minutes long. Every person participated in four sessions with two new co-participants in each session. The differences in enlisted grade were controlled by assignment of subjects to session with persons of their own status.

DESIGN

Couch and Carter (6) have demonstrated in a factor analysis of the rated behavior of individuals in group interaction that three orthogonal factors

1 Other aspects of this research have been reported in other papers. Problems of reliability of scoring and consistency of subject performance were discussed in Borgatta & Bales (5). Problems concerning the effect of task differences of experience, and the "accumulation of a common culture" are discussed in Borgatta & Bales (4). The effects of participation with various types of co-participants, and a rationale for reconstituting groups are presented in Borgatta & Bales (3). The relationships among sociometric measures, interaction performance, ratings by superiors, intelligence, and selected variables are discussed in Borgatta (2).

account for the major portion of the variance in these ratings. The factors have been identified as: (*1*) *Group goal facilitation;* (*2*) *Individual prominence;* and (*3*) *Group sociability*. More simply, the factors may be identified as Task ability, Individual assertiveness, and Social acceptability. For this study, using the Couch and Carter experience, along with that accrued from other sources, we attempted to measure the factors as follows:

FACTOR I: *Task ability*—(a) leadership rating received from coparticipants on a task criterion; (b) the I.Q. score as measured by the Science Research Associates Primary Mental Abilities.

FACTOR II: *Individual assertiveness*—the total activity rate of the individual in terms of the number of initiated acts per unit of time (using Bales' category system 1).

FACTOR III: *Social acceptability*—the sociometric popularity as determined by choices received on a criterion of "enjoyed participation with."

It is our notion that a *great man* would need to possess each of the three independent qualities to a substantial degree. With this fusion of qualities the great man is able to satisfy the major role demands and personality needs of group members. In this study we have defined the great man in terms of a product of the four measures mentioned above. The product of the scores is used rather than a sum to emphasize the requirement of a *simultaneous* occurrence of the qualities. Some sample computations of the product index used are shown in Table 1.

Great men were selected on the basis of their performance in the first session. The top eleven such persons were chosen, each participating in a separate group. That is, there was no case of two great men together in a first session. Our choice of eleven persons was arbitrary and based on the assumption that only about the top tenth of the total sample would satisfy the criterion of "greatness." In the three subsequent sessions when two great men participated together, that three-man group was eliminated from the sample; this reduced our number from 33 to 25. We did this because the term "great man group" implies a group with a *single* great man as all-around leader.

Before examining other hypotheses, a point of concern for this study is whether a person who performs as a great man in the first session does so by virtue of the particular composition of his group, or whether it is a function of relatively stable characteristics of his personality which determine his "greatness" in any group in which he participates. If there is no stability in performance, our subsequent hypotheses are meaningless.

We have no post-meeting estimates of productivity or satisfaction. However, we have indices of interaction in the group which have face validity as bearing on productivity and satisfaction.

(a) For the satisfactory performance of a group in relation to a complex or general task, a large number of suggestions which are acceptable to the group must be made. An index which is a reasonable *a priori* estimate of this kind of task facilitation is the simultaneous presence of high rates of giving suggestion and showing agreement in the group as a whole.

TABLE I

Some Sample Factor Product Indices

SUBJECT IDENTIFICATION	FACTOR I TASK ABILITY		FACTOR II INDIVIDUAL	FACTOR III SOCIAL	PRODUCT INDEX
(ordered by index)	(a) Leadership	(b) I.Q. (percentile)	(c) Assertiveness	(d) Acceptability	(a) (b) (c) (d) (in 1,000's)
1	4	97	161	2	124.9
2	4	96	145	2	111.4
3	4	98	126	2	98.8
4	4	81	152	2	98.5
5	4	78	151	2	94.2
6	3	88	175	2	92.4
7	4	78	135	2	84.2
8	4	96	106	2	81.4
9	4	68	144	2	78.3
10	4	70	121	2	67.8
11	4	54	145	2	62.6
.					
.					
.					
102	1	4	117	2	0.9
103	3	2	94	1	0.6
104	1	4	46	2	0.4
105	1	1	99	2	0.2
106 *	0	8	75	0	0.0
107	0	1	25	1	0.0
108	0	12	16	0	0.0
.					
.					
.					

* There were twenty-one persons with a product-index of 0.

Again, for this index we use a product relationship so that both must be high in order for the index to be high. The total number of suggestions was multiplied by the total number of agreements (Bales' category 4 times category 3). This gives a rough measure of the degree to which a given group reaches consensus on proposed solutions to the task problem.

(b) A high rate of showing tension (Bales' category 11) is a fairly direct indication of difficulty in the interaction process. It is usually a sign of anxiety and withdrawal from participation by the individual. High rates of showing tension in the group are probably associated with low satisfaction, although the relationship may not be linear.

(c) An indication of a friendly atmosphere in a group is a high rate of interaction in the positive social emotional categories, showing solidarity and showing tension release. In this case, our measure is the sum of these (Bales' category 1 plus category 2), indicating the amount of warmth expressed in the group.

HYPOTHESES

Hypothesis (*1*): *Great men* will tend to remain *great men* over a series of sessions.

Hypothesis (*2*): Sessions in which *great men* participate will have a higher product rate of suggestion and agreement (index: time rate of giving suggestion times rate of giving agreement).

Hypothesis (*3*): Sessions in which *great men* participate will have lower time rates of showing tension than those in which they do not participate.

Hypothesis (*4*): Sessions in which *great men* participate will have higher time rates of showing solidarity and tension release than those in which they do not participate.

Results

Hypothesis (*1*): The top eleven persons (of a total sample of 123) defined by the product index of the first session were followed through the subsequent sessions, and the frequency with which they appeared within the top eleven ranks of the product index in the second, third and fourth sessions was noted. Of the eleven persons, eight were in the top ranks in the second and third sessions, and seven were still in top rank in the fourth session, which is a remarkably stable performance. This pattern, based on Chi Square tests, is significant beyond .001 level. The hypothesis is emphatically supported.

The results of the remaining hypotheses are presented in Table 2.

Hypothesis (*2*): When the first sessions in which the great men participated were examined, it was found that they were significantly higher than the residual category of first sessions in terms of the product rate of agreement and suggestion. When subsequent sessions in which they participated were examined, it was found that the product index of agreement and suggestion for the sessions remained significantly higher than those in which the great men did not participate. The hypothesis is emphatically supported.

Hypothesis (*3*): Sessions from which great men were selected showed less tension than the residual first sessions as expected. The difference in the predicted direction was significant when subsequent sessions in which great men participated were compared to those in which they did not. The hypothesis is supported.

Hypothesis (4): When the first sessions in which great men participated were compared with the remaining first sessions with regard to amount of positive affect shown, it was found that the "great man" sessions were significantly higher. In the subsequent sessions the difference remained significant. The hypothesis is emphatically supported.

TABLE 2

Mean Rates of Interaction for Great Man Groups and Non Great Man Groups: Identification of Great Men Based on First Session

	SESSION 1	SESSIONS 2, 3, 4
Product Rate of Giving Suggestion and Agreement:		
Great Man Groups	867 (N = 11)	530 (N = 25)
Non Great Man Groups	566 (N = 31)	362 (N = 95)
(value of t)	(5.98)*	(2.43)*
Rate of Showing Tension		
Great Man Groups	9.4 (N = 11)	11.7 (N = 25)
Non Great Man Groups	14.1 (N = 31)	16.4 (N = 95)
(value of t)	(1.41)	(1.79)*
Rate of Showing Solidarity and Tension Release		
Great Man Groups	39.6 (N = 11)	28.6 (N = 25)
Non Great Man Groups	19.7 (N = 31)	22.2 (N = 95)
(value of t)	(3.98)*	(1.65)*

* $\alpha \leq .05$, one tail test.

DISCUSSION

The stability with which great men, chosen on the basis of their first session performance, retain top position in subsequent groups is impressive.

To the extent that our hypotheses are supported, it is suggested that great men selected on the basis of their first session continue to have an influence on the relatively superior performance of the groups in which they subsequently participate.

The evidence is quite clear that those groups containing a great man have higher product-rates of giving suggestions and agreements. Insofar as one has any reason to believe that this is related to the quality of solutions, the "productivity" of these groups is likely to be increased relative to the groups without great men.

To the extent that a lack of showing tension is an indication of smooth functioning, groups with great men appear to show less inhibited response to the task situation with less anxiety and withdrawal from active participation. This may indicate greater satisfaction with the group. Further evidence of this is seen by the greater amount of positive social emotional behavior, reflecting friendly interpersonal relationships among the members of the group.

Thus, it may be said that great men tend to make "great groups" in the sense that both major factors of group performance—productivity and satisfaction of the members—are simultaneously increased.

CONCLUSION

In general, the great man principle of group composition appears to have much to recommend it. Further study [3] should focus on testing some of the underlying assumptions of the various principles of group composition, especially in terms of the differential effect of the leadership structures on group performance.

REFERENCES

1. Bales, R. F. *Interaction process analysis.* Cambridge, Mass.: Addison-Wesley, 1950.
2. Borgatta, E. F. Analysis of social interaction and sociometric perception. *Sociometry*, 1954, 17, 7–32.
3. Borgatta, E. F., & Bales, R. F. Interaction of individuals in reconstituted groups. *Sociometry*, 1953, 16, 302–320.
4. Borgatta, E. F., & Bales, R. F. Task and accumulation of experience as factors in the interaction of small groups. *Sociometry*, 1953, 16, 239–252.
5. Borgatta, E. F., & Bales, R. F. The consistency of subject behavior and the reliability of scoring in interaction process analysis. *Amer. sociol. Rev.*, 1953, 18, 566–569.
6. Carter, L. F. Leadership and small group behavior. In M. Sherif, & M. O. Wilson (Eds.), *Group relations at the crossroads.* New York: Harper, 1953. Pp. 257–284.

3 A study is now in progress under the direction of Robert F. Bales in which groups composed according to the role differentiation principle will be compared with groups composed according to the great man rationale.

A NOTE ON THE

Type

IN WHICH THIS BOOK IS SET

THE TEXT *of this book was set on the Linotype in* JANSON, *a recutting made direct from type cast from matrices made by Anton Janson. Whether or not Janson was of Dutch ancestry is not known, but it is known that he purchased a foundry and was a practicing type-founder in Leipzig during the years 1660 to 1687. Janson's first specimen sheet was issued in 1675. His successor issued a specimen sheet showing all of the Janson types in 1689. His original matrices are now in the possession of the Stempel foundry, Frankfurt am Main.*

His type is an excellent example of the influential and sturdy Dutch types that prevailed in England prior to the development by William Caslon of his own incomparable designs, which he evolved from these Dutch faces. The Dutch in their turn had been influenced by Garamond in France. The general tone of Janson, however, is darker than Garamond and has a sturdiness and substance quite different from its predecessors. It is a highly legible type, and its individual letters have a pleasing variety of design. Its heavy and light strokes make it sharp and clear, and the full-page effect is characterful and harmonious.